OXFORD **READERS**

# The British Empire

**Jane Samson** is Assistant Professor in the Department of History
and Classics at the University of Alberta, Edmonton. She is editor, with
Alan Frost, of *Pacific Empires: Essays in Honour of Glyndwr Williams*
(1999) and author of *Imperial Benevolence: Making British Authority in the
Pacific Islands* (1998).

# OXFORD **READERS**

The Oxford Readers series represents a unique resource which brings together extracts of texts from a wide variety of sources, primary and secondary, on a wide range of interdisciplinary topics.

OXFORD **READERS**

# The British Empire

*Edited by* Jane Samson

OXFORD
UNIVERSITY PRESS

# OXFORD

UNIVERSITY PRESS

Great Clarendon Street, Oxford OX2 6DP

Oxford University Press is a department of the University of Oxford.
It furthers the University's objective of excellence in research, scholarship,
and education by publishing worldwide in

Oxford New York

Athens Auckland Bangkok Bogotá Buenos Aires Cape Town
Chennai Dar es Salaam Delhi Florence Hong Kong Istanbul Karachi
Kolkata Kuala Lumpur Madrid Melbourne Mexico City Mumbai Nairobi
Paris São Paulo Shanghai Singapore Taipei Tokyo Toronto Warsaw

with associated companies in Berlin Ibadan

Oxford is a registered trade mark of Oxford University Press
in the UK and in certain other countries

Published in the United States
by Oxford University Press Inc., New York

British Library Cataloguing in Publication Data

Data available

Library of Congress Cataloging in Publication Data

Data available

ISBN 0–19–289293–2

1 3 5 7 9 10 8 6 4 2

Typeset in Dante
by RefineCatch Limited, Bungay, Suffolk
Printed in Great Britain by
TJ International Ltd, Padstow, Cornwall

# Preface

One of imperialism's most divisive legacies lies in the realm of language, especially the language of representation. The British empire circled the globe between the eighteenth and twentieth centuries, and during that time racial and cultural terminology changed extensively. Historical material often contains language that is considered unacceptable today. But the problem goes further than that: terms that are used proudly in one country today might cause grave offence in another. For example, Australia's aboriginal peoples are reclaiming the word 'black' at the same time as 'black' is being rejected in favour of 'African American' in the United States. 'Native' peoples in Canada would probably be surprised to know how offended Africans would be to be called 'Natives'. An expression that is insisted upon in one place might be considered racist in another.

The issue of descriptive terminology was therefore a difficult one to resolve for this volume. American usage is becoming more widespread, but to refer to black Loyalists during the American Revolution as 'African Americans' is clearly inappropriate; they identified as British subjects. Black people in Britain, the West Indies, and elsewhere refer to themselves in a variety of ways, but 'black' is a common reference in most cases. A similar example concerns Canada's indigenous population. Rather than calling themselves 'Amerindians', as in the United States, they are First Nations, Natives, or First Peoples. In another case, people of south Asian descent in Canada are usually called 'East Indians' to distinguish them from West Indians (in the Caribbean) and Native Indians (or First Nations). This last example actually tells the story of European imperialism in miniature. Believing they had found Asia—'the Indies'—Christopher Columbus and his successors labelled the indigenous Caribbean peoples 'Indians', and the whole region became known as the 'West Indies' in English. Soon the entire indigenous population of the Americas also became known as 'Indians'. As British rule spread through South Asia, the various peoples of that region became known collectively as 'Indians' despite their wide variety of political or ethnic identities. Even in the south Pacific, explorers like Captain Cook referred to island peoples and Australian aborigines as 'Indians'. At the heart of this process of identification was the assumption that Europeans had a right to label non-Europeans. It is no wonder that, in the post-colonial world, the search for acceptable collective names is both passionate and controversial. Wishing to be sensitive to this complexity, I have not imposed uniform terms in my headnotes or introductions. Instead I have used terminology that, to the best of my knowledge, would be considered acceptable to the peoples concerned.

I owe many people my thanks for their support and assistance during the preparation of this book. Chris Bayly of Cambridge University, and George Miller of OUP, gave me the opportunity to write the book. Peter Marshall, Katherine Prior, and Glyndwr Williams read chapters, uncovered new sources, and made many valuable suggestions and criticisms. Staff at the British Library, the Institute of Commonwealth Studies library, the National Maritime Museum, and the library of the University of Alberta, gave me invaluable assistance. Fiona Kinnear, my editor for the completion of the project, showed great patience during my move from the UK to Canada. Thanks must also go to my husband Simon for his never-failing support, and to my son Alexander who very kindly delayed his arrival until after I had finished a draft of the manuscript. I would like to dedicate this book to him.

# Contents

## 2. The Eighteenth Century

## 3. The Nineteenth Century

## 4. The Twentieth Century

# List of Maps

# Introduction

## Empire and identity

The British empire expanded and declined over a period of five centuries. It was the largest territorial empire in world history. For these reasons it is difficult—perhaps foolish—to try to uncover a general theme that can be traced through the whole story. Nevertheless, an organizing principle of some sort is a great help for students and teachers alike, and for this volume I have chosen the theme of identity.

Historians once assumed that countries, and their populations, progressed naturally towards modern nationhood and citizenship. Lately these concepts have been questioned, and most scholars today see identities—whether national, racial, or cultural—as having been created by historical circumstances including imperialism. To put it simply: the British empire changed the way people saw and defined themselves. British colonies often contained groups of people who had never before shared a common political destiny; the British empire also featured mass migrations which introduced large numbers of immigrants into parts of the world where they had never lived before. Countries like Canada or Malaysia acquired what we now call 'multicultural' populations which contained everything from indigenous peoples to British or European immigrants and the descendants of immigrant workers from India, China, and elsewhere. These groups acquired a new identity—'British subjects'—and that identity itself changed after independence to become 'Canadians' or 'Malaysians'.

It is easy to see why this new, national identity was so effective at first. Even in a colony ruled by foreigners, with artificial boundaries that took no account of traditional indigenous groupings, a national identity was supremely useful in creating a unified fight for independence. After independence was achieved it provided a focus for unity and optimism about the new country's future as a modern nation state.

But what it means to be a Canadian or a Malaysian today is by no means straightforward, as ethnic tensions in both countries (and many others) prove. People of different cultural backgrounds, or with different standards of living, can disagree about what the characteristics of the national identity should be. What should the national language be? Should there be one or more official religions? Is democratic rule important? These questions did not go away after independence from Britain was achieved, and as a result historians are able to see identities as changeable and controversial rather than fixed or inevitable. By using the theme of identity and linking it with the story of the

British empire, this book can provide insight into many of today's most important international debates.

Identities in Britain itself were also influenced by empire. The different peoples of the British Isles came together when they went overseas, and this helped create a collective 'British' identity at home. 'Britishness' eventually began to include peoples from other parts of the world when Indians, Africans, and others migrated to Britain in increasing numbers during the twentieth century. Finally, their empire gave British people an international role that was, for a time, uniquely powerful. The development and decline of that imperial identity took place over time and was subject to the same challenges that confronted identities in the colonies. As in the colonies, different groups in Britain itself had their own ideas about what the empire was for, and whether or not it was a good thing. The empire could be both unifying and divisive: a paradox which helps to explain why the story of empire is so fascinating, and its legacy so complicated.

## The making of Britain

Before going into detail about Britain's imperial identity, the domestic identity of 'Britain' itself needs explanation. The word reflects centuries of English expansion beginning in the middle ages when the Normans and their successors began colonizing parts of Wales and Ireland. The Tudor monarchs brought both countries directly under the English Crown during the sixteenth century, although the Crown's actual control was confined to particular areas only. The English and Scottish thrones were themselves combined in 1603 when James VI of Scotland succeeded Elizabeth Tudor, and by this time English and Scottish Protestants had settled in northern Ireland. After the union of parliaments with Scotland in 1707, the word 'Britain' became a convenient way of referring to the new political entity of England, Wales, and Scotland.

Ireland's relationship to Britain varied considerably: although Henry VIII and his successors claimed the kingship of Ireland there was a separate Irish parliament until 1801. In that year a new name—'United Kingdom'—had to be invented to reflect the union of parliaments between Britain and Ireland; today, Northern Ireland remains part of the United Kingdom. Even after these centuries of political change, many people today (especially in North America, in my experience) still refer to the United Kingdom as 'England'. In the past, Scots and others also used the word 'English' to identify and distinguish themselves from, say, Spaniards in the Americas or Indians in south Asia. It was a convenient shorthand revealing England's dominance in the making of Britain.

## Britain's imperial identity

This domestic background was intimately connected with the development of the British empire. England's experience of conquest and settlement in Ireland formed a blueprint for its early plantation colonies in the Americas and West Indies; these early colonies, then, were technically 'English' colonies before 1603. After the union of crowns in that year, Scotland had a direct political stake in overseas expansion, and Scots, Welsh, and Irish emigrated along with the English to the settlement colonies. By the time 'Britain' came into being in 1707 there was already a 'British empire' composed of settlers, labourers, and traders drawn from all parts of the British Isles. This joint participation did much to solidify political and cultural ties at home, and those ties made it easier for all Britons to participate in the building of empire. In other words, Britain and its empire created a definition of Britishness much larger than a merely domestic national identity.

The 'Britishness' of the British empire may have been established by the eighteenth century, but this did not mean that British perceptions of the empire were straightforward or unchanging. What was the empire for? How should it be run and by whom? Debates about these questions raged throughout the empire's history. The early empire was closely connected with the British Crown's power and privileges: a very different type of empire from a later one which favoured free trade and large-scale emigration. By the twentieth century a dual empire had developed consisting of self-governing settler colonies like Canada and tropical colonies like India governed undemocratically through doctrines of trusteeship and 'development' theory. Thus the identity and purpose of empire could alter radically over time, and one of the most notable characteristics of the British empire was its remarkable adaptability in the face of change.

Culture influenced those changes as much as political or economic factors did. For example, the evangelical Christian revival of the eighteenth and early nineteenth centuries helped to inspire the anti-slavery and missionary movements. Empire was always about commerce, but now it was about being Christian and humane as well. Changing ideas about race were also important: black people, once divided into Christian and non-Christian categories by the British, became increasingly identified with slavery and inferiority regardless of their religious beliefs. By the later nineteenth century, scientific racism offered the British a new way of relegating non-Europeans to an apparently permanent status of subordination.

Crises also affected imperial identities. The loss of the American colonies in 1783, the Indian Rebellion of 1857, and Britain's diminished international status after the Second World War are examples of events which intensified debate about the nature and future of empire. When other European powers began building extensive empires of their own during the late nineteenth century, the British began speaking of an 'Anglo-Saxon' empire in order to distinguish it from other European ethnic identities such as Gallic (French) or Teutonic (German). During this time the British approved of American expansion in the Philippines and other former Spanish colonies because the United States shared their superior 'Anglo-Saxon' destiny.

The British were not always in control of this process of identity formation, however. It is true that they categorized colonial populations in ways that fit with current notions about what the empire was for. The same group of people could be variously identified as collaborators to be courted, enemies to be defeated, commercial opportunities to be exploited, or victims to be protected. But these identities could be challenged or replaced by others fashioned by colonial peoples themselves. British settlers could develop identities different from, and even at odds with, their domestic British counterparts. As we will see, the American colonists often appealed to a shared 'Englishness' when demanding greater liberty from British government regulation; the different political factions in America were normally labelled 'Whigs' and 'Tories', as they were in Britain. Later, during the War of Independence, the colonists abandoned this shared identity in favour of a distinction between 'Americans' and 'British'.

Non-Europeans had an even wider range of options because they already had their own indigenous identities when the British first arrived. Such peoples could see themselves in various ways after colonial rule began. The ancient ties of kinship, religion, or tribe still persisted, but these could be combined with—or even overturned by—newer ones. This was often a necessity when indigenous peoples were confronted with the dislocations of the colonial period. A good example of a hybrid traditional-modern identity was the Maori King movement in mid-nineteenth-century New Zealand. There was no centralized political identity among the Maori before the British came, but increasing British settlement created the need for a co-ordinated Maori reponse. The result was the emergence of a Maori king as a symbol of unity, and the creation of a new, unified identity for the land itself: 'Maoridom' or, more recently, 'Aotearoa' as a substitute for the European 'New Zealand'.

Even the end of empire was bound up with changing identities. The British often delayed self-government for non-European populations in the name of protective trusteeship. Later, the multiracial identity of the Commonwealth allowed a more equitable relationship to emerge. In the colonies, nationalisms were developing which rejected British imperialism while exploiting many of its characteristics: the use of English, the centralizing effect of railways and printing presses, and the impact of Western political philosophies. These hybrid nationalisms have left the post-colonial world with many dilemmas. Having rejected the identity of 'British subject', nationalist movements were faced, after independence, with the problem of promoting national unity in populations divided by gender, race, class, religion, and language.

In many cases these divisions were aggravated, and even created by, colonial rule. The importation of African, south Asian, and Chinese labour produced dramatic demographic and social change in many British colonies. Once they achieved self-government, Canada and Australia both passed anti-Chinese legislation meant to rid their new nations of unwelcome Asian elements. After independence in the former African colonies of Kenya and Uganda, their south Asian populations were forcibly expelled in the name of 'Africanization'. The common factor in each of these cases is the role of empire in moving large numbers of people around the globe with unpredictable results, and one of the most acute political challenges of the twenty-first century will be the tension between competing local, national, and international identities. An understanding of imperial history is essential for the full complexity of this problem to be understood.

There is yet another dimension to the relationship between imperialism and national identity. Unlike its tropical colonies in Africa, Asia, or the Pacific islands, Britain's colonies of settlement acquired self-government rapidly and peacefully in the nineteenth century, and full independence by 1931. Britain saw Canada, South Africa, Australia, and New Zealand as evidence of its superiority to empires such as Spain's, which had gained independence only after civil war. But this triumphant story of peaceful British settlement and self-rule in the so-called white Dominions was (and is) deceptive. During the nineteenth century the indigenous populations of these countries were increasingly excluded from the developing process of nationalism and self-government. Indigenous peoples were denied the vote until the 1960s in Canada and Australia, and their numbers and culture were devastated by aggressive assimilation policies and the effects of disease and poverty. South Africa, self-governing after 1910, adopted the racial segregation system known as *apartheid* which severely limited the civil rights of non-Europeans; only in 1994 were the first non-racial elections held in South Africa. In such countries, a double colonization can be said to have taken place. The European colonists and their descendants tended to focus on themselves and their struggle for political independence from Britain, obscuring the fact that this process had excluded the original inhabitants. Many indigenous activists today would argue that, apart from South Africa, the former Dominions have not yet begun decolonization within their own borders.

But it would be wrong to dwell only on the divisive legacy of empire. Many of the features of globalization—free trade, long-range communications, and the widespread use of English—have their roots in the massive imperial expansion of the eighteenth and nineteenth centuries. An important global political organization—the Commonwealth of Nations—is also a legacy of empire. Composed of almost all of Britain's former colonies, its ongoing popularity comes from a combination of shared history and common future aspirations. During the twentieth century the Commonwealth has been, variously, a white Dominions club, a testing ground for racial tolerance, a matrix for sporting, educational, and technological exchanges, and a human rights forum. It has successfully reinvented imperial relationships to suit the needs of post-colonial states. Although the current British monarch is the symbolic head of the Commonwealth, Britain itself has played an increasingly low-key role in the organization, and at its remarkable biennial heads of government meetings, the leaders of its member states go on retreat together without the usual entourage of advisers and media. The tiniest Pacific island nations meet on equal terms with the heads of the most populous and influential members. There is no doubt that the Commonwealth's origins are imperial, but its activities confirm that global connections can convey benefits as well as injustices.

## Why an empire reader?

I have been struck by the large number of readers on theories of imperialism—especially post-colonial literary theory—that are available to students today, and puzzled by the absence of affordable collections of historical material. In other words, students and their teachers can easily find out what today's intellectuals think about empire, but must turn to older works, or burrow in archives, in order to access texts from the age of empire itself.

One reason for the decline in document readers is undoubtedly the decreasing popularity of political and economic history; today's academic climate tends to favour literary or cultural approaches. There is a perception (misguided in my opinion) which sees political and economic history as increasingly irrelevant to the study of empire. But important as culture is, it cannot be magically uncoupled from other aspects of society, and trade can be as vital a part of identity formation as literature.

Let me explain what my own approach has been. Like detectives, historians can learn much by 'following the money', and the economic policies of the British empire, like those of any global organization, had an enormous effect on world history. I have therefore paid close attention to the changing economic underpinning of the empire, taking the story right up to the 'development' policies which are still the subject of so much controversy in international relations today. Political and legal sources are no less essential if identity issues are to be fully explored. Here we find the definitions of race, citizenship, land rights, education objectives, and official language policies that were so critical to distinctions between 'us' and 'them'. I agree with those who say that cultural artefacts also have much to tell us, and for that reason I have included extracts of poetry and fiction in this collection. It is my hope that a wide range of types of material, rather than a more exclusive focus, will give students a better sense of the enormous complexity of empire.

Because this volume covers such a vast chronological and geographical subject, my document selections were inevitably arbitrary and specialists will, no doubt, lament the neglect of their own special fields of interest. But if I can give students a broad overview of British imperialism, and provide instructors with a resource to supplement other readings, then I will have achieved my purpose. My hope is that teachers of world history, colonialism, and nationalism will all find this book useful.

This reader is divided into four roughly chronological chapters. Each chapter has a general introduction placing the British empire into a world history context, and individual sections then take up themes or issues from a range of perspectives. Most chapters combine a number of extracts from contemporary material with analysis by a leading historian; these are meant to provide additional information, to cover areas not dealt with by the contemporary material, and to introduce students to various theories about the motives and means of imperial expansion.

The only exception to this pattern is Chapter 4 on the twentieth century. Because decolonization was so rapid, and took place relatively recently, theories of decolonization are still in the developmental stages. There is a growing secondary literature on the end of empire, but it was not always possible to find material on the particular case studies and comparisons I wished to make. For this reason, several secondary extracts have been placed with some contemporary material in the first section of Chapter 4. The remaining sections compare decolonization in colonies of various types using a larger than usual number of contemporary extracts. This format allowed me to introduce students to general questions about decolonization in the first section, and then to delve into the nationalisms, conflicts, and special circumstances of the various case studies I chose. For practical reasons I decided to confine the story to the period leading up to independence in each country described, and I concentrated on colonies that became independent between 1947 and 1980. Britain still retains a handful of tiny dependencies, and even its former colonies still struggle with the legacy of imperialism. Perhaps, in this sense, the story of the British empire has no clear ending.

# Chapter 1

## The Early Empire

### INTRODUCTION

**W**e have seen that the word 'Britain' reflects a long history of conquest, colonization, and consolidation. As British influence expanded overseas this process continued on a larger scale, and the acquisition of an empire became an important feature of British identity. Some features of this imperial identity would remain remarkably constant, based as they were on the geography of the British Isles. The ocean was England's means of communication, trade, and warfare with the outside world, and England's first empire was an empire of the sea.

The Portuguese led European overseas exploration and trade in the fifteenth century, and English sailors often joined Portuguese voyages to west Africa, Asia, and Brazil. But by the sixteenth century the greatest colonial power was Spain, whose conquests in the Caribbean and central/south America were vast; Spain then acquired control of the Portuguese empire when it incorporated Portugal itself between 1580 and 1640. The Dutch were active, too, dominating the East Indies spice trade and ousting the Portuguese from most of the west African coast by the end of the sixteenth century.

England's ventures were modest by comparison: a brief exploration of the north-east North American seaboard by John Cabot in 1497; summer settlements in Newfoundland for the north Atlantic fishery; and exploration/privateering voyages against the Spanish by men like Francis Drake and Walter Raleigh. England's defeat of the Spanish Armada in 1588 encouraged further expansion, but the Dutch presence in south-east Asia forced the English East India Company to obtain footholds in south Asia to gain access to the valuable spice trade.

Meanwhile, the united Spanish/Portuguese monarchy proved unable to prevent incursions in its traditional areas of influence. The expansion of Dutch and English influence in Africa was a case in point. Portuguese exploration and trade with Africa flourished in the fifteenth century, and there were a chain of Portuguese outposts along the African coasts, trading for gold, ivory, spices, and slaves. But these small settlements led a precarious existence: isolated, devastated by disease, and dependent on the goodwill of neighbouring African leaders. After its conquest by Spain, Portugal saw its overseas interests neglected in favour of Spanish colonies, and the Dutch and

English (among others) were quick to take advantage of this situation. An English trading post at Cormantine in west Africa was augmented by the seizure of Cape Coast Castle from the Dutch in 1664. By this time the slave trade was driving European expansion in west Africa; Portugal's domination of the trade to the Spanish American colonies—Spain had no base of its own in Africa—declined during its struggle for independence from Spain in the early seventeenth century. Spain was forced to turn to the Protestant maritime powers, Holland and England, to maintain its supply of African slaves. This ready market, plus that of its own plantation colonies in the West Indies and North America, allowed several English chartered companies and a large number of individual traders to build up England's share of the slave trade.

England's first successful plantation in North America was Virginia, refounded (after several false starts) in 1607. Modelled on the plantations owned by English and Scots in Ireland, the Virginia settlement—like all of Britain's early settlements in the Americas—was based on British royal patronage. Groups of merchants, aristocrats, and gentry obtained grants of land from the Crown which gave permission to settle colonists and begin farming. The same process characterized British expansion in the West Indies where islands claimed by Spain, such as Barbados, were colonized by the British during the 1620s and 1630s. Britain also took the Spanish colony of Jamaica by force in 1655. By the end of the seventeenth century British plantations were growing a wide variety of crops including tobacco and sugar. In return for the granting of land, the British government required the colonists to trade exclusively with Britain and one another, and to use only British shipping. Even after most of the merchant venturers had relinquished control, and the colonies became virtually self-contained settlements, the restrictions on non-British trade and transport remained. This economic exclusiveness—known as protectionism—was a prominent characteristic of the early British empire.

England's other trans-Atlantic colonies were not always founded for purely commercial reasons. Newfoundland was occupied only during the fishing season. English Puritans, Quakers, and Catholics established settlements in what is now the north-eastern United States, attempting to create godly communities based on particular social and theological principles. The first of these colonies was at Plymouth in 1620. But these idealistic settlements took place within the usual context of international rivalry and economics. They were bulwarks of Englishness between the Spanish territories to the south, and New France (later Quebec) to the north. They were also reinforcements against the Dutch, whose creation of 'New Netherland' around the Hudson River had threatened to divide areas of influence that England regarded as its own.

The seventeenth century featured several wars between Britain and the Netherlands, and a British victory in 1664 renamed New Amsterdam as New York, giving Britain control of the entire north-eastern seaboard (see Map 1).

By 1700 there were eleven English colonies along this coast, from Maine to the Carolinas. France, however, retained a strong inland presence from its bases in New France and Acadia. To counter this, and to claim a larger share of the profitable fur trade, Charles II chartered the Hudson's Bay Company in 1670 to exploit all of the lands drained by rivers flowing into the Bay: a third of the North American continent. From bases established in the hinterland, it was hoped, England could circumvent the French settlements and find a Northwest Passage to the Pacific Ocean and the riches of Asia. The inevitable clash with France in North America, in the Pacific, and elsewhere, would dominate the eighteenth-century empire.

## I.I  AN EMPIRE OF THE SEA

In the earliest English voyages of exploration we can see close connections between the English Crown, seaborne trade, and imperial expansion. King Henry VII despatched John Cabot in 1497 to investigate the Atlantic coast of what is now Canada, but Cabot's findings were minimal (Extract 1). It was during the sixteenth century that explorers, fishermen, and traders enhanced England's knowledge of the overseas world. By Queen Elizabeth's reign and the time of Shakespeare, the framework for an imperial identity was already in place: maritime power, the quest for prestige, and a sense of Protestant destiny (Extract 2). The defeat of the Spanish naval armada, and the decline of Portuguese influence at the hands of the Dutch in the sixteenth century, provided England with opportunities for expansion.

By the beginning of the seventeenth century, England's imperial activities became more systematic as chartered companies of merchant adventurers began exploiting overseas resources and, for the first time, established territorial claims (with local consent) around their small trading outposts in Asia and Africa. Many of these companies were short-lived but others, notably the East India Company (EIC) established in 1600, would become wealthy and influential (Extract 3). The EIC is a good example of a monopolistic company whose charter prohibited trading by any other organization within its huge territory in the Indian and Pacific Oceans. In other parts of the empire, especially in North America and the West Indies, the Crown still controlled the framework for trade, but too many people were involved for monopolies to be enforced. The relationship between trade and settlement was also different in various parts of the early empire. The plantations of North America and the West Indies required settlement, but the fur trade of the Hudson's Bay Company could be conducted mainly through existing indigenous networks. In Asia and west Africa, too, the English did business with existing economic and political systems.

The early modern empire is often called 'mercantilist' because of the prominent role of the State in encouraging commerce for the benefit of the nation and the Crown. After the disruptions of the Civil War and Inter-regnum of 1642–60, one of the first acts of Charles II was to strengthen the Crown's control of imperial commerce (Extract 4). England would monopolize the transportation and importation of colonial produce through its chartered companies in the East, and the enforced used of English domestic shipping in the Atlantic, and in return overseas settlements would enjoy exclusive access to English markets and goods. The seventeenth century 'Laws of Trade', which included the new Navigation Act, codified this policy for the first time and culminated in the creation of a Board of Trade in 1696 to oversee and regulate colonial affairs.

The key was the identification of empire with the State. Imperial commerce brought revenue to the Crown and gave England exclusive access to its own supplies of valuable imports like spices, tobacco, and sugar. These imports produced customs and excise revenues, filling royal coffers depleted by war. The protectionist system also generated an immense network of patronage, allowing monarchs to reward their friends and raise additional funds. Historian Hilary Beckles explains how the West Indian colonies became the 'hub' of English trans-Atlantic commerce during this period (Extract 5).

Schemes for North American plantations also developed during Elizabethan times. In the wake of the explorations (and privateering depredations) of men like Francis Drake and Walter Raleigh, Queen Elizabeth made small but significant challenges to Spain's domination of the Americas. Under the patronage of Raleigh and others, Richard Hakluyt collected accounts of English voyages to the New World, and promoted the establishment of English settlements in North America (Extract 6). These would be plantations like the West Indian ones, and the growing of tobacco and other products would make them profitable (Extract 7). But they were also islands of English Protestantism in a New World dominated by Spanish and French Catholicism. John Smith, an early explorer of the area he named 'New England', called on his countrymen to challenge Spanish supremacy in the Americas and claimed that, by founding an empire in New England, England itself would be restored through a renewal of its spirit of Protestant enterprise and an expanding maritime trade (Extract 8).

**1**   **A Venetian**

> There is no surviving account by John Cabot himself about his explorations in North America. Cabot was originally from Venice, and this letter home from a Venetian in London gives one of very few descriptions of Cabot's activities; the letter was written on 23 August 1497.

That Venetian of ours who went with a small ship from Bristol to find new islands has come back and says he has discovered mainland [*terra firma*] 700 leagues away, which is the country of the Grand Khan [*Gram Cam*], and that he coasted it for 300 leagues and landed and did not see any person; but he has brought here to the king certain snares [*luzi*] which were spread to take game and a needle for making nets [*uno agoda far rede*], and he found certain notched [or felled] trees [*al'boti tajati*] so that by this he judges that there are inhabitants. Being in doubt he returned to his ship; and he has been three months on the voyage; and this is certain. And on the way back he saw two islands, but was unwilling to land, in order not to lose time, as he was in want of provisions. The king here is much pleased at this; and he [Cabot] says that the tides are slack [*le aque è stanchi*] and do not run as they do here. The king has promised him for the spring ten armed ships as he [Cabot] desires and has given him all the prisoners to be sent away, that they may go with him, as he has requested; and has given him money that he may have a good time until then. And he is with his Venetian wife and his sons at Bristol. His name is Zuam Talbot and he is called the Great Admiral [*el gran armirante*] and vast honour is paid to him and he goes dressed in silk, and these English run after him like mad, and indeed he can enlist as many of them as he pleases, and a number of rogues as well. The discoverer of these things planted on the land which he has found a large cross with a banner [*bandiera*] of England and one of St Mark, as he is a Venetian, so that our flag [*confalone*] has been hoisted very far afield.

[*Source*: David B. Quinn, ed., *New American World: a documentary history of North America to 1612* (New York: Arno Press, 1979), vol. 1, p. 96.]

## 2    William Shakespeare

Playwright William Shakespeare wrote this speech for the character of John of Gaunt, in *Richard II* (1597), proclaiming the English rejection of royal tyranny and England's identity as a maritime power. The speech became one of the best-known expressions of English nationalism.

> This royal throne of kings, this sceptred isle,
> This earth of majesty, this seat of Mars,
> This other Eden, demi-paradise,
> This fortress built by nature for herself
> Against infection and the hand of war,
> This happy breed of men, this little world,
> This precious stone set in the silver sea,
> Which serves it in the office of a wall,
> Or as a moat defensive to a house,
> Against the envy of less happier lands [. . .]
>
> This blessed plot, this earth, this realm, this England,
> This nurse, this teeming womb of royal kings,
> Feared by their breed, and famous by their birth,
> Renowned for their deeds as far from home,
> For Christian service and true chivalry,
> As is the sepulchre in stubborn Jewry

Of the world's ransom, blessed Mary's Son:
This land of such dear souls, this dear, dear land
Dear for her reputation through the world [. . .]
[*Source*: John M. Lothian, ed., William Shakespeare, *Richard II*
(Oxford: Clarendon Press, 1938), pp. 59–60.]

## 3   East India Company Charter

Queen Elizabeth I granted this charter to the East India Company in
1600. Note the powers of land disposal and revenue collection that were
granted, and the ambitious mandate stretching from Asia and Africa
across the Pacific. The EIC was never able to exploit such an extensive
monopoly and would concentrate its activities on south and south-east
Asia.

We greatly tendering the Honour of our Nation, the Wealth of our People,
and the Encouragement of them, and others of our loving Subjects in their
good Enterprizes, for the Increase of our Navigation, and the Advancement
of lawful Traffick, to the Benefit of our Common Wealth, . . . go give and
grant unto our said loving Subjects, . . . That they and every of them from
henceforth be, and shall be one Body Corporate and Politick, in Deed and in
Name, by the Name of *The Governor and Company of Merchants of London,
Trading into the East-Indies*, . . . capable in Law to have, purchase, . . . and
retain, Lands, Rents, Priviledges, Liberties, Jurisdictions, Franchises and
Hereditaments of whatsoever Kind, Nature and Quality so ever they be . . .
And also to give . . . and dispose Lands . . . and to do and execute all and
singular other Things. [. . .]

    And further, all such the Apprentices, Factors, or Servants of them and of
every of them, which hereafter shall be employed, by The Said *Governor and
Company*, in the said Trade of Merchandize, of or to the *East-Indies*, beyond
the Seas, or any other the Places aforesaid, in any Part of the said East-Indies,
or other the Places aforesaid, shall and may, by the Space of Fifteen Years,
from the Feast of the Birth of our Lord God last past, before the Date
thereof, freely traffick and use the Trade of Merchandize, by Seas, in and by
such Ways and Passages already found out and discovered, or which hereafter
shall be found out and discovered, as they shall esteem and take to be fittest,
into and from the said East-Indies, in the Countries and Parts of Asia and
Africa, and into and from all the Islands, Ports, Havens, Cities, Creeks, Towns,
and Places in Asia and Africa, and America, or any of them, beyond the Cape
of Bona Esperanza [*Good Hope*] to the Streights of Magellan, where any Trade
or Traffick of Merchandize may be used or had, and to and from every of
them. [. . .]

And by virtue of our Prerogative Royal, which we will not in that Behalf have argued, or brought in Question, we straitly charge, command and prohibit . . . all the Subjects of us . . . that none of them, directly or indirectly, do visit, haunt, frequent or trade, traffick or adventure, by way of Merchandize, into or from any of the said East-Indies, or into or from any the Islands, Ports, Havens, Cities, Towns or Places aforesaid, other than The said Governor and Company . . . and such particular Persons as now be, or hereafter shall be of that Company, their Agents, Factors and Assigns, during the said Term of Fifteen Years, unless it be by and with such Licence and Agreement of the said Governor and Company.

> [*Source*: A. F. Madden and D. K. Fieldhouse, eds, '*The Empire of the Bretaignes*', *1175–1688:*
> *The Foundations of a Colonial System of Government*, vol. 1 of *Select documents on the*
> *constitutional history of the British Empire and Commonwealth* (hereafter *SDBE*)
> (Westport and London: Greenwood Press, 1985), pp. 234, 235 6, 237.]

## 4    Navigation Act 1660

The *Navigation Act* of 1660 revived and reinforced earlier Acts designed to promote English commerce and to protect it from competition with other European countries.

*For the increase of shipping and encouragement of the navigation of this nation, wherein, under the good providence and protection of God, the wealth, safety and strength of this kingdom is so much concerned:* Be it enacted that . . . no goods or commodities whatsoever shall be imported into or exported out of any lands, islands, plantations or territories to his Majesty belonging or in his possession, or which may hereafter belong unto or be in the possession, of his Majesty, his heirs and successors, in Asia, Africa or America in any other ship or ships, vessel or vessels whatsoever, but in such ships or vessels as do truly and without fraud belong only to the people of England or Ireland, dominion of Wales or town of Berwick upon Tweed, or are of the built of and belonging to any the said lands, islands, plantations or territories, as the proprietors and right owners thereof, and whereof the master and three fourths of the mariners at least are English. [. . .]

And it is further enacted . . . That no goods or commodities whatsoever, of the growth or manufacture of Africa, Asia, America, or of any part thereof, or which are described or laid down in the usual maps or cards of those places, be imported into England, Ireland, or Wales, islands of Guernsey and Jersey, or town of Berwick upon Tweed, in any other ship or ships, vessel or vessels whatsoever, but in such as do truly and without fraud belong only to the people of England or Ireland, dominion of Wales, or town of Berwick upon Tweed or of the lands, islands, plantations or territories in Asia, Africa or America, to his Majesty belonging, as the proprietors and right owners thereof, and whereof the master, and three fourths at least of the mariners are *English* . . . [. . .]

No sugars, tobacco, cotton wool, indicoes, ginger fustick, or other dying wood, of the growth, production or manufacture of any English plantation in America, Asia or Africa, shall be shipped, carried, conveyed or transported from any of the said English plantations to any land, island, territory, dominion, port or place whatsoever, other than to such other English plantations as do belong to his Majesty, his heirs and successors, or to the Kingdom of England, or Ireland, or principality of Wales, or town of Berwick upon Tweed, there to be laid on shore . . . [. . .]

[*Source*: Madden and Fieldhouse, *Empire of the Bretaignes*, pp. 386–9.]

## 5   Hilary McD. Beckles

Eric Williams, the historian who became the Prime Minister of Trinidad and Tobago, described the West Indian islands as 'the hub of Empire'. Certainly by the end of the seventeenth century commentators on Empire such as Charles Davenant, Josiah Child, and Dalby Thomas judged the West Indian islands to be Britain's most profitable overseas investment. Eighteenth-century analysts of colonial trade and economic growth developed this argument in relation to profitability in the sugar plantation economy. For Adam Smith, the place of sugar among colonial produce was clear: 'the profits of a sugar plantation in any of our West Indian colonies are generally much greater than those of any other cultivation that is known either in Europe or America'. 'The Sugar colonies', noted Arthur Young, 'added above three million [pounds] a year to the wealth of Britain.' In our own time, however, there has been widespread agreement that the sugar colonies were dismal social failures.

In 1600 England's interests in these 'small scraps of land' seemed 'more an opposition program' characterized by erratic, but violent, assault upon Spanish settlements and trade than the projection of a clearly defined policy of colonization. Raiding and plundering became the norm, and represented what seemed to be the extent of English capabilities, attracting considerable capital from the investing community. English merchants thus proved themselves ready to invest in long-distance projects, even in politically volatile areas, once the returns were good.

During the twenty years of war with Spain, 1585–1604, there was 'no peace beyond the line', and the value of prize money brought to England from the Caribbean ranged between £100,000 and £200,000 per year. Privateering, linked directly to contraband trades, continued to be important well into the century. It had an impact on everyday life in Jamaica (which came into English possession following Cromwell's Western Design of 1655–56 on Spanish possessions in the West Indies), especially as returns contributed to local financing of the agricultural economy. The Elizabethan state, for tactical political reasons, had not wished publicly to support such Caribbean operations, but individual adventurers were confident that they had the means to solve any problem which might be encountered in the Americas, and they could call on financially experienced courtiers and gentlemen to organize and invest in these ventures.

In these approaches to colonization, the English followed the Dutch, who had formulated ground-plans to trade and settle in the Caribbean. The Guiana coasts, located between Spanish settlements on the Orinoco and Portuguese possessions on the Amazon, attracted English as well as Dutch attention. In 1604, nine years after Ralegh's effort, Charles Leigh attempted a settlement on the Wiapoco. There were others: Harcourt's attempt (1609–13), Ralegh's (1617–18), and Roger North's (1619–21). An important outcome of these operations was the opportunity to survey the Windward and Leeward Islands, which the Spanish had left neglected and undefended.

The Spanish had attached little economic value to the Lesser Antilles because the islands could not yield large quantities of precious metals, and the English who first became involved in individual islands also encountered determined opposition from the Kalinagos (Caribs) similar to that which had discouraged the Spaniards. The turning-point was Thomas Warner's visit to St Christopher (St Kitts) in 1622. Warner was a participant in North's Guiana project, and considered St Christopher ideally suited for the establishment of tobacco plantations. A group of mariners, led by John Powell, touched at Barbados in 1625 en route from the Guianas, and made similar observations. Warner and Powell returned to England to seek financial backing for a novel type of English colonizing activity [. . .].

Failed attempts at a Guiana settlement marked the beginning of a new approach by England to Caribbean colonization. The financial collapse of the Virginia Company in 1624 had resulted in a management takeover by the Crown which signalled a greater determination to convert commercial enterprises into permanent settlement. The furthering of agricultural settlements financed by joint-stock companies, syndicates, and individuals symbolized the beginning of a conceptual triumph over the long-standing tradition of piracy. At the same time, it brought to the centre of the colonizing mission powerful groups of nobles and gentry who saw this as a new arena in which to compete for royal patronage, and some became participants in a 'patent war' for control of overseas territories. For example, on

2 July 1625 James Hay, Earl of Carlisle, was issued a grant by Charles I of the 'Caribbean Islands', and on 25 February 1628 the Earl of Pembroke obtained a grant from the King for the same territories. A violent and bloody struggle ensued between settlement parties despatched to the islands by both nobles, and it was only further royal intervention which settled the conflict in favour of Carlisle.

In the next decade the Caribbean islands experienced a veritable 'swarming of the English' as more settlers established themselves in the West Indies than in any single mainland colony. This was in spite of the political and constitutional chaos which resulted from clashes between rival patents. What survived these conflicts, significantly, were the three principles that constituted the legacy of the failed Virginia Company: the option of a permanently settled community; the production for export of agricultural crops; and the idea that propertied Englishmen in far-flung colonies had an inalienable right to self-government. The aggressive promotion and defence of this legacy made the islands a place which held out greater prospects of glamour, excitement, danger, and quick profit than any mainland colony.

Given the opportunity, these earliest English colonial sponsors would probably have followed their Spanish enemies into establishing some sort of feudal system, by subjecting the aboriginal population and establishing themselves as lords living on tributes, as they preferred the search for gold and silver to agricultural production for the export trade. By the 1620s these opportunities were no longer available. Hopes of easy gold and the myth of Ralegh's El Dorado had subsided. It was clear that successful colonization in the Caribbean would be based on agriculture and trade.

The English established colonies at St Christopher in 1624, Barbados in 1627, Nevis in 1628, and Montserrat and Antigua in 1632. Previous to the campaign of 1655–56, when Oliver Cromwell added Jamaica to the list of English possessions, these small islands were the backbone of England's seaborne Empire, and the primary location of capital accumulation in the Americas. The economic importance of these islands far surpassed that of Puritan New England, but that is not to say that Puritans were not interested in the West Indies. Individual Puritans, including members of the prominent Winthrop and Downing families, spent some time in the West Indies, but collectively Puritans never attained the political power necessary to promote the West Indies as a location for New Jerusalem evangelism. Even at Providence Island, off the coast of Nicaragua, where they financed a settlement and secured political control, the culture of piracy and smuggling, as well as cruel exploitation of unfree labour, transcended considerations of building a religious utopia and rendered their community indistinguishable from those of other European settlers in neighbouring islands.

By 1640 the English had gained a demographic advantage in the Caribbean over other European nations. The islands attracted more settlers than mainland colonies up to 1660, which suggests that they were perceived as the destinations that held the best prospects for material and social advancement. The white population grew rapidly up to about 1660 when it reached 47,000, constituting some 40 per cent of all the whites in Britain's transatlantic colonies. Gemery's estimates suggest that of the total of 378,000 white emigrants to America between 1630 and 1700, 223,000 (about 60 per cent) went to the colonies in the wider Caribbean.

Economic depression and political turmoil of the 1620s and early 1630s, and the effective marketing of the colonies as places of opportunity for all classes, constituted a winning formula for pro-emigration agents. The population of Barbados in particular rose sharply during the 1630s, advancing sevenfold between 1635 and 1639. No other colony rivalled Barbados as a destination for settlers during this period. The West Indies also forged ahead of the mainland colonies in the expansion of economic activities. Investment and trade increased in direct relation to population growth, and West Indian capitalists were able to secure in the early years the greater share of labourers leaving both Ireland and Britain for America.

The organization of staple production—tobacco and cotton—in the formative years depended upon the labour of thousands of British indentured labourers. Unlike the islands acquired by the Spanish in the Greater Antilles, the Lesser Antilles lacked a large indigenous population which could be reduced to servitude. In the absence of a native labour force such as had been exploited by the Spaniards in Mexico and Peru, the obvious alternative supply of workers was found through the importation of indentured servants. This meant—as it also did in the Chesapeake—that the producer who commanded most servants was the individual most likely to succeed. [. . .]

Reports from the West Indies during the second half of the century indicate the steady advance of sugar cultivation, although sugar monoculture was certainly not the case in these islands. Contests for the best lands in Jamaica between sugar farmers, cash-crop producers, and cattlemen remained as intense as that between agriculturalists and contraband traders for control of official policy with respect to the colony's development. Piracy and contraband also remained attractive in Jamaica as a means of wealth accumulation, despite the ascendancy of the agricultural trades which the mercantilist intellectuals considered to be the only sustainable source of wealth. The cultivation of cacao, which had been pursued on Jamaica by the Spaniards, was persisted in by some English planters, and it was the profits made from cacao that made it possible for some of them to become involved with sugar production. Efforts were also made to cultivate sugar on the four Leeward islands of Antigua, Montserrat, Nevis, and St Christopher, but none of these became a major sugar producer in the seventeenth century despite the fact that the planters in all these areas were lured by the Barbados model. Less suitable agricultural terrain, and the high cost of constructing the mill, the boiling house, and the curing house that was necessary on every sugar plantation, go some way towards explaining the limited advance of sugar production into the Lesser Antilles. The more weighty disincentive, however, would have been the close location of these islands to the Caribbean settlements of other European powers. Their consequent exposure to attack by European rivals made them altogether more risky places for the high capital investment that sugar required than Barbados and Jamaica. Instead of the monocrop production of sugar that came to characterize Barbados after the 1650s, the Lesser Antilles persisted with more mixed economic activity that included the production of indigo, tobacco, ginger, cotton, domesticated cattle, and fish as well as sugar.

The reorganization of economic activity in Barbados and the Leewards is generally referred to as 'The Sugar Revolution'. The cultivation of sugar cane on large plantations on Barbados steadily displaced the growing of tobacco, cotton, and indigo on smaller farms, and supplemented these activities on the other islands. Sugar planting, with its larger labour- and capital-equipment needs, stimulated demand for bigger units. Landowners enclosed on tenants, and small freeholders were bought out, and pushed off. As a result, land prices escalated and there was a rapid reduction in the size and output of non-sugar producers. In most islands some small-scale farmers continued to occupy prime lands, maintaining a cash-crop culture on the margins of plantations. But small farmers found it difficult to compete as tobacco and cotton prices fell and their operations often proved unprofitable. By the 1680s the 'sugar islands' had lost their reputation as hospitable places for propertyless European migrants, while the progress of sugar cultivation on the island of Barbados effected a more rapid and more total manipulation of the natural environment than occurred anywhere else in the Atlantic that came under English control during the course of the seventeenth century. [. . .]

Englishmen had entered the Caribbean rather tentatively, but by the beginning of the eighteenth century they were confident and in effective control. The first enemy, the Spanish, had early become reconciled to the English presence in the Lesser Antilles, and later surrendered Jamaica without much of a fight. The Dutch had consolidated a considerable commercial empire after 1621, when their West India Company was formed and 'parented' pioneering English settlers. By 1650 the English, now feeling secure and ambitious, bit the Dutch hand that had fed them, first in 1652–54 and then in a series of trade wars in 1665–67 and 1672–74. Turning to the French, the English assaulted settlers and harassed traders in the wars of 1666–67 and 1689–97. Finally, in 1713 they succeeded in crushing French resistance and captured the prime prize: the *Asiento* contract to supply slaves to the Spanish colonies.

The English developed the islands as major economies in their own right, but also as part of the Atlantic trading system. The islands were valuable to the economic viability of the mainland colonies, with commodity trade between the two being of vital importance to English merchants. Trading connections in rum, foodstuffs, construction materials, sugar, and slaves contributed to the perception of the islands as the 'hub of Empire'. While English merchants had established global trading networks, the West Indies were central to their operations, and were represented as such in the first depictions of what came to be called 'the English [after 1707, the British] empire in America'. The islands absorbed more slaves over time, and produced a more lucrative commodity than any other region in colonial America. The Atlantic system, as an economic order centred on the slave-plantation complex, was therefore revolutionized in the seventeenth century. The sugar estate was the hub of this network in the movements of labour, capital, and management. The West Indies thus occupied a special place in the development of what ultimately became the British Empire.

[*Source:* Hilary McD. Beckles, 'The "Hub of Empire": The Caribbean and Britain in the Seventeenth Century', in Nicholas Canny, ed., *The Origins of Empire: British Overseas Enterprise to the Close of the Seventeenth Century*, vol. 1 of *The Oxford History of the British Empire* (Oxford and New York: Oxford University Press, 1998), hereafter *OHBE*, pp. 218–23, 225–6, 239.]

## 6    Richard Hakluyt

Richard Hakluyt published this *Discourse of Western Planting* in 1585, before the defeat of the Spanish Armada, when England was concerned about the power of the Spanish empire. The *Discourse* also promoted the economic and cultural advantages of colonization.

1. That this westerne discoverie will be greately for thinlargement of the gospell of Christe whereunto the Princes of the refourmed relligion are chefely bounde amongest whome her ma$^{tie}$ ys principall.

2. That all other englishe Trades are growen beggerly or daungerous, especially in all the kinge of Spayne his Domynions, where our men are dryven to flinge their Bibles and prayer Bokes into the sea, and to forsweare and renownce their relligion and conscience and consequently theyr obedience to her Ma$^{tie}$.

3. That this westerne voyadge will yelde unto us all the commodities of Europe, Affrica, and Asia, as far as wee were wonte to travell, and supply the wantes of all our decayed trades.

4. That this enterprise will be for the manifolde imploymente of nombers of idle men, and for bredinge of many sufficient, and for utterance of the greate quantitie of the commodities of our Realme.

5. That this voyage will be a great bridle to the Indies of the kinge of Spaine and a meane that wee may arreste at our pleasure for the space of tenne weekes or three monethes every yere, one or twoo hundred saile of his subjectes shippes at the fysshinge in Newfounde lande.

6. That the mischefe that the Indian Threasure wrought in time of Charles the later Emperor father to the Spanishe kinge, is to be had in consideration of the Q. moste excellent Ma^tie, leaste the contynuall commynge of the like threasure from thence to his sonne, worke the unrecoverable annoye of this Realme, whereof already wee have had very dangerous experience.

7. What speciall meanes may bringe kinge Phillippe from his high Throne, and make him equal to the Princes his neighbours, wherew^th all is shewed his weakenes in the west Indies.

8. That the lymites of the kinge of Spaines domynions in the west Indies be nothinge so large as ys generally ymagined and surmised, neither those partes w^ch he holdeth be of any such forces as ys falsly geven oute by the popishe Clergye and others his fautors, to terrifie the Princes of the Relligion and to abuse and blynde them.

9. The Names of the riche Townes lienge alonge the sea coaste on the northe side from the equinoctialle of the mayne lande of America under the kinge of Spayne.

10. A Brefe declaracion of the chefe Ilands in the Bay of Mexico beinge under the kinge of Spaine, w^th their havens and fortes, and what commodities they yelde.

11. That the Spaniardes have executed most outragious and more then Turkishe cruelties in all the west Indies, whereby they are every where there, become moste odious unto them, whoe woulde joyne w^th us or any other moste willingly to shake of their moste intollerable yoke, and have begonne to doo it already in dyvers places where they were Lordes heretofore.

12. That the passage in this voyadge is easie and shorte, that it cutteth not nere the trade of any other mightie Princes, nor nere their Contries, that it is to be perfourmed at all tymes of the yere, and nedeth but one kinde of winde, that Ireland beinge full of goodd havens on the southe and west sides, is the nerest parte of Europe to yt, w^ch by this trade shall be in more securitie, and the sooner drawen to more Civilitie.

13. That hereby the Revenewes and customes of her Ma^tie bothe outwardes and inwardes shall mightely be inlarged by the toll, excises, and other dueties w^ch w^thoute oppression may be raised.

14. That this action will be greately for thincrease, mayneteynaunce and safetie of our Navye, and especially of greate shippinge w^ch is the strengthe of our Realme, and for the supportation of all those occupacious that depende upon the same.

15. That spedie plantinge in divers fitt places is moste necessarie upon

these luckye westerne discoveries for feare of the daunger of being prevented by other nations w<sup>ch</sup> have the like intentions, w<sup>th</sup> the order thereof and other reasons therw<sup>th</sup>all alleaged.

16. Meanes to kepe this enterprise from overthrowe and the enterprisers from shame and dishono<sup>r</sup>.

17. That by these Colonies the Northwest passage to Cathaio and China may easely quickly and perfectly be searched oute aswell by river and over-lande, as by sea, for proofe whereof here are quoted and alleaged divers rare Testymonies oute of the three volumes of voyadges gathered by Ramusius and other grave authors.

18. That the Queene of Englande title to all the west Indies, or at the leaste to as moche as is from Floride to the Circle articke, is more lawfull and righte then the Spaniardes or any other Christian Princes.

19. An aunswer to the Bull of the Donacion of all the west Indies graunted to the kinges of Spaine by Pope Alexander the vi<sup>th</sup> whoe was himselfe a Spaniarde borne.

20. A brefe collection of certaine reasons to induce her Ma<sup>tie</sup> and the state to take in hande the westerne voyadge and the planting there.

21. A note of some thinges to be prepared for the voyadge w<sup>ch</sup> is sett downe rather to drawe the takers of the voyadge in hande to the presente consideracion then for any other reason for that divers thinges require preparation longe before the voyadge, w<sup>th</sup>oute w<sup>ch</sup> the voyadge is maymed.

[*Source*: Roberta Marx Delson, ed., *Readings in Caribbean History and Economics: An Introduction to the Region* (New York, London and Paris: Gordon and Breach Science Publishers, 1981), pp. 33–6.]

---

## 7  Ralph Lane

Ralph Lane, one of the colonists from the first (abortive) attempt to establish an English settlement in Virginia, reported to Richard Hakluyt on 3 September 1585 with an optimistic account of the colony's prospects.

In the meane while you shall understand that since sir Richard Greenvils departure from us, as also before, we have discovered the maine to bee the goodliest soile under the cope of heaven, so abounding with sweete trees, that bring such sundry rich and most pleasant gummes, grapes of such greatnes, yet wild, as France, Spaine nor Italy hath no greater, so many sortes of Apothecarie drugs, such severall kindes of flaxe, and one kind like silke, the same gathered of a grasse, as common there as grasse is here. And now within these few dayes we have found here a Guinie wheate, whose eare yeeldeth corne for bread, 400. upon one eare, and the Cane maketh very good and perfect suger, also Terra Samia, otherwise Terra sigillata. Besides that, it is the goodliest and most pleasing territorie of the world (for the soile is of an huge unknowen greatnesse, and very wel peopled and towned, though savagelie) and the climate so wholesome, that we have not had one sicke, since we touched land here. To conclude, if Virginia had but Horses and Kine in some reasonable proportion, I dare assure my selfe being inhabited with English, no realme in Christendome were comparable to it. For this alreadie we find, that what commodities soever Spaine, France, Italy, or the East parts do yeeld unto us in wines of all sortes, in oiles, in flaxe, in rosens, pitch, frankenscence, currans, sugers, & such like, these parts do abound with y$^e$ growth of them all, but being Savages that possesse the land, they know no use of the same. And sundry other rich commodities, that no parts of the world, be they West or East Indies, have, here we finde great abundance of. The people naturally most curteous, & very desirous to have clothes, but especially of course cloth rather than silke, course canvas they also like wel of, but copper carieth y$^e$ price of all, so it be made red. Thus good Master Hakluyt and master H. I have joyned you both in one letter of remembrance, as two that I love dearely well, and commending me most hartily to you both, I commit you to y$^e$ tuition of the almighty.

[*Source*: Quinn, *New American World*, vol. 3, p. 293.]

## 8    Captain John Smith

Captain John Smith explored what is now the north-eastern coast of the United States, and promoted the area as a site for English colonization; it was he who named this region 'New England'. As in Hakluyt's writings, rivalry with Spain is a prominent theme of Smith's argument.

It would bee an historie of a large volume, to recite the adventures of the Spanyards, and Portugals, their affronts, and defeats, their dangers and miseries; which with such incomparable honour and constant resolution, so farre beyond beleefe, they have attempted and indured in their discoveries and plantations, as may well condemne us, of too much imbecillitie, sloth, and negligence: yet the Authors of those new inventions, were held as ridiculous, for a long time, as now are others, that doe but seek to imitate their unparalleled vertues. And though we see daily their mountaines of wealth (sprong from the plants of their generous indevours) yet is our sensualitie and untowardnesse such, and so great, that wee either ignorantly beleeve nothing; or so curiously contest, to prevent wee knowe not what future events; that wee either so neglect, or oppresse and discourage the present, as wee spoile all in the making, crop all in the blooming; and building upon faire sand, rather then rough rockes, judge that wee knowe not, governe that wee have not, feare that which is not; and for feare some should doe too well, force such against their willes to be idle or as ill. And who is he hath judgement, courage, and any industrie or qualitie with understanding, will leave his Countrie, his hopes at home, his certaine estate, his friends, pleasures, libertie, and the preferment sweete England doth afford to all degrees, were it not to advance his fortunes by injoying his deserts? whose prosperitie once appearing, will incourage others; but it must be cherish- || ed as a childe, till it be able to goe, and understand it selfe; and not corrected, nor oppressed above its strength, ere it knowe wherefore. A child can neither performe the office, nor deedes of a man of strength, nor indure that affliction He is able; nor can an Apprentice at the first performe the part of a Maister. And if twentie yeeres bee required to make a child a man, seven yeares limited an apprentice for his trade; if scarce an age be sufficient to make a wise man a States man; and commonly, a man dies ere he hath learned to be discreet: If perfection be so hard to be obtained, as of necessitie there must bee practice, as well as theorick: Let no man much condemne this paradox opinion, to say, that halfe seaven yeeres is scarce sufficient, for a good capacitie, to learne in these affaires, how to carrie himselfe: and who ever shall trie in these remote places the erecting of a Colony, shall finde at the ende of seaven yeares occasion enough to use all his discretion; and, in the Interim all the content, rewards, gaines, and hopes will be necessarily required, to be given to the beginning, till it bee able to creepe, to stand, and goe, yet time enough to keepe it from running, for there is no feare it will grow too fast, or ever to any thing; except libertie, profit, honor, and prosperitie there found, more binde the planters of those affaires, in devotion to effect it; then bondage, violence, tyranny, ingratitude, and such double dealing, as bindes free men to become slaves, and honest men turne knaves: which hath ever bin the ruine of the most popular || commonweales; and is verie unlikelie ever well to begin in a new.

Who seeth not what is the greatest good of the Spanyard, but these new conclusions, in searching those unknowne parts of this unknowne world? By which meanes hee dives even into the verie secrets of all his Neighbours, and the most part of the world: and when the Portugale and Spanyard had found the East and West Indies; how many did condemn themselves, that did not accept of that honest offer of Noble Columbus? who, upon our neglect, brought them to it, perswading our selves the world had no such places as they had found; and yet ever since wee finde, they still (from time to time) have found new Lands, new Nations, and trades, and still daily dooe finde both in Asia, Africa, Terra incognita, and America; so that there is neither Soldier nor Mechanick, from the Lord to the begger, but those parts afforde them all imploiment; and discharge their Native soile, of so many thousands of all sorts, that else, by their sloth, pride, and imperfections, would long ere this have troubled their neighbours, or have eaten the pride of Spaine it selfe.

Now he knowes little, that knowes not England may well spare many more people then Spaine, and is as well able to furnish them with all manner of necessaries. And seeing, for all they have, they cease not still to search for that they have not, and know not; It is strange we should be so dull, as not maintaine that which wee have, and pursue that wee knowe. Surely I am sure many would taste it ill, to bee abridged of the titles and honours of their predecessors: when if but truely they would judge themselves; looke how inferior they are to their noble vertues, so much they are unworthy of their honours and livings: which never were ordained for showes and shadowes, to maintaine idlenesse and vice; but to make them more able to abound in honor, by heroycall deeds of action, judgement, pietie, and vertue. What was it, They would not doe both in purse and person, for the good of the Commonwealth? which might move them presently to set out their spare kindred in these generous designes. Religion, above all things, should move us (especially the Clergie) if wee were religious, to shewe our faith by our workes; in converting those poore salvages, to the knowledge of God, seeing what paines the Spanyards take to bring them to their adulterated faith. Honor might move the Gentrie, the valiant, and industrious; and the hope and assurance of wealth, all; if wee were that we would seeme, and be accounted. Or be we so far inferior to other nations, or our spirits so far dejected, from our auncient predecessors, or our mindes so upon spoile, piracie, and such villany, as to serve the Portugall, Spanyard, Dutch, French, or Turke (as to the cost of Europe, too many dooe) rather then our God, our King, our Country, and our selves? excusing our idlenesse, and our base complaints, by want of imploiment; when heere is such choise of all sorts, and for all degrees, in the plan- || ting and discovering these North parts of America.

[*Source*: John Smith, 'A Description of New England', in *Travels and works of Captain John Smith: President of Virginia and Admiral of New England 1580–1631* (Edinburgh: J. Grant, 1910), pp. 348–50.]

## 1.2 SLAVERY

**B**y the time England entered the African slave trade, the European bond-age of non-European peoples was already well established. The Portuguese were the first to establish extensive trading contacts with west Africa, where slavery was already practised and could be encouraged in order to meet the growing European demand for colonial labour. This coincided with the decline, through disease and extermination, of the indigenous peoples of the West Indies, and the discovery in the Americas that the indigenous population could not always provide an adequate labour supply.

Another crucial factor was the introduction of sugar cultivation to British (and other) colonies in the West Indies. Plantations had experimented with a variety of crops, but by the later seventeenth century sugar was becoming dominant in the Caribbean: in Jamaica in 1671 there were 57 sugar plantations; by 1684 there were 246. Sugar was a highly labour-intensive crop, and such was the demand for slaves that several nations launched expeditions to compete with Portuguese slavers on the west African coast; the voyages of John Hawkins (Extract 9) were the first such ventures by England. Portugal was in a dominant position at first, and its coastal bases, or 'factories', sprang up to co-ordinate the collection of slaves from the interior and their sale to European traders. After ousting Portugal from many of these bases during the sixteenth century, the Dutch and their African allies expanded the trade, and England began establishing factories of its own. The first of these was established at Cormantine in 1651; a larger outpost, Cape Coast Castle, was won from the Dutch in 1664, a year after the Company of Royal Adventurers into Africa (later refounded as the Royal African Company) had its charter renewed and expanded. The new charter included the first specific mention of slaving as an aspect of England's African operations. Captains employed by the Company would sail for west Africa with a supply of trade goods, exchange these with an African leader for slaves at one of the factories (Extract 10), and take the notorious 'Middle Passage' across the Atlantic to the West Indies or North America, where the slaves would be sold in exchange for tobacco or sugar for the return trip to England (Extract 11). Many English sailors died of disease or malnutrition on these voyages, but mortality was much higher among the slaves confined below decks (Extract 12). The Royal African Company took 89,200 slaves from the African coast between 1673 and 1689 of which about 20,000 died during the crossing.

In the seventeenth century, the Company sold the vast majority of its slaves to Jamaica and Barbados; only later would the North American colonies begin to import slaves in large numbers, and they tended to buy them from the West Indies rather than directly from Africa (Extract 13). In the meantime, Britain supplemented its own colonial trade through obtaining a monopoly, the *asiento*, on trade with Spain's colonies, including the slave trade. These economic developments were directly related to an increasing identification of Africans with slavery; this, in turn, prompted Europeans to justify themselves by referring to alleged African social and cultural inferiority. England's white colonists had once made a distinction between Christian and non-Christian Africans: only non-Christians could be enslaved. But by the mid-seventeenth century, blacks in the colonies had to prove their status as free men (Extract 14). This was an important shift in identity. Hakluyt had envisioned free settlements invigorated by hardworking and patriotic Protestantism, but by the end of the seventeenth century, many of Britain's colonies were already deeply divided by race (Extract 15).

## 9   Sir John Hawkins

Sir John Hawkins, later treasurer of the Royal Navy, sailed to west Africa in 1562 on the first documented English slaving expedition. Note that his potential market was the Spanish West Indies.

Master John Hawkins having made divers voyages to the Iles of the Canaries, and there by his good and upright dealing being growen in love and favour with the people, informed himselfe amongst them by diligent inquisition, of the state of the West India, whereof hee had received some knowledge by the instructions of his father, but increased the same by the advertisements and reports of that people. And being amongst other particulars assured, that Negros were very good marchandise in Hispaniola, and that store of Negros might easily bee had upon the coast of Guinea, resolved with himselfe to make triall thereof, and communicated that devise with his worshipfull friendes of London: namely with Sir Lionell Ducket, Sir Thomas Lodge, M. Gunson his father in law, sir William Winter, M. Bromfield, and others. All which persons liked so well of his intention, that they became liberall contributors and adventurers in the action. For which purpose there were three good ships immediately provided: The one called the *Salomon* of the burthern of 120. tunne, wherein M. Hawkins himselfe went as Generall: The second the *Swallow* of 100. tunnes, wherein went for Captaine M. Thomas Hampton: and the third the *Jonas* a barke of 40. tunnes, wherein the Master supplied the Captaines roome: in which small fleete M. Hawkins tooke with him not above 100. men for feare of sicknesse and other inconveniences, whereunto men in long voyages are commonly subject.

With this companie he put off and departed from the coast of England in the moneth of October 1562. and in his course touched first at Teneriffe, where hee received friendly intertainment. From thence he passed to Sierra Leona, upon the coast of Guinea, which place by the people of the countrey is called Tagarin, where he stayed some good time, and got into his posses-sion, partly by the sworde, and partly by other meanes, to the number of 300 Negros at the least, besides other merchandises which that countrey yeeldeth. With this praye hee sayled over the Ocean sea unto the Iland of Hispaniola, and arrived first at the port of Isabella: and there hee had reasonable utter-ance of his English commodities, as also of some part of his Negros, trusting the Spaniards no further, then that by his owne strength he was able still to master them. From the port of Isabella he went to Puerto de Plata, where he made like sales, standing alwaies upon his guard: from thence also hee sayled to Monte Christi another port on the North side of Hispaniola, and the last place of his touching, where he had peaceable traffique, and made vent of the whole number of his Negros: for which he received in those 3 places by way of exchange such quantitie of merchandise, that hee did not onely lade his owne 3 shippes with hides, ginger, sugars, and some quantities of pearles, but he fraighted also two other hulkes with hides and the like commodities, which hee sent into Spaine. And thus leaving the Iland, he returned and disemboqued, passing out by the Ilands of the Caycos, without further entring into the bay of Mexico, in this his first voyage to the West India. And so with prosperous successe and much gaine to himselfe and the aforesayde adventurers, he came home, and arrived in the moneth of September 1563.

[*Source*: Elizabeth Donnan, ed., *Documents Illustrative of the History of the Slave Trade to America* (New York. Octagon Books, 1965), vol. 1, pp. 45–7.]

## 10    Olaudah Equiano

Olaudah Equiano was one of the most famous black abolitionists of the eighteenth century. Having purchased his freedom after a lifetime of slavery, he published his memoirs in 1789 in hopes of drawing attention to slavery's evils. This account of his capture in west Africa shows the combination of indigenous and European factors involved; Equiano had several African masters before being sold to a British trader on the coast.

My father, besides many slaves, had a numerous family of which seven lived to grow up, including myself and a sister who was the only daughter. As I was the youngest of the sons I became, of course, the greatest favourite with my mother and was always with her; and she used to take particular pains to form my mind. I was trained up from my earliest years in the art of war, my daily exercise was shooting and throwing javelins, and my mother adorned me with emblems after the manner of our greatest warriors. In this way I grew up till I was turned the age of 11, when an end was put to my happiness in the following manner. Generally when the grown people in the neighbourhood were gone far in the fields to labour, the children assembled together in some of the neighbours' premises to play, and commonly some of us used to get up a tree to look out for any assailant or kidnapper that might come upon us, for they sometimes took those opportunities of our parents' absence to attack and carry off as many as they could seize. One day, as I was watching at the top of a tree in our yard, I saw one of those people come into the yard of our next neighbour but one to kidnap, there being many stout young people in it. Immediately on this I gave the alarm of the rogue and he was surrounded by the stoutest of them, who entangled him with cords so that he could not escape till some of the grown people came and secured him. But alas! ere long it was my fate to be thus attacked and to be carried off when none of the grown people were nigh. One day, when all our people were gone out to their works as usual and only I and my dear sister were left to mind the house, two men and a woman got over our walls, and in a moment seized us both, and without giving us time to cry out or make resistance they stopped our mouths and ran off with us into the nearest wood. [. . .]

The first object which saluted my eyes when I arrived on the coast was the sea, and a slave ship which was then riding at anchor and waiting for its cargo. These filled me with astonishment, which was soon converted into terror when I was carried on board. I was immediately handled and tossed up to see if I were sound by some of the crew, and I was now persuaded that I had gotten into a world of bad spirits and that they were going to kill me. Their complexions too differing so much from ours, their long hair and the language they spoke (which was very different from any I had ever heard) united to confirm me in this belief. Indeed such were the horrors of my views and fears at the moment that, if ten thousand worlds had been my own, I would have freely parted with them all to have exchanged my condition with that of the meanest slave in my own country. [. . .]

When I recovered a little I found some black people about me, who I believed were some of those who had brought me on board and had been receiving their pay; they talked to me in order to cheer me, but all in vain. I asked them if we were not to be eaten by those white men with horrible looks, red faces, and loose hair. They told me I was not, and one of the crew brought me a small portion of spirituous liquor in a wine glass, but being afraid of him I would not take it out of his hand. One of the blacks therefore took it from him and gave it to me, and I took a little down my palate, which instead of reviving me, as they thought it would, threw me into the greatest consternation at the strange feeling it produced, having never tasted such any liquor before. Soon after this the blacks who brought me on board went off, and left me abandoned to despair.

[*Source*: Paul Edwards, ed., *The Interesting Narrative of the Life of Olaudah Equiano, or Gustavus Vassa the African, Written by Himself* (London: Heinemann, 1967; first publ. 1789), pp. 15–16, 25–6.]

## 11 Invoice, Royal African Company ship *Swallow*

Table 1 overleaf is an invoice for goods to be traded for slaves from the Royal African Company's ship *Swallow* in 1679. Table 2 shows to whom the slaves were sold at the British West Indian colony of Nevis.

[*Source*: Donnan, *Documents of the Slave Trade*, vol. 1, pp. 256–7.]

## 12 Captain Phillips

The disease and suffering experienced by slaves aboard the *Hannibal* in 1693–4 were typical of such voyages. Note Captain Phillips' observations about the transfer of smallpox from the immune Europeans to the non-immune Africans.

Having bought my compliment of 700 slaves, *viz.* 480 men and 220 women, and finish'd all my business at Whidaw, I took my leave of the old king, and his cappasheirs, and parted, with many affectionate expressions on both sides, being forced to promise him that I would return again the next year, with several things he desired me to bring him from England; and having sign'd bills of lading to Mr. Peirson, for the negroes aboard, I set sail the 27th of July in the morning, accompany'd with the *East-India Merchant*, who had bought 650 slaves, for the island of St. Thomas, with the wind at W.S.W. [. . .]

Having completed all my business ashore in fourteen days that I lay here, yesterday in the afternoon I came off with a resolution to go to sea. Accordingly about six in the evening we got up our anchors, and set sail for Barbadoes, being forc'd to leave the *East-India merchant* behind, who could not get ready to sail in nine or ten days; which time I could not afford to stay, in respect to the mortality of my negroes, of which two or three died every day, also the small quantity of provisions I had to serve for my passage to Barbadoes . . .

*Table 1: Invoice of goods laden abord the 'Swallow' Capt. Evan Seys Commander for accompt of the Royall African Company of England Bound for New Callabar their to take in 220 Negroes And consigned unto said Capt. Evans Seys.*

|  |  |  |  | l. | s. | d. |
|---|---|---|---|---|---|---|
| Iron 2000 barrs wt. 25 tons at £15:5:0 |  |  |  | 381 | 5 | 0 |

Copper barrs. 5 chests

| | barrs | cwt. | qr. | lb. | | | |
|---|---|---|---|---|---|---|---|
| 44 | 200 | 2 : 0 : 06 | | | | | |
| 45 | 200 | 2 : 0 : 07 | | | | | |
| 46 | 200 | 2 : 0 : 06 | | | | | |
| 47 | 200 | 2 : 0 : 08 | | | | | |
| 48 | 200 | 2 : 0 : 07 | | | | | |
| | 1,000 | 10 : 0 : 06 at £6:3 | | | 65 | 07 | 1 |

Cowries, 3 barrells

| | cwt. | qr. | lb. | | | | | |
|---|---|---|---|---|---|---|---|---|
| 130 | 2 : 0 : 14 | Tare | 20 | | | | | |
| 131 | 2 : 0 : 04 | ,, | 19 | | | | | |
| 160 | 2 : 0 : 21 | ,, | 22 | | | | | |
| | 6 : 1 : 11 | ,, | 61 | | | | | |
| tare | 2 : 05 | | | | | | | |
| | 5 : 3 : 06 net at £3:7 | | | | 19 | 08 | 10 | |

Beeds, 1 chest

29 { 26 bunches white wt. 76 at 13 *d*. £4:02:4
    { 17 ditto christall wt. 48 ,, 15 *d*. £3:00: —         7   02   4

Manelloes 1 bunch black

| | cwt. | qr. | lb. | | | | |
|---|---|---|---|---|---|---|---|
| 5,000 rings wt. 1 : 2 : 25 net at £3:5 | | | | 5 | 11 | 11 | |
| For customs and all other charges | | | | 7 | 00 | 6 | |

1 box 2 scarlett laced coates } for presents £5:08:5
    2 white hatts laced    }        £2:05          7   13   5

Negroe Provitions

| | | | |
|---|---|---|---|
| 1 hhd. and 1 Runlett qt. 76 galls. fine spiritts | £11:10 | | |
| 6 hhds. beanes | 7:05 | | |
| 1 hhd. flour | 3:10 | | |
| 1 hhd. pease | 1:15 | | |
| 2 puncheons and 1 barrell | 6:10 | | |
| 1 barrell qt. 1 tobacoe | 2:19 | | |
| 1 barrell qt. 7 gross pipes | 0:09 | | |
| 1 hhd. vineger | 3:05 | | |
| 1 hhd. salt | 1:02 | | |
| 22½ stock fish at £6-3 and 1 puncheon beef, £3:5 | 9:00 | 47 | 13 | 0 |

                                                     539   2   2

Table 2: *Accompt of Sales of 71 Negroes Sould out of the Shipp 'Swallow' Capt. Evan Says Commander For Accompt of the Royall African Company of England.*

| | MEN | WOMEN | BOYS | GIRLS | LBS. OF SUGAR |
|---|---|---|---|---|---|
| Sir W. Stapleton at 3000 | 4 | | | 1 | 15,000 |
| George Cruff | S | | 1 | | 2,800 |
| James Walker | 4 | 3 | 1 | | 26,600 |
| Moses Leavermore 2 at 3800, 1 at 2800 | 1 | 1 | 1 | | 10,400 |
| Edward Parsons | 3 | 1 | 2 | | 19,200 |
| John Pope | S | 0 | 1 | | 2,800 |
| John Chapman | | 0 | 1 | | 2,000 |
| John Williams | 1 | | | | 3,500 |
| Thomas Weekes | 1 | 1 | 1 | | 9,500 |
| John Syms | 2 | 1 | | | 10,800 |
| Humphrey Heywood | | 2 | | | 7,000 |
| Nath. Harris | 3 | 1 | | | 14,000 |
| Joseph Crisp | 2 | 7 | | 2 | 32,200 |
| David Howels | 2 | 2 | | | 13,800 |
| Walter Clarke | 1 | | | | 3,500 |
| Hurly Welch | | 1 | | | 3,500 |
| John Wighall | 1 | | | | 3,200 |
| Hurly Jackman | | 1 | | | 1,700 |
| Robert Ellin | | 1 | | | 1,200 |
| Phillip Sullivan | 1 | | | | 1,080 |
| John Jeffries | 1 | | | | 3,500 |
| Edward Harris | | 1 | | | 3,000 |
| Capt. Evan Seys | 1 | | | | 2,560 |
| William Meede | 3 | 6 | | | 8,181 |
| | 31 | 29 | 7 | 4 | 199,721 |

Allowed by the Ma'r for the overplus of his Fr'tt etc.       736

200,457

| | |
|---|---|
| Men | 31 |
| Women | 29 |
| Boys | 7 |
| Girls | 4 |
| — | 36 |
| 71 | — |
| 3 | 104 commission |
| 16 | 6 freight |
| — | — |
| 91 | 10 |
| 6 dead | |
| — | |
| 97 | |

Note that the 2 boys and 2 girls marked with S the mast'r pretended was his and his mates for which noe Fr'tt or commiss'n was allowed him.

WILL'M FREEMAN
HENRY CARPENTER
ROBERT HELMES

We spent in our passage from St. Thomas to Barbadoes two months eleven days, from the 25th of August to the 4th of November following: in which time there happen'd much sickness and mortality among my poor men and negroes, that of the first we buried 14, and of the last 320, which was a great detriment to our voyage, the royal African company losing ten pounds by every slave that died, and the owners of the ship ten pounds ten shillings, being the freight agreed on to be paid them by the charter-party for every negroe deliver'd alive ashore to the African company's agents at Barbadoes; whereby the loss in all amounted to near 6560 pounds sterling. The distemper which my men as well as the blacks mostly die of, was the white flux, which was so violent and inveterate, that no medicine would in the least check it; so that when any of our men were seiz'd with it, we esteem'd him a dead man, as he generally proved. I cannot imagine what should cause it in them so suddenly, they being free from it till about a week after we left the island of St. Thomas. And next to the malignity of the climate, I can attribute it to nothing else but the unpurg'd black sugar, and raw unwholesome rum they bought there, of which they drank in punch to great excess, and which it was not in my power to hinder, having chastis'd several of them, and flung overboard what rum and sugar I could find [. . .] . . .

The negroes are so incident to the small-pox, that few ships that carry them escape without it, and sometimes it makes vast havock and destruction among them: but tho' we had 100 at a time sick of it, and that it went thro' the ship, yet we lost not above a dozen by it. All the assistance we gave the diseased was only as much water as they desir'd to drink, and some palm-oil to anoint their sores, and they would generally recover without any other helps but what kind nature gave them.

One thing is very surprizing in this distemper among the blacks, that tho' it immediately infects those of their own colour, yet it will never seize a white man; for I had several white men and boys aboard that had never had that distemper, and were constantly among the blacks that were sick of it, yet none of them in the least catch'd it, tho' it be the very same malady in its effects, as well as symptoms, among the blacks, as among us in England, beginning with the pain in the head, back, shivering, vomiting, fever, etc. But what the small-pox spar'd, the flux swept off, to our great regret, after all our pains and care to give them their messes in due order and season, keeping their lodgings as clean and sweet as possible, and enduring so much misery and stench so long among a parcel of creatures nastier than swine; and after all our expectations to be defeated by their mortality. No gold-finders can endure so much noi-some slavery as they do who carry negroes; for those have some respite and satisfaction, but we endure twice the misery; and yet by their mortality our voyages are ruin'd, and we pine and fret our selves to death, to think that we should undergo so much misery, and take so much pains to so little purpose.

[*Source*: Donnan, *Documents of the Slave Trade*, vol. 1, pp. 408–10.]

## 13 Peter Kalm

> Swedish botanist Peter Kalm toured the American colonies and published an account of his travels in 1770 including the following observations about the labour supply in Pennsylvania. After discussing free and indentured labour, he turns to a third type: slaves.

The *negroes* or blacks constitute the third kind. They are in a manner slaves; for when a negro is once bought, he is the purchaser's servant as long as he lives, unless he gives him to another, or sets him free. However, it is not in the power of the master to kill his negro for a fault, but he must leave it to the magistrates to proceed according to the laws. Formerly the negroes were brought over from Africa, and bought by almost everyone who could afford it, the Quakers alone being an exception. But these are no longer so particular and now they have as many negroes as other people. However, many people cannot conquer the idea of its being contrary to the laws of Christianity to keep slaves. There are likewise several free negroes in town, who have been lucky enough to get a very zealous Quaker for their master, and who gave them their liberty after they had faithfully served him for a time.

At present they seldom bring over any negroes to the English colonies, for those which were formerly brought thither have multiplied rapidly. In regard to their marriage they proceed as follows: in case you have not only male but likewise female negroes, they may intermarry, and then the children are all your slaves. But if you possess a male negro only and he has an inclination to marry a female belonging to a different master, you do not hinder your negro in so delicate a point, but it is of no advantage to you, for the children belong to the master of the female. It is therefore practically advantageous to have negro women. A man who kills his negro is, legally, punishable by death, but there is no instance here of a white man ever having been executed for this crime. A few years ago it happened that a master killed his slave. His friends and even the magistrates secretly advised him to make his escape, as otherwise they could not avoid taking him prisoner, and then he would be condemned to die according to the laws of the country, without any hopes of being saved. This leniency was granted toward him, that the negroes might not have the satisfaction of seeing a master executed for killing his slave. This would lead them to all sorts of dangerous designs against their masters and to value themselves too much.

The negroes were formerly brought from Africa, as I mentioned before, but now this seldom happens, for they are bought in the West Indies, or American Islands, whither they were originally brought from their own country. It has been found that in transporting the negroes from Africa directly to these northern countries, they have not such good health as when they come gradually, by shorter stages, and are first carried from Africa to the West Indies, and from thence to North America. [. . .]

The price of negroes differs according to their age, health and ability. A full grown negro costs from forty pounds to a hundred of Pennsylvania currency. There are even examples that a gentleman has paid a hundred pounds for a black slave at Philadelphia and refused to sell him again for the same money. A negro boy or girl of two or three years old, can hardly be gotten for less than eight or fourteen pounds in Pennsylvania money. Not only the Quakers but also several Christians of other denominations some-times set their negroes at liberty. This is done in the following manner: when a gentleman has a faithful negro who has done him great services, he some-times declares him independent at his own death. This is however very expensive; for they are obliged to make a provision for the negro thus set at liberty, to afford him subsistence when he is grown old, that he may not be driven by necessity to wicked actions, or that he may fall a charge to any-body, for these free negroes become very lazy and indolent afterwards. But the children which the free negro has begot during his servitude are all slaves, though their father be free. On the other hand, those negro children which are born after the parent was freed are free. The negroes in the North American colonies are treated more mildly and fed better than those in the West Indies. They have as good food as the rest of the servants, and they possess equal advantages in all things, except their being obliged to serve their whole lifetime and get no other wages than what their master's good-ness allows them. They are likewise clad at their master's expense. On the contrary, in the West Indies, and especially in the Spanish Islands, they are treated very cruelly; therefore no threats make more impression upon a negro here than that of sending him over to the West Indies, in case he will not reform. It has likewise been frequently found by experience that when you show too much kindness to these negroes, they grow so obstinate that they will no longer do anything but of their own accord. Therefore a strict discipline is very necessary, if their master expects to be satisfied with their services.

[*Source*: Willie Lee Rose, ed., *A Documentary History of Slavery in North America* (New York, London and Toronto: Oxford University Press, 1976), pp. 47–9.]

## 14 Fernando

Fernando, a black servant in a Virginian household, found that his claim to be an indentured servant, and his identity as a Christian, were insufficient to prevent him from being declared a slave by the county court in 1667. Unfortunately the record of his appeal to the General Court was destroyed.

Whereas Fernando a Negro sued Capt. [John] Warner for his freedome pretending hee was a Christian and had been severall yeares in England and therefore ought to serve noe longer than any other servant that came out of England accordinge to the custome of the Country and alsoe Presented severall papers in Portugell or some other language which the Court could not understand which he alledged were papers From severall Governors where hee had lived a freeman and where hee was home. Wherefore the Court could find noe Cause wherefore he should be free but Judge him a slave for his life time, From which Judgement the said Negro hath appealled to the fifth day of the next Generall Court.

[*Source*: Warren M. Billings, ed., *The Old Dominion in the Seventeenth Century: A Documentary History of Virginia, 1606–1689* (Chapel Hill: University of North Carolina Press, 1975), p. 169.]

## 15 Winthrop D. Jordan

In scanning the problem of *why* Negroes were enslaved in America, certain constant elements in a complex situation can be readily, if roughly, identified. *It may be taken as given* that there would have been no enslavement without economic need, that is, without persistent demand for labor in underpopulated colonies. Of crucial importance, too, was the fact that Africans in America were relatively powerless. In themselves, however, these two elements will not explain the enslavement of Indians and Negroes. The pressing need in America was labor, and Irish, Scottish, and English servants were available. Most of them would have been helpless to ward off outright enslavement if their masters had thought themselves privileged to enslave them. As a group, though, masters did not think themselves so empowered. Only with Indians and Africans did Englishmen attempt so radical a deprivation of liberty—which brings the matter abruptly to the most difficult and imponderable question of all: what was it about Indians and Negroes which set them apart from Englishmen, which rendered them *different*, which made them special candidates for degradation?

To ask such questions is to inquire into the *content* of English attitudes, and unfortunately there is little evidence with which to build an answer. It may be said, however, that the heathen condition of Negroes seemed of considerable importance to English settlers in America—more so than to English voyagers upon the coasts of Africa—and that heathenism was associated in some settlers' minds with the condition of slavery. Clearly, though, this is not to say that English colonists enslaved Africans merely because of religious difference. In the early years, the English settlers most frequently contrasted themselves with Negroes by the term *Christian*, though they also sometimes described themselves as *English*. Yet the concept embodied by the term *Christian* embraced so much more meaning than was contained in specific doctrinal affirmations that it is scarcely possible to assume on this basis that Englishmen set Negroes apart because they were heathen. The historical experience of the English people in the sixteenth century had made for fusion of religion and nationality; the qualities of being English and Christian had become so inseparably blended that it seemed perfectly consistent to the Virginia Assembly in 1670 to declare that 'noe negroe or Indian though baptised and enjoyned their owne Freedome shall be capable of any such purchase of christians, but yet not debarred from buying any of their owne nation.'

From the first, then, the concept embedded in the term *Christian* seems to have conveyed much of the idea and feeling of *we* as against *they*: to be Christian was to be civilized rather than barbarous, English rather than African, white rather than black. The term *Christian* itself proved to have remarkable elasticity, for by the end of the seventeenth century it was being used to define a kind of slavery which had altogether lost any connection with explicit religious difference. In the Virginia code of 1705, for example, the term sounded much more like a definition of race than of religion: 'And for a further christian care and usage of all christian servants, *Be it also enacted* . . . That no negroes, mulattos, or Indians, although christians, or Jews, Moors, Mahometans, or other infidels, shall, at any time, purchase any christian servant, nor any other, except of their own complexion, or such as are declared slaves by this act.' By this time 'Christianity' had somehow become intimately and explicitly linked with 'complexion.' The 1705 statute declared 'That all servants imported and brought into this country, by sea or land, who were not christians in their native country . . . shall be accounted and be slaves, and as such be here bought and sold notwithstanding a conversion to christianity afterwards.' As late as 1753 the Virginia slave code anachronistically defined slavery in terms of religion when everyone knew that slavery had for generations been based on the racial and not the religious difference.

It is worth making still closer scrutiny of the terminology which Englishmen employed when referring both to themselves and to the two peoples they enslaved, for this terminology affords the best single means of probing the content of their sense of difference. The terms *Indian* and *Negro* were both borrowed from the Hispanic languages, the one originally deriving from (mistaken) geographical locality and the other from human complexion. When referring to the Indians the English colonists either used that proper name or called them *savages*, a term which reflected primarily their view of Indians as uncivilized. In significant contrast, the colonists referred to *negroes*, and by the eighteenth century to *blacks* and to *Africans*, but almost never to African *heathens* or *pagans* or *savages*. Most suggestive of all, there seems to have been something of a shift during the seventeenth century in the terminology which Englishmen in the colonies applied to themselves. From the initially most common term *Christian*, at mid-century there was a marked shift toward the terms *English* and *free*. After about 1680, taking the colonies as a whole, a new term of self-identification appeared—*white*.

So far as the weight of analysis may be imposed upon such terms, diminishing reliance upon *Christian* suggests a gradual muting of the specifically religious elements in the Christian-Negro distinction in favor of secular nationality. Negroes were, in 1667, 'not in all respects to be admitted to a full fruition of the exemptions and impunities of the English.' As time went on, as some Negroes became assimilated to the English colonial culture, as more 'raw Africans' arrived, and as increasing numbers of non-English Europeans were attracted to the colonies, English colonists turned increasingly to what they saw as the striking physiognomic difference. In Maryland a revised law prohibiting miscegenation (1692) retained *white* and *English* but dropped the term *Christian*—a symptomatic modification. By the end of the seventeenth century dark complexion had become an independent rationale for enslavement: in 1709 Samuel Sewall noted in his diary that a 'Spaniard' had petitioned the Massachusetts Council for freedom but that 'Capt. Teat alledg'd that all of that Color were Slaves.' Here was a barrier between 'we' and 'they' which was visible and permanent: the black man could not become a white man. Not, at least, as yet.

What had occurred was not a change in the justification of slavery from religion to race. No such justifications were made. There seems to have been, within the unarticulated concept of the Negro as a different sort of person, a subtle but highly significant shift in emphasis. A perception of Negro heathenism remained through the eighteenth and into the nineteenth and even the twentieth century, and an awareness, at very least, of the African's different appearance was present from the beginning. The shift was an alteration in emphasis within a single concept of difference rather than a development of a novel conceptualization. Throughout the colonies the

terms *Christian*, *free*, *English*, and *white* were for many years employed indis-
criminately as synonyms. A Maryland law of 1681 used all four terms in one
short paragraph.

Whatever the limitations of terminology as an index to thought and feeling, it seems likely that the English colonists' initial sense of difference from
Africans was founded not on a single characteristic but on a cluster of qualities which, taken as a whole, seemed to set the Negro apart. Virtually every
quality in 'the Negro' invited pejorative feelings. What may have been his
two most striking characteristics, his heathenism and his appearance, were
probably prerequisite to his complete debasement. His heathenism alone
could not have led to permanent enslavement since conversion easily wiped
out that failing. If his appearance, his racial characteristics, meant nothing to
the English settler, it is difficult to see how slavery based on race ever
emerged, how the concept of complexion as the mark of slavery ever entered
the colonists' minds. Even if the English colonists were most unfavorably
struck by the Negro's color, though, blackness itself did not urge the complete debasement of slavery. Other cultural qualities—the strangeness of his
language, gestures, eating habits, and so on—certainly must have contributed
to the English colonists' sense that he was very different, perhaps disturbingly
so. In Africa these qualities had for Englishmen added up to *savagery*; they
were major components in that sense of *difference* which provided the mental
margin absolutely requisite for placing the European on the deck of the slave
ship and the African in the hold.

The available evidence (what little there is) suggests that for Englishmen
settling in America, the specific religious difference was initially of greater
importance than color, certainly of much greater relative importance than for
the Englishmen who confronted Negroes in their African homeland. Perhaps
Englishmen in Virginia, tanning seasonally under a hot sun and in almost
daily contact with tawny Indians, found the Negro's color less arresting than
they might have in other circumstances. Perhaps, too, these first Virginians
sensed how inadequately they had reconstructed the institutions and practices of Christian piety in the wilderness; they would perhaps appear less as
failures to themselves in this respect if compared to persons who as Christians were *totally* defective. Perhaps, though, the Jamestown settlers were told
in 1619 by the Dutch shipmaster that these 'negars' were heathens and could
be treated as such. We do not know. The available data will not bear all the
weight that the really crucial questions impose.

Of course once the cycle of degradation was fully under way, once slavery
and racial discrimination were completely linked together, once the engine of
oppression was in full operation, then there is no need to plead lack of
knowledge. By the end of the seventeenth century in all the colonies of the
English empire there was chattel racial slavery of a kind which would have
seemed familiar to men living in the nineteenth century. No Elizabethan

Englishman would have found it familiar, though certain strands of thought and feeling in Elizabethan England had intertwined with reports about the Spanish and Portuguese to engender a willingness on the part of English settlers in the New World to treat some men as suitable for private exploitation. During the seventeenth century New World conditions had enlarged this predisposition, so much so that English colonials of the eighteenth century were faced with full-blown slavery—something they thought of not as an institution but as a host of ever present problems, dangers, and opportunities.

[*Source*: Winthrop D. Jordan, *The White Man's Burden: Historical Origins of Racism in the United States* (New York: Oxford University Press, 1974), pp. 50–4.]

## 1.3  COLONIAL IDENTITIES

In the West Indies and North America, England 'planted' colonies of settlement that were very different from its trading outposts in Asia or Africa. In those parts of the world, indigenous trade networks allowed the English to operate from small, coastal communities; tropical diseases also discouraged settlement. England's trans-Atlantic colonies, on the other hand, were plantations based on the Irish model: in need of land and labour. This inevitably raised the question of indigenous sovereignty and land rights, divisive issues which remain unresolved today in most former colonies. In the seventeenth century, English law claimed that indigenous sovereignty needed to be respected only if the inhabitants were Christian; if not, England (or any other European country) could conquer the country and overthrow its native laws after conquest (Extract 16). Non-Christian native people could be identified as alien and lawless: a powerful justification for dispossession.

In the early stages of colonization, indigenous populations could force English traders or settlers to deal with them as sovereign peoples, but tensions increased as immigration grew. England's first permanent settlement in North America, Virginia, came into conflict with local Amerindian groups as soon as its settlers began occupying too much land. Virginia's economy began revolving around tobacco (Extract 17), grown to free English smokers from dependency on Spanish supplies, and tobacco quickly exhausted the soil. As the colonial population grew and its trade prospered, the need for land increased and there was open conflict with Amerindians from 1622 onward (Extract 18). The Virginian government's attempts to conciliate Native leaders angered many settlers, particularly after tobacco prices began to fall. The indigenous population, already considered 'lawless' in English legal theory, now became identified as a hindrance to the expansion and prosperity of Virginia and the other colonies. Sooner or later, a similar process characterized Native/settler relations throughout North America.

Not all of the early English settlements were founded entirely as commercial operations, though all of them depended on trade for their livelihood. A theocratic colony was established in 1620 at Plymouth (Extract 19) and other colonies of conscience were founded later. Although these colonies identified themselves as exclusive communities dedicated to God, historian David Cressy warns against too much generalization about 'Puritans' (Extract 20). Of the *Mayflower* colonists at Plymouth there were only 35 members of an identifiable Puritan congregation, with 67 other migrants ranging from entrepreneurs to vagrants. Contemporary records also show a diversity of nationalities and motives among settlers to all the early American colonies (Extract 21). But the majority of the colonists were of British

ancestry, and often identified themselves collectively as 'English' to distinguish themselves from other Europeans, Amerindians, or Africans.

English governments were keen to centralize the control of colonial matters, and charters were sometimes revoked in favour of direct rule. In 1624
Virginia became the first settlement to be governed directly by the Crown,
and a 'Dominion of New England' was created in the years 1685–8. This
centralising tendency, along with 'Laws of Trade' like the Navigation Act, produced deep resentment and forms part of the background to the American
Revolution. But the West Indies were also affected by it; Barbados and
Jamaica grew particularly restive. During the English Civil War and the
Cromwell Republic, the Barbadians sought (in vain) to obtain free trade and
self-government after identifying these as key aspects of an English identity
(Extract 22). Colonists there, and in Jamaica, complained that England was
treating them as it would the Irish, exploiting them economically and deny-
ing them political rights. But increasing sugar production meant dependence
on African slave labour, and this meant that West Indian communities were
already diverging from the 'ancient English' identity they sought to uphold.

## 16    Calvin's Case

Calvin's Case, heard in 1608 by the court of King's Bench in England,
was a landmark judgment defining issues of English jurisdiction over
persons born outside England (Calvin was a Scot claiming property in
England). The judgment also declared that the law of Christian
nations should prevail if they conquered non-Christian territory, and
this theory would stand until overturned by the Chief Justice, Lord
Mansfield, in the eighteenth century (Extract 42).

An alien is a subject that is born out of the allegiance of the king and under
that of another, and can have no real or personal action concerning land . . .

[Every man was either a subject born, or (temporarily or perpetually) an
alien friend or similarly an alien enemy. All pagans were perpetual enemies to
Christendom in law and the law presumed they will not be converted.]

And upon this ground there is a diversity between a conquest of a kingdom of a Christian king, and the conquest of a kingdom of an infidel; for if a
king come to a Christian kingdom by conquest, seeing that he hath 'vitae et
necis potestatem', he may at his pleasure alter and change the laws of that
kingdom, but until he doth make an alteration of those laws, the ancient laws
of that kingdom remain. But if a Christian king should conquer a kingdom
of an infidel, and bring them under his subjection, there ipso facto the laws of
the infidel are abrogated; for that they be not only against Christianity, but

against the law of God and of nature, contained in the Decalogue: and in that case, until certain laws be established amongst them, the king by himself, and such judges as he shall appoint, shall judge them and their causes according to natural equity, in such sort as kings in ancient time did with their king-doms, before any certain municipal laws were given, as before hath been said.

[*Source*: Madden and Fieldhouse, *Empire of the Bretaignes*, p. 36.]

## 17   Ralphe Hamor

Ralphe Hamor, author of *A True Discourse of the Present Estate of Virginia* (1614) paid tribute to John Rolfe's successful experiments in tobacco growing. Tobacco would become the foundation of the colonial economy before prices declined later in the century, but Rolfe is probably better known for his marriage to the high-ranking Amerindian woman Pocahontas.

The valuable commoditie of Tobacco of such esteeme in England (if there were nothing else) which every man may plant, and with the least part of his labour, tend and cure will returne him both cloathes and other necessaries. For the goodnesse whereof, answerable to *west-Indie Trinidado* or *Cracus* [i.e., Caraccas] (admit there hath no such bin returned) let no man doubt. Into the discourse wherof, since I am obviously entred, I may not forget the gentle-man, worthie of much commendations, which first tooke the pains to make triall thereof, his name Mr. John *Rolfe*, *Anno Domini* 1612. partly for the love he hath a long time borne unto it, and partly to raise commodity to the adven-turers, in whose behalfe I witnesse and vouchsafe to holde my testimony in beleefe, that during the time of his aboade there, which draweth neere upon six yeeres, no man hath laboured to his power, by good example there and worthy incouragement into England by his letters, then he hath done . . .

[*Source*: Billings, *The Old Dominion in the Seventeenth Century*, p. 36.]

## 18   Edward Waterhouse

Initial relations between settlers and Amerindians in Virginia were mainly peaceful, and descriptions of them were usually condescend-ing but sympathetic. A major change came in 1622 when 347 men, women, and children were killed during a surprise attack on the British settlement. The negative language of this account by Edward

Waterhouse would dominate colonial accounts of Native people after the massacre.

The last *May* there came Letters from *Sir Francis Wiat* [i.e., Wyatt] *Governor* in VIRGINIA, which did advertise that when in *November* last [1621] he arived in VIRGINIA, and entred upon his Government, he found the Country setled in a peace (as all men there thought) sure and unviolable, not onely because it was solemnly ratified and sworne, and at the request of the Native King stamped in Brasse, and fixed to one of his Oakes of note, but as being advantagious to both parts; to the Savages as the weaker, under which they were safely sheltred and defended; to us, as being the easiest way then thought to pursue and advance our projects of buildings, plantings, and effecting their conversion by peaceable and fayre meanes. And such was the conceit of firme peace and amitie, as that there was seldome or never a sword worne, and a Peece seldomer, except for a Deere or Fowle. By which assurance of securitie, the Plantations of particular Adventurers and Planters were placed scatteringly and straglingly as a choyce veyne of rich ground invited them, and the further from neighbors held the better. The houses generally set open to the Savages, who were alwaies friendly entertained at the tables of the English, and commonly lodged in their bed-chambers. The old planters (as they thought now come to reape the benefit of their long travels) placed with wonderfull content upon their private dividents, and the planting of particular Hundreds and Colonies pursued with an hopefull alacrity, all our projects (saith he) in a faire way, and their familarity with the Natives, seeming to open a faire gate for their conversion to Christianitie. [. . .]

[O]n the Friday morning (the fatal day) the 22 of *March*, as also in the evening, as in other dayes before, they came unarmed into our houses, without Bowes or arrowes, or other weapons, with Deere, Turkies, Fish, Furres, and other provisions, to sell, and trucke with us, for glasse, beades, and other trifles: yea in some places, sate downe at Breakfast with our people at their tables, whom immediately with their owne tooles and weapons, eyther laid downe, or standing in their houses, they basely and barbarously murthered, not sparing eyther age or sexe, man, woman or childe; so sodaine in their cruell execution, that few or none discerned the weapon or blow that brought them to destruction. In which manner they also slew many of our people then at their severall workes and husbandries in the fields, and without their houses, some in planting Corne and Tobacco, some in gardening, some in making Bricke, building, sawing, and other kindes of husbandry, they well knowing in what places and quarters each of our men were, in regard of their daily familiarity, and resort to us for trading and other negotiations, which the more willingly was by us continued and cherished for the desire we had of effecting that great master-peece of workes, their conversion. And by this meanes that fatall Friday morning, there fell under the

bloudy and barbarous hands of that perfidious and inhumane people, contrary to all lawes of God and men, of Nature and Nations, three hundred
forty seven men, women, and children, most by their owne weapons; and not
being content with taking away life alone, they fell after againe upon the
dead, making as well as they could, a fresh murder, defacing, dragging, and
mangling the dead carkasses into many pieces, and carrying some parts away
in derision, with base and bruitish triumph.

[*Source*: Billings, *The Old Dominion in the Seventeenth Century*, pp. 220–1.]

## 19  William Bradford

The 'Mayflower Compact' described the hopes of settlers who
had left the port of Plymouth in 1620 on the ship *Mayflower*; this
account was written by a *Mayflower* passenger, William Bradford.
They founded a new settlement near Cape Cod under the nominal
protection of the Virginia Company.

I . . . begin with a combination made by them before they came ashore; being
the first foundation of their government in this place. Occasioned partly by
the discontented and mutinous speeches that some of the strangers amongst
them had let fall from them in the ship: 'That when they came ashore they
would use their own liberty, for none had power to command them, the
patent they had being for Virginia, and not for New England which belonged
to another government with which the Virginia Company had nothing to do.'
And partly that such an act by them done, this their condition considered,
might be as firm as any patent and in some respects more sure.

The form was as followeth: In the name of God, Amen. We, whose names
are underwritten, the loyal subjects of our dread Sovereign Lord King James,
by the grace of God of Great Britain, France and Ireland, King, Defender of
the Faith, [*& c*]. Haveing undertaken for the glorie of God and the advancement of the Christian faith and honour of our King and countrie, a voyage to
plant the first colonie in the northerneparts of Virginia, doe, by these presents, solemnly and mutually in the presence of God and one of another,
covenant and combine ourselves togeather unto a civill body politick for our
better ordering and preservation and furtherance of the ends aforesaid; and
by vertue hereof to enact, constitute and frame such just and equall lawes,
ordinances, acts, constitutions and offices from time to time as shall be
thought most meete and convenient for the generall good of the colonie,
unto which we promise all due submission and obedience. In witness
whereof we have hereunder subscribed our names at Cape Codd, the 11th of

November in the year of the raigne of our Soveraigne Lord King James of England, France and Ireland the eighteenth and of Scotland the fiftie fourth.

[*Source*: Madden and Fieldhouse, *Empire of the Bretaignes*, vol. 1, pp. 278–9.]

<br>

## 20    David Cressy

Whereas religion drove Puritan ministers and lay enthusiasts to Massachusetts (providing, at least, the most explicit, the most accessible and certainly the most venerable interpretation of their actions), secular factors and even casual incidents guided the recruitment of others. It is not necessary to agree with John Smith, Henry Dade or Philip Vincent to recognize the private and secular components of migrant motivation. Disastrous harvests (especially in 1629 and 1630), a collapsing cloth industry, rising poor rates, popular disturbances and the recurrence of plague (in 1625 and in 1636–7) no doubt contributed to the feeling that these were dark days. Although there is no evidence to link these conditions directly with emigration, the cumulative miseries of Charles I's reign (no worse than those of Elizabeth's reign) may have inclined some people to move when the opportunity of New England beckoned.

Unaware that there would be either Plymouth separatists or Massachusetts Puritans, Captain Smith had written, 'I am not so simple to think that ever any other motive than wealth will ever erect there a commonwealth, or draw company from their ease and humours at home, to stay in New England.' Time proved Smith wrong in this regard, but he also appreciated the intangible benefits that might attract people to America. Smith sketched these advantages in one of the earliest evocations of the American dream.

Here are no hard landlords to rack us with high rents or extorting fines, nor tedious pleas in law to consume us with their many years disputations for justice, no multitudes to occasion such impediments to good orders as in popular states . . . Here every man may be master of his own labour and land . . . and if he have nothing but his hands he may set up his trade, and by industry grow rich.

Religious and secular migrants alike might be affected by these views, which would compound rather than displace their other motivations.

Disreputable motives brought more than a handful of migrants to New England. Some were escaping prosecution, debts or vengeance at home, and accepted emigration as the lesser evil. In 1639 the inhabitants of Newbury, Massachusetts, pondered the problem of Walter Allen, a newcomer from Bury in England who had allegedly fathered two bastard children in the last

five years. Allen 'came over hither because he could no longer abide in Bury',
but he found life no sweeter in New England. Other newcomers in the 1630s
included Robert Wright, a sometime linen draper in Newgate market and
after that a brewer on the Bankside and on Thames Street; he was allegedly
wanted in London 'for clipping the king's coin'. Another was 'Sir' Christopher Gardiner, adventurer, fraud and bigamist, who had abandoned two
wives in London and was living in Massachusetts with Mary Groves, 'a
known harlot'. One more was William Schooler, a vintner of London, who
not only had 'been a common adulterer, as he himself did confess', but
'had wounded a man in duel'. Schooler had fled first to the Low Countries
before migrating to New England, abandoning his wife on the other side
of the ocean. Despite the godly environment he ran further into crime in
Massachusetts, and was hung for raping and killing a maidservant.

Such notorious migrants were moved by neither religious purity nor economic opportunities. They demonstrate that New England, despite its
religious orientation, played host to a diverse people with motives of all sorts.
The migrant stream was mixed in its morality and circumstances, as Bradford
and Winthrop well recognized. My intention in drawing attention to these
disreputable colonists is not to substitute the secular for the religious, rene-
gades for saints, but rather to illustrate the variety of personality and experience in a community that is still often presented as homogeneous, upright
and dour. The Schoolers and Allens were no more typical than the Winthrops
and Mathers. [. . .]

Unsuitable and unregenerate settlers repeatedly violated the godly calm of
New England. Problems of profanity, drunkenness and tobacco-puffing
stained the winter of 1632. 'Wicked persons', not only servants, brought
down upon themselves the 'evident judgement of God' as well as the outrage
of the Puritan leaders. The early court records teem with incidents of
irreligion, drunkenness, profanity, lechery and worse. In one of the most
extreme cases, George Spencer was charged at New Haven with 'prophane,
atheistical carriage, in unfaithfulness and stubbornness to his master, a course
of notorious lying, filthiness, scoffing at the ordinances, ways and people of
God', culminating in his bestiality with a pig. An anxious committee of
ministers asked him 'whether he did use to pray to God. He answered, he had
not since he came to New England, which was between four or five years
ago'. Spencer admitted that he had scoffed at the Lord's day, calling it Lady's
day, but denied all the rest. However, he could not gainsay the record of his
bad character, or the evidence of a monstrous piglet, to which he allegedly
showed a telling paternal resemblance. George Spencer was executed at New
Haven in April 1642.

The battle saw victories as well as defeats, which may explain how New
England developed as a Puritan society despite the flaws and exceptions in the
'Puritan migration'. Conceiving the settlement in religious terms, the leaders

constantly struggled to bring their population into conformity with their ideals. The colonies were organized and controlled by the godly party, who once they were in power began to make their own rules. Puritan magistrates and Puritan ministers dominated social and political life. The Puritan alliance between court house and pulpit created a religious culture unparalleled in the English-speaking world. Secular migrants, who had chosen New England for social or economic reasons, found themselves at a distinct disadvantage if they did not join a church. Church membership, a visible symbol of belonging, paved the way for social, political and economic success. A conversion experience, and the ability to testify to it, became the prerequisite for admission to a church. Under the pressure of powerful Puritan preaching, in an environment dominated by Puritan magistrates, it would not be surprising if a sizeable proportion of the settlers experienced 'conversion'. Whether shallow and hypocritical or deeply passionate, Puritanism grew more readily in the environment of New England than back home.

[*Source*: David Cressy, *Coming Over: migration and communication between England and New England in the seventeenth century* (Cambridge and New York: Cambridge University Press, 1987), pp. 98–100, 101–2.]

## 21  John Oldmixon

This account by John Oldmixon contains the first published use of the phrase 'British empire', but it also describes the multicultural population of the American colonies.

We have seen enough of the Measures of the Persecutors in *England*, to know what Reason the first Planters had to settle here. Great Numbers of them, at all Hazards, transported themselves to *New-England*, to enjoy there the Liberty of Conscience refused them at home, which multiply'd this Colony much faster than any other . . . That the additional Increase has been equal within these 30 Years, to any the like Increase after the Toleration in *England*, will not be question'd by those that are acquainted with the Transportations thither, I mean not criminal, especially from *Ireland*, from whence it is said 10000 *Scotch Presbyterian* families have transported themselves to *America* since the Death of King *William* . . .

At a little Distance from *Philadelphia* is a pleasant Hill, very well wooded, on the Banks of the *Schuylkill*, called *Fair Mount*. *Wioco*, half a Mile from the Town, is a *Swedish* settlement, where the people of that Nation have a *Meeting-house* for Religion . . . the *Swedes* have another Meeting-house at *Tenecum* . . .

*Mountjoy* is a Manor that belonged to a Daughter of Mr. *Pen* [founder of the colony of Pennsylvania] . . . 'Tis inhabited by *English* and *Dutch*, and is the next Place for Bigness and Trade to *Philadelphia*, containing now between 5 and 600 Houses well built. Here live and thrive many Merchants and Tradesmen; the Church has a large Conregation, mostly *Welsh*.

[In Virginia] Besides the *English* Inhabitants, there are now several hundreds of *French* Refugee Families, who were sent thither by King *William*. These Refugees had a very rich Territory assigned them, twenty Miles above the Falls of *James* River, on the South-side of the River, formerly the Habitation of a War-like Nation of the *Indians*, call'd the *Monachans*; and the Town where the *French* Protestants settled, is call'd the *Monachan* Town.

[In Georgia in 1735] *Tomochichi* and other *Indian* Chiefs re-embark'd on board the *Prince of Wales*, commanded by Capt. *George Dunbar*, who was bound for *Georgia* with a Transport of *Salzburghers*, *German* Protestant Refugees . . . In the beginning of *January* following, about 150 *Scotch* Highlanders arrived at *Savanah*, designed to settle on the Frontiers of that Colony next the *Spaniards*.

[*Source*: John Oldmixon, *The British Empire in America* (London: Brotherton *et al.*, 1710; orig. publ. 1708), vol. i, pp. 226, 227, 302, 303, 427, 534, 535.]

## 22    Petition of the Barbadian assembly to Parliament

The Barbadian Assembly petitioned Parliament on 11 December 1659 (at the end of the Richard Cromwell's regime in Britain) to obtain more control over their own economy and government.

1. That wee may enjoy and have confirmed . . . by a law etc: antient libertys, priviledges, customes, constitutions, and laws, fixed in the primary settlement and wherein our . . . interests are onley dependant, together with, our articles made on the Rendition of this Island, to this authority according to a letter from the Council of State, dated the 14th of October 1652.

2. That no offices whatsoever relating to this Island (except the Governor) may be imposed on us, by gift, grant, patent, commission, or otherwise, howsoever, but bee and remaine to the government here, to bee nominated, chosen and dependant thereon, . . .

3. That in case wee may be thought worthy to be obliged by any principal freedome you may reasonably condiscend unto: that we may have a confirmation of liberty here (by a law, or your commission) for the representative body of the people to choose a governor out of the freeholders of this island and one out of every parish to bee his assistant and joyne with him in the execuson of government: and in case of the governor's death to elect a new

governor and councill, or if otherwise that the representation of this island may bee expressed and nominated in your commission to be a parte of the government joyntly and equall with the governor.

4. That in regard the generality of the people here, are poore and the necessary defense of this place is required in this remote parte, might exhaust the very uttmost gaine and profit of theire labours, that all fines, mulcts, amercements, fellons goods, forfeitures, whatsoever may bee and remaine to the disposing of the government here, for publicke and necessary use to the defense of the place.

5. That in regard wee are English Men, and should bee reputed to the Comonwealth, no other than as one of her ports (as of Bristol to London) that all customs on goods exported, from England to this colony may bee taken of, and that wee may bee enfranchised with all trade generally, equal with any people of England. And that no monopolizes, companyes, societyes, or other incroachments bee continued or permitted in any trade relating to this island, but in regard the necessary existence of this place requires some more than ordinary freedome in order to its production. That all nations in amity may bring us provisions, servants, horses, slaves, mares, or cattle, whether of theire growth, or not, and that the Act made in October 1650 restrayning all manner of trade with us bee repealed.

6. That forasmuch as great prejudices have befallen us, by the presumptiousnes and refractiousness of comanders of men or war, victuallers, and other vessells, that it bee confirmed to us that all comanders of shipps arriving here may conform to the lawes and customes of this place, by entry of bonds, not to carry of any debitors, servants, slaves, but submit to the government here, on seizures or other business here transacted, as finally as at any port of England.

7. That in all treatyes forraingne, this colony may bee comprized . . . that all advantages may attain to us as a good member of the Comonwealth, equal with other the partes, or people of the English nation.

8. That the government here, by governor, councel and assembly may have power to make such necessary lawes for the good of this place and people, as intrench not, or repugne any penal law, or statutes of this nation, or derogatory to this authority and government of the Comon wealth of England.

9. That wee may have power to appoint a little mint-house within this island for coyning of money, equal with New England and Jamaica, and to raise all forreigne money.

10. That you will be pleased to accept these our desires as singly fought for, in reference to the best and real good of this island, and not out of any disrespect to the person of our governor, at present confirmed over us, whose integrity to your Honours hath beene ever very eminent amongst us.

[Source: Madden and Fieldhouse, Empire of the Bretaignes, vol. 1, pp. 375–6.]

# Chapter 2

## The Eighteenth Century

### INTRODUCTION

**B**y the end of the seventeenth century British influence had grown, especially in the Atlantic world, at the expense of Spain and the Netherlands.
Britain's growing share of the slave trade, and its expanding plantations,
generated wealth and led to substantial growth in Britain's port towns: British
shipping in the Atlantic and Indian oceans would increase sixfold between the
end of the seventeenth century and 1815. Increasing numbers of Britons (and
other Europeans) were emigrating to the American colonies, which reached a
population of 2,300,000 by 1770. But in other parts of the world Britain's role
was still similar, even inferior, to that of other countries. Many European
nations had trading outposts on the African coasts, and the Dutch had a
settlement colony in south Africa. Britain was only one of several countries
with trading privileges in India, and in south-east Asia the Dutch were still
dominant. Spanish and Portuguese colonies stretched across south, central,
and southern North America while Spain's galleons crossed the Pacific to the
Philippines. It was by no means obvious that Britain would create a substantial empire in any of these these areas, but during the eighteenth century
several successful wars would combine with scientific and commercial
exploration to create imperial opportunities for Britain.

The Netherlands had been Britain's primary maritime rival during the later
seventeenth century, but this changed after the accession in 1688 of Mary II
and her Dutch husband William of Orange. By the turn of the century
British foreign policy had France in its sights and a series of wars with France
and its allies would erode their empires in Britain's favour. The Treaty of
Utrecht (1713) transferred Acadia (now Nova Scotia in Canada) and the vast
fur trading area of Hudson Bay to the British along with Newfoundland, the
cornerstone of the lucrative north Atlantic cod fishery. Utrecht also gave
Britain the exclusive right to provide slaves and other goods for Spain's colonies. At the end of the Seven Years War in 1763, the Treaty of Paris transferred Cape Breton Island (now in Nova Scotia) and Quebec to the British
along with some West Indian islands, the Spanish colonies in Florida, and the
vast area between the Appalachian mountains and the Mississippi River.

Shortly afterwards the British empire experienced an enormous military
defeat: the loss of the American colonies after their declaration of independ-

ence in 1776. Some historians have described this as the end of the first British empire, and the beginning of a new one based on eastern trade. Today, historians see more continuity than disruption between these two periods. It is true that the Americans and their allies defeated the British in the American colonies themselves, but it is also true that Britain defeated those allies, especially France, in other parts of the world. Like the Seven Years War, the American War of Independence became global in scope, with the empires of Britain, France, the Netherlands, and Spain all drawn into the conflict. In this wider arena Britain won territorial gains in India as well as trade concessions from the Dutch in south-east Asia. Even in the Atlantic world the British recovered dominance; trade with the new United States quickly exceeded pre-independence levels. In the Pacific, Britain successfully challenged Spain over trading rights on the north-west coast of North America in 1789. And colonies of settlement were never abandoned. To the west of Quebec a new colony, Upper Canada, was created to accommodate an influx of Loyalists and other migrants from the United States. Britain also established a settlement for freed slaves and black Loyalists at Sierra Leone in west Africa in 1787, and a penal colony on the east coast of Australia in 1788. The Canadian and Australian settlements soon expanded and additional colonies would be founded across their respective continents in the nineteenth century.

In the meantime, Britain's trading operations in India had become a substantial empire of military and political power. All of Britain's imperial wars involved a complex network of alliances, including indigenous peoples, and in India the role of local politics was crucial. The military genius of Robert Clive, commander of the East India Company's army in the 1750s, was an important factor in the massive expansion of EIC territory during the eighteenth century. Clive's alliances with Indian princes within the declining Mughal empire, and his successful defeat of French-allied Indian forces, gave him an Indian political identity as well as a British commercial one. When the Mughal emperor gave him the *diwani*, or civil government, of the vast and wealthy territory of Bengal in 1765, Clive and the EIC became Indian rulers. The implications for Britain's future role in India were vast: no longer simply a trading company, the EIC presented Britain with a new (and not necessarily welcome) set of political responsibilities in south Asia.

At the end of the eighteenth century Britain was again at war with France, and by the time of Napoleon's final defeat in 1815 Britain had gained yet more imperial territory in the West Indies and south Africa (see Map 2). The Cape Colony (later South Africa), along with increased trading rights in south-east Asia, were gains from the Dutch which would become bases for further expansion in both regions.

## 2.1 NEW HORIZONS

**B**ritain's Crown-dominated protectionist trading system always had its critics, but in the eighteenth century a more vigorous debate began about the economics of empire. Many believed that free trade should replace the old, monopolistic system. Some traders had always been willing to defy the regulations, and now their cause was taken up at the highest intellectual and political level. The Scottish philosopher Adam Smith was an advocate of free trade; he also questioned the profitability of empire under the existing system. Colonies were expensive, especially when wars were fought to acquire or defend them, and Smith believed that only unrestricted global commerce would justify the expenditure. The loss of the American colonies sharpened his views considerably (Extract 23). Free trade would not be fully implemented until the nineteenth century, but from the late eighteenth century onward mercantilism came under increasing attack. Widespread exploration merged with the free trade debate to create a sense of global opportunity for a Britain beginning to be transformed by the industrial revolution.

Scientific curiosity and innovation, both characteristics of the European Enlightenment, combined with Britain's increasing maritime power. Voyages of exploration usually involved a combination of state and private interests, as when Captain James Cook and the gentleman scientist, Joseph Banks, set out for the south Pacific in 1768, or when the African Association was formed in 1788 to encourage inland exploration in west Africa (Extract 24). Sometimes these ventures led to formal colonization: the convict settlement of New South Wales in Australia was founded in 1788 partly on the recommendation of Banks (Extract 25). The Pacific was a particularly important new field of scientific and commerical endeavour, and despite the efforts of the East India Company (Extract 26) free trade quickly became predominant in the north Pacific, and between Australia and New Zealand. But Britain's zeal for exploration was not only about commerce or national prestige. The empire was also becoming an empire of knowledge where everything from coastlines and wind patterns to animals and plants was being observed, catalogued, and analysed. The process of mapping itself, now much more accurate thanks to Britain's invention of the chronometer for measuring longitude, allowed the British to perceive the globe as an integrated whole. But this empire of science was never as objective as its practitioners believed. The literary and cultural theorist Edward Said has suggested that British descriptions of the non-European world owed more to European preconceptions than to facts (Extract 27).

Britain's struggle with the Netherlands, familiar since the seventeenth century, continued when the Dutch allied themselves with France during several eighteenth-century conflicts. For the first time Britain was able to expand into the Dutch strongholds of southern Africa and south-east Asia. The Dutch Cape Colony had been founded in 1652; Britain's interest in it revolved around the superb port at Cape Town which dominated the major maritime route between India and Europe (Extract 28). The British also enhanced their presence in south-east Asia, establishing a strategic port settlement at Singapore in 1819 (Extract 29).

## 23 Adam Smith

Adam Smith described his vision of imperial economics in *An Inquiry into the Nature and Causes of the Wealth of Nations* (1776), denouncing protectionist policies and calling for free trade.

To found a great empire for the sole purpose of raising up a people of customers, may at first sight appear a project fit only for a nation of shop keepers. It is, however, a project altogether unfit for a nation of shopkeepers; but extremely fit for a nation whose government is influenced by shopkeepers. Such statesmen, and such statesmen only, are capable of fancying that they will find some advantage in employing the blood and treasure of their fellow-citizens, to found and maintain such an empire. [. . .]

The maintenance of this monopoly has hitherto been the principal, or more properly perhaps the sole end and purpose of the dominion which Great Britain assumes over her colonies. In the exclusive trade, it is supposed, consists the great advantage of provinces, which have never yet afforded either revenue or military force for the support of the civil government, or the defence of the mother country. The monopoly is the principal badge of their dependency, and it is the sole fruit which has hitherto been gathered from that dependency. Whatever expence Great Britain has hitherto laid out in maintaining this dependency, has really been laid out in order to support this monopoly. The expence of the ordinary peace establishment of the colonies amounted, before the commencement of the present disturbances, to the pay of twenty regiments of foot; to the expence of the artillery, stores, and extraordinary provisions with which it was necessary to supply them; and to the expence of a very considerable naval force which was constantly kept up, in order to guard, from the smuggling vessels of other nations, the immense coast of North America, and that of our West Indian islands. The whole expence of this peace establishment was a charge upon the revenue of Great Britain, and was, at the same time, the smallest part of what the dominion of the colonies has cost the mother country. If we would know the amount of the whole, we must add to the annual expence of this peace establishment the interest of the sums which, in consequence of her considering her colonies as provinces subject to her dominion, Great Britain has upon different occasions laid out upon their defence. We must add to it, in particular, the whole expence of the late war, and a great part of that of the war which preceded it. The late war was altogether a colony quarrel, and the whole expence of it, in whatever part of the world it may have been laid out, whether in Germany or the East Indies, ought justly to be stated to the account of the colonies. It amounted to more than ninety millions sterling, including not only the new debt which was contracted, but the two shillings in the pound additional land tax, and the sums which were every year borrowed from the sinking fund. The Spanish war which began in 1739, was principally a colony quarrel. Its principal object was to prevent the search of the colony ships which carried on a contraband trade with the Spanish main. The whole expence is, in reality, a bounty which has been given in order to support a monopoly. The pretended purpose of it was to encourage the manufactures, and to increase the commerce of Great Britain. But its real effect has been to raise the rate of mercantile profit, and to enable our merchants to turn into a branch of trade, of which the returns are more slow and distant than those of the greater part of other trades, a greater proportion of their capital than they otherwise would have done; two events which if a bounty could have prevented, it might perhaps have been very worth while to give such a bounty.

Under the present system of management, therefore, Great Britain derives nothing but loss from the dominion which she assumes over her colonies.

[*Source*: George Bennett, *The Concept of Empire: From Burke to Attlee, 1774–1947* (London: A. and C. Black, 1953), pp. 43–4, 45–7.]

## 24    The African Association: 'Plan of the Association'

The African Association was formed by a group of gentlemen who hoped to encourage the British exploration of the interior of Africa. This 'Plan of the Association', presented at its first meeting in 1788, shows the global perspective and concern for scientific prestige of the Association.

Of the objects of inquiry which engage our attention the most, there are none, perhaps, that so much excite continued curiosity, from childhood to age; none that the learned and unlearned so equally wish to investigate, as the nature and history of those parts of the world, which have not, to our knowledge, been hitherto explored. To this desire the Voyages of the late

Captain Cook have so far afforded gratification, that nothing worthy of research by Sea, the Poles themselves excepted, remains to be examined; but by Land, the objects of discovery are still so vast, as to include at least a third of the habitable surface of the earth: for much of Asia, a still larger proportion of America, and almost the whole of Africa, are unvisited and unknown.

In Asia there are few extensive districts of which we are wholly ignorant; but there are many of which we are imperfectly informed; and to our knowledge of several of these, the expected publication of the Travels of Mr. Forster, in the service of the East India Company, may bring material improvement. [. . .]

To our knowledge of America, a large and valuable addition may soon be expected; for several of the inhabitants of Canada had the spirit, about two years since, to send, at their own expense, different persons to traverse that vast continent, from the river St. Lawrence westward to the opposite ocean.

While, in this manner, the circle of our knowledge with respect to Asia and America is gradually extending itself, and advancing towards perfection, some progress has been made in the discovery of particular parts of Africa: for Dr. Sparman's Narrative has furnished important information, to which will soon be added that of Mr. Patterson, whose account of his travels and observations in the southern parts of Africa is already in the press; and if a description of the still more extended travels of Colonel Gordon, the present commander of the Dutch troops at the Cape of Good Hope, should be given to the public, the southern extremity of the African peninsula may perhaps be justly considered as explored. Mr. Bruce also, it is said, is preparing for the press an account of the knowledge which he has obtained on the eastern side of that quarter of the globe.

But notwithstanding the progress of discovery on the coasts and borders of that vast continent, the map of its interior is still but a wide extended blank, on which the geographer, on the authority of Leo Africanus, and of the Xeriff Edrissi the Nubian author, has traced, with a hesitating hand, a few names of unexplored rivers and of uncertain nations.

The course of the Niger, the places of its rise and termination, and even its existence as a separate stream, are still undetermined. Nor has our knowledge of the Senegal and Gambia rivers improved upon that of De la Brue and Moore; for though since their time half a century has elapsed, the falls of Felu on the first of these two rivers, and those of Baraconda on the last, are still the limits of discovery.

Neither have we profited by the information which we have long possessed, that even on the western coasts of Africa, the Mahometan faith is received in many extensive districts, from the tropic of cancer southward to the line. That the Arabic, which the Mussulman priests of all countries understand, furnishes an easy access to such knowledge as the western Africans are able to supply, is perfectly obvious; as it also is, that those Africans must, from the nature of their religion, possess, what the traders to the coast ascribe to them, an intercourse with Mecca. But although these circumstances apparently prove the practicability of exploring the interior parts of Africa, and would much facilitate the execution of the plan, yet no such efforts have hitherto been made. Certain however it is, that, while we continue ignorant of so large a portion of the globe, that ignorance must be considered as a degree of reproach upon the present age.

Sensible of this stigma, and desirous of rescuing the age from a charge of ignorance, which, in other respects, belongs so little to its character, a few individuals, strongly impressed with a conviction of the practicability and utility of thus enlarging the fund of human knowledge, have formed the plan of an Association for promoting the discovery of the interior parts of Africa.

[*Source*: Robin Hallett, ed., *Records of the African Association 1788–1831* (London: Thomas Nelson and Sons, 1964), pp. 42, 43–5.]

## 25    Joseph Banks

Joseph Banks was president of the Royal Society when he gave evidence before the Committee of the House of Commons on Transportation, 1 April 1779. He had travelled to Australia on Captain Cook's first voyage. Note Banks's optimism about the climate and potential profitability of the proposed new settlement.

*Joseph Banks*, Esquire, being requested, in case it should be thought expedient to establish in a colony of convicted felons in any distant part of the globe, from whence their escape might be difficult, and where, from the fertility of the soil, they might be enabled to maintain themselves, after the first year, with little or no aid from the mother country, to give his opinion what place would be most eligible for such settlement? informed your Committee *that* the place which appeared to him best adapted for such a purpose, was Botany Bay, on the coast of New Holland, in the Indian Ocean, which was about seven months voyage from England; that he apprehended there would be little probability of any opposition from the natives, as, during his stay there, in the year 1770, he saw very few, and did not think there were above fifty in all the neighbourhood, and had reason to believe the country was very thinly peopled; those he saw were naked, treacherous, and armed with lances, but extremely cowardly, and constantly retired from our people when they made the least appearance of resistance: he was in this bay in the end of April and beginning of May 1770, when the weather was mild and moderate; that the climate, he apprehended, was similar to that about Toulouse, in the south of France, [. . .] there were no beasts of prey, and he did not doubt but our oxen and sheep, if carried there, would thrive and increase; there was great plenty of fish, he took a large quantity by hauling the seine, and struck several stingrays, a kind of skate, all very large; one weighed 336 pounds. The grass was long and luxuriant, and there were some eatable vegetables, particularly a sort of wild spinage; the country was well supplied with water; there was abundance of timber and fuel, sufficient for any number of buildings, which might be found necessary. Being asked, how a colony of that nature could be subsisted in the beginning of their establishment? he answered, they must certainly be furnished, at landing, with a full year's allowance of victuals, raiment, and drink; with all kinds of tools for labouring the earth, and building houses; with black cattle, sheep, hogs, and poultry; with seeds of all kinds of European corn and pulse; with garden seeds; with arms and ammunition for their defence; and they should likewise have small boats, nets, and fishing-tackle; all of which, except arms and ammunition, might be purchased at the Cape of Good Hope; and that afterwards, with a moderate portion of industry, they might, undoubtedly, maintain themselves without any assistance from England. He recommended sending a large number of persons, two or three hundred at least; their escape would be very difficult, as the country was distant from any part of the globe inhabited by Europeans. And being asked, whether he conceived the mother country was likely to reap any benefit from a colony established in Botany Bay? he replied, if the people formed among themselves a Civil Government, they would necessarily increase, and find occasion for many European commodities; and it was not to be doubted, that a tract of land such as New Holland, which was larger than the whole of Europe, would furnish matter of advantageous return.

[*Source*: Vincent Harlow and A. F. Madden, *British Colonial Developments 1774–1834: Select Documents* (Oxford: Clarendon Press, 1953), pp. 426–8.]

## 26  Alexander Dalrymple

Alexander Dalrymple's 'Memorandum on Trade to the South Seas and the North West Coast of America', 23 February 1791. Dalrymple, an EIC official who would become Hydrographer to the Admiralty, was promoting the Company as the best agent for British commercial expansion in the Pacific.

I have heard from more than one person that it is in the contemplation of Ministers, by way, it is alleged, of profiting by the Spanish Convention, to open the trade to the South Seas, and the North West Coast of America, to all ships that may choose to proceed thither without any other restriction, than giving bond to conform to the articles of the Convention: that all such vessels shall be allowed to proceed to China, to dispose of their cargoes, and by way of inducing the East India Company to give their consent, it is proposed the amount of these cargoes shall be paid into the Company's cash for bills on England, and perhaps they may offer to bring home teas at a low freight. . . .

The obvious motive for the measure in contemplation is the extension of trade.

I will readily admit that the free trade of the South Seas would be of the utmost value to this manufacturing and commercial country. But without considering how far a smuggling trade should be encouraged, I am confident a free ingress into the South Seas, of every vessel giving bond to conform to the terms of the Convention, would not be the means to obtain that commerce, but would be the ruin of more adventures than it would enrich. [. . .]

The 2d point is the fur trade of the North West Coast of America.

Of all trades none so much requires to be under regulation as the fur trade. One of two things must take place; either the number of furs may be obtained to any extent? or the number to be obtained must be limited? In the 1st case the value at the foreign market must be greatly depreciated, by an unbounded and unregulated influx: in the other a competition must raise the value beyond measure at the place of purchase; and the adventures being without mutual communication, the number of purchasers on the coast would be either too great to obtain cargoes, or too small to take off the furs collected, which would throw the trade infallibly into the hands of the Spaniards at their settlements, or of the Americans who have already engaged in that branch of trade, and unless we profit by the advantage of our possessions in Hudson's Bay, which would secure us a shorter cut, the Americans will certainly beat us out, as they can sail so much cheaper than we; and as it is a branch of trade that does not require a great capital.

I have in the Memoir on the fur trade, already pointed out the mode of securing the fur trade to this country by the cooperation of the East India and Hudson's Bay Companies, and this plan might be made a merit of, with the Spaniards as effectually preventing disputes. I am confident everyone fully conversant with the subject will perceive that it would be ruinous to the Southern Fishery to blend fishery and commerce. . . .

I do not question that our commerce in the East may be greatly extended; and I also readily admit that it is incumbent on the Company to endeavour extending their commerce; but I contend that the Company are more competent to extend the commerce to effect, than any chance adventurers, who are deterred from prosecuting a trade if the first attempt fails, which is always most likely to happen in the ignorance of the assortment, proper for an unknown market, and of the character and disposition of the rulers; and should chance be in favour of the first adventurer the public is kept in ignorance; whereas a failure of the first attempt by the Company may prevent a like mishap, if the Company are stimulated to action by Government; for I acknowledge that corporate bodies naturally require stimulation.

[*Source*: Harlow and Madden, *British Colonial Developments*, pp. 36–8.]

## 27    Edward W. Said

On a visit to Beirut during the terrible civil war of 1975–1976 a French journalist wrote regretfully of the gutted downtown area that 'it had once seemed to belong to . . . the Orient of Chateaubriand and Nerval.' He was right about the place, of course, especially so far as a European was concerned. The Orient was almost a European invention, and had been since antiquity a place of romance, exotic beings, haunting memories and landscapes, remarkable experiences. Now it was disappearing; in a sense it had happened, its time was over. Perhaps it seemed irrelevant that Orientals themselves had something at stake in the process, that even in the time of Chateaubriand and Nerval Orientals had lived there, and that now it was they who were suffering; the main thing for the European visitor was a European representation of the Orient and its contemporary fate, both of which had a privileged communal significance for the journalist and his French readers.

Americans will not feel quite the same about the Orient, which for them is much more likely to be associated very differently with the Far East (China and Japan, mainly). Unlike the Americans, the French and the British—less so the Germans, Russians, Spanish, Portuguese, Italians, and Swiss have had a long tradition of what I shall be calling *Orientalism*, a way of coming to terms with the Orient that is based on the Orient's special place in European Western experience. The Orient is not only adjacent to Europe; it is also the place of Europe's greatest and richest and oldest colonies, the source of its civilizations and languages, its cultural contestant, and one of its deepest and most recurring images of the Other. In addition, the Orient has helped to define Europe (or the West) as its contrasting image, idea, personality, experience. Yet none of this Orient is merely imaginative. The Orient is an integral part of European *material* civilization and culture. Orientalism expresses and represents that part culturally and even ideologically as a mode of discourse with supporting institutions, vocabulary, scholarship, imagery, doctrines, even colonial bureaucracies and colonial styles. In contrast, the American understanding of the Orient will seem considerably less dense, although our recent Japanese, Korean, and Indochinese adventures ought now to be creating a more sober, more realistic 'Oriental' awareness. Moreover, the vastly expanded American political and economic role in the Near East (the Middle East) makes great claims on our understanding of that Orient.

It will be clear to the reader (and will become clearer still throughout the many pages that follow) that by Orientalism I mean several things, all of them, in my opinion, interdependent. The most readily accepted designation for Orientalism is an academic one, and indeed the label still serves in a number of academic institutions. Anyone who teaches, writes about, or researches the Orient—and this applies whether the person is an anthropologist, sociologist, historian, or philologist—either in its specific or its general aspects, is an Orientalist, and what he or she does is Orientalism. Compared with *Oriental studies* or *area studies*, it is true that the term *Orientalism* is less preferred by specialists today, both because it is too vague and general and because it connotes the high-handed executive attitude of nineteenth-century and early-twentieth-century European colonialism. Nevertheless books are written and congresses held with 'the Orient' as their main focus, with the Orientalist in his new or old guise as their main authority. The point is that even if it does not survive as it once did, Orientalism lives on academically through its doctrines and theses about the Orient and the Oriental.

Related to this academic tradition, whose fortunes, transmigrations, specializations, and transmissions are in part the subject of this study, is a more general meaning for Orientalism. Orientalism is a style of thought based upon an ontological and epistemological distinction made between 'the Orient' and (most of the time) 'the Occident.' Thus a very large mass of writers, among whom are poets, novelists, philosophers, political theorists, economists, and imperial administrators, have accepted the basic distinction between East and West as the starting point for elaborate theories, epics, novels, social descriptions, and political accounts concerning the Orient, its people, customs, 'mind,' destiny, and so on. *This* Orientalism can accommodate Aeschylus, say, and Victor Hugo, Dante and Karl Marx. A little later in this introduction I shall deal with the methodological problems one encounters in so broadly construed a 'field' as this.

The interchange between the academic and the more or less imaginative meanings of Orientalism is a constant one, and since the late eighteenth century there has been a considerable, quite disciplined—perhaps even regulated—traffic between the two. Here I come to the third meaning of Orientalism, which is something more historically and materially defined than either of the other two. Taking the late eighteenth century as a very roughly defined starting point Orientalism can be discussed and analyzed as the corporate institution for dealing with the Orient—dealing with it by making statements about it, authorizing views of it, describing it, by teaching it, settling it, ruling over it: in short, Orientalism as a Western style for dominating, restructuring, and having authority over the Orient. I have found it useful here to employ Michel Foucault's notion of a discourse, as described by him in *The Archaeology of Knowledge* and in *Discipline and Punish*, to identify Orientalism. My contention is that without examining Orientalism as a discourse one cannot possibly understand the enormously systematic discipline by which European culture was able to manage—and even produce—the Orient politically, sociologically, militarily, ideologically, scientifically, and imaginatively during the post-Enlightenment period. Moreover, so authoritative a position did Orientalism have that I believe no one writing, thinking, or acting on the Orient could do so without taking account of the limitations on thought and action imposed by Orientalism. In brief, because of Orientalism the Orient was not (and is not) a free subject of thought or action. This is not to say that Orientalism unilaterally determines what can be said about the Orient, but that it is the whole network of interests inevitably brought to bear on (and therefore always involved in) any occasion when that peculiar entity 'the Orient' is in question. How this happens is what this book tries to demonstrate. It also tries to show that European culture gained in strength and identity by setting itself off against the Orient as a sort of surrogate and even underground self.

Historically and culturally there is a quantitative as well as a qualitative difference between the Franco-British involvement in the Orient and—until the period of American ascendancy after World War II—the involvement of every other European and Atlantic power. To speak of Orientalism therefore is to speak mainly, although not exclusively, of a British and French cultural enterprise, a project whose dimensions take in such disparate realms as the imagination itself, the whole of India and the Levant, the Biblical texts and the Biblical lands, the spice trade, colonial armies and a long tradition of colonial administrators, a formidable scholarly corpus, innumerable Oriental 'experts' and 'hands', an Oriental professorate, a complex array of 'Oriental' ideas (Oriental despotism, Oriental splendor, cruelty, sensuality), many Eastern sects, philosophies, and wisdoms domesticated for local European use—the list can be extended more or less indefinitely. My point is that Orientalism derives from a particular closeness experienced between Britain and France and the Orient, which until the early nineteenth century had really meant only India and the Bible lands. From the beginning of the nineteenth century until the end of World War II France and Britain dominated the Orient and Orientalism; since World War II America has dominated the Orient, and approaches it as France and Britain once did. Out of that closeness, whose dynamic is enormously productive even if it always demonstrates the comparatively greater strength of the Occident (British, French, or American), comes the large body of texts I call Orientalist.

[*Source*: Edward W. Said, *Orientalism* (New York: Pantheon, 1978), pp. 1–4.]

**28    East India Company officials**

> East India Company officials wrote to Lord Hillsborough, Secretary of State for the Northern Department, on 25 October 1781. They explained the importance to the India trade of capturing the Cape of Good Hope from the Dutch; note their hopes that the EIC would dominate commercial activities at the Cape once it was in British hands.

But the question, my Lord, is not simply whether we shall attempt the Cape of Good Hope for the sake of conquest, or merely to distress the enemy; it involves another of the utmost consequence, namely, whether, by leaving an enemy in possession of the Cape, we shall submit to lose the Island of St. Helena; be deprived of every place of refreshment and supply for the King's and Company's homeward-bound ships; or continue liable to all those dangers which may justly be expected to our shipping from an active and enterprising enemy so near that Island; and the extreme danger they must ever be in, whilst such enemy holds the Cape of Good Hope, is so evident that the smallest attention to the route to and from India must demonstrate the proposition and render the consideration truly alarming. We know the attack of the Island has been in contemplation, and if an enemy had arrived there in time it must have been fatal to the Company's eighteen ships and perhaps to His Majesty's ships which are now so happily arrived in safety.

That the power possessing the Cape of Good Hope has the key to and from the East Indies, appears to us self-evident and unquestionable. Indeed we must consider the Cape of Good Hope as the Gibraltar of India. This circumstance, my Lord, has not been felt during the long peace subsisting between Great Britain and the States General; but the present rupture with the Dutch has totally changed the scene, and rendered the possession of the Cape of the last importance. No fleet can possibly sail to or return from India without touching at some proper place for refreshment, and, in time of war, it must be equally necessary for protection. [. . .]

The Island of St. Helena, even in time of peace, has scarcely been able to accommodate the Company's ships. During times of war with France that island has been constantly assisted from the Cape. This resource being utterly cut off, the future consequences must be so serious that we crave leave to offer it as our clear opinion, that not only the Company's possessions in India, but also the immense trade between Britain and that part of the world will be hazarded and in extreme danger, if the Dutch and French are permitted to hold possession of the Cape of Good Hope. And it is our further opinion, and however prematurely offered, we most humbly hope your Lordship will have the goodness to pardon us, if, in the warmth of our zeal for the interest of the East India Company and for the prosperity of the nation, we presume to suggest that in case of success against the Cape of Good Hope, this great national object cannot be so secured as to prevent further inconvenience and danger, if ever the Dutch are again permitted to hold exclusive possession of a place so important to our possessions in the East, to our commercial concerns in general, and consequently to the welfare of Great Britain. There is room sufficient for both nations at the Cape of Good Hope. The present crisis demonstrates to us the necessity of the East India Company being permitted to have a permanent establishment there, sufficient to enable us at all times to supply our ships and those of His Majesty with all necessary refreshment, and also in time of war to afford them the most ample protection.

[*Source*: Harlow and Madden, *British Colonial Developments*, pp. 5–7.]

## 29    Sir Stamford Raffles

Sir Stamford Raffles wrote this letter on 10 June 1819 after becoming governor of the British trading outpost on Sumatra in what is now Indonesia. On his advice the EIC would purchase the port of Singapore, a small town in those days, from the Sultan of Johore.

You will probably have to consult the map in order to ascertain from what part of the world this letter is dated . . .

I shall say nothing of the importance which I attach to the permanence of the position I have taken up at Singapore: it is a child of my own. But for my Malay studies I should hardly have known that such a place existed: not only the European, but the Indian world was also ignorant of it.

I am sure you will wish me success; and I will therefore only add that if my plans are confirmed at home, it is my intention to make this my principal residence, and to devote the remaining years of my stay in the East to the advancement of a colony which, in every way in which it can be viewed, bids fair to be one of the most important, and at the same time one of the least expensive and troublesome, which we possess. Our object is not territory, but trade; a great commercial emporium, and a *fulcrum*, whence we may extend our influence politically as circumstances may hereafter require. By taking immediate possession, we put a *negative* to the Dutch claim of exclusion, and at the same time revive the drooping confidence of our allies and friends. One free port in these seas must eventually destroy the spell of Dutch monopoly; and what *Malta* is in the West, that may *Singapore* become in the East.

[*Source*: Harlow and Madden, *British Colonial Developments*, p. 73.]

## 2.2 THE AMERICAN REVOLUTION

The British debate about free trade was of particular interest in the American colonies. The colonists were growing in number (see Map 3) and self-confidence, but were unable to trade where they wished. Colonial produce had to be shipped in British vessels, to and from British ports, and the desirable Asian trade was controlled by the British EIC. The colonists were proud of their social and political achievements in America, and resented British attempts to make them pay taxes towards the cost of their defence, since they sent no representatives to the British parliament. They worried that Britain's policy of reserving land for Amerindians would restrict the westward expansion of their settlements (Extract 30), and after 1763 many of them feared the influence of the new, French-speaking, Catholic members of the British empire in Quebec.

Britons themselves debated the economic and political status of the American colonies, especially with regard to taxation without representation (Extract 31). This was not a predicament unique to the colonies: Britain itself was not yet a democracy, and political reformers saw colonial policy as a reflection of the outdated domestic political system. Some British observers identified the American protests as typically 'English': based on traditional perceptions of English liberty, entrepreneurship, and assertiveness (Extract 32). King George III and the government, however, believed that Britain's authority in the colonies was paramount, and affirmed their right to tax and regulate them. In a review of historical theories about the American Revolution, historian John Shy concludes that the American élite became increasingly alienated by this attitude, and when Britain began taking punitive measures to restore authority, the élite was able to mobilize popular opinion in favour of a declaration of independence (Extract 33).

Colonial resentment turned into defiance, war, and the proclamation of a new nation—the United States of America—in 1776 (Extract 34). In American history the War of Independence (1775–83) is often seen, understandably, as a British–American conflict. To understand its wider significance in British imperial history, however, we have to acknowledge the range of alliances and goals that turned this colonial war into a global conflict. Even in North America the war was multinational and multiracial. Promised their freedom in return for serving with the British forces, many slaves fought against the new republic, but slaves and free blacks also fought against the British. Amerindians were also found on both sides of the conflict (Extract 35). The colonial population as a whole was also divided although most supported independence and were prepared to make any sacrifice necessary (Extract 36).

After the entry of France, Spain, and the Netherlands against Britain, the worldwide empires of these countries became involved, putting Britain under enormous pressure on a number of fronts. In North America itself, tactical errors combined with attrition to make the war effort increasingly costly and ineffective: Britain had over 50,000 troops at the height of the conflict and still could not make headway against the new republic and its allies. British politicians, sensitive to increasing public criticism, chose to surrender. But as we know, Britain could offset the loss of the American colonies against significant gains in other parts of the world. Loyalists swelled the population of the Canadian colonies; of particular interest are the black Loyalists who found themselves discriminated against in British North America (Extract 37). Many eventually chose to emigrate to the new British colony of Sierra Leone in west Africa instead.

Meanwhile, Britain's economic relationship with the United States strengthened, and by the twentieth century the Americans had become Britain's most important military allies. The American Revolution allowed the United States to pursue an ongoing relationship with Britain on its own terms, and eventually the United States would surpass its former mother country in everything from economic strength to international influence.

## 30   Matthew Smith and James Gibson

'A Remonstrance from the Pennsylvania Frontier' by Matthew Smith and James Gibson dated 13 February 1764. The petitioners identify themselves with Englishmen and English political and legal rights; they were particularly concerned about the perceived leniency of the British home government towards crimes committed by Amerindians.

We, Matthew Smith and James Gibson, in behalf of ourselves and His Majesty's faithful and loyal subjects, the inhabitants of the frontier counties of Lancaster, York, Cumberland, Berks, and Northampton, humbly beg leave to remonstrate and to lay before you the following grievances, which we submit to your wisdom for redress.

1. We apprehend that as freemen and English subjects, we have an indisputable title to the same privileges and immunities with His Majesty's other subjects who reside in the interior counties of Philadelphia, Chester, and Bucks, and therefore ought not to be excluded from an equal share with them in the very important privilege of legislation. Nevertheless, contrary to the Proprietor's Charter and the acknowledged principles of common justice and equity, our five counties are restrained from electing more than ten representatives, viz., four for Lancaster, two for York, two for Cumberland, one for Berks, and one for Northampton; while the three counties (and city)

of Philadelphia, Chester, and Bucks, elect twenty-six. This we humbly conceive is oppressive, unequal, and unjust, the cause of many of our grievances, and an infringement of our natural privileges of freedom and equality; wherefore we humbly pray that we may be no longer deprived of an equal number with the three aforesaid counties, to represent us in Assembly.

2. We understand that a bill is now before the House of Assembly, wherein it is provided that such persons as shall be charged with killing any Indians in Lancaster County, shall not be tried in the county where the fact was committed, but in the counties of Philadelphia, Chester, or Bucks. This is manifestly to deprive British subjects of their known privileges, to cast an eternal reproach upon whole counties, as if they were unfit to serve their country in the quality of jurymen, and to contradict the well-known laws of the British nation in a point whereon life, liberty, and security essentially depend, namely, that of being tried by their equals in the neighborhood where their own, their accusers', and the witnesses' character and credit, with the circumstances of the fact, are best known, and instead thereof putting their lives in the hands of strangers who may as justly be suspected of partiallity to, as the frontier counties can be of prejudices against Indians; and this, too, in favour of Indians only, against His Majesty's faithful and loyal subjects. Besides, it is well known that the design of it is to comprehend a fact committed before such a law was thought of. And if such practices were tolerated, no man could be secure in his most valuable interests. We are also informed to our great surprize, that this bill has actually received the assent of a majority of the House, which we are persuaded could not have been the case had our frontier counties been equally represented in Assembly. However, we hope that the Legislature of this Province will never enact a law of so dangerous a tendency, or take away from His Majesty's good subjects a privilege so long esteemed sacred by Englishmen.

3. During the late and present Indian wars, the frontiers of this Province have been repeatedly attacked and ravaged by skulking parties of the Indians, who have with the most savage cruelty murdered men, women, and children without distinction, and have reduced near a thousand families to the most extream distress. It grieves us to the very heart to see such of our frontier inhabitants as have escaped savage fury with the loss of their parents, their children, their wives or relatives, left destitute by the public, and exposed to the most cruel poverty and wretchedness while upwards of an hundred and twenty of the savages who are with great reason suspected of being guilty of these horrid barbarities under the mask of friendship, have procured themselves to be taken under the protection of the government, with a view to elude the fury of the brave relatives of the murdered, and are now maintained at the public expence. Some of these Indians now in the barracks of Philadelphia, are confessedly a part of the Wyalusing Indians, which tribe is now at war with us, and the others are the Moravian Indians, who, living

amongst us under the cloak of friendship, carried on a correspondence with our known enemies on the Great Island. We cannot but observe with sorrow and indignation that some persons in this Province are at pains to extenuate the barbarous cruelties practised by these savages on our murdered brethren and relatives, which are shocking to human nature, and must pierce every heart but that of the hardened perpetrators or their abettors, nor is it less distressing to hear others pleading that although the Wyalusing tribe is at war with us, yet that part of it which is under the protection of the government may be friendly to the English and innocent.

[*Source*: S. E. Morison, ed., *Sources and Documents llustrating the American Revolution 1764–1788* (Oxford: Clarendon, 1923), pp. 9–11.]

## 31    William Pitt and George Grenville

William Pitt, the future Prime Minister, debates taxation in the American colonies with George Grenville, the current Chancellor of the Exchequer during the House of Commons debate on the 'Address of Thanks for the King's Speech', 14 January 1766.

*Mr. Pitt* . . . It is my opinion, that this kingdom has no right to lay a tax upon the colonies. At the same time, I assert the authority of this kingdom over the colonies, to be sovereign and supreme, in every circumstance of government and legislation whatsoever. They are the subjects of this kingdom, equally entitled with yourselves to all the natural rights of mankind and the peculiar privileges of Englishmen, equally bound by its laws, and equally participating of the constitution of this free country. The Americans are the sons, not the bastards, of England. [. . .]

There is an idea in some, that the colonies are virtually represented in this House. I would fain know by whom an American is represented here? Is he represented by any knight of the shire, in any county in this kingdom? Would to God that respectable representation was augmented to a greater number! Or will you tell him, that he is represented by any representative of a borough—a borough, which perhaps, its own representative never saw. This is what is called, 'the rotten part of the constitution'. It cannot continue the century; if it does not drop, it must be amputated. The idea of a virtual representation of America in this House is the most contemptible idea that ever entered into the head of a man; it does not deserve a serious refutation.

The Commons of America, represented in their several assemblies, have ever been in possession of the exercise of this, their constitutional right, of giving and granting their own money. They would have been slaves if they had not enjoyed it. At the same time, this kingdom, as the supreme governing and legislative power, has always bound the colonies by her laws, by her regulations, and restrictions in trade, in navigation, in manufactures, in everything, except that of taking their money out of their pockets without their consent. . . .

*Mr. Grenville* . . . I cannot understand the difference between external and internal taxes. They are the same in effect, and only differ in name. That this kingdom has the sovereign, the supreme legislative power over America, is granted. It cannot be denied; and taxation is a part of that sovereign power. It is one branch of the legislation. It is, it has been exercised, over those who are not, who were never represented. It is exercised over the India Company, the merchants of London, the proprietors of the stocks, and over many great manufacturing towns. [. . .]

When I proposed to tax America, I asked the House, if any gentleman would object to the right; I repeatedly asked it, and no man would attempt to deny it. Protection and obedience are reciprocal. Great Britain protects America; America is bound to yield obedience. If not, tell me when the Americans were emancipated? When they want the protection of this kingdom, they are always very ready to ask it. That protection has always been afforded them in the most full and ample manner. The nation has run itself into an immense debt to give them their protection; and now they are called upon to contribute a small share towards the public expense, an expence arising from themselves, they renounce your authority, insult your officers, and break out, I might almost say, into open rebellion. The seditious spirit of the colonies owes its birth to the factions in this House. Gentlemen are careless of the consequences of what they say, provided it answers the purpose of opposition. We were told we trod on tender ground: we were bid to expect disobedience. What was this, but telling the Americans to stand out against the law, to encourage their obstinacy with the expectation of support from hence? Let us only hold out a little, they would say, our friends will soon be in power. Ungrateful people of America! Bounties have been extended to them. When I had the honour of serving the Crown, while you yourselves were loaded with an enormous debt, you have given bounties on their iron, their hemp, and many other articles. You have relaxed, in their favour, the Act of Navigation, that palladium of the British commerce; and yet I have been abused in all the public papers as an enemy to the trade of America.

[*Source*: Madden and Fieldhouse, *The Classical Period of the first British Empire, 1689–1783*, vol. 2 of SDBE, pp. 534–6.]

## 32    Edmund Burke

Edmund Burke was an Irish-born statesman and political reformer who delivered this 'Speech on Conciliation with America' on 22 March 1775. Its radical proposals included the repeal of taxation legislation offensive to the colonists. Burke welcomed the 'English' identity which prompted them to seek greater economic and political freedom.

In this Character of the Americans, a love of Freedom is the predominating feature, which marks and distinguishes the whole: and as an ardent is always a jealous affection, your Colonies become suspicious, restive, and untractable, whenever they see the least attempt to wrest from them by force, or shuffle from them by chicane, what they think the only advantage worth living for. This fierce spirit of Liberty is stronger in the English Colonies probably than in any other people of the earth; and this from a great variety of powerful causes; which, to understand the true temper of their minds, and the direction which this spirit takes, it will not be amiss to lay open somewhat more largely.

First, the people of the Colonies are descendants of Englishmen. England, Sir, is a nation, which still I hope respects, and formerly adored, her freedom. The Colonists emigrated from you, when this part of your character was most predominant; and they took this biass and direction the moment they parted from your hands. They are therefore not only devoted to Liberty, but to Liberty according to English ideas, and on English principles. Abstract Liberty, like other mere abstractions, is not to be found. Liberty inheres in some sensible object; and every nation has formed to itself some favourite point, which by way of eminence becomes the criterion of their happiness. It happened, you know, Sir, that the great contests for freedom in this country were from the earliest times chiefly upon the question of Taxing. Most of the contests in the ancient common wealths turned primarily on the right of election of magistrates; or on the balance among the several orders of the state. The question of money was not with them so immediate. But in England it was otherwise. On this point of Taxes the ablest pens, and most eloquent tongues, have been exercised; the greatest spirits have acted and suffered. In order to give the fullest satisfaction concerning the importance of this point, it was not only necessary for those who in argument defended the excellence of the English constitution, to insist on this privilege of granting money as a dry point of fact, and to prove, that the right had been acknowledged in ancient parchments, and blind usages, to reside in a certain body called an House of Commons. They went much further; they attempted to prove, and they succeeded, that in theory it ought to be so, from the particular nature of a House of Commons, as an immediate representative of the people; whether the old records had delivered this oracle or not. They took infinite pains to inculcate, as a fundamental principle, that, in all monarchies, the people must in effect themselves mediately or immediately possess the power of granting their own money, or no shadow of liberty could subsist. The Colonies draw from you as with their life-blood, these ideas and principles. Their love of liberty, as with you, fixed and attached on this specific point of taxing. Liberty might be safe, or might be endangered in twenty other particulars, without their being much pleased or alarmed. Here they felt its pulse; and as they found that beat, they thought themselves sick or sound. I do not say whether they were right or wrong in applying your general arguments to their own case. It is not easy indeed to make a monopoly of theorems and corollaries. The fact is, that they did thus apply those general arguments; and your mode of governing them, whether through lenity or indolence, through wisdom or mistake, confirmed them in the imagination, that they, as well as you, had an interest in these common principles. [. . .]

The Americans will have no interest contrary to the grandeur and glory of England, when they are not oppressed by the weight of it; and they will rather be inclined to respect the acts of a superintending legislature, when they see them the acts of that power, which is itself the security, not the rival, of their secondary importance. In this assurance, my mind most perfectly acquiesces; and I confess, I feel not the least alarm, from the discontents which are to arise, from putting people at their ease; nor do I apprehend the destruction of this empire, from giving, by an act of free grace and indulgence, to two millions of my fellow citizens, some share of those rights, upon which I have always been taught to value myself.

It is said indeed, that this power of granting vested in American assemblies, would dissolve the unity of the empire; which was preserved, entire, although Wales, and Chester, and Durham, were added to it. Truly, Mr. Speaker, I do not know what this unity means; nor has it ever been heard of, that I know, in the constitutional policy of this country. The very idea of subordination of parts, excludes this notion of simple and undivided unity. England is the head; but she is not the head and the members too. Ireland has ever had from the beginning a separate, but not an independent, legislature; which, far from distracting, promoted the union of the whole. Every thing was sweetly and harmoniously disposed through both Islands for the conservation of English dominion, and the communication of English liberties. I do not see that the same principles might not be carried into twenty Islands, and with the same good effect. This is my model with regard to America, as far as the internal circumstances of the two countries are the same. I know no other unity of this empire than I can draw from its example during these periods, when it seemed to my poor understanding more united than it is now, or than it is likely to be by the present methods.

[*Source*: W. M. Elofson and John A. Woods, eds, *Party, Parliament, and the American War 1774–1780*, vol. 3 of *The Writings and Speeches of Edmund Burke* (Oxford: Clarendon Press, 1996), pp. 119–121; 158.]

## 33    John Shy

Whether or not one accepts the view that revolution is an extraordinary phenomenon, akin to collective madness, with people acting in ways they could barely imagine in the relative calm of normal political and social intercourse, revolution lays a heavy burden on the historian. For decades American settlers and British officials had disagreed, as people do in every political system, about a variety of major and minor points of conflict, but the Imperial system had functioned remarkably well. By 1763 Great Britain and her Empire were admired throughout an Enlightened Europe for their stability, prosperity, and liberty. And yet, within little more than a decade, the Empire broke down in an ugly civil war, triggered by Americans behaving in a frenzy of revolutionary zeal to build anew from the wreckage of the old. How to explain it? Some would say that revolution is not so extraordinary, although its onset is always shocking. The American colonies had been growing rapidly, as well as visibly away from British rule; thoughtful observers knew that separation was inevitable. Equally predictable was British determination to prevent separation, by war if necessary. Again the circle of explanation leads back to war; the prospect as well as the reality of war became the catalysts for revolution. Whichever view one takes of revolution—a collective frenzy, or the continuation of normal politics by other means—the American Revolution challenges the historical imagination.

With vast new territories to defend and govern, from Hudson Bay to the Gulf of Mexico, and over the Appalachians to the Mississippi, an unprecedented military garrison for mainland North America seemed obviously required in 1763. But fifteen regiments of British troops scattered over half a continent would add heavy annual expenses to the gigantic financial burden left by the war, and Americans whose future had been secured by the war might reasonably be expected to contribute to their cost. A new military force might also be used to regulate volatile relations with the Indian occupants of the new territories, policing traders whose sharp methods in the past had provoked Indian retaliation, and controlling the speculators and squatters whose relentless quest for land claimed by the Indians had been an even more serious cause of native disaffection. Whether troops and warships stationed in America might also assist in more effective enforcement of Imperial trade laws, whose flagrant violation by colonial merchants and sea-captains had been so visible in the last years of the war, was less clear, but it was at least an interesting idea. Such was the British mental baggage carried into the post-war period.

Americans, delighted by the dream finally realized of French and Spanish removal, heartened by Britain's wartime generosity, and proud of their own considerable contribution to final victory, looked forward to a golden age in which an enlightened mother country would gently guide the growth of her colonial children. An ever more numerous people, secure in their British liberty, and granted by decades of Imperial precedent a large measure of autonomy, would carry the Empire westward to the glory and profit of all Imperial subjects, British and American. In a word, Americans were never more British than in 1763.

These two differing outlooks were bound to clash, but an inevitable post-war economic recession in America, and a perhaps equally predictable period of political turmoil in Britain, sharpened conflict when it came. Pitt, his talents unsuited to peace, lost power as victory was secured, but lurked dangerously on the flank of successive post-war governments, ready to deploy his charisma for or against, as the mood took him. Americans loved him, and he claimed to love them, although his speeches did not always speak pure affection. In 1763–64, when the government took the first steps to restrict American migration on to lands west of the Appalachian crest, to curb the use of paper money, and to tighten the rules of colonial trade while incidentally raising a revenue that would help defray the new costs of Empire, Pitt did not object, but Americans did, vociferously.

The strong negative response in the colonies after 1763 to what appear to be modest changes in Imperial governance has puzzled historians. The white population of the American colonies was arguably the most gently governed, lightly taxed, least oppressed people in the eighteenth-century Western world. In 1763 its future looked bright. So why the explosion of discontent that eventually became full-scale revolution?

The best answer lies with those Americans who had been allowed to govern the colonies since their settlement under more or less benign royal supervision: a small minority of families in every colony, from New England to Georgia, often descended from the first settlers of the colony, more affluent, better educated, well known, experienced in governing, and inter-married. This colonial élite had managed their numerous, mobile, fecund, contentious, and increasingly diverse and dispersed constituents not by means of armed force, of which there was virtually none, but by consent and accommodation. Their importance in the political and economic success of the Empire as effective brokers between London, provincial capitals, and the

American grass roots can hardly be exaggerated. And yet their role and position were tenuous, not established by statute or royal charter, but based like so much else in the British constitution on long precedent and tacit understanding. [. . .]

Even more difficult and contentious questions for historians have arisen from their need to explain American popular response. The real stake in these contested Imperial issues for ordinary American families is not self-evidently clear, and yet their response would be vital to the eventual outcome. Why were colonial leaders so successful in mobilizing popular resistance to new British policies? A few historians have argued that the question is badly posed, because popular American dislike for an intrusive British presence actually pushed leaders further and faster than they intended to go; but most concur that the role of leadership was determinative. Then how account for the successful organization of popular energies in a society where all authority was weak, and individualistic behaviour commonplace?

These questions hardly arose for earlier historians, steeped in the legend of national origins. But the professionalization of historiography had by the early decades of the twentieth century formulated two different sets of answers. One was most succinctly set forth in 1924 by the Yale historian Charles M. Andrews: revolution arose from the very Englishness of the Imperial polity. Decentralized, loose jointed, and guided by the principles of 1688, the Imperial constitution had allowed Americans to persuade themselves that their elective Assemblies were Houses of Commons in miniature, protecting the rights as Englishmen of every New Englander, New Yorker, Virginian, and Carolinian. No effective rebuttal from Britain had lent credibility to these mistaken ideas. So the years of Imperial reform after 1763 inevitably brought confrontation, and Americans, incapable of adapting their ideas to new Imperial realities, rebelled.

Charles Beard, who began to transform American historical consciousness in 1913, offered a different answer. He and his many disciples explained all political behaviour in terms of economic interest. Explaining the American Revolution was as simple as describing the conflicts of economic interest between Great Britain and the American colonies.

Dissatisfaction with both answers was evident before the middle of the twentieth century. Economic explanation had too many logical and evidentiary weaknesses, and a nagging sense of incompleteness clung to what may be called the alternative Whig-Imperial version. Relentlessly, a new answer emerged from the work of Bernard Bailyn at Harvard, his student Gordon Wood, and a growing number of followers. By an imaginative rereading of texts well known for two centuries, they stressed the explanatory force of ideology.

Unlike the pallid constitutional theories emphasized by Andrews, ideology for Bailyn and Wood is a powerful fusion of belief and emotion, a deeply implanted quasi-religious sense of reality pervading colonial America, a belief-system that when challenged, as it was by British measures after 1763, predictably exploded into revolution. This explanation, centered on the twinned though reciprocally antagonistic concepts of liberty and power, has proved highly persuasive, in part at least because it readily explains both élite and mass behaviour leading up to 1776, as well as a great deal else about American history afterward.

This digression into historiography is necessary because not all are convinced that ideology answers all the important questions about the American Revolution. A recent major work by a distinguished journalist-historian on the Revolution recasts it as 'a struggle for power', blending the older explanations of Andrews and Beard while giving almost no attention to ideology. To the question of popular mobilization it should be noted that on only three brief occasions was popular response strongly consensual: against the Stamp Act in 1765, against the so-called Coercive or Intolerable Acts in 1774, and during most of the first year of open warfare, 1775–76. For the rest of a twenty-year struggle division, doubt, and apathy were as characteristic as popular enthusiasm or unanimity. That an estimated one out of every four or five white Americans rejected the Revolution should not be forgotten. To the persistent question about popular response, the best answers are still agnostic.

[*Source*: John Shy, 'The American Colonies, 1748–1783', in P. J. Marshall, ed., *The Eighteenth Century*, vol. 2 of *OHBE*, pp. 307–9, 310–312.]

## 34   The American Declaration of Independence

Britons had often denounced despotism and tyranny in Europe, and had overthrown two of their own kings using similar language. Here the accusations are levelled against George III and his government by the newly proclaimed United States of America on 4 July 1776.

When in the Course of human events, it becomes necessary for one people to dissolve the political bands which have connected them with another, and to assume among the Powers of the earth, the separate and equal station to which the Laws of Nature and of Nature's God entitle them, a decent respect to the opinions of mankind requires that they should declare the causes which impel them to the separation.

We hold these truths to be self-evident, that all men are created equal, that they are endowed by their Creator with certain unalienable Rights, that among these are Life, Liberty and the pursuit of Happiness. That to secure these rights, Governments are instituted among Men, deriving their just powers from the consent of the governed. That whenever any Form of Government becomes destructive of these ends, it is the Right of the People to alter or to abolish it, and to institute new Government, laying its foundation on such principles and organizing its powers in such form, as to them shall seem most likely to effect their Safety and Happiness. Prudence, indeed, will dictate that Governments long established should not be changed for light and transient causes; and accordingly all experience hath shown, that mankind are more disposed to suffer, while evils are sufferable, than to right themselves by abolishing the forms to which they are accustomed. But when a long train of abuses and usurpations, pursuing invariably the same Object evinces a design to reduce them under absolute Despotism, it is their right, it is their duty, to throw off such Government, and to provide new Guards for their future security. Such has been the patient sufferance of these Colonies; and such is now the necessity which constrains them to alter their former Systems of Government. The history of the present King of Great Britain is a history of repeated injuries and usurpations, all having in direct object the establishment of an absolute Tyranny over these States. [. . .]

In every stage of these Oppressions We have Petitioned for Redress in the most humble terms: Our repeated Petitions have been answered only by repeated injury. A Prince, whose character is thus marked by every act which may define a Tyrant, is unfit to be the ruler of a free People.

Nor have We been wanting in attention to our British brethren. We have warned them from time to time of attempts by their legislature to extend an unwarrantable jurisdiction over us. We have reminded them of the circumstances of our emigration and settlement here. We have appealed to their native justice and magnanimity, and we have conjured them by the ties of our common kindred to disavow these usurpations, which, would inevitably interrupt our connections and correspondence. They too have been deaf to the voice of justice and of consanguinity. We must, therefore, acquiesce in the necessity, which denounces our Separation, and hold them, as we hold the rest of mankind, Enemies in War, in Peace Friends.

We, therefore, the Representatives of the united States of America, in General Congress, Assembled, appealing to the Supreme Judge of the world for the rectitude of our intentions, do, in the Name, and by Authority of the good People of these Colonies, solemnly publish and declare, That these United Colonies are, and of Right ought to be Free and Independent States; that they are Absolved from all Allegiance to the British Crown, and that all political connection between them and the State of Great Britain, is and ought to be totally dissolved; and that as Free and Independent States, they have full Power to levy War, conclude Peace, contract Alliances, establish Commerce, and to do all other Acts and Things which Independent States may of right do. And for the support of this Declaration, with a firm reliance on the Protection of Divine Providence, we mutually pledge to each other our Lives, our Fortunes and our sacred Honor.

[*Source*: Francis Newton Thorpe, ed., *The Federal and State Constitutions, Colonial Charters, and other Organic Laws of the . . . United States of America* (Washington: Government Printing Office, 1909), vol. 1, pp. 3–6.]

## 35   Letter from Philadelphia (from an unknown author)

This letter of 6 December 1776 was printed in the *Morning Chronicle and London Advertiser*. Note that, at this point, colonial identities still revolve around familiar ethnic and political terminology; the two sides have not yet divided into 'British' and 'American'.

We have just come to hand, by express from Virginia, that Ld. Dunmore had issued a Proclamation, declaring all Negroes and servants free that belonged to men in arms for the defence of their country; that he had beat the Provincials in two skirmishes; the particulars are only known to the Congress, which we fear are not very favourable. Great numbers of people, white and black, had repaired to the King's standard, which he had hoisted. As there are in Norfolk many of his sc——ly countrymen, English Tories, and others, no better, and thro' the country, in the neighbouring counties of Aromack, Hampton, and others on the western shore, many gentlemen wavering, we should not wonder at their being awed to follow this Jacobite Scotch fortunist to their ruin. Little do they or he know what force we are preparing. [. . .]

The Scotch and Irish people there are hand in hand with us, and very spirited. We do not expect much aid from Annapolis, as the most able people there (except the Carrols) are creatures, tools of government and Tories; many of which are already fled to your degenerate land for safety; particularly three of the Delanys, Dr. Stewart and his sons, your old friend T. C. Williams, and A. Stewart, who last year made their peace with a burnt offering of their brig and tea. No doubt but you will see them in Bristol; they may think themselves happy in being out of the way; for be assured, men of their sentiments have not much security for their lives and properties here. But to return; there is but little doubt of our united forces soon giving a good account of Lord Dunmore, which we pray most ardently for. We have nothing to fear but from the Asia, a sixty gun ship, lying at New York, that the Captain may have information of the destination of our fleet, and endeavour to interrupt them at our Capes. Hell itself could not have vomitted any thing more black than his design of emancipating our slaves; and unless he is cut off before he is reinforced, we know not how far the contagion may spread.

The flame runs like wild fire through the slaves, who are more than two for one white in the Southern Colonies. The subject of their nocturnal revels, instead of music and dancing, is now turned upon their liberty. I know not whence these troubles may lead us. If our friends in England are not able to oblige the ministry to give way, we are lost; and already gone too far to retract with safety.

[*Source*: Margaret Wheeler Willard, ed., *Letters on the American Revolution 1774–1776* (Port Washington, NY: Kennikat Press, 1925), pp. 231–2, 233.]

## 36 Letter from Maryland (from a female correspondent)

Male politicans and soldiers were by no means the only Americans who defied the British government. In this letter of 2 December 1775 a woman in Annapolis, Maryland lists the household sacrifices she is prepared to make in the name of patriotism. The account of burning a ship refers to an incident at Annapolis in 1774 modelled after the better-known 'Boston Tea Party'.

Pray what are your ministry doing? Making a rod for their own backs; for they never will enslave the brave Americans. We have done with you; the non-importation took place yesterday; and now you shall see how we can do without you; we can live as well as need to be: but I cannot tell how we shall dress: I have cloaths enough for some time, but have no pins to put them on; but never fear, I shall have my share of what there are. There is no more tea to be drank here, but very good coffee. The 19th of last October we burned a ship, tea and all; for which you'll, I suppose, send us some red-coats.

[*Source*: Wheeler, *Letters on the American Revolution*, pp. 22–3.]

## 37 Thomas Peters

Thomas Peters had been a sergeant in the Regiment of Guides and Pioneers during the War of Independence and, like many black Loyalists, had been promised land in one of the Canadian colonies after the war. Tired of waiting, he petitioned the British Secretary of State, William Grenville, to ask for land elsewhere in the empire.

The humble Memorial and Petition of Thomas Peters a free Negro and late a Serjt. in the Regiment of Guides and Pioneers serving in North America under the Command of Genl. Sir Henry Clinton on Behalf of himself and others the Black Pioneers and loyal Black Refugees hereinafter described Sheweth

That your Memorialist and the said other Black Pioneers having served in North America as aforesaid for the Space of seven years and upwards, during the War, afterwards went to Nova Scotia under the Promise of obtaining the usual Grant of Lands and Provision.

That notwithstanding they have made repeated Applications to all Persons in that Country who they conceived likely to put them in Possession of the due Allotments, the said Pioneers with their Wives and Children amounting together in the whole to the Number of 102 People now remain at Annapolis Royal have not yet obtained their Allotments of Land except one single Acre of land each for a Town Lot and tho' a further Proportion of 20 Acres each Private man (viz) about a 5th part of the Allowance of Land that is due to them was actually laid out and located for them agreeable to the Governor's Order it was afterwards taken from them on Pretence that it had been included in some former Grant and they have never yet obtained other Lands in Lieu thereof and remain destitute and helpless.

That besides the said 102 People at Annapolis who have deputed your Memorialist to represent their unhappy Situation there is also a Number of free Black Refugees consisting of about 100 Families or more at New Brunswick in a like unprovided and destitute Condition for tho' some of them have had but a Part of their Allowance of Land offered to them it is so far distant from their Town Lots (being 16 or 18 miles back) as to be entirely useless to them and indeed worthless in itself from its remote situation.

That the said two Descriptions of People having authorized and empowered your Memorialist to act for them as their Attorney he has at much Trouble and Risk made his way into this Country in the Hope that he should be able to procure for himself and his Fellow Sufferers some Establishment where they may attain a competent Settlement for themselves and be enabled by their industrious exertions to become useful subjects to his Majesty.

That some Part however of the said Black People are earnestly desirous of obtaining their due Allotment of Land and remaining in America but others are ready and willing to go wherever the Wisdom of Government may think proper to provide for them as free Subjects of the British Empire.

Your Memorialist therefore (most honble Sir) humbly prays that you will most humanely consider the Case of your Memorialist and the said other Black People and by laying the same before his Majesty or otherwise as you shall deem most proper that they may be afforded such Relief as shall appear to be best adapted to their Circumstances and Situation.

[*Source*: Christopher Fyfe, *Sierra Leone Inheritance* (London: Oxford University Press, 1964), pp. 118–19.]

## 2.3 CONQUEST AND IDENTITY

The eighteenth century gave Britain victories and dilemmas in equal measure. The earlier empire had consisted primarily of plantation colonies in North America and the West Indies; British trade with Africa and Asia was confined to coastal outposts similar to those of other European countries. By 1815, however, Britain was ruling over millions of non-English-speaking peoples, most of them in south Asia: an unprecedented development for which there was no existing policy. It had also lost political control over the American colonies, prompting some historians to talk about a 'swing to the east' in imperial policy. This view makes it seem as though the American colonies were all that really mattered in British North America; on the contrary, the acquisition of Quebec (see Map 4) created political and philosophical problems that would profoundly affect the future governance of the empire.

After the Seven Years War the British government proclaimed the rule of English law in Quebec while affirming the rights of Native people beyond the areas of French settlement (Extract 38). This seemed logical because of Britain's traditional suspicion of the French in North America: in 1755 French-speaking Acadians had been expelled from the new British colony of Nova Scotia. The proclamation of 1763 also reflected the British government's wish to reward Native leaders for their military assistance. As a result, the proclamation pleased few non-Natives in North America. But restricted access to Native land infuriated settlers in the ever-growing American colonies while the overthrow of French law alienated the Québécois (Extract 39). Britain had not thought carefully enough about how to rule a non-British population; the situation in Quebec demanded a new way of thinking about the relationship between power and cultural difference. Critics of the 1763 proclamation, such as the Chief Justice, Lord Mansfield, insisted that local laws were not automatically invalidated by military conquest (Extract 40). The British government was forced into an about-turn, affirming in the Quebec Act (1774) that the French language and civil law, along with the Roman Catholic faith, would be protected by the British colonial authorities. Now it was English-speaking settlers in Quebec, and in the American colonies, who felt alienated and the Quebec Act would join their growing list of grievances against the British (Extract 41). Once again, a purely 'English' identity was harder and harder to sustain in the changing eighteenth-century empire. The transition from 'Englishmen' to 'British subjects' was under way: a political rather than an ethnic identity.

The debate about Quebec had profound implications for other parts of the British empire. Similar issues were arising in West Indian islands acquired from France. In a famous judgment in 1774 Lord Mansfield established that existing law was not overturned by conquest; only by subsequent legislation

(Extract 42). The Cape Colony, surrendered by the Dutch, was another test case. The British took over a well-established Afrikaner society with its own language, legal system, and culture. At the Cape there was no hasty proclamation of British cultural dominance; instead, the colonial authorities released a series of directives permitting the use of Afrikaans in official proceedings and retaining the traditional Dutch civil courts (Extract 43). The British had learned a valuable lesson in Quebec.

But what of the indigenous populations of these areas? In southern Africa the British quickly found themselves in conflict with Africans disturbed by the accelerating pace of European settlement. In British North America, as Daniel K. Richter explains, Native Indians experienced an erosion of their influence by the end of the eighteenth century as the profitable fur trade moved westward (Extract 44). During the nineteenth and twentieth centuries indigenous peoples would be increasingly marginalized, seen—at best—as helpless dependants rather than allies.

## 38    Royal Proclamation, 1763

> The Royal Proclamation of 7 October 1763 was made after the end of the Seven Years' War to reinforce the Crown's control of new territories in North America.

And whereas it will greatly contribute to the speedy settling our said new Governments, that our loving Subjects should be informed of our Paternal care, for the Security of the Liberties and Properties of those who are and shall become Inhabitants thereof, We have thought fit to publish and declare, by this our Proclamation, that We have, in the Letters Patent under our Great Seal of Great Britain, by which the said Governments are constituted, given express Power and Direction to our Governors of our said Colonies respectively, that, so soon as the State and Circumstances of the said Colonies will admit thereof, they shall, with the Advice and Consent of the Members of our Council, summon and call General Assemblies within the said Governments respectively, in such Manner and Form as is used and directed in those Colonies and Provinces in America which are under our immediate Government; and We have also given Power to the said Governors, with the Consent of our said Councils, and the Representatives of the People so to be summoned as aforesaid, to make, constitute, and ordain Laws, Statutes, and Ordinances for the Public Peace, Welfare, and good Government of our said Colonies, and of the People and Inhabitants thereof, as near as may be agreeable to the Laws of England, and under such Regulations and Restrictions as are used in other Colonies; and in the mean Time, and until such Assemblies can be called as aforesaid, all Persons inhabiting in or resorting to our said Colonies may confide in our Royal Protection for the Enjoyment of the Benefit of the Laws of our Realm of England; for which Purpose We have given Power under our Great Seal to the Governors of our said Colonies respectively to erect and constitute, with the Advice of our said Councils respectively, Courts of Judicature and Public Justice within our said Colonies for hearing and determining all Causes, as well Criminal as Civil, according to Law and Equity, and as near as may be agreeable to the Laws of England, with Liberty to all Persons who may think themselves aggrieved by the Sentences of such Courts, in all Civil Cases, to appeal, under the usual Limitations and Restrictions, to Us in our Privy Council. [. . .]

And whereas it is just and reasonable, and essential to our Interest, and the Security of our Colonies, that the several Nations or Tribes of Indians with whom We are connected, and who live under our Protection, should not be molested or disturbed in the Possession of such Parts of our Dominions and Territories as, not having been ceded to or purchased by Us, are reserved to them, or any of them, as their Hunting Grounds,—We do therefore, with the Advice of our Privy Council, declare it to be our Royal Will and Pleasure, that no Governor or Commander in Chief in any of our Colonies of Quebec, East Florida, or West Florida, do presume, upon any Pretence whatever, to grant Warrants of Survey, or pass any Patents for Lands beyond the Bounds of their respective Governments, as described in their Commissions; as also that no Governor or Commander in Chief in any of our other Colonies or Plant-ations in America do presume for the Present, and until our further Pleasure be known, to grant Warrants of Survey, or pass Patents for any Lands beyond the Heads or Sources of any of the Rivers which fall into the Atlantic Ocean from the West and North West, or upon any Lands whatever, which, not having been ceded to or purchased by Us as aforesaid, are reserved to the said Indians, or any of them.

[*Source*: Ramsay Muir, ed., *The Making of British India 1756–1858* (Manchester: Manchester University Press, 1915), pp. 5–6, 8–9.]

---

**39**  **'Petition of divers of the French inhabitants of the province of Quebec'**

This petition dated December 1773 appealed for an end to the policies established by the Proclamation of 1763, and promised loyalty to the Crown.

In the year 1764, your Majesty thought fit to put an end to the military government of this province, and to establish a civil government in its stead. And from the instant of this change we began to feel the inconveniences which resulted from the introduction of the laws of England, which till then we had been wholly unacquainted with. Our former countrymen, who till that time had been permitted to settle our civil disputes without any expense to us, were thanked for their services, and dismissed; and the militia of the province, which had till then been proud of bearing that honourable name under your Majesty's command, was laid aside. It is true indeed we were admitted to serve on juries; but at the same time we were given to understand, that there were certain obstacles that prevented our holding places under your Majesty's government. We were also told that the laws of England were to take place in the province, which, though we presume them to be wisely suited to the regulation of the mother-country for which they were made, could not be blended and applied to our customs without totally overturning our fortunes and destroying our possessions. [. . .]

Vouchsafe, most illustrious and generous sovereign, to dissipate these fears and this uneasiness, by restoring to us our ancient laws, privileges, and customs, and to extend our province to its former boundaries. Vouchsafe to bestow your favours equally upon all your subjects in the province, without any distinction! Preserve the glorious title of sovereign of a free people: a title which surely would suffer some diminution, if more than an hundred thousand new subjects of your Majesty in this province, who had submitted to your government, were to be excluded from your service, and deprived of the inestimable advantages which are enjoyed by your Majesty's ancient subjects. [. . .]

We conclude by entreating your Majesty to grant us, in common with your other subjects, the rights and privileges of citizens of England. Then our fears will be removed, and we shall pass our lives in tranquillity and happiness, and shall be always ready to sacrifice them for the glory of our prince and the good of our country.

[*Source*: Arthur Berriedale Keith, ed., *Speeches and Documents on British Colonial Policy 1763–1917* (Oxford: Oxford University Press, 1961), pp. 32–4.]

## 40    Lord Mansfield

The Chief Justice, Lord Mansfield, wrote to George Grenville, Chancellor of the Exchequer, on 24 December 1764. Mansfield believed that the Royal Proclamation's imposition of British law was illegal.

Since I saw you I have heard from the King in general, and afterwards more particularly, but very distinctly, from some persons who visited me last night, of a complaint concerning a civil government and judge sent to Canada. Is it possible that we have abolished their laws, and customs, and forms of judicature all at once?—a thing never to be attempted or wished. The history of the world don't furnish an instance of so rash and unjust an act by any conqueror whatsoever: much less by the Crown of England, which has always left to the conquered their own laws and usages, with a change only so far as the sovereignty was concerned. Where other changes have happened, as in Ireland, they have been the work of a great length of time, many emergencies, and where there was a pale of separation between the conquerors and conquered, and the former only conquered by their own laws at first, Berwick [and] the conquests made by Edward III, and yielded by the treaty of Bretigny, retained their own municipal laws. Minorca does now. Is it possible that a man *sans aveu*, without knowing a syllable of their language or laws, has been sent over with an English title of magistracy unknown to them, the powers of which office must consequently be inexplicable, and unexecutable by their usages?

For God's sake learn the truth of the case, and think of a speedy remedy. I was told last night that the penal statutes of England concerning Papists are to be held in force in Canada.

The fundamental maxims are, that a country conquered keeps her own laws, 'till the conqueror expressly gives new. A colony which goes from hence to settle in a waste country, if they have an express constitution by charter, (or so far as that is silent), carries with them such part of the laws of England as is adapted to, and proper for their situation.

A very small part of the Common or Statute Law of England is law there by this maxim. Ecclesiastical Laws, Revenue Laws, Penal Laws, and a thousand other heads, do not bind there by implication, though in force here at the time of their settlement.

Perhaps the principal parts of this Report may be untrue, but I am so startled at it that I cannot help writing to you: you may easily learn from the Board of Trade whether there has been any act from hence to send them over in a lump a new and unknown law.

[*Source*: Madden and Fieldhouse, *Classical Period of the First British Empire*, pp. 16–17.]

## 41 'Petition for the repeal of the Quebec Act'

This petition of 12 November 1774 set out the grievances of the English-speaking inhabitants of Quebec. They defined themselves as 'British' in contrast to the French 'Canadians' (compare Extract 77).

That, under the sanction of his Majesty's royal proclamation, bearing date the seventh day of October, in the year of our Lord one thousand seven hundred and sixty-three, which graciously promises to all persons inhabiting in, or resorting to, this province, his royal protection for the enjoyment of the benefit of the laws of the realm of England, until assemblies should be called therein, they did come and settle themselves in this province, having entrusted their own properties, as well as very considerable sums of their friends, in goods and merchandize, from Great Britain, and entrusted the same into the hands of the Canadians, as well for the purpose of internal trade in the province, as for outsets in carrying on the traffic of furs and peltries in the Indian countries and fisheries below Quebec, many of them having purchased lands and houses, and been employed in agriculture, and the exportation of grain and other produce to foreign markets, to the great benefit and emolument of the said province, which has flourished chiefly by the industry and enterprising spirit of the said subjects, who, under the protection of British laws, and by the assistance of annual supplies of British manufactures, and other goods and merchandize obtained upon credit from the merchants of Great Britain, have been enabled to carry on at least four parts in five of all the imports and exports which are principally made in British bottoms, the latter consisting of furs, peltries, wheat, fish, oil, potash, lumber, and other country produce: and for the more convenient carrying on the said trade and commerce, they have built wharfs and store-houses at a very great expense, insomuch that the property, real and personal, now in British hands, or by them entrusted to Canadians at a long credit, is one half of the whole value of the province, exclusive of the wealth of the different communities [. . .] And whereas an act of parliament has lately passed, entituled, 'An act for the making more effectual provision for the government of the province of Quebec in North America,' which is said to have been passed upon the principles of humanity and justice, and at the pressing instance and request of the new subjects, signified to his Majesty by an humble petition setting forth their dislike to the British laws and form of government, and praying, in the name of all the inhabitants and citizens of the province, to have the French institutes in their stead, and a total abolition of trials by jury, together with a capacity of holding places of honour and trust in common with his Majesty's ancient subjects. We crave leave to inform your honourable house, that the said petition was never imparted to the inhabitants in general (that is) the freeholders, merchants, and traders, who are equally alarmed with us at the Canadian laws being to take place, but was in a secret manner carried about and signed by a few of the seigneurs, chevaliers, advocates, and others in their confidence, at the suggestions, and under the influence of their priests; who, under colour of French laws, have obtained an act of parliament which deprives his Majesty's ancient subjects of all their rights and franchises, destroys the Habeas Corpus act, and the inestimable privilege of trial by juries, the only security against the venality of a corrupt judge, and gives unlimited power to the governor and council to alter the criminal laws; which act has already struck a damp upon the credit of the country, and alarmed all your humble petitioners with the just apprehensions of arbitrary fines and imprisonment, and which, if it takes place, will oblige them to quit the province, or, in the end, it must accomplish their ruin, and impoverish or hurt their generous creditors, the merchants in Great Britain, &c. To prevent which, your petitioners most humbly pray that the said act may be repealed or amended, and that they may have the benefit and protection of the English laws, in so far as relates to personal property; and that their liberty may be ascertained according to their ancient constitutional rights and privileges heretofore granted to all his Majesty's dutiful subjects throughout the British empire.

[*Source*: Keith, *Speeches and Documents*, pp. 66–7, 68–9.]

## 42    Lord Mansfield

> One of the most far-reaching decisions made by Lord Mansfield was in the 1774 case Campbell vs. Hall. Campbell was suing a British customs collector in the West Indian colony of Grenada (won from France during the Seven Years War), and Mansfield made it clear that existing laws remained after conquest although the British Crown could alter them later. He dismissed the 'absurd' principle of *Calvin's Case* (see Extract 16).

I will state the propositions at large:

1. A country conquered by the British arms becomes a dominion of the King in the right of his crown, and therefore necessarily subject to the legislative power of the Parliament of Great Britain.

2. The conquered inhabitants once received into the conqueror's protection become subjects; and are universally to be considered in that light, not as enemies or aliens.

3. Articles of capitulation, upon which the country is surrendered, and treaties of peace by which it is ceded, are sacred and inviolate, according to their true intent and meaning.

4. The law and legislation of every dominion equally affects all persons and property within the limits thereof, and is the true rule for the decision of all questions which arise there. Whoever purchases, sues, or lives there, puts himself under the laws of the place, and in the situation of its inhabitants. An Englishman in Ireland, Minorca, the Isle of Man, or the Plantations, has no privilege distinct from the natives while he continues there.

5. The laws of a conquered country continue in force until they are altered

by the conqueror. The justice and antiquity of this maxim are incontrovertible; and the absurd exception as to pagans mentioned in Calvin's case, shows the universality and antiquity of the maxim. That exception could not exist before the Christian era, and in all probability arose from the mad enthusiasm of the Crusades. In the present case the capitulation expressly provides and agrees that they shall continue to be governed by their own laws, until his Majesty's pleasure be further known.

[*Source*: Keith, *Speeches and Documents*, pp. 40–2.]

## 43  Lord Charles Somerset

The Lieutenant-Governor of the Cape, Lord Charles Somerset, passed this ordinance on 13 December 1826 to mitigate an earlier directive proclaiming that English would be the exclusive language used in the courts. Somerset had also authorized the existing Dutch courts to hear civil cases; only criminal charges would have to be heard before the new British courts.

Whereas it is expedient to postpone the period at which the use of the English Language is to be exclusively adopted in all the Courts of Justice in this Colony, until such Arrangements shall be made as may facilitate the introduction of this beneficial measure, and render its utility at once certain and permanent; and whereas many of these Arrangements have, from unavoidable causes, been delayed, and are yet wanting: Be it therefore enacted, That so much of the Proclamation of the 5th day of July 1822, as directs that the English Language shall be used in all Judicial Acts and Proceedings of the several Courts of Justice in this Colony, from and after the 1st day of January 1827, shall be, and is hereby repealed, and declared void, and of no effect; and that it shall and may be lawful to continue to use the Dutch Language in the Proceedings of those Courts where it is now used; anything in the said Proclamation of the 5th day of July 1822, to the contrary notwithstanding.

II. Provided always, and be it hereby enacted, That it shall and may be lawful for the Governor of this Colony, for the time being, by Proclamation to be made and published at any time after the passing of this Ordinance, to direct and order that the English Language be used in the Judicial Acts and Proceedings of all or any of the Courts of Justice in this Colony, at such subsequent period as to him shall seem fit.

[*Source*: George McCall Theal, ed., *Records of the Cape Colony: from Feburary 1793 to April 1831* (London: Government of the Cape Colony, 1897), p. 107.]

44   **Daniel K. Richter**

In the early 1760s Britain's victory temporarily removed any incentive to acknowledge Native American interests or to observe long-standing rituals of collective diplomacy. 'Our superiority in this war rendered our regard to this people still less, which had always been too little', a contemporary commentator rued. 'Decorums, which are as necessary at least in dealing with barbarous as with civilised nations, were neglected.'

Throughout Indian country tempers flared as the British Commander-in-Chief, Jeffrey Amherst, sought to confine inter-cultural trade to army posts, to ban the sale of weapons and ammunition entirely, and to halt the expensive custom of diplomatic gift-giving. In this context, the Delaware religious figure Neolin found receptive audiences in the Ohio Country and the *pays d'en haut* for a nativist message of cultural self-reliance symbolized by a ritual renunciation of European goods. One of Neolin's many disciples was the Ottawa leader Pontiac, who envisioned the expulsion of the British from the Great Lakes region and (along with much of the region's Franco-American and *métis* population) hoped for the restoration of French hegemony. In May 1763 Pontiac initiated what became a six-month siege of the British garrison at Detroit. Almost simultaneously, but apparently without central direction, other Indian forces attacked posts throughout the north-west; only Niagara, Pittsburgh, and, in the end, Detroit survived. The British regained superiority by late 1763, although fighting continued for two more years. Ironically, the very lack of European trade goods and weapons that Neolin advocated contributed to the Indians' defeat.

After 'Pontiac's War', financial and practical considerations made British officials more conciliatory. The policy shift began with the Royal Proclamation of 1763 which, to the extent it established a boundary between Europeans and natives that followed the Appalachian Mountains, conformed to the principles of the Treaty of Easton and to long-standing aims of Native American leaders. In almost no other way, however, did the Proclamation—to the extent Native Americans understood it—satisfy their demands. On the one hand, the royal government proved powerless to prevent squatters from traversing the line. On the other, whatever guarantees it offered were couched in language that assumed British, rather than Indian, ownership of 'the extensive and valuable acquisitions, in America secured to our Crown by the late definitive treaty of peace'. Indeed, the creation of the new colonies of East and West Florida and Quebec in those territories was the Proclamation's main item of business. [. . .]

The stage was set, then, for a mad scramble among British interests for control of Kentucky and for a potential renewal of nativist resistance among disfranchised Cherokees and Ohio Country Indians. Matters came to a head in 1774, when agents of the Virginia Governor Lord Dunmore provoked a war between Virginians settled at Pittsburgh and the Shawnees in order to pre-empt the competing claims of Pennsylvanians and the promoters of a proposed new 'Vandalia' colony. At the Treaty of Camp Charlotte, a Shawnee faction was forced to acknowledge Virginia's ownership of Kentucky. The signatories, however, by no means spoke for all Shawnees—much less all Cherokees or Ohio Country Indians—and the death of Sir William Johnson in 1774 threatened to plunge the entire Northern Superintendency into disarray.

Before the implications of these developments became clear, the declaration of United States independence fundamentally changed the diplomatic calculus by reintroducing the balance-of-power potential of 'the Modern Indian Politics'. Paradoxically, however, the British found themselves in the position formerly assumed by the French. At Montreal, in what was now the province of Quebec, the replacement of the French 'Father' by a British one had begun well before 1776. Scottish merchants used their transatlantic connections to drive Franco-American competitors from the market, but for the retail end of their commerce they relied on the same *voyageurs* as had their predecessors. In the garrisons of trading posts in the *pays d'en haut*, red coats merely replaced white, and necessity produced within the army a group of interpreters and agents increasingly skilled in the Native American diplomatic protocols that Amherst had so recently scorned.

The United States, meanwhile, filled the place of the mid-century Indians' British 'Brethren'. As had been the case before Independence, the conflicting economic imperatives of agricultural expansion and peaceful trade rested uneasily with a diplomatic need to play the 'deed game' in a situation where the Congress wrestled with thirteen state governments, private economic interests, and ungovernable backcountry whites for control of relations with the Native American population. Within this strange-yet-familiar diplomatic framework, Indian leaders attempted to remain neutral, while various factions kept open lines of communication to British and 'Americans' alike. Militants sought to seize the opportunity to ally with the British and regain lost territories; others argued caution on the basis of a generalized distrust of Europeans, the folly of what might prove a self-destructive war, the imperative to keep trading connections intact, or the need to accommodate whomever the eventual victor might be.

As the American War for Independence proceeded, almost no Native American groups managed perfect neutrality, but few unanimously joined the British and still fewer the United States. Along the St Lawrence, the former *sauvages domiciliés*—now called by the British 'the Seven Nations of Canada'—resumed their not-to-be-taken-for-granted role as military buffers.

Little such caution was to be found in the Ohio Country, however, with its tradition of nativist pan-Indianism, its recent memories of Fort Stanwix and Dunmore's War, and its ceaseless onslaught of settlers from Virginia and Pennsylvania; anti-United States militants easily prevailed in most, but not all, villages. The frontier war that resulted (or rather continued with hardly a break from 1774 on) entailed ferocious atrocities on both sides and reached its peak in the early 1780s, after fighting between British and US forces had mostly ceased elsewhere. [. . .]

When Britain acknowledged the independence of the United States of America in the Peace of Paris of 1783, the Crown's negotiators ignored the network of Indian alliances built up since 1763. The treaty made no mention whatsoever of Indians and simply transferred to the United States ownership of all territory south of the Great Lakes, east of the Mississippi, and north of the Floridas. Britain's Native American allies reacted with disbelief, as they confronted a victorious republic eager to claim their lands by what it deemed a right of conquest. From the Cherokee country southward, the British abandonment was virtually complete, and only slightly tempered by the reintroduction of a counterbalance to United States power in Spanish Florida. As the Creek leader Alexander McGillivray understated, 'to find ourselves and Country betrayed to our Enemies and divided between the Spaniards and Americans is Cruel and Ungenerous'.

Farther northward, the Treaty of Paris had less immediate impact, as raids and counter-raids scarred Kentucky and the Ohio Country without reference to European diplomacy. At the same time, the continued British military occupation of Detroit and other western posts in defiance of the Paris Treaty prolonged economic support for Indian militants. Moreover, from the Governor of Quebec, Sir Frederick Haldimand, down through the ranks of agents stationed in Indian country, British officers shared the sense of betrayal so prevalent among the Native Americans they had fought beside for nearly a decade, and they worked to mitigate the disaster. In 1784 the Governor granted Britain's refugee Iroquois allies a substantial tract of land on the Grand River in present-day Ontario; ultimately roughly half of the Iroquois population followed Brant to new homes there. From that base, Brant worked with Indian leaders from throughout the Ohio Country and *pays d'en haut* to create a Western Confederacy to carry on the struggle against the United States and defend an Ohio River border with the new republic.

The Quebec government remained officially neutral as the Western Confederacy defeated US armies led by Josiah Harmar in 1790 and Arthur St Clair in 1791. Still, the British agents who participated in the Confederacy's councils and obstructed United States efforts to negotiate a settlement gave every impression that troops would support the Indians in a crisis. In August 1794 the western war reached its climax with General Anthony Wayne's methodical march toward the Confederacy's centres on the Maumee River. Yet when Indian forces who had failed to repulse the invaders at the battle of Fallen Timbers sought refuge at the British post on the Maumee, its commander, fearing he could not resist an attack by Wayne, closed the gates against them. Thus left, as the Delaware leader complained, 'in the lurch', the Confederacy's forces abandoned the field and turned Wayne's relatively minor victory into a major triumph. Over the winter, as word arrived of Jay's Treaty requiring British withdrawal from the western posts, the various nations and factions of the Confederacy—like other abandoned British allies a decade earlier—coped with betrayal as best they could, having, in the words of British Indian agent Alexander McKee, 'lost all hopes of the interference of the government'. The result in the summer of 1795 was the Treaty of Greenville, which yielded most of the present state of Ohio to the United States.

For nearly two decades after the Greenville Treaty the focus of British–Indian relations shifted away from its traditional diplomatic and geographic centres in eastern North America. At the turn of the nineteenth century cutthroat competition among agents of the Hudson Bay, North-West, and several smaller fur companies emphasized commercial expansion north and westward of the Great Lakes toward the Rocky Mountains. The War of 1812, however, briefly retrained British attention south of the Lakes. Facing massive US emigration beyond the long-defunct Greenville Treaty line, Indians throughout the region had been mobilized by a new wave of nativism preached by the Shawnee prophet Tenskwatawa and his brother Tecumseh, who emerged, like Pontiac before him, as the most visible leader of a decentralized political and military movement. Tecumseh of course welcomed British aid, but, well aware of previous betrayals, he directed most of his energies toward the peoples of his home region and toward alliances with like-minded leaders of the Cherokees and Creeks to the southward. In 1813 the ignominious performance of British troops at the Battle of the Thames, in which Tecumseh lost his life, drove home to his followers a now familiar lesson. At the Peace of Ghent in 1814 Britain's Indian allies again were left to make the best terms they could with the United States.

[*Source*: Daniel K. Richter, 'Native Peoples of North America and the Eighteenth-Century British Empire', in Marshall, *The Eighteenth Century*, pp. 363–4, 366–7, 368–9.]

## 2.4 THE PROBLEM OF INDIA

The debate about ruling large numbers of non-British people was more pointed in India than anywhere else in the empire during the eighteenth century. The Mughal empire, which had ruled substantial parts of south Asia for centuries, was beginning its final collapse. Warfare in or between various princely states in India now involved Europeans as well—after all, they had trading interests to protect or enhance—but was conducted using mainly Indian troops (*sepoys*). The East India Company had built up its own *sepoy* army, and under the leadership of Robert Clive it enjoyed a series of unprecedented military successes (see Map 5). Most notable was Clive's defeat of the forces of the Nawab of Bengal at the Battle of Plassey in 1757 and the subsequent acquisition of the civil government, or *diwani*, of Bengal.

The *diwani* meant that for the first time the EIC was actually ruling (and taxing) Indians, a development which would eventually lead to wider British involvement, and to acrimonious debate about the Company's identity and purpose in India (Extract 45). Should it confine itself to commercial matters, or should it wield political influence in the subcontinent? If the latter, should it rule according to Indian custom or should it bring Christianity, western government, and British law to India? Indian leaders themselves began to fear that the Company's military victories foreshadowed an end to their political independence (Extract 46).

By the time Warren Hastings became Governor of Bengal in 1772 further conquests had increased the EIC's wealth and political authority. Like his predecessors, Hastings believed that Indian legal, taxation and landholding practices should be retained under British supervision (Extract 47). Hastings' respect for Indian culture, and his willingness to exploit (rather than over-turn) aspects of Indian government, provoked an outcry. In 1784 the government of William Pitt passed an India Act designed to give the British government a role in deciding EIC policy. This failed to satisfy Hastings' critics; he was recalled to Britain, and impeached in 1788 (Extract 48). During his long trial Parliament received petitions from Indians defending Hastings against the charges of tyranny and corruption (Extract 49). British opinion was itself divided between those who believed that the EIC should avoid policies which would change Indian society, and those who hoped that the Company would sponsor missionaries and attempt to Westernize India. The growing evangelical revival in Britain had considerable influence on the debate, and so did the economic and political reformers. Advocates of free trade attacked the EIC as the largest and richest of the monopolistic chartered companies. Political radicals saw EIC rule as a symbol of absolute rulership, corruption, and arrogance, believing that the empire in India was morally offensive (Extract 50). It was clear that British domestic issues were influencing, and being influenced by, the debate about Britain's imperial identity and responsibility.

Although Warren Hastings was eventually acquitted, the EIC appointed successors who would redirect the course of EIC policy. Taxation on land, the heart of EIC revenues in Bengal, was reorganized under the 'Permanent Settlement' of 1793 (Extract 51) in a process which replaced relatively flexible indigenous landowning traditions with a fixed system under British supervision. Other reforms followed aimed at creating a more British administration in India. At the heart of this transformation was a profound change in British conceptions of Indians during the eighteenth century. Once defined as commercial and political allies (or rivals) with an ancient civilization, they were now identified as cultural inferiors requiring guidance and reform. In his description of Indian society's response to this change (Extract 52), Rajat Kanta Ray quotes a Mughal poet who wrote, 'This age is not like that which went before it. The times have changed, the earth and sky have changed'.

## 45   Richard Becher

Richard Becher, an EIC officer, wrote to the governor of Bengal on 24 May 1769 about the corruption of taxation in Bengal. Observations such as his would lead to increased British regulation and supervision of revenue in future.

It must give pain to an Englishman to have Reason to think that since the accession of the Company to the *Diwani* the condition of the people of this Country has been worse than it was before; and yet I am afraid the Fact is undoubted; . . . this fine Country, which flourished under the most despotic and arbitrary Government, is verging towards its Ruin . . . [. . .]

When the English received the grant of the *Diwani* their first consideration seems to have been the raising of as large sums from the Country as could be collected, to answer the pressing demands from home and to defray the large Expences here. The *Zeminders* not being willing or able to pay the sums required, *Aumils* have been sent into most of the Districts. These *Aumils* on their appointment agree with the Ministers to pay a fixed sum for the Districts they are to go to, and the man that has offered most had generally been preferred. What a destructive system is this for the poor Inhabitants. The *Aumils* have no Connection or natural Interest in the Welfare of the Country where they make the Collections, nor have they any certainty of holding their Places beyond the Year: the best recommendation they can have is to pay up their *Kistbundi* punctually, to which purpose they fail not to rack the Country whenever they find they cannot otherwise pay their *Kists* and secure a handsome sum for themselves. . . . These *Aumils* also have had no check on them during the time of their Employment; they appoint those that act under them; so that during the Time of the Year's Collection their power is absolute. There is no . . . likelihood of complaints till the poor *Ryot* is really drove to Necesity by having more demanded of him than he can possibly pay. Much these poor wretches will bear rather than quit their Habitations to come here to complain, especially when it is to be considered that it must always be attended with loss of time, risk of obtaining Redress, and a Certainty of being very ill-used should the *Aumil's* influence be sufficient to prevent the poor Man's obtaining justice or even access to those able to grant it to him. On this destructive Plan and with a continual Demand for more Revenue have the collections been made ever since the English have been in possession of the *Diwani*.

[*Source*: Muir, *The Making of British India*, pp. 92–4.]

## 46   John Holwell

John Holwell, magistrate for Calcutta, had been acting governor when the Nawab of Bengal (Siraj-Uddaula) captured the city in 1756, and he was one of only four survivors of the prison known as the 'Black Hole of Calcutta'. He reported to the EIC directors on 30 November 1756 quoting advice that the Nawab's grandfather had given Siraj-Uddaula concerning European involvement in India.

'My life has been a life of war and stratagem: for what have I fought, to what have my councils tended, but to secure you, my son, a quiet succession to my *subadari*? My fears for you have for many days robbed me of sleep. I perceived who had power to give you trouble after I am gone hence. . . . Keep in view the power the European nations have in the country. This fear I would also have freed you from if God had lengthened my days.—The work, my son, must now be yours. Their wars and politicks in the Telinga country should keep you waking. On pretence of private contests between their kings they have seized and divided the country of the King and the goods of his people between them. Think not to weaken all three together. The power of the English is great; . . . reduce them first; the others will give you little trouble, when you have reduced them. Suffer them not, my son, to have fortifications or soldiers: if you do, the country is not yours.'

[*Source*: Muir, *The Making of British India*, pp. 40–1.]

## 47   Warren Hastings

Warren Hastings, governor of Bengal, wrote to the Chief Justice, Lord
Mansfield, on 21 March 1774 about the sophistication of Indian law.

Among the various plans which have been lately formed for the improvement
of the British interests in the provinces of Bengal, the necessity of establishing a new form of judicature, and giving laws to a people who were supposed
to be governed by no other principle of justice than the arbitrary wills, or
uninstructed judgments, of their temporary rulers, has been frequently suggested; and this opinion I fear has obtained the greater strength from some
publications of considerable merit in which it is too positively asserted that
written laws are totally unknown to the Hindus or original inhabitants of
Hindustan. From whatever cause this notion has proceeded, nothing can be
more foreign from truth. I presume, my Lord, if this assertion can be proved,
you will not deem it necessary that I should urge any argument in defence of
their right to possess those benefits under a British and Christian administration which the Mahomedan government has never denied them. It would be a
grievance to deprive the people of the protection of their own laws, but it
would be a wanton tyranny to require their obedience to others of which they
are wholly ignorant, and of which they have no possible means of acquiring a
knowledge. . . . It was judged advisable for the sake of giving confidence to
the people, and of enabling the Courts to decide with certainty and despatch,
to form a compilation of the Hindu laws with the best authority which could
be obtained; and for that purpose ten of the most learned *pundits* were invited
to Calcutta from different parts of the province, who cheerfully undertook
this work, have incessantly laboured in the prosecution of it, and have already,
as they assure me, completed it, all but the revisal and correction of it.

  This code they have written in their own language, the Sanscrit. A translation of it is begun under the inspection of one of their body into the Persian
language, and from that into English. The two first chapters I have now the
honour to present to your Lordship with this, as a proof that the inhabitants
of this land are not in the savage state in which they have been unfairly
represented, and as a specimen of the principles which constitute the rights
of property among them. . . . With respect to the Mahomedan law, which is
the guide at least of one fourth of the natives of this province, your Lordship
need not be told that this is as comprehensive, and as well defined, as that of
most states in Europe, having been formed at a time in which the Arabians
were in possession of all the real learning which existed in the western parts
of this continent.

[*Source*: Muir, *The Making of British India*, pp. 144–5.]

## 48   Edmund Burke

The House of Lords began impeachment proceedings against Warren
Hastings in February 1788, and this speech by the Tory MP Edmund
Burke is one of the most famous in parliamentary history.

My Lords, the first thing in considering the character of any Governor is to
have some test by which it may be tried. And we conceive here that when a
British Governor is sent abroad, he is sent to pursue the good of the people as
much as possible in the spirit of the Laws of this Country, which intend in all
respects their conservation, their happiness, and their prosperity. These are
the principles upon which Mr Hastings was bound to govern, and upon
which he is to account for his conduct here. [. . .]

But he has told your Lordships in his defence, that actions in Asia do not
bear the same moral qualities as the same actions would bear in Europe. My
Lords, we positively deny that principle. I am authorized and called upon to
deny it. And having stated at large what he means by saying that the same
actions have not the same qualities in Asia and in Europe, we are to let your
Lordships know that these Gentlemen have formed a plan of Geographical
morality, by which the duties of men in public and in private situations are
not to be governed by their relations to the Great Governor of the Universe,
or by their relations to men, but by climates, degrees of longitude and
latitude, parallels not of life but of latitudes. [. . .]

Mr Hastings comes before your Lordships not as a British Governor,
answering to a British Tribunal, but as a Soubahdar, as a Bashaw of three tails.
He says: I had an arbitrary power to exercise; I exercised it. Slaves I found the
people; slaves they are. They are so by their Constitution; and if they are, I
did not make it for them. I was unfortunately bound to exercise this arbitrary
power, and accordingly I did exercise it. It was disagreeable to me, but I did
exercise it, and no other power can be exercised in that Country. This, if it be
true, is a plea in Bar. But I trust and hope your Lordships will not judge by
Laws and institutions, which you do not know, against those Laws and
institutions which you do know, and under whose power and authority Mr
Hastings went out to India. Can your Lordships patiently hear what we have
heard with indignation enough, and what, if there were nothing else, would
call actions which are justified upon such principles to your Lordships Bar,
that it may be known whether the Peers of England do not sympathize with
the Commons in their detestation of such doctrine? Think of an English
Governor tried before you as a British subject, and yet declaring that
he governed upon the principles of arbitrary power. This plea is, that he
did govern there upon arbitrary and despotic, and, as he supposes, Oriental

principles. And as his plea is boldly avowed and maintained and as, no doubt, all his conduct was perfectly correspondent to these principles, these principles and that conduct must be tried together. [. . .]

I impeach Warren Hastings, Esquire, of High Crimes and Misdemeanours.

I impeach him in the name of the Commons of Great Britain in Parliament assembled, whose parliamentary trust he has betrayed.

I impeach him in the name of all the Commons of Great Britain, whose national character he has dishonoured.

I impeach him in the name of the people of India, whose laws, rights and liberties he has subverted, whose properties he has destroyed, whose Country he has laid waste and desolate.

I impeach him in the name and by virtue of those eternal laws of justice which he has violated.

I impeach him in the name of human nature itself, which he has cruelly outraged, injured and oppressed, in both sexes, in every age, rank, situation and condition of life.

[*Source*: P. J. Marshall, ed., *India: The Launching of the Hastings Impeachment 1786–1788*, vol. 6 of *The Writings and Speeches of Edmund Burke* (Oxford: Clarendon, 1991), pp. 344–5, 346–7, 459.]

---

**49**  **Addresses from inhabitants of Benares, India**

Many Indians wrote in support of Hastings during the impeachment trial. The first of these two addresses was written by the inhabitants of Benares; the second by the pundits, brahmins, and other religious leaders of Benares. Hastings' governance in the Indian tradition, and his support for Hindu temples, would have confirmed the suspicions of his critics.

## From the inhabitants of Benares

He laid the foundations of justice and the pillars of the law. In every shape, we, the inhabitants of this country, during the time of his administration, lived in ease and peace. We are therefore greatly satisfied with and thankful to him. As the said Mr. Hastings was long acquainted with the modes of government in these regions, so the inmost purpose of his heart was openly and secretly, indeed, bent upon those things which might maintain inviolate our religious advances and persuasions, and guard us in even the minutest respect from misfortune and calamity. In every way he cherished us in honour and credit.

## From the Pundits and other Brahmins of Benares

Whenever that man of vast reason, the Governor-General, Mr. Hastings, returned to this place, and people of all ranks were assembled, at that time he gladdened the heart of every one by his behaviour, which consisted of kind wishes and agreeable conversation, expressions of compassion for the distressed, acts of politeness, and a readiness to relieve and protect every one alike without distinction. To please us dull people, he caused a spacious music gallery to be built, at his own expense, over the gateway of the temple of Veesmaswar, which is esteemed the head jewel of all places of holy visitation. He never at any time, nor on any occasion, either by neglecting to promote the happiness of the people, or by looking with the eye of covetousness, displayed an inclination to distress any individual whatsoever.

[*Source:* Muir, *The Making of British India*, pp. 164–5.]

---

## 50 William Cobbett

William Cobbett was an essayist and political commentator. He was particularly critical of the expansion of the empire in south Asia and its cost in British lives and revenue. Writing in April 1808 he laments the decades of war in India which had swollen the EIC's territory there.

The recent intelligence from India, or, 'our Empire in the East', is of a gloomy complexion, in my sight, only inasmuch as it gives an account of the loss of a great number of English officers and soldiers. It may serve to make men reflect justly on the nature of the wars we carry on in India; and may lead them to the conclusion, so much to be desired, namely, that the possession of that country is a terrible evil. This, it seems, is to be *the last* war; but, we have been told the same thing for more than thirty years past. There is a constant, never-ceasing war in India. There is not always actual fighting; but, there are always going on preparations for fighting. What right, in God's name, what right have we to do this? How is it possible for us to justify our conduct, upon any principle of morality? Conquests in India are not at all necessary to either our safety or our comfort. There is no glory attending such conquests and their accompanying butcheries. We must be actuated by a sheer love of gain; a sheer love of plunder. I really believe, that the history of the whole world does not afford an instance of a series of aggressions so completely unjustifiable and inexcusable.

[*Source:* G. D. H. and Margaret Cole, eds., *The Opinions of William Cobbett* (London: Cobbett Publishing Co., 1944), p. 258.]

## 51   Lord Cornwallis

The Governor-General, Lord Cornwallis, explains his plans, under the
Permanent Settlement, for the role of *zamindars*, the traditional collectors of land revenue. By making them landholders, with permanent responsibility for particular areas, Cornwallis and the EIC altered
local government in Bengal and elsewhere.

In a country where the landlord has a permanent property in the soil it will
be worth his while to improve that property; at any rate he will make such an
agreement with them (his tenants) as will prevent their destroying it. But
when the lord of the soil himself, the rightful owner of the land, is only to
become the farmer for a lease of ten years, and if he is then to be exposed to
the demand of a new rent, which may perhaps be dictated by ignorance or
rapacity, what hopes can there be, I will not say of improvement, but of
preventing desolation? Will it not be his interest, during the early part of that
term, to extract from the estate every possible advantage for himself; and if
any future hopes of a permanent settlement are then held out, to exhibit his
lands at the end of it in a state of ruin? I am not only of opinion that the
*zemindars* have the best right, but from being persuaded that nothing could be
so ruinous to the public interest as that the land should be retained as the
property of the Government, I am also convinced that, failing the claim of
right of the *zemindars*, it would be necessary for the public good to grant a
right of property in the soil to them, or to persons of other descriptions.

It is the most effectual mode for promoting the general improvement of
the country, which I look upon as the important object for our present
consideration.

I may safely assert that one-third of the Company's territory in Hindostan
is now a jungle inhabited only by wild beasts. Will a ten years' lease induce
any proprietor to clear away that jungle, and encourage the *ryots* to come and
cultivate his lands, or lose all hopes of deriving any benefit from his labour,
for which perhaps by that time he will hardly be repaid? . . .

It is for the interest of the State that the landed property should fall into
the hands of the most frugal and thrifty class of people, who will improve
their lands and protect the *ryots*, and thereby promote the general prosperity
of the country.

[*Source*: Muir, *The Making of British India*, pp. 186–7.]

52 **Rajat Kanta Ray**

With the creation by 1793 of Cornwallis's 'government-by-regulations', in Bengal the Company's rule, at least for an élite, ceased to be arbitrary and predatory and became predictable. In what was known as the Permanent Settlement, the taxation assessment on the land of Bengal was fixed for ever, at what was initially a high level, and rights to land were thereby created that could be bought and sold. Money invested in land was permanently secure. Unable to pay the assessment, many old landholders were forced to sell out; those who bought from them were in a sense throwing in their lot with the British. The élite who could use the new legal system were also guaranteed personal security and absolute rights to property through the Company's courts, even against the government itself.

While it was beginning to offer positive inducements to Indians to ally with it, the Company was also putting its own house in order. Pitt's India Act and a subsequent Act of 1786 unified the British state in India under the Governor-General's command. The Governor-General now had clear authority over the other Presidencies and over his own Council. No longer, as the Chief Justice of India had observed, might a whole Presidency be involved in domestic discord with the enemy at the gate and 'the Government General' a tame spectator of the confusion.

The young Wellington grasped the significance of these developments for the balance of power in India when he saw that the Company's government was now guided by 'all the rules and systems of European policy', whereas the Indian powers, especially the Marathas, hardly knew of such rules and systems, for 'the objects of their policy are always shifting'.

Tipu Sultan, who dimly realized the awesome power of European technology and organization, sought to graft some aspects of it to his state by developing an army with fire-power, government manufacture of armaments, and state management of commercial factories and banking establishments. But Cornwallis hemmed him in by securing the military co-operation of the Nizam and the Marathas in 1792, and Wellesley cut short his experiments in 1799. He had injured the Company's trade by placing an embargo, and had sought an alliance with the French. Tipu was killed when the British took his capital, and the occupation of his territories by the British army brought Arthur Wellesley's forces within striking-distance of Poona, at a critical moment when civil war between Holkar and Sindia paralyzed the internal mechanisms of the Maratha confederacy. Governor-General Lord Wellesley's massive intervention destroyed that confederacy (an abortive attempt to revive it led to the extinction of the Peshwa's state in 1818) and substituted the hegemony of the East India Company for the 'balance of power'.

For Wellesley and that generation, the symbol of this hegemony was possession of the Red Fort and at Delhi its blind Emperor. Wellesley adverted to 'the importance of securing the person and nominal authority of the Mogul against the designs of France, and the encrease of reputation of the British name, which would result from affording an honourable asylum to the person and family of that injured and unfortunate monarch'. But once the Red Fort was in British hands, he saw 'no obligation imposed upon us, to consider the rights and claims of his Majesty Shah Aulum as Emperor of Hindustan'.

The political hegemony of the East India Company visibly transformed the conditions of Indian trade and finance. With more revenues than before—an impressed Persian chronicler who had served in the Imperial treasury at the Red Fort estimated that Lord Wellesley had increased the wealth of the Company's territory from Rs. 70 million worth of revenue to Rs. 150 million, that is, £15 million—the Company authorities were in a position to clip the wings of the Indian bankers and to break out of the irksome dependence on their *hundis*. These instruments were relegated to inland Indian business, the so-called bazaar, as the Company floated public loans at as low a rate as 6 per cent, and eventually at 5 per cent, on the basis of heightened public confidence.

Part of this confident public was the growing body of non-official Europeans gathered around the houses of agency for the conduct of the private trade. The other part was the emerging Indian public of the Presidency towns, presided over by the landholders and the leaders of the Indian business communities that dealt with the British: Bengali *banians* of Calcutta, the Tamil *dubashes* of Madras, and the Parsee brokers of Bombay, whose function was to act as the intermediaries between the European agency houses and the Indian bazaar.

The favoured agency houses, which had come forward with large loans in the Maratha War, replaced the Company in the commanding heights of India's exchange economy. As the Company's exports of Indian cotton textiles to Europe ceased after the Charter Act of 1813, the agency houses laid out nearly £5 million to develop indigo, cotton, silk, and opium as alternative export items. This fostered a triangular colonial trade between India, China, and Britain, and in the process provided a broader channel for the flow of remittances to England. The compulsory supply of white personnel and services by Britain to India, the shipments of cotton and opium from India to China, and the exports of tea from China to Britain defined an indirect and less disruptive circuit for the transmission of India's tribute to Britain. [. . .]

As the once-prosperous Mughal towns withered away, and while the colonial port cities grew slowly, there sprang into a prominence a brand of late Mughal poetry called the *Shahr-i-Ashob*, or Town in Lament, with *inqilab* [social disruption (ed.)] at the centre of its theme. The Mughal troopers, lamented the poet Rasikh of Patna, were so afflicted by poverty that they could not command even a toy clay horse. Yet another poet of Patna, Jauhri, saw with shock the cavalry of 'lalas and baboos' (parvenus serving the English) going forth with a tumult through the town. It was a time, the poets complained, when everything had been 'turned upside down', and all were subject to 'the impression of changing fortune'. The flippant art of love, cultivated by cavaliers and courtesans in the decaying Mughal towns, was coloured by the fickleness of fortune:

> I told her the story of my heart: she listened for a while, and said
> I have to go. But you can stay; sit there, and go on with your tale.

The hours spent in the company of the *Saki* might blunt the edge, but would not altogether wipe out the injury done to self-esteem by the humiliating denial of the high offices of the state and the rigid exclusion from the positions of power. A collective racial degradation was implicit in the social revolution that had occurred. 'The greatest men formerly', wrote the Judge and Magistrate of Midnapore in Bengal in response to a query from Wellesley's government, 'were the Musalman rulers, whose places we have taken, and the Hindoo zemindars—These two classes are now ruined and destroyed—The natives mostly looked up to, are our Omlah [subordinate officers] and our domestics: these are courted and respected: they must necessarily be the channel, through which every suitor and every candidate looks up for redress and preferment.'

This was *inqilab*, and of a sort that the Muslim gentry (*ashraf*) of the reduced Mughal towns could not but rage over. The manner in which the men in charge of the affairs of the powerful English households (*mutasaddis*) treated visiting Indian gentlemen of ancient and illustrious families filled Ghulam Husain Khan with indignation at 'a variety of affronts and indignities'. The 'aversion' and 'disdain' which he saw the English evince for the company of the natives, exposed to his view a political hegemony which was at the same time a racial monopoly: 'they are come at last to undervalue the Hindustanees, and to make no account of the natives from the highest to the lowest; and they carry their contempt so far, as to employ none but their own selves in every department and in every article of business, esteeming themselves better than all others put together.'

On this point, Raja Ram Mohun Roy and the new generation of Hindu gentry (*bhadralok*) in Calcutta were at one with Saiyid Ghulam Husain Khan and the older generation of Muslim noblemen (*umara*) of Patna and Murshidabad, however profoundly the Raja would differ from the Saiyid regarding the benevolence of the Mughal and the injustice of the English.

The better classes of the natives of India [so ran an Indian petition to Parliament drafted by Ram Mohun Roy] are placed under the sway of the Honourable East India Company, in a state of political degradation which is absolutely without a parallel in their former history. For even under the Mahomedan conquerors, such of your petitioners as are Hindoos, were not only capable of filling but actually did fill numerous employments of trust, dignity and emolument, from which under the existing system of the Honourable Company's government, they are absolutely shut out.

The colonial rationale for the disfranchisement of a whole race—'Asiatic treachery and falsehood' (Wellesley), 'the perverseness and depravity of the natives of India in general' (John Malcolm)—derived from a particular construction of the native character which induced the Utilitarian philosopher at India House to reflect gravely, 'In India there is no moral character'. The proneness of the natives to 'mendacity and perjury' was for the philosopher James Mill the major obstacle to ensuring justice through the courts of law. Had he possessed Ram Mohun Roy's insight into the matter, he would have seen what his more acute Indian contemporary grasped: that it was the existing system of English judges and native pleaders which promoted the crime of perjury to such an extent as to make it impossible to distinguish what was true from what was not. The English judges treated the native pleaders and officers of the court with contempt, while the latter looked up to the judges as humble dependants of a master rather than independent advocates of the rights of their clients. 'And the whole are so closely leagued together, that if a complaint is preferred to a higher authority against the judge (he having the power of promoting or ruining the prospects of Native officers and pleaders) they are all ready to support him and each other to the defeat of justice, by false oaths and fabricated documents.'

Indian reactions to the establishment of British hegemony ranged from the inclination of the doctors of Islamic law (ulama) to reject the whole system, to the design of the English-educated Hindus to turn its internal rules to the advantage of their countrymen. The essence of the system, as Wellesley explained to the Court of Directors in 1800, was the rule of the law. He was acquainted with those who rejected that law and its rule altogether; he hardly yet anticipated those who might try and turn that law upon its giver.

[*Source*: Rajat Kanta Ray, 'Indian Society and the Establishment of British Supremacy, 1765–1818', in Marshall, *The Eighteenth Century*, pp. 521–5.]

# Chapter 3

## The Nineteenth Century

### INTRODUCTION

After its defeat of Napoleonic France in 1815, Britain became the world's dominant naval and commercial power. Its territorial empire was larger than ever (see Map 2), and technological innovation would combine with capital investment to continue the process of imperial expansion even beyond formal colonial borders. This process, known as 'informal empire', drew countries like Siam (now Thailand) into Britain's sphere of influence even though they remained technically independent. Britain also took advantage of a series of nationalist wars which terminated Spain's enormous empire in the Americas during the early nineteenth century. British army and navy officers advised the nationalists, and the newly independent Latin American republics often rewarded Britain with trade privileges and the use of strategic ports. Argentina, in particular, would become the site of intensive British investment.

Sheer lack of competition allowed Britain to sustain this dominant position throughout the early and mid-nineteenth century; a period often said to feature a 'Pax Britannica'. There was little that was peaceful about the process of imperial expansion, as we will see, but the Royal Navy's extensive mapping and policing made maritime trade safer than it had ever been before. Although France and Russia also went through expansionist phases, this did not bring about a return to the near-constant European warfare of the eighteenth century. Only during the later nineteenth century would competition from other powers challenge Britain's commercial and imperial pre eminence. Britain was especially worried about the so-called Great Game— Russian encroachment in Afghanistan and other areas near India—and allied with other countries against Russia during the Crimean War of 1854–6. But for the most part the nineteenth century saw an unprecedented freedom from British military expenditure in Europe.

At home, the Industrial Revolution was transforming Britain into a commercial superpower. No other country would industrialize to the same extent before the 1870s, giving Britain a near-monopoly on the production of manufactured goods. But this did not mean that Britain could afford to ignore the outside world. The growing British population required imported food from Europe and the United States; British factories required imported raw materials. Although the expanding empire could meet some of these needs, the empire was not self-sufficient. These developments revived the free trade debate of the late eighteenth century and, this time, the old mercantilist system was almost completely overturned. Free trade suited Britain well for most of the century; only after the 1870s, when other industrializing powers threatened British commercial dominance, did protectionism begin to appeal once again to British statesmen and industrialists.

At the end of the nineteenth century this new atmosphere of competition prompted a 'new imperialism'. Germany and the United States had consolidated politically and economically, enabling them to industrialize and to challenge Britain's predominance in manufacturing. They wished to enhance their status, and the identity of an international 'Power' in the late nineteenth century depended on the acquisition of an empire. Various European nations, including Germany, scrambled to divide the 'unclaimed' areas of Africa and the Pacific between them. The United States expanded through informal imperialism in Latin America (where it surpassed Britain in investment and political influence) and by acquiring Cuba, the Philippines, and other territories after the Spanish–American war in 1898. Japan, meanwhile, was fighting a series of expansionist wars in east Asia and beginning the industrialization of its economy. Not to be outdone, the British also increased their imperial territory and the British empire had almost reached its greatest extent by 1914 (see Map 6).

The challenges of the late nineteenth century created an intensified imperial rivalry and prompted new interpretations of Britain's imperial identity. At the political level ideas about protectionism, imperial federation, and joint imperial defence were proposed. At the popular level, the images and literature of empire found an enthusiastic audience due to increased literacy and the proliferation of inexpensive books and newspapers. Empire-wide societies such as the scouting movement helped to express this renewed popular support for imperialism, and the sense of rivalry with Germany and other nations only served to make British nationalism more aggressive and xenophobic than ever.

## 3.1 TRADE AND EMPIRE

Whatever else the British empire was about, it was always about trade. Economics were a vital part of imperial identity and growth, and the empire (especially in India) was a source of wealth and a field for investment. When we compare the nineteenth century with earlier periods we can see how readily the British could reinvent the commercial basis of empire in order to accommodate changing economic philosophies in Britain itself.

By 1850 the triumph of free trade capitalism was virtually complete. Some of the biggest of the old chartered companies still traded—the Hudson's Bay Company, for example—but they enjoyed little of their former predominance. The role of the British state had also declined, reflecting a belief in laissez-faire economics, or what might be called 'deregulation' today. Given the American colonists' hostility to British economic interference in the eighteenth century, it was ironic that several of Britain's remaining colonies should now mourn the passing of the old, exclusive system. Agricultural producers like Canada worried about losing the security of protective tariffs (Extract 53). But free trade also encouraged increased capital investment, spread imperial profits through a growing commercial élite, and prompted innovation. For example, the first use of steam vessels for upriver trading in west Africa was in a series of privately financed ventures by Macgregor Laird in the 1830s.

Older organizations like the East India Company were forced to become more competitive; even though the EIC retained a monopoly on the China trade until 1833 it worked hard to acquire other sources of that great British beverage, tea. British imports of tea were steadily increasing during the early nineteenth century, and the Chinese would accept only specie, usually silver, in payment. One solution to the problem was to develop a trade in opium. Another was to obtain tea plants for cultivation on British territory. The Chinese were understandably reluctant to allow plants to leave the country, but the British used intermediaries to obtain them by stealth and to create plantations for their cultivation in India (Extract 54). Similar manœuvres created plantations for chincona (for malaria prevention) in India, rubber in Malaya, and many other examples of global plant transfer and exploitation.

As ever, the labour supply failed to keep pace with commercial expansion, and after the abolition of slavery throughout the empire in 1833 the British needed to find alternatives to African slave labour. Only free labour would satisfy Britain's new identity as a humanitarian empire, and a return to the indenture system seemed ideal. Once used to bring Irish and British workers to the American and West Indian colonies, indentures exchanged a fixed period of labour for transportation, payment, food, and housing. By the nineteenth century south Asians and Chinese were seen as ideal labourers and 1,475,000 people signed official indentures to work in Britain's colonies between 1834 and 1920. Of course the recruitment and employment process was open to abuse (Extract 55), and a series of investigations produced regulatory legislation at intervals (Extract 56). But the eventual decline of indenture did not come from British initiatives: it was the 'White Australia' policy in the early twentieth century, and racist legislation in Canada and South Africa, that drastically reduced Asian and Pacific island labour in those countries. Later, pressure from the Indian nationalist movement would discourage south Asian indentures in Africa and south-east Asia.

The nineteenth century also featured a range of technological developments which assisted British expansion. By the middle of the century steam technology had transformed British passenger and cargo shipping, reducing travel time and permitting easier and safer inshore and upriver voyages. Telegraphy combined with submarine cable technology to create a global communications system linking the far-flung British empire (Extract 57). Railways proliferated, permitting greater access to the interior of colonies, especially in Africa (Extract 58), which had previously tended to revolve around coastal settlements. Building on the strategic and economic gains of the eighteenth century, the nineteenth-century empire combined political and cultural will with the technological means of bringing vast new areas under British rule. These developments also helped create the 'informal empire' which was such a vital part of Britain's growing power and prosperity (Extract 59).

## 53   W. E. Gladstone

W. E. Gladstone, as Secretary of State for the Colonies, wrote to the Governor-General of Canada on 3 June 1846 about free trade and empire. Canadian traders were alarmed about the end of British protectionism, and Canada would sign a reciprocal trade treaty with the United States in 1854.

Her Majesty's Government conceive that the protective principle cannot with justice be described as the universal basis, either of the general connexion between the United Kingdom and its colonies, or even of their commercial connexion. There is a large and important group of the colonies of this country, having a very extended commerce, and one of a peculiarly British character, in relation to which the protective system has at no time exercised a powerful influence, and in relation to which at present it has little more than a nominal existence. I speak of the Australian colonies: and it cannot fail to be remarked, that while these are the most distant, and therefore, according to the suppositions of many, the most in need of commercial preference, they have also made the most rapid progress, and have thus most effectually belied that necessity. It is true, indeed, that a part of their material prosperity may be ascribable to the supply of penal labour; but this is far from affording an explanation of the case, since perhaps the most remarkable instances of vigorous and rapid growth among the Australian possessions of Her Majesty have been instances in which penal labour has been altogether unknown. The energy of the colonists has, without doubt, under Divine Providence, been the main cause of their singular advancement; stimulated, but not overborne by distance, and aided, not repressed, by the enjoyment of commercial freedom. The same energies, with less disadvantage of distance to contend against, will, it may be confidently predicted, have a similar effect in developing the resources of British North America, and not with less, but rather with the more signal success, when capital, industry and skill shall be left to take their own spontaneous direction, and to turn to account, as individual prudence shall suggest, the abundant materials and instruments of wealth which the bounty of Heaven has bestowed. [. . .]

It appears to be the impression of the Assembly that some great revolution of prices is likely to occur, as the consequence of the pending changes in the law, which will deprive the Canadian farmer of all hope of remuneration for his surplus produce. But the Canadian farmer is advancing from year to year in capital and in science; and, to say nothing of the great advantages he cannot fail to derive from improved communications, it would surely be rash to assert, nor probably do the Assembly in their address intend to imply, that his industry must be paralysed unless he shall continue to receive the precise amount of average payment for his grain that he has hitherto received for it. Doubtless the alarm which has been excited has reference to the idea of some sudden, great and permanent reduction of price, to follow the repeal of the British Corn Law. Without pretending to estimate too nicely the momentary or the occasional effects of that measure, Her Majesty's Government cannot but admit that they could better appreciate at least certain presumptive, though far from demonstrative, grounds for the alarm of the Canadian agriculturist in regard to the future fortunes of the colony if they shared in such an anticipation. To some reduction of average and usual price, from the removal of artificial restraints, they are disposed to look forward; but when they consider the steady and rapid growth of population in the corn-producing countries of the globe, they cannot but be persuaded that it would be unwise, whether in the friends or the opponents of commercial relaxation, to recommend or dissuade it on the ground of any great revolution in permanent prices to be operated by it; and their expectations of advantage, sanguine as these anticipations are, have reference in a greater degree to the increased steadiness of the market, and to the vigour which general trade will derive from the removal of restraints upon the exchange of commodities, and agriculture, from the cessation of all artificial influence disturbing the balance of its several pursuits, and from the wholesome stimulus that competition, which in farming pursuits can scarcely become overwrought, rarely fails to impart to industry.

[*Source*: Kenneth N. Bell and W. Morrell, *Select Documents on British Colonial Policy 1830–1860* (Oxford: Clarendon Press, 1968), pp. 339–40.]

## 54    Dr Wallick

> The botanist Dr Wallick reported his 'Observations on the Cultivation of the Tea Plant for Commercial Purposes, in the mountainous part of Hindustan' on 3 February 1832 for Charles Grant, president of the Board of Control for Indian Affairs. Dependent on China for most of its tea supplies, Britain was anxious to cultivate Chinese tea on British territory in India.

From what has been advanced in speaking of the general rules that are to be observed in all our endeavours to naturalize the plants of foreign and distant climates, it is obvious that we cannot expect to succeed, unless we pay strict attention to those laws of nature in the distribution of the plants on the surface of the earth, which have been traced by the labours of some of the first naturalists and agriculturists; and on the other hand, it must be allowed, that vague and unsatisfactory experiments, such as those were which have been enumerated above, ought not to have any weight in the solution of the problem, whether the tea plant admits of being advantageously cultivated in foreign countries for commercial or agricultural purposes. The time has arrived when this question has assumed a more than ordinary degree of interest; and there exist territories within the British dominions in the East Indies, agreeing so perfectly with those of the tea provinces, that no doubt can be entertained of their being capable of producing tea equal to the best kinds ever obtained from China; unless, indeed, it should be contended, that the plant differs from all others on a point in which the whole vegetable kingdom has been found to agree, and that it forms an exception to one of the most beautiful laws of nature. [. . .]

I have already had occasion to observe that a species of camellia grows wild in Nipal, and in publishing an account of it in 1818, I noticed that a tea shrub was thriving vigorously in a garden at Katmandu, 10 feet in height, and producing plentiful flowers and fruits during the last four months of the year. During my visit to that capital some years afterwards, I saw the shrub, and I ascertained that the seeds of it had been brought from Pekin by the return of one of the triennial embassies which are sent to China by the Goorka government.

If we take all these concurring circumstances into due consideration, we may surely entertain sanguine hopes, that under a well-directed management the tea plant may at no distant period be made an object of extensive cultivation in the Honourable East India Company's dominions, and that we shall not long continue dependent on the will and caprice of a despotic nation for the supply of one of the greatest comforts and luxuries of civilized life.

[*Source*: Great Britain, *Parliamentary Papers* 1831–1832, vol. X, part II, 'Affairs of the East India Company' [735-II], p. 668.]

## 55   'Bibee' Zuhoorun

Former indentured servant 'Bibee' Zuhoorun testifies before a Parliamentary committee on 20 September 1838. She was from India and had worked in Mauritius for two and half years without pay before returning home. Fewer women sought indenture than men, and those who did might have sexual harrassment added to the usual worries about pay, housing and transport.

[N]ot one of the Coolies would remain there if they could help it; every one would leave if there was a land journey; not one would advise any of their friends to go there. I have received injury, I have lost my castes even my mother will not drink water from my hand or eat with me; but God is my witness I speak the truth, I am not telling a lie. I complained three times at the police, but I was only put in the house of correction once, and that was because I stated my determination not to do work; I was sent there until a ship was ready; if I was to starve and could not live by begging, I would rather die in the street than go back there; it is a country of slaves; the negroes are slaves there; I was sitting in a tailor's shop at Bhowanipore when this Junglee Haldad and the baboo came to me, and said, 'If you want service, there is a lady and gentleman going about five days' journey by sea; if you have a mind to go, we can get you a place;' that very day they gave me 20 rupees and took 10 back. At the end of the year, when found I got no wages, what could I do? [. . .]

Dr. Boileau's house was about six miles from the city; I never was allowed to go there; what could I buy? I had no money. My mistress was kind to me at first, but my master said something to her which changed her behaviour to me. My master said I told a lie in charging him with wishing me to lie with him. I used frequently to run away to his wife and tell her all this, and then he used to say I lied, and beat me; at last, about six months before I left the island, she was very angry, and never came near him at all. I do not know her age, but the child was about four years old. My mistress did not believe her husband. Dr. Boileau had two black Caffre girls; they were good-natured, and often did work for me which I could not do without losing my caste; if he saw them, he would beat them too. I told them what my master wanted; they said, 'He is a bad fellow, he serves every body so.'

[*Source*: Great Britain, *Parliamentary Papers* 1841, vol. XVI, 'Report of the Committee Appointed . . . to Inquire into the Abuses alleged to exist in exporting . . . Hill Coolies and Indian Labourers, of various Classes, to other Countries . . . ' [45], pp. 45–6.]

## 56   Report of Government of India on indenture

The Indian government's report on indenture in 1839 recommended a regulated system in order to prevent corruption and abuse.

We conceive it to be distinctly proved beyond dispute, that the Coolies and other natives exported to Mauritius and elsewhere were (generally speaking) induced to come to Calcutta by misrepresentation and deceit, practised upon them by native crimps, styled duffadars and arkotties, employed by European and Anglo-Indian undertakers and shippers, who were mostly cognizant of these frauds, and who received a very considerable sum per head for each Coolie exported.

That if the natives in the interior, Hill Coolies or others, had been distinctly made aware that they were to go beyond seas to a great distance, and to remain absent for five years, it is probable that not one, or at least that very few, would have been induced to take such an engagement.

That the Coolies seem generally to have been induced, by the duffadars and others employed in that business, to come to Calcutta by being persuaded that they should find employment as peons under the Company, work on the public roads, or as gardeners, porters, &c.

That in the cases of the Hill Coolies especially, and in many other instances, the parties were really incapable of understanding the nature of the contracts they were said to have entered into, even when an opportunity of explanation had been afforded apparently sufficient for the purpose.

That in despite of the regulations of 1837 and the interference of the police, an impression was successfully created and maintained up to the date of the suspension of the trade among the Coolies, that they would be liable to penal consequences if they expressed dissatisfaction at being sent on board ship; and this seems to have induced them, both previous to their departure and after their return, to suppress the mention of their grievances wherever they conceived themselves interrogated by government officers.

That kidnapping prevailed to a very considerable extent; and the Coolies, while kept in Calcutta itself and its neighbourhood, were actually in a state of close imprisonment. [. . .]

It appears in evidence that no restraint has at any time existed on the emigration of women, yet very few have gone. The Mauritias government has really been desirous that they should be sent; but I think it may be fairly inferred that the planters have not. The result of the emigration that has already taken place has been most disastrous to the families of those who have emigrated; and it is shown by the memorandum furnished to the Land-holders' Society by Mr. Taylor, and printed in the Appendix to the Calcutta Report [. . .], that the districts of Bancoorab and Maunbhoom have been burdened with a vagrant and mendicant population of paupers, composed of the deserted families of emigrant Coolies.

On the subject of the condition of the Coolies in Mauritius, there is contradictory evidence. Mr. Onslow, of the Madras Civil Service, the Rev. Mr. Garstin, Dr. Wise, Captains Mackenzie and Rayne (all unexceptionable witnesses in point of good faith, character and veracity), bear testimony to their general healthy appearance and their apparent contentment, and seem to consider them as improved in condition. The natives, however, who have returned, with the exception of one Ramdeen, gave evidence the other way. It must be admitted, on such questions, these persons, however ignorant, are really the best judges. The European gentlemen would, from their own position in society, and their natural dispositions, associate probably only with planters of the superior classes and of humane tempers, and whose treatment of their Coolie labourers would, it may be reasonably presumed, be liberal and considerate. And when an opinion is pronounced that the condition of a Coolie is bettered at Mauritius, it should be first ascertained what that condition was in India, and what is the condition of his wife and children, or those of his family dependent upon him, when left behind. Any benefit derived from the superiority of climate at Mauritius or elsewhere may, we think, very reasonably be put out of question, as a mere European notion. It is clear, however, that if the contracts be fulfilled with perfect good faith, the individual Coolie temporarily betters his condition by emigrating to Mauritius, because he gets higher money wages, and food and clothing found him beside, though he has to work harder than in India. But it is clear also from the evidence, that the contracts, generally speaking, are not fulfilled by the planters. The conclusion of our minds from the whole evidence is, that these contracts have been strictly and literally fulfilled in no instance. Under good masters, there may be substantial fulfilment in good faith, as far as the circumstances of the island, in respect of imports of the kind of food stipulated for, permit (an equivalent being provided when the thing stipulated for cannot be afforded). In the majority of cases, however, there is nothing like that kind of performance shown; but, on the contrary, rice and salt and clothing seem to be all that the Coolies do actually receive from bad masters; and no money wages at all seem to be paid in the majority of instances. The average rate of wages paid to Hill Coolies and others at European factories and establishments in Bengal, Tirhoot, Assam and Goruckpore is three and a half rupees to five rupees a month; less than three rupees is rarely paid; and they very often receive four rupees. These wages, when received by Dhangas or Hill Coolies, are sufficient to enable them to save money to return periodically and every year to their families. [. . .]

We are convinced, in fine, that no laws or regulations likely to be passed, short of making the whole land and sea transport of Coolies government services, superintended by government officers and medical men, will suffice to prevent great misery and distress, even on this side of the Cape, and that if West Indian voyages be permitted, the waste of human life and misery that will fall on the Coolies exported under the name of free labourers will approach to those inflicted on the negro in the middle passage by the slave trade. The numbers of Coolies exported to Demerara, Berbice and Essequibo, to Trinidad, Jamaica and the West India Islands generally, would probably be very great; the cost of the voyage there and back would be very heavy, particularly if short terms of contract were enforced, and the impossibility of preventing exportation (whether professedly regulated or merely illicit) from foreign European ports and native territories in India complete. We think the latter consideration quite decisive against the expediency of re-opening the trade, when we reflect that in addition to Danish there are Portuguese and French ports and territories from which a very large exportation could easily be organized. A prohibition to receive Coolies into British colonies in foreign vessels might no doubt be enforced, but the exportation to foreign colonies could not be checked, except by long negotiations, if it were once begun, and our government would have no reason to urge for remonstrance or interference that could not be answered by a reference to its own example, and on the general and abstract principles, that it is always an advantage to all countries where labour is dear to import it from those where labour is cheap; and that it is the right of all men to trade in free labour, and especially of him whose only property is his capacity to labour, to sell that commodity to the best profit.

It seems to us that the permission to renew this traffic would weaken the moral influence of the British Government throughout the world, and deaden or utterly destroy the effect of all future remonstrances and negotiations respecting the slave trade; and this effect would ensue, however stringent, minute or restrictive might be the regulations ordained to check abuses.

Regulations would be met by other regulations, specious and unobjectionable in form; the difference would be in the execution and in the good faith of the framers.

[*Source*: Great Britain, *Parliamentary Papers* 1841, vol. XVI, 'Report of the Committee Appointed . . . to Inquire into the Abuses alleged to exist in exporting . . . Hill Coolies and Indian Labourers, of various Classes, to other Countries . . .' [45], pp. 5, 6–7, 9–10.]

**57** **'Imperial telegraphs',** *The Quarterly Review*

British telegraph cables circled the world by the beginning of the twentieth century, creating a global communications system known as the 'All-Red Route' because it travelled entirely through British territory.

The science of submarine telegraphy was, in fact, fairly well worked out many years ago; and the Pacific cable may be regarded as but an extension of what has already been done, though involving special arrangements and precautions. The difficulties that were raised remind one, however, of the incredulity manifested in regard to the first Atlantic cable, but with this difference, that in the earlier case there were practically no applicable data to go upon. It may be doubted, indeed, whether the Pacific cable would ever have been laid but for the vigour of the present Colonial Secretary. The scheme was coldly looked on until Mr Chamberlain took it in hand as part of a great national and imperial policy. He recognised its importance as a link for bringing the Empire into direct telegraphic connexion for political, commercial, and strategic purposes. In practically annihilating space, the telegraph is one of the strongest links between distant countries; and its importance from a sentimental point of view is by no means to be despised. There is no question that direct and unbroken imperial telegraphy can do much, not only to stimulate commercial activity between the mother-country and the colonies, but also to strengthen that sense of unity and that community of feeling and policy on which the cohesion of the Empire, under present conditions, depends.

[*Source*: 'Imperial Telegraphs', *The Quarterly Review*, no. 394 (1903), pp. 364–83.]

## 58    Charles Eliot

> The British believed that only Europeans were capable of improving
> and developing African natural and human resources, and were proud
> of their ability to survey landscapes and create the borders of new
> countries.

Probably the Uganda Railway is to the general public the best-known feature
in East Africa. Never perhaps has a railway been so prominent, and so completely dominated all surrounding interests. And rightly so. It is not an
uncommon thing for a line to open up a country, but this line has literally
created a country. As a civilised territory and a possible residence for Europeans, East Africa may be said to have come gradually into existence at exactly
the same rate as the rails advanced, and at present the most important
question that can be asked about any locality is, How far is it from the line?

The whole enterprise offers the most extraordinary example of the pluck
and luck which characterise the British race, and also of our happy-go-lucky
methods. It may probably be said, with justice, that every other nation would
have shrunk from the task, but also that every other nation would have
executed it in a more business-like way. Yet whatever criticisms may be made
on the circumstances of construction, and especially on the cost, no one can
deny that the result is successful and useful.

[*Source*: Charles Eliot, *The East Africa Protectorate* (London:
Edward Arnold, 1905), pp. 208, 209.]

## 59    Martin Lynn

British expansion overseas between 1820 and 1880 was extensive, and its
nature a major point of controversy at home. For contemporaries the question was how far expansion overseas should be welcomed, given its implications for domestic society and politics. Expense, economy, retrenchment,
the 'condition of England', and corruption were but some of the issues tied
up in this. While much of the argument focused on Britain's existing colonial
holdings and reform of the relationship between these and Britain itself,
discussion also addressed the nature of Britain's influence beyond the colonies
and its impact on the British economy. [. . .]

Free trade, defined in the broadest sense of allowing the free play of
the market, was seen as central to this process of expansion. Free trade was

the vehicle for 'world bettering' as well as for the expansion of British economic interests overseas. It was the means whereby Britain's role in the wider world could best be shaped. Yet the value of this expansion overseas and the place of free trade in it remained controversial, particularly early in the century. In origin the debate about free trade was an argument about the nature of Britain's domestic society, the place within it of land, commerce, industry, and finance, and the role of the State in economic affairs. However, the overseas dimensions to this were clearly considerable. The benefits of free trade were seen as twofold. First, it would stimulate the growth of British manufacturing. It would help other countries to earn sterling through increased exports of food and raw materials to Britain and would enable them to buy more British manufactures. It would encourage the international division of labour, and enhance Britain's comparative advantage in the world economy. Free trade, in short, would enable Britain to become and remain 'the workshop of the world'.

Tightly coupled to this was a second idea, of capitalism as a moral force. Free trade would help civilize the world through the spread of enterprise and the work ethic. This was related to ideas of progress towards a moral goal, defined largely in terms of British cultural norms. The spread of British trade and investment overseas was thus seen as good in its own right; it brought with it enterprise, progress, and civilization. Free trade would encourage moral regeneration, allowing economically 'backward' nations to develop their resources and throw off outdated élites while encouraging the development of capitalist classes through the moral dimensions of industry and capital accumulation. This was seen as being to the benefit of the areas on the receiving end of British intervention, whether or not they realized it. That this might also be to the gain of British economic interests was regarded as incidental, since free trade, it was argued, was to the benefit of all. In this sense free trade became the quintessential characteristic of the early Victorian view of the world, combining moral commitment with material self-interest. [. . .]

[But] the triumph of free trade ideas in the mid-nineteenth century did not in practice imply an end to government intervention overseas in defence of British economic interests. Rather, the issue was how best should such intervention be undertaken and how far, in practice, should the government go in its support of those interests. Certainly the gaining of free trade treaties to open up a region's commerce, encouragement for the spread of trade, and the general promotion of free trade principles were accepted as central government aims. Yet there were limits to the government's role, particularly when it came to supporting private interests. First, public duty should never become confused with private gain. In Palmerston's words, 'it is the business of the Government to open and to secure the roads for the merchant', but no more. Indeed, one influential study of Foreign Office policy in this period suggests that *laissez-faire* and free trade were taken literally by a Foreign Office that defined its role in 'securing roads' before the 1880s very narrowly. Hostile to supporting individual bondholders or traders, it was only prepared to intervene on behalf of British economic interests overseas where such interests reinforced existing British political concerns. Secondly, the free trade treaties the Foreign Office pushed for were restricted to 'equal favour and open competition' for all powers. Their function was to open up markets to outsiders, protect British traders and financiers under international law, and guarantee that British trade and finance would receive equal treatment with that of other European states. The 'Open Door' was open for everyone. There was no policy here of obtaining exclusive privileges for Britain.

British policy was less selfless, however, than might appear. The government did not need to go beyond the 'Open Door' to obtain exclusive privileges in this period; the British economy's success made it possible to entertain ambitions of dominating large areas of the globe almost by default. Given the favourable international situation and that Britain's industrial and financial lead was so great, opening an area to outside influences by treaty was often sufficient to ensure that British trade and finance, rather than any rival's, would be paramount in that region. Opening economies to outside commerce by promoting free trade was *de facto* a policy of expanding British influence. [. . .]

The centrality of free trade ideas in British ambitions for the wider world in these years can be seen in several regions outside the colonial Empire that were particularly the focus of British economic interest: Latin America, China, the Ottoman empire, and parts of Africa. British ambitions in Latin America were clear, at least before the 1860s: in Castlereagh's words, it was the 'opening to our manufactures of the markets of that great continent'. The collapse of Spanish and Portuguese rule clearly offered possibilities to a power like Britain that could dominate South American waters and that had already been establishing an important presence in the region's commerce, but this required governmental action. Thus, it has been argued, between the 1830s and the 1860s the British government pursued an interventionist policy in Latin America designed to remove barriers to the intrusion of British trade and finance, to eradicate the slave trade, and to protect British economic interests. Officials intervened on numerous occasions. For example, in 1845, as in 1806–07, British forces intervened in the River Plate. British forces were also used in the landing at Callao in 1839 and the Mexico intrusion of 1861–62. On other occasions the mere presence of the Royal Navy was sufficient to obtain compliance, as off Peru in 1857 on behalf of bondholders, and against Chile in 1863. British pressure helped the creation of Uruguay, while Palmerston used the navy to threaten Brazil over the slave trade in 1848–49. From the 1830s to the 1860s the government clearly showed its willingness to intervene assertively in Latin America to open 'the markets of that great continent'. [. . .]

Similarly in China, British ambitions were to open this potential market of a quarter of humankind to British economic intrusion. Again the hope was that 'world bettering' and British economic ambitions would go hand in hand. The British government's involvement in the region grew sharply, with repeated interventions between the 1830s and 1860s. Chinese reluctance to open their economy to the 'foreign devils' from the West clashed with Britain's ambitions for free trade and demands for recognition and equal status. Such clashes culminated in the so-called Opium War of 1839–42, the seizure of Hong Kong, and the attempt to open China's economy to western trade and finance through the Treaty of Nanking (Nanjing) in 1842. The resulting five 'treaty ports', the 'concessions', and the principle of extra-territoriality were central to British ambitions in China. A further assault on China was launched in 1847 and again, this time with French involvement, between 1856 and 1860, culminating in the establishment of further treaty ports and concessions. [. . .]

The Ottoman empire was a further region where Britain entertained political and economic ambitions. Leaving aside the Balkan provinces of the empire, two areas were of particular importance to Britain: Turkey itself and Egypt. The strategic importance of Turkey, primarily because of concerns about the route to India, can be seen in British involvement in its defence against Muhammad Ali, ruler of Egypt, in 1839 and against Russia in 1853–56 during the Crimean War. Britain's aim was to gain a breathing space whereby Ottoman administration, its army, and its economy could be reformed and its independence thereby preserved. It was, said Palmerston, of 'utmost importance' to Britain to keep the Ottoman empire an independent state. [. . .]

As British ambitions to regenerate Turkey's economy through free trade ran into difficulties, Egypt grew in strategic and economic importance, particularly after the opening of the Suez Canal in 1869 and as illustrated by Benjamin Disraeli's purchase of the Khedive's shares in the Canal company in 1875. Britain's aims were to counter French influence in Egypt by opening its economy to British enterprise. Thereby, felt the Earl of Clarendon, later Foreign Secretary, Britain could secure 'the overland communication with India . . . the progress of civilization and the development of the commercial resources of the East'. Under Muhammad Ali (1805–48), Egypt had experienced considerable economic growth. His modernization policies focused on protection and a strong state sector in the economy: government-run factories produced textiles, sugar, glass, and paper, while the state monopolized exports. With increased agricultural output, particularly in cotton, their centrepiece from the 1830s, these initially successful policies were undermined by the 1838 treaty: it seriously affected Muhammad Ali's state-run factories, and demolished state monopolies, compelling Egypt's rulers to rely increasingly on foreign loans. Large-scale borrowing ensued, particularly from British sources, accompanied by an influx of westerners protected under the Capitulations. As in China, indigenous jurisdictions were increasingly eroded under western pressures. [. . .]

Tropical Africa too held an important place in the British government's designs. Here British commercial and political involvement grew markedly in these years. Again British aims centred on the spread of free trade—usually couched in terms of the moral imperatives of the anti-slave trade campaign—which became critical to ambitions of regenerating the continent and developing an important trading partner for British industry. This 'dream of tropical wealth' meant that particularly during the period from the 1840s to the 1860s, and notably under the impact of Palmerston, a growing British involvement on both sides of the continent—in areas as different as the Niger, Dahomey, Abyssinia, and Zanzibar—was encouraged. Here consul and anti-slaving naval officer worked to support the British presence in the form of trader and missionary. Palmerston encouraged expeditions to the Niger in 1841 and 1857; the mission to Dahomey in 1850; the assault on Lagos in 1851 and its annexation ten years later; the creation of a Consulate at Massawa in 1847; and the actions against the Zanzibar slave trade in the early 1840s. The abolition of slave trading on both sides of the continent would be followed, it was hoped, by a surge in legitimate trade leading to economic rewards for Britain and the march of civilization for Africa.

Between 1815 and 1880 British policy-makers intervened frequently in these four regions to support British political and economic interests. In all of them ideas of 'world bettering' and British economic benefits were tightly intertwined in the shape of market capitalism. The seizure of colonies was largely—though by no means entirely—eschewed and the emphasis was placed on establishing positions whereby British influence could be increased and the region's economy opened up to outside trade and investment via the free trade treaty. Where necessary this was undertaken by force, with the seizure of bases such as Hong Kong and the establishment of naval power like the anti-slaving squadrons off West and East Africa, used to maintain British leverage. From such points, Consuls and Political Agents could promote the provisions of free trade treaties and facilitate the spread of British trade and investment into their respective regions, thereby creating a burgeoning realm of British influence overseas.

[*Source*: Martin Lynn, 'British Policy, Trade, and Informal Empire in the Mid-Nineteenth Century', in Andrew Porter, ed., *The Nineteenth Century*, vol. 3 of *OHBE*, pp. 101–3, 105–6, 109–14.]

## 3.2   REFORM AND EMPIRE

During the nineteenth century the evangelical Christian revival combined with a new seriousness in public service to promote a reassessment of Britain's imperial purpose. As the historian Andrew Porter explains, the identity of trustee and protector was at its most powerful in the anti-slavery and aboriginal rights movements (Extract 60). When the anti-slavery movement began at the end of the eighteenth century, abolitionists had tended to be evangelical Christians who believed that slavery was a sin for which Britain must atone. Part of that atonement involved the abolition of slavery itself, but equally important was the sending of missionaries to west Africa, and the introduction of alternative sources of trade (Extract 61). Meanwhile, the supporters of slavery argued that slaves enjoyed a higher standard of living than the indigenous inhabitants of Africa (Extract 62). But they fought a losing battle against political will and popular opinion; in 1833 slavery was abolished throughout the British empire, and Royal Navy captains were despatched to sign treaties with African leaders worried about securing alternative sources of income (Extract 63). The navy found a new, peacetime purpose on anti-slavery patrol, taking heavy casualties from tropical fevers and conducting dangerous rescue missions when slavers attempted to jettison their human cargo before being boarded.

British missionaries spread around the world during this period, and although they made little progress in south Asia, they produced large numbers of converts in some areas of Africa and the south Pacific. Missionaries also promoted British trade by introducing Western economic and labour practices, and by encouraging the import of British-made clothing and manufactured goods (Extract 64). Missions also brought English-language education and Western medicine to large numbers of non-Europeans; it is important to note, however, that missionaries were often opposed to actual colonization, preferring to retain control of contact between Western and non-Western societies.

Missionaries had been admitted to India since the beginning of the nineteenth century, but had little success. Westernization tended to come from government initiatives and as Britain's south Asian empire expanded (see Map 7) there was much debate about what kind of education system should be introduced. Some argued that indigenous languages and traditions should be followed, but the advocates of Westernization promoted English-style education as a means of cultural advancement and the creation of a common means of communication (Extract 65). Muslim and Hindu laws were selectively incorporated into new Indian law codes, but the British unequivocally rejected aspects of Indian tradition that they disagreed with, such as child marriage and widow suicide (*sati*). Even the political radicals who criticized colonial rule in Canada or Australia were still in favour of imperialism when it involved India. Although 'Christianization and Civilization' was meant to be benevolent, it was based on an unquestioned sense of cultural superiority.

British humanitarians regarded this new empire of conscience as a triumphant story of progress, but their activities created problems as well as solutions. Even at the time, some of them realized that Westernization would inevitably lead to demands for Western political rights (Extract 66) as it was already doing in the settler colonies (see Chapter 3, section 3.3). There were also problems associated with the success of the anti-slavery campaign, especially in the West Indies. Understandably reluctant to continue labouring on the plantations where they had been slaves, blacks wanted to purchase their own farmland and the colonial government was slow to make such land accessible and affordable (Extract 67). Indentured labourers from India were introduced to meet the plantation labour shortage, but the problems of land distribution and economic decline would haunt the West Indies for generations. In west Africa the introduction of plantations and Western culture, seen as liberating by most Britons, could be perceived as threatening by Africans (Extract 68). The British felt that there was a vast difference between the old days of economic exploitation and the new, paternalistic empire, but to colonial subjects the change might only mean that alien rule had intensified.

## 60    Andrew Porter

The literature available on the nature and achievements of the anti-slavery movement, on the dynamic kaleidoscopic alliance of reforming interests which propelled it, and its engagement with government and colonial interests is impossible to summarize briefly. Nevertheless, the movement's main phases of development are clear. Its rapid parliamentary progress between 1787 and 1792 gave way to prolonged frustration, as war with France seriously impeded further action. The argument for delaying, until peace was restored, what all parties agreed would be a far-reaching measure, was endorsed in a parliamentary resolution in 1795. Popular agitation for this as for other reforming causes was severely curtailed by fears of radical revolution and the restrictive legislation from 1795 onwards. Pitt's government was preoccupied with the war, divided internally, and consequently reluctant to take up a contentious issue which lacked the Crown's support. Humanitarians' shortage of effective economic arguments for abolition remained a serious weakness. Not until the disappearance of Addington's ministry in 1804, the major shift in the fortunes of war following France's naval defeat at Trafalgar, a temporary glut of sugar, and the political upheaval which brought the Ministry of All Talents into office was progress possible. Renewed popular agitation, the development by abolitionists of arguments which presented ending the trade as damaging to the French and part of wartime strategy, and the abolitionist sympathies of Whig ministers underpinned the legislation of 1805–07 which ended British involvement in the trade. [. . .]

The appointment of a Whig ministry in November 1830, the return of more MPs committed to reform or emancipation, and erosion of the West Indian interest at the elections of 1830 and 1832 favoured the abolitionists. Still more so did the Jamaican rebellion of December 1831, followed as it was by fierce retribution against the slaves, attacks on missionaries blamed for the mayhem, and the destruction of their chapels. As in 1823, the evangelical and nonconformist world was fully roused, as were other humanitarians. Petitions to Parliament favouring immediate emancipation outstripped those for parliamentary reform. The first proposals for a bill came from Lord Howick at the Colonial Office in summer 1832, and an act was passed the following August. Slaves in Britain's colonies were emancipated as from 1 August 1834; subject to varying periods of 'apprenticeship' to their former masters, all would be completely free in 1840. Slave-owners were compensated for their loss of property in slaves from a fund of £20 million established by the government and paid for by metropolitan taxpayers.

The implications of this bald outline for the relationship of humanitarian activity and Britain's Imperial experience are several. As with the definition of trusteeship concerning India, so too the development of an anti-slavery movement had a symbiotic relationship with Empire. Had British slaving and slave-ownership not existed in a context where British authority could plausibly be asserted to restrain it, British humanitarianism would have lacked such clear direction and purpose. Abolitionists could cajole and threaten, but without a government willing and capable of acting, humanitarian outcries were ineffectual. Empire provided the sphere within which benevolent government action was most readily conceivable, with the result that humanitarians rarely questioned the continued existence of territorial Empire, and throughout the century frequently supported extensions of British authority if that would serve their purposes. In practice, their assumptions about universal rights necessitated removing limits to Imperial sovereignty. In the same way, imperialists pointed to their association with humanitarian policies as further justifying the maintenance and expansion of colonial territory. With abolition and emancipation behind them, despite the limitations of both measures, humanitarians were always able to believe in the possibility of success; the tradition of Wilberforce, Buxton, and Sturge had to be maintained, and their achievements might be repeated. After 1833 governments, always under pressure from conflicting interests, could express their sympathy with humanitarian goals even when disinclined or unable to promote them effectively. [. . .]

As the political reform and slavery debates receded, the mid-1830s saw determined attempts to redirect humanitarian efforts towards peoples untouched by the Atlantic slave trade but nevertheless suffering severely from uncontrolled British expansion. Where once India had loomed large, by 1830 the Khoisan and Bantu peoples of southern Africa, Australian Aborigines, New Zealand's Maoris, and Pacific islanders were attracting attention. The elements of the general problem were clear: British traders, established settlers and new emigrants, seamen, and others in these regions were increasingly in conflict with the indigenous peoples. Under conditions where greed, ignorance, and fear outweighed goodwill; where neither party recognized or understood the political authority and social conventions of the other; where distant governments could not enforce their will, even if they possessed the nominal legal right to do so; where the liquor, arms, and opium trades flourished; there, lawlessness, the right of the strongest, retaliation, and revenge flourished. Where colonial frontiers were ill-defined or non-existent, the geographical extent of British colonial authority even over British subjects was uncertain. Tales of atrocities multiplied and were magnified in the telling, further increasing the general insecurity.

Moved by events in southern Africa, where the Imperial government finally reversed the Cape Governor's decision to retain Queen Adelaide Province after the war of 1834, the House of Commons was persuaded to have a committee examine the whole problem in 1836–37. The evidence taken convinced the committee that 'the effect of European intercourse . . . has been, upon the whole, hitherto a calamity upon the native and savage nations', that Europeans were generally at fault where conflicts occurred, and that immediate government intervention was essential. Non-intervention and the absence of regulation served no national interest. 'On the contrary, in point of economy, of security, of commerce, of reputation, it is a short-sighted and disastrous policy. As far as it has prevailed, it has been a burthen upon the empire. [. . .]

The Report was paternalistic in tone, and took for granted Britain's self-evident superiority. Nevertheless, it was deeply critical of the consequences of British neglect and expatriate activities; well aware of the practical difficulties of legislation and enforcement; and worried about principles of equity as between different cultural groups. Given the appalling prospect that, without intervention, conditions would deteriorate as emigration increased, and noting that British strength often rendered indigenous groups unable 'to resist any encroachments, however unjust, however mischievous, which we may be disposed to make', the Committee tried to define the principles of a system which would as far as possible 'enforce the observance of their [indigenous] rights'. [. . .]

These recommendations should not be dismissed as merely rhetorical or cosmetic. The Report identified clearly the areas and issues which were to pre-occupy British administrators throughout the century. In the light of solutions canvassed at the time, its failure to take more seriously the possibility of further restricting or even prohibiting land transfers may seem short-sighted. However, such a course was precluded by belief in its practical impossibility, as well as confidence in the likelihood and advantages of assimilation. Other ideal alternatives were also seen as impractical. Although 'the safety and welfare of an uncivilized race require that their relations with their more cultivated neighbours should be diminished rather than multiplied', British citizens could not be confined to barracks anywhere within the Empire. Even officially negotiated treaties were 'rather the preparatives . . . for disputes than securities for peace', given 'the superior sagacity which the European will exercise in framing, in interpreting, and in evading them'. Britain's strength and Imperial authority were often incapable of translation into the precise and competent exercise of power. At the time, the Committee's carefully considered suggestions were regarded as imperfect but the best available. [. . .]

Although the 1840s opened promisingly, the achievements to 1870 were often disappointing. Earlier conventional wisdom was either disproved or at least seriously questioned. In West Africa, legitimate trade was not driving out the slave trade—and not simply because it lacked strength or appeal, as Buxton had argued in 1839. The balance of advantage against the slave trade was frequently unclear, and Britain's use of force to decide the issue increased. It became difficult for humanitarians to sustain their optimistic belief that a temporary push with government assistance would everywhere tip the balance in favour of free and prosperous enterprise. Slavery and the trade in Africa remained an intractable and—if travellers' reports were believed—growing problem, unamenable to existing British naval and diplomatic activity. The greater efficiency of free over slave labour was not borne out by the Caribbean colonies' experience, and the terms available for free labour were often unattractive to freed slaves and indigenous people. The consequence for the British and Foreign Anti-Slavery Society was a decade of debilitating argument as to whether or not colonial produce should continue to receive preferential treatment in Britain's markets, or be compelled to compete on a free and equal basis with slave-grown produce from elsewhere. The Free Traders' victory by 1854 indicated a loss of commitment to the West Indian cause. [. . .]

The position of the Aborigines' Protection Society was no better. Hodgkin, another Quaker as well as ethnologist and professional physician, remained Secretary until 1866, but seems to have had neither time nor contacts sufficient to his increasingly complicated task. By the end of the 1840s it was clear that Imperial initiatives were having only limited and temporary success. The Aboriginal Protectors appointed in New South Wales and Western Australia (1838–39) after ten years had evidently failed. In New Zealand the early optimism soon evaporated. Confidence was only partially restored by Governor Grey (1846–52), and at the expense of shifting to an overtly assimilationist policy towards the Maori. Moreover, the conflict over land purchases from Maoris remained unresolved, and Grey's ability to negotiate with them, as well as his administrative command, proved beyond his successors.

For those pinning their hopes on the principles of the 1837 Report, however, there were still more fundamental obstacles. Prominent were democratic political institutions and the growth of colonial self-government. Ironically, the same representative electoral practices which enabled the humanitarians to put pressure on the Imperial government to act, once transferred to the colonies worked against humanitarian aims. This came as no surprise in the mid-century. West Indian Assemblies had fought to ward off amelioration and circumvent the Emancipation Act; the Cape Colony's less popularly based Legislative Council tried the same in its 1834 Vagrancy Act. For these reasons the 1837 Report, and by then also the Imperial government, had favoured removing such matters from popular control; but the line proved impossible to hold. The Imperial authorities found the political demand for settler self-government undeniable. Although in Natal responsible government was delayed on the humanitarian ground that such a small white community could not be trusted with power over blacks, this was exceptional. Before 1870 all settler colonies had acquired sufficient financial power to enable them to shape policy towards indigenous populations more or less as they wished. Expenditure on native peoples called for in 1837, and to some extent institutionalized by a Governor such as Grey both in New Zealand and the Cape, was cut to the bone. Legislation, carefully framed to avoid Imperial disallowance, and embodying employment conditions or qualifications for political involvement akin to those in Britain, established patterns of labour law and political rights favourable to white minorities. Everywhere indigenous customary rights to land were steadily extinguished.

[*Source*: Andrew Porter, 'Trusteeship, Anti-Slavery, and Humanitarianism', in Porter, *The Nineteenth Century*, pp. 202–3, 204, 207, 208–9, 211, 212–13.]

## 61    Thomas Fowell Buxton

Thomas Fowell Buxton carried on the British anti-slavery campaign after the death of its founder, William Wilberforce. Note Buxton's views of race: though supremely condescending, his writings also insisted that Africans shared the same basic nature and responses as Europeans.

One part of our national debt to Africa has already been acknowledged by the emancipation of our colonial slaves. There remains yet, however, a larger debt uncancelled,—that of restitution to Africa itself. We shall have much difficulty in ascertaining the amount of this obligation. Had we the means of discovering the total number of the sufferers whose miseries we have caused, or could we form the faintest idea of the nature and extent of the woes which are justly chargeable upon us as a nation, the duty of making reparation to Africa would be obvious. [. . .]

I repeat, that a stronger proof we cannot have, that it is the duty of the people of this empire to take up the cause upon Christian grounds, as a measure of atonement for the injuries we have done to her, as the only means now within our power of making restitution to her still degraded population; and as the most successful implement for uprooting from its very foundations that gigantic and accursed tree, which for ages has nourished beneath its shadow lamentation, and mourning, and woe.

Let but the people of this Christian country take up this cause *as a duty*, nationally and religiously, and no difficulties, however great, can, with the Divine blessing, hinder its success.

Nationally and religiously, the duty is plain. We have been put in trust with Christianity,—we have been the depositaries of a pure and holy faith, which inculcates the most expanded benevolence, and yet have not only neglected, as a nation, to confer upon Africa any real benefit, but have inflicted upon it a positive evil. Covetousness has dimmed our moral perceptions of duty, and paralysed our efforts, during many generations; and now that the nation has awakened from its lethargy, it is high time to act up to the principles of our religion.

Africa still lies in her blood. She wants our missionaries, our schoolmasters, our bibles, all the machinery we possess, for ameliorating her wretched condition. Shall we, with a remedy that may safely be applied, neglect to heal her wounds? Shall we, on whom the lamp of life shines, refuse to disperse her darkness?

[*Source*: Thomas Fowell Buxton, *The African Slave Trade and its Remedy* (London: Dawsons, 1968; orig. publ. 1839), pp. 512, 513.]

## 62    Edward Long

West Indian planters like Long argued that Africans enjoyed a higher standard of living as British-owned slaves than they had in their home villages. But beneath these rationalizations, published in 1774, lay assumptions about African racial inferiority that could be expressed with shocking brutality.

The planters of this island have been very unjustly stigmatized with an accusation of treating their Negroes with barbarity. Some alledge [sic], that these slave-holders (as they are pleased to call them, in contempt) are law-less bashaws, West-India tyrants, inhuman oppressors, bloody inquisitors, and a long &c. of such pretty names. The planter, in reply to these bitter invectives, will think it sufficient to urge, in the first place, that *he* did not make them slaves, but succeeded to the inheritance of their services in the same manner as an English squire succeeds to the estate of his ancestors; and that, as to his Africans, he buys their services from those who have all along pretended a very good right to sell [and] that it cannot be for his interest to treat his Negroes in the manner represented; but that it is so to use them well, and preserve their vigour and existence as long as he is able . . . [. . .]

I will assert, in my turn, and I hope without inconsistency or untruth, that there are no men, no orders of men in Great-Britain, possessed of more disinterested charity, philanthropy, and clemency, than the Creole gentlemen of this island [. . .] [Their] authority over [slaves] is like that of an antient [sic] patriarch: conciliating affection by the mildness of its exertion, and claim-ing respect by the justice and propriety of its decisions and discipline, it attracts the love of the honest and good; while it awes the worthless into reformation . . . [. . .]

That in the native Africans' sale of Negroes to our shipping, various frauds have been committed, and persons improperly and unjustly sold; that mer-chants of ships have been inhuman; that planters have been wantonly cruel, may be supposed from the enormity of crimes seen every day in the most civilized states. To these abuses efficacious remedies should be applied [. . .] But, to say the truth, it must be confessed, that the difference between the condition of the Negroes in general in Africa, and in our colonies, is so great, and so much happier in our colonies, that they themselves are very sensible of it. . . . [. . .]

[But] among men of so savage a disposition, as that they scarcely differ from the wild beasts of the wood in their ferocity of their manners, we must not think of introducing polished rules and refinements. [. . .] Such men must be managed at first as if they were beasts; they must be tamed, before they can be treated like men.

[*Source*: Edward Long, *The History of Jamaica* (London: T. Lowndes, 1774), vol. 2, pp. 267, 269, 271, 399–401.]

## 63 Conference on board Her Majesty's ship *Bonnetta*

West African leaders were keenly aware of the devastation caused by slavery, but concerned about exactly what would replace it as the mainstay of their economies; many of them demanded (and got) substantial cash payments from the British government.

King Pepple, of Bonny, accompanied by Anna Pepple, by his Juju man or high priest, and Hee Chee, Anna Pepple's secretary, for the first time went on board a man-of-war, for the purpose of paying a visit to Captain Craigie, where he was received with the usual salutes. [. . .]

Captain Craigie then proceeded to read to King Pepple and suite the despatch of Lord Palmerston dated 14th April, 1838, relative to Slave abolition, and strongly impressed upon His Majesty that part which states that treaties had already been made between England and other African Princes for the purpose of putting an end to the Slave Trade, and that in those cases the Articles of Treaty had been faithfully maintained.

Captain Craigie assured the King that England ever dispensed justice, and would encourage the lawful commerce of the Bonny in every way; that she would send out ships in abundance for their palm-oil and other products; and if the Bonny men directed their attention properly to these, he was certain they could easily get rich without exporting slaves.

Captain Craigie further told His Majesty that the Queen of England wished to make a friendly agreement with the King of Bonny to put an end to Slave exportation; and moreover added that his mistress was determined to put a stop to it at all hazards.

The King, Anna Pepple, and the Juju man for some time remained silent; their countenances, however, were indicative of their consternation; the idea of making such a proposal seemed to them to be incomprehensible. At length Anna Pepple said—

'If we cease to sell slaves to foreign ships, our principal source of wealth will be gone; the English were our first customers, and the trade has since been our chief means of support.'

*Captain Craigie.* 'How much would you lose if you gave up selling slaves for exportation?'

*Anna Pepple.* 'Too much—very much—we gain more by one slave-ship than by five palm-oil ships.'

*Hee Chee, Anna Pepple's Secretary.* 'We depend entirely on selling slaves and palm-oil for our subsistence; suppose then the Slave Trade done away with, the consumption of palm-oil in England to stop, the crop to fail, or that the English ships did not come to the Bonny, what are we to do? we must starve, as it is contrary to our religion to cultivate the ground.'

*Captain Craigie.* 'There need be no apprehension of the demand for palm-oil in England ceasing, or of English ships not coming out to the Bonny to take from you your products in exchange for British merchandize; but if you can show clearly that your losses will be so great by giving up slave exportation, I think it possible that the Queen of England may in some measure remunerate you for such loss. I have no authority whatever to make any agreement with you with regard to such compensation, I only wish to know if you are disposed to treat for the abolition of the Slave Trade, to enable me to represent your views and demands thereon to my own Government.'

*Juju Man.* 'Suppose a Spanish ship's coming to Bonny with goods to exchange for slaves; are we to send her away? This morning you made a breakfast for me, and as I was hungry it would have been foolish not to have eaten; in like manner, if the Spanish ship had things which we stood in need of, it would be equally foolish not to take them.'

*Captain Craigie.* 'How would the abolition of the slave exportation so materially affect you?'

*King Pepple.* 'It would affect myself and chiefs thus—

'First, by stopping the revenues arising from slaves being exported.

'Secondly. Our own profit on slaves, and that arising from piloting slave-ships up and out of Bonny would be lost.'

*Captain Craigie.* 'I again assure you that the Slave Trade must be stopped. Not one vessel can escape from the Bonny, as you will know from "Scout's" blockade of the river in 1836 and 1839. If it becomes necessary, I shall anchor a vessel off Juju Point, and to pass her you are aware will be impossible; but as the English Government always adopt the principle of putting an end to evils by friendly agreements than by compulsion, and as it is that they may be disposed, if your requests are within reasonable limits, to make you an annual "dash," or remuneration, for a term of years (perhaps five years), how much would you consider to be sufficient?'

After some consultation among themselves, Hee Chee, Anna Pepple's Secretary, said, 'The King will take 4000 dollars yearly.'

*Captain Craigie.* 'As I said before, I am not authorized to treat for any sum, but I am certain that 4000 dollars would be considered too much; indeed I would not venture to propose more than 2000 dollars. If you will say that this sum (for the time above specified) will be sufficient, I shall lay the matter before the English Government.'

[*Source*: 'Conference on board Her Majesty's ship "Bonetta"', 11 March 1839 in Great Britain, *Parliamentary Papers*, vol. LXIV, 'Papers relating to engagements entered into by King Pepple and the Chiefs of the Bonny' [970], pp. 2–3.]

## 64 John Williams

The missionary John Williams worked in the south Pacific islands during the early nineteenth century and advocated combining Christianization with the promotion of British commerce.

From these facts it will be apparent, that, while our best energies have been devoted to the instruction of the people in the truths of the Christian religion, and our chief solicitude has been to make them wise unto salvation, we have, at the same time, been anxious to impart a knowledge of all that was calculated to increase their comforts and elevate their character. And I am convinced that the first step towards the promotion of a nation's temporal and social elevation, is to plant amongst them the tree of life, when civilization and commerce will entwine their tendrils around its trunk, and derive support from its strength. Until the people are brought under the influence of religion, they have no desire for the arts and usages of civilized life; but that invariably creates it. [. . .] The females had long observed the dress of the Missionaries' wives, but while heathen they greatly preferred their own, and there was not a single attempt at imitation. No sooner, however, were they brought under the influence of religion, than all of them, even to the lowest, aspired to the possession of a gown, a bonnet, and a shawl, that they might appear like Christian women [. . .]

Nor are the heathen the only parties benefited by such exertions. The whole civilized world, and our own countrymen especially, share the advantages [. . .] we may simply glance at the commercial advantages which have resulted and are still resulting from these labours. In the South Sea Islands alone, many thousands of persons are at this moment wearing and using articles of European manufacture, by whom, a few years ago, no such article had been seen: indeed, in the more advanced stations, there is scarcely an individual who is not attired in English clothing, which has been obtained in exchange for native produce. Thus we are benefited both in what we give and in what we receive.

[*Source*: John Williams, *A Narrative of Missionary Enterprise* (London: John Snow, 1841), pp. 152–3.]

## 65  Sir Charles Trevelyan

Sir Charles Trevelyan was a former member of the Bengal Civil Service who published his views on Indian education in 1838.

[The Education Committee's] object is to fill the minds of the liberally educated portion of the people with the knowledge of Europe, in order that they may interpret it in their own language to the rest of their countrymen. For this purpose, while, on the one hand, the pupils are encouraged to acquire the various kinds of information which English literature contains, and to form their taste after the best English modes; on the other, every endeavour is used to give them the habit of writing with facility and elegance in their native languages. [. . .]

If English is to be the language of education in India, it follows, as a matter of course, that it will be the scientific language also, and that terms will be borrowed from it to express those ideas for which no appropriate symbols exist in the popular dialects. The educated class, through whom European knowledge will reach the people, will be familiar with English. They will adopt the English words with which they are already acquainted, and will be clear gainers by it, while others will not be losers. The introduction of English words into the vernacular dialects will gradually diminish the distance between the scientific and popular language. It will become easier for the unlearned to acquire English, and for the learned to cultivate and improve the vernacular dialects. The language of India will be assimilated to the languages of Europe, as far as the arts and sciences and general literature are concerned; and mutual intercourse and the introduction of further improvements will thus be facilitated. And, above all, the vernacular dialects of India will, by the same process, be united among themselves. This diversity of language is one of the greatest existing obstacles to improvement in India. But when English shall everywhere be established as the language of education, when the vernacular literature shall every where be formed from materials drawn from this source, and according to models furnished by this prototype, a strong tendency to assimilation will be created. Both the matter and the manner will be the same. Saturated from the same source, recast in the same mould, with a common science, a common standard of taste, a common nomenclature, the national languages, as well as the national character, will be consolidated; the scientific and literary acquisitions of each portion of the community will be at once thrown into a common stock for the general good; and we shall leave an united and enlightened nation, where we found a people broken up into sections, distracted by the system of caste, even in the bosom of each separate society, and depressed by literary systems, devised much more with a view to check the progress, than to promote the advance, of the human mind. No particular effort is required to bring about these results. They will take place in the natural course of things by the extension of English education, just as the inhabitants of the greater part of Europe were melted down into one people by the prevalence of the Roman languages and arts. All that is required is, that we should not laboriously interpose an obstacle to the progress of this desirable change by the forced cultivation of the Sanskrit and Arabic languages. [. . .]

To promote the spread of knowledge among our subjects is undoubtedly one of the most sacred duties which has devolved on us as the rulers of India: but I cannot admit the correctness of the test by which the Oriental party would determine the kind of knowledge to be taught. Is it meant that we are bound to perpetuate the system patronised by our predecessors, merely because it was patronised by them, however little it may be calculated to promote the welfare of the people? If it be so, the English rule would be the greatest curse to India it is possible to conceive. Left to themselves, the inherent rottenness of the native systems must, sooner or later, have brought them to a close. But, according to this view of the subject, the resources of European skill are to [be?] employed in imparting to them a new principle of duration: knowledge is to be used to perpetuate ignorance—civilisation to perpetuate barbarism; and the iron strength of the English Government to bind faster still the fetters which have so long confined the native mind. This is a new view of our obligations; and, if it be a just one, it is to be hoped that in pity to our subjects we shall neglect this branch of our duties. Fortunately for them, we have not thought it incumbent on us to act on this rule in other departments of administration. We have not adopted into our system bar- barous penal enactments and oppressive modes of collecting the revenue because they happened to be favourites with our predecessors.

The test of what ought to be taught is, truth and utility. Our predecessors consulted the welfare of their subjects to the best of their information: we are bound to do the same by ours. We cannot divest ourselves of this responsibility: the light of European knowledge, and the diffusive spirit of European benevolence give us advantages which our predecessors did not possess. A new class of Indian scholars is rising under our rule, more numer- ous and better instructed than those who went before them; and, above all, plans are in progress for enlightening the great body of the people as far as their leisure will permit—an undertaking which never entered into the imagination of any of the former rulers of India.

[*Source*: Charles E. Trevelyan, *On the Education of the People of India* (London: Longman, Orme, Brown, Green and Longmans, 1838), pp. 47, 124–5, 141–2.]

## 66   Thomas Babington Macaulay

Some reformers realized that Westernization would inevitably lead to demands for self-government in India, although they believed that this lay far in the future. Member of Parliament and historian, Thomas Babington Macaulay, was a keen advocate of British-style education and government in India and was about to become legal adviser to the Governor-General of India when he made this speech on 10 July 1833.

To the great trading nation, to the great manufacturing nation, no progress which any portion of the human race can make in knowledge, in taste for the conveniences of life, or in the wealth by which those conveniences are produced, can be matter of indifference. It is scarcely possible to calculate the benefits which we might derive from the diffusion of European civilisation among the vast population of the East. It would be, on the most selfish view of the case, far better for us that the people of India were well governed and independent of us, than ill governed and subject to us—that they were ruled by their own kings, but wearing our broad cloth, and working with our cutlery, than that they were performing their salams to English collectors and English Magistrates, but were too ignorant to value, or too poor to buy, English manufactures. To trade with civilized men is infinitely more profitable than to govern savages. That would, indeed, be a doting wisdom, which, in order that India might remain a dependency, would make it an useless and costly dependency—which would keep a hundred millions of men from being our customers in order that they might continue to be our slaves. [. . .]

Are we to keep the people of India ignorant in order that we may keep them submissive? Or do we think that we can give them knowledge without awakening ambition? Or do we mean to awaken ambition and to provide it with no legitimate vent? Who will answer any of these questions in the affirmative? Yet one of them must be answered in the affirmative, by every person who maintains that we ought permanently to exclude the natives from high office. I have no fears. The path of duty is plain before us: and it is also the path of wisdom, of national prosperity, of national honour.

The destinies of our Indian empire are covered with thick darkness. It is difficult to form any conjecture as to the fate reserved for a state which resembles no other in history, and which forms by itself a separate class of political phenomena. The laws which regulate its growth and its decay are still unknown to us. It may be that the public mind of India may expand under our system till it has outgrown that system; that by good government we may educate our subjects into a capacity for better government, that, having become instructed in European knowledge, they may, in some future age, demand European institutions. Whether such a day will ever come I know not. But never will I attempt to avert or to retard it. Whenever it comes, it will be the proudest day in English history. To have found a great people sunk in the lowest depths of slavery and superstition, to have so ruled them as to have made them desirous and capable of all the privileges of citizens would indeed be a title to glory all our own. The sceptre may pass away from us. Unforeseen accidents may derange our most profound schemes of policy. Victory may be inconstant to our arms. But there are triumphs which are followed by no reverses. There is an empire exempt from all natural causes of decay. Those triumphs are the pacific triumphs of reason over barbarism; that empire is the imperishable empire of our arts and our morals, our literature and our laws.

[*Source*: Bennett, *The Concept of Empire*, pp. 72–3, 74–5.]

## 67    Lord Glenelg

> The West Indian economies had been dependent on slavery and many questions remained after slavery had been abolished. Charles Grant, Lord Glenelg, as Secretary of State for the Colonies in 1836, was clearer about the problems than the solutions.

It would appear that a country is then in its most prosperous state, when there is as much labour in the market as can be profitably employed. In new countries, where the whole unoccupied territory belongs to the Crown, and settlers are continually flowing in, it is possible, by fixing the price of fresh land so high as to place it above the reach of the poorest class of settlers, to keep the labour-market in its most prosperous state from the beginning. This precaution, by ensuring a supply of labourers at the same time that it increases the value of the land, makes it more profitable to cultivate old land well than to purchase new. The natural tendency of the population to spread over the surface of the country, each man settling where he may, or roving from place to place in pursuit of virgin soil, is thus impeded. The territory, expanding only with the pressure of population, is commensurate with the actual wants of the entire community. Society, being thus kept together, is more open to civilizing influences; more directly under the control of government; more full of the activity which is inspired by common wants, and the strength which is derived from the division of labour, and altogether is in a sounder state, morally, politically, and economically, than if left to pursue its natural course.

This policy has of late years been pursued with very good results in our North American and Australian colonies; and there is no doubt that it may be applied with advantage in the West Indies also. It cannot indeed be expected to be either so simple or so effectual in its operation, owing to the existing relations of West Indian society contracted under a different system; to the alternately neglected and exhausted state in which the long operation of an opposite policy has left the already appropriated territory; to the unnatural condition of the labouring population, and to the artificial channels in which productive industry has hitherto been confined. It is probable that the particular regulations which have been found to answer in the possessions alluded to, may not be applicable to so different a state of things. Of this, however, within the limits of your government, you are the most competent judge. I have therefore to request that you will take the matter into your earliest consideration; and that you will then submit to me in detail the arrangements which you may recommend as best calculated to carry the views of His Majesty's Government into effect in the colony under your care.

[*Source*: Circular from Lord Glenelg to the governors of the West Indian colonies, 30 January 1836 from Great Britain, *Parliamentary Papers*, vol. XV, 'Report from the Select Committee on Negro Apprenticeship in the Colonies' [560], pp. 224–5.]

## 68   Chinua Achebe

The Nigerian novelist Chinua Achebe has tried to capture the negative response to British missionary involvement in west Africa. For many Africans, the arrival of missionaries had a significance far beyond their stated purpose of conversion: they also brought intensive and threatening commercial, political and cultural change.

Umuofia had indeed changed during the seven years Okonkwo had been in exile. The church had come and led many astray. Not only the low-born and the outcast but sometimes a worthy man had joined it. Such a man was Ogbuefi Ugonna, who had taken two titles, and who like a madman had cut the anklet of his titles and cast it away to join the Christians. The white missionary was very proud of him and he was one of the first men in Umuofia to receive the sacrament of Holy Communion, or Holy Feast as it was called in Ibo. Ogbuefi Ugonna had thought of the Feast in terms of eating and drinking, only more holy than the village variety. He had therefore put his drinking-horn into his goatskin bag for the occasion.

But apart from the church, the white men had also brought a government. They had built a court where the District Commissioner judged cases in ignorance. He had court messengers who brought men to him for trial. Many of these messengers came from Umuru on the bank of the Great River, where the white men first came many years before and where they had built the centre of their religion and trade and government. These court messengers were greatly hated in Umuofia because they were foreigners and also arrogant and high-handed. They were called *kotma*, and because of their ash-coloured shorts they earned the additional name of Ashy-Buttocks. They guarded the prison, which was full of men who had offended against the white man's law. Some of these prisoners had thrown away their twins and some had molested the Christians. They were beaten in the prison by the *kotma* and made to work every morning clearing the government compound and fetching wood for the white Commissioner and the court messengers. Some of these prisoners were men of title who should be above such mean occupation. They were grieved by the indignity and mourned for their neg-lected farms. As they cut grass in the morning the younger men sang in time with the strokes of their matchets:

> *Kotma* of the ash buttocks,
> He is fit to be a slave
> The white man has no sense,
> He is fit to be a slave

The court messengers did not like to be called Ashy-Buttocks, and they beat the men. But the song spread in Umuofia.

Okonkwo's head was bowed in sadness as Obierika told him these things.

'Perhaps I have been away too long,' Okonkwo said, almost to himself. 'But I cannot understand these things you tell me. What is it that has happened to our people? Why have they lost the power to fight?'

'Have you not heard how the white man wiped out Abame?' asked Obierika.

'I have heard,' said Okonkwo. 'But I have also heard that Abame people were weak and foolish. Why did they not fight back? Had they no guns and matchets? We would be cowards to compare ourselves with the men of Abame. Their fathers had never dared to stand before our ancestors. We must fight these men and drive them from the land.'

'It is already too late,' said Obierika sadly. 'Our own men and our sons have joined the ranks of the stranger. They have joined his religion and they help to uphold his government. If we should try to drive out the white men in Umuofia we should find it easy. There are only two of them. But what of our own people who are following their way and have been given power? They would go to Umuru and bring the soldiers, and we would be like Abame.' He paused for a long time and then said: 'I told you on my last visit to Mbanta how they hanged Aneto.'

'What has happened to that piece of land in dispute?' asked Okonkwo.

'The white man's court has decided that it should belong to Nnama's family, who had given much money to the white man's messengers and interpreter.'

'Does the white man understand our custom about land?'

'How can he when he does not even speak our tongue? But he says that our customs are bad; and our own brothers who have taken up his religion also say that our customs are bad. How do you think we can fight when our own brothers have turned against us? The white man is very clever. He came quietly and peaceably with his religion. We were amused at his foolishness and allowed him to stay. Now he has won our brothers, and our clan can no longer act like one. He has put a knife on the things that held us together and we have fallen apart.'

'How did they get hold of Aneto to hang him?' asked Okonkwo.

'When he killed Oduche in the fight over the land, he fled to Aninta to escape the wrath of the earth. This was about eight days after the fight, because Oduche had not died immediately from his wounds. It was on the seventh day that he died. But everybody knew that he was going to die and Aneto got his belongings together in readiness to flee. But the Christians had told the white man about the accident, and he sent his *kotma* to catch Aneto. He was imprisoned with all the leaders of his family. In the end Oduche died and Aneto was taken to Umuru and hanged. The other people were released, but even now they have not found the mouth with which to tell of their suffering.'

The two men sat in silence for a long while afterwards.

[*Source*: Chinua Achebe, *Things Fall Apart* (Heinemann: London, 1984), pp. 123–5.]

## 3.3 THE BRITISH DIASPORA

The Victorian spirit of reform and improvement affected Britain's colonies of settlement, too. By the early nineteenth century emigration had increased, especially to British North America (later Canada; see Map 8) and to new colonies in Australia and New Zealand (Maps 9 and 10). A group known as the 'Colonial Reformers' were keen advocates of organized emigration, and began calling for government measures to organize land sales and the labour supply (Extract 69). The Reformers, who also tended to be free trade supporters, encouraged the involvement of the private sector, particularly with regard to the transportation of emigrants. Their critics argued that nothing could justify additional imperial expansion: it was too expensive, both financially and morally. Such critics were in the minority, however, and the popularity of emigration itself was making the debate academic. Between 1853 and 1920 a total of 5,400,000 Britons emigrated to the colonies from England, Wales, and Scotland; most of them went to Canada. Irish people living in Britain are included in these totals, and there was also direct migration from Ireland to the colonies in Canada and Australia.

Emigrants made long, often dangerous voyages by sea and faced shipboard conditions of widely varying quality (Extract 70). A series of Passenger Acts introduced government inspections and health standards, but newly arrived immigrants were warned against expecting unemployment assistance (Extract 71). However, most immigrants welcomed freedom and adventure in their new homelands (Extract 72). They particularly enjoyed the looser class structure of the colonies, and many became conspicuously upwardly mobile through land ownership (Extract 73). Although people were encouraged to emigrate as families, men outnumbered women in the settlement colonies and special female emigration campaigns were conducted to redress the balance (Extract 74). The widespread presence of white women and children was new: during the fur trade period in English Canada, and at the convict settlements in Australia, men had predominated. Historians have debated the significance of the shifting gender balance in the nineteenth century, particularly with regard to relations between the British and indigenous peoples (Extract 75).

Demands for greater self-government grew along with the settler population, and they found support among the advocates of political reform in Britain itself (Extract 76). British governments were anxious to avoid another American Revolution, but (as with imperial expansion in the late eighteenth century) there was no blueprint for creating radical new forms of colonial government. How could a multicultural patchwork of colonies, such as those in British North America, come together to govern themselves (Extract 77)? How could a colony be self-governing and still part of the empire? Canada's transition to a self-governing federation in 1867 encouraged constitutional experimentation in the other settlement colonies; British imperial identity had expanded to accommodate—for white British subjects—a high degree of political independence (Extract 78).

But this new face of empire was inevitably linked with another development: the increasing social and political exclusion of the indigenous populations of settler colonies. Even the term 'settler colony' implies that the population consisted of settlers, but on the contrary: Canada, Australia, New Zealand, and South Africa were already inhabited by peoples whose economic and military assistance had often been essential to British activities. In North America, the British had relied on indigenous allies during every war, including the war of 1812 against the United States. But the arrival of so many new British immigrants led to demands for increased land sales and resource exploitation; colonial governments began creating reserves for indigenous peoples while designating other land as 'waste' and therefore available for sale (Extract 79). In Australia the resulting racial alienation took a particularly violent form: although some Aborigines worked for the new cattle and sheep properties, others were driven from the land and even deliberately murdered (Extract 80). Britain was proud of the peaceful transition to self-government in the settlement colonies, but the ongoing resentment of their indigenous peoples is also understandable. Their cultures paid a heavy price for Victorian imperial progress. While demands for the vote were met for white males during the nineteenth century, the indigenous populations of Canada and Australia would not be included in the franchise until the 1960s. As for the colonies in Asia and Africa, authoritarian paternalism—not self-government—was the order of the day.

## 69   Edward Gibbon Wakefield

Edward Gibbon Wakefield was a leader of the Colonial Reform movement, and believed that Britain's colonies of settlement should be not only retained, but expanded. Here Wakefield, pretending to be a British emigrant to Australia, discusses the crucial issues of land and labour in 1849.

In many colonies, and in quite modern times, neither capital nor labour has always obtained a high remuneration. Algeria, I believe, is one of them. A list of them would contain most of the colonies, lately dependencies, of Spain in South America. In the newest English colony, New Zealand, profits have at times been low, most of the capitalists for the time being were ruined, and a large proportion of the labourers were thrown out of employment, by causes altogether independent of any excess of capital in proportion to labour, or of labour in proportion to capital. The cause of the mischief in such cases, is one that has at all times prevailed over the greatest portion of the world; it is insecurity of property. If there is not a fair prospect of enjoying the proper fruits of enterprise and industry, enterprise and industry are feeble: they are paralysed if there is a well-founded fear of never enjoying their fruits; of reaping instead nothing but loss and disappointment. Security of property is the indispensable foundation of wealth, let all other circumstances be what they may. Security of property depends wholly on government. In order, therefore, that profits and wages should be constantly high in a colony, it is essential that the colony should be tolerably well governed; well enough, that is, to hold out a fair prospect that enterprise and industry will enjoy their proper fruits. In all the cases that I can call to mind, of low profits and low wages in a colony, not occasioned by the disturbing causes above mentioned, the cause has been a stagnation of enterprise and industry, arising from insecurity of property; and the insecurity of property arose from defective or vicious government. I lay it down as an axiom therefore, that tolerably good colonial government is an essential condition of that state of continual high profits and high wages, which moderately well-governed colonies exhibit.

Provided, then, that care is taken to prevent temporary gluts of either capital or labour in very young colonies, and provided also that colonial government is tolerably good, it may be affirmed with confidence, that neither too much capital nor too many people can be sent to a colony; for the more of both the colony receives, the more readily will fresh importations of capital and people find profitable employment; certainly without any decrease, perhaps with an increase, in the rates of profit and wages.

[*Source*: Edward Gibbon Wakefield, *A View of the Art of Colonization* (Oxford: Clarendon Press, 1914), pp. 81–2.]

## 70   G. M. Douglas

Privately hired emigrant shipping produced a wide variation in the health and safety of emigrants, as this 1842 report on migration to Canada shows.

I have the honour to submit, for the information of his Excellency the Governor-general, the accompanying tabular Return (A.) of sick emigrants admitted, discharged, and died at the quarantine hospital, Grosse Isle, for the season ending October 31st. On comparing the same with the admissions,

&c. of previous years (B.), it will be seen that the proportion of sick to the number of emigrants arrived has been somewhat greater this year than last. The mortality of passengers on the voyage has not, however, been so great; while the number of deaths on ship-board last year was 222 out of 28,060 emigrants, or 0.79 per cent; the number this year has been 302 out of 44,584, or 0.67 per cent.; as in former years, the great majority of these deaths were infants at the breast, young children, and aged persons. The loss of infant life on the passage is very great every year, and is readily accounted for from the circumstance of the mothers, upon whom the children depend for support, being placed under circumstances in every way most unfavourable to affording it. She is in most instances from the country, accustomed to respire pure air, and to take active exercise; from this state she is transferred to the hold of a vessel, where she suffers from sea-sickness, is anxious and alarmed, and her food and water in many cases bad and unwholesome; from these causes the infant, deprived of its usual supply of nourishment, pines and dies from inanition. Aged persons, or those in second childhood, are obnoxious to the same causes, and suffer in proportion. A greater number of the deaths took place this year on board of emigrant vessels that were in their passage out in the early part of May; at which time a succession of severe gales of wind from the S. W. were encountered by all those at that time in long. 30° to 40° W. One gale, which lasted from the 4th to the 6th May, was so violent, as to oblige the emigrant vessels exposed to it to keep their hatches battened down for upwards of 48 hours; during which time much suffering was experienced by the poor people; deprived of fresh air, of the means of cooking, and their *morale* affected by the dread of shipwreck. Many of these vessels arrived with loss of bulwarks, boats, and galleys, and in all cases with a greater proportion of sickness and deaths than those not exposed to the fury of the gale.

This season, as in former years, wherever measles and small-pox broke out on board of crowded vessels, the mortality has been very great. Among the worst cases, I would instance the ship Mountaineer, from Liverpool, among whose passengers both these diseases raged, and the number of deaths was 32 out of 505. These passengers suffered also from a deficiency of food, and were reduced to the utmost extremity when they arrived at Grosse Isle; I was under the necessity of admitting 41 to hospital. On board of the bark Ayrshire, from Dublin and Newry, there were 25 deaths out of 428. In the Renfrewshire, from Glasgow, 16 out of 554. In the Compton, from Liverpool, 12 out of 320. In the Minstrel, from Liverpool, 10 out of 180. On board of all these vessels both measles and small-pox prevailed extensively, and had the usual effect of vitiating the atmosphere of the hold, and causing fever amongst those of the adult passengers who were not obnoxious to the contagion of these specific diseases. [. . .]

As offering a favourable contrast to the above recited instances of suffering and deaths, I beg to allude to the case of 23 passenger vessels that arrived at the quarantine station on 3d July. There were on board of these ships upwards of 5,000 emigrants, out of which number I had occasion to send only six to hospital, and but 15 deaths had taken place on the voyage. This comparative absence of sickness and deaths in so large a body of people of all ages, was owing entirely to the extremely favourable weather experienced on their transit to this country. The passage of these vessels did not on an average exceed 30 days, during the whole of which time the weather was never such as to prevent the passengers being on deck. Some of the shipmasters declared they might have made the passage in an open boat, the sea was so smooth and the wind so light; during the 10 years of my official connexion with the quarantine department of the province, I have never witnessed so large a body of emigrants arrive in such good health. The number of births of emigrants on the voyage out, and at the quarantine station, amounted this year to 117; two of these cases were twins; in the great majority of these cases both mother and child did well; two deaths in child-birth took place.

[*Source*: G. M. Douglas, medical superintendent at Quebec to Rawson W. Rawson of the Governor-General's office, 1 December 1842 from Great Britain, *Parliamentary Papers* 1843, vol. XXXIV, 'Papers Relating to Emigration' [291], pp. 28, 29.]

## 71 'For the Information of Emigrants'

These extracts from a notice to immigrants arriving at Montreal make it clear that the government would not support the homeless or unemployed. Land purchase incentives, and an expanding railway network, helped encourage new colonists westward into Upper Canada (now Ontario) and eventually into the central prairies.

There is nothing of more importance to emigrants, on arrival at Quebec, than correct information on the leading points connected with their future pursuits. Many, especially single females and unprotected persons in general, have suffered much from a want of caution, and from listening to the opinions of interested and designing characters, who frequently offer their advice unsolicited. To guard emigrants from falling into such errors, they should, immediately on their arrival at Quebec, proceed to the office of the chief agent for emigrants, where persons desirous of proceeding to any part of Canada will receive every information relative to the lands open for settlement, routes, distances and expenses of conveyance; where also labourers, artisans or mechanics, will be furnished, on application, with the best directions in respect to employment, the places at which it is to be had, and the rate of wages. [. . .]

Small capitalists in search of cleared farms are invited to call at this office, where they will be furnished with the descriptions of a number of farms in various stages of improvement, situated in different sections of the province, many of which combine the advantages of being in the neighbourhood of churches, schools, post-offices, grist and saw mills; and from their vicinity to Quebec and Montreal, the highest market-price may always be obtained for any surplus produce.

On the route from Quebec to their destination they will find many plans and schemes offered to their consideration; but they should disregard such statements, unless well satisfied of their correctness. On all occasions when emigrants stand in need of advice, application should be made to the Government agents, who will gratuitously furnish every requisite information.

Ample notice having now been given, as well in Great Britain and Ireland as in Canada, that an Act has been passed by the Legislature, in which it is expressly stipulated that the emigrant tax levied under its authority should be applied only to the relief of destitute sick emigrants, all parties are, therefore, distinctly informed that no relief whatever will be afforded out of this fund, unless in cases of sickness; and that, therefore, for the future, no free passage will be given. [. . .]

Emigrants should remain about the towns as short a time as possible after arrival. By their proceeding at once into the agricultural districts, they will be certain of meeting with employment more suitable to their habits; those with families will also more easily procure the necessaries of life, and avoid the hardships and distress which is experienced by a large portion of the poor inhabitants in our large cities during the winter season. The chief agent will consider such persons as may loiter about the ports of landing to have no further claims on the protection of Her Majesty's agents, unless they have been detained by sickness or some other satisfactory cause.

[*Source*: 'For the Information of Emigrants' in 1850, from Great Britain, *Parliamentary Papers* 1851, vol. XL, 'Papers Relative to Emigration' [348], pp. 5–6.]

## 72 Daniel Quigley

Many emigrants left Britain with their families but others, especially single men, went out alone. In this letter of 22 April 1893 to his sister Susanna in Belfast, Irish emigrant Daniel Quigley sends news of himself and his brothers from Australia.

I am sorry that I am not in a position to give you the desired information as to Willy['s] whereabouts. About 5 years ago I heard from him; he was at a place in the north west of Queensland about 2,000 miles from here. If I remember right it was the Seatopa gold fields he was on at the time he wrote me. I have not heard from him since nor of him from anyone.

I often see the Joseph of our family in the form of our oldest brother Patrick, but as he and the writer has not spoken for the past 13 years, any information that he could give me on the subject I am not likely to get, but in this case I will get a friend of mine to interview him on the subject of Willy's whereabouts. I will write to my friends in the different Queensland gold fields and see if I can find him; as soon as I can get any trace of him I will let you know at once. There is very little doubt but he is all right in some of the colonies; I suppose by this he is hitched to some of the banana women in the north or west of Queensland with a family of his own and quite forgotten that he left an old mother in the Emerald Isle to mourn his loss or to dream about his death or otherwise. However old gairl you can make yourself quite easy in your mind for he will turn up some day all right, perhaps with a big nugget in his fob[?] and half a dozen of young Bells with him and Mrs. Bell but let us hope that she won't be black as I was very near getting hitched up to a black myself. There is nothing impossible for a colonial in the back blocks to be up to, but for fear you should think that I married a black princess or an old jin for to colonize myself, I will get Mrs. D. Quigley to send you her photo and that of my gairl, Doris Bell Quigley aged three and a half years and my son, so she say, Charles Banister who was 1 year and 6 months at the time the pictures were taken. I got married in June 1889 and of course those two are the result of that union. Do you think that I got hitched up too young; of course they say that the older we get the foolisher we become.

I have been all over the country where Willy is now, some nineteen years ago and I may be able to find him out: to advertise for him might be useless, for I have been in places where we never seen a newspaper from Christmas to the next Christmas. I am sorry to hear that you have been troubled but Burns said that man was made to mourn and I suppose he meant woman too.

[Source: Patrick O'Farrell, ed., Letters from Irish Australia, 1825–1929 (Sydney: New South Wales University Press, 1984), pp. 58–9.]

---

**73   Testimony of a labourer who became a landowner, Australia**

One of the greatest attractions of emigration was the relative ease of land ownership, and therefore of upward social mobility, in the colonies. Class boundaries were much more fluid, as this testimony from Australia shows.

Came to this country in 1839; on landing, my money and property were worth about £30; was engaged two days after my arrival, at 24s. per week, afterwards 30s.—out of this I got my own food; when I had been three months in service, was engaged as overseer; commenced for myself with the sum of £40, on a clearing lease of ten acres, rent £10 a year; this land I have since purchased for £70; have about half the sum paid; I have 3 horses, 2 carts, and a dray, 10 goats, a number of poultry, and have a tolerable house of my own; I employ two labourers, giving them board and lodgings, and 8s. a week; if I had the capital I could employ more with profit to myself; my young children I send to school, and pay 6d. per week each.

[*Source*: C. M. H. Clark, ed., *Select Documents in Australian History 1788–1850*, vol. 1 (Sydney: Angus and Robertson, 1950), p. 201.]

## 74   Advertisement for women migrants to Australia

All of the settlement colonies featured populations with fewer white women than men; the Australian colonies, several of which had begun as penal settlements, had a particularly large imbalance. Emigration societies in Britain began advertising for single young women willing to migrate.

### NOTICE TO YOUNG WOMEN

Desirous of bettering their condition by an Emigration to New South Wales.

In New South Wales and Van Diemen's Land there are very few women compared with the whole number of people, so that it is impossible to get women enough as Female Servants or for other Female Employments. The consequence is, that desirable situations, with good wages, are easily obtained by Females in those Countries; but the Passage is so long that few can pay the expence of it without help. There is now, however, the following favourable opportunity of going to New South Wales.

The Committee has been formed in London for the purpose of facilitating Emigration, which intends to send out a Ship in the course of the Spring, expressly for the conveyance of Female Emigrants, under an experienced and respectable Man and his Wife, who have been engaged as Superintendents. The parties who go in that Vessel must be *Unmarried Women or Widows*; must be *between the ages of 18 and 30*; and must be of *good health and character*. They must also be *able to pay* £6 towards the expense of their Passage. The remainder of the expense will be paid by the Society. Every arrangement will be made for the comfort of the Emigrants during the voyage; and Medical Assistance provided: they will also be taken care of on their first landing in the Colonies; and they will find there, ready for them, a list of the different situations to be obtained, and of the wages offered, so that they may at once see the different opportunities of placing themselves. The women sent out in this manner will not be bound to any person whatsoever, but will be, to all intents and purposes, Free Women.

Persons who, on reading this Notice, may desire to emigrate in the manner pointed out, should apply by Letter to the 'Emigration Committee, 18, Aldermanbury, London'. If the Letter be sent by General Post, it should be sent under a cover addressed to 'The Under Secretary of State, Colonial Department, London'. It will be proper that the Application should be accompanied by recommendations from the Resident Minister of the Parish, and from any other respectable persons to whom the Applicant may be known; the same recommendations should state the fact that the Applicant will be able to pay £6, when she shall receive notice that it is time to embark.

All Applications made in the foregoing manner, will be answered; and it is requested that Parties will apply without delay, as the fine teak-built ship, 'Bussorah Merchant', 530 tons burthen, now in the London Docks, is appointed to sail on the 13th April next expressly with Female Emigrants selected by the Committee.

[*Source*: Clark, *Select Documents in Australian History*, pp. 183–4.]

## 75    Margaret Strobel

'It's a well-known saying that the women lost us the Empire. It's true,' stated Sir David Lean in 1985, repeating a sentiment found in scholarly works. Histories of the nineteenth- and twentieth-century empires virtually ignore European women. If they are mentioned at all, their arrival is seen to have contributed to the deterioration of the relationship between the European administrator and those he governed. A noted specialist in Indian history draws a strikingly misogynistic picture of these women:

As women went out in large numbers, they brought with them their insular whims and prejudices, which no official contact with Indians or iron compulsion of loneliness ever tempted them to abandon. [They were] too insular in most cases to interest themselves in alien culture and life for its own sake.

In this view, a wife drew a man away from his official responsibilities; a family made demands on his time. The presence of supposedly vulnerable women provided a reason to fear the alleged sexual appetites of indigenous men, while the arrival of wives occasioned a decline in the incidence of indigenous mistresses, from whom administrators learned much about colonial society and culture. Finally, English wives in substantial numbers made possible the creation of an exclusive group, socially distanced from indigenous peoples and containing its own hierarchy. In her role as hostess, the wife led the rituals that maintained this boundary and internal hierarchy.

Although this view of the role of European women in the empire dominates the literature on British India, it appears as well with regard to both French and British Africa, British Malaya, Papua, Fiji, and the Solomon Islands. The myth ignores the longstanding practice of populating newly conquered lands with European men and women to sustain European institutions and society. Where the goal was rule (in India, Southeast Asia, the Pacific Islands, and most of Africa) rather than settlement (as in the New World or South Africa), European women were valued less.

Rather than blaming European women for the growing rift between white and nonwhite populations in the empires, recent historians tend to see their arrival as coinciding with other developments in colonial society: intensified appropriation of indigenous land and/or labor, a heightened racial prejudice, the growth of evangelical Christianity with its ethnocentrism and attack on nonmarital and nonmonogamous liaisons, a shortage of administrative personnel, and the increased numbers of women *and* men. [. . .]

From among various European colonizers, we know most about British attitudes toward sexuality in their colonies, although there is some evidence that other colonial powers were less anxious about interracial sexual relationships. Until the late eighteenth century, British residents in India found both intermarriage and the existence of a Eurasian community more acceptable than was later the case. With the free entry of missionaries from 1813 on came criticism of taking Indian mistresses. Official thinking manifested a great ambivalence. Administrators justified the sexual availability of indigenous women for the British army and administrators on the grounds of keeping men virile and heterosexual, essential components of rule that reflected the power of the Raj itself. Yet toward the turn of the century, as colonial rule proceeded and racial prejudices deepened, the need to reinforce social distance overcame concerns about sexual access. The official mind linked control of sexual behavior to social order and disorder generally. Hence British officers, particularly political officers who were to exhibit exemplary behavior, must avoid sexual contact with indigenous women. By the 1860s, having Indian concubines or wives was disapproved. [. . .]

In the early period of African colonization, the presence of concubines surprised no one. A London official claimed that 'the practice of cohabitation with native women has been and is extremely common throughout West and East Africa; indeed I am informed that of the unmarried white officials there is only a small percentage who have abstained entirely from the practice.'

The perils of transition when one's wife came out are illustrated by a story circulated in West Africa about 1910:

One D[istrict] C[ommissioner] arrived with] his new spouse [at] his boma late at night and promptly went to bed. About four in the morning his cook walked boldly into the room, lifted the mosquito net sheltering the exhausted sleepers, soundly slapped the lady on her bottom and said, 'Leave now, missi, time to go back to the village.'

By 1909 the issue of concubinage came to a head. Perhaps recognizing the ubiquity and causes of concubinage, the British Colonial Office did not respond until it was pressured following an incident in Kenya. There, the antics of a district officer with a young African woman attracted the attention of the sole European woman in the district and her husband. When the district commissioner only lost one year of seniority and was forbidden to be in charge of a district for a mere two years, the couple complained to the secretary of state for the colonies. The resulting circulars, issued in 1909, prohibited liaisons with indigenous women in various parts of the empire. This edict caused less hardship in India than in the newer British colonies in Africa. By 1845 'the presence of English women was taken for granted' in India, but in Accra (present-day Ghana) there were only four European women on the eve of World War I. In the Federated Malay States, the decline in concubinage following World War I was linked not only to the circular, but also to the increased number of European women there, from a ratio of forty women per hundred men in 1911 to fifty per hundred by 1921. But the presence of European women did not automatically curtail concubinage. One wife of a district officer in Malawi in the late 1940s divorced her husband because he continued to keep his African 'wives' in the house.

Thus attitudes toward sexual liaisons between European men and indigenous women changed both with pressure from such advocates of more strict sexual morals as missionaries and with the increased size of the European community in a particular colony. Despite the official policy articulated for the British Empire in 1909, the notion remained in some circles that in the 'good old days' concubinage had facilitated a better relationship between ruler and ruled. [. . .]

European male sexual fear and jealousy of non-European men's relationships with European women spanned the colonies. In general, nineteenth-century British men viewed Hindu men as lascivious and feared they attracted English women. In one case, both professional and sexual jealousies of British physicians formed the basis of charges raised in 1859 in India against a Eurasian physician, Dr. Gillies. Breaking the prohibition against intimacy across racial boundaries, Gillies was accused of removing an English woman's sheet and touching her body in the course of assisting her in child-birth. [. . .]

Sexual fear on the part of Europeans reached its height in 1926 in Papua,

New Guinea, where Lieutenant-Governor Hubert Murray signed legislation that specified the death penalty (with no possible alternative) for rape or *attempted* rape. Although the law, known as the White Woman's Protection Ordinance, did not specify the race of the assailant, it was understood to apply to an indigenous man attacking a white woman. The law stood until the repeal of all discriminatory legislation in 1958. At the time of its passage, no white woman had been raped in Papua, although some had been touched in their bedrooms by male servants, and a white nurse had been attacked. The passage of this ordinance, the most extreme response to a supposed threat of 'Black Peril,' resulted from white male settlers' agitation in a small and isolated European community. White women had little to do with its passage. Various residents, white and Papuan, gave racist explanations in identifying the source of the problem (mission-educated male servants— uppity natives) or sexist ones (white women who, by their behavior, invited attack). But neither of these analyses explains the interest of white males in passing the law or its unprecedented harshness. Fundamentally, the ordin- ance, like most responses to 'Black Peril' threats, resulted from the con- tradictory feelings of racial superiority and vulnerability and the sexual projection of white males on colonized men.

In sum, the myth of destructive women contains two aspects that pertain to sexuality. First, in interfering with the European male's access to indigen- ous concubines, European women, it is argued, contributed to the creation of greater distance between the communities. Concubinage entailed physical proximity and intimacy in a context of inequality. The same can be said of the mistress/servant relationship, yet the increased number of households established by and servants hired by incoming European women is not seen as contributing to the developing of ties with the indigenous community. In fact, social distance was created by attitudes of superiority exhibited by both European women and men in the colonies. To single out European women's dislike for concubinage as the source of social distance is to leave unquestioned the inequality of the colonizing male/colonized female concu- bine relationship. The fact that such a structurally unequal relationship has been taken as evidence of closeness between the two communities indicates how little understanding there was and is of gender and power in the dynam- ics of colonialism. Only if one ignores the element of subordination in a concubinage relationship can it be read as closeness.

Second, European women's presence, it is thought, aroused the sexual appetites of indigenous men, and women had then to be protected from the latter; this situation of sexual competition increased the distance between European and indigenous men. The contradictory nature of this formulation reveals clearly the underlying sexism of the myth itself. If concubinage enhanced the relationship of colonizer and colonized, then why should not voluntary sexual liaisons between European women and indigenous men do the same? Because they confounded the fundamental belief that women should be subordinate to men, and a wife from the racially superior group threatened that subordinate status. On the question of the sexual assault of European women by indigenous men, the dreaded 'Black Peril,' the picture is ambiguous. In Papua, European men rather than women agitated for the passage of the harsh legislation. Reminiscences of former colonial wives often do not mention their fear of indigenous men. On the other hand, in 1907 during one of the South African 'Black Perils,' the Associated Women's Organizations of the Transvaal requested that the government enact segregation as a protection against assaults on women. Whether or not women participated in efforts to prevent real or imagined assaults, the notion that they needed male protection fit nicely into the imperial and sexist ideologies of the day.

[Source: Margaret Strobel, White Women and the Second British Empire (Bloomington: Indiana University Press, 1991), pp. 1–4, 5–7.]

## 76   John Stuart Mill

Settlers demanding more political control over their own affairs were supported in Britain by political philosophers like John Stuart Mill. Mill and the other colonial reformers advocated self-government (for white colonial populations only) as part of a confident British empire.

It is now a fixed principle of the policy of Great Britain, professed in theory and faithfully adhered to in practice, that her colonies of European race, equally with the parent country, possess the fullest measure of internal self-government. They have been allowed to make their own free representative constitutions by altering in any manner they thought fit, the already very popular constitutions which we had given them. Each is governed by its own legislature and executive constituted on highly democratic principles. The veto of the Crown and of Parliament, though nominally reserved, is only exercised (and that very rarely) on questions which concern the empire, and not solely the particular colony. How liberal a construction has been given to the distinction between imperial and colonial questions, is shown by the fact, that the whole of the unappropriated lands in the regions behind our American and Australian colonies, have been given up to the uncontrolled disposal of the colonial communities; though they might, without injustice, have been kept in the hands of the Imperial Government, to be administered for the greatest advantage of future emigrants from all parts of the empire. Every Colony has thus as full power over its own affairs, as it could have if it were a member of even the loosest federation; and much fuller than would belong to it under the Constitution of the United States, being free even to tax at its pleasure the commodities imported from the mother country. Their union with Great Britain is the slightest kind of federal union; but not a strictly equal federation, the mother country retaining to itself the powers of a Federal Government, though reduced in practice to their very narrowest limits. This inequality is, of course, as far as it goes, a disadvantage to the dependencies, which have no voice in foreign policy, but are bound by the decisions of the superior country. They are compelled to join England in war, without being in any way consulted previous to engaging in it.

[*Source:* John Stuart Mill, *Considerations on Representative Government* (London: Parker, Son, and Bourn, 1861), pp. 322–3.]

## 77   Lord Durham

Lord Durham, Governor-General of Canada, produced a report on the Canadian situation, but speaks less formally in this letter of 1838. Note that he refers to the English-speaking population as 'British'; only the French-speakers are called 'Canadians' (compare Extract 41). Both groups sought greater self-government and had produced political rebellions during the previous year.

The information which my residence here has enabled me to obtain as to the condition of the two Canadas is of such a nature as to make me doubt whether, if I had been fully aware of the real state of affairs in this part of the world, any considerations would have induced me to undertake so very difficult a task as is involved in my mission. [. . .]

The first point to which I would draw your attention, being one with which all others are more or less connected, is the existence of a most bitter animosity between the Canadians and the British; not as two parties holding different opinions and seeking different objects in respect to Government, but as different races engaged in a national contest. [. . .]

It was long before the Canadians perceived that their nationality was in the course of being over-ridden by a British nationality. When the Constitutional Act bestowed on them a representative system, they were so little conversant with its nature, and so blind to the probable results of British emigration, that they described the constitution as a 'machine Anglaise pour nous taxer,' and elected to the House of Assembly almost a majority of Englishmen. But with the progress of British intrusion, they at length discovered, not only the uses of a representative system, but also that their nationality was in danger; and I have no hesitation in asserting that of late years they have used the representative system for the single purpose of maintaining their nationality against the progressive intrusion of the British race. They have found the British pressing upon them at every turn, in the possession of land, in commerce, in the retail trade, in all kinds of industrious enterprize, in religion, in the whole administration of government, and though they are a stagnant people, easily satisfied and disinclined to exertion, they have naturally resisted an invasion which was so offensive to their national pride.

The British, on the other hand, impeded in the pursuit of all their objects, partly by the ancient and barbarous civil law of the country, and partly by the systematic opposition of the Canadians to the progress of British enterprize, have naturally sought to remove those impediments, and to conquer, without much regard to the means employed, that very mischievous opposition. The actual result should have seemed inevitable. The struggle between the two races, conducted as long as possible according to the forms of the constitution, became too violent to be kept within those bounds.

[*Source*: Durham to Glenelg, 9 August 1838 in Great Britain, *Parliamentary Papers* 1839, vol. XXXII, 'Copies of Extracts of Correspondence relative to the Affairs of British North America' [2], pp. 152, 153.]

## 78   P. J. Marshall

In the period from 1783 to 1870 there can be no doubt of Britain's ambitions, or, to be more exact, of many British people's ambitions. Britain was a restless society. British people were leaving the British Isles, seeking commercial advantages and propagating their values throughout the world. A considerable part of this restless energy spilt over beyond the bounds of the British empire, but its most lasting memorial was an expanding empire of rule. If always essentially British in fundamentals, this empire took very different forms in different parts of the world.

### Colonies of settlement

When Britain conceded American independence in 1783, Quebec and Nova Scotia formed the nucleus of the colonies that constituted Britain's remaining stake on the North American continent—British North America. The population of these colonies was swelled by the arrival of about 50,000 'loyalists'— people who for various reasons had chosen to leave the rebellious colonies and continue to live under British authority. Those loyalists who moved to Quebec introduced a major non-French element to the province for the first time. In 1791 the English-speaking districts of Quebec were turned into a separate province of Upper Canada from which modern Ontario has grown. Over the fifty years after the ending of the European wars in 1815, more than a million British immigrants entered the provinces, although more than half of those eventually moved down to the United States. Of those who remained in British North America, the majority settled in Upper Canada. The old Quebec, later Lower Canada, was dominated by French-speakers. Even if they received no new immigrants, their natural rate of population increase was still spectacular. The French Canadians remained a strongly cohesive community, preserving their language, their Roman Catholicism, and parts of their own legal system. But although the French continued to dominate Quebec, continuous immigration from Britain meant that the French Canadians were no more than a powerful minority in British North America as a whole by the mid-nineteenth century.

The British North American colonies were the proving ground for systems of government considered appropriate for sizeable white communities anywhere within the British empire. British policy was generally to ensure an adequate degree of imperial authority—exercised by a Governor appointed in London—over what were regarded as essential matters, while letting the colonists run their own affairs in all other respects through their own assemblies or local parliaments with as little interference as possible. Close supervision over colonies of white settlement was never desired. In the Canadian colonies by the middle of the nineteenth century and later in other colonies dominated by whites, most of the Governor's powers came to be exercised by local ministers who could command a majority in the Assembly. This was the system eventually known as 'responsible government', under which British colonies became for all intents and purposes internally self-governing, while remaining within the empire and accepting British control over their relations with foreign countries. In retrospect, responsible government was a device of which the British came to be very proud. It seemed to combine freedom for the inhabitants of British colonies to run their own affairs with guarantees that imperial links would survive and therefore that a British identity would be preserved.

Responsible government was first achieved in British North America but not without difficulty. So long as there was a French majority in Canada, the British were wary of handing over real power to a local leadership that might not ultimately prove to be loyal to Britain. (A part of the French population had even taken up arms in revolt in 1837.) The British strategy was first of all to try to bring the provinces of British North America together in a larger block. The larger the unit, the smaller would be the French component in it and the greater would be its chances of resisting the seduction of being absorbed into the great republic to the south. A prosperous, stable, united Canada could stand on its own and make its own terms with the United States. In 1840 English-speaking Upper Canada and Quebec (or Lower

Canada), with its French-speaking majority, were joined together. It was becoming clear that a new French leadership was willing to cooperate with English-speaking Canadian politicians, on the implied condition that Quebec would keep its religion, language, and identity within a union. This union was enlarged by the act creating the Canadian Confederation of 1867, patiently engineered by Canadian politicians with encouragement from London, which united the Canadas and the two main maritime provinces. The act made specific provision for the new Canada to incorporate all the lands claimed to the west by Britain, including the territory of British Columbia on the Pacific in 1871.

In 1788 a British colony was established in a part of the world totally remote from any European colonizing enterprise in the past. After a pro-digious journey round the Cape of Good Hope and across the Indian Ocean, a fleet of eleven vessels containing 736 convicted criminals, a Governor and some officials, and an escort of marines founded a British colony on the eastern coast of Australia in what later became New South Wales. This was to be the first European settlement of any kind in Australasia, an area about which very little was known in Europe. The site for which the first fleet was aiming had been visited in 1770 by Captain James Cook as he sailed up the coast of Australia on the first of his great voyages of exploration into the Pacific. The briefest of calls into what was named Botany Bay suggested that it might be a habitable location for Europeans. Seventeen years later a British government chose to act on that suggestion and dispatch the fleet.

This was a stroke of extraordinary boldness, not to say foolhardiness. Although New South Wales in fact turned out to be an environment in which European settlers would eventually flourish, the British government had no sure knowledge as to what conditions there would be like, and the new colony only survived its initial problems with a great deal of good fortune. Why then did British ministers run such risks? One widely held view is that they were playing for high imperial stakes—that they considered it important for British interests to establish a base somewhere in the Pacific and that the convicts were the best means of getting a new colony off the ground. While it seems to be beyond doubt that British ministers were to some degree interested in the possibilities of the Pacific, no conclusive evidence has yet been found to support theories that settlement in Australia in 1788 was sought primarily for commercial or strategic ends. The traditional explan-ation that New South Wales was colonized to provide a convict settlement is more plausible. Transportation was an important part of the British penal system. Convicts had been transported in the past to colonial America but after the revolution America was no longer available. No alternative destin-ation could be found, in spite of determined efforts to do so, and very large numbers of convicts awaiting transportation were accumulating in Britain. They had to go somewhere—New South Wales was where they went. That is not the whole explanation for the founding of white Australia, but it seems still to be the major factor.

Once the new colony was established, the British government continued to pour out convicts, some 160,000 of them, without significant interruption until 1852. Who the convicts were, how they were treated, and what sort of society emerged among them are all subjects of lively debate. What is beyond question is that they were the basis on which the first two Australian colonies, New South Wales and Van Diemen's Land (Tasmania), were built.

From the landing of the first fleet, non-convict 'free' settlers also went to Australia. Their numbers gradually increased as the opportunities for making a new life in Australia began to become apparent. Australia offered the resources of the Pacific Ocean, particularly seals and whales, convict labour, and an abundance of land from which a thinly-spread Aborigine population—probably around 750,000 on the eve of the first white settlement— could be displaced. (This settlement was accompanied by more violence from whites and more resistance by Aborigines than was once assumed.) The land was used in particular for raising sheep, wool being a cargo whose value in relation to its bulk was sufficient to defray the costs of the immense voyage. By the 1830s Australia was becoming a major supplier of wool to the British textile industry.

The cost of the long haul out to Australia, by comparison with the relatively short trip across the Atlantic, always limited 'free' emigration from Britain. But enough people were encouraged to move, often by schemes of assisted passages in which there was some degree of government involvement, to enable new colonies to be established without convicts. In 1826 settlement began in Western Australia. The new colony of South Australia was sanctioned by act of Parliament in 1834. In the same year settlers from Van Diemen's Land moved across the straits to take up land in what is now Victoria. The success of that settlement was revolutionized by the great gold discoveries of the 1850s, which brought waves of new immigrants to the workings in Victoria and New South Wales. The white population of the Australian colonies jumped from 437,665 in 1851 to over a million in 1861.

Some whites from New South Wales crossed over into New Zealand to use it as a base for voyages into the Pacific and to trade with the Maoris. By the 1830s the lands of New Zealand were coming to be of interest to groups in Britain who wanted to ship out emigrants. In 1840 the British government intervened to try to impose a new order in New Zealand. It was annexed for Britain and white settlement under regulation was officially sanctioned, while under the Treaty of Waitangi guarantees were given to Maori representatives. The new order had eventually to be imposed by force. Maoris resisted the loss of land and of their capacity to rule themselves and proved to be very formidable fighters. In a series of Maori Wars and other skirmishes from 1845 to 1872 British regiments were fully extended and often badly mauled. The outcome of the wars and of the continuing flow of new British immigrants into New Zealand, stimulated by gold rushes in South Island, was to reduce the Maoris to a minority of the total population. By 1870 there were 250,000 whites to some 50,000 Maoris.

As in Quebec, when the British annexed the Cape of Good Hope in 1806 they acquired new European subjects who were not of British origin—in this case the Afrikaners, a population of about 30,000, who, outside the considerable port of Cape Town, were for the most part thinly scattered as farmers (hence 'boers') across a wide area. In addition to the Afrikaners, the Cape was also inhabited by its indigenous people, the Khoikhoi, by slaves brought in by the Dutch, and by communities of people of mixed race. On the frontiers of the area claimed by the Dutch, there were formidable African peoples, especially the Xhosa on the eastern Cape frontier, who disputed the further expansion of European settlement.

Until the great discoveries of minerals in the later nineteenth century, South Africa was not regarded as a major economic asset and it attracted relatively few British immigrants. British interests in this highly complex society were at first mainly limited to maintaining a stable order around the strategically vital harbour of Cape Town, the half-way house to India. Stability was not, however, easy to ensure. At any time rural Afrikaners were inclined to migrate in search of fresh grazing land. Under the British they felt that they had added incentives to move. Some found British rule alien and heavy-handed, a threat to the distinctiveness of their culture and institutions and especially to their labour supply: the British eventually abolished slavery throughout the empire, while imposing regulations on other forms of labour. Instead of rebelling, as some French Canadians had done in 1837, a part of the Afrikaner population took itself away from British jurisdiction by trekking out of the Cape into apparently vacant land to the north. Between 1836 and 1846 about 14,000 Afrikaners embarked on the Great Trek. Their migration created fresh problems for the British. The lands of the north were not of course vacant. They were claimed by African peoples with whom the Afrikaners came into violent conflict. War in the interior, which threatened to spread south into British territory, was added to the more or less endemic war with the Xhosa on the eastern frontier. After a brief attempt to bring under control the new Afrikaner republics of the Orange Free State and the South African Republic (Transvaal), the British for the time being more or less washed their hands of the interior, leaving the trekkers alone. Nearer the coast, however, British involvement continued to be expensive and unrewarding, as a series of Kaffir Wars were fought against the Xhosa and Natal was annexed.

At the Cape, in the Australian colonies, and in New Zealand the British established constitutional arrangements on the same principles as they had done in British North America. Essential imperial control was to be maintained, but otherwise the white communities were to rule themselves as far as possible. Initially elected assemblies were established and eventually the government of the colonies was made 'responsible' to these assemblies as in Canada. Most Australian colonies got responsible government in 1855, New Zealand in 1856, and the Cape in 1872. As with British North America, the British were also concerned to see individual colonies merge into larger and, it was hoped, more stable units, capable of undertaking their own defence. The Australian colonies were not, however, to come together until 1901. The intractable problems of uniting the old British colonies of the Cape and Natal with the Afrikaner republics of the Orange Free State and the Transvaal were not to be overcome until after South Africa had been convulsed by war at the end of the century.

By 1870 British politicians could take some satisfaction from the growth and development of colonies in Canada, South Africa, Australia, and New Zealand. They had stayed within the imperial fold, while developing their own local autonomies. Even the French Canadians and the majority of Afrikaners who remained at the Cape had been kept within the empire. A part at least of the civilizing mission that the Victorians had set themselves had been fulfilled: British values had been preserved in 'British' communities overseas. In terms of wealth and power, Britain stood to gain too. The growth of the white population in Australia, Canada, and New Zealand was to make them by the late nineteenth century 'steady and faithful allies' (as Grey had put it in 1853) of real value to Britain as sources of high-quality military manpower in future wars. As their economies grew, and that of South Africa was transformed by gold and diamonds, their value as trading partners with Britain and as homes for British investment was to grow enormously.

There was, however, a blot on the record of success. The protection of vulnerable non-European peoples was another part of the Victorian civilizing mission. By and large Britain had abandoned this part of its mission in what were emerging as 'white' colonies. British opinion had taken very little notice of the problems of the native American population of Canada or of Australian Aborigines. The Maoris of New Zealand and the Khoikhoi and the Africans of South Africa had, however, featured prominently in the concerns of British humanitarians. The attitudes of British governments had reflected some of this concern, but in the end Britain was not willing to go very far in interposing its authority on their behalf against the wishes of the dominant white communities, and indeed had provided the military power through which these wishes had been enforced. The Xhosa of the eastern Cape in South Africa and the Maoris of New Zealand, for example, had lost their lands as a result of defeat by British forces.

[Source: P. J. Marshall, '1783–1870: An Expanding Empire', in P. J. Marshall, ed., The Cambridge Illustrated History of the British Empire (Cambridge: Cambridge University Press, 1996), pp. 34–43.]

## 79   Lord Glenelg

By the 1830s Native peoples came under pressure to sign treaties making land available for sale to British and other European immigrants. The Colonial Secretary, Lord Glenelg, writing to the Governor-General of Canada on 22 August 1838, distinguished between 'waste' land (available for sale) and shrinking Native territories that would soon become known as 'reserves'.

The Condition of the Indians as to Education is far from creditable to British Rule. Under the French Government that People were placed under the special Care of the Jesuit Missionaries, a Class of Men of whom it must be admitted, that whatever may have been their Delinquencies in the Old World, they have in the New, been known chiefly as the Protectors and Civilizers of a Race forsaken or trampled upon by all beside. It is Time for us to emulate their Example, and to supply, however tardily, the Place of the Instructors of whom our Conquests have deprived the original Possessors of the Soil. You will accordingly take into immediate Consideration the best Means of 'establishing and maintaining Schools among them in which the Rudiments of Education shall be taught, joined, if possible, with Instruction in Agriculture and some of the Handicrafts; and in order to promote these Objects' you are authorized, if you think fit, to direct that some of the Medals or Ornaments now given as Presents should be reserved, and hereafter be 'converted into Prizes for Proficiency in Learning, or for Industry and Success in Agriculture.' [. . .]

With respect to the Settlement of the Indians, I cannot but agree in the Conclusion at which the Committee arrive:—'Upon the whole, however, it would seem to the Committee to be more advisable to endeavour to form compact Settlements of such as may be so disposed upon Lands not very remote from older Settlements, allowing, however, such as may be willing to take separate Locations elsewhere to follow their own Choice, and giving them agricultural Implements, but no other Description of Presents.'

[*Source*: Great Britain, *Parliamentary Papers* 1839, vol. XXXIV, 'Correspondence relating to the Indians in Canada' [323], pp. 6–7.]

## 80   Nancy and Anzac Munnganyi

Perceived as less advanced than North American Indians or other indigenous peoples, Australian Aborigines had never been acknowledged as occupants of the land: there were no treaties in Australia.

The stories of Nancy and Anzac Munnganyi refer to the late nine-teenth century and include accounts of deliberate poisoning.

Jack Jangari, now of Wyndham but formerly of Pigeon Hole, spoke of poison:

Well it was early days. I was in the Pigeon Hole yet when I was a kid. I was in the Pigeon Hole. When I was first coming there, and there was one cook, I forget [the name of] that cook who was there. He made a big stew for those boys, in the big oven. And he put a strychnine. And that's why they called it Poison Creek. That's the place. Fancy putting strychnine in the big oven, for the boys [who] were working. Poor buggers eh?

Nancy, too, spoke of poison. She was not born when this incident occurred, but she had the story from her relations who survived:

At Innesvale, in the bush there . . . oh, they used to be hunting for people there too . . . And hunting, and they got the whole lot. Take them back to station, Dela-mere. Girl and woman, and [their] husbands, you know. Big mob of people. He made them work, and they worked good way.

And that story from my mother, you know. When my mother was young, my uncle [mother's brother] was young too; they were working there. When they fin-ished work, helping that man good way, and that cook put the strychnine in the tucker. Poison them, you know.

Soon as they have, oh, that much hungry, too, you know, from working. They went there. And they had a good feed. Plenty sugar, and strychnine there. As soon as they were finished, and that man came, shot them there now where they were working.

You know, they couldn't walk now. Oh, nother mob got a good idea. They ate mud. Ate that mud, vomit it back again. My mother was there. My uncle got shot right in the water. He jumped in the water. Still they found him in the water. They shot him.

And they kept those girls there, women, they gave them a feed [no poison]. One old fellow got shot . . . guts shot. Still he ran, running along that big hill there, just breaking bushes there, put his guts back in, and stuff them with that grass . . . He was still alive. And he went to—he didn't come back to Delamere Station. [. . .]

People got in the way just by staying at home. Anzac Munnganyi explained that there was no place, ultimately, to which people could flee:

White man just really put it over Aborigines. Aborigines didn't want to go ask him: 'where you been borning?' Where's his country? White man just came up and picked the land straight away. Every place . . .

And the whiteman put the strychnine. That's at this Camfield River, this Mudbura mob. My father was working, and he looked that idea there for whitefellow. All right, couple of blokes died just like a dog from that strychnine. That'd be Mudbura mob, from Camfield River. That's the old story, early days. No lie. My father was working. Not only my father. Everywhere, all the old people.

They reckon it's one story, every way. Ngarinmanpurru, Bilinara, Nungaliwurru, Wardaman, Warlpiri, Walman, they know. Because whitefellow never do only one place this way. Every way [they were] shooting. All around the Wave Hill, Warlpiri, Walman, Gurindji, Nyining, Jiyal, Walmayarri, Bilinara, Wolayijurung, Ngarinmanpurru, Nungaliwurru, Wardaman, all round. Right up where this Yanyula, Binbinga, Ngalurunga, Jingulu, Wampayi, same thing. They try it in the Territory every way. That's the story we know from Top End—old people were losing all the people every way. Aboriginal never got away.

[Source: Deborah Bird Rose, *Hidden Histories: black stories from Victoria River Downs, Humbert River and Wave Hill Stations* (Canberra: Aboriginal Studies Press, 1991), pp. 45–7.]

## 3.4   EMPIRE CONTESTED

The non-European peoples of the British empire were by no means passive witnesses of imperial expansion. Although the nineteenth century was supposed to feature a 'Pax Britannica', it actually involved an almost continuous series of colonial wars. These conflicts caution us against overemphasizing the confident, relentless expansion of British power and serve to remind us of the strong resistance to imperialism in many quarters. This section examines three types of conflict: a commercial war to force open new markets for British goods in China; a major colonial rebellion in India; and a war over land rights and race relations in the settlement colony of New Zealand. Each war was distinctive, but they all shared a common theme: defeat by an empire able to deploy the latest technology, and to reinforce troops and supplies (Extract 81).

Indigenous resistance took place for a number of reasons, one being the rejection of British demands for increased trade. The Chinese 'Opium Wars' are a case in point. As we know, Britain was anxious to increase access to Chinese markets in order to reduce the need to pay for tea with silver. British merchants had been trading Indian opium in China since the eighteenth century, but by the early nineteenth century the scale of trade had grown sufficiently to alarm the Chinese government (Extract 82). But large-scale smuggling operations continued when it became clear that the colonial government of India (still run by the EIC) was doing little to respect China's wishes. When the Chinese began seizing British property and restricting the movements of traders at the port of Canton, the British merchants called on Britain to force China to grant freer trade (Extract 83). Britain launched successful naval attacks on the Chinese coast in the years 1839–42 to protect its citizens, but in truth it was protecting its ability to force trade on an unwilling foreign government (Extract 84). There would be further resistance to the British, and other Western nations, in the nineteenth and twentieth centuries, and in each case the Chinese were defeated by Western military technology, and by the declining power of their own central government. From bases in Hong Kong, Canton, and other 'Treaty Ports' forced open after military defeat, the British and other Westerners were able to impose their will without actually ruling China directly: a good example of 'informal empire'.

In India, resentment about Westernization combined with rapid political change to produce a widespread rebellion in 1857. The immediate cause was a rumour about the use of animal fats on rifle cartridges: beef fat, forbidden to Hindus, and pork fat, forbidden to Muslims. But what began as a mutiny in some regiments of the EIC army quickly escalated to include a number of forms of resistance including renewed loyalty to the Mughal Emperor

(Extract 85), or local political manœuvring designed to restore rights lost to the EIC (Extract 86). Britain's initial response to the rebellion was savage (Extract 87), especially after stories circulated about the rape and murder of British women and children.

By 1858 the official policy had become more conciliatory. In that year the EIC's political authority was replaced by direct rule from London, and Queen Victoria reassured her Indian subjects about Britain's benevolent intention to improve and protect India (Extract 88). But despite the government's promise to separate the state from missionary activities, this imperial benevolence still meant an escalating process of Westernization. By the later nineteenth century, that Westernization had helped to create a new Indian nationalism and increasing demands for independence.

What is usually called 'The Maori War' was actually one of several conflicts in mid nineteenth century New Zealand, and refers to the largest clash between 1860 and 1868. In 1860 matters came to a head during a dispute between Maori chiefs about the legitimacy of a land sale to the colonial government; the chiefs opposed to the sale gathered their warriors and attacked British forces at Taranaki (see Map 10) with unexpected success (Extract 89). Their rebellion was endorsed by the Maori King, the son of a chief elected by the King movement in the 1840s to symbolize a new Maori sense of unity in the face of colonization, and he became a powerful focus of loyalty during the war (Extract 90). The conflict soon spread to other parts of New Zealand. The British home government did not take Maori nationalism particularly seriously, and although they had hoped to avoid open war, they were prepared to enforce British authority at all costs. Once the war had been won, the New Zealand government seized millions of acres of land belonging to the defeated tribes; this land was then sold to settlers (Extract 91).

## 81   David Killingray

The vast imperial possessions acquired by the European powers in the late nineteenth century were gained largely by armed force. That Eurocentric phrase 'Scramble for Africa' marks what was in fact a continental-scale process of war and subjugation to establish alien control over African polities and economies. Armed force was also needed to extend and maintain the colonial presence in what were often troublesome possessions. In certain areas of Africa (eg. Mauritania, Libya, Angola, Sudan) primary resistance continued well into the 1930s. Although colonial law and order was threatened by occasional revolts and acts of communal violence, by 1914 large areas of Africa, particularly British West Africa, were relatively passive. By the outbreak of the Great War, European rule in Africa was often very tentative and most colonies were thinly administered and policed. Europeans acted as Imperial managers while African rulers, especially under systems of indirect rule, continued to be the effective governors of much of African political and economic life.

European empires in Africa were gained principally by African mercenary armies, occasionally supported by white or other colonial troops. In what Kipling described as 'savage wars of peace' the bulk of the fighting was undertaken by black soldiers whose disciplined firepower and organization invariably defeated numerically superior African armies. At the start of the period under consideration breech loading rifles, metallic cartridges, Gatling machine guns and light mobile artillery had become part of the armaments of European, and European led, armies in Africa. By 1914 the weight and effectiveness of firepower had increased greatly, communication systems had progressed to radio telegraphy, and air power was also beginning to be used in colonial wars. As a result numerically larger African armies were usually decimated in open battle by explosive shells, machine guns and rapid concentrated rifle fire. Proportionately the slaughter was immense. At Atbara, in the 1898 campaign to conquer the Sudan, the Khalifa's forces lost 7,000 killed to the British-Egyptian losses of some 600; later at Kurari (Omdurman) more than 11,000 Sudanese peasants were killed in battle against Kitchener's forces which lost 140 men. The once powerful emirates of Northern Nigeria rapidly succumbed to superior British firepower. Sokoto, with an army variously estimated at 6,000 to 30,000, but possessing few rifles, was defeated at Burmi in 1903 by a colonial force of under 500 men. The battle lasted ninety minutes; British casualties numbered a handful, the Sokoto dead lay in hundreds.

European and colonial armies occasionally suffered humiliating and severe defeats at the hands of Africans. In 1879 the Zulu surprised and completely annihilated a British force at Isandhlawana; Hicks Pasha's force advancing up the Nile was wiped out at El Obeid by the Khalifa's forces in November 1883, while Ethiopia gained a decisive victory over the Italians at Adowa in 1896 and so preserved her independence for a further forty years. And in 1921 a Spanish army in Morocco received a crushing defeat at Anual at the hands of the Rif. These were exceptions largely brought about by incompetent leadership, raw recruits, a disdain for the enemy, and involving an element of tactical surprise. In open battle African armies could rarely successfully compete with even small European led armies. However, in guerilla warfare Africans were often strikingly successful. Whereas most large centralized states surrendered after an initial confrontation and defeat, certain small, and also acephalous, polities kept up a long drawn-out military struggle against alien rule. Good examples are the Igbo, the Herero, and the Nandi. [. . .]

In the years 1871–1914 French, British and Portuguese military activity was largely confined to fighting colonial wars. Strategic and tactical lessons learned by the French in Algeria and Indo-China, and by the British in India, the Nile Valley and South Africa, served as models for West African campaigns. In both open and forested country the square formation was employed, encircling reserves and non-combatants, and presenting an armed wall against any developing movements to flank or rear by the enemy. 'Savage warfare', as it was sometimes called, produced an influential body of literature which also informed military thinking and strategic ideas in Europe. The lessons of colonial warfare led to organizational changes in the British Army and the creation of a Service Corps concerned with supply.

Two other related themes can be briefly dealt with at the end of this section: attitudes to colonial warfare, and the costs. Mangin argued that 'we conducted wars without hate; the *sofa* who fought against us yesterday was the tirailleur of tomorrow'. 'Savage warfare' is a truism more often than a description of colonial warfare. Colonial military campaigns were often extremely violent. In West Africa most tended to be relatively short and fairly decisive, although long and destructive operations were required to break the resistance of certain groups of people. In the process great suffering and destruction was inflicted. Claude MacDonald informed the Foreign Office about the plight of Brass, in Southern Nigeria, as a result of colonial conquest: 'towns are destroyed; trade almost ruined; women and children starving in the bush; hundreds have been killed; smallpox has been raging'.

African and colonial warfare had its rules but they were different from those advocated and practiced in European, or 'civilized', warfare. Dum Dum bullets, shelling civilian targets, killing the wounded on the battlefield, the shooting of prisoners, and the seizure of loot and slaves all appear in the catalogue of West African colonial wars in the late nineteenth century. Punitive expeditions destroyed crops and stores and lifted cattle, leaving villagers to starve as a salutary lesson for resistance or revolt. There is no way of calculating the numbers killed as a consequence of colonial war. Certainly no part of West Africa suffered European depredations to the extent of Southern Tanzania following the Maji Maji rebellion of 1905–07. However, one positive outcome was that over large areas of West Africa after 1900 a measure of peace was imposed and maintained under colonial rule.

It is not uncommon to argue that Christian missions welcomed colonial conquest in West Africa. There were always those who hailed colonial campaigns as 'righteous wars' and who argued that 'a sword of steel often goes before a sword of the spirit'. Equally there were those who denounced war and violence. In Europe liberals and humanitarians and commercial interests condemned the employ of 'savage mercenaries' and 'nigger-hunting campaigns'. John Holt, the Liverpool merchant, argued that West Africa wars disrupted trade and killed potential customers.

In financial terms colonial wars imposed a heavy burden on local colonial administration rather than on metropolitan treasuries. Colonies were expected to be financially self-supporting and their revenues consequently often bore the heavy costs of defence and the campaigns of conquest. In the Gold Coast in 1898 military expenditure consumed over thirty percent of total government revenue, while for a period of twenty-five years the colony was saddled with repaying a loan advanced from London to cover the Asante expedition of 1895–96. African societies were rarely able to sustain long wars; they possessed neither the technology nor the economic base to do so. Serious short-term costs came when war disrupted trade and production. Colonial conquest certainly had long-term effects on regional economies although not all were negative; the colonial presence also encouraged trade and production albeit often in new directions.

[*Source*: David Killingray, 'Colonial Warfare in West Africa 1870–1914', in J. A. de Moor and H. L. Wesseling, eds., *Imperialism and War: Essays on Colonial Wars in Asia and Africa* (Leiden: E. J. Brill, 1989), pp. 146–8, 156–8.]

## 82   Lin, Imperial Commissioner

The Chinese emperor decided to ban the opium trade in 1839 and his representative at Canton issued an edict to all foreigners in China on 18 March 1839 threatening the seizure of opium from their warehouses. The tone of the edict, equating foreigners with barbarism, was typical of the attitude of Chinese officials at the time.

Lin, High Imperial Commissioner of the Celestial Court, a Director of the Board of War, and Governor of Hookwang, issues his commands to the foreigners of every nation, requiring of all full acquaintance with the tenour thereof.

It is known that the foreign vessels, which come for a reciprocal trade to Kwangtung, have derived from that trade very large profits. This is evidenced by the facts,—that, whereas the vessels, annually resorting hither, were formerly reckoned hardly by tens, their number has of late years amounted to a hundred and several times ten: and that whatever commodities they have brought, none have failed to find a full consumption; whatever they may have sought to purchase, never have they been unable readily to do so. Let them but ask themselves, whether between heaven and earth, any place affording so advantageous a commercial mart is elsewhere to be found? It is because our Great Emperors, in their universal benevolence, have granted you commercial privileges, that you have been favoured with these advantages. Let our ports once be closed against you, and for what profits can your several nations any longer look? Yet more,—our tea and our rhubarb—seeing that, should you foreigners be deprived of them, you therein lose the means of preserving life,—are without stint or grudge granted to you for exportation, year by year, beyond the seas. Favours never have been greater!

Are you grateful for these favours? You must then fear the laws, and in profit for yourselves, must not do hurt to others. Why do you bring to our land the opium, which in your lands is not made use of, by it defrauding men of their property, and causing injury to their lives? I find that with this thing you have seduced and deluded the people of China for tens of years past: and countless are the unjust hoards that you have thus acquired. Such conduct rouses indignation in every human heart, and it is utterly inexcusable in the eye of celestial reason.

The prohibitions formerly enacted by the Celestial Court against opium, were comparatively lax; and it was yet possible to smuggle the drug into the various ports. Of this the Great Emperor having now heard, his wrath has been fearfully aroused, nor will it rest till the evil be utterly extirpated. Whoever among the people of this inner land deals in opium, or establish houses for the smoking of it, shall be instantly visited with the extreme penalties of the laws; and it is in contemplation to render capital also the crime of smoking the drug. [. . .]

I proceed to issue my commands. When these commands reach the said foreign merchants, let them with all haste pay obedience thereto; let them deliver up to Government every particle of the opium on board their store-ships. Let it be ascertained by the Hong merchants, who are the parties so delivering it up, and what number of chests, as also what total quantity in catties and taels, is delivered up under each name. Let these particulars be brought together in a clear tabular form, and be presented to Government, in order that the opium may all be received in plain conformity thereto, that it may be burnt and destroyed, and that thus the evil may be entirely extirpated. There must not be the smallest atom concealed or withheld.

At the same time, let these foreigners give a bond, written jointly in the foreign and Chinese languages, making a declaration to this effect:—'That their vessels, which shall hereafter resort hither, will never again dare to bring opium with them; and that should any be brought, as soon as discovery shall be made of it, the goods shall be forfeited to Government, and the parties shall suffer the extreme penalties of the law: and that such punishment will be willingly submitted to.'

I have heard that you foreigners are used to attach great importance to the word 'good faith.' If then you will really do as I, the High Commisioner, have commanded,—will deliver up every particle of the opium that is already here, and will stay altogether its future introduction,—as this will prove also, that you are capable of feeling contrition for your offences, and of entertaining a salutary dread of punishment, the past may yet be left unnoticed. I, the High Commissioner, will, in that case, in conjunction with the Governor and

Lieutenant-Governor, address the throne, imploring the Great Emperor to vouchsafe extraordinary favour, and not alone to remit the punishment of your past errors, but also, as we will further request, to devise some mode of bestowing on you his imperial rewards, as an encouragement of the spirit of contrition and wholesome dread thus manifested by you. After this, you will continue to enjoy the advantages of commercial intercourse; and, as you will not lose the character of being 'good foreigners,' and will be enabled to acquire profits and gain wealth by an honest trade, will you not, indeed, stand in a most honourable position?

If, however, you obstinately adhere to your folly, and refuse to awake; if you think to make up a tale covering over your illicit dealings, or to set up as a pretext, that the opium is brought by foreign seamen, and the foreign merchants have nothing to do with it; or to pretend craftily that you will carry it back to your countries, or will throw it into the sea; or to take occasion to go to other provinces in search of a door of consumption; or to stifle inquiry by delivering up only one or two-tenths of the whole quantity: in any of these cases, it will be evident that you retain a spirit of contumacy and disobedience, that you uphold vice and will not reform. Then, although it is the maxim of the Celestial Court to treat with tenderness and great mildness men from afar, yet, as it cannot suffer them to indulge in scornful and contemptuous trifling with it, it will become requisite to comprehend you also in the severe course of punishment prescribed by the new law.

[*Source*: 'Edict from the Imperial Commissioner', from Great Britain, *Parliamentary Papers* 1840, vol. XXXVI, 'Correspondence relating to China' [223], pp. 350–1.]

---

## 83   Petition from British residents of Canton

> The British residents of Canton, including a number of Indian merchants, appealed to the British government for protection, insisting that the interests of commerce should prevail over local sovereignty. The recipient of the petition, the Foreign Secretary, Lord Palmerston, was a vigorous defender of British interests overseas.

We do not attempt to deny the unquestionable right of the Chinese Government to put a stop to the importation of opium, and have readily signed an agreement to abstain from that trade at Canton, on the first requisition of the Government to that effect; but we think your Lordship will perceive that long prescription had hitherto given foreigners ample reason to question the sincerity of the Chinese Government with regard to the discontinuance of the importation; and that, under any circumstances, that Government cannot be justified, by the lax observance of prohibitions, and open connivance of its officers, in at one time fostering a trade involving several millions sterling, and at another rendering its pursuit a pretext for spoliation. [. . .]

We deem it also an imperative duty to assure your Lordship most solemnly of our firm conviction, that the public approval, on the part of Her Majesty's Government, of this prompt interposition of Her Majesty's Representative, and the early adoption of such measures as the wisdom of Her Majesty's advisers may determine on, with regard to our future relations with the Chinese empire, can alone avert the occurrence of similar, or even more violent outrages.

[*Source*: Memorial by British Residents at Canton to Viscount Palmerston, 23 May 1839 from *Parliamentary Papers* 1840, vol. XXXVI, 'Correspondence relating to China' [223], pp. 418–20.]

## 84  Treaty of Nanking, 1842

The Treaty of Nanking was signed on 29 August 1842 and its provisions reveal the scope of the Chinese defeat. Britain's demands were not for political control in China, but rather for enormous commercial concessions and war reparations.

His Majesty the Emperor of China agrees, that British subjects, with their families and establishments, shall be allowed to reside, for the purpose of carrying on their mercantile pursuits, without molestation or restraint, at the cities and towns of Canton, Amoy, Foochowfoo, Ningpo, and Shanghai. [. . .]

It being obviously necessary and desirable that British subjects should have some port whereat they may careen and refit their ships when required, and keep stores for that purpose, His Majesty the Emperor of China cedes to Her Majesty the Queen of Great Britain, &c., the Island of Hong-Kong, to be possessed in perpetuity by Her Britannick Majesty, her Heirs and Successors, and to be governed by such laws and regulations as Her Majesty the Queen of Great Britain, &c., shall see fit to direct. [. . .]

The Emperor of China agrees to pay the sum of six millions of dollars, as the value of the opium which was delivered up at Canton in the month of March, 1839, as a ransom for the lives of Her Britannick Majesty's Superintendent and subjects, who had been imprisoned and threatened with death by the Chinese High Officers. [. . .]

The Government of China having compelled the British merchants trading at Canton to deal exclusively with certain Chinese merchants, called Hong Merchants (or Co-Hong) [. . .] His Imperial Majesty further agrees to pay to the British Government the sum of three millions of dollars, on account of debts due to British subjects by some of the said Hong Merchants, or Co-Hong, who have become insolvent, and who owe very large sums of money to subjects of Her Britannick Majesty. [. . .]

The Government of Her Britannick Majesty having been obliged to send out an expedition to demand and obtain redress for the violent and unjust proceedings of the Chinese High Authorities towards Her Britannick Majesty's Officer and subjects, the Emperor of China agrees to pay the sum of twelve millions of dollars, on account of the expences incurred.

[*Source*: Great Britain, *Parliamentary Papers* 1844, vol. LI, 'Treaty between Her Majesty and the Emperor of China' [521], p. 4.]

## 85    Charles Theophilus Metcalfe

> Mainodin Hassan Khan was an Inspector of Police at Delhi before the rebellion, and became a colonel in one of the new regiments professing loyalty to the Mughal Emperor. He was pardoned after the rebellion ended. A British friend of the Khan and member of India's colonial government, Charles Theophilus Metcalfe, published the Khan's version of events for posterity.

On the 17th of February, 1856, the British annexed Oude. They little antici-pated the result. Thousands of men in the service of the King were thereby thrown out of employment, and were deprived of the means of livelihood. The worse the administration had been, the greater was the multitude of soldiers, courtiers, police, and landholders, who had fattened on it.

Those who had petitioned the English for redress were the poor and the oppressed. But the oppressors saw in British rule their own suppression. Oude was the birthplace of the Purbeah race, and these feelings of dissatis-faction affected the whole Purbeah race in the service of the British Govern-ment. To the native mind the act of annexation was one of gross injustice, and provoked a universal desire for resistance.

The King, and all those connected with him, although bowing to the hand of fate, became henceforward the bitter enemies of the English. At this time there were stationed at Lucknow two regiments, the 19th and the 34th, which were in the pay of the English Government. They had frequent consultations together on the injustice of the step which had been taken, and on the resistance which should be offered, and the attempts which should be made to create a rebellion for the purpose of overthrowing the British authority. It so happened that at the time of the annual change of regiments in 1857 one of these two regiments was sent to Berampur, the other to Barrackpur. Both these regiments were full of bitterness towards the English Government, and from them letters were written to other Purbeah regiments. The 34th took the lead. These letters reminded every regiment of the ancient dynasties of Hindustan; pointed out that the annexation of Oude had been followed by the disbandonment of the Oude army, for the second time since the connection of the English with Oude; and showed that their place was being filled by the enlistment of Punjabís and Sikhs, and the formation of a Punjab army. The very bread had been torn out of the mouths of men who knew no other profession than that of the sword. The letters went on to say that further annexations might be expected, with little or no use for the native army. Thus was it pressed upon the Sepoys that they must rebel to reseat the ancient kings on their thrones, and drive the trespassers away. The welfare of the soldier caste required this; the honour of their chiefs was at stake.

[*Source*: Charles Theophilus Metcalfe, ed., *Two Native Narratives of the Mutiny in Delhi* (Westminster: Archibald Constable & Co., 1898), pp. 36–8.]

## 86 Nana Sahib's Proclamation

Nana Sahib had been trying to claim the throne of the Hindu kingdom of Maratha through his adoptive father; the Marathas had been defeated by the EIC and their nominal ruler (and his successors) were promised a valuable pension. The EIC had rejected Nana Sahib's claim in 1853 and when the Indian rebellion broke out he allied himself with the Mughal imperial family and called for all Marathas to support the uprising against the British.

It is well known that in these days all the English have entertained these evil designs, first to destroy the religion of the whole Hindostani army and then to make the people Christians by compulsion. Therefore we, solely on account of our religion, have combined with the people, and have not spared alive one infidel, and have re-established the Delhi dynasty on these terms, and thus act in obedience to orders and receive double pay. Hundreds of guns and a large amount of treasure have fallen into our hands; therefore it is fitting that whoever of the soldiers and people dislike turning Christians should unite with one heart and act courageously, not leaving the seed of these infidels remaining. For any quantity of supplies delivered to the army the owners are to take the receipts of the officers; and they will receive double payment from the Imperial Government. Whoever shall in these times exhibit cowardice, or credulously believe the promises of those impostors the English, shall very shortly be put to shame for such a deed; and, rubbing the hands of sorrow, shall receive for their fidelity the reward the ruler of Lucknow got. It is further necessary that all Hindoos and

Mussulmans unite in this struggle, and, following the instructions of some respectable people, keep themselves secure, so that good order may be maintained, the poorer classes kept contented, and they themselves be exalted to rank and dignity; also, that all, so far as it is possible, copy this proclamation, and dispatch it everywhere, so that all true Hindoos and Mussulmans may be alive and watchful, and fix in some conspicuous place (but prudently to avoid detection), and strike a blow with a sword before giving circulation to it.

[*Source*: P. J. O. Taylor, *A Companion to the 'Indian Mutiny' of 1857* (Delhi: Oxford University Press, 1996), pp. 239–40.]

## 87   Letter to the Editor of *The Times*

A letter to the editor of *The Times* described the execution of EIC army mutineers at Peshawar by tying them to the muzzles of artillery guns and firing shells to dismember them. This humiliating death deprived both Muslims and Hindus of proper burial rites.

A force of Europeans with guns was sent round the forts, one of which, Meerdan, was held by the 55$^{th}$ Native Infantry in open mutiny; they tried to escape when our force appeared, and some got off to Swat; the others were made prisoners (150 were killed on the spot), tried by drumhead court-martial, and instantly shot. [. . .] Some of the 200 prisoners of the 55$^{th}$ have been tried, and we blew 40 of them away from our guns in the presence of the whole force three days ago; a fearful but necessary example, which has struck terror into their souls. [. . .] Such a scene I hope never again to witness—human trunks, heads, legs, arms, &c, flying about in all directions. [. . .] Trials are going on, and the mutineers will never forget the lesson taught at Peshawur. It is not my business to contrast or compare with scenes elsewhere. I trust and believe we have done what duty demands.

[*Source*: *The Times*, 14 June 1857, p. 7.]

## 88   Royal Proclamation, 1858

Near the end of the rebellion in 1858, after the British government had taken control of Indian territory away from the EIC, Queen Victoria issued a proclamation meant to reassure her new Indian subjects. Note the promise not to impose Christianity, and the offer (severely restricted in practice) of civil service posts to Indians.

Firmly relying Ourselves on the truth of Christianity, and acknowledging with gratitude the solace of Religion, We disclaim alike the Right and the Desire to impose our Convictions on any of Our Subjects. We declare it to be Our Royal Will and Pleasure that none be in any wise favoured, none molested or disquieted by reason of their Religious Faith or Observances; but that all shall alike enjoy the equal and impartial protection of the Law. . . . And it is Our further Will that, so far as may be, Our Subjects, of whatever Race or Creed, be freely and impartially admitted to Offices in Our Service, the Duties of which they may be qualified, by their education, ability, and integrity, duly to discharge.

We know, and respect, the feelings of attachment with which the Natives of India regard the Lands inherited by them from their Ancestors; and We desire to protect them in all Rights connected therewith, subject to the equitable demands of the state; and We will that generally, in framing and administering the Law, due regard be paid to the ancient Rights, usages, and Customs of India. [. . .]

Our Clemency will be extended to all Offenders, save and except those who have been, or shall be, convicted of having directly taken part in the Murder of British Subjects. [. . .] To all others in Arms against the Government, We hereby promise unconditional Pardon, Amnesty, and Oblivion of all Offence against ourselves, Our Crown and Dignity, on their return to their homes and peaceful pursuits.

[*Source*: Great Britain, *Parliamentary Papers* 1908, vol. LXXIV, 'Copies of . . . the Proclamation of the late Queen Victoria on the 1st day of November 1858 to the Princes, Chiefs, and People of India' [324], pp. 2–3.]

## 89   Major Thomas Nelson

British soldiers found the Maori to be formidable foes, as this 1860 report of a failed attack on a Maori *pa*, or fortified settlement, shows.

I have the honour to inform you, for the information of the Colonel commanding, that, in reference to your letter of yesterday's date, I moved out this morning at 5 o'clock with the detail noted in the margin, to attack the new pahs in the mounds on the south-east of the camp, and returned from thence to camp at half-past 11 a.m.

The attack was commenced by the artillery at 7 a.m., at a range of 400 yards to the north-west of the pahs. A breach was, however, not made in the large pah of a sufficient size to justify me in ordering the men to assault it. During the time the artillery was playing on the pah, large bodies of Maories were seen advancing from the rear and occupying in extended order a ditch and bank about 400 yards in advance of our right flank, from which they kept up a constant fire.

Seeing there was no means of entering the pah, I immediately ordered an advance towards the ditch and bank just mentioned, which was made in a most continued and gallant manner, until the men reached a deep ravine with an entrenchment behind, and which they found impossible to pass, it being defended by two if not even three large bodies of Maories, who were almost entirely concealed behind it, and another entrenchment in rear, as well as the very high fern. Here a desperate and destructive fire was opened upon us, and most gallantly returned.

Our skirmishers being far fewer in number, and exposed in a much greater degree than the enemy, I deemed it desirable to direct them to join the main body; and our ammunition being nearly expended, I withdrew the whole of the men, and returned to camp in regular order.

I regret to have to report that the casualties have been numerous; but when, as it is supposed, the whole of W. King's natives came down to support the Waikatos in the pahs,—the whole amounting apparently to about 800 men (foremost among whom was an European, who was shot dead),—it cannot be considered that the number is great in proportion to those opposed to us.

Among the deaths I have to lament that of Lieutenant Brooke, 40th Regiment, who fell in the noble discharge of his duty, and 29 non-commissioned officers and men of the different corps; among the wounded, Captain Seymour, R.N., severely, and 33 non-commissioned officers and men of the different corps. I enclose a return of casualties. The loss of the rebels, from personal observations, must have been very great.

[*Source*: Major Thomas Nelson to the brigade commanding officer at Taranaki, 27 June 1860 in Great Britain, *Parliamentary Papers* 1860, vol. XLVII, 'Papers relating to New Zealand', p. 81.]

## 90   William Thompson (Te Waharra)

A Maori chief, William Thompson (Te Waharra), writes to another chief, urging him to hold fast to his principles during the war. Note how apparently liberal laws on intermarriage are interpreted by Te Waharra as a threat to Maori survival.

To all the Natives of Whanganui. I have heard from Aaron (Arona) about your determination to retain possession of the land; that is good; be strong to hold your lands.

There are three things we must hold to: The Almighty, the King, and the Land.

The Governor is about going your way; when he gets there, do you demean yourselves like the Ngarara (lizard or other reptile), which, on beholding humankind, remains silent. Be cautious of the wolf; the wolf is the Governor, who is trying to beguile (or deceive) us.

There are two laws which will shortly be made known to us, one is for the white man to intermarry with the Maori, the result of which will be the destruction of our position and appearance as the Maori people; the other law is the establishment of schools, so that we may be taught the European language; this will also tend to our subversion as a race as at present constituted (our likeness will be destroyed).

Another system of the Governor's is the appointing of Maori Magistrates, and paying them 50 *l*. per annum.

The reason why I do not visit you is because I am busily engaged, otherwise I should follow the Governor's example, and visit all parts of the Islands.

[*Source*: Te Waharra to Rio, 30 April 1862 in Great Britain, *Parliamentary Papers* 1863, vol. XXXVIII, 'Papers relating to the affairs of New Zealand' [467], p. 4.]

## 91   Governor Bowen

> The British took advantage of their victory to seize millions of acres of land belonging to the tribes who had been defeated. Governor Bowen, reflecting on the legacy of the Maori War, compared its outcome with the English colonization of Ireland, and with the defeat of Scottish Highlanders in the eighteenth century.

During my tour in the Waikato (to the more important incidents of which I have now referred), I visited the remains of the Maori pahs and field-works, especially those at Mere-Mere and at Rangariri, before which so many of our officers and soldiers fell. An English high-road now traverses, and the posts and wires of the electric telegraph surmount the mouldering trenches and rifle-pits, already overgrown with wild shrubs and fern. I am assured that the Colonial Government will take measures for the proper preservation of the graveyards at Rangariri and the other scenes of former contests, where many British soldiers rest near their Maori foemen.

I annex a map on which Major Heaphy, v.c., has described the confiscated lands, where the military settlements have been planted, and also the territory of King Tawhiao and his immediate adherents, now enclosed by an *aukáti*, or boundary, which no European is allowed to cross on pain (after due warning) of death. Your Grace will, of course, recognize in the Maori *aukáti* a 'pale,' in the sense familiar in Irish history, with this important difference, however, that in Ireland the 'pale' was set up by the colonists against the natives, whereas in New Zealand it is set up by the natives against the colonists. It has been often observed that it is a lamentable fact that, after all the expenditure of blood and treasure which has taken place in this country, the Queen's writ can hardly be said to run in the purely Maori districts of New Zealand in the reign of Queen Victoria, any more than it ran in the Celtic districts of Ireland in the reign of Queen Elizabeth, and in the Celtic districts of Scotland in the reign of Queen Anne. Indeed a close historical parallel has been frequently drawn between the social condition of the Maori Highlands at the present day, and that of the Scotch Highlands down to the middle of the 18th century, when a general reconstruction of society followed the suppression of the rebellion of 1745, and the subsequent breaking up of the system of clanship, and abolition of tribal tenures, and of the hereditary authority of the chiefs. It is well known that the regular troops and the colonial forces fought with the accustomed gallantry and success of English soldiers throughout the recent war, whenever they encountered the Maoris in the open field, and whenever they could bring them to close combat in the fortified *pahs*; but owing to the great difficulties presented by the mountains and forests of the interior of New Zealand, to the Maori system of fighting in *tanas*, or war parties, dispersed over a wide extent of natural fastnesses, and to a variety of other causes, there has been no Culloden in New Zealand history.

[*Source*: Great Britain, *Parliamentary Papers* 1868–69, vol. XLIV,
'Papers relating to New Zealand' [59], pp. 132–3.]

## 3.5 THE 'NEW IMPERIALISM'

**B**ritain faced new circumstances after 1870 which eroded the international dominance it had enjoyed since 1815, and brought it into increasing conflict with rival imperial powers. In response, British policymakers (and the general public) promoted a more aggressive imperialism to ensure that Britain did not fall behind. These developments prompt many textbooks to regard the late nineteenth and early twentieth centuries as the 'age of empire' and Britain's renewed imperial expansion as a 'new imperialism'. But when we consider the long history of the British empire we can also see the 'new imperialism' as another of Britain's periodic reassessments of the empire's identity and purpose; a new theme on an old tune (Extract 92).

British domestic politics reflected the new urgency in imperial policy-making. The leader of the opposition, Benjamin Disraeli, spoke in 1872 of the need for greater imperial pride, reinventing his Conservative party as the promoter and defender of empire (Extract 93). As prime minister, Disraeli would pursue an assertive imperialism which was popular with the newly expanded voting population, and which alarmed the more cautious Liberals and their leader, William Gladstone. It was Disraeli, however, who captured the mood of the times: even the Liberals found themselves embroiled in expansionist policies by the 1880s. For example, Disraeli's government acquired a large number of shares in the new Suez Canal and by the 1880s this financial interest was threatened by nationalist uprisings and instability in the Egyptian government. Gladstone, who won the 1880 election in part through his opposition to Disraeli's aggressive foreign policy, found himself with no choice but to order the invasion of Egypt in 1882 (Extract 94).

International factors also contributed to the new imperialism, especially the loss of British pre-eminence in naval, economic, and international political matters. New nations were becoming imperial powers. The 'scramble for Africa' at the end of the nineteenth century (see Map 11) took place at a series of European conferences where, to keep the peace in Europe, politicians drew arbitrary borders and apportioned new colonies to satisfy national egos. In Africa itself, the agents of empire obtained new lands and trading rights through treaties that were sometimes of doubtful integrity (Extracts 95 and 96).

The increased pace of expansion sparked new conflicts with indigenous populations, and even the advocates of imperialism began to lament its cost (Extract 97). By the end of the nineteenth century and the coming of the South African War it seemed to some that the empire had become little more than an elaborate investment protection scheme (Extract 98). For others, the changing times presented Britain with an opportunity to reinvent its empire, enabling it to compete effectively for prestige abroad and votes at home

(Extract 99). This group, sometimes known as 'the imperialists', gathered around the Conservative politician, Joseph Chamberlain, in the 1890s and created a programme of imperial reform. Most of their ideas would be too radical for Chamberlain's Conservative colleagues to accept, particularly the idea of an Imperial Parliament with direct representation by the self-governing settler colonies (called Dominions by the early twentieth century). But Chamberlain's economic plans found greater favour (Extract 100). Free trade had been Britain's dominant commercial ideology for most of the century, but free trade was now allowing American and German goods to undercut British commerce. Chamberlain advocated free trade within the British empire, but with tariffs imposed on goods produced outside it: a return to the old concept of protectionism. He also promoted a formal 'development' policy whereby investors would help create more effective economies and infrastructure in the colonies. Both schemes would be implemented in the early twentieth century. Chartered companies also reappeared, encouraging the private sector to shoulder the burden of colonial investment without the need for formal British rule; Cecil Rhodes's British South African Company was one of the best known of these. In most cases, however, the companies proved unable to handle the cost and conflict of expansion and their areas of influence became colonies in any case.

Chamberlain and the other 'imperialists' wanted to create a more efficient empire, and part of this new image involved what became known as 'indirect rule' (Extract 101). Because the empire was expanding so fast, particularly in Africa and the Pacific islands, the cost of administering it was also increasing. To keep that cost down, the concept of trusteeship was expanded from its earlier, humanitarian roots. The legacy of Charles Darwin had contributed to ideas about racial determinism in Britain, and late Victorian trusteeship assumed that non-European peoples needed to have their affairs run for them. Indirect rule involved the use of indigenous leadership and traditional forms of taxation and land ownership under British supervision. This helped reduce the cost of imperial administration and, in many cases, the power of indigenous élites was increased in the process. Well into the twentieth century the British would point to trusteeship and indirect rule as evidence of the benevolent, collaborative face of empire. But they were storing up trouble for the future. As historian Sir John Seeley noted in the 1880s, Britain's imperial power was undermining the future ability of non-Europeans to govern themselves (Extract 102).

**92** **P. J. Marshall**

What was strikingly new about the later nineteenth century was the intensity of public debate about empire. Central to this debate was concern about how Britain now stood in relation to other European powers.

## The challenge overseas

It was becoming obvious that in many parts of the world Britain would no longer enjoy the free hand that it had been able to take for granted for so long. Anxieties about American dominance of the western hemisphere abated, but old fears about Russian territorial expansion in Asia became much more acute in the 1870s. In 1873 the Russians established their control over Khiva, the last of the major independent khanates of Central Asia. By 1884 they were firmly established on the borders of Afghanistan and a railway network was being constructed, which, the British feared, could sustain a powerful Russian army within easy striking distance of India.

By the 1880s assumptions that, because of Britain's absolute naval supremacy, the only serious threats to the empire would be from powers able to attack British colonies overland no longer seemed to be valid. The naval building of France and Russia caused anxiety in the 1880s. By the end of the century Germany was embarking on the first of its programmes of naval expansion and Japan, Italy, and the United States were also all acquiring fleets of modern warships. In 1897, in spite of a great expansion of the British fleet, the battleships of the other powers outnumbered the Royal Navy by ninety-six to sixty-two. Britain had lost its naval monopoly.

Thus from the 1880s other powers were acquiring the means to support probes into areas where Britain had not faced serious competition before, especially in the Far East and in Africa. In South East Asia the foothold established by the French in the 1860s in Indochina (Vietnam) was pushed outwards towards southern China and Siam (Thailand). The French were joined by the Germans in seeking commercial concessions and grants of coastal enclaves from the Chinese. Germany also claimed territory in the Pacific, occupying part of New Guinea. Russia joined Germany and France in disputing what had effectively been British commercial and diplomatic dominance of China's relations with the outside world. In 1891 the Russians started to build a great railway across Siberia. They claimed Manchuria as their special sphere and, like the French and Germans, they took over a coastal enclave.

In Africa south of the Sahara more assertive French policies became evident in 1879. Expansion from old coastal trading settlements gathered momentum in the 1880s and 1890s, culminating by the end of the century in a vast French territorial empire in tropical Africa. In 1884–85 the Germans were also challenging Britain in Africa: their initial annexations became the colonies of South West Africa (Namibia), Tanganyika (Tanzania), and Togo and Cameroon in West Africa.

## The challenge in Europe

To many British people, the more active roles being played by the French, Germans, and Russians outside Europe were symptoms of much deeper changes on the continent itself. The appearance of increasing numbers of German merchants selling German goods and supported on occasions by German cruisers throughout the world was just one manifestation of the great transformation of Germany. By far the most spectacular and threatening evidence of this transformation was the overwhelming of France in war in 1871 and the completion of German unity in the same year. The new Germany had clearly harnessed great industrial power and a highly efficient state machinery to waging war with an altogether new intensity. In eighteen days, over a million German soldiers had been mobilized and 462,000 of them had moved into France. France was defeated, but it reformed its armed forces and tried to recover its position in Europe and the world. Tsarist Russia was engaged in a transformation much more uneven and much less total than Germany's, but still impressive. A great European war in which the survival of Britain or of its fundamental interests would be at stake had seemed a remote possibility after the defeat of Napoleon. Now it no longer seemed so remote. Were such a war to break out would Britain be capable of holding its own with the new leviathans? [. . .]

Even if cold winds had not been blowing out of Europe, the empire's economic contribution to Britain would have been re-examined in the later nineteenth century. However, the belief that military power now depended on industrial strength gave this re-examination a much keener edge. A number of developments were strengthening Britain's economic links with the world outside Europe. More and more of Britain's food and of the raw materials for its industry came from such sources, though not necessarily from the empire. Half of the food that British people ate was imported by 1914. By the end of the nineteenth century Britain needed to import most of the wheat it consumed. Here the empire was a major supplier: by 1913 nearly half the wheat imported into Britain came from the empire. The proportion of British exports going to countries created by European colonization overseas (Latin America as well as the British colonies of settlement) increased from 21.2 per cent in 1871–75 to 28.5 per cent in 1909–13 and the proportion going to African and Asian markets rose from 31.6 per cent to 36.2 per cent. By contrast, Europe's share declined slightly and that of the United States fell markedly.

Increasing British trade with countries outside Europe was made possible by a number of developments in the later nineteenth century. The steamship and the railway brought down the costs of moving commodities around the world. Cheap communications enabled the farmers of the colonies of settlement to exploit their advantages—above all, their access to an abundance of cheap land—over the farmers in Europe. Many of the improvements in communications across the world, such as the great railway networks of North and South America or Australasia, were to a large extent financed by Britain. Between 1870 and 1914 British savings were invested overseas on a massive and totally unprecedented scale. Little of this investment, probably only some 13 per cent, went to Europe. Over half of it went to North and South America and 16 per cent to Australasia. Only small amounts went to Africa outside South Africa or indeed to any other tropical area. In short, the British invested overwhelmingly in countries of recent white settlement, whether they were British colonies or not. Although only 40 per cent of total investment went to the empire, the heavy concentration of this imperial investment on colonies of settlement (Australia, Canada, New Zealand, and South Africa) still did much to stimulate their rapid development. Even more rapid development in the future would, it was hoped, be brought about by appropriate British policies. [. . .]

## The partitions of Africa and South East Asia

Until late in the nineteenth century, Britain's interests anywhere in Africa north of the Limpopo or throughout South East Asia were confined to West African coastal enclaves, such as Sierra Leone, The Gambia, or a string of forts on the Gold Coast (Ghana), and to Singapore, Malacca, and Penang on the Malay coast. Trading networks, such as those on the Niger river, penetrated further inland, but the British presence was still a strictly limited one. Yet by 1900 Britain had acquired huge territorial possessions in both areas. A string of British colonies had been established in East and Central Africa as well as in West Africa. The British had also occupied Egypt and the Sudan. In South East Asia the British had extended their authority over the whole Malay peninsula and had conquered the kingdom of Burma.

Traditionally, Britain's spectacular territorial gains in the last quarter of the nineteenth century have been explained in one of two ways. One view is that Britain acted to secure the resources and markets of the tropics for its increasingly hard-pressed industries; the other view is that Britain's aim was to protect vital strategic interests. Neither explanation on its own survives close examination. By most standards the stakes in these spectacular partitions were not very high. Quite valuable trades were already being carried on in some areas, such as the palm oil trade of the Niger or the tin trade of the Malay states. Should these trades be seriously threatened, they were certainly worth protecting from Britain's point of view, but they hardly justified massive annexations. Egypt, which had a large population and a sophisticated economy and where large sums had already been invested by western concerns, including British ones, was the only major economic asset at stake. The strategic importance of the control of Egypt was also obvious and it had been enhanced by the construction of the Suez canal. But it required some ingenuity to invest most of the rest of the territory about to be partitioned with much strategic significance.

Rather than attempt any overall explanation of the partitions, it is important to recognize that conditions varied markedly between the 1880s and the 1890s. The story of the partitions is one of gathering momentum: in the 1880s annexations were still limited; they became unrestrained in the 1890s.

In the 1880s, the British appeared to be reacting to the initiatives of other powers. As France and Germany made new claims, Britain felt compelled to match them by defining its own claims to areas where British traders had usually been operating for many years. Most interpretations date the partition of Africa as starting with French actions between 1879 and 1882—an expedition from Senegal towards the upper Niger and the ratification of a treaty with an African ruler on the Congo. German interventions followed in 1884. British responses in the 1880s were generally limited and hesitant. Counter claims were put forward and Britain participated in the Berlin conference of 1885 which tried to limit expansion and define claims. When Britain claimed territory, there was a strong preference for using private bodies—companies to which the British government awarded charters, entitling them to occupy and administer territory. The Royal Niger Company was chartered in 1886 to implement British claims on the Niger. In 1888 the Imperial British East African Company took over territory allocated to Britain in East Africa by the agreement with Germany of 1886. Cecil Rhodes's British South Africa Company was chartered in 1889 to occupy the future Rhodesia (Zimbabwe) and exclude Afrikaners or other Europeans from the area. A company was chartered for the administration of British claims to North Borneo in 1881. In Malaya British authority was also established by indirect means as a series of treaties were signed from 1874 to take rulers under British protection.

In Egypt British intervention was direct and involved the dispatch of considerable forces of the Crown to bombard Alexandria and to invade Egypt in 1882. Even here the British claimed to be acting on the defensive, arguing that law and order had broken down under a new Egyptian regime. The Egyptian army was defeated at the battle of Tell el-Kebir. Egypt never formally became a British colony as such: it was 'occupied' by Britain and what purported to be its own administration was placed under close British supervision. [. . .]

The other major act of British aggression in the 1880s was a war against

Burma. The kingdom of Burma had already lost territory to Britain, but in 1885 the Viceroy of India used his army in the way that his predecessors had done so often to subdue what he regarded as a recalcitrant neighbour, in whom the French showed some interest.

Egypt and Burma apart, British acquisitions of territory during the 1880s were generally conducted in a low-key manner: limited gains were made, usually avoiding major confrontations with other powers. In the 1890s British policy was more assertive. The outlines of the future colonies of the Gold Coast and Nigeria began to be filled in by forceful actions against African peoples. On the Niger French claims were brusquely rebuffed in a sharp crisis. In 1885 the British had pulled back from the Sudan, even though General Gordon had perished in the withdrawal, an episode that attracted intense public concern and much resentment against a government that was accused of allowing him to die a Christian martyr's death. In 1896 the government of Lord Salisbury decided that the Sudan must now be conquered. A powerful expeditionary force under General Kitchener drove south from Egypt and destroyed the forces of the Islamic Mahdist regime in the Sudan in 1898 at Omdurman. As in West Africa, there was now to be no compromise with French claims. The French tried to establish their right to the Upper Nile by sending a small expeditionary force overland from West Africa to a village called Fashoda in 1898. The British insisted that the French withdraw. War was the alternative if they did not. The French accepted the situation and withdrew.

Britain's role in the partition of Africa is often depicted as the 'new' British imperialism in action overseas. For the 1880s at least, this is misleading. Throughout the decade, outside Egypt, the British edged forward cautiously, making piecemeal gains. Only the death of Gordon seems to have aroused deep public concern. For the 1890s, however, there is a much closer connection between imperial attitudes at home and what happened in Africa. Serious imperialists were primarily concerned with reuniting the dispersed British race, not with conquering African territory. Nevertheless, the Conservative government elected in 1895 was committed to maintaining Britain's position in every part of the world, almost regardless of cost. Challenges must be faced, by force if necessary. The French yielded to the threat of force on the Niger and the Nile. The Afrikaners did not. The ensuing South African War with its cost and eventual unpopularity was a great setback for imperial idealism.

Wars and threats of war over Africa in the 1890s, together with ambitious programmes to reconstruct the empire and thus to regenerate Britain itself, are striking new developments in the history of the British empire. But by 1914 the British empire had not been reconstructed and in the newly acquired territories, apart from Egypt, very little had been done to create effective administrations or to realize such economic potential as they might possess.

The continuities between the period 1870 to 1914 and the earlier nineteenth
century are in fact more striking than the changes.

[*Source*: P. J. Marshall, '1870–1918: The Empire under Threat', in Marshall, *Cambridge
Illustrated History of the British Empire*, pp. 54–7, 72–6.]

## 93 Benjamin Disraeli

Benjamin Disraeli (later Earl of Beaconsfield) was leader of the opposition Conservative Party when he gave this speech at the Crystal
Palace on 24 June 1872. In it he stated that only the Conservatives
were the true party of empire, playing on the increasing popularity of
imperialism among ordinary Britons.

If you look to the history of this country since the advent of Liberalism—
forty years ago—you will find that there has been no effort so continuous, so
subtle, supported by so much energy, and carried on with so much ability and
acumen, as the attempts of Liberalism to effect the disintegration of the
Empire of England. And, gentlemen, of all its efforts, this is the one which
has been the nearest to success. Statesmen of the highest character, writers of
the most distinguished ability, the most organised and efficient means, have
been employed in this endeavour. It has been proved to all of us that we have
lost money by our Colonies. It has been shown with precise, with mathematical demonstration, that there never was a jewel in the Crown of England
that was so truly costly as the possession of India. How often has it been
suggested that we should at once emancipate ourselves from this incubus!
Well, that result was nearly accomplished. When those subtle views were
adopted by the country under the plausible plea of granting self-government
to the Colonies, I confess that I myself thought that the tie was broken. Not
that I for one object to self-government; I cannot conceive how our distant
Colonies can have their affairs administered except by self-government.

But self-government, in my opinion, when it was conceded, ought to have
been conceded as part of a great policy of Imperial consolidation. It ought to
have been accompanied by an Imperial tariff, by securities for the people of
England for the enjoyment of the unappropriated lands which belonged to
the Sovereign as their trustee, and by a military code which should have
precisely defined the means and the responsibilities by which the Colonies
should be defended, and by which, if necessary, this country should call for
aid from the Colonies themselves. It ought, further, to have been accompanied by the institution of some representative council in the metropolis,
which would have brought the Colonies into constant and continuous relations with the Home Government. All this, however, was omitted because

those who advised that policy—and I believe their convictions were sincere—looked upon the Colonies of England, looked even upon our connection with India, as a burden upon this country; viewing everything in a financial aspect, and totally passing by those moral and political considerations which make nations great, and by the influence of which alone men are distinguished from animals.

Well, what has been the result of this attempt during the reign of Liberalism for the disintegration of the Empire? It has entirely failed. But how has it failed? Through the sympathy of the Colonies for the Mother Country. They have decided that the Empire shall not be destroyed; and in my opinion no Minister in this country will do his duty who neglects any opportunity of reconstructing as much as possible our Colonial Empire, and of responding to those distant sympathies which may become the source of incalculable strength and happiness to this land.

[*Source*: George Earle Buckle, *The Life of Benjamin Disraeli: Earl of Beaconsfield* (London: John Murray, 1920), vol. 4, pp. 194–5.]

## 94 Lord Cromer

By 1882 the government of Egypt was breaking down under nationalist pressure, and the Prime Minister, Gladstone, ordered an invasion to protect British interests in the Suez Canal. Evelyn Baring, Earl Cromer, ruled Egypt under a nominal native government.

Egypt may now almost be said to form part of Europe. It is on the high road to the far East. It can never cease to be an object of interest to all the Powers of Europe, and especially to England. A numerous and intelligent body of Europeans and of non-Egyptian Orientals have made Egypt their home. European capital to a large extent has been sunk in the country. The rights and privileges of Europeans are jealously guarded, and, moreover, give rise to complicated questions, which it requires no small amount of ingenuity and technical knowledge to solve. Exotic institutions have sprung up and have taken root in the country. The Capitulations impair those rights of internal sovereignty which are enjoyed by the rulers or legislatures of most States. The population is heterogeneous and cosmopolitan to a degree almost unknown elsewhere. Although the prevailing faith is that of Islam, in no country in the world is a greater variety of religious creeds to be found amongst important sections of the community.

In addition to these peculiarities, which are of a normal character, it has to be borne in mind that in 1882 the army was in a state of mutiny; the Treasury was bankrupt; every branch of the administration had been dislocated; the ancient and arbitrary method, under which the country had for centuries been governed, had received a severe blow, whilst, at the same time, no more orderly and law-abiding form of government had been inaugurated to take its place.

Is it probable that a Government composed of the rude elements described above, and led by men of such poor ability as Arábi and his coadjutors, would have been able to control a complicated machine of this nature? Were the Sheikhs of the El-Azhar Mosque likely to succeed where Tewfik Pasha and his Ministers, who were men of comparative education and enlightenment, acting under the guidance and inspiration of a first-class European Power, only met with a modified success after years of patient labour? There can be but one answer to these questions. Sentimental politicians may consider that the quasi-national character of Arábi's movement gives it a claim to their sympathies, but others who are not carried away by sentiment may reasonably maintain that the fact of its having been a quasi-national movement was one of the reasons which foredoomed it to failure; for, in order to justify its national character, it had to run counter, not only to the European, but also to the foreign Eastern elements of Egyptian government and society. Neither is it in the nature of things that any similar movement should, under the present conditions of Egyptian society, meet with any better success. The full and immediate execution of a policy of 'Egypt for the Egyptians,' as it was conceived by the Arábists in 1882, was, and still is impossible.

[*Source*: Lord Cromer, *Modern Egypt* (New York: Macmillan, 1908), vol. i, pp. 326–7.]

## 95   Treaty between Lo Bengula and agents of Cecil Rhodes

Cecil Rhodes was one of the best-known late Victorian imperialists. As head of the British South Africa Company he exploited territory obtained by treaty with African rulers such as Lo Bengula of Matabeleland and Mashonaland. This transaction of 1888 was named the 'Rudd concession' after one of Rhodes' agents.

Know all men by these presents, that whereas Charles Dunell Rudd, of Kimberley; Rochfort Maguire, of London; and Francis Robert Thompson, of Kimberley, have covenanted and agreed . . . to pay me . . . the sum of one hundred pounds sterling, British currency, on the first day of every lunar month; and further, to deliver at my royal kraal one thousand Martini-Henry breech-loading rifles, together with one hundred thousand rounds of suitable ball cartridges . . . and further to deliver on the Zambesi River a steamboat with guns suitable for defensive purposes, or in lieu of the said steamboat, should I elect, to pay to me the sum of five hundred pounds sterling, British currency. On the execution of these presents, I, Lo Bengula, King of Matabeleland, Mashonaland, and other adjoining territories ... do hereby grant and assign unto the said grantees ... the complete and exclusive charge over all metals and minerals situated and contained in my kingdoms ... together with full power to do all things that they may deem necessary to win and procure the same and to hold, collect, and enjoy the profits and revenues, if any, derivable from the said metals and minerals, subject to the aforesaid payment; and whereas I have been much molested of late by divers persons seeking and desiring to obtain grants and concessions of land and mining rights in my territories, I do hereby authorize the said grantees ... to exclude from my kingdom ... all persons seeking land, metals, minerals, or mining rights therein, and I do hereby undertake to render them all such needful assistance as they may from time to time require for the exclusion of such persons, and to grant no concessions of land or mining rights ... without their consent and concurrence ... This given under my hand this thirtieth day of October, in the year of our Lord 1888, at my royal kraal.

[*Source*: Louis Snyder, *The Imperialism Reader; documents and readings on modern expansionism* (Princeton, NJ: Van Nostrand, 1962).]

## 96   Appeal of Lo Bengula to Queen Victoria

The year after he granted the 'Rudd concession', Lo Bengula's people raised concerns about the fairness of the treaty and local British missionaries encouraged him to appeal to Queen Victoria. But in the meantime, Rudd and his colleagues proceeded with their mining activities and the British government chose not to interfere.

Some time ago a party of men came to my country, the principal one appearing to be a man called Rudd. They asked me for a place to dig for gold, and said they would give me certain things for the right to do so. I told them to bring what they could give and I would show them what I would give. A document was written and presented to me for signature. I asked what it contained, and was told that in it were my words and the words of those men. I put my hand to it. About three months afterwards I heard from other sources that I had given by that document the right to all the minerals of my country. I called a meeting of my *Indunas* [councillors], and also of the white men and demanded a copy of the document. It was proved to me that I had signed away the mineral rights of my whole country to Rudd and his friends. I have since had a meeting of my *Indunas* and they will not recognise the

paper, as it contains neither my words nor the words of those who got it. . . .
I write to you that you may know the truth about this thing.

[*Source*: Snyder, *Imperialism Reader*, p. 220.]

## 97    Rudyard Kipling

The poet and novelist Rudyard Kipling, often stereotyped as an
uncritical advocate of imperialism, was keenly aware of the empire's
unwelcome presence in much of the non-European world, and of its
cost in British lives. For him, Britain's imperial obligations were a
bitter but necessary burden.

### The White Man's Burden
#### 1899

Take up the White Man's burden—
    Send forth the best ye breed—
Go bind your sons to exile
    To serve your captives' need;
To wait in heavy harness,
    On fluttered folk and wild—
Your new-caught, sullen peoples,
    Half-devil and half-child.

Take up the White Man's burden—
    In patience to abide,
To veil the threat of terror
    And check the show of pride;
By open speech and simple,
    An hundred times made plain,
To seek another's profit,
    And work another's gain.

Take up the White Man's burden—
    The savage wars of peace—
Fill full the mouth of Famine
    And bid the sickness cease;
And when your goal is nearest
    The end for others sought,
Watch Sloth and heathen Folly
    Bring all your hope to nought.

Take up the White Man's burden—
    No tawdry rule of kings,
But toil of serf and sweeper—

The tale of common things.
The ports ye shall not enter,
   The roads ye shall not tread,
Go make them with your living,
   And mark them with your dead.

Take up the White Man's burden—
   And reap his old reward:
The blame of those ye better,
   The hate of those ye guard—
The cry of hosts ye humour
   (Ah, slowly!) toward the light:—
'Why brought ye us from bondage,
   Our loved Egyptian night?'

Take up the White Man's burden—
   Ye dare not stoop to less—
Nor call too loud on Freedom
   To cloak your weariness;
By all ye cry or whisper,
   By all ye leave or do,
The silent, sullen peoples
   Shall weigh your Gods and you.

Take up the White Man's burden—
   Have done with childish days—
The lightly proffered laurel,
   The easy, ungrudged praise.
Comes now, to search your manhood
   Through all the thankless years,
Cold, edged with dear-bought wisdom,
   The judgment of your peers!

[*Source: Collected Verse of Rudyard Kipling* (Toronto: The Copp,
Clark Company, 1906), pp. 215–17.]

---

## 98   J. A. Hobson

The British intellectual J. A. Hobson saw imperial expansion as a calculated support for capitalist expansion: a theory which would inspire V. I. Lenin, among others. Theories of capitalist imperialism continue to thrive a century after Hobson's publication in 1902.

Although the new Imperialism has been bad business for the nation, it has been good business for certain classes and certain trades within the nation.

The vast expenditure on armaments, the costly wars, the grave risks and embarrassments of foreign policy, the checks upon political and social reforms within Great Britain, though fraught with great injury to the nation, have served well the present business interests of certain industries and professions.

It is idle to meddle with politics unless we clearly recognise this central fact and understand what these sectional interests are which are the enemies of national safety and the commonwealth. We must put aside the merely senti-mental diagnosis which explains wars or other national blunders by outbursts of patriotic animosity or errors of statecraft. Doubtless at every outbreak of war not only the man in the street but the man at the helm is often duped by the cunning with which aggressive motives and greedy purposes dress them-selves in defensive clothing. There is, it may be safely asserted, no war within memory, however nakedly aggressive it may seem to the dispassionate his-torian, which has not been presented to the people who were called upon to fight as a necessary defensive policy, in which the honour, perhaps the very existence, of the State was involved.

The disastrous folly of these wars, the material and moral damage inflicted even on the victor, appear so plain to the disinterested spectator that he is apt to despair of any State attaining years of discretion, and inclines to regard these natural cataclysms as implying some ultimate irrationalism in politics. But careful analysis of the existing relations between business and politics shows that the aggressive Imperialism which we seek to understand is not in the main the product of blind passions of races or of the mixed folly and ambition of politicians. It is far more rational than at first sight appears. Irrational from the standpoint of the whole nation, it is rational enough from the standpoint of certain classes in the nation. A completely socialist State which kept good books and presented regular balance-sheets of expenditure and assets would soon discard Imperialism; an intelligent *laissez-faire* demo-cracy which gave duly proportionate weight in its policy to all economic interests alike would do the same. But a State in which certain well-organised business interests are able to outweigh the weak, diffused interest of the community is bound to pursue a policy which accords with the pressure of the former interests. [. . .]

It is not too much to say that the modern foreign policy of Great Britain has been primarily a struggle for profitable markets of investment. To a larger extent every year Great Britain has been becoming a nation living upon tribute from abroad, and the classes who enjoy this tribute have had an ever-increasing incentive to employ the public policy, the public purse, and the public force to extend the field of their private investments, and to safeguard and improve their existing investments. This is, perhaps, the most impor-tant fact in modern politics, and the obscurity in which it is wrapped has constituted the gravest danger to our State. [. . .]

Such is the array of distinctively economic forces making for Imperialism, a large loose group of trades and professions seeking profitable business and lucrative employment from the expansion of military and civil services, and from the expenditure on military operations, the opening up of new tracts of territory and trade with the same, and the provision of new capital which these operations require, all these finding their central guiding and directing force in the power of the general financier.

The play of these forces does not openly appear. They are essentially parasites upon patriotism, and they adapt themselves to its protecting colours. In the mouth of their representatives are noble phrases, expressive of their desire to extend the area of civilisation, to establish good government, promote Christianity, extirpate slavery, and elevate the lower races. Some of the business men who hold such language may entertain a genuine, though usually a vague, desire to accomplish these ends, but they are primarily engaged in business, and they are not unaware of the utility of the more unselfish forces in furthering their ends. Their true attitude of mind was expressed by Mr. Rhodes in his famous description of 'Her Majesty's Flag' as 'the greatest commercial asset in the world'.

[*Source*: J. A. Hobson, *Imperialism: A Study* (London: Unwin Hyman, 1938; orig. publ. 1902), pp. 46–7, 53–4.]

## 99 Earl of Rosebery

The proliferation of popular organizations such as the Royal Colonial Institute demonstrates the appeal of empire to all classes of British society. In this speech to the Institute in 1893, the Foreign Secretary, the Earl of Rosebery, drew on Anglo-Saxon racial superiority, and the need to compete with other peoples, as a justification for continued expansion.

Since 1868 the Empire has been growing by leaps and bounds. That is, perhaps, not a process which everybody witnesses with unmixed satisfaction. It is not always viewed with unmixed satisfaction in circles outside these islands. There are two schools who view with some apprehension the growth of our Empire. The first is composed of those nations who, coming somewhat late into the field, find that Great Britain has some of the best plots already marked out. To those nations I will say that they must remember that our colonies were taken—to use a well-known expression—at prairie value, and that we have made them what they are. We may claim that whatever lands other nations may have touched and rejected and we have cultivated and improved are fairly parts of our Empire, which we may claim to possess by an indisputable title. But there is another ground on which the extension of our Empire is greatly attacked, and the attack comes from a quarter nearer home. It is said that our Empire is already large enough and does not need extension. That would be true enough if the world were elastic, but, unfortunately, it is not elastic, and we are engaged at the present moment in the language of mining in 'pegging out claims for the future'. We have to consider not what we want now, but what we shall want in the future. We have to consider that countries must be developed either by ourselves or some other nation, and we have to remember that it is part of our responsibility and heritage to take care that the world, as far as it can be moulded by us, shall receive the Anglo-Saxon and not another character. . . . We have to look forward beyond the chatter of platforms and the passions of party to the future of the race of which we are at present the trustees, and we should in my opinion grossly fail in the task that has been laid upon us did we shrink from responsibilities and decline to take our share in a partition of the world which we have not forced on, but which has been forced upon us.

[*Source*: *The Times*, 2 March 1893, p. 8.]

**100**   **Joseph Chamberlain**

> Supporters of the 'new imperialism', especially the Colonial Secretary, Joseph Chamberlain, promoted the reorganization of imperial policy, defence, and finances in order to make the empire more profitable and efficient. Chamberlain's idea of an imperial free-trade zone was supported by the Dominions, but not put into effect until the twentieth century (see Chapter 4).

I have laid down four propositions which I think cannot be controverted. The first is that there is a universal desire among all the members of the Empire for a closer union between the several branches, and that, in their opinion as in ours, this is desirable—nay, it is essential for the existence of the Empire as such. My second proposition is that experience has taught us that this closer union can be most hopefully approached in the first instance from its commercial side. My third proposition is that the suggestions which have hitherto been made to us, although we know them to have been made in good part, are, when considered from the point of view of British interests, not sufficiently favourable to be considered by this country. My fourth proposition is that a true Zollverein for the Empire, that a free trade established throughout the Empire, although it would involve the imposition of duties against foreign countries, and would be in that respect a derogation from the high principles of free trade and from the practice of the United Kingdom up to the present time, would still be a proper subject for discussion and might probably lead to a satisfactory arrangement if the colonies on their part were willing to consider it. ('Hear, hear,' and cheers.)

[*Source*: Joseph Chamberlain, *Foreign and Colonial Speeches* (London: Routledge and Sons, 1897), pp. 172–3.]

## 101 Lord Lugard

> The British hoped that by collaborating with indigenous political leaders they could tap into traditional social and legal systems and govern through 'indirect rule'. The most famous advocate of this system was Frederick, Lord Lugard, who became Governor-General of Nigeria in 1914.

Both the Arabs in the east and the Fulani in the west are Mohamedans, and by supporting their rule we unavoidably encourage the spread of Islam, which from the purely administrative point of view has the disadvantage of being subject to waves of fanaticism, bounded by no political frontiers. In Nigeria it has been the rule that their power should not be re-established over tribes which had made good their independence, or imposed upon those who had successfully resisted domination.

On the other hand, the personal interests of the rulers must rapidly become identified with those of the controlling Power. The forces of disorder do not distinguish between them, and the rulers soon recognise that any upheaval against the British would equally make an end of them. Once this community of interest is established, the Central Government cannot be taken by surprise, for it is impossible that the native rulers should not be aware of any disaffection.

This identification of the ruling class with the Government accentuates the corresponding obligation to check malpractices on their part. The task of educating them in the duties of a ruler becomes more than ever insistent; of inculcating a sense of responsibility; of convincing their intelligence of the advantages which accrue from the material prosperity of the peasantry, from free labour and initiative; of the necessity of delegating powers to trusted subordinates; of the evils of favouritism and bribery; of the importance of education, especially for the ruling class, and for the filling of lucrative posts under Government; of the benefits of sanitation, vaccination, and isolation of infection in checking mortality; and finally, of impressing upon them how greatly they may benefit their country by personal interest in such matters, and by the application of labour-saving devices and of scientific methods in agriculture. [. . .]

I have throughout these pages continually emphasised the necessity of recognising, as a cardinal principle of British policy in dealing with native races, that institutions and methods, in order to command success and promote the happiness and welfare of the people, must be deep-rooted in their traditions and prejudices. Obviously in no sphere of administration is this more essential than in that under discussion, and a slavish adherence to any particular type, however successful it may have proved elsewhere, may, if unadapted to the local environment, be as ill-suited and as foreign to its conceptions as direct British rule would be.

[*Source*: Lord Lugard, *The Dual Mandate in British Tropical Africa* (London: Frank Cass and Company, 1965; orig. publ. 1922), pp. 210–11.]

## 102   Sir John Seeley

Historian Sir John Seeley gave a series of lectures in the 1880s arguing that Britain had two empires: an empire of settlement leading to peaceful self-rule in the Dominions, and an empire in India which was governed undemocratically. He explained this paradox using a theory of reluctant (and therefore disorganized) British imperialism. He shrewdly diagnosed the lack of a cohesive national identity in India, and blamed Britain for enhancing the problem and therefore making continued British rule necessary.

The colonies and India are in opposite extremes. Whatever political maxims are most applicable to the one, are most inapplicable to the other. In the colonies everything is brand-new. There you have the most progressive race put in the circumstances most favourable to progress. There you have no past and an unbounded future. Government and institutions are all ultra-English. All is liberty, industry, invention, innovation, and as yet tranquillity. Now if this alone were Greater Britain, it would be homogeneous, all of a piece; and, vast and boundless as the territory is, we might come to understand its affairs. But there is at the same time another Greater Britain, surpassing this in population though not in territory, and it is everything which this is not. India is all past and, I may almost say, has no future. What it will come to the wisest man is afraid to conjecture, but in the past it opens vistas into a fabulous antiquity. All the oldest religions, all the oldest customs, petrified as it were. No form of popular government as yet possible. Everything which Europe, and still more the New World, has outlived still flourishing in full vigour; superstition, fatalism, polygamy, the most primitive priestcraft, the most primitive despotism; and threatening the northern frontier the vast Asiatic steppe with its Osbegs and Turcomans. Thus the same nation which reaches one hand towards the future of the globe and assumes the position of mediator between Europe and the New World, stretches the other hand towards the remotest past, becomes an Asiatic conqueror, and usurps the succession of the Great Mogul.

How can the same nation pursue two lines of policy so radically different without bewilderment, be despotic in Asia and democratic in Australia, be in the East at once the greatest Mussulman Power in the world and the guardian of the property of thousands of idol-temples, and at the same time in the West be the foremost champion of free thought and spiritual religion, stand out as a great military Imperialism to resist the march of Russia in Central Asia at the same time that it fills Queensland and Manitoba with free settlers? Never certainly did any nation, since the world began, assume anything like so much responsibility. [. . .]

Our acquisition of India was made blindly. Nothing great that has ever been done by Englishmen was done so unintentionally, so accidentally, as the conquest of India. There has indeed been little enough of calculation or contrivance in our colonisation. When our first settlers went out to Virginia and New England, it was not intended to lay the foundations of a mighty republican state. But here the event has differed from the design only in degree. We did intend to establish a new community, and we even knew that it would be republican in its tendency; what was hidden from us was only its immense magnitude. But in India we meant one thing, and did quite another. Our object was trade, and in this we were not particularly successful. War with the native states we did not think of at all till a hundred years after our first settlement, and then we thought only of such war as might support our trade; after this time again more than half a century passed before we thought of any considerable territorial acquisitions, [. . .]

It is possible to hold that England would be better off now had she founded no such Empire at all, had she remained standing, as a mere merchant, on the threshold of India, as she stands now on that of China. But the abandonment of India is an idea which even those who believe that we shall one day be driven to it are not accustomed to contemplate as a practical scheme. There are some deeds which, though they had been better not done, cannot be undone. A time may conceivably come when it may be practicable to leave India to herself, but for the present it is necessary to govern her as if we were to govern her for ever. Why so? Not mainly on our own account. [. . .] [A] condition of anarchy seems almost to have been chronic in India since Mahmoud, and to have been but suspended for a while in the Northern half by Akber and Shah Jehan.

India then is of all countries that which is least capable of evolving out of itself a stable Government. And it is to be feared that our rule may have diminished what little power of this sort it may have originally possessed. For our supremacy has necessarily depressed those classes which had anything of the talent or habit of government. The old royal races, the noble classes, and in particular the Mussulmans who formed the bulk of the official class under the Great Moguls, have suffered most and benefited least from our rule. This decay is the staple topic of lamentation among those who take a dark view of our Empire; but is it not an additional reason why the Empire should continue? Then think of the immense magnitude of the country; think too that we have undermined all fixed moral and religious ideas in the intellectual classes by introducing the science of the West into the midst of Brahminical traditions. When you have made all these reflexions you will see that to withdraw our Government from a country which is dependent on it and which we have made incapable of depending upon anything else, would be the most inexcusable of all conceivable crimes and might possibly cause the most stupendous of all conceivable calamities. [. . .]

There is then no Indian nationality, though there are some germs out of which we can conceive an Indian nationality developing itself. It is this fact, and not some enormous superiority on the part of the English race, that makes our Empire in India possible. If there could arise in India a nationality-movement similar to that which we witnessed in Italy, the English Power could not even make the resistance that was made in Italy by Austria, but must succumb at once. For what means can England have, which is not even a military state, of resisting the rebellion of two hundred and fifty millions of subjects? Do you say, as we conquered them before, we could conquer them again? But I explained that we did not conquer them. I showed you that of the army which won our victories four-fifths consisted of native troops. That we were able to hire these native troops for service in India, was due to the fact that the feeling of nationality had no existence there. Now if the feeling of a common nationality began to exist there only feebly, if, without inspiring any active desire to drive out the foreigner, it only created a notion that it was shameful to assist him in maintaining his dominion, from that day almost our Empire would cease to exist.

[*Source*: John Seeley, *The Expansion of England* (Leipzig: Tauchnitz, 1884), pp. 186–8, 189, 206–7, 237–8.]

# Chapter 4

## The Twentieth Century

### INTRODUCTION

**H**istorians disagree about exactly when the decline of the British empire began. Some point to the insecurities of the 1880s and 1890s; others prefer the South African War as a landmark. Most see the First World War as a crucial turning point, and all agree that by the time the Second World War was over Britain was no longer a superpower. After that, widespread decolonization was inevitable. During the first half of the twentieth century, however, the empire also showed signs of remarkable loyalty to Britain, and British policy by no means readily accepted the possibility of rapid decolonization. The empire remained enormously popular among ordinary people in Britain until after the Second World War. Even in the colonies of settlement, where definitions of citizenship were shifting from 'British subject' to 'Canadian' or 'Australian', most people were aware of their part in a global imperial network. Nevertheless, by the 1960s Britain was forced to accept the eventual loss of its imperial identity.

Meanwhile, far from appearing to be an empire in decline, the British empire actually grew to its largest extent during the early twentieth century. Although Britain had been concerned about imperial rivalry since the 1880s it was still optimistic about the internal cohesiveness of its own empire. By the beginning of the century, several chartered companies had gone bankrupt, prompting the government to take charge of them as 'protectorates' (a name that reflected the current doctrines of development and indirect rule). The First World War, despite its cost in human life, ended with an expanded British empire ruling over several former German and Ottoman territories. The entry of the United States into the First World War in 1917 had been a crucial part of the Allied victory, and during the peace negotiations of 1918–19 it seemed that the USA, under President Woodrow Wilson, intended to play a large role in international affairs in the future. Wilson had great hopes for the new League of Nations that he helped to create, but American political opinion still favoured isolationism, and during the 1920s and 1930s Britain and other western European countries still dominated the international political stage. This position was enhanced by the relative weakness of a Russia still rebuilding after the revolution of 1917 and subsequent civil war. This situation would not last. After 1945 only two superpowers—the USA and the USSR—dominated the developing cold war.

By the time the pace of British decolonization increased in the 1960s a clear pattern had emerged: a reduced commitment to empire at home, developing nationalisms in the colonies, and Britain's insistence on democratic majority rule before independence would be granted. Nationalism had begun much earlier in the Dominions, and their identities as independent states had been confirmed by the Statute of Westminster in 1931. India's nationalist movement began during the late nineteenth century, splitting into Muslim and Hindu variations later. In most of Asia, Africa, and the Pacific, however, nationalism was still developing by the time decolonization took place. New identities such as 'Nigerian' or 'Fijian' were promoted by a political élite anxious for independence, but were not necessarily understood the same way by men and women of the various races and cultures contained within the state's borders. Most of Britain's colonies were modern creations, their borders drawn without regard to indigenous political or cultural groupings, and their populations altered by the impact of disease, the slave trade, warfare, and immigration. Nationalist movements therefore faced a double challenge. They struggled to create independent states out of political entities that had been created by colonialism itself, and they attempted to forge a new identity that disparate peoples and cultures could share. But labels such as 'Malaysian' or 'Kenyan' often masked rather than resolved the problem of societies fragmented by race, ethnicity, social rank, and gender. The British sometimes created federations to overcome the problem, hoping for the same success that Canada, Australia, and South Africa had enjoyed. But the federations proposed for Africa and the West Indies were short-lived at best, and it became clear that decolonization in these areas would proceed state by state.

Because Britain insisted on the establishment of democratic majority rule before granting independence, political élites in the colonies needed to overcome their differences to some extent. Some could not, as in the Palestinian mandate. Others did, but only temporarily, as in India before partition. In other cases such as Malaysia or Zimbabwe consensus came only after civil war. In some former colonies democracy made its first appearance at the time of decolonization, but has been under threat since.

We must consider these post-colonial conditions when we ask whether or not British decolonization was peaceful. It is true that British imperial history contains nothing comparable to the hideous collapse of the former Belgian Congo, the 1954–62 French war in Algeria, or the drawn-out battle for independence in Portuguese Angola in the 1970s. This is something of which the British are justifiably proud. But all empires cast long shadows. Border disputes, communal violence, and economic inequality were produced by local circumstances, but also by imperialism itself. Perhaps it was inevitable that the massive and long-lasting British empire would make an impact too profound for easy resolution.

## 4.1 THE END OF EMPIRE?

There were critical voices amid the popular imperialism of the early twentieth century, not least because of the controversy generated by the 'Scramble for Africa', and by the increasing visibility of colonial wars. The advent of the telegraph, combined with on-the-spot reporting for Western newspapers, gave imperial warfare an unprecedented immediacy and by the end of the nineteenth century critics were deploring the cost in human life and suffering (Extract 103). Marxist theories connecting capitalism with imperialism, especially in the writings of J. A. Hobson and the Russian revolutionary leader V. I. Lenin, provided a new dimension for debate about empire's purpose and morality. But empire had always been controversial, and criticism at home was a relatively minor reason for the actual dissolution of empire in the twentieth century.

It is important to realize how popular the empire still was during the early twentieth century: the historian John M. Mackenzie demonstrates how it pervaded all aspects of popular culture from the late nineteenth century to the 1930s (Extract 104). The concept of colonial development, introduced by Chamberlain's 'new imperialism', gained favour in the early twentieth century and was still in force in the 1950s (Extract 105). The early twentieth-century empire cultivated a constructive image whose symbol was often the District Officer: the imperial man-on-the-spot who attempted, usually with the greatest sincerity, the impossible task of modernization without trauma (Extract 106). The Dominions, completely independent after 1931, chose to remain in close association with Britain through the developing structure of the British Commonwealth.

By the end of the Second World War, however, the British people had decided to remake and revitalize their nation. The victory of the Labour Party in 1945 committed Britain to the creation of a welfare state, and to rapid decolonization in India (Extract 107). After Indian independence in 1947 nationalists in most other British colonies began demanding similar treatment. By 1980 almost all of them had succeeded. The process of decolonization was never straightforward, however, and some British politicians resisted the loss of imperial power. The Suez Crisis of 1956, when Britain and France conspired with Israel in an attempt to thwart Egypt's nationalization of the Suez Canal, was probably the last gasp of old-fashioned imperial ambition (Extract 108). But widespread public protest about Suez demonstrated that British domestic identity was changing: imperialism seemed old-fashioned now when compared with contemporary interest in American popular culture, and Britain's relationship with Europe. After Suez, the new Prime Minister, Harold Macmillan, toured Africa and talked about 'winds of change'; during the 1960s almost all of Britain's remaining colonies would achieve independence.

Meanwhile, the United States and the Soviet Union were creating an international dynamic very different from the old pattern of European imperial rivalry. Both nations officially encouraged decolonization, yet both also sought to take newly independent countries into their spheres of influence. Britain was no longer a global power in this new, cold war world. This transition from global empire to second-rank nation has taken place so recently that theories about decolonization are still in the developmental stage (Extract 109). But was decolonization actually the end of empire?

The Commonwealth might be further evidence of empire's ability to reinvent and even subvert itself to meet new needs. What began as an exclusive club for the white Dominions had always contained the potential for something more (Extract 110). As the pace of decolonization grew in the 1960s and 1970s it became clear that, far from rejecting the Commonwealth as irrelevant, former colonies in Africa and Asia wished to join and transform it. They did this so successfully, and the resulting institution is so popular, that even without British participation the Commonwealth would continue to thrive (Extract 111). Is the Commonwealth an outdated relic of imperialism, or a unique, democratic international forum?

## 103   Wilfred Blunt

Wilfred Blunt, a diplomat and writer, was particularly critical of Britain's involvement in Egypt and the Sudan in the 1880s. As the twentieth century opened he regarded the legacy of imperialism with horror.

The old century is very nearly out, and leaves the world in a pretty pass, and the British Empire is playing the devil in it as never an empire before on so large a scale. We may live to see its fall. All the nations of Europe are making the same hell upon earth in China, massacring and pillaging and raping in the captured cities as outrageously as in the Middle Ages. The Emperor of Germany gives the word for slaughter and the Pope looks on and approves. In South Africa our troops are burning farms under Kitchener's command, and the Queen and the two Houses of Parliament and the bench of bishops thank God publicly and vote money for the work. The Americans are spending fifty millions a year on slaughtering the Filipinos; the King of the Belgians has invested his whole fortune on the Congo, where he is brutalizing the negroes to fill his pockets. The French and Italians for the moment are playing a less prominent part in the slaughter, but their inactivity grieves them. The whole white race is reveling openly in violence, as though it had never pretended to be Christian. God's equal curse on them all! So ends the famous nineteenth century into which we were so proud to have been born.

[*Source*: Snyder, *Imperialism Reader*, p. 147.]

## 104 John M. Mackenzie

From the perspective of the late twentieth century, it is hard to recognize the pervasiveness and power of the British Empire in the thought and imagination of many sections of the British public. Yet there have been echoes in the Falklands War in 1982; there has been the continuing fascination of the entertainment media with many aspects of the Imperial experience; and most recently there has been the prominence given to the handover of Hong Kong to China in 1997. Serious and scholarly interest in Imperial matters has also led to the development of programmes to collect oral, visual, and written material about colonial experiences while a Museum of the British Empire and Commonwealth has been established in Bristol. In still wider perspective, British officials such as those at the Colonial or India Offices were not the only people to be connected to the enterprise of Empire. Many more British people had a knowledge of the Empire because of personal, professional, religious, and cultural experiences.

Thousands of British families had friends or relatives who had emigrated to the Dominions, or who had served or were serving in other parts of the dependent Empire as civil servants, teachers, missionaries, engineers, or in such technical trades as driving locomotives, and of course as soldiers in the British army. Imperial perceptions were not confined to Cheltenham and other genteel places where retired Imperial servants congregated. All social classes were influenced in different ways. The churches of the country and their Sunday schools were a constant source of information about Empire, as missionaries 'on furlough' preached about their work, showed magic-lantern slides, and urged their hearers to contribute generously to medical, educational, and evangelical work throughout the Empire. The missionary commitment to medicine as well as educational work helped to popularize the notion that Western medicine and Western-trained doctors were heroically tackling the most feared tropical diseases and the scourge of maternal and infant mortality. Medicine was thus seen to parallel the perceived moral and spiritual force of the work of Christian missions.

In the various institutions of higher education, Empire was also a pervasive theme—through the teaching of specifically Imperial history, through the university-based training of new cohorts of civil servants in such disciplines as law and languages, and through the teaching of technical skills intimately linked to the Imperial experience. As well as medicine and hygiene, these included forestry, agriculture, surveying, engineering, and anthropology.

The Empire increasingly came to the British public in new and often dramatic ways: through the cinema newsreel and through the press, with its coverage of colonial crises and constitutional developments. British people were, for example, well aware of the 1919 Amritsar shooting in northern India, which generated heated domestic debate. As constitutional reform and eventually decolonization became imminent, the British people were aware of Asian and African politicians visiting London for Round Table Conferences. Among the earliest of such visitors was Mahatma Gandhi, who in 1931 took care to stay in London's East End and to visit the cotton mills as well as to talk in universities and schools. By so many and varied means did the Empire become an integral aspect of British culture and imagination.

There were also specific ways in which groups and individuals sought to popularize Empire more consciously. These included great public exhibitions, consumer propaganda, popular literature, particularly adventure stories written for boys and girls, and 'imperial cinema', both in the shape of newsreels and educational productions, and through romantic and adventure stories. [. . .]

There is a paradox about these activities during these years. On the one hand, the growth in numbers and range of activities of the wide variety of Imperial societies represented a great deal of energy. One Dominions Secretary, J. H. Thomas, pointed out in 1932 that there were thirty-three Imperial and patriotic societies. Many attempts at amalgamation failed, and such diversity would ultimately prove a great weakness. On the other hand, anti-Imperial sentiment was equally fragmented, and radical groups supporting anti-colonial policies tended to be small and often 'marginal to the political process'. Nevertheless, intellectuals and nationalists from the Indian and dependent Empire were able to make contact with sympathetic individuals and factions as well as with each other, and the interaction had considerable significance for future decolonization.

That the cultural, political, and economic relations of the Empire were somehow regarded as above controversy and party politics is well illustrated by the attitude of the BBC. The Corporation, founded in 1923 and dominated until 1938 by its first Director-General, John Reith, viewed the Empire as a significant source of broadcasting material and a topic of central concern to national life, one which could be turned to nationalist, moral, and quasi-religious ends. Reith had an almost mystical approach to the Empire, which he regarded as the most successful example of internationalism and peaceful coexistence in modern times. In this his thinking was close to that of such diverse figures as J. C. Smuts, Robert Baden-Powell, and George Bernard Shaw. It followed that the medium of radio could contribute to the cohesion of British subjects and of the worldwide family of English-speaking peoples. One of the first successful outside broadcasts was that of the opening speech of George V at the Wembley Exhibition in 1924. Thereafter the BBC was involved in every national event and in the many pageants and exhibitions which contributed to the Imperial ethos. It carried special Empire Day programmes, and frequently broadcast talks, features, and poetry relating to the Empire. In 1932 it began a tradition of Christmas broadcasts associated with the King's Christmas messages, which included contributions from colonial territories around the world. [. . .]

The teaching of Imperial ideas in schools did not arise immediately from the 'New Imperialism' of the 1870s and 1880s. Although there were texts in the nineteenth century for teachers and pupils on the development of the British Empire, it was not until the 1890s that education codes and teacher manuals began to stress the importance of the Empire and its associated adventure tradition in conveying concepts of national identity and pride to schoolchildren. From that period, the Empire became a focus for teaching in geography, history, aspects of English (readers often included Imperial poetry and prose), and religious studies. Geography had a notable immediacy because of exploration and the consequent discussion of natural resources, the character of indigenous peoples, and the capacity of technology to exploit global riches.

It was this sense of a historic geographical mission, sometimes traced to medieval times, sometimes to the heroic era of the Tudors and Stuarts, which was conveyed in so much Imperial poetry, including that of Tennyson, Kipling, Newbolt, Austin, Noyes, and Masefield. Similarly, the fiction of Empire, particularly that of Captain Marryat, W. H. G. Kingston, R. M. Ballantyne, Henry Rider Haggard, G. A. Henty, and R. L. Stevenson was regarded as suitable reading material for the young by day schools, Sunday schools, and youth organizations. The history and the contemporary life and work of the Christian missions could also be linked to the same national enterprise: the lives of Christian heroes, such as David Livingstone, General Charles Gordon, Mary Slessor, and many others continued to be related to the adventure tradition in pursuit of the moral examples and self-sacrifice associated with the Empire.

Although a generation of scholars was beginning to react against it, Sir John Seeley's *The Expansion of England* of 1883 remained in print. His vision of Empire as the logical and inseparable outcome of English dominance within Britain had a considerable influence on teachers and school textbooks. Although many school texts reflected changing conditions in emphasizing the internationalist and trusteeship aspects of the Imperial mission, others upheld the view that the Tudor period marked the origins of the British Empire, or insisted that the eighteenth century should be studied essentially as an era of colonial wars. The vast majority of publishers continued to take a pride in Empire for many decades thereafter. There are few, if any, dissident voices within school geography and history texts, for to take a contrary line would inevitably have been seen as unpatriotic. No school or local authority could take such a risk. The satirical work, 1066 and All That, first published in 1930, was reacting against a tradition of history teaching in the period.

Imperial studies had also become more common in universities. The Rhodes and Beit Trustees had been active in funding chairs and lectureships in London and Oxford. The Colonial Service increasingly sent recruits for language, anthropological, and other training to these institutions of higher education, as well as to the recently founded School of Oriental and African Studies. As in technical and medical services, the old traditions of amateurism were being replaced by attempts to develop professionalism in the colonial world, though most historians of Empire, such as A. P. Newton, Basil Williams, and Sir Reginald Coupland, continued to write within an Imperial moralistic tradition.

If school texts and most university studies reveal little hint of anti-Imperial sentiment or the rise of colonial nationalism until well after the Second World War, juvenile literature continued to exploit many of the themes which had made it such a successful area of publishing in the late nineteenth century. Celebrated journals and comics, such as the Boy's Own Paper, Gem, Magnet, and Union Jack, continued publication throughout this period and carried many of the same sort of adventure stories set within the colonial context as they had done in the last decades of the nineteenth century. While many more boys from the Dominions, and also India, began to appear at Frank Richards's Greyfriars School, they still embarked on colonial adventures in Africa, Canada, and elsewhere during the holidays. [. . .]

The celebration of Empire Day became an annual event in the majority of schools, and was fostered by features on the BBC and in the Radio Times. It was enhanced by marches and band performances in most towns. Perhaps its main impact was in offering a half-day holiday from school. The Empire Youth Movement and its observances never had the same impact and was restricted to a privileged few in the cities and towns in Britain and the Dominions. Yet these movements grew during this period, and secured more extensive funding and support. Their lavish annual reports and other publications indicate that the ideology of Empire was not experiencing a sudden and dramatic death. On the contrary, the international economic crisis and the continuing desire for security at home and Empire abroad seem to have created an Indian summer in the dissemination of Imperial ideas. There was a continuing disposition to turn national and royal events into great Imperial extravaganzas. [. . .]

Films with an 'Imperial' content attracted an immense public. The tradition of using the works of popular writers or of celebrating heroic patriotic action overseas began early and continued in the inter-war period (for example, A. E. W. Mason's *The Four Feathers* was first made during the First World War, Rider Haggard's *She* was filmed in 1925, and a film about Livingstone was produced in the same year). The 1930s became the classic decade of Imperial spectaculars. Hollywood companies were as active as British filmmakers in celebrating the Empire. Paramount's *The Lives of a Bengal Lancer* (1935, only loosely based on Francis Yeats-Brown's book, *Bengal Lancer*, published in 1930) was a blockbusting success on both sides of the Atlantic and stimulated many imitations. Cinemagoers seemed to be enthralled by melodramatic actors clothed in colourful, and often inauthentic, uniforms in exotic settings. Other Imperial epics flowed, slightly incongruously, out of Hollywood, such as *Clive of India* (1935), *Wee Willie Winkie* (1937), *Storm over Bengal* (1938), *The Sun Never Sets*, *Gunga Din*, and *Stanley and Livingstone* (the last three all 1939).

In Britain, Alexander and Zoltan Korda made *Sanders of the River* (after a novel by Edgar Wallace, 1935), *The Drum* (1938), and *The Four Feathers* (1939, both after A. E. W. Mason), while Michael Balcon at Gaumont British produced *Rhodes of Africa* and *The Great Barrier* (both 1936), as well as *King Solomon's Mines* (after Rider Haggard, 1937). Noted stars acted in Imperial extravaganzas: on the British side Gracie Fields appeared in a musical, *We're Going to Be Rich* (1937), set in the South African gold-fields, and on the American the child star Shirley Temple appeared in *Wee Willie Winkie*, *Susannah of the Mounties*, and *The Little Princess* (all 1939). The tradition was maintained by *The Four Just Men* (1939), based on an Edgar Wallace thriller about a plot to seize the Suez Canal, and such Kipling material as *Elephant Boy*, the *Jungle Book* (1942), and *Soldiers Three* and *Kim* (1951). So successful was the 1930s' formula that it continued through the 1950s and 1960s, with such successes as *Storm over Africa* and *Storm over the Nile* (1953 and 1955), *Khyber Patrol*, *King of the Khyber Rifles*, and *West of Zanzibar* (all 1954), *North-West Frontier* (1959), *Zulu* (1963), and *Khartoum* (1966), to mention only a few.

Such films represented an extraordinary Indian summer in the popular culture of Empire. They all projected myth rather than reality, an adventure tradition suffused with an ideology dating from the 1890s: with a sense of mission, and of economic opportunity, of the superiority of Western science, technology, administrative, and military capacity with all its attendant racial prejudice. Films in the context of Empire offered their vast audiences not only escapist entertainment but also a sense of security, as well as feelings of pride and achievement. They reflected assumptions of racial and cultural superiority. They constituted the most significant evidence for the argument that the public was little infected with anti-Imperial sentiment. The emotional power of these films was great. Even Bertolt Brecht found himself being seduced by *Gunga Din*, and a critic in the *New York Times* described *The Four Feathers* as 'an imperialist symphony'. George Orwell regarded the movies and the radio as two of the prime reasons for the absence of true working-class dissent within Britain.

In his analyses of British society in this period, Orwell noted that a chasm had opened up between the ideas of the intelligentsia and the cultural interests of the masses. Among the latter, he singled out patriotism, the Empire, breeding, honour, and discipline, all suffused with reverence for the monarchy. Thus, it seems to be one of the apparent curiosities of British Imperial history that, when the Empire encountered the economic, political, and constitutional crises that would ultimately bring it down, British domestic culture came to emphasize colonial relationships as never before. There were several reasons. There is often a time-lapse in ideas filtering into popular culture. New entertainment technologies, such as cinema and radio, cling to tested ways to ensure their success. The practitioners of the techniques of propaganda, advertising, and public relations stuck to eternal verities around which a national consensus had formed. It was, after all, an ethos which could be portrayed as combining both a national and an individual ethic. The loss of this moral force may well have been a vital contributor to the acceptance of decolonization.

All this is not to suggest that a gullible public was duped. No one forced people to visit exhibitions, purchase comics, journals, and books, participate in pageants, national ceremonies, or Empire Day Movement activities, switch on their radios, or flock to the cinema. People were partly conditioned by a rise in living standards. The public sought consolation in what often felt like threatening times, and had the sense of participating in a worldwide enterprise which seemed, despite the intellectual jeremiads of the day, to represent success. The realm of politics and ideology were inseparably linked to the Empire.

One acute social observer, looking back from the vantage-point of the 1980s, remembered that his village classroom as a boy in the 1920s 'was steeped in officially sanctioned nationalism. The world map was red for the Empire and dull brown for the rest, with Australia and Canada vastly exaggerated in size by Mercator's projection. The Greenwich meridian placed London at the centre of the world. Empire Day and 11 November [Armistice Day marking the Allied victory at the end of the First World War] ritualized an established national supremacy.' At the time when this memory was recorded the processes of decolonization had already eroded most of the specifically Imperial aspects of popular British culture. The longer-term legacies of colonial connections, however, were significantly changing the face of British society. After the Second World War waves of immigrants from the West Indies, and then from India, Pakistan, and eventually Bangladesh (formerly East Pakistan), settled in Britain, clustering in its big urban areas. As a result, despite tightening controls on new immigration, Britain became increasingly a multi-ethnic society. This ethnic diversity became even more manifest with the birth of second and third generations of once-immigrant families. The cultural repercussions of migration were soon clearly visible—in the building of Hindu temples and of mosques, in the change in school curricula to acknowledge the multiracial and multi-religious origins of pupils, in the burgeoning of Indian and Pakistani corner shops and restaurants, and, more darkly, in the growth of racial tensions. Ironically, a post-colonial metropolitan society and culture now found itself more deeply marked by the long-term effects of Imperial connections than in earlier generations when Empire seemed real but remote.

> [*Source*: John M. Mackenzie, 'The Popular Culture of Empire in Britain', in Judith M. Brown and Wm. Roger Louis, eds., *The Twentieth Century*, vol. 4 of *OHBE*, pp. 212–13, 218–19, 220–2, 225, 228–31.]

## 105   Henry Hopkinson

> Henry Hopkinson, the British Minister of State for Colonial Affairs at the United Nations, spoke to the UN on 21 October 1952 about British colonial policy. Note that the 'new imperialist' concept of colonial development was still alive and well.

Britain is proud of her achievements in the Colonial field. Around the table of the United Nations sit the representatives of a dozen famous countries which at one time or another were under British administration. Now they are sovereign states, in most cases associated with Britain and each other in the Commonwealth.

Along with this pride in her past and present achievements, Britain carries a sure optimism about the future. Her aim is to bring greater health and happiness to millions of men, women and children, and to lead them on to true self-government. Britain is convinced that the premature abandonment of dependent territories would only lead to conditions of political insecurity and economic disorganization, but that by helping to build an association of stable self-governing communities she will be making a great contribution to the strength of the free world. This policy is clearly as beneficial to the Colonial territories themselves as it is to Britain and the rest of the democratic nations, for without international peace and economic stability no country can hope to attain personal liberty or material prosperity. There are many things still to be done, but Britain is determined, even at the cost of sacrifices by her own people, that this work shall be carried through. [. . .]

To the extremist, dependent status is an anachronism which should be ended immediately, without thought of the consequences to the territory 'liberated'. When these matters are discussed in an entirely political atmosphere political considerations prevail, and the social, racial and economic factors affecting the people's welfare are passed over. Britain considers it her duty to prevent the dependent peoples from becoming the sport of international politics.

If a territory is too unproductive to feed its people, too undeveloped to administer itself, or too disunited and weak to resist aggression, to abandon it to a nominal 'freedom' would, so far from being an act of benevolence, be one of disservice. 'Our critics,' said Sir Alan Burns, an experienced Colonial administrator who has represented the United Kingdom on the Trusteeship Council, 'are sometimes impatient because they do not see suddenly flowering a fully self-sufficient central administration, based on the pure principle of democracy. Such a flower, without roots, would perish.'

The peoples of the less developed territories have many problems— illiteracy, soil erosion, malnutrition, labor conditions—in which there cannot be too much world-wide interest. But these problems are best examined on the international level by expert technical bodies, where without regard to considerations based on political or constitutional status, standards of achievement can be considered on a world basis.

'The peoples of the non-self-governing territories,' Sir Anthony Eden told the United Nations Assembly on 11th November, 1952, 'need the help which the Colonial powers are able to give them, until they can stand on their own feet. Without that help these peoples cannot enjoy conditions of economic and social stability. The modern practice of Colonial administration is designed to bring them this assistance, and to guide them towards self-government. It is a partnership between the weak and the strong. Warring tribes of diverse kinds are welded into nations. Law is established and justice and respect for human rights, replacing the rule of the jungle and the despot.'

[*Source*: Snyder, *Imperialism Reader*, pp. 129–30, 131–2.]

## 106   Kenneth Bradley

> Kenneth Bradley was a district officer in Northern Rhodesia (now Zambia) and Tanganyika (now Tanzania) after the First World War. He recounts some of his experiences in the Mwangazi district of Tanganyika and praises the system of trusteeship.

We are camped to-night close to the Portuguese border, which, such was the habit of our fathers when the scramble for Africa was at its height, has been cut in a dead straight line for a hundred miles or more regardless of all natural landmarks or tribal boundaries. After endless disputes about trespass by the poor bewildered natives on either side, a Commission sat, or rather walked, and now the frontier is marked for all to see by a ride through the bush which marches, straight as a die, up hill and down dale for all the hundred miles.

The Achewa, an enormous tribe, used to live all over this part of Africa. The predecessor of the present Undi, the Paramount Chief, lived in Portuguese territory, and his people covered all the land as far north as Lake Nyasa and as far west as the escarpment of the Luangwa valley. Then the marauding Angoni came and stole the best land they had, about Fort Jameson and the lake shore. Then the white men came and divided it all up again, and the poor creatures find themselves living in three separate countries. [. . .]

I used to spend a great deal of my time in the bad old days of Direct Rule, when the chief was of no account, going round each village hut by hut, exhorting apathetic savages to re-thatch and sweep and clean. I do not do this any more. It is not that my exhortations were entirely wasted, nor that I have grown lazy and cynical with the years. I still have as great a belief in the potentialities of the African as ever I had. With, however, the institution of Indirect Rule the position of the District Officer has altered entirely. He is no longer the ruler of individual lives and the oppressor of the village lazybones. The chief is being taught to rule again, and my job is to guide him, and to get *him* to do the work. So now I sit at a distance and watch Mwangala with a fatherly eye as he goes from hut to hut, praising, exhorting, or cursing as the case demands. The villages are on the whole cleaner here than they were ten years ago, and the number of originally or ambitiously designed huts has increased.

It is, rightly, a very slow process, and I am, as a matter of fact, coming to the conclusion that it is one which the individual District Officer or Chief can do little to accelerate. The ever-increasing contact of the village native with 'civilization' is doing the job far more effectually. I am prepared to wager that every outstanding house I have seen on this tour is the work of someone who has come back from working on the copper mines or in the towns of Southern Rhodesia. [. . .]

The first thing the Angoni did with their money when they achieved a Native Treasury was to start a school. The Ngoni father may be reactionary and tiresome about windows in his hut, rubbish-pits, latrines, or selling his cattle, but he differs not a whit from his Chewa cousin in his enthusiasm about education. Let my son be educated, he says, and then he will be able to get a better-paid job, and my rake-off from his salary will be correspondingly greater. So the Angoni set aside funds and appointed a committee: one chief, the Superintendent of Native Education, myself, and the headmaster, as soon as one could be found. That was early in 1938. By September the nuclei of the buildings were up, and the teachers appointed. Pupils were enrolled, and within a week there were seventy-five names on the books, forty-five boarders and thirty day children. The school was opened with ceremony, and work began. [. . .]

On the still morning air I could hear the high chanting of a tribal song. *God save the King* is positively the only European tune allowed in the school, just as no English history is taught until the children have been thoroughly grounded in the history of their own tribe and of Northern Rhodesia.

One of the Chief's Elders comes once a week to teach the children Ngoni law and custom, they learn tribal dances, and we hope before long to arrange for the teaching of Ngoni handicrafts. We are trying to be very practical in our policy of bringing the children up to be good Angoni as well as educated citizens of a British Commonwealth of Nations.

[*Source*: Kenneth Bradley, *The Diary of a District Officer* (London: Thomas Nelson and Sons, 1947; orig. publ. 1943), pp. 31–2, 194, 195–6.]

## 107   British Labour Party conference resolution, 1942

The British Labour Party passed this resolution in hopes of committing a potential Labour government to widespread decolonization. The Attlee government was actually very cautious, promising independence only for India.

This Conference considers that the time has arrived for a restatement of the principles of the Labour Party as applied to the government of the colonies and to the status of colonial peoples.

This should be a charter of freedom for colonial peoples abolishing all forms of imperialist exploitation and embodying the following main principles:

(1)  All persons who are citizens of the colonial commonwealth should be considered to possess and be allowed to enjoy equality of political, economic, and social rights in the same way as the citizens of Great Britain.
(2)  The status of colony should be abolished and there should be substituted for this that of States named according to the country in which they are situated and having an equal status with the other nations of the commonwealth.
(3)  In all colonial areas there should be organised a system of democratic government, using the forms of indigenous institutions in order to enable the mass of people to enter upon self-government by the modification of existing forms of colonial administration in conformity with these principles.
(4)  In all colonial areas, in Africa and elsewhere, where the primitive systems

of communal land tenure exist, these systems should be maintained and land should be declared inalienable by private sale or purchase. All natural resources should be declared public property and be developed under public ownership.

(5) A commonwealth council of colonial peoples should be set up on which each former colonial state should be represented in accordance with the number of its population, but giving also special attention to the representation of national groups within each State.

[*Source*: Snyder, *Imperialism Reader*, p. 168.]

108 **Anthony Nutting**

Anthony Nutting was the Minister of State for Foreign Affairs in the Conservative government led by Prime Minister Anthony Eden. Here he recalls discussions at a meeting with French officials on 14 October 1956 at which Eden's obsession with defeating Nasser became clear. There is no reference to American or other international opinion: Eden believed that Nasser was purely a European imperial problem.

Gazier then proceeded to ask us what would be Britain's reaction if Israel were to attack Egypt. Eden replied that this was a very difficult question. The Tripartite Declaration [of 1950] would presumably be invoked, and this would involve us as signatories.

'But would you resist Israel by force of arms?' Gazier asked. To this Eden replied with a half-laugh that he could hardly see himself fighting for Colonel Nasser! Then, casting his mind back to the 1954 agreement about the Suez base, he turned to me and said, 'Didn't your agreement say something about our not being obliged to send troops if Egypt was attacked by Israel?'

I replied that . . . this provision only governed our rights to return to the base and did not in any way nullify our obligations under the Tripartite Declaration to resist any attack across the armistice borders of Israel and the Arab world. We had reaffirmed these obligations publicly on countless occasions before and since the 1954 agreement had been signed, and there was no getting away from them.

Eden looked somewhat crestfallen at this. But a moment later he could scarcely contain his glee when Glazier reminded him that the Egyptians had recently contended that the Tripartite Declaration did not apply to Egypt . . .

'So that lets us off the hook,' Eden said excitedly, 'We have no obligation, it seems, to stop the Israelis attacking the Egyptians.' . . .

Challe then proceeded to outline what he termed a possible plan of action for Britain and France to gain physical control of the Suez Canal. The plan, as he put it to us, was that Israel should be invited to attack Egypt across the Sinai Peninsula and that France and Britain, having given the Israeli forces enough time to seize all or most of Sinai, should then order 'both sides' to withdraw their forces from the Suez Canal, in order to permit an Anglo-French force to intervene and occupy the Canal on the pretext of saving it from damage by fighting.

[*Source*: Scott Lucas, ed., *Britain and Suez: The lion's last roar*
(Manchester: Manchester University Press, 1996), pp. 75–6.]

## 109   John Darwin

By contrast with other great empires in world history which sank slowly through various stages of decay, the break-up of the British empire was remarkably sudden and complete. Despite the economic and military strains of the inter-war years and the terrible battering at German, Italian and Japanese hands in the Second World War, it had re-emerged in 1945 territorially intact. Vast swathes of the world map were still painted red; countries like Egypt and Iraq, though technically independent, were as much under Britain's thumb as before the war. Twenty-five years later, on the eve of Britain's third and successful bid to join the European Community, the areas of the world still under British rule or domination had been reduced to a handful of dots on the map, and those colonies that remained, like Hong Kong, Gibraltar and the Falkland Islands, were viewed in London as a burden of embarrassment to be shed as quickly as possible. By that time Britain had long since been eclipsed as a military power by the United States and the Soviet Union, and as an economic power also by Germany, France and Japan. Sterling crises and the renunciation of a strategic role east of Suez—once the playground of British sea power—signalled that the substance as well as the forms of power had melted away.

The end of empire was not only remarkably rapid: it was also surprisingly undisruptive in British politics. For France and Portugal, the withdrawal from empire coincided with constitutional upheaval at home. In Britain, the calm of public attitudes remained unbroken (except, briefly, at the time of Suez), perhaps because of a curious consensus that regarded giving up colonial rule as unavoidable, but of little real significance for the mainsprings of British world power. Britain passed from its imperial to its post-imperial age without a serious shock, and without the great discontinuities in political and diplomatic attitudes which were so marked in almost every other European country after 1945. Indeed, the manner of its passing was not the least of the legacies of empire.

But the absence of impassioned debate over the end of empire or of an agonizing reappraisal of the bases of a post-imperial role should not make us think that the last phase of empire had little influence on British politics or foreign policy. In fact, the management of Britain's imperial interests outside Europe dominated the making of British foreign policy for fifteen years after 1945. Continuing faith in an economic future based upon close commercial relations with Commonwealth countries encouraged an arrogant dismissiveness towards the prospects of a European Common Market in the 1950s. Failure to dispose of small, far-off colonies plunged Britain into a dangerous conflict in the 1980s and still threatens it with grave international difficulties in the 1990s. For all the coolness with which imperial retreat seemed to be viewed by British politicians of all parties, it would be a great mistake to suppose that the way in which the British gave up their empire did not have an extraordinarily pervasive influence over their external relationships and economic fortunes after 1945.

Only in the last few years has it begun to be possible to view this process unsentimentally and with some sense of perspective. In many writers the end of empire still arouses strong emotions. To most the end of colonial rule was a moral victory to be celebrated: to a few a disaster to be deplored. In the memoirs of politicians it was an act of statesmanship to be boasted about. More popular writing still invites the reader to combine a frisson of guilt at colonialist misdeeds with complacent relief that all turned out well in the end. But as we move further from Britain's imperial age, we can look at events with greater detachment, and as the archives open up gain more insight into the thought and actions of politicians and officials at home and abroad. Contrary to a widespread impression, we still know very little about the calculations which led British governments to promote self-government in colonial territories and then to accept a rapid acceleration towards full independence. We know little about the pressures upon them from foreign governments, particularly the United States, or from business interests at home. Our knowledge of the growth and strength of nationalist movements in the colonies is patchy and often unreliable.

Even when these gaps in our knowledge are filled up, we will still find the causes of the break-up of the British empire a puzzle. It will not be enough to trace the steps by which dozens of different colonies came to attain full sovereignty. We will need the answers to more difficult questions: why did the British yield independence to so many widely different communities with near simultaneity? Why should colonial nationalisms have been so much more difficult to contain after 1945? What was the influence of new ideologies and political values in the post-war world at home as well as in the colonies? What were the effects of economic weakness on Britain's attitude to its imperial role and on its ability to sustain it? Why did the independence the British granted turn out in most cases to lead to a much more complete separation from the mother-country than had been expected? When, indeed, did empire end?

The 'end of empire' is in fact a deceptively enigmatic phrase. In reality, it is not only difficult to say exactly when empire did end, but what precisely that empire was. Historians have long recognized that the British approach to empire was flexible and pragmatic. In the heyday of their imperial power, the British had been ready to concede almost complete autonomy to their settlement colonies on the understanding that they would remain satellites in a British world system. Similarly, they had been content to leave some of their most important economic partners in the less developed regions of the world entirely independent politically while they fulfilled the economic func-tions of a colony. Even countries that were regarded as of key strategic importance might be left technically independent provided that Britain enjoyed a dominant position in their external relations. The countries col-oured red on the map were not considered intrinsically more valuable than those left outside the 'formal empire'. The British 'empire' was a consti-tutional hotch-potch of independent, semi-independent and dependent coun-tries, held together not by formal allegiance to a mother-country but by economic, strategic, political or cultural links that varied greatly in strength and character. Thus using a purely constitutional yardstick to judge whether empire had ended or not would be highly misleading, and might tell us little or nothing about the real relationship between Britain and the territory concerned.

In this discussion of the causes of the imperial break-up, a looser and more flexible definition is used. For practical purposes, British leaders equated empire with the exercise of global power and treated their formal empire of dependent territories as components of a world system strategically depend-ent on Britain, economically complementary to Britain and culturally under its influence. So long as constitutional change made no difference to these fundamentals, British policy makers were able to regard it as an inconvenient, sometimes distasteful, necessity, but not of over-riding importance. Even when certain territories unequivocally seceded from the sphere of British influence (like Burma in 1948), this could be regarded with equanimity pro-vided the rest of the system looked secure. Of course, after 1945, not only did an increasing number of colonial territories become independent in a consti-tutional sense, but the whole imperial system of formal rule and informal influence gradually disintegrated as the British lost the means, and perhaps the will, to hold it together. By 1960 'empire' in the looser sense used here was on the ropes. By 1970 it was dead. Arguably, we may see the seeds of imperial decline before 1939, or even before 1914. But if by the 'end of empire' we mean the final disintegration of an imperial system pivoted on British military and economic power, then it was in the post-war years that collapse began, and not until after 1960 that it was complete.

The object of this short book is not to provide a narrative of the process of imperial break-up, or even a full examination of its causes: either would require a much larger book. Nor is there space to consider the elusive question of the *effects* of the end of empire on post-colonial Britain. What is presented here is a discussion of the most widely favoured explanations for Britain's imperial decline and fall.

Thus far theories of decolonization have tended to emphasize the importance of one or other of the three main arenas of political, economic and ideological change. Some locate the vital causes of dissolution in the mother-country itself, seeing declining power, economic weakness or a redefinition of national interests as the motor of change. On this view, empire was given up either because it was felt to be too burdensome or because it no longer served any economic or strategic purpose. In some older versions of this metropolitan theory, great emphasis is laid on the liberalism of official attitudes and the farsighted intention of British statesmen to transform colonies into free states (at just the right moment) and the empire into a Commonwealth of free and equal members.

In large part this may be dismissed as implausible special pleading by politicians and bureaucrats writing in vain old age and too easily tempted to reconcile their memories and their reputations. But in its more sophisticated versions, the argument that Britain gave up its empire without much of a fight because it had ceased to be worth fighting for, the metropolitan theory is not so easily disposed of. The fact of Britain's great reorientation politically, economically and strategically towards Europe, and the fragile unity of the nationalist movements thrown against colonial rule, combine to suggest that the British colonial empire was liberated more by the indifference of its masters than by the struggles of its subjects. But, as we shall see in later chapters, there are important grounds for doubting whether a metropolitan theory of imperial disengagement provides a satisfactory explanation, and for wondering whether a conscious reappraisal of the kind it assumes really *preceded* the break-up of the imperial system.

The second major theory is compellingly simple. It is based on the contrast between a world of six or seven great powers before 1939 and the 'bi-polar' world after 1945, in which world affairs were dominated by two superpowers. In such a world, argues this international theory, there could be no place for a middle-rank power clinging hopelessly to the prerogatives of a bygone age. Britain was, relatively, far too weak after 1945 to maintain a world system. Moreover, the superpowers were both hostile to old-style imperialism (though for different reasons) and determined to supplant it with their own varieties of influence. The crunch came at Suez in 1956, when the paratroop diplomacy of the old colonial powers was denounced by the United States and the Soviet Union, and notice served that Britain could no longer act unilaterally in the Third World to prop up its own global influence. Indeed, within little more than a decade of the crisis, the British had renounced a world role.

Quite clearly, the *force majeure* of international politics powerfully affected the stability of Britain's post-war empire and threatened its cohesion. In crucial aspects after 1945 Britain was dependent on American support and goodwill. Over certain issues, notably the future of Palestine in 1945–8, Britain found the pressure of American wishes irresistible. But it is too crude to see the British simply abandoning their empire as a result of a superpower squeeze. Neither the United States nor the Soviet Union was in a position to apply this kind of pressure generally in the first fifteen years after 1945, or necessarily wished to do so. Nor did the rise of the superpowers lead British statesmen to abandon their own project for a great international association centred on Britain. Nor is it clear that progress towards self-government in British colonies was to any significant degree the result of external pressure by a superpower. International factors undoubtedly played a vital, if indirect, role and certainly undermined the stratagems of British leaders. But their influence must be carefully qualified.

The third theory is the 'peripheral' theory of decolonization. In its cruder form it argues that the British empire was disrupted by the nationalism of its subjects, who were mobilized against colonial rule *en masse* and whose opposition made it unworkable. As we will see, there are grounds for doubting whether nationalism (however powerful and decisive in certain cases) really was the crucial factor in instigating Britain's imperial retreat generally. There are strong arguments against attributing to colonial political movements the strength and cohesion perceived by historians chiefly concerned to celebrate 'nation-building' in new states, or romantically attracted to the charismatic political leaders who emerged in the post-war Third world. In the broader setting of a 'peripheral' theory, however, the force of local colonial pressures becomes much more credible. We can see how colonial administrators stirred up powerful opposition by their post-war policies, and alienated their essential allies in colonial society. Unable to insulate colonial societies from external influences, harried by insistent demographic and ecological pressures and handicapped by a skeletal administrative structure, the colonial rulers teetered on the brink of losing control and sometimes fell over it. Fear of anarchy drove them out, amid a welter of hasty bargains with self-styled nationalists—the only plausible successors who could take over the reins of state power. The question remains, however, whether local, colonial difficulties of this kind were really enough to drive the British into abandoning their empire.

It is perhaps obvious that no simple or single cause will be sufficient to account for the break-up of such a vast, variegated and far-flung empire as the British. Those interested in the history of particular regions or countries may be more impressed by their distinctive character and circumstances than by similarities with the experience of other colonial regions. But in making sense of the phase when colonial rule, or informal 'semi-colonial' domination, by Britain came to an end, it is wise to weigh the influence of metropolitan, international and colonial politics before reaching any firm conclusions. As is suggested in the final chapter, the most convincing explanation for the dissolution of the imperial system as a whole, or the 'end of empire' in an individual colony, is likely to be found by tracing the ways in which events at each level ricocheted off each other to produce a pattern of decolonization that was, in the British case, of unexpected completeness.

[*Source:* John Darwin, *The End of the British Empire: The Historical Debate* (Oxford: Blackwell, 1991), pp. 1–7.]

## 110 Jan Christiaan Smuts

Jan Christiaan Smuts, an Afrikaner war hero, was prime minister of South Africa during the First World War. A speech he made in London on 15 May 1917 contained the first public use of the phrase 'British Commonwealth'.

I think the very expression 'Empire' is misleading, because it makes people think that we are one community, to which the word 'Empire' can appropriately be applied. Germany is an Empire. Rome was an Empire. India is an Empire. But we are a system of nations. We are not a State, but a community of States and nations. We are far greater than any Empire which has ever existed, and by using this ancient expression we really disguise the main fact that our whole position is different, and that we are not one State or nation or empire, but a whole world by ourselves, consisting of many nations, of many States, and all sorts of communities, under one flag.

We are a system of States, and not a stationary system, but a dynamic evolving system, always going forward to new destinies. Take the position of that system to-day. Here you have the United Kingdom with a number of Crown Colonies. Besides that you have a large Protectorate like Egypt, an Empire by itself. Then you have a great Dependency like India, also an Empire by itself, where civilisation has existed from time immemorial, where we are trying to see how East and West can work together. These are enormous problems; but beyond them we come to the so-called Dominions, independent in their government, which have been evolved on the principles of your free constitutional system into almost independent States, which all belong to this community of nations, and which I prefer to call 'the British Commonwealth of Nations.' [. . .]

What I feel in regard to all the empires of the past, and even in regard to the United States, is that the effort has always been towards forming one nation. All the empires we have known in the past and that exist to-day are founded on the idea of assimilation, of trying to force human material into one mould. Your whole idea and basis is entirely different. You do not want to standardise the nations of the British Empire; you want to develop them towards greater, fuller nationality. These communities, the offspring of the Mother Country, or territories like my own, which have been annexed after the vicissitudes of war, must not be moulded on any one pattern. You want them to develop freely on the principles of self-government, and therefore your whole idea is different from anything that has ever existed before. That is the fundamental fact we have to bear in mind—that this British Commonwealth of nations does not stand for standardisation or denationalisation, but for the fuller, richer, and more various life of all the nations comprised in it.

Even the nations which have fought against it, like my own, must feel that their cultural interests, their language, their religion, are as safe and as secure under the British flag as those of the children of your own household and your own blood. It is only in proportion as this is realised that you will fulfil the true mission which is yours. Therefore it seems to me that there is only one solution, and that is a solution supplied by our past traditions—the traditions of freedom, self-government, and of the fullest development for all constituent parts of the Empire.

[*Source*: Jan Christiaan Smuts, *War-time speeches: a compilation of public utterances in Great Britain* (London: Hodder & Stoughton, 1917), pp. 26–7, 28–9.]

## 111   W. David McIntyre

Arnold Smith, the first Secretary-General, may have found it 'harder to describe than to operate', but the Commonwealth now fulfils the qualifications of an international organization. It has a symbolic head, an agreed membership, a Secretariat and Secretary-General, principal and subordinate organs and agencies, budgets, a legal personality, diplomatic privileges and immunities. Through an impressive series of declarations, it has well publicized purposes and principles. Though it has no charter or written constitution, the first of the modern declarations in 1949 was, in the view of Sir William Dale (formerly legal adviser to the British Foreign and Commonwealth Office) of 'a constituent nature', giving the Commonwealth 'a rudimentary, autochthonous constitution'. Subsequent elaborations by the declarations of the 1970s and 1980s were seen by Stephen Chan (a New Zealander now an academic in Britain, and before that a member of the staff of the Commonwealth Secretariat) as providing 'a dynamic constitutional structure that derives from international conditions and the Commonwealth response to them'. This is a far cry from the traditional approach but it echoes the British habit of constitution-making by convention rather than statutory instrument, even if it represents a somewhat loose approach to constitutionalism.

To base objections to the contemporary Commonwealth on the doctrine of the equality of each member country is to be guilty of an anachronistic literal-mindedness. Equality of *status* was never meant to imply equality of *function*. Discrepancies between the size, wealth, population and power of Britain and the original Commonwealth members were always great. The doctrine of equality (which was accepted before sovereign equality was actually achieved) referred to an equal voice in political discourse. Another type of equality was affirmed in 1981 by Arnold Smith, when he recalled in his memoirs that 'the shafts of light that illuminated the thinking and subsequent actions of Commonwealth countries have come as often from the leaders of the smaller and newer states, as from the older and larger countries'. Increasingly equality came to have wider meanings. Quite small members (e.g. Singapore) can make qualitatively valuable contributions.

In the sporting arena team games, which were once instruments of imperialist ideology, became powerful vehicles for popular nationalism. England, the original home of cricket, was soon equalled and often surpassed by Australia, even before Federation; later by the West Indies, a group of very small countries; later still by India, which has the Commonwealth's largest population. In rugby, too, New Zealand with a small population and Australia with comparatively small rugby-playing constituency soon equalled and bettered the British.

In the very different field of technical assistance, the 'volunteers abroad' organizations of the four older Commonwealth members accept equality of local pay to ensure the equal sharing of circumstances. For the provision of the majority of its experts, the Commonwealth Fund for Technical Co-operation arranges attachments from one developing country to another, rather than from developed to developing members.

In considering the utility of the contemporary Commonwealth recognition must, now, be given to three fundamental new features. First of all, a far reaching transformation took place in the quarter-century after the founding of the Secretariat in 1965. Henceforth the 'legacy of empire' approach needed to be abandoned in favour of an evaluation of the importance of the association to its members collectively and individually. Secondly, recognition needs to be accorded to the unique 'depth' of the association's existence. Analysis of constitutional, political and inter-governmental activities have often been made to the exclusion of the diverse endeavours of persons other than politicians and officials. We need, today, to bring into focus an association of states which, although bearing many traces of its historic genesis, has been re-created institutionally and operationally over the past twenty-five years. Above all it has, unlike other groupings of states, an independently-generated voluntary, private, professional, cultural and sporting life, which enriches, and cannot be separated from an understanding of, the whole. This gives the Commonwealth its unique character.

Thirdly, and more controversially, consideration must be given to recent attempts at consolidation and 'recomposition'. A major part of the trans-formations wrought since 1965 have involved the 'de-Britannicizing' of the Commonwealth. Institutions and agencies which were formerly part of the centralized empire, under British sovereignty and administrative control, have become, instead, the property of the association as a whole, co-ordinated by its Secretariat and subject to supervision by the Heads of Government collectively, especially at their biennial meetings (the CHOGMs). New institu-tions like the Commonwealth Foundation and the Commonwealth Fund for Technical Co-operation (CFTC) were launched on a multi-lateral basis. At the same time, a second trend which became evident, especially from the mid-1970s onwards, was the 'globalizing' of Commonwealth endeavours, as the Secretariat made links with other international bodies, as Commonwealth agencies worked towards wider goals and some organizations admitted non-Commonwealth members. Accompanying this trend was a third, that of 'regionalization', whereby nearly all the members, not least Britain, became involved in, and gave high priority in their foreign and trade policies to, regional organizations. At the voluntary, sporting and professional levels, too, most of the associations were also organized at the regional level. And few of the regional organizations are exclusive to the Commonwealth.

These centrifugal tendencies represented a salutary and necessary phase in the final transition from an imperial matrix. But there are now signs of a quest for consolidation and recomposition in both the 'width' and 'depth' of the association. The formation of the African-Caribbean-Pacific (ACP) group-ing for negotiating with the European Community, with its own Secretariat in Brussels, transcended the three regions involved. The Commonwealth Secretariat has organized inter-regional consultations. Excessive concern for Africa in the 1970s prompted 'super-regional' conferences for Asia and the Pacific, but they were short-lived. There are suggestions that regional health secretariats and youth centres might serve wider Commonwealth functions.

There has also been a long-standing endeavour, tried in the 1970s, and revived in the 1980s, to embrace the vast area of voluntary, private, profes-sional and philanthropic activity and provide linkages to the official sphere. The boundaries are already blurred. Some professional organizations are semi-official, a few inter-governmental with membership confined to public servants, even though they function as autonomous associations. Conversely, some independently-created professional organizations are used to operate official Commonwealth programmes.

The attempt to use modern communications technology to link voluntary organizations through liaison units and to co-ordinate and expand distance education may be seen as part of this trend towards 'recomposition'. It is highly important in the sense that tapping the drive and expertise of the extensive voluntary and private sector to the service of the association may facilitate fruitful new avenues of consultation and co-operation. It also gives grounds for caution at the possibility of undue government interference or excessive bureaucratization. Co-ordination of information, however, may lead to an acceptable institutional balance within the network. [. . .]

We also need to look at the popular aspects of the Commonwealth—the arts festivals, youth programmes, societies devoted to creating understanding between peoples and—the subject which attracts the greatest mass interest— sports. We need to consider why Commonwealth arts festivals were late in starting and remain somewhat tenuous in organization and why sports organ- izations have been so conservative. The desire to 'keep politics out of sport' led many sporting bodies to maintain sporting contacts with South Africa, which embarrassed their governments and even jeopardized other sports events, like the Commonwealth Games. When we come to the Games we see that the rise of Third World sporting achievement is not matched by a willingness to approve (with one exception) venues outside the original Commonwealth countries. Finally, possibly the single most popular aspect of the Commonwealth, in terms of media coverage, mass identification and symbolism, there is the role of the Queen as Head of the Commonwealth and monarch of seventeen member states. That the most traditional of British institutions should have proved so unassumingly and elegantly adaptive is perhaps an unexpected example of the 'modernity of tradition'. Although this has not been without disapproval in Britain, controversy over the Head of the Commonwealth in the 1980s served, in the event, to clarify and underline the significance of the Queen's position.

Traditionalists and pragmatists in Britain may question the utility of the Commonwealth as a major adjunct to British policy. When the main trans- formations of the past twenty-five years are understood in context, however, the width and depth in the multilateral nature of the association, its activities and aims, stand out in clearer focus. [. . .]

The first landmark, the fortieth anniversary of which was celebrated in the papers of the 1989 CHOGM, was India's decision to become a republic, coupled with its desire to stay in the Commonwealth. This necessitated agreement about a new concept of association by the other members and, also, a new role for the monarchy. Constitution-making for India and the prospect of a smooth progress towards full independence for a united India had floundered on the rocks of communal rivalry and, once the post-war Labour Government in Britain had decided on a time-table for the transfer of power, partition became inevitable. A quick solution was found by the granting of independence to the new Dominions of India and Pakistan in 1947, leaving the details of their constitutions to be worked out by the new regimes. In the following year Ceylon also became a Dominion, but Burma became a republic outside the Commonwealth. The Republic of Eire signified the same intention so it could sever for ever the last connexion with the British Crown.

However, Pandit Nehru wanted India to stay in the Commonwealth even though it would become a republic. He hoped that, if India made provision for 'Commonwealth citizenship', agreed not to treat the citizens of other members as aliens and accepted the King as 'first citizen' of the Commonwealth and the 'fountain-head of honour', a republic would be acceptable. Attlee agreed, but the British Law Officers and the Foreign Office clung to a narrowly legal view of allegiance to the Crown. From the old Dominions, Peter Fraser of New Zealand deplored the possibility of a 'watered-down' or a 'flabby' or a 'Kingless' Commonwealth. Others suggested a more flexible approach. The King might be accepted as the symbol of unity and free association. A way out was suggested by Gordon-Walker, then Secretary of State for Commonwealth Relations: let there be mutual declarations of intent—one by India indicating that it wished to remain a member and one by the rest saying that they agreed. In the end, a special conference of Prime Ministers in 1949 produced a single declaration, which remains one of the major 'constituent' or 'declaratory' documents of the association. In the preamble paragraph (based-upon and awkwardly echoing 1926) the eight governments, who were 'united as Members of the British Commonwealth of Nations and owe a common allegiance to the Crown, which is the symbol of their free association', indicated that they had considered the impending constitutional changes. India's intention to become a 'sovereign independent republic' was then stated. It also desired to continue in 'full membership of the Commonwealth of Nations' and accepted the King as the symbol of the free association of the members and 'as such Head of the Commonwealth'. The government of the other members, the basis of whose membership was 'not hereby changed', then signified their acceptance. Thus the precedent for republican membership was established. In a minute, unpublished at the time, Liaquat Ali Khan of Pakistan got an assurance that further such requests would be entertained.

Above all the monarchy's role had been adapted in an imaginative way. While remaining the symbol of the free association the King now took on the new role as Head of the Commonwealth. The particular phraseology adopted (and the insertion of 'as such', which amused George VI in spite of his many misgivings) was at the insistence of Dr Daniel Malan of South Africa, who also secured another unpublished minute to the effect the role implied no constitutional power. If the new formula had taken two years of careful negotiation, it paved the way for a further twenty-six republics in the next forty years. From 1948 to 1957 the Commonwealth went through its 'Euro-South Asian phase', with membership standing at eight.

The second landmark was the 'Wind of Change' and the coming of the black Commonwealth. By 1962 membership had doubled to sixteen. Several elements comprised this phase. Throughout the 1950s and the early 1960s the British, having announced the goal of colonial self-government, still doubted that many dependencies could ever become full members of the Commonwealth. Problems of size and viability led to a search for alternative forms of 'statehood'. There was consideration of a 'two tier', even a 'four tier' Commonwealth. But in 1957 Ghana became the first black member. Harold Macmillan's 'wind of change' tour of Africa in 1960, beginning in Ghana and culminating in a much-noticed speech to the South African parliament in Cape Town, indicated that the independence of the larger African colonies was imminent. Nigeria followed soon after in 1960; Sierra Leone and Tanganyika in 1961.

An entirely new dimension was also reached with the independence of Cyprus (with a population of only half-a-million) in 1960 and that of Jamaica and Trinidad (following the demise of the West Indies Federation) in 1962. A very significant change had occurred without public debate. Clearly the size threshold for membership had been relaxed. This meant that the potential membership of the Commonwealth suddenly changed beyond recognition. And South Africa quit. Ostensibly this was because of the need for other members to accept a change to republican status for the Union, but actually because of opposition to its racial policies. This also gave further emphasis to the new character of the 'multi-racial association'.

This meant that a third landmark was passed in the mid-1960s. The unexpected prospect of a vastly increased membership and a certain puzzlement and loss of direction in Whitehall prompted the British Government to seek new forms of co-operation, which might engage the imagination of the new African and island states. A programme entitled 'The Way Ahead' was prepared for the 1964 Prime Minister's meetings, including the idea of a Commonwealth Foundation jointly funded by the member states. These proposals were, however, overtaken by the initiative of Milton Obote of Uganda and Kwame Nkrumah of Ghana, who proposed a Commonwealth Secretariat, a suggestion which was actually implemented in 1965. But this innovation was, in turn, partly overshadowed at first by the Rhodesian revolt later in the year. It meant that the first Prime Ministers' meetings organized by the new secretariat, in 1966, involved bitter recriminations over Rhodesia. There was therefore a dual break with the past. On the one hand, the comparatively smooth transition of colonies to independence by negotiation was dramatically breached by the Rhodesian settlers; on the other hand, a new shared organ of co-ordination had been created to detach the Commonwealth from Whitehall.

The fourth landmark came as a consequence of these breaks. From 1966 to 1969 there was an unusually long interval between Prime Minister's meetings as the British sought to avoid further confrontations over Rhodesia. Meanwhile the Secretariat and the Foundation began to find their feet and still more small states achieved independence and sought full membership. When the meetings resumed in 1969 the communiqué was still headed (as they had been since 1944) 'Meeting of Commonwealth Prime Ministers' but the text began 'Commonwealth Heads of Government met . . .' Five new members attended (only one with a population as big as one million) bringing the total to twenty-eight, which made it 'one of the biggest consultative gatherings of Heads of Government . . . since the signature of the United Nations Charter'. It was also the last but one to date to be held in London. Singapore provided the venue in 1971 and for this meeting the title became 'Commonwealth Heads of Government Meeting'. Here (at the first CHOGM) the adoption of a Declaration of Principles; the formal creation of the Commonwealth Fund for Technical Co-operation; the discussion of Britain's impending entry into the European Communities; the absence of the Queen, and the new venue, all served to emphasise the 'de-Britannicizing' process that had begun in the 1960s.

A fifth landmark was also passed by 1971. The attendance of the first Pacific island states heralded another expansion in the membership. In the 1970s and 1980s twenty-one new members were to join. Of these, Bangladesh had a very large population (and its membership was balanced by Pakistan's withdrawal early in 1972) and Zimbabwe's was also large. But the other nineteen new members were, with the exception of Papua New Guinea, all very small states with a combined population of only about two-and-a-half million. While the membership doubled in this way between the 1960s and the 1980s, professional organizations encouraged by the Foundation proliferated and new regional organizations also became established. In these two decades the shape and functioning of the Commonwealth had changed out of all recognition by comparison with the post-war years.

[*Source*: W. David McIntyre, *The Significance of the Commonwealth, 1965–90* (London: Macmillan, 1991), pp. 4–7, 8–9, 16–19.]

## 4.2 THE EMPIRE AT WAR

Three important conflicts, the South African War and the First and Second World Wars, revealed both the strength and the vulnerability of the British empire in the early twentieth century. The British empire declined as it had begun: for a number of reasons, and over a period of time. But there were some important historical turning points, and there is no doubt that the South African War (sometimes called the Boer War) was one of the most significant of these.

The South African War of 1899–1902 was symptomatic of the British empire's ambiguous success. Slavery had been abolished in the Cape Colony in 1833 and this, among other things, prompted a large number of Afrikaners (sometimes called Boers in older English texts) to move northward in a 'Great Trek'. They then established two independent Afrikaner republics: the Transvaal (also known as the South African Republic) and the Orange Free State. By the end of the nineteenth century the British had forcibly annexed the Transvaal and the expansionist Cape Colony premier, Cecil Rhodes, had pushed British interests northward into what would become Southern and Northern Rhodesia. In 1895 Rhodes tried to encourage a coup in the Transvaal; the 'Jameson Raid' failed miserably, Rhodes was forced to resign, and Afrikaner opinion hardened against the British (Extract 112).

Some African groups joined with the British against the Afrikaners, but more significant was the widespread support from the Dominions and colonies. Colonial troops had been involved in imperial wars before, but never on such a large scale. The British government was immensely gratified by what it saw as an imperial war effort against a common enemy (Extract 113). But British tactics in South Africa quickly became controversial: Afrikaner fighters pioneered what became known as 'guerrilla' warfare and the British responded by burning civilian farms and confiscating livestock (Extract 114). They also created the first modern concentration camps by rounding up Afrikaner women and children, incarcerating them in hopes of forcing their menfolk to surrender. Although the war produced intense patriotism in Britain and the Dominions, the moral controversy it generated also gave ammunition to empire's critics.

The First World War was less immediately controversial. When Britain declared war on Germany in 1914 the entire British empire was automatically involved. Troops from all over the empire volunteered to serve under British command; the response from the Dominions was particularly strong (Extract 115). But even there dissenting voices were heard, notably French Canadians and Afrikaners, who resented Britain's control of foreign policy. Even among supporters of the war effort there was a growing sense of national—as well as imperial—pride (Extract 116). In India, where nationalist movements had been growing since the late nineteenth century, wartime regulations and austerity measures antagonized those who had hoped that Indians would have greater control over their own government. Nevertheless, many Indians found reasons to support the war effort and Indian troops were deployed in almost every theatre of war (Extract 117). There is no doubt that the human and natural resources of empire helped Britain and its allies defeat Germany, and no doubt that after 1918 the British empire was larger than ever. The League of Nations granted mandates in Iraq, Palestine, and elsewhere to Britain with instructions to bring these countries quickly to independence; Britain also acquired former German or Ottoman colonies such as Tanganyika (now Tanzania).

Much had changed by the time the empire was again at war in 1939. The Dominions, now fully independent, made their own declarations of war; although their support for Britain was still enthusiastic they would now insist on more control over their own troops. Australia, feeling betrayed and vulnerable after the fall of Singapore in 1942, was prepared to turn to the United States for protection if necessary (Extract 118). In the meantime support from the empire, especially from Canada, had helped Britain to survive Hitler's attempted maritime blockade and aerial bombardment in 1940 (Extract 119). Despite the crucial importance of the eventual entry of the United States and the Soviet Union into the war, the role of Britain's empire had been significant from the beginning.

The dependent colonies, as in 1914, were automatically at war along with Britain, but this time their nationalist movements were more vigorous. Wartime austerity, forced labour (especially in Africa), and the military weakness demonstrated by Britain at Singapore all enhanced demands for independence. Although many colonial subjects volunteered for military service, the British were in no doubt about the need to make greater political and economic concessions as soon as the war was over (Extract 120). By 1945 a number of other factors were also in play: a devastated British economy, the prominence of the United States, the looming capitalist–communist confrontation, and the election in Britain of a Labour government pledged to grant Indian independence. In historian Keith Jeffery's words, 'the ultimate cost of defending the British Empire during the Second World War was the Empire itself' (Extract 121).

## 112   President Steyn of the Orange Free State

In October 1899 President Steyn of the Orange Free State called on
Afrikaners to defend themselves against British aggression. Note
the fear that Britain would admit 'Hottentots' (blacks) to the
colonial legislature.

*Appeal to Afrikanders. Address to compatriots on both sides of the Orange River.*
Asks them to decide what they will do in the uncertain future. Recites England's proceedings with regard to Slachtersnek, Diamond Fields, Jameson
Raid. England desires to avenge Amajuba, and destroy Afrikander nation.
Owing to existence of two independent Afrikander Republics, the Afrikander
in the English Colonies is still tolerated. If Republics fall into hands of England, Boers of Cape Colony and Natal will be disarmed. Hottentots will sit
with them in Parliament. 'Wherefore men belonging to our race that live
under the British flag, know and understand full well that the destruction of
the Boer Republics means the destruction of the Afrikander nation; if the
Republics go under, the Afrikander will merely be referred to as a nation that
once existed. Know that in that event England's iron yoke will press upon
and plague you to the last day. Wherefore, I ask: will you allow England
to employ your Colony, your money, your cattle, yea, even yourselves, to
destroy your brothers and compatriots? Afrikanders be true to your people.'

[*Source*: Great Britain, *Parliamentary Papers* 1900, vol. LVI, 'Further Correspondence
Relating to Affairs in South Africa' [Cd. 43], p. 41.]

## 113   Joseph Chamberlain

Canada, like many other parts of the empire, supported the British
during the South African War and contributed troops to what it
regarded as an imperial campaign. Here Joseph Chamberlain, as
Colonial Secretary, thanks the Governor-General of Canada for
this enthusiastic Canadian support.

I received from you on the 2nd instant a copy of an Approved Minute of the
Dominion Privy Council, dated the 14th of October, 1899, in which your
Ministers authorized the equipment and despatch of 1000 volunteers for
service with the Imperial troops in South Africa.

The great enthusiasm and the general eagerness to take an active part in
the military expedition which has unfortunately been found necessary for the
maintenance of British rights and interests in South Africa have afforded

much gratification to Her Majesty's Government and the people of this country. The desire thus exhibited to share in the risks and burdens of Empire has been welcomed, not only as a proof of the staunch loyalty of the Dominion, and of its sympathy with the policy pursued by Her Majesty's Government in South Africa, but also as an expression of that growing feeling of the unity and solidarity of the Empire which has marked the relations of the Mother Country with the Colonies during recent years.

The thanks of Her Majesty's Government are specially due to your Ministers for the cordial manner in which they have undertaken and carried through the work of organizing and equipping the Canadian contingent.

[*Source*: Joseph Chamberlain to the Earl of Minto, 15 November 1899 in Great Britain, *Parliamentary Papers* 1900, vol. LVI, 'Correspondence relating to the Despatch of Colonial Contingents to South Africa' [Cd. 787], p. 28.]

## 114   Field-Marshal Lord Roberts

The British commander-in-chief, Lord Roberts, issued this proclamation on 16 June 1900 explaining that Afrikaner civilians were now considered to be military targets. This decision, along with the Afrikaner commando tactics of communications disruption and ambush, contributed to the 'total war' concept of twentieth-century warfare.

## Proclamation

Whereas small parties of raiders have recently been doing wanton damage to public property in the Orange River Colony and South African Republic by destroying railway bridges and culverts and cutting the telegraph wires, and whereas such damage cannot be done without the knowledge and connivance of the neighbouring inhabitants and the principal civil residents in the districts concerned;

Now, therefore, I, Frederick Sleigh, Baron Roberts, of Kandahar and Waterford, K.P., G.C.B., G.C.S.I., G.C.I.E., V.C., Field-Marshal, Commander-in-Chief of Her Majesty's Troops in South Africa, warn the said inhabitants and principal civil residents that, whenever public property is destroyed or injured in the manner specified above, they will be held responsible for aiding and abetting the offenders. The houses in the vicinity of the place where the damage is done will be burnt and the principal civil residents will be made prisoners of war.

[*Source*: Great Britain, *Parliamentary Papers* 1900, vol. LVI, 'Proclamations Issued by Field-Marshal Lord Roberts in South Africa' [Cd. 426], p. 10.]

## 115    Private Ernest White

A nurse at the 4th London General Hospital kept an autograph book in which Private Ernest White of the South African force wrote this poem on 13 March 1915. His clumsy verses show an ordinary soldier's view of imperial loyalty. Despite the recent South African War, South Africans of all backgrounds served with distinction in the First World War.

> We're the same in far South Africa
> As you are in London Town,
> And we're proud of dear old England
> For her feats have won renown.
> So we came along to help you
> With mingling pride and joy,
> And we've tried to do our duty
> With our gallant Blighty Boys.
>
> So hands across the sea boys
> Feet on British ground,
> Motherhood and brotherhood
> All the Empire around.
> I shall soon be sailing homeward
> Far across the sea,
> But I could never forget the Friendship
> I made in Dear Old Blighty.

[*Source*: Manuscript autograph book of G. M. Livorder, private collection, printed with permission from S. J. Dowsey.]

## 116    Australia's military contribution in the First World War

Australia's attitude towards its military contribution in the First World War, reflected in this 1916 comment, shows how the conflict fostered nationalism as well as imperial solidarity. Massive Australian casualties during the disastrous Gallipoli operation of 1915 produced 'ANZAC Day', an annual commemoration which is still Australia's one truly national day.

The price of nationhood must be paid in blood and tears; there is no country that truly loves its flag which has not made the supreme sacrifice—which has not freely offered up the lives of its best and bravest for a dream, for an ideal, for a solemn purpose. It is the fortune of Australia to find her true soul in a great and glorious struggle to preserve the liberties of the smaller nations, to crush a despotic militarism which would awe and subjugate the rest of the world. Anzac Day, which we have celebrated for the first time, and celebrated, we hope, in a solemn and thoughtful mood, means more to us than an immortal charge up the cliffs of Gallipoli. Whilst it reminds us of the valour of our dead heroes, who live in lonely graves on classic ground, it reminds us, too, in a much greater degree, of the day Australians really knew themselves. Before the Anzacs astonished the watching nations, our national sentiment was of a flabby and sprawling character. We were Australian in name, and we had a flag, but we had been taught by our politicians not to trust ourselves— we were constantly admonished by our daily journals to remember that we were nothing better than a joint in the tail of a great Empire. [. . .]

Anzac Day has changed all that. The Australian flag has been brought from the garret and has been hoisted on a lofty tower in the full sight of its own people. No matter how the war may end—and it can only end one way—we are at last a nation, with one heart, one soul, and one thrilling aspiration.

[*Source*: F. K. Crowley, ed., *Modern Australia in Documents* (Melbourne: Wren, 1973), vol. 1, p. 255.]

## 117   Letters by Indian soldiers

These brief extracts from letters by Indian soldiers show a range of responses to military service in the First World War. In the first (withheld by the censor), a Pathan Muslim writes to his family, warning them about bad conditions and poor leadership in his regiment. The second letter focuses on the enhancement of ethnic prestige through military service, and the third sees battle as an opportunity for release from the Hindu cycle of reincarnation. The fourth extract shows a Muslim soldier's decision to adopt some aspects of Western culture.

[i] My brethren, for the sake of God and His Prophet do not come over here, for our people have no *izzat*, and nowadays we have two sirdars, Naslim Khan and Sarbaland Khan, who are such bad men as I have never come across before. If you can preserve your lives, stay in India. [. . .]

[ii] What we all have to say to you is this—that you should serve the Government loyally and well. God will reward you, and you will increase the reputation of our people. The Marathas are as a mountain and cannot be moved. Do not show your back to the enemy, for your religious teaching forbids this. [. . .]

[iii] You must not be in the least bit anxious. This material universe is merely

an illusion, because just in the same way as you weep so do my father, brother and sister. But this is a useless proceeding on your part, because at such a time as this, even if my life should be lost, it should cause you all intense joy. First, for many days I have eaten the salt of the Government. Second, such an opportunity to die is never likely to recur. Such a death is a true liberation from future birth. Not only is this so for me alone; but it is the same for all heroes. Everyone knows this, but you should take it into your careful consideration and tell others. [. . .]

[iv] My own eyes have been opened since I came to Europe, and I have entirely altered the views which I held before. I wring my hands with regrets that I did not set myself to acquire learning, but regrets are of no avail now. I missed my chance and I am now well in years. If I live to return, and if God gives me children, I will fashion their lives according to my new ideas. Please God, I will give them a good education, whether they be sons or daughters. When I was in Hindustan and used to hear of anyone going to England for education, or even of anyone setting himself to acquire complete education in Hindu stani, I used myself to say 'these people lose their religion and return as Christians'. Now that I have come here, I realize how wrong I was in my ideas. There is no question at all of religion—it is education alone which makes them wise, and teaches them to hate and abandon those habits and customs in our country which are improper, and to live according to their new ideas.

[*Source*: David Omissi, ed., *Indian Voices of the Great War: Soldiers' Letters, 1914–18*
(Houndmills: Macmillan, 1999), pp. 88–9, 324–5.]

**118**   **John Curtin**

> In this speech to the Australian nation in December 1941, the
> Prime Minister, John Curtin, outlined his strategy in response to
> the humiliating British defeat at Singapore and the entry of the
> United States into the war.

Without any inhibitions of any kind, I make it quite clear that Australia looks to America, free of any pangs as to our traditional links or kinship with the United Kingdom.

We know the problems that the United Kingdom faces. We know the constant threat of invasion. We know the dangers of dispersal of strength, but we know, too, that Australia can go and Britain can still hold on.

We are, therefore, determined that Australia shall not go, and we shall exert all our energies towards the shaping of a plan, with the United States as its keystone, which will give to our country some confidence of being able to hold out until the tide of battle swings against the enemy.

Summed up, Australian external policy will be shaped toward obtaining Russian aid, and working out, with the United States, as the major factor, a plan of Pacific strategy, along with British, Chinese and Dutch forces.

[*Source*: Crowley, *Modern Australia in Documents*, vol. 2, p. 51.]

## 119   Winston Churchill

During the war the eloquent speeches of the Prime Minister, Winston Churchill, inspired English-speakers around the world. Here, on 30 June 1943, he draws on traditional imagery of Britain as an island-fortress (compare with Extract 2) supported by its empire and other allies.

Alone in history, the British people, taught by the lessons they had learned in the past, have found the means to attach to the Motherland vast self-governing Dominions upon whom there rests no obligation, other than that of sentiment and tradition, to plunge into war at the side of the Motherland.

None of these Dominions, except Southern Ireland, which does not under its present dispensation fully accept Dominion status, has ever failed to respond, with all the vigour of democratic institutions, to the trumpet-call of a supreme crisis, to the overpowering influences and impulses that make Canada, that make Australia—and we have here in Dr. Evatt a distinguished Australian—that make New Zealand, and South Africa send their manhood across the ocean to fight and die. [. . .]

In the vast sub-continent of India, which we trust will presently find full satisfaction within the British Commonwealth of Nations, the martial races and many others have thronged to the Imperial standards. . . . Many scores of thousands of troops have been drawn from the immense tropical spaces, or from lonely islands nursed by the waves of every sea. Many volunteers there were for whom we could not find arms. Many there are for whom even now we cannot find opportunities. But I say that the universal ardour of our Colonial Empire to join in this awful conflict, and to continue in that high temper through all its ups and downs, is the first answer that I would make to those ignorant and envious voices who call into question the greatness of the work we are doing throughout the world, and which we shall still continue to do.

The time came when this loosely and variously knit world-spread association, where so much was left unwritten and undefined, was confronted with the most searching test of all. The Mother Country, the home of the kingship, this famous island, seemed to enter the very jaws of death and destruction. [. . .]

It was proved that the bonds which unite us, though supple as elastic, are stronger than the tensest steel. Then it was proved that they were the bonds of the spirit and not of the flesh, and thus could rise superior alike to the most tempting allurements of surrender and the harshest threats of doom. In that dark, terrific and also glorious hour we received from all parts of His Majesty's Dominions, from the greatest and from the smallest, from the strongest and from the weakest, from the most modern to the most simple, the assurance that we would all go down or come through together. You will forgive me if on this occasion, to me so memorable, here in the heart of mighty London, I rejoice in the soundness of our institutions and proclaim my faith in our destiny.

[*Source*: Bennett, *The Concept of Empire*, pp. 417, 418.]

## 120    Colonial Office memorandum

The Colonial Office was aware that wartime inflation and deprivation would provoke dissent in Britain's African colonies. This memorandum was written in February 1943 in order to plan an agenda for post-war economic development and increased self-government.

If the threat of war continues to recede from West Africa, one of the results may be that questions which educated Africans would otherwise have been content to leave until after the war may be pressed upon our attention at an earlier date. The questions to which I refer are those connected with the aspirations of the Africans to be given an opportunity of playing a much fuller and more influential part in the administration of the territories to which they belong.

For the reasons set out briefly below it seems desirable to prepare in advance for this possibility so as to be able to confront an incipient agitation with a definite plan of action by His Majesty's Government.

No practicable scheme will satisfy the extremists and the ill-informed people who encourage them in this country, but the realization that His Majesty's Government know what they mean to do and are in earnest about doing it should have a steadying effect which will be much needed. But it is important not to delay too long. [. . .]

From time to time members of His Majesty's Government have referred in general terms to the benevolent intentions of His Majesty's Government towards the Colonial peoples, and hitherto it has not apparently been thought really necessary to do more than to express sentiments of this kind from time to time, while dealing *ad hoc* with any particular grievance or symptom of discontent as it arises in some concrete form, or even, on occasion, anticipating a demand by some more or less innocuous concession. To judge, however, from what has appeared from time to time since the outbreak of war in the West African newspapers, African opinion amongst the small body of politically-minded African referred to above is becoming less and less easily satisfied with such methods.

It is not suggested that a continuance of the present opportunist policy is likely to result in serious and widespread disaffection or opposition to British administration in West Africa. What is to be feared is rather a widening breach between the European and the African as the latter becomes more educated, and an increasing sense of frustration on his part. The result of such a tendency might well be to hamper very considerably the efforts of His Majesty's Government for the general social betterment of the African races. In a word, our success in raising the standard of life, in the widest sense of the term, of the African is likely to be largely dependent upon the extent to which we can associate him as an active, intelligent and enthusiastic collaborator in the task of his own betterment.

Action is required along three main lines:

(1) The provision of greatly increased educational facilities. This is fundamental to all the rest.
(2) Greatly increased employment of Africans in the public administration and municipal government. This is clearly dependent upon the extent to which the increased educational facilities can produce men and women of the right type and with the right training.
(3) A progressive education of the African in the handling of public affairs, whether in Municipal Councils or in Legislative Councils. This is in some ways the most difficult problem of all. It is impossible to deal with it adequately in such a memorandum as this, but for the present purpose it may suffice to suggest that the line of approach should be to make political progress for the African far more closely dependent upon the two factors referred to above than has been the practice in the past.

Moreover it seems not unlikely that the confidence of the educated African in the good faith of His Majesty's Government may, to some extent, be affected by the general economic scheme into which the West African Colonies will have to be fitted in the post-war world. This is a problem which clearly cannot be discussed now.

[*Source*: Richard Rathbone, ed., *Ghana*, vol. 1 of *British Documents on the End of Empire* (London: HMSO, 1992), pp. 24–5.]

**121**    **Keith Jeffery**

What impact did the Second World War have on the Empire? It is possible to argue that the war caused no substantive change; it merely accelerated and accentuated existing trends. In terms of constitutional development, so this argument goes, self-government and independence would have happened anyway. The war, if it had any real impact at all, simply affected the timing of these reforms. In contrast to this approach, it may be that the war produced objective changes that would not otherwise have happened; that the war made things significantly different. Certainly, at the time many observers felt that the sheer scale of the conflict was irrevocably changing the Empire. In 1942 the Governor of Uganda, Sir Charles Dundas, comparing the war to that of 1914–18, asserted that it would have 'an even more rousing influence, chiefly political and social, and it will be sheer blindness not to foresee the logical consequences'.

Constitutional change is easy to map, since it played a relatively small part in Imperial wartime policy-making. In the dependent Empire, domestic politics, with a few significant exceptions, were generally kept in a kind of suspended animation. Pending the end of the war, governments throughout the Empire went to sometimes extravagant lengths to suppress domestic criticism. In Canada and Australia the (pacifist) Jehovah's Witnesses were proscribed. Much more seriously, the 'Quit India' movement in 1942, which produced the gravest challenge to British rule since 1857, was swiftly and unambiguously crushed by the authorities in New Delhi.

The only major constitutional alteration during the war occurred in Jamaica, which was granted full internal self-government in 1944 with a House of Representatives elected by universal adult suffrage. New constitutions in British Guiana, the Gold Coast, and Nigeria established Legislative Councils with, for the first time, unofficial majorities. In 1940 and 1942 constitutional schemes offering 'Dominion Status' to India were put forward, reflecting both the extent of internal political challenge to the Raj and the vital military and strategic importance of the subcontinent. In July 1943 the Secretary of State for the Colonies, Oliver Stanley, told Parliament that the British government was 'pledged to guide Colonial people along the road to self-government within the framework of the British Empire'. Stanley disingenuously claimed that this had always been British policy, but it had never hitherto been stated in such unequivocal terms.

It may be, however, that the precise *nature* of proposed constitutional and political change was affected by the war and wartime conditions. It has been argued, for example, that the *war* made partition inevitable in India and that

British techniques of divide and rule that were applied to sustain the war effort favoured the Muslim League at the expense of Congress. Writing in the winter of 1944–45, one observer asserted that the expanding Muslim bourgeoisie, itself underpinned by the flourishing wartime economy, was sharpening Muslim separatism. The general impact of the conflict and the demands imposed by the Government of India in the interests of the war were clearly destabilizing. 'The convulsions and constraints of the war', wrote Manzoor Ahmad, 'produced fragmentation in the Indian political set-up and brought to the surface disruptive and disintegrating forces undermining national unity'. In the view of another historian, the war 'finally broke the hold of the leaders of Congress and the Muslim League over their respective followings', and also deprived the British of that 'initiative and ability to control events which was the vital underpinning of their plans to advance India to the status of a Dominion'.

For the 'old' Dominions, the war, as the First World War had done, did much to enhance their autonomy. The war enabled Canada to carve out 'a new stature as a middle power'. In 1939, argues John Granatstein, Canada was 'a colony in everything but name'. Six years later 'the nation, for a brief period, was as independent and powerful as it would ever be'. The way in which the war was fought, particularly after the United States entered the conflict, widened the Dominions' diplomatic horizons and forged new alliances, sometimes in conjunction with Britain, but in some cases involving the Dominions alone. The intra-Imperial links and the exclusive, bilateral relationships that individual Dominions had with London, and that collectively constituted the 'Empire' before 1939, were supplemented, perhaps even superseded, by new linkages with Washington, even before the United States became a belligerent. The Canadian–United States agreement made at Ogdensburg, New York, in August 1940 established a 'Permanent Joint Board on Defence'. This agreement, together with an economic arrangement concluded a year later at F. D. Roosevelt's residence at Hyde Park, inextricably linked the defences and economies of the two nations. Australia travelled a similar route. After the fall of Singapore, Australia itself feared invasion and gravitated closer than before towards the United States. From April 1942 the American General Douglas MacArthur took command of all Allied forces in the South-West Pacific area, and became the Australian government's chief military adviser. In effect, the Australian war effort was 'subsumed in the enormous US military machine'.

The effect of the war as a catalyst for change can be observed in its social impact throughout the Empire. The expansion of economic activity, some measure of prosperity, and the presence of sometimes large numbers of service personnel in training camps and in transit certainly had an unsettling effect in many colonies. The strains of war contributed to a situation in the Bahamas that erupted into rioting during which three people died in Nassau in June 1942. The war had destroyed the tourist industry and thrown many Bahamians out of work. Although the construction of an Anglo-American military base offered the possibilities of employment, the contractors had determined only to offer low wages to local workers, who responded with protest. One skilled worker, urged with destroying a Union Jack, explained, 'I willing to fight under the flag, but I ain't gwine starve under the flag'. In Kenya white settlers moaned about increasing African insolence. 'The chief cause of it', wrote one to the *Mombasa Times* in September 1942, 'is the misguided, over-zealous friendliness and undignified attitude of the Forces.'

It has been argued that the experience of enlistment and military service, frequently overseas, had a 'modernizing' and radicalizing impact on those involved. Returning soldiers, for example, were often in the vanguard of demands for political change in the Colonial Empire. F. M. Bourret has stressed the 'psychological effect which wider contacts with world affairs' had upon West Africans. 'Though the number of Gold Coast servicemen was small in relation to the population,' she continues, 'their influence after demobilization was all out of proportion to their numbers'. The pace of political reform in the colony was sharply accelerated following a wave of disturbances precipitated by a rally of ex-soldiers in Accra in February 1948. A government inquiry into the disturbances concluded that 'the large number of African soldiers returning from service with the Forces, where they had lived under different and better conditions, made for a general communicable state of unrest'. 'Such Africans,' continued the report, 'by reason of their contacts with other peoples including Europeans had developed a political and national consciousness.'

Increased employment—there was a growing urban wage-earning class—and the acquisition of new skills in both civilian and military sectors were important in promoting African political consciousness. For Kenyan soldiers this development has been ascribed in part to military service: 'the acquisition of good health and simple technical skills from the army played a far larger part in the political awakening of the African masses than the occasional sight of militant nationalism in the Middle or Far East.' In Tanganyika there was some agitation by demobilized soldiers. A group of ten ex-servicemen petitioned the colonial administration in July 1946, concerned that 'the freedom we have fought for is not going to be given to us . . . The Tanganyika Government should realize that we have been fighting for our own freedom and not for imperial purposes.' Nevertheless, it appears that most of the returning African soldiers simply 'faded rapidly back to the land'. On balance, those who had stayed at home were more active in post-war politics than those who had served in the army during the war.

The Japanese victories following Pearl Harbor provided new opportunities for armed opponents to British rule. The most outstanding example of this was the Indian National Army (INA) first commanded by Mohan Singh and later led by Subhas Chandra Bose. Canvassing for recruits among demoralized Indian prisoners-of-war captured in Malaya and Singapore, the nationalists secured quite a good response. Many men felt, in the words of one later INA brigade commander, that they had been 'handed over like cattle by the British to the Japs'. By the summer of 1943 Bose had an army of 11,000, with a further 20,000 in training. But the INA did not achieve any great military success; its chief significance was to demonstrate quite explicitly to the British that Indian loyalty to the British Empire—even among soldiers—could not necessarily be relied upon in all circumstances. In occupied Burma, which was granted a measure of independence by the Japanese in 1943, the Burma National Army under its leader Aung San at first took the Japanese side but later defected to the Allies. During the war the British themselves actually provided military training for some anti-imperialists. The Malay Chinese, Chin Peng, for example, among other Communists, was trained in subversion and sabotage techniques by the covert action specialists of Special Operations Executive for operations against the Japanese. As leader of the 'insurrection' in Malaya that commenced in 1948, Chin Peng used these very skills against the British, initially with some success.

There were economic changes too. Industrial development and the exploitation of resources left many parts of the Empire more economically self-sufficient than before. The demands of the war stimulated Indian industrialization and prompted concern about the long-term damage this might do to British interests. In 1941 the leading industrialist, Lord Rootes, warned of 'the detrimental effects' of possible Indian automobile manufacturing on the British car industry 'in the period after the war'. There was a massive expansion in the exploitation of tropical resources, especially after the fall of Malaya. Bulk-purchasing schemes were set up for almost all major exports, such as Northern Rhodesian copper, West Indian bananas, Palestine citrus, Ceylonese tea, and East African cotton and sisal. Although the increased demand for these commodities might bring local prosperity, some—for example, much of the West African cocoa crop—were never exported at all. The purchases were simply made as an indirect subsidy to the growers in order to prevent social or economic hardship.

Governments throughout the Empire became more interventionist in support of the war effort. Both the 'colonial state' and individual colonial administrations became more 'managerial'. The Tanganyikan government, for example, was under pressure from above—London urging it to deliver—and from below, as it became more indispensable to the running of the colonial economy and to the satisfying of internal economic and political demands. The same processes are identifiable in India, where the recruitment and provisioning of armed forces, economic mobilization, rationing, and widespread requisitioning caused the state to penetrate more deeply than ever before into Indian society. This growth of the state might not have happened without the pressures of war, which dramatically converted colonial governments into more-or-less enthusiastic Keynesians. The enhanced role of the state was certainly a continuing legacy of the war.

This was matched by the Colonial Office's growing conviction of the merits of government-sponsored 'development' and welfare schemes, which were intended to enhance economic efficiency and productivity, improve living standards, and, it was hoped, reduce social, and perhaps political, unrest in the colonies, while demonstrating to the world (especially the United States) Britain's commitment to what might be called 'constructive imperialism'. The 1940 Colonial Development and Welfare Act was a much-vaunted, though practically not very effective, demonstration of this new commitment. As the tide of war turned in the Allies' favour, these developments were intensified by a new 'colonial mission', articulated by Oliver Stanley into a bipartisan policy which sought to reshape the Imperial system on the basis of equal relationships and common economic and social benefits.

Sterling balances, and the sterling area, represented another legacy of the war, which in the case of India unambiguously demonstrated power shifts within the Empire. The pressures of the conflict welded the rather loose pre-war sterling bloc into a closely integrated monetary association that survived for twenty years after the war. It also helped secure Britain's economic position in the world. But the sterling balances which Dominions and colonies alike built up in London reflected more clearly than anything else the cost of the war to Britain. As Lord Keynes put it, the 'principles of good housekeeping' had, for good reasons, been thrown 'to the winds' during the war, when British expenditure on defence and war supplies was almost entirely based on credit. This resulted in territories which had owed Britain money before the war emerging as creditors in 1945. Arising from the 1939 Defence Expenditure Agreement, over £1,300 million of India's enormous contribution to the Imperial war effort was charged up to Britain.

The Second World War saw the apotheosis of the British Empire, yet it contained elements of both the best and the worst in the Imperial relationship. During the war it was clearly demonstrated that colonial control depended ultimately on force, albeit applied by Britain in pursuit of national survival. On one level, a seamless robe of force and coercion linked the British response to external and internal challenges. D-Day, El Alamein, and Imphal thus share an Imperial relationship with the suppression of the 1942 Indian uprising, the British occupation of Iraq, Syria, and Iran, and the shooting by police and military of strikers in the Northern Rhodesian Copper Belt in March 1940 or in the Bahamas in June 1942. The increased authoritarianism of wartime Imperial control was but one manifestation of 'rule by the sword'.

The corollary to this was that, where force failed—as in Asia—the Empire was gravely, if not fatally, injured. The failure by Britain to protect Imperial subjects had a long-term effect. In Sarawak, for instance, although a battalion of British-officered Punjabis held out after the Japanese landings from 19 December 1941 until 3 April 1942, the local people were consigned to almost four years of enemy occupation. 'For liberation from the "evil oppression" of the Japanese', writes one historian, 'the people of Sarawak turned, not to the British, who had let them down, but to their own efforts as guerrillas . . . and to soldiers of the 9th Australian Division.' But for some the shared experience of war appeared to have consolidated the Empire. In November 1946 Lord Alanbrooke, the wartime Chief of the Imperial General Staff, told the Royal Empire Society that the war had strengthened the 'family' bonds of the Commonwealth, and he expressed the hope that 'those bonds which have held this British family together will continue to grow in strength'.

On the more positive side there was some constitutional advance. Self-government, the precise meaning of which remained unclear, was promised, most immediately to India, but the principle, though not the timing, was conceded for the Colonial Empire. 'Partnership' and 'colonial development' became maxims for the future. In part, these promises were prompted by the need to secure internal support for the war effort throughout the Empire and to reassure the Americans that the British Empire was not actually very imperial at all. There were those, however, who conceived a higher purpose for colonial development and self-government. The old Colonial Office hand, Sir John Shuckburgh, identified a 'new angle of vision' towards colonial problems, 'which, if it did not originate with the War, was greatly accentuated by wartime conditions and reactions'. He argued that European colonial administrators had now to 'collaborate with Colonial peoples, not, as in the past, merely to direct them . . . Inter-racial co-operation must be the keynote of Colonial policy.' 'We are', he concluded in his unpublished 'Colonial Civil History of the War', 'in fact engaged in a race against time; and the prize of victory will not be the perpetuation, but the honourable interment of the old system'. Yet, honourable or not, the 'interment' of the British Imperial system was an inevitable consequence of the 1939–45 conflict. The means by which the immense resources of the Empire were channelled into an extra-ordinary collective war effort unleashed social and political expectations that in the end could not be accommodated, even within a reformed colonial system such as that envisaged by Oliver Stanley and his successors in the Labour government. Paradoxically, the ultimate cost of defending the British Empire during the Second World War was the Empire itself.

[*Source*: Keith Jeffery, 'The Second World War', in Brown and Louis, eds., *The Twentieth Century*, pp. 320–7.]

## 4.3  THE PIONEERS: INDIA/PAKISTAN AND GHANA

Opinion about Britain's role in India might have changed over time, but there was no doubt that India was the 'jewel in the crown' of the British empire. One of its viceroys, Lord Curzon, said in 1901 that 'As long as we rule in India we are the greatest power in the world. If we lose it we shall drop straight away to a third rate power'. India's huge population, and its profitability, made its fate of central importance in the story of decolonization.

British advocates of greater Indian self-government were in the minority during the nineteenth century, but it is important to note that the Indian National Congress (INC), a model for later nationalist movements elsewhere, was founded in 1885 by a mixed group of Indians and British who promoted moderate appeals for self-government. The INC soon became Indian dominated, but remained moderate at the beginning of the twentieth century. Nationalist demands for greater political responsibility were often made in a spirit of imperial loyalty (Extract 122). But by 1914 only 5 per cent of the members of the Indian Civil Service were Indians. The First World War intensified nationalism in India; political protest grew more forceful, and the colonial government reacted defensively (Extract 123).

By the 1930s the INC became more radical, calling for independence as soon as possible (Extract 124). The political and spiritual leader, Mohandas Gandhi, warned that the INC's campaign of civil disobedience was an indication of the passion with which Indians were prepared to pursue their freedom (Extract 125). The majority view in Britain, however, was that India was not ready for independence and that Britain would betray its trusteeship role if it acceded to the INC's demands (Extract 126). This condescension infuriated the nationalists, and during the Second World War a sometimes-violent 'Quit India' movement gathered momentum in the subcontinent. The war itself was assisting the nationalists by revealing British military weakness against the Japanese at Singapore: Asians had defeated the supposedly invincible imperial forces.

With hopes for independence running higher than ever, debate was also increasing about the nature of an independent India. Muslims were particularly anxious about their possible status in a Hindu-dominated population. In 1940 the president of the Muslim League, M. A. Jinnah, announced the goal of a separate Muslim state—Pakistan—and therefore raised the possibility of partition (Extract 127). In 1945 the new Labour government in Britain promised Indian independence and despatched Lord Louis Mountbatten, the last Viceroy, to negotiate it. Three things became clear: independence could not be delayed, it would require partition (see Map 12), and it would lead to bloodshed. Even before independence day on 14 August 1947 the riots and mass migrations began as Hindus, Muslims, Sikhs, and others attacked one another or fled their homes for the 'right' side of the newly drawn borders (Extract 128). New nations were also created, with less violence, in Sri Lanka (formerly Ceylon) and Burma in 1948.

The rise of the INC was closely watched by nationalist movements elsewhere in the British empire, especially by the Western-educated élite of the Gold Coast, now Ghana (see Map 13). Like the early INC, west African nationalists originally sought greater self-government within the empire (Extract 129). After the Second World War, Gold Coast nationalism became more radical and was linked with socialism by Kwame Nkrumah who founded the Convention People's Party in 1949 (Extract 130). Britain's colonial development policy was inadequate to meet the demands of a new generation who wanted their wartime efforts repaid with full independence. Riots in the capital, Accra, in 1948 were prompted by this growing frustration, and by farmers' resentment about Britain's interventionist development policies on the native-owned cocoa plantations.

By the mid-1950s Britain realized that the pace of self-government in the Gold Coast would have to accelerate and talk of Africans 'not being ready' was replaced by pragmatism about the inevitability of independence (Extract 131). But like India, the Gold Coast contained various religious and ethnic groupings who were united by their desire to end British rule, but concerned about how their different interests would be represented in the government of the new nation (Extract 132). In Ghana and in many other former British colonies, the solution was perceived to be the continuation of British judicial, professional, and government systems under African leadership; the retention of imperial administrative and ceremonial structures would, it was hoped, provide a sense of unity and shared heritage. After constitutional compromises had been worked out, the new state of Ghana was celebrated on 9 March 1957 (Extract 133). The relatively smooth decolonization of Ghana and its acceptance into the Commonwealth paved the way for independence in Nigeria in 1960 and Sierra Leone in 1961. But periods of dictatorship and civil war have shown how difficult the achievement of unity and democracy has been in these countries.

## 122    Sir Satyendra Sinha

Sir Satyendra Sinha was a Bengali lawyer and the first Indian member of the Viceroy's Council. As Under-Secretary for India in the British Cabinet he sought equality with the Dominions for India on 6 April 1917 at the Imperial War Conference.

Sir, I should like, while supporting this Resolution, to make what I consider to be a merely verbal alteration, because I am certain that it could not be intentionally meant to exclude India, especially after the Resolution which this Conference has already passed. I therefore propose that we should add to the Resolution, in the second paragraph, after the words 'upon a full recognition of the Dominions as autonomous nations of an Imperial Commonwealth,' the words 'and of India as an important portion of the same.' The Resolution was drafted, of course, with special reference to the Self-governing Dominions, but, as I said, it could not have been intended to exclude India from participation in the arrangements which are recommended for the purpose of representation in foreign policy and in foreign relations. The foreign policy and the foreign relations of the Empire are to a very large extent concerned with India, and, therefore, it is only right that India should be represented in all consultations for the purpose of dealing with such foreign policy and foreign relations. As a corollary to that amendment I propose another consequential one, namely, that instead of the words, 'should recognize their right to an adequate voice in foreign policy and in foreign relations,' in order to make it perfectly clear, we should say, 'in order to recognize the right of the Dominions and of India to an adequate voice in foreign policy,' and so on. It is with some diffidence that I address the Conference and ask for this amendment to be made, but I do so principally on the assurance that it is bound to be acceptable, having regard to the attitude of the Conference already with regard to India ... [...] India has in a peculiar degree a sense of loyalty to the person and throne of the Monarch in England, and it would, therefore, give the greatest satisfaction to my countrymen that this Conference should unequivocally express its declaration that the monarchial form of government, as it is, is the best suited to the requirements of the Empire.

[*Source*: A. F. Madden and John Darwin, eds., *The Dominions and India since 1900*, vol. 6 of *SDBE* , p. 40.]

## 123   The 'Crawling Order'

> Post-war unrest prompted a large demonstration in the north Indian town of Amritsar in 1919, and a white female doctor was attacked. The local British authorities panicked, sending in the troops (killing about 400 unarmed Indians) and using 'The Crawling Order' to humiliate the local population.

Among the orders passed by General Dyer at Amritsar was an order that has been styled 'Crawling Order.' This order was passed on the 19th April, eight days after General Dyer had arrived and four days after the declaration of martial law. This order was passed with reference to a street where Miss Sherwood had been brutally attacked on the 10th April by the mob. The street is narrow, but of considerable length, and has abutting on it on both sides houses of different dimensions. The order was to the effect that no Indians should be allowed to pass through the street, but if they wanted to pass they must go on all fours, and pickets were placed at certain points in the street to enforce obedience to this order. . . .

General Dyer says that he did not expect that anybody would pass through the street and subject himself to this order of going on all fours. It was, however, a very curious coincidence that within a few minutes after he had passed the order and put the pickets, twelve persons had to be arrested for being insolent and he ordered them to be taken into custody, and the police took them through that street and the picket enforced the crawling order on them. . . .

Sir Michael O'Dwyer disapproved of this order and telephoned to General Beynon to have the order withdrawn as he considered it an improper order; and he informed the Viceroy as to what he had done in the matter.

[*Source*: Snyder, *Imperialism Reader*, p. 420.]

---

## 124   The Indian National Conference's 'Independence Day Resolution'

The INC grew more impatient during the inter-war period, issuing a statement known as the 'Independence Day Resolution' on 20 January 1930.

Jawaharlal Nehru, the Congress President, has instructed all Provincial Committees that they should arrange to get the following resolution of the Working Committee translated into their respective provincial languages, and distribute it widely throughout the provinces. The President also asks that this resolution should be read at and explained to the meetings proposed to be held in connection with these celebrations, and that those present should be asked to signify their assent to it by a show of hands.

We believe that it is the inalienable right of the Indian people, as of any other people, to have freedom to enjoy the fruit of their toil, and have the necessities of life so that they may have full opportunities of growth. We believe also that, if any Government deprives the people of these rights and oppresses them, the people have the further right to alter it or to abolish it.

## India's debasement

The British Government in India has not only deprived the Indian people of their freedom, but has debased it economically, politically, culturally, and spiritually. We believe that India must sever the British connection and attain *purna swarajya*, or complete independence.

India has been ruined economically. The revenue derived from our people is out of all proportion to our income. Our average income is seven pies per day. Of the heavy taxes we pay, 20 per cent is raised from the land revenue derived from the peasantry, and 3 per cent from the salt tax, which falls most heavily on the poor. Village industries, such as hand spinning, have been destroyed, leaving the peasantry idle for at least four months in the year and dulling their intellect for want of handicrafts. Nothing has been substituted, as in other countries, for crafts thus destroyed.

The Customs and currency have been so manipulated as to heap further burdens on the peasantry. The British manufactured goods constitute the bulk of our imports. The Customs duties betray a clear partiality for the British manufactures, and the revenue from them is used, not to lessen the burden on the masses, but for sustaining a highly extravagant administration. Still more arbitrary has been the manipulation of the exchange ratio, which has resulted in millions being drained from the country.

## Political

Politically, India's status has never been so reduced as under the British régime. No reforms have given real political power to the people. The tallest of us have to bend before foreign authority. The rights of free expression of opinion and free association have been denied to us, and many of our countrymen are compelled to live in exile abroad, and cannot return to their homes. All administrative talent is killed, and the masses have to be satisfied with petty village offices and clerkships.

Culturally, the system of education has torn us from our moorings and our training has made us hug the very chains that bind us spiritually. Compulsory disarmament has made us unmanly, and the presence of an alien army of occupation, employed with deadly effect to crush in us the spirit of resistance, has made us think that we cannot look after ourselves, or put up a defense against foreign aggression or even defend our homes and families from the attacks of thieves and robbers and miscreants.

## The mandate

We hold it to be a crime against man and God to submit any longer to the rule that has caused this disaster to our country. We recognise, however, that the most effective way of gaining our freedom is not through violence. We will, therefore, prepare ourselves by withdrawing, so far as we can, all voluntary association from the British Government and will prepare for civil disobedience, including non-payment of taxes.

We are convinced that if we can but withdraw our voluntary help, and stop the payment of taxes without doing violence, even under provocation, the end of this inhuman rule is assured. We, therefore, hereby solemnly resolve to carry out the Congress instructions issued from time to time for the purpose of establishing *purna swarajya*.

[*Source*: Snyder, *Imperialism Reader*, pp. 440–1.]

## 125  Mohandas Gandhi

> Mohandas Gandhi attended a British conference on Indian consti-
> tutional reform in 1931. In this statement made on 30 November he
> warned the conference that the INC's demand for independence
> would have to be met.

The Congress represents the spirit of rebellion. I know that the word 'rebellion' must not be whispered at a Conference which has been summoned in order to arrive at an agreed solution of India's troubles through negotiation. Speaker after speaker has got up and said that India should achieve her liberty through negotiation, by argument, and that it will be the greatest glory of Great Britain if Great Britain yields to India's demands by argument. But the Congress does not hold that view, quite. The Congress has an alternative that is unpleasant to you. [. . .]

For the sake of liberty people have fought, people have lost their lives, people have killed and have sought death at the hands of those whom they have sought to oust. The Congress then comes upon the scene and devises a new method not known to history, namely, that of civil disobedience, and the Congress has been following that method up. But again I am up against a stone wall and I am told that it is a method that no government in the world will tolerate. [. . .] I suggest to you, Prime Minister, it is too late today to resist this, and it is this thing which weighs me down, this choice that lies before them, the parting of the ways probably. I shall hope against hope, I shall strain every nerve to achieve an honourable settlement for my country if I can do so without having to put the millions of my countrymen and countrywomen and even children through this ordeal of fire.

[*Source*: *Parliamentary Papers* 1931–32, vol. VIII, 'Indian R.T.C. (Second Session): Proceedings' [Cmd. 3997], pp. 391–2.]

## 126    Winston Churchill

This speech by Winston Churchill on 23 February 1931 on the
prospect of Indian independence demonstrates the paternalism of
most British political opinion at the time.

At present the Government of India is responsible to the British Parliament,
which is the oldest, the least unwise and the most democratic parliament in
the world. To transfer that responsibility to this highly artificial and restricted
oligarchy of Indian politicians would be a retrograde act. It would be a
shameful act. It would be an act of cowardice, desertion and dishonour. It
would bring grave material evils, both upon India and Great Britain; but it
would bring upon Great Britain a moral shame which would challenge for
ever the reputation of the British Empire as a valiant and benignant force in
the history of mankind.

The faithful discharge of our duty in India is not only a cause, but a
symbol. It is the touchstone of our fortunes in the present difficult time. If we
cannot do our duty in India, be sure we shall have shown ourselves unworthy
to preserve the vast Empire which still centres upon this small island. The
same spirit of unimaginative incompetence and weak compromise and
supine drift will paralyse trade and business and prevent either financial
reorganisation or economic resurgence. What we require to do now is to
stand erect and look the world in the face, and do our duty without fear or
favour.

[*Source*: Bennett, *The Concept of Empire*, p. 404.]

## 127    M. A. Jinnah

M. A. Jinnah, president of the Muslim League, made a momen-
tous announcement in his presidential address of 1940: the League
would insist on the partition of India and the establishment of an
independent Muslim state.

The problem in India is not of an inter-communal character but manifestly of
an international one, and it must be treated as such. So long as this basic and
fundamental truth is not realised, any constitution that may be built will
result in disaster and will prove destructive and harmful not only to the
Musalmans but to the British and Hindus also. If the British Government are
really in earnest and sincere to secure peace and happiness of the people of

the sub-continent, the only course open to us all is to allow the major nations separate homelands by dividing India into 'autonomous national states'. There is no reason why these states should be antagonistic to each other. On the other hand, the rivalry and the natural desire and efforts on the part of one to dominate the social order and establish political supremacy over the other in the government of the country will disappear. It will lead more towards natural goodwill by international pacts between them, and they can live in complete harmony with their neighbours. This will lead further to a friendly settlement all the more easily with regard to minorities by reciprocal arrangements and adjustments between Muslim India and Hindu India, which will far more adequately and effectively safeguard the rights and interests of Muslims and various other minorities.

It is extremely difficult to appreciate why our Hindu friends fail to understand the real nature of Islam and Hinduism. They are not religions in the strict sense of the word, but are, in fact, different and distinct social orders, and it is a dream that the Hindus and Muslims can ever evolve a common nationality, and this misconception of one Indian nation has gone far beyond the limits and is the cause of most of your troubles and will lead India to destruction if we fail to revise our notions in time. [. . .]

. . . The present artificial unity of India dates back only to the British conquest and is maintained by the British bayonet, but termination of the British regime, which is implicit in the recent declaration of his Majesty's Government, will be the herald of the entire break-up with worse disaster than has ever taken place during the last one thousand years under Muslims. Surely that is not the legacy which Britain would bequeath to India after 150 years of her rule, nor would Hindu and Muslim India risk such a sure catastrophe.

[*Source*: Cyril Philips, ed., *The evolution of India and Pakistan, 1858 to 1947: select documents* (London: Oxford University Press, 1964), pp. 353–4.]

**128   Sir Penderel Moon**

> Sir Penderel Moon was revenue minister for Bahawalpur in north-western India at the time of partition in 1947. In this account of a partition-related massacre the victims are Hindus, but his published reminiscences emphasize that Muslims, Sikhs, and others were victimized in other parts of the country.

Being a colony town, Hasilpur was the headquarters of a number of revenue and colony officials, including two naib-tahsildars. There was also a police station with a sub-inspector in charge. We drove into the main bazaar, fully expecting some of these functionaries to be waiting to meet us. But there was not a soul to be seen. The bazaar was silent and deserted. We drove into the mandi and then out again and round the outside of the town, and at last we found someone who told us that the thanedar and all the Hindus had gone away to 'old' Hasilpur—a village lying about two miles to the north of the new town. I think neither of us had ever heard of its existence. We were shown the general direction in which it lay and were soon bumping along a sandy, sunken and twisty lane that was said to lead to it. I thought we were never going to reach it; and then, almost unexpectedly, we suddenly came upon it—a small but ancient village, rising up on a slight eminence, but concealed from view by big clumps of tall-growing reeds. Along its curving western side there was a belt, fifty to one hundred yards wide, of open sandy ground between the houses and the cultivated fields. Our road took us along this western side with the sandy belt on our left. As we drove along, I thought I saw well ahead of us some heaps of manure scattered about on this stretch of sand and nearer, though about seventy yards off and close to the edge of the fields, a couple of men seemed to be lying on the ground. I glanced towards Gurmani, murmuring, 'Why are those men lying over there?' and saw on his face a look of incredulous horror as he gazed out of the window of the car.

'They're corpses,' I exclaimed, answering my own question; and now, to my amazement, the heaps of manure took shape as heaps of human bodies. In twos and threes and sixes and tens, more and more came into view as we rounded the curve of the village, till at the north-western corner, close to the main entrance leading up into it, they lay 'Thick as autumnal leaves that strew the vale of Vallambrosa'. Men, women and children, there they were all jumbled up together, their arms and legs akimbo in all sorts of attitudes and postures, some of them so life-like that one could hardly believe that they were really dead. I was forcibly reminded of pictures that I had seen as a child of Napoleonic battlefields; and there was perhaps some reason for this in that all these people had in fact been shot down by rifle fire.

We got out of the car and walked slowly up into the village, too stunned to speak. We had heard reports of trouble at Bahawalnagar and Chishtian, but not a rumour of disturbances at Hasilpur, still less of such a massacre as this. It came, to me at least, as a staggering shock, sweeping away entirely, and for many days to come, the light-hearted and almost frivolous mood of the morning.

Near the top of the village, in a large two-storied building, we found the thanedar and a throng of women and children whose sobbing and whimpering swelled to a deafening crescendo of mingled grief and resentment as soon as they caught sight of us. It was hard to endure. In an open space outside there lay two or three wounded men under an ill-contrived awning of tattered sacking. One of them, almost stark naked, was literally covered with blood and an old woman was pathetically fanning his face and trying to keep the flies off him. We could do nothing to help.

Someone had noticed Brigadier Marden's car standing outside the village when we arrived, so we knew that he must be somewhere about the place. We were inquiring where he was when he himself appeared, dressed in uniform and carrying a tommy-gun. I did not at all like this last feature for in my opinion there was no reason for the commander of the troops to go about with anything more than a revolver. We commented on the hideous slaughter which Marden told us had only occurred that morning. He then said that at Bahawalnagar, from where he had just come, there had also been grave disturbances and heavy casualties. With a very serious face, he drew Gurmani aside and said he wanted to speak to him alone. I guessed at once what he was going to say and my guess was almost immediately confirmed for, in a few moments, Gurmani called me to where they were standing and said, 'Marden says the troops are unreliable.'

[*Source*: Penderel Moon, *Divide and Quit: An Eyewitness Account of the Partition of India* (Delhi: Oxford University Press, 1998), pp. 134–5.]

### 129   Petition of the National Congress of British West Africa

The National Congress of British West Africa (founded in 1919) was one of many African nationalist organizations modelled on the Indian National Congress. Here the NCBWA petitions the British government on 19 October 1920 for greater self-government. Note that the organization was mainly professional in composition.

*That* apart from the fact that the National Congress of British West Africa represents substantially the *intelligentsia* and the advanced thought of British West Africa, and that the principles it stands for are some of those fundamental ones that have always actuated communities that have arrived at the stage of national consciousness, it also represents the bulk of the inhabitants of the various indigenous communities and with them claims, as sons of the soil, the inherent right to make representations [as] to existing disabilities, and to submit recommendations for the necessary reforms: *That* your Petitioners would respectfully beg leave to point out that in asking for the franchise, the people of British West Africa are not seeking to copy a foreign institution. On the contrary, it is important to notice that the principle of electing representatives to local councils and bodies is inherent in all the [political] systems of British West Africa, which are essentially democratic in nature, as may be gathered from standard works on the subject: *That*, further, according to the African system, no Headman, Chief, or Paramount Ruler has an inherent right to exercise Jurisdiction unless he is duly elected by the people to represent them, and that the appointment to political offices also entirely depends upon the election and the will of the people: *That* such being the British West African system of representation, the arrangement by which the Governor of a Crown Colony nominates whom he thinks proper to represent the people, cannot but strike them as a great anomaly and does constitute a grievance and a disability which they now respectfully pray may be remedied.

[*Source*: Frederick Madden and John Darwin, eds., *The Dependent Empire, 1900–1948: Colonies, Protectorates, and Mandates*, vol. 7 of *SDBE* (Westport and London: Greenwood Press, 1994), p. 660.]

## 130   Kwame Nkrumah

Kwame Nkrumah became the first prime minister of Ghana before independence in 1957. Here he makes a 'Declaration to the Colonial Peoples of the World' in 1945 at the Pan-African Congress in Manchester, UK. Nkrumah drew much inspiration from Marxist interpretations of imperial history and economics.

The duty of any worthwhile colonial movement for national liberation, however, must be the organization of labour and of youth; and the abolition of political illiteracy. This should be accomplished through mass political education which keeps in constant contact with the masses of colonial peoples. This type of education should do away with that kind of intelligentsia who have become the very architects of colonial enslavement.

Then, the organizations must prepare the agents of progress, must find the ablest among its youth and train their special interests (technological, scientific and political) and establish an education fund to help and to encourage students of the colonies to study at home and abroad, and must found schools of its own for the dissemination of political education. The main purpose of the organization is to bring about the final death of colonialism and the discontinuance of foreign imperialist domination. The organization must root itself and secure its basis and strength in the labour movement, the farmers (the workers and peasantry) and the youth. This national liberation movement must struggle for its own principles and to win its aims.

It must have its own press. It cannot live separately from, nor deviate from the aims and aspirations of the masses, the organized force of labour, the organized farmers, and the responsible and cogent organization of youth. These form the motive force of the colonial liberation movement and as they develop and gain political consciousness, so the drive for liberation leaves the sphere of mere ideas and becomes more real.

The peoples of the colonies know precisely what they want. They wish to be free and independent, to be able to feel themselves on an equal with all other peoples, and to work out their own destiny without outside interference, and to be unrestricted to attain an advancement that will put them on a par with other technically advanced nations of the world. Outside interference does not help to develop their country. It impedes and stifles and crushes not only economic progress, but the spirit and indigenous enterprise of the peoples themselves. [. . .]

Thus the goal of the national liberation movement is the realization of complete and unconditional independence, and the building of a society of peoples in which the free development of each is the condition for the free development of all.

PEOPLES OF THE COLONIES, UNITE: The working men of all countries are behind you.

> [*Source*: Kwame Nkrumah, *Towards Colonial Freedom: Africa in the struggle against world imperialism* (London: Heinemann, 1962), pp. 41–2, 43.]

## 131   Report by member of staff of the Governor of the Gold Coast

A member of the governor's staff reported in a brutally pragmatic way on 21 July 1956 about the results of the recent general election in the Gold Coast. Just six years previously Nkrumah had been imprisoned for sedition.

The Colonial Office have just woken up to the (locally) well-known fact that Nkrumah and his main lieutenants have misappropriated public funds and have connived at, and possibly organised, the murder of opponents. They are professing to be much concerned. This is rather absurd at this stage of proceedings. Admittedly Arden-Clarke keeps them starved of intelligence: and he is rather naturally unable to realise the extent to which Nkrumah is double faced and has shaped his behaviour deliberately to create a good impression: and as Governor he has had a duty to emphasise the hopeful side of the picture. But ministerial corruption has long been common knowledge and the West African experts in the C.O. make annual liaison visits here for a month or so. The comforting myth that the Gold Coast was likely to be a well-behaved child that would be a credit to its parent has always, as you know, seemed to me to bear little relation to facts. The Government is in the hands of knaves. As African rogues go, they are not very bad ones: they have their saving graces: and it would probably be impossible to muster a dozen honest men in politics to replace them. The practical question now is not whether they are good or bad, but whether we can maintain reasonable working relations with them.

On this fundamental question greater familiarity has, in the last six months, made me rather more hopeful about the future. At first the shock of the immaturity and questionable characters of the political leaders, and the absence of qualified African officials to take over from the retiring expatriates, made it difficult to see the reassuring features of the scene. The main asset is the good humoured and easy going outlook of the African: with time, careful handling and extreme patience, it should be possible to lead him to recognize where the country's interests lie: and these fortunately coincide with our own. But it will be uphill work over a long period, in which we shall have to take a lot of trouble and be prepared to go to some expense. We cannot rest on our colonial laurels and leave the young buck to go his own way. In India, Pakistan and Ceylon the administrations were in responsible hands and we could wait and see. Here the impulsiveness, venality and ignorance of Ministers make their actions highly unpredictable and add up to a large measure of irresponsibility, and we must, so far as possible, take steps to safeguard our position. Unless we succeed in establishing our own influence more firmly, Ministers will be easy game for unscrupulous foreigners, playing up with flattery, gifts and promises, served in a congenial atmosphere of anti-Colonial hymn singing. The main question is how much time there will be for salutary Commonwealth influences to work before the Gold Coast has entrenched herself amongst disreputable friends elsewhere.

[*Source*: Richard Rathbone, ed., *Ghana* (London: HMSO, 1992), vol. 2, pp. 292–3.]

---

**132**   **British Cabinet memorandum**

Many of Ghana's post-independence problems, especially ethnic and religious divisions, were foreshadowed in this British Cabinet memorandum of 7 February 1957 on the new Ghanaian constitution.

*The Colonial Secretary* said that the purpose of his recent visit to Accra had been to allay the disquiet among the Ashanti and the tribes in the Northern territories that their local traditions and institutions would not be preserved under the new Constitution for Ghana. A satisfactory agreement had been reached as a result of his intervention. The Prime Minister of the Gold Coast, Dr. Nkrumah, however, had subsequently proposed to adopt certain provisions which would nullify the safeguards introduced to cover the interests of the Ashanti and the Northern territories. It had been necessary for two Gold Coast Ministers, Mr. Gbedemah and Mr. Botsio, to pay an urgent visit to London. After further discussion, agreement on all points had been restored, and every possible step had been taken to entrench in the actual Constitution safeguards for the rights of the tribal and regional peoples. The White Paper setting out the Constitutional proposals for the Gold Coast would be published forthwith.

The Cabinet would welcome the gracious suggestion by H.R.H. the Duchess of Kent that she should extend her forthcoming visit to the Gold Coast on the occasion of the independence celebrations in order to visit the Ashanti and Northern territories. Such a visit would do much to allay inter-regional suspicions, and would make an important contribution towards a successful start for Ghana as an independent State.

[*Source*: Rathbone, *Ghana*, vol. 2, p. 409.]

## 133   'The Birth of Ghana'

> Reporting 'The Birth of Ghana' on 9 March 1957 this Ghanaian newspaper emphasized the presence of British-derived institutions in the new government, and the British ceremonial of the political handover.

Ghana's judges, in their wigs and red robes, filed in to take their places behind the dais; a jubilant Prime Minister was greeted by his supporters with the new slogan, 'Serve Ghana Now'; Dr. Busia, Leader of the Opposition, though a sick man, came from Ashanti to play his part; and when Sir Charles and Lady Arden-Clarke entered the Chamber in state there was a full muster of M.Ps. [. . .]

The parliamentary proceedings began when Sir Emmanuel Quist, in his magnificent Speaker's robes, entered. Mr. Ayensu, the Clerk, who was a prominent figure in his wig and gown, read the proclamation and the prayers and then went to the entrance to lead Sir Charles and his party in again. The Speaker went to the entrance to conduct the Duchess's party which was led by Major Aferi of the Ghana Regiment and Superintendent Ababio of the Ghana police. The Duchess's long white gown, orders and decorations and magnificent diamonds made her a fitting representation for a Queen, and as she took her seat there was dead silence. [. . .]

The House then got down to work, to give overseas visitors a model exhibition of parliamentary proceedings. Mr. Chapman was re-elected Deputy Speaker after a proposal by the Government, seconded by the

Opposition. Dr. Nkrumah then in a short speech moved an address in reply to the Speech from the Throne. He emphasised the value of the Commonwealth link, thanked overseas visitors and friends and recorded his gratification that they were parting from the imperial power with the warmest feelings of friendship. The Opposition interjected in traditional manner and particularly applauded references to corruption. Dr. Busia impressed everybody with his carefully worded analysis of colonialism which he joined with a message of thanks to the British and others from overseas who had helped to build up Ghana. And so the meeting ended—a magnificent and magnificently managed piece of international publicity for Ghana: but also an affirmation that independence meant no complete break with the past but only the shedding of bonds no longer tolerable.

[Source: West Africa no. 2082, 9 March 1957, p. 219.]

## 4.4 SETTLER MINORITIES: KENYA AND ZIMBABWE

**B**ritain had anti-slavery and commercial treaties with coastal east Africans since the early nineteenth century, and explorers like the Scottish missionary David Livingstone had promoted greater British involvement in the interior in the 1860s. Germany was also interested in the area and the two countries agreed on spheres of influence in 1886; by 1895 Britain had established the East African Protectorate. After the First World War, Britain also ruled the former German colony of Tanganyika, now Tanzania, as well (see Map 13).

British East Africa (known as Kenya from the early twentieth century) contained a vocal minority of European settlers, most of them British (Extract 134). Kenya's coffee plantations were lucrative and worked by African labourers; however, south Asians predominated on the railways and in the commercial sector. By the time demands for self-government arose in the early twentieth century, both whites and Indians wanted to know what their political and civil rights would be under the oft-repeated British principle of African majority rule (Extract 135).

It was already clear by the 1930s that land disputes between settlers and Africans, especially the Kikuyu of the fertile Highlands region, were going to dominate any discussion of political reform (Extract 136). This made Kenya very different from India, or Ghana, where most prime land remained in indigenous hands. By the 1950s urbanization was combining with grievances about forced labour during the Second World War, and with the ongoing land question, to produce unprecedented resentment among the Kikuyu. Mau-Mau was the result: an oathtaking movement aimed at restoring Kikuyu cultural and political integrity (Extract 137). A state of emergency was proclaimed from 1952 to 1959 during which 95 whites and about 14,000 Africans were killed; Africans actually bore the brunt of Mau-Mau hostility (Extract 138). British troops ruthlessly suppressed the movement, and the colonial government used its emergency powers to imprison African nationalist leaders like Jomo Kenyatta of the Kenya African National Union (Extract 139).

British opinion was divided about what to do next, fearing that rapid independence would plunge Kenya into civil war, knowing that continued British rule might have the same result. But a choice had to be made, and it seemed better to compromise with African nationalists than to risk alienating them; besides, the neighbouring countries of Tanzania (1961) and Uganda (1962) were on the road to independence. The British therefore needed someone to negotiate with who was more or less representative of African opinion in Kenya. Like so many other nationalist leaders, Kenyatta had been imprisoned by the British only to be released, consulted, and eventually recognized as leader of his newly independent country. Events in Kenya moved quickly: Kenyatta was released in 1961 and became president just two years later.

The decolonization of South Rhodesia was delayed even longer due to the greater number and determination of its European settlers, who numbered 220,000 out of a population of about three and a quarter million in 1964. Rhodesian land ownership was even more controversial than its Kenyan counterpart. The most fertile land tended to be in white hands because of treaties signed by Cecil Rhodes's British South Africa Company and other organizations in the late nineteenth century. As in Kenya, the British delayed independence because the settlers opposed African majority rule while the African nationalists would accept nothing less than full democratic representation. The split between these two views was so great that they had different national identities: the whites were Rhodesians; the blacks were Zimbabweans, named after the ancient African empire of Great Zimbabwe. This historic African identity was reflected in the name of the nationalist organisation ZAPU, the Zimbabwe African People's Union, led by the politically moderate Joshua Nkomo (Extract 140).

Frustrated by Britain's refusal to give them control of Rhodesia, the settlers turned to the radical Rhodesian Front and its leader Ian Smith for solutions. In 1965 Smith's government made a unilateral declaration of independence—the first of its kind in the British empire since the American declaration of 1776 (Extract 141). This radicalized the African nationalists, who turned to the more militant leader Robert Mugabe and declared open warfare on Smith's racist regime; Mugabe eventually formed the breakaway Zimbabwe African National Union (ZANU) which he still leads today.

Smith's regime was able to resist a Commonwealth and United Nations boycott by accepting assistance from ex-Commonwealth member South Africa, and British political opinion was divided about the morality of compromising with white Rhodesia. This equivocation alienated Mugabe's ZANU and he began seeking support from China and the Soviet Union. Later, Mugabe would explain that he sought to create an African socialism; not Soviet or Chinese communism (Extract 142). He pointed to the case of North Rhodesia (now Zambia) which had decolonized relatively peacefully in 1964 under socialist leadership.

Mugabe eventually convinced the British that he was the man they needed to lead an independent Zimbabwe. Like so many new post-independence leaders he had successfully made the transition from political prisoner to statesman. Ironically, it was Margaret Thatcher who, in 1980, agreed to hand over the government of the new Zimbabwe to an avowed socialist (Extract 143). As in Kenya, some white settlers chose to leave after independence, but most did not and land distribution remains a serious problem in Zimbabwe.

## 134    Elspeth Huxley

Novelist Elspeth Huxley believed in Kenya's destiny as European-run country. In her autobiography she describes her Kenyan girl-hood and her recollections of race relations.

We set off in an open cart drawn by four whip-scarred little oxen and piled high with equipment and provisions. No medieval knight could have been more closely armoured than were Tilly and I, against the rays of the sun. A mushroom-brimmed hat, built of two thicknesses of heavy felt and lined with red flannel, protected her creamy complexion, a long-sleeved white blouse clasped her by the neck and a heavy skirt of khaki drill fell to her booted ankles.

I sat beside my mother, only a little less fortified in a pith helmet and a starched cotton dress. The oxen looked very thin and small for such a task but moved off with resignation, if not with speed, from the Norfolk hotel. Everything was dusty; one's feet descended with little plops into a soft, warm, red carpet, a red plume followed every wagon down the street, the dust had filmed over each brittle eucalyptus leaf and stained the seats and backs of rickshaws waiting under the trees.

We were going to Thika, a name on a map where two rivers joined. Thika in those days—the year was 1913—was a favourite camp for big-game hunters and beyond it there was only bush and plain. If you went on long enough you would come to mountains and forests no one had mapped and tribes whose languages no one could understand. We were not going as far as that, only two days' journey in the ox-cart to a bit of El Dorado my father had been fortunate enough to buy in the bar of the Norfolk hotel from a man wearing an Old Etonian tie. [. . .]

Tilly went on squashing ticks while a great many Africans in red blankets, with a good deal of shouting and noise, stowed our household goods in the cart. There was a mountain of boxes, bundles and packages. On top was perched a sewing machine, a crate of five Speckled Sussex pullets and a lavatory seat. The pullets had come with us in the ship from Tilbury and Tilly had fed them every day and let them out on the deck for exercise.

Robin, my father, did not come with us in the cart. He was there already, locating the land and, Tilly hoped, building a house to receive us. A simple grass hut could be built in a couple of days, but this needed organization, and Tilly was not counting on its being there.

'I only hope that if he builds one, he will do so on the right farm,' she said.

Farm was of course the wrong word. My father had picked out on a map five hundred acres of blank space with a wriggling line, presumed to be a river, on each side. [. . .]

Robin got a map from the Land Office with a lot of lines ruled on it, from which the position of our holding could be deduced. Nothing had been properly surveyed. The boundary between the land earmarked for settlement and land reserved for the Kikuyu was about a mile away.

'Any amount of labour,' Roger Stilbeck had said. 'You've only got to lift your finger and in they come. Friendly enough, if a bit raw. Wonderfully healthy climate, splendid neighbours, magnificent sport, thousands of years of untapped fertility locked up in the soil. I congratulate you, my dear fellow, I really do. You've been lucky to get this opportunity. Buck Ponsonby was bitterly disappointed. Best of luck, and look us up when you come in for the races. Keep in touch, old man.' [. . .]

We had with us in the cart a cook-cum-houseboy called Juma lent to us, as a great favour, by Roger Stilbeck to see us in. He was used to grander ways and, the farther we travelled from Nairobi, the more disapproving he became of the local inhabitants, who to me looked as wild and exciting as the gazelles and antelopes.

'They are small like pigeons,' he said loftily. 'They eat chickens, which make them cowardly. Look at their legs! Thin like a bustard. And their women are like donkeys, with heads as smooth as eggs. They are not to be trusted. Why do you wish to live amongst such stupid people? Here your crops will not prosper, your cattle will die . . .' [. . .]

'These oxen,' Juma grumbled, 'they are as old as great-grandmothers, their legs are like broken sticks, this driver is the son of a hyena and lacks the brains of a frog. When the new moon has come we shall still be travelling in this worthless cart.'

'No more words,' Tilly said snappily. Juma had a patronizing air that she resented, and she doubted if he was showing enough respect. Those were the days when to lack respect was a more serious crime than to neglect a child, bewitch a man or steal a cow, and was generally punishable by beating. Indeed respect was the only protection available to Europeans who lived singly, or in scattered families, among thousands of Africans accustomed to constant warfare and armed with spears and poisoned arrows, but had themselves no barricades, and went about unarmed. This respect preserved them like an invisible coat of mail, or a form of magic, and seldom failed; but it had to be very carefully guarded. The least rent or puncture might, if not immediately checked and repaired, split the whole garment asunder and expose its wearer in all his human vulnerability. Kept intact, it was a thousand times stronger than all the guns and locks and metal in the world; challenged, it could be brushed aside like a spider's web. So Tilly was a little sensitive about respect, and Juma was silenced.

[*Source*: Elspeth Huxley, *The Flame Trees of Thika: Memories of an African Childhood*
(London: Chatto and Windus, 1959), pp. 5, 6, 7, 13, 14–15.]

**135   Memorandum from British Colonial Secretary**

Kenya's population included a substantial minority of south Asians, but this 1932 memorandum by the British Colonial Secretary made it clear that Britain regarded Kenya as a colony in trust for the African population. After independence the Kenyan government would expel the south Asians in the name of Africanization.

The history of the position of Indians in Kenya up to the end of the late war may be summarised briefly. There have been Indian merchants established along the East African Coast for a long time, and, with the opening up of Uganda and Kenya, and particularly with the development of British administration in those countries during the last thirty-eight years, Indian traders have penetrated into the interior. Many Indian artisans and labourers employed in the construction of the Uganda Railway remained to engage in commerce, and, at the beginning of the present century, the number of Indians in Kenya was greatly increased by the arrival of artisans, clerks and small traders. [. . .]

It was the question of the ownership of land in the Highlands which first brought Indian and European interests into conflict. The Highlands, less the area in that region reserved for Africans, amount to about one-tenth of the total area of the Colony and Protectorate, and they are in climate unique in the great belt of Tropical African possessions of the Crown. There were a few European settlers from about 1897, but the encouragement of their immigration into the country as a matter of policy may be dated from 1902. From that time the influx of European settlers increased steadily. [. . .]

The African population of Kenya is estimated at more than 2½ millions; and according to the census of 1921, the total number of Europeans, Indians and Arabs in Kenya (including officials) were 9,651, 22,822 and 10,102 respectively.

Primarily, Kenya is an African territory and His Majesty's Government think it necessary definitely to record their considered opinion that the interests of the African natives must be paramount, and that if, and when, those interests and the interests of the immigrant races should conflict, the former should prevail. [. . .] In the administration of Kenya His Majesty's Government regard themselves as exercising a trust on behalf of the African population, and they are unable to delegate or share this trust, the object of which may be defined as the protection and advancement of the native races.

[*Source: Parliamentary Papers* 1932, vol. XVIII, 'Indians in Kenya' [Cmd. 1922], pp. 4, 10–11.]

## 136   Koinange Mbiyu

The Kikuyu chief Koinange Mbiyu travelled to London to testify
before a Parliamentary committee on British East Africa on 28
April 1931. His primary concern was the acquisition by Europeans
of the best farmland in the Highlands.

I regard this Committee now as my father, but I want you, the members of
the Committee, to remember that whereas I am regarding you, and therefore
the Government, as my father, my mother is my land and the country in
which I was born [. . .] In Kiambu District about 1911, 1912–14 native land
called 'Githaka' was taken by the Government and sold to Europeans. The
Government promised the natives that it would compensate them—
Rs.50,550—for the land. But they have still not yet been paid [. . .] The chief
trouble is that the country is big enough, but it was divided up without
enough forethought, by somebody who did not understand [. . .] The trouble
is that a number of the actual clans who were landowning families had their
land alienated over their heads, with them on the land, and eventually pres
sure was brought to bear to make them leave it, and that is why they have had
to go away, far from their own country, as Squatters [. . .] They see that there
are cases where a European has 10 square miles, whereas a native is well over
100 to the square mile, while they are being trained and taught to develop
their agriculture, and while they are being educated, their cry is 'If we are
educated in this way where are we going to develop?'

[Source: Parliamentary Papers 1930–31, vol. VII [Cmd. 156], pp. 400–2.]

## 137   British memorandum on Mau-Mau

A British view of Mau-Mau is summarized in this official
memorandum from 1952. Note that the colonial administration
recognized the importance of factors such as urbanization, land
ownership, and agricultural modernization.

The Government and people of Kenya are faced with a challenge to law,
order and progress not from the Africans of Kenya as a whole, but from the
Mau Mau, an organisation within one tribe, the Kikuyu, but strongly opposed
by a large and growing proportion of the Kikuyu themselves. The first duty
of the Government is to restore law and order, to apprehend and punish
those guilty of the many and bestial crimes committed by the Mau Mau

against Africans and others alike, and of organising the Mau Mau movement itself. Only then can progress towards political advancement and interracial cooperation be resumed.

The exact nature and origin of the Mau Mau movement are in some respects obscure. It is almost entirely a Kikuyu movement, and it appears to derive from certain peculiarities of the Kikuyu tradition and tribal organisation. This tradition is permeated with witchcraft, which has always played a very important part in Kikuyu tribal customs, particularly in relation to the use of land. It has indeed been suggested that the Mau Mau movement represents, in part, a last effort by witch-doctors to retain their influence in face of the advance of education and civilisation. Furthermore, traditionally, tribal custom in the Kikuyu has forbidden military age-groups to engage in most forms of agriculture, these being left to women, children and old men.

The East African tribes have adapted themselves with varying degrees of success to the disappearance of tribal warfare as a normal practice, but in none has difficulty with the younger age groups been quite as acute as among the Kikuyu. This is partly due to the fact that the tribe has been particularly affected by the urban influence of Nairobi, where young men of the Kikuyu have drifted in considerable numbers. The problem of young and able-bodied men with insufficient socially sanctioned employment, subject to the disturbing influence of an urban civilisation and meretricious attractions of urban life, is one to which an answer is still being sought in many parts of the world . . . [. . .]

One of the most obvious facets of the Mau Mau organisation is that it is violently anti-European, and much play is made in its propaganda with the existence of the so-called 'White Highlands.' The main problem confronting African farmers is in fact not so much an absolute shortage of land (much of the land in the Reserves is not being cultivated to full productivity) but the necessity of carrying out the difficult transfer from a primitive shifting subsistence agriculture to a much more productive system of fixed agriculture, which is essential if higher standards of living are to be achieved. . . . Great efforts have been made by the Government to teach new methods and many Africans have taken full advantage of them, not only as regards food crops for consumption but also as regards export crops, such as tea, coffee, and pyrethrum. . . . Advances have taken place in the Kikuyu reserve as elsewhere, but the Mau Mau leaders have among other things stirred up opposition to improved agriculture and have gone so far as to incite people to destroy contour terraces and other improvement works. In this respect the Mau Mau movement resembles that of the loom-breakers at the time of the Industrial Revolution in England, and stands in the way of the economic advance of the Kikuyu people—and of all Africans in Kenya.

[*Source:* Snyder, *Imperialism Reader*, pp. 501–3.]

## 138 Interviews with Mau-Mau members

In these interviews with Mau-Mau members we hear Africans describe the mixed motives of the movement. Hostility towards Africans perceived as colonial collaborators was as strong a factor as antagonism towards Europeans.

A gang member, who had not wanted to participate, reflects the view of the population and saw only tragedy. The following are extracts from several interviews.

I had joined Mau Mau 'for *umoja*', not for killing. Local members of Mau Mau did not meet together, they were waiting for a *Kiama kia Moscou* which said that it was not going to wait. I cannot tell more about them, [ordinary Mau Mau members] were afraid of them because they could kill you so it was better to know nothing and not to ask. I heard that they also spoke with two sides. I heard that some joined the CID and that is why they called themselves *kia Moscou*. . . .

The Committee in Nairobi told people to kill the Headman and they were giving shs 100/– to each of us. . . . Because they killed the wrong ones they were not paid.

I do not like killing, even of —, but they found me in the garden. . . .

They killed [Gitau] because he was an enemy of [Kimani, principal leader] they had had litigation. These . . . people who wanted to kill came together with about 25 others. . . . [They] intended to kill the headman and — a Homeguard from Kibichoi who used to beat people like . . . They came at [homestead of a Kimani member] and stayed there until dark.

They were asked by her [his wife] to kill — [an agricultural instructor] because he reported them of not making good terraces. They went for him and they killed him. They then started their journey to [the Headman]. They had asked — to be a watchman. He did not like that. So he called [a] Homeguard . . . to stay with him in his house so he could be a witness that he did not take part. [They] heard people coming so [they] ran away and started shouting, using a whistle. They [the gang] got annoyed. They tried to follow him but failed. That is why they went to [his homestead] and killed his wife and child. Then [one of Kimani] told the others that someone of Gitau had been troubling his wife, so . . . they went to that [Gitau house] and killed him and his children and wife. But he lived and so did his wife. They then went all away and ran.

He felt caught between the threat of the security forces and the *Muhimu*, which would kill them for not having followed orders.

. . . We all ran away because we thought we are Mau Mau, most of Mau Mau were killed and will be killed if they did something wrong, so we ran away.

[*Source*: Greet Kershaw, *Mau Mau from below* (Oxford: James Currey, 1997), pp. 256–7.]

**139**   **Jomo Kenyatta**

At his trial for suspected Mau-Mau activity in 1953, Jomo Kenyatta denied the charges and gave this outline of his hopes for a peaceful transition to independence.

Early in 1947, when I was very busy in the activities of schools, I came to know about and joined the Kenya African Union. At the annual meeting in June, I was elected as President. The aims of KAU were to unite the African people of Kenya; to prepare the way for introduction of democracy in Kenya; to defend and promote the interests of the African people by organizing and educating them in the struggle for better working and social conditions; to fight for equal rights for all Africans and break down racial barriers; to strive for extension to all African adults of the right to vote and to be elected to parliamentary and other representative bodies; to publish a political newspaper; to fight for freedom of assembly, press and movement.

To fight for equal rights does not mean fighting with fists or with a weapon, but to fight through negotiations and by constitutional means. We do not believe in violence at all, but in discussion and representation.

We feel that the racial barrier is one of the most diabolical things that we have in the Colony, and we see no reason at all why all races in this country cannot work harmoniously together without any discrimination. If people of goodwill can come together, they can eliminate this evil. God put everybody into this world to live happily, and to enjoy the gifts of Nature that God bestowed upon mankind. During my stay in Europe—and especially in England—I lived very happily, and made thousands of good friends. I do not see why people in this country cannot do the same thing. To my mind, colour is irrelevant.

Some time ago, I invited about 40 Europeans to meet me, and spent a whole day with them at our school at Githunguri. One of them said they expected to be chased away; then he apologised for the hatred that he had felt for us, and for believing that we hated the Europeans. That was a common attitude of many settlers who had never met me. I told him I was just an ordinary man, striving to fight for the rights of my people, and to better their conditions, without hating anybody.

[*Source*: Jomo Kenyatta, *Suffering without bitterness: the founding of the Kenya nation* (Nairobi: East Africa Publishing House, 1968), pp. 27–8.]

## 140    Joshua Nkomo

Joshua Nkomo, president of the Zimbabwe African People's Union (ZAPU), addressed the UN Special Committee on Decolonization on 19 March 1962. He provided an African perspective on Rhodesian history and called for a conciliatory approach to race relations and eventual independence.

In 1914 there was a war. Two things happened. We were told that the world was faced by a threat from maniacs in Germany who threatened the world with oppression. We came by the thousands and we fought in that war. While we were fighting in 1914, the remaining settlers changed the law and gave majority seats in the Legislative Council in our country to elected members. Elected by whom? By the settlers and no reference was made to the African people. Here we are dealing with a question of consent. We are dealing with a question of who is the person in Southern Rhodesia. If you talk of the peoples of Southern Rhodesia, about whom are you talking, Britain? That is our question to the British. They tell the world and they tell you that the people decided. [. . .]

By the Land Apportionment Act, the vicious law in our country which became the basis of exploitation and degradation of our people, our land was divided into two categories, European and African. Southern Rhodesia then had not moved to Europe, it was still in Africa, but we had and we still have European areas in Southern Rhodesia today. Of course, the land that was declared European was that fertile land which the peoples of Southern Rhodesia had—that is, the peoples of the Zimbabwe, that is Southern Rhodesia now; our country is named after Rhodes, but the real name of the country is Zimbabwe, the Kingdom of Monomotapa. Now, those areas which people had inhabited for years were declared European and some remote areas never before inhabited by people were declared African. [. . .]

It was clear that the policies followed by the settlers were racist. I have said, and I must emphasize, that we of the Zimbabwe African Peoples' Union and, indeed, the whole of the African population is not racist; we are not against any person. We are against the oppression of men by men. We never can and never shall tolerate such a policy.

[*Source*: Aquino de Bragança and Immanuel Wallerstein, eds., *The African liberation reader: documents of the national liberation movements* (London: Zed Press, 1982), vol. 2, pp. 6, 7.]

**141**  **Ian Smith**

> The Prime Minister, Ian Smith, declared independence in 1965
> in order to maintain white control in Rhodesia. At this press
> conference on 13 December 1968 he explained the policy of his
> government and answered questions about the possibility of
> African majority rule.

When I spoke at the Bulawayo Trade Fair earlier this year, I was at pains to give my thinking on this very important question when I said that I believed that in Rhodesia we had to live with our history and whether we liked it or not, I believed that partition such as that which took place in Israel, India or South Africa, was simply not a practical proposition in Rhodesia. One has simply to look at the patch-work quilt effect of our Land Apportionment map to realize this. On the other hand, the traditional separate development policy of Rhodesia is possible and, indeed, has proved successful. An excellent example of this is our Land Apportionment policy which has been praised by many people and, in fact, was included in our 1961 Constitution at the request of the British Government. Under this policy, half the land belongs to the African and half to the European but, and this is the significant point, there must be a central Government at the top. It is a policy which is unique to Rhodesia and one which has proved itself over the years. [. . .]

Next, I would like to turn to the economic scene in order to correct certain mis-representations which are abroad. It will be clear to those of you who were here around 1959 to 1962 that we are witnessing a revival of the old gang of those days who, aided and abetted by the Argus Group, tried to talk Rhodesians into agreeing that we had no option but to hand our country over and, what's more, that this should be done sooner rather than later. People were talking about whether this should be done in five years or 10 years, and it appeared as if the objective was to bring it about as soon as possible.

You will also remember that this was responsible for breaking the confidence of Rhodesians, particularly when they knew what had happened to so many other countries in Africa to the north of us. It was as a result of this that we saw Rhodesians streaming out of our country in their thousands. Some people went because they had lost their jobs; but, worse still, there were others who abandoned their jobs and went because they had lost confidence in the future of their country. We saw good people from countries to the north of us, trekking through Rhodesia, unwilling to stay because they could see no future for the European and his civilization here.

Fortunately, all this has changed, but it took time and it was a far from easy task; it took the advent of the Rhodesian Front to power and their Declaration of Independence to stop the rot; to put right all the wrongs which had been done; to establish through unilateral action our independence, which our predecessors misled us into believing that they had negotiated for us, in exchange for the 1961 Constitution. [. . .]

Q. But in your assessment then Mr. Prime Minister, blacks would not probably be fit for black majority rule within your lifetime?

A. I don't believe in black majority rule ever in Rhodesia, not in a thousand years. I repeat, I believe in black and whites working together. If one day it's white and the next day it's black, I believe we will have failed and I think it will be a disaster for Rhodesia.

[*Source*: Government of Rhodesia, *For the Record* (Salisbury: Government Printer, 1968), pp 1–2, 2–3, 13.]

## 142    Robert Mugabe

Robert Mugabe, who had accepted arms and other assistance from the Soviet Union, took great pains in a series of newspaper interviews in 1978 to explain that he was a Zimbabwean socialist rather than a Soviet-style communist.

**Tempo**: The Western press is presently running an 'anti-communist' campaign. At the same time they are portraying the Patriotic Front as a 'communist' creation.

**Mugabe**: This is absolute nonsense. We are not a creation of the Soviet Union or Cuba; we are a creation of Zimbabwe. Our army is a manifestation of the nationalist desires of our people, a product of the history of our country.

We began with non-violent struggle. When we understood this wouldn't work, we changed our tactics to boycotts, strikes, and demonstrations. When these didn't work, we moved to sabotage against property without destruction of human life. When this failed, we decided on the armed struggle and formed ZANU.

At that point, in 1963, there was a division in the nationalist movement. But, at the same time as ZANU, ZAPU also began to organize for armed struggle. We shared conviction in the cause of liberation through armed struggle.

We contacted our progressive friends and allies for assistance. The Soviets gave us aid, as did the entire international socialist community. ZAPU trained militants in Cuba and, after 1967, so did we. But though we trained cadres in the socialist countries, this did not transform our army into a Russian or Chinese army.

Our war is supported by the progressive world. And it is true that our objective is the liquidation of imperialism and colonialism. But it is the Zimbabwean people who are fighting the war. No one can deny us the right to seek aid from our friends and allies. But it will always be Zimbabweans who direct the struggle. [. . .]

**Tempo**: How does the Patriotic Front see the state being built by the Zimbabwean people after independence is achieved?

**Mugabe**: We view the armed struggle as a means of achieving peace in our country, not as an instrument for killing and indiscriminate violence. It is an instrument which we can use to make revolutionary changes. This has been made necessary by the fact that the colonial power (Britain) has handed over its role to the colonists that established a fascist order in our country, oppressing our people. The peasants have become poorer and the working class has been exploited to the point where the worker is almost a slave.

Through the means of armed struggle we will set up a democratic state. There will have to be a major socio-economic transformation. The legal system will have to be changed immediately in order to lay the basis for the transformation of our nation toward socialism. Oppression must give way to peace. Once peace has been established, we'll make some changes to enable the workers to take power and control the means of production. The peasants will start to organize collectives and communal villages.

At that point the state will be not only an instrument of peace, but also a guarantee that the revolutionary process will continue. That is why we say that the armed struggle becomes a socio-economic struggle to serve the people's needs.

[*Source*: Liberation Support Movement, *Zimbabwe: The Final Advance, Documents on the Zimbabwe Liberation Movement* (Oakland, CA: Liberation Support Movement Press, 1978), pp. 28–9, 31.]

---

**143**   **The Commonwealth Heads of Government Meeting, 1979**

General Olusegun Obasanjo of Nigeria and the former British foreign minister Sir Michael Palliser recalled the conversion of the British Prime Minister, Margaret Thatcher, in support of Mugabe.

*What led you to wield that club of an economic boycott, immediately before Lusaka?*

Before that meeting at Lusaka, we had taken certain steps to make it clear to the British government that we were not going to stand for a half-solution, or half-cocked measures, as far as Rhodesia was concerned. We placed the ultimate responsibility for the solution squarely on the British government. So, now we had taken some economic measures to bring it vividly home to the British government that we *were* indeed holding them responsible. We left what you might call the 'trump card'— the taking over of BP, its operations in the field, its exploration and its downstream operation of marketing—to the eve of the Lusaka Commonwealth leaders' conference. I believe that was crucial. [. . .]

*Lord Walston, in the House of Lords debate on Rhodesia in July, very shortly before Mrs Thatcher made her statement in Canberra, said that Britain had not been allowed to tender for one very large and important contract worth five hundred million pounds, because of the Prime Minister's statement in Canberra.*

That is true. We *did* prevent British companies from tendering for contracts and supplies. As I said, we laid out a plan, and it had just started to unfold. The British government was angered by our action, and at the same time realized that the time had come when they must move along the line. President Kaunda told me that when Mrs Thatcher arrived in Lusaka, before the measures we took had been announced, she had given President Kaunda to understand the British were not going beyond the mandate they had for Rhodesia in the British general election.

*'I will not be bullied', she said.*

Yes. 'I will not be bullied.' But, I believe Nigeria's contribution to her change of mind was substantial. We had intended to take a strong position. I had never met Mrs Thatcher, and I wanted to impress our intention on somebody who knew her, and the sort of person she was. That opportunity came with [Australian Prime Minister] Malcolm Fraser's visit. I believe that Malcolm Fraser, who came here on his way to the Lusaka conference, and with whom I had a real heart to heart discussion, helped her to move in the direction that we eventually did.

*Long after these events, you wrote a letter to the Financial Times in London, in 1986, in which you expressed views about 'Mrs Thatcher's instincts being at war with her logic'. What bearing do you believe that may have had at the time?*

Those who know her very well have said that her first instinct is always wrong. She needs strong persuasion, a really strong person, to persuade her to another, and *right*, instinct. I believe that is what happened at Lusaka. Her first *instinct* was wrong. I have no doubt about that. But she was persuaded, and she took the right decision. I believe she has no regret for what she did. One must praise Mrs Thatcher. For a political leader to change his, or her, mind in the face of reality is a mark of statesmanship. I have tremendous regard for her. [. . .]

No doubt it is easy to exaggerate or sentimentalize the importance of such things, but the intimacy of President Kaunda's small study, with the senior members of the Commonwealth gathered there so closely, can hardly have failed to influence the minds of the participants. Anyhow, it was in that room, with the bookshelves behind Kaunda's chair lined with unopened, indeed uncut, pages of the voluminous works of Lenin, that Zambia's President recalled 'a turning point'. [. . .]

While several strands of thinking in Britain have come to see it as an inherited burden, tinged with obsolesence, 'the Commonwealth' had put a hard-headed case to the Prime Minister. As **Sir Michael Palliser** makes clear, Mrs Thatcher had been impressed by that at Lusaka, and by the absence of modish hypocrisies from the African leaders.

Although we tend to think of the Lusaka meeting as exclusively 'African', and obviously its main purpose was to try and lead up to a *Rhodesian* constitutional conference, it was also dealing with a lot of *other* Commonwealth problems which cut across the discussion on Africa. There was a full range of other things—the standard Commonwealth agenda—which tended to chop the Lusaka conference up a bit. That meant it was also a broader process of education for Mrs Thatcher in the nature of the Commonwealth.

I'm not going to try and explain 'the nature of the Commonwealth' in thirty seconds, because 'the nature of the Commonwealth' is still totally ill-understood by most people, in this country and elsewhere. I would not pretend to understand it myself, completely. But there is no doubt that this was an educative process, more generally—and, not just in 'Africa'. I say this because I do think it played some part in a change in *attitude* by the Prime Minister towards the Commonwealth. There was a greater understanding of the value of the Commonwealth as an instrument, and as an organization: therefore, of the desirability of keeping the Commonwealth in play; of winning support within the Commonwealth for what we wanted to do in Africa— and in Rhodesia. Here again—it is the same thing—one should not underestimate the extent to which that influence operates on the *African* Commonwealth leaders. One of the extraordinary things about the Commonwealth is that, in spite of all the rows, and the fights, which go on every time they meet, there is a desire to keep the Commonwealth together. The heads of government *enjoy* meeting. I have got no doubt about that at all. Take a country like Pakistan for example, which has left the Commonwealth—but which *longs* to come back in. The Commonwealth is a strange animal, which does have this effect on people when they meet. You get some very sharp exchanges, yet there is a general feeling that it is a *valuable* coming together of people and ideas, and with a shared language. All that, I think, played its part.

[*Source*: Michael Charlton, *The last colony in Africa: diplomacy and the independence of Rhodesia* (Oxford: Oxford University Press, 1990), pp. 44–56, 56, 57.]

## 4.5 PEOPLES AND BORDERS: PALESTINE AND MALAYSIA

After the First World War the British empire expanded to include several Middle Eastern territories mandated by the League of Nations (see Map 14). During the war Britain had made contradictory promises in the Middle East: T. E. Lawrence, 'Lawrence of Arabia', had pledged self-government for Arabs willing to help Britain against the Turks and Germans, while the Sykes-Picot agreement of 1916 secretly divided much of the area between Britain and France. Meanwhile, the British Foreign Secretary, Arthur Balfour, had been impressed by the arguments of Zionists seeking the re-establishment of a Jewish nation in Palestine (Extract 144), and in 1917 he issued a declaration pledging Britain to the support of a Jewish 'national home' while declaring support for existing Palestinian political and civil rights (Extract 145). Problems surfaced immediately. Was such a 'national home' going to become a sovereign Jewish state? Zionists hoped that it was, and Jewish emigration to Palestine steadily increased. The Muslim and Christian population pressed the British (unsuccessfully) for precise definitions about how their rights would be protected (Extract 146). Knowing that it had to bring Palestine to independence as quickly as possible under the terms of the mandate, Britain began to worry about the divisive effect of continuing Jewish immigration. After a serious uprising by Muslims in 1936 Britain began imposing immigration quotas (Extract 147): a doubly serious decision in light of the increasingly violent anti-semitism of the Nazi and other regimes in Europe.

One possible solution was the partition of Palestine along racial and cultural lines, but a series of investigations concluded that this would not produce politically or economically viable states. The government decided that ongoing British rule was the lesser of two evils: a situation that pleased nobody, the British included (Extract 148). The Second World War suspended constitutional discussions, but after the war Britain came under pressure from the United Nations, and the United States, to resolve the Palestinian dilemma. Jewish nationalists, unwilling to risk further delay, forced Britain's hand by proclaiming the state of Israel in 1948. A regional war broke out immediately and, unable to cope, Britain handed the area over to United Nations supervision. Israeli–Palestinian conflict continues to this day.

In south-east Asia Britain faced one of its greatest unification challenges: several scattered territories and islands stretching from the Malay states south of Thailand to the northern part of the island of Borneo (see Map 15). These had been acquired by treaty during the nineteenth century, and most of them were ruled indirectly through indigenous sultanates; before the Second World War there was little sense of unity even though the group of mainland colonies was usually referred to as a single unit: 'Malaya'. Then, after the Japanese conquest of Singapore in 1942, Britain lost both trust and respect in the eyes of Malay nationalists.

After the war Britain was anxious to maintain influence in Malaya: its rubber exports were vital to the economic recovery of the empire, Singapore was an important Royal Navy base, and (like the United States) Britain worried about growing communist influence in the region. The government also realized that Malaya would have to be granted independence sooner rather than later. But what was Malaya's identity as a potential nation? The indigenous Malays were mainly Muslim with Christian and other minorities, but the population also included large numbers of south Asians and Chinese: the legacy of indentured labour and extensive migration (Extract 149). The British worried about this lack of ethnic cohesion, but agreed to a constitution granting special privileges to Malays in 1948 when it created the Federation of Malaya. But the federal solution, so beloved of British colonial administrators, would provide only a temporary respite from ethnic tensions.

In the meantime, communism was providing a focus for disaffected groups in south-east Asia, especially sections of Malaya's Chinese population. Militants in the Malayan Communist Party initiated a guerrilla campaign that forced the colonial government into a declaration of emergency in 1948 (Extract 150). British and Commonwealth troops helped to restore order and to wage a 'hearts and minds' campaign to reassure the population about the government's benevolent intentions. Ironically, the success of this strategy would encourage the United States to think that they could win a similar victory in Vietnam.

But the problem of integration in Malaya remained unresolved (Extract 151). The Alliance Party led by Tunku Rahman drew up a new constitution in 1956 which still reserved privileges such as land ownership for indigenous Malays (Extract 152), yet the Alliance Party won a massive majority in the general election; the British felt they had no choice but to press forward to independence in 1957 and welcome Malaya into the Commonwealth (Extract 153). But Singapore, with its 75 per cent Chinese population, refused to join the federation until 1963 when the country was renamed 'Malaysia'. Even a loose federal relationship proved unworkable and Singapore seceded to become an independent republic in 1965.

## 144    Chaim Weizmann

Zionist leader Chaim Weizmann describes the Jews' desire to return to their ancient homeland.

What has produced this particular mentality of the Jews which makes me describe the Jewish race as a sort of disembodied ghost—an entity and yet not an entity in accordance with the usual standards which are applied to define an entity? I believe the main cause which has produced the particular state of Jewry in the world is its attachment to Palestine. We are a stiff-necked people and a people of long memory. We never forget. Whether it is our misfortune or whether it is our good fortune, we have never forgotten Palestine, and this steadfastness, which has preserved the Jew throughout the ages and throughout a career that is almost one long chain of inhuman suffering, is primarily due to some physiological or psychological attachment to Palestine. We have never forgotten it nor given it up. We have survived our Babylonian and Roman conquerors. The Jews put up a fairly severe fight and the Roman Empire, which digested half of the civilized world, did not digest small Judea. And whenever they once got a chance, the slightest chance, there the Jews returned, there they created their literature, their villages, towns, and communities. And, if the Commission would take the trouble to study the post-Roman period of the Jews and the life of the Jews in Palestine, they would find that during the nineteen centuries which have passed since the destruction of Palestine as a Jewish political entity, there was not a single century in which the Jews did not attempt to come back.

[*Source:* Chaim Weizmann, *The Jewish People and Palestine* (London: Zionist Organisation, 1939), p. 12.]

## 145    Arthur Balfour

'The Balfour Declaration' of 2 November 1917 was published as an open letter from the Foreign Secretary, Arthur Balfour, to Lord Lionel Rothschild. Balfour had consulted the American and French governments before printing the declaration, but note the conflicting promises it makes.

I have much pleasure in conveying to you, on behalf of his Majesty's Government, the following declaration of sympathy with Jewish Zionist aspirations which has been submitted to, and approved by, the Cabinet:—

'His Majesty's Government view with favour the establishment in Palestine of a national home for the Jewish people, and will use their best endeavour to facilitate the achievement of this object, it being clearly understood that nothing shall be done which may prejudice the civil and religious rights of existing non-Jewish communities in Palestine, or the rights and political status enjoyed by Jews in any other country'.

I should be grateful if you would bring this declaration to the knowledge of the Zionist Federation.

[*Source: The Times*, 9 November 1917, p. 7.]

---

## 146   Memorandum from Arab delegation and Winston Churchill's reply

> Arab representatives submitted a memorandum to Winston Churchill in March 1921 outlining their point of view. Churchill was making a visit of inquiry to Palestine, and his reply to the Arabs simply referred them back to the Balfour Declaration, declaring that Britain would uphold it.

The Arabs did not dislike the Turk because he was a Turk, neither did he love the Englishman because he was British; he hated the one because he desired complete independence, and he loved the other hoping and believing that the Englishman would help him to attain his goal . . . Palestine, one of our most sacred lands, has been isolated for a thought-out purpose, and this has been the reward of the Allies to the Arabs for their fidelity and the blood they sacrificed . . . Today the Arabs' belief in England is not what it was . . . If England does not take up the cause of the Arabs, other Powers will. From India, Mesopotamia, the Hedjaz and Palestine the cry goes up to England now. If she does not listen then perhaps Russia will take up their call some day, or perhaps even Germany. For though today Russia's voice is not heard in the councils of the nations, yet the time must come when it will assert itself . . .

Had Zionists come to Palestine simply as visitors, or had matters remained as before the war, there would be no question of Jew or non-Jew. It is the idea of transforming Palestine into a home for the Jews that Arabs resent and fight against. The fact that a Jew is a Jew has never prejudiced the Arabs against him. Before the war Jews enjoyed all the privileges and rights of citizenship. The question is not a religious one. For we see that Christians and Moslems alike, whose religions are not similar, unite in their hatred of Zionism . . .

In replying to the Delegation, Churchill said:

It is manifestly right that the Jews, who are scattered all over the world, should have a national centre and a national home where some of them may be reunited. And where else could that be but in this land of Palestine, with which for more than 3,000 years they have been intimately and profoundly associated? We think it will be good for the world, good for the Jews and good for the British Empire. But we also think it will be good for the Arabs who dwell in Palestine, and we intend that it shall be good for them, and that they shall not be sufferers or supplanted in the country in which they dwell or denied their share in all that makes for its progress and prosperity. And here I would draw your attention to the second part of the Balfour Declaration which solemnly and explicitly promises to the inhabitants of Palestine the fullest protection of their civil and political rights. I was sorry to hear in the paper you have just read that you do not regard that promise as of value. It seems to be a vital matter for you and one to which you should hold most firmly and for the exact fulfilment of which you should claim. If the one promise stands, so does the other; and we shall be judges as we faithfully fulfil them both.

[*Source*: Doreen Ingrams, ed., *Palestine Papers 1917–1922: Seeds of Conflict* (London: John Murray, 1972), pp. 118–19.]

## 147   Report of Palestine Royal Commission

After the 1936 uprising Britain began restricting Jewish immigration to Palestine despite the fact that increasing numbers of Jews were trying to flee persecution in Europe.

The continued impact of a highly intelligent and enterprising race, backed by large financial resources, on a comparatively poor indigenous community, on a different cultural level, may produce in time serious reactions. Can it be the duty of the Mandatory or indeed is it in the interests of the National Home itself to allow immigrants to come into the country in large numbers without any regard to an increasing hostility which from time to time finds expression in violent disorder? The issue is quite plain and should be squarely faced by everyone concerned. Do the Jewish people really wish that Palestine should afford a refuge to the maximum number of Jews which can be economically absorbed if the result is constant rebellion and repression? And, determined as we believe they are to fulfil the obligations undertaken in the Mandate, do the British people really wish that British lives should continue to be sacrificed to that end? We suggest that these questions can only be answered in the affirmative if it can be demonstrated beyond a doubt that there is no other way in which justice can be done and good faith maintained. [. . .]

Our recommendations are:

(i) Immigration should be reviewed and decided upon political, social and psychological as well as economic considerations. [. . .] A political 'high level' should be fixed at 12,000 a year for the next five years, to include Jews of every category. [. . .]

(ii) The definition of dependency should be revised. [. . .]
(iii) The abolition of certain categories dealing with members of the liberal professions and craftsmen, and the revision of the conditions governing the free entry of capitalists. [. . .]
(iv) The final allocation of immigration certificates should be subject to the approval of the High Commissioner.

[*Source*: Great Britain, Colonial Office, *Palestine Royal Commission: Report* (London: HMSO, 1937), pp. 221, 274.]

**148    Statement of the British Government on Palestine**

Forced to attempt to clarify its position with regard to the establishment of a Jewish homeland, the British government issued a statement on the future of the mandate in November 1938. Its proposed conference failed to reach agreement.

His Majesty's Government, after careful study of the Partition Commission's report, have reached the conclusion that this further examination has shown that the political, administrative and financial difficulties involved in the proposal to create independent Arab and Jewish States inside Palestine are so great that this solution of the problem is impracticable.

His Majesty's Government will therefore continue their responsibility for the government of the whole of Palestine. They are now faced with the problem of finding alternative means of meeting the needs of the difficult situation described by the Royal Commission which will be consistent with their obligations to the Arabs and the Jews. His Majesty's Government believe that it is possible to find these alternative means. They have already given much thought to the problem in the light of the reports of the Royal Commission and of the Partition Commission. It is clear that the surest foundation for peace and progress in Palestine would be an understanding between the Arabs and the Jews, and His Majesty's Government are prepared in the first instance to make a determined effort to promote such an understanding. With this end in view, they propose immediately to invite representatives of the Palestinian Arabs and of neighbouring States on the one hand and of the Jewish Agency on the other, to confer with them as soon as possible in London regarding future policy, including the question of immigration into Palestine. As regards the representation of the Palestinian Arabs, His Majesty's Government must reserve the right to refuse to receive those leaders whom they regard as responsible for the campaign of assassination and violence.

His Majesty's Government hope that these discussions in London may help to promote agreement as to future policy regarding Palestine. They attach great importance, however, to a decision being reached at an early date. Therefore, if the London discussions should not produce agreement within reasonable period of time, they will take their own decision in the light of their examination of the problem and of the discussions in London, and announce the policy which they propose to pursue.

[*Source*: Great Britain, *Palestine: Statement by His Majesty's Government in the United Kingdom* (London: HMSO, 1938), p. 4.]

## 149   Ch'en Chia-keng

Ch'en Chia-keng ('Tan Kah-Kee' in older references) was a Chinese intellectual and political leader in colonial Malaya. Here he describes the racial situation between the two world wars.

In the 1930's, during the depression, unemployment was constantly on the increase among men and women; the situation was particularly bad for the Overseas Chinese work force. The government of Malaya, for the benefit of the natives, improved irrigation, gave financial aid to people to plant paddy, and set the goal of self-sufficiency in grain production. The natives were given every kind of encouragement to engage in farming. However, native Malayans are lazy and unambitious, so the government's efforts met with minimal success. The Straits government in Singapore established a Chinese Secretariat, a special government agency to handle matters concerning its Chinese residents. Within the Secretariat was an advisory council. It was called the Chinese Advisory Board. There were 30 members, most of whom had originally come from China and they were appointed by the Secretariat for Chinese Affairs. They had no fixed terms of office and many of them were permanent appointees. When meetings were held they were chaired by the Secretary for Chinese Affairs. Although the Advisory Board had been set up, it was a token organization to gain the support of the Chinese. I was a Board member for several years [1923–33]. During the depression the natives had gained the right to cultivate paddy, but the Chinese had not been able to do so. However, the Chinese comprised half of the population of Malaya, and if Malaya was to become self-sufficient in food grains, it would be very difficult to attain this goal without them. Because of this, I proposed equal treatment for everyone and my motion was passed by the Board and submitted by the Secretary for Chinese Affairs to a higher level of government. Nothing came of my motion, and so I resigned from the Board. However, more and more Overseas Chinese continued to lose their jobs. Apart from those who had enough money to pay their passages home, each month tens of thousands were financed by the government to return to China. This serves to show how great the government's desire was to get rid of the Chinese!

[*Source*: A. H. C. Ward *et al.*, eds., *Memoirs of Tan Kah-Kee* (Singapore: Singapore University Press, 1994), pp. 277–8.]

## 150   Petition of plantation owners in Malaysia

European rubber plantation owners grew increasingly concerned about their safety and petitioned the colonial government for decisive action. The speaker at this meeting was H. H. Facer, a planters' representative. Note that Chinese labour contractors were also the targets of violence.

Now we do know out there that the subversive elements—call them Communists or what you will—are mainly of Chinese nationality, but they have been wise enough to use as their dupes Indians who may be classed as British nationals. We are quite convinced in our own minds that the use of these dupes is part of their planned procedure, for they know that those British nationals will not be banished. They give the orders, the stooges carry them out.

Having enjoyed immunity for so long, the criminal elements are coming out into the open. There are reports in the press of armed gangs appearing in the streets of small towns armed and unmasked. In Rengam village several murders were committed in sight of the police station. This will give you an idea of how bold they are getting. The police have advised planters to go about armed, and on a number of estates protection is given. This action is necessary even on estates where there is no dispute with labour at all. It bears out the statement of the O.S.P.C. which I read to you that the body responsible for the trouble does propose to make a move to eliminate Europeans. I can say that when I left Malaya, although there was no panic amongst planters they were definitely apprehensive as to the future. If you consider their situation living practically alone miles away from their neighbours, and many of them with no telephones, you will appreciate that they just haven't a chance if gangsters come along. There is no warning that the gangsters will be at a certain house at a certain time. You will understand the apprehension of the planters who do not know whether they are next on the list. In the case of the murders which were committed on the day I left, the subordinate staff in the office were told 'we are out for Europeans' and they were not molested, in fact they were told to go away.

Now, representations have been made to the High Commissioner that this would happen if stronger measures were not taken. I do not propose to enlarge on that point as Mr. Palmer and Mr. Shearn were among those who conveyed the warnings and they will no doubt inform you on that. I would like to say that not only are Europeans threatened. I have here a letter which was sent to the British Advisor, Johore Bahru by a union of contractors:—

'We most respectfully beg to bring the following facts for your urgent consideration and assistance.

Our Union represents about 60 Contractors who control over 6,000 rubber estate workers within the District of Johore Bahru.

Since the middle of the last month a lot of unrest has been caused in many estates in the Johore Bahru district and especially since the beginning of this month several cases of murder and criminal intimidations have also come to our knowledge. It is believed that Communist agitators are responsible for fatal attacks on some unarmed Contractors.

Our work has been mainly to assist the rubber producing Companies to keep peace and order in estates within our control. Since all these murders and criminal intimidations are the handiwork of the Communist agitators, we Contractors have had no peace of mind. We are in constant fear of being attacked while we supervise work during the day or while we are asleep at home. Most of the Communists pose as labourers and it is not possible for us to ascertain those who possess firearms.

In view of the above mentioned circumstances and in view of the fact that most of us are unarmed, we shall be very much obliged if you will be good enough to consider the matter sympathetically and see your way to give us adequate protection against similar dastardly attacks. If this is not practicable at an early date, we shall have no alternative but to abandon our contract work which may seriously affect the financial stability of the country.'

I have referred to the danger to Europeans—now the Chinese contractors are threatened, the men who provide the labour for the estates.

[*Source*: A. J. Stockwell, ed., *Malaya* (London: HMSO, 1995), vol. 3, pp. 22–3.]

## 151    Sir D. MacGillvray

The British hoped that a secular state school system would help to create a unified sense of Malayan nationalism and reduce ethnic differences; this memorandum on schools was produced by Sir D. MacGillvray on 14 July 1955 during the run-up to full self-government.

The different races in Malaya think of themselves primarily as Malays, Chinese or Indians and only secondarily, if at all, as Malayans. No plans for defence against communist aggression from without and subversion from within can have a full chance of success so long as the people are thus left without a common outlook on fundamental questions. It is therefore urgently necessary to create a united Malayan nation, aware and proud of being Malayan. This is not to say that a new and united Malaya would, by its mere existence, necessarily prevent the country from going communist or from seeking to join the neutrals. But it would provide one of the essential conditions—probably the most important—under which efforts to hold Malaya for the West would have a good chance of success.

The process of nation-building, although recognised as essential by the authorities and some sections of local opinion, has so far made slow progress. The situation can be radically changed by one means only, reforms in the educational system which will make it an effective stimulant to national consciousness. The need is for schools, dedicated to promoting Malayan unity, in which children of all races may grow up together, learning each his mother-tongue as a subject of study but being taught through the medium of a common language. The common language must be the *lingua franca* of the country, English. Only thus can racial exclusiveness, at present fostered by the vernacular system of education which predominates in Malaya, be broken down.

The desirability of building new schools of this kind has been officially accepted since the enactment of the Education Ordinance of 1952, in which they are described as 'English-medium National Schools'. But, owing partly to Chinese opposition and partly to lack of money, only one such National School has so far been brought into existence. [. . .]

The Federation Government have not the money to pay for this scheme. Moreover, although an elected Government in the Federation would be happy enough, if funds were available, to sanction expenditure of this order on education, it is unlikely that it would willingly devote the money to building schools of this particular kind. If, therefore the scheme is to go through Her Majesty's Government must bless it and 'underwrite' it financially. It is hoped that after the elections the new Government may be persuaded to proceed with the scheme from local resources on the understanding that Her Majesty's Government, when considering year by year the general financial needs of the country, would take the cost of this scheme into account, as they already take account of certain other of the Federation's financial commitments.

[*Source*: Stockwell, *Malaya*, vol. 3, pp. 132–3.]

## 152   Tunku Abdul Rahman

> Tunku Abdul Rahman would become the first prime minister of
> independent Malaya in 1957. In this memorandum he outlined his
> hopes for a British constitutional commission, hoping to allay fears
> about Malay and Islamic favouritism in his Alliance party. But a
> paragraph on the special position of Malays caused alarm among
> non-Malays, and in the British government.

We, the Alliance, comprise the three main political parties in the Federation
of Malaya: the United Malays National Organisation, the Malayan Chinese
Association and the Malayan Indian Congress, which have allied themselves
into a single movement for the sacred purpose of achieving independence for
this country. With 'Merdeka within 4 years' as our main platform, we were
returned to power by the electorate at all levels from local to Federal Councils with unprecedented success. We, therefore, represent the great majority
of the population of the Federation of Malaya.

The political testament, which we set out below, reflects the firm desire of
the majority of the peoples of this country for a form of government which
will ensure freedom, equality and unity of the new nation. We, therefore,
desire that the future constitution of this country must provide for the establishment of a sovereign and fully independent State in which the people shall
enjoy freedom and equality. This constitution shall also provide for a stable
democratic government and ensure, peace and harmony amongst all its
peoples. [. . .]

### Common nationality

The constitution should provide for nationality laws that would build a
peaceful and stable independent federation, with a contented and unified
people whose loyalty is unquestioned and undivided, so that, in due course,
the country can take its proper place in the comity of nations. To achieve this
end, it is essential to have a nationality law which provides for a common
nationality, to the exclusion of all others. [. . .]

### Special position of Malays

While we accept that in independent Malaysia, all nationals should be
accorded equal rights, privileges and opportunities and there must not be
discrimination on grounds of race or creed, we recognize the fact that the
Malays are the original sons of the soil and that they have a special position
arising from this fact, and also by virtue of the treaties made between the

British Government and the various sovereign Malay States. The Constitution should, therefore, provide that the Yang di-Pertuan Besar should have the special responsibility of safeguarding the special position of the Malays. In pursuance of this, the Constitution should give him powers to reserve for Malays a reasonable proportion of lands, posts in the public service, permits to engage in business or trade, where such permits are restricted and controlled by law, Government scholarships and such similar privileges accorded by the Government; but in pursuance of his further responsibility of safeguarding the legitimate interests of the other communities, the Constitution should also provide that any exercise of such powers should not in any way infringe the legitimate interests of the other communities or adversely affect or diminish the rights and opportunities at present enjoyed by them.

[*Source*: 'Political testament of the Alliance', 25 September 1956 in Stockwell, *Malaya*, vol. 3, pp. 307, 312, 315.]

| 153 | **Sir P. Liesching** |

British ministers hoped to avoid a repetition of the confrontation between South Africa and Britain over Ghana's application to join the Commonwealth; both Ghana and Malaya became Commonwealth members in 1957. In this letter the UK High Commissioner recognizes that it would be South Africa, and not the non-white former colonies, that would find itself increasingly marginalized.

Now that Ghana has been accepted by the Union Government, not without hesitation and difficulty, as a fellow member of the Commonwealth, I have been considering the prospects opened up for us here by the near approach to independence of the next candidate for membership, namely the Federation of Malaya.

It might be thought that the principle of accepting these colonies as Commonwealth members has now been swallowed by the Union and that since that awkward corner has been turned there will be no great difficulty in the future. This comforting conclusion might in the case of Malaya find support from the reflection that she is remote and non-African and that her independence will have none of the direct impact on South Africa that the emergence of Ghana will inevitably have, and is indeed already having. But the conclusion is, of course, far wide of the mark. Commonwealth membership for non-White countries, implying an eventual preponderance of non-White Prime Ministers at Commonwealth Prime Ministers meetings, is a matter of intense interest to Union Ministers—and could well in the long run be decisive for their attitude to the Commonwealth connexion. [. . .]

No doubt the Union Government's views on these matters are unacceptable to us and there is, I assume, no possibility of Malaya's progress to independence and Commonwealth membership being impeded on their account. But it is equally true that, unless we regard the Union's relationship with the Commonwealth as of no account, some attention must be paid to her Government's views. [. . .]

In the longer term the Union's continued membership of the Commonwealth is still an open question. The recent comments of Dr. Odendaal, the new National Party leader in the Transvaal (on which I shall be reporting separately) sufficiently indicates [sic] that the objective of the extreme Nationalists in that important province is still to take the Republic out of the Commonwealth—though that is by no means the end of the matter. On our side it may be that we are moving towards a situation in which we might ourselves be content to see her outside. But all this is for the longer term.

[*Source*: Sir P. Liesching to the Commonwealth Relations Office,
14 March 1957 in Stockwell, *Malaya*, vol. 3, pp. 364–5.]

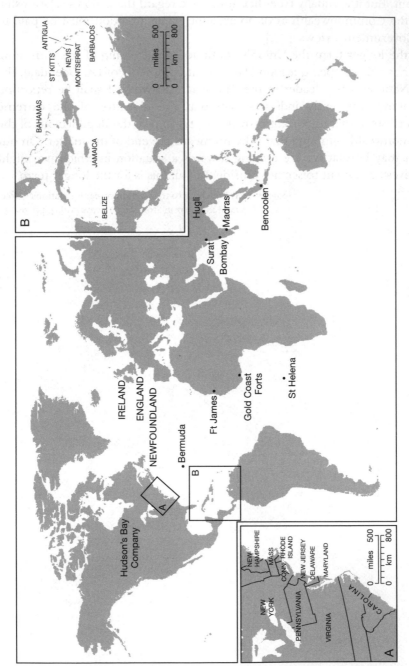

MAP 1.   England Overseas in 1689

**Inset B labels:** BAHAMAS, BELIZE, JAMAICA, ST KITTS, NEVIS, MONTSERRAT, ANTIGUA, BARBADOS
0 miles 500 / 0 km 800

**Main map labels:** Hudson's Bay Company, NEWFOUNDLAND, IRELAND, ENGLAND, Bermuda, Ft James, Gold Coast Forts, St Helena, Surat, Bombay, Hugli, Madras, Bencoolen

**Inset A labels:** NEW HAMPSHIRE, MASS, CONN, RHODE ISLAND, NEW YORK, NEW JERSEY, DELAWARE, PENNSYLVANIA, MARYLAND, VIRGINIA, CAROLINA
0 miles 500 / 0 km 800

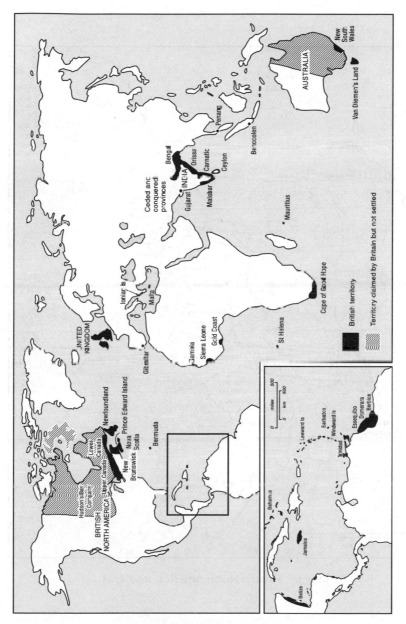

MAP 2. The British Empire in 1815

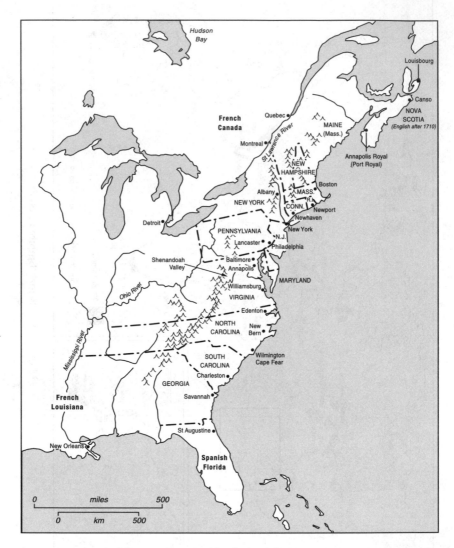

**Map 3.** Eastern North America, 1690–1748

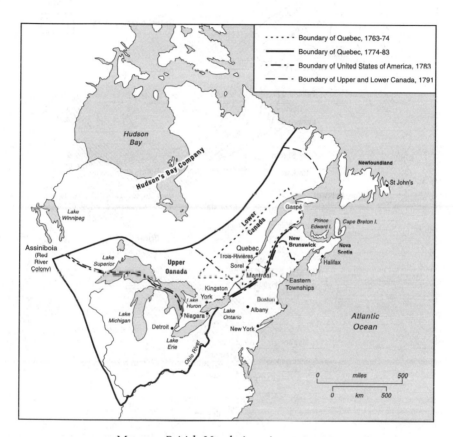

**Legend:**
- ······ Boundary of Quebec, 1763-74
- ——— Boundary of Quebec, 1774-83
- —·—·— Boundary of United States of America, 1783
- ——— Boundary of Upper and Lower Canada, 1791

Hudson
Bay

Hudson's Bay Company

Newfoundland

St John's

Lake
Winnipeg

Gaspé

Prince
Edward I.    Cape Breton I.

Lower Canada

Assiniboia
(Red
River
Colony)

Lake
Superior

Upper
Canada

Quebec
Trois-Rivières
Sorel

New
Brunswick

Nova
Scotia

Halifax

Montreal

Kingston

York

Lake
Huron

Eastern
Townships

Lake
Michigan

Niagara

Lake
Ontario

Boston

Albany

Detroit

Atlantic
Ocean

Lake
Erie

Ohio River

New York

0        miles        500

0        km        500

MAP 4.    British North America, 1760–1815

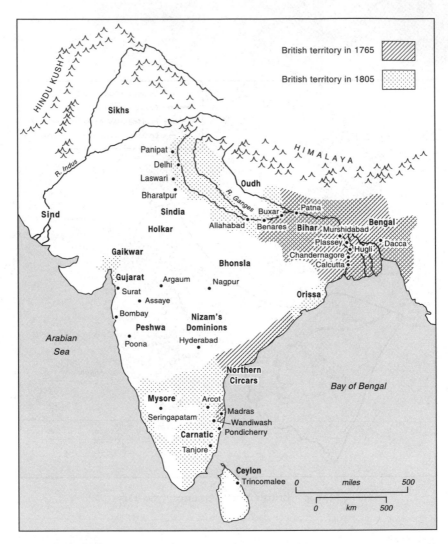

HINDU KUSH

Sikhs

R. Indus

HIMALAYA

Panipat

Delhi

Laswari

Bharatpur

Oudh

Sindia

R. Ganges

Buxar

Patna

Holkar

Allahabad

Benares

Bihar

Bengal

Sind

Murshidabad

Plassey

Dacca

Chandernagore

Hugli

Gaikwar

Calcutta

Gujarat

Argaum

Nagpur

Bhonsla

Surat

Assaye

Orissa

Bombay

Nizam's
Dominions

Arabian
Sea

Peshwa

Hyderabad

Poona

Northern
Circars

Bay of Bengal

Mysore

Arcot

Madras

Seringapatam

Wandiwash

Pondicherry

Carnatic

Tanjore

Ceylon

Trincomalee

0        miles        500

0        km        500

MAP 5.    The Growth of British Territorial Empire in India

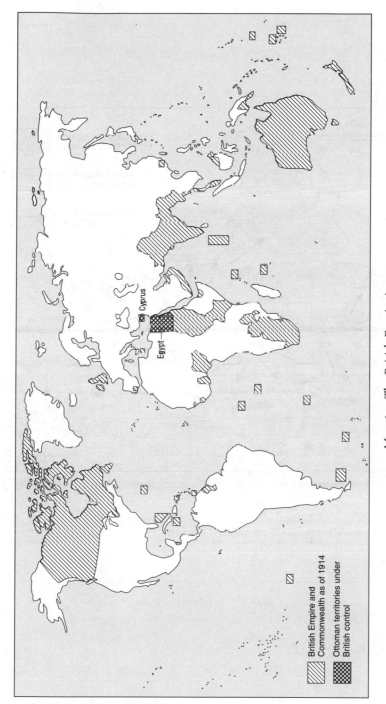

Cyprus

Egypt

British Empire and
Commonwealth as of 1914

Ottoman territories under
British control

MAP 5.   The British Empire in 1914

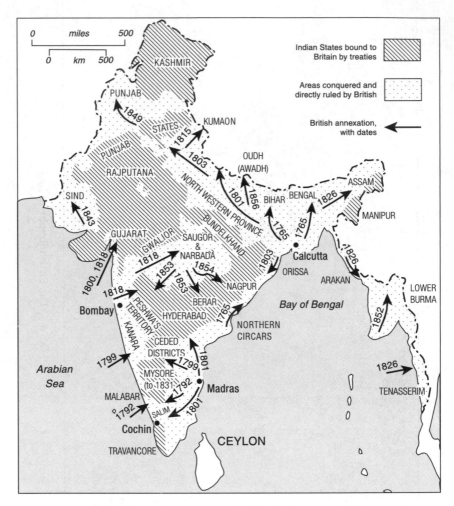

KASHMIR

*miles* 500

*km* 500

Indian States bound to
Britain by treaties

Areas conquered and
directly ruled by British

British annexation,
with dates

PUNJAB
*1849*
STATES
KUMAON
*1815*
*1803*
OUDH
(AWADH)
PUNJAB
RAJPUTANA
NORTH WESTERN PROVINCE
*1801*
*1856*
BIHAR
BENGAL
*1826*
ASSAM
SIND
*1843*
BUNDELKHAND
MANIPUR
GUJARAT
GWALIOR
SAUGOR
&
NARBADA
*1818*
*1853*
*1854*
*1803*
*1765*
Calcutta
*1800, 1818*
*1818*
PESHWA'S
TERRITORY
*1853*
BERAR
*1765*
NAGPUR
ORISSA
ARAKAN
LOWER
BURMA
Bombay
HYDERABAD
Bay of Bengal
KANARA
NORTHERN
CIRCARS
*1852*
Arabian
Sea
*1799*
CEDED
DISTRICTS
*1799*
*1801*
MYSORE
(to 1831)
*1792*
Madras
*1826*
MALABAR
*1792*
SALIM
*1801*
TENASSERIM
Cochin
TRAVANCORE
CEYLON

MAP 7.    Pre-Mutiny India

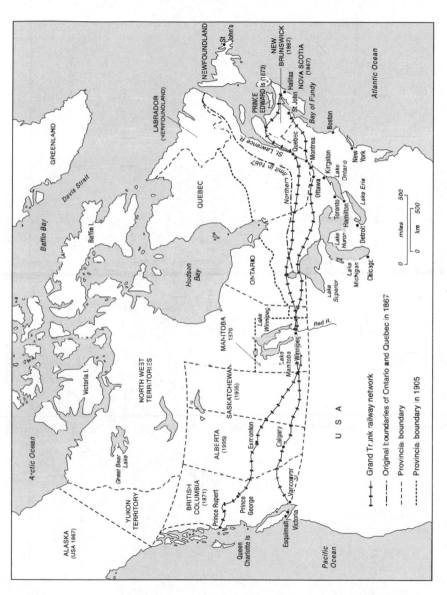

MAP 8. Canada, to 1905

Grand Trunk railway network
Original boundaries of Ontario and Quebec in 1867
Provincial boundary
Provincial boundary in 1905

ALASKA (USA 1867)
YUKON TERRITORY
BRITISH COLUMBIA (1871)
NORTH WEST TERRITORIES
ALBERTA (1905)
SASKATCHEWAN (1905)
MANITOBA 1870
ONTARIO
QUEBEC
LABRADOR (NEWFOUNDLAND)
NEWFOUNDLAND
GREENLAND

Arctic Ocean
Great Bear Lake
Victoria I.
Baffin I.
Baffin Bay
Davis Strait
Hudson Bay
Lake Winnipeg
Lake Manitoba
Queen Charlotte Is.
Prince Rupert
Prince George
Esquimalt
Victoria
Vancouver
Edmonton
Calgary
Winnipeg
Red R.
Lake Superior
Lake Michigan
Lake Huron
Lake Erie
Lake Ontario
Chicago
Detroit
Hamilton
Toronto
Ottawa
Kingston
Montreal
Quebec
St. Lawrence R.
Northern (built in 1867)
New York
Boston
Bay of Fundy
St. John
Halifax
PRINCE EDWARD Is (1873)
NEW BRUNSWICK (1867)
NOVA SCOTIA (1867)
St John's
Atlantic Ocean
Pacific Ocean
U S A

miles 500
km 500
0

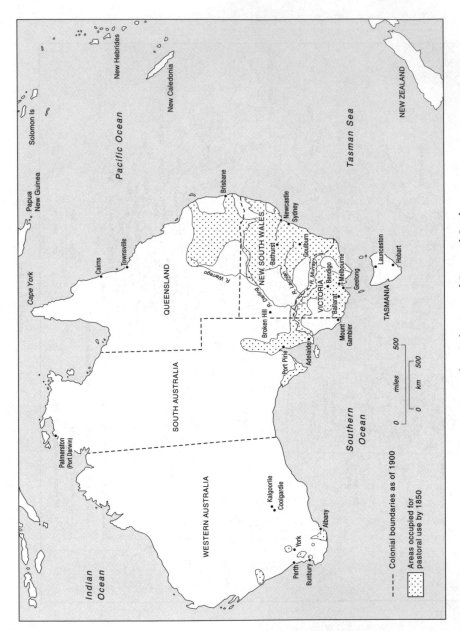

MAP 9. Australia: Colonies and Pastoral Settlement

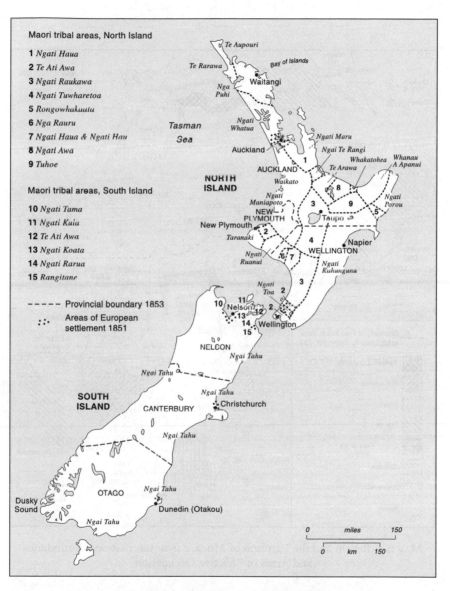

Maori tribal areas, North Island

**1** *Ngati Haua*
**2** *Te Ati Awa*
**3** *Ngati Raukawa*
**4** *Ngati Tuwharetoa*
**5** *Rongowhakuutu*
**6** *Nga Rauru*
**7** *Ngati Haua & Ngati Hau*
**8** *Ngati Awa*
**9** *Tuhoe*

Maori tribal areas, South Island

**10** *Ngati Tama*
**11** *Ngati Kuia*
**12** *Te Ati Awa*
**13** *Ngati Koata*
**14** *Ngati Rarua*
**15** *Rangitane*

---- Provincial boundary 1853
⋰ Areas of European settlement 1851

*Te Aupouri*
*Te Rarawa*
Bay of Islands
Waitangi
*Nga Puhi*
Tasman Sea
*Ngati Whatua*
Auckland
*Ngati Maru*
*Ngai Te Rangi*
*Whakatohea*
*Whanau A Apanui*
*Te Arawa*
**1**
AUCKLAND
NORTH ISLAND
*Waikato*
**8**
*Ngati Maniapoto*
*Ngati Porou*
**3**
**9**
**5**
NEW PLYMOUTH
New Plymouth
*Taranaki*
**2**
Taupo
**4**
*Ngati Ruanui*
**6 7**
WELLINGTON
Napier
*Ngati Kuhungunu*
*Ngati Toa*
**2**
**3**
**11**
**10**
Nelson
**13**
**12**
**2**
**14**
Wellington
**15**
NELSON
*Ngai Tahu*
*Ngai Tahu*
SOUTH ISLAND
CANTERBURY
*Ngai Tahu*
Christchurch
*Ngai Tahu*
Dusky Sound
OTAGO
*Ngai Tahu*
Dunedin (Otakou)
*Ngai Tahu*

0        miles        150
0        km        150

MAP 10.   New Zealand: Native Peoples and White Settlers

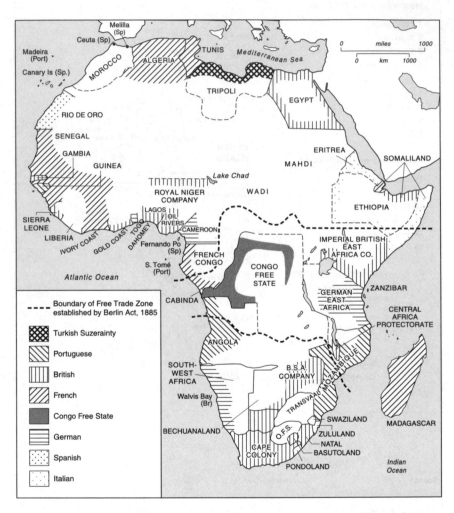

Melilla
(Sp)
Ceuta (Sp)
Madeira
(Port)
Canary Is (Sp.)
MOROCCO
ALGERIA
TUNIS *Mediterranean Sea*
TRIPOLI
EGYPT
RIO DE ORO
SENEGAL
GAMBIA
GUINEA
*Lake Chad*
ROYAL NIGER
COMPANY
WADI
ERITREA
MAHDI
SOMALILAND
ETHIOPIA
SIERRA
LEONE
LIBERIA
IVORY COAST
GOLD COAST
TOGO
DAHOMEY
LAGOS
OIL
RIVERS
CAMEROON
Fernando Po
(Sp)
S. Tomé
(Port)
FRENCH
CONGO
IMPERIAL BRITISH
EAST
AFRICA CO.
ZANZIBAR
*Atlantic Ocean*
CABINDA
CONGO
FREE
STATE
GERMAN
EAST
AFRICA
CENTRAL
AFRICA
PROTECTORATE
ANGOLA
SOUTH-
WEST
AFRICA
B.S.A.
COMPANY
MOZAMBIQUE
Walvis Bay
(Br)
TRANSVAAL
MADAGASCAR
BECHUANALAND
O.F.S.
SWAZILAND
ZULULAND
NATAL
BASUTOLAND
*Indian
Ocean*
CAPE
COLONY
PONDOLAND

0    *miles*    1000
0    km    1000

- - - Boundary of Free Trade Zone
established by Berlin Act, 1885

Turkish Suzerainty

Portuguese

British

French

Congo Free State

German

Spanish

Italian

MAP II.   Britain and the Partition of Africa, *c*.1891: International Boundaries
and Areas of Effective Occupation

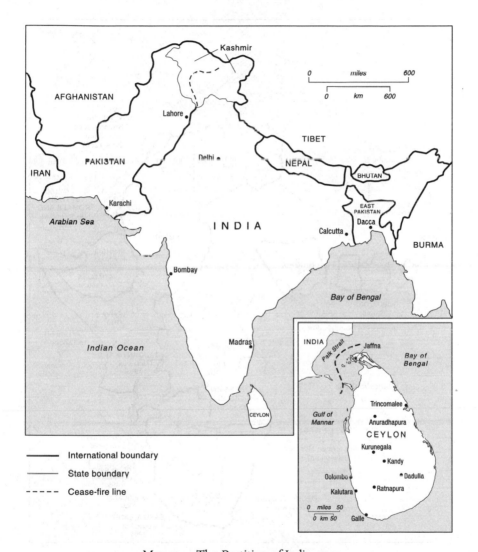

MAP 12.   The Partition of India, 1947

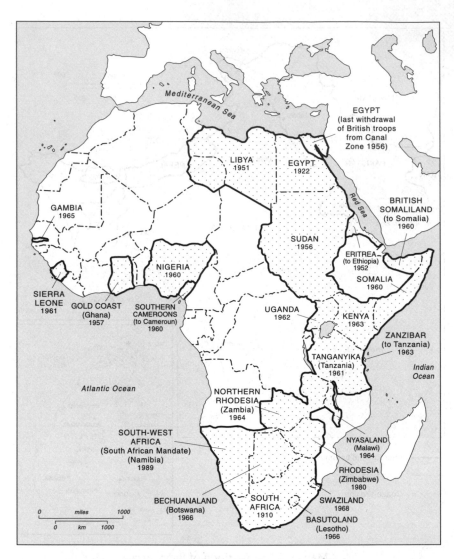

MAP 13. British Decolonization in Africa

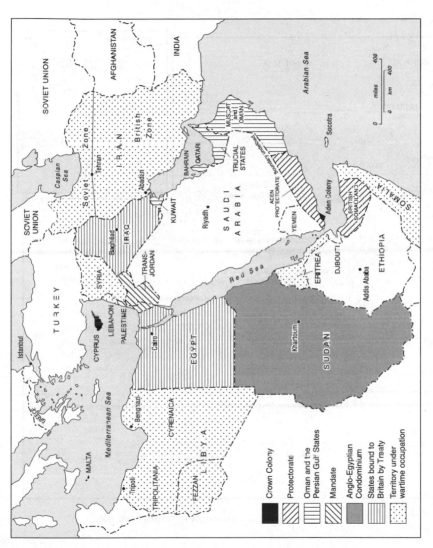

MAP 14. The Middle East in 1945

Crown Colony

Protectorate

Oman and the
Persian Gulf States

Mandate

Anglo-Egyptian
Condominium

States bound to
Britain by Treaty

Territory under
wartime occupation

MAP 15.   British Decolonization in South-East Asia

# Chronology

| DATE | BRITAIN AND EUROPE | THE AMERICAS AND CARIBBEAN | AFRICA | ASIA AND THE PACIFIC |
|---|---|---|---|---|
| 1497 | | John Cabot's first voyage to North America | | |
| 1558 | Accession of Elizabeth I | | | |
| 1564 | | | John Hawkins's slaving voyages begin | |
| 1576 | | Martin Frobisher explores Newfoundland | | |
| 1577 | | | | Francis Drake circumnavigates the globe |
| 1584 | | Walter Raleigh's expedition to South America | | |
| 1585 | | First Virginia settlement | | |
| 1588 | England defeats the Spanish Armada | | | |
| 1600 | | | | English East India Company chartered |

*Chronology—cont.*

| DATE | BRITAIN AND EUROPE | THE AMERICAS AND CARIBBEAN | AFRICA | ASIA AND THE PACIFIC |
|---|---|---|---|---|
| 1603 | Accession of James I and the Union of Crowns | | | |
| 1607 | | First permanent Virginia settlement | | |
| 1612 | | Settlement of Bermuda begins | | |
| 1618 | Thirty Years War 1618–48 | | | |
| 1620 | | Voyage of the *Mayflower* | | |
| 1622 | | The 'Virginia Massacre' | | |
| 1627 | | Colonization of Barbados | | |
| 1632 | | | Cormantine and other slave depots established on west African coast | |
| 1639 | | | | Grant of Madras to England |
| 1642 | English Civil War 1642–6 | | | |
| 1651 | First Navigation Act | | | |
| 1655 | | Jamaica taken from Spain | | |

|  |  | | |
|---|---|---|---|
| 1660 | Restoration of Charles I | | |
| 1661 | White population of Virginia reaches 24,000 | | England gains Bombay |
| 1662 | | Company of Royal Adventurers into Africa (later Royal African Company) enters the slave trade | |
| 1664 | England conquers New Netherland | | |
| 1670 | Hudson's Bay Company chartered | | |
| 1688 | The 'Glorious Revolution'; accession of William and Mary in 1689 | | |
| 1690 | | | England founds trading port at Calcutta |
| 1696 | Board of Trade established | | |
| 1698 | | Slave trade opened to private traders | |
| 1707 | Act of Union between England and Scotland | | |
| 1713 | Treaty of Utrecht | | |

*Chronology—cont.*

| DATE | BRITAIN AND EUROPE | THE AMERICAS AND CARIBBEAN | AFRICA | ASIA AND THE PACIFIC |
|---|---|---|---|---|
| 1740 | | | | George Anson's circumnavigation begins |
| 1744 | | | | British/French hostilities begin in India |
| 1756 | Seven Years War 1756–63 | | | Nawab of Bengal captures Calcutta |
| 1757 | | | | Robert Clive defeats Nawab at Battle of Plassey |
| 1760 | | New France surrenders | | |
| 1761 | | | | Capture of French settlement at Pondicherry |
| 1763 | Treaty of Paris | | | |
| 1765 | | Stamp Act to tax colonies; riots in America (Act repealed in 1766) | | Mughal Emperor grants Britain *diwani* of Bengal |
| 1768 | | | | Start of Captain James Cook's first voyage |
| 1773 | | The 'Boston Tea Party' | | |

|  |  |
|---|---|
| 1774 | Quebec Act recognizes Catholicism and French civil law |
| 1775 | War of American Independence 1775–83 |
| 1776 | Declaration of American Independence |
| 1783 | Treaty of Versailles |
| 1784 | Loyalist settlement in Canada; India Act passed to create some government control |
| 1786 | First British settlement on Malay coast at Penang |
| 1787 | Sierra Leone established as settlement for freed slaves |
| 1788 | African Association founded; Trial of Warren Hastings begins; establishment of penal colony of New South Wales |
| 1790 | 'Nootka Crisis' with Spain over north Pacific trade |
| 1791 | Canada Act establishes colonies of Upper and Lower Canada |

*Chronology—cont.*

| DATE | BRITAIN AND EUROPE | THE AMERICAS AND CARIBBEAN | AFRICA | ASIA AND THE PACIFIC |
|------|--------------------|-----------------------------|--------|----------------------|
| 1793 | French Revolutionary War 1793–1802 | | | Macartney embassy to China |
| 1795 | | | British occupation of Cape of Good Hope | |
| 1799 | | | | British conquest of Mysore |
| 1802 | Treaty of Amiens | | | |
| 1803 | Napoleonic War 1803–15 | | | |
| 1807 | Abolition of the slave trade | | | |
| 1812 | 1812–14 war with USA over border with Canada | | | |
| 1813 | | | | East India Company Charter Act opens the India trade and permits missionaries |
| 1815 | Treaty of Vienna | | | |
| 1819 | | | | Stamford Raffles acquires Singapore |

|  | | | |
|---|---|---|---|
| 1824 | Britain recognizes independent republics in Latin America | | |
| 1829 | | | Entire Australian continent declared British territory |
| 1833 | Britain seizes Falkland Islands / Abolition of slavery throughout the empire | | EIC monopoly on China trade abolished |
| 1837 | Rebellions in Upper and Lower Canada 1837–8 | | |
| 1839 | | | First Opium War begins with China |
| 1840 | Colonial Land and Emigration Commission appointed | | Treaty of Waitangi makes New Zealand a British colony |
| 1842 | | | Treaty of Nanking ends first Opium War with China |
| 1844 | | Britain begins direct rule in Gold Coast | |
| 1846 | Western USA/BNA border set at 49th parallel | | |
| 1849 | Navigation Acts repealed | | |

| DATE | BRITAIN AND EUROPE | THE AMERICAS AND CARIBBEAN | AFRICA | ASIA AND THE PACIFIC |
| --- | --- | --- | --- | --- |
| 1853 | | | David Livingstone traverses African continent | |
| 1857 | | | | Indian Rebellion begins |
| 1858 | | | | End of Indian Rebellion; direct rule of India begins |
| 1860 | | | | Maori War begins |
| 1867 | | BNA Act creates the Canadian confederation | | |
| 1874 | Benjamin Disraeli becomes Prime Minister | | Suez Canal opens | Britain annexes Fiji |
| 1876 | Queen Victoria is made 'Empress of India' | Canadian Pacific Railway completes cross-country link | Egypt's bankruptcy results in Anglo-French control | |
| 1877 | | | Britain annexes the Transvaal | |
| 1880 | Machine guns and semi-automatic rifles proliferate | | | |
| 1881 | | | | British North Borneo Company chartered |

|  | | |
|---|---|---|
| 1882 | Britain bombards Alexandria and occupies Egypt | |
| 1884 | West Africa Conference in Berlin outlines spheres of influence | |
| 1885 | Death of General Gordon in the Sudan | Indian National Congress formed |
| | Colonial Defence Committee established | |
| 1886 | Anglo-German agreement on spheres of influence in eastern Africa | Britain annexes Burma |
| | Colonial and Indian Exhibition held in London | |
| 1888 | Imperial British East Africa Company chartered | Sarawak, North Borneo, and Brunei become British protectorates |
| 1889 | British South Africa Company chartered | |
| | Conference in Berlin outlines spheres of influence in the Pacific | |
| 1891 | Anglo-Portuguese treaty outlines spheres of influence in south-east Africa | |
| 1895 | 'Jameson Raid' on Transvaal; East African Protectorate established | |
| | Joseph Chamberlain becomes Secretary of State for the Colonies | |

*Chronology—cont.*

| DATE | BRITAIN AND EUROPE | THE AMERICAS AND CARIBBEAN | AFRICA | ASIA AND THE PACIFIC |
|---|---|---|---|---|
| 1898 | | Spanish–American War | Anglo-French Agreement on west Africa | |
| 1899 | | Canada and other colonies contribute troops to South African War | South African War 1899–1902 | German–British convention outlines rights in Pacific islands |
| 1901 | Public rejoicing over relief of Mafeking in south Africa; death of Queen Victoria | | Britain annexes Asante in west Africa | Australian colonies combine into the Commonwealth of Australia |
| 1902 | Preferential tariffs agreed with Canada, Australia, and NZ | | | Pacific Cable completes all-British global telegraph system |
| 1906 | | | | Muslim League formed in India |
| 1907 | Self-governing colonies now called 'Dominions'; Dominions department created within Colonial Office | | | |

|  | | | |
|---|---|---|---|
| 1910 | First Imperial Conference held in London (1911) | Union of South Africa established | |
| 1911 | First Imperial Conference held in London | | |
| 1912 | | African National Congress founded in South Africa | |
| 1914 | First World War 1914–18; Canada automatically at war | Unification of Northern and Southern Nigeria; Britain makes Egypt a protectorate; African colonies automatically at war | Australia, New Zealand, India, and Pacific island colonies automatically at war |
| 1917 | Imperial War Conference agrees to include India; United States enters the war | | |
| 1919 | Treaty of Versailles creates League of Nations and mandate system | 'Balfour Declaration' promises national homeland for Jews | 'Amritsar Massacre' in India |
| 1920 | | National Congress of British West Africa formed | |
| 1922 | | Britain recognizes Egyptian independence but retains control of Suez Canal | |

*Chronology—cont.*

| DATE | BRITAIN AND EUROPE | THE AMERICAS AND CARIBBEAN | AFRICA | ASIA AND THE PACIFIC |
|------|--------------------|-----------------------------|--------|----------------------|
| 1925 | Dominions Office separates from Colonial Office | | | |
| 1929 | Colonial Development Act passed | | | |
| 1930 | Round Table Conference on India | | | Gandhi leads 'Salt March' civil disobedience campaign |
| 1931 | Statute of Westminster grants full independence to Dominions | | | |
| 1932 | Ottawa Conference establishes 'Imperial Preference' tariff system | | | Gandhi imprisoned; Indian National Congress banned |
| 1936 | Death of King George V; abdication crisis of Edward VIII; accession of George VI | | Arab revolt in Palestine | |

|  | | | |
|---|---|---|---|
| 1939 | Second World War 1939–45 | Canada declares war independently | Australia and New Zealand declare war independently |
| 1941 | | United States enters the war | South Africa declares war independently |
| 1942 | | | Japan captures Singapore |
| 1945 | Clement Attlee's Labour government elected | | |
| 1947 | | | Independence of India and Pakistan |
| 1948 | | Beginning of apartheid era in South Africa; Britain withdraws from Palestine; riots in Gold Coast | Gandhi assassinated; state of emergency declared in Malaya |
| 1951 | | | ANZUS defence treaty between Australia, New Zealand, and USA |
| 1952 | Accession of Queen Elizabeth II | Mau-Mau rebellion in Kenya | |
| 1956 | | Suez Crisis | |
| 1957 | | Ghanaian independence | Malayan independence |

| DATE | BRITAIN AND EUROPE | THE AMERICAS AND CARIBBEAN | AFRICA | ASIA AND THE PACIFIC |
|---|---|---|---|---|
| 1960 | | | Nigerian independence; Sharpeville Massacre in South Africa | |
| 1961 | Britain unsuccessfully applies to join European Economic Community (EEC) | | Sierra Leone and Tanzania independent; South Africa leaves the Commonwealth | |
| 1962 | | Independence of Jamaica and Trinidad | Ugandan independence; arrest of Nelson Mandela, leader of ANC in South Africa | Independence of Western Samoa in south Pacific |
| 1963 | | | Independence of Kenya and Zanzibar | |
| 1964 | | | Malawi (Nyasaland) and Zambia (Northern Rhodesia) become independent | |
| 1965 | Commonwealth Secretariat established in London | | Gambia and Lesotho independent | Cook Islands independence |

|  |  |
|---|---|
| 1966 | Independence of Guyana and Barbados |
| 1966 | Lesotho (Basutoland) and Botswana (Bechuanaland) independent |
| 1968 | Independence of Mauritius and Swaziland |
| 1968 | Nauru independent |
| 1970 | Independence of Fiji |
| 1973 | Britain joins EEC |
| 1978 | Independence of Tuvalu (Ellice Islands) |
| 1979 | Election of Conservative government under Margaret Thatcher |
| 1979 | Lancaster House conference on Rhodesia |
| 1979 | Independence of Kiribati (Gilbert Islands) |
| 1980 | Zimbabwe (Rhodesia) becomes independent |
| 1980 | Independence of Vanuatu (New Hebrides) |
| 1982 | Britain defeats Argentinian forces after invasion of the Falkland Islands |
| 1994 | Nelson Mandela elected President of South Africa; South Africa rejoins the Commonwealth |
| 1997 | Britain returns Hong Kong to Chinese rule |

# Select Bibliography

GENERAL OVERVIEWS

C. A. BAYLY, *Imperial Meridian: The British Empire and the World 1780–1830* (London; New York: Longman, 1989).

P. J. CAIN and A. G. HOPKINS, *British Imperialism: Innovation and Expansion 1688–1914* (London: Longman, 1993).

——*British Imperialism: Crisis and Deconstruction 1914–1990* (London: Longman, 1993).

R. HYAM, *Britain's Imperial Century, 1815–1914: A Study of Empire and Expansion*, 2nd edn. (London: Macmillan, 1993).

LAWRENCE JAMES, *The Rise and Fall of the British Empire* (London: Abacus, 1995).

DENIS JUDD, *Empire: The British Imperial Experience, from 1765 to the Present* (London: HarperCollins, 1996).

T. O. LLOYD, *The British Empire 1558–1995*, 2nd edn. (Oxford; New York: Oxford University Press, 1996).

WM. ROGER LOUIS, ed., *The Oxford History of the British Empire*, 5 vols. (Oxford: Oxford University Press, 1998/1999).

P. J. MARSHALL, ed., *The Cambridge Illustrated History of the British Empire* (Cambridge: Cambridge University Press, 1996).

J. MORRIS, *Heaven's Command: An Imperial Progress* (London: Faber, 1973); *Pax Britannica: The Climax of an Empire* (London: Faber, 1968); *Farewell the Trumpets: An Imperial Retreat* (London: Faber, 1978).

A. N. PORTER, ed., *Atlas of British Overseas Expansion* (London: Routledge, 1991).

BERNARD PORTER, *The Lion's Share: A Short History of British Imperialism 1850–1995*, 3rd edn. (London; New York: Longman, 1996).


THE EARLY EMPIRE

BERNARD BAILYN and PHILIP D. MORGAN, *Strangers within the Realm: Cultural Margins of the First British Empire* (Chapel Hill, NC: University of North Carolina Press, 1991).

A. CALDER, *Revolutionary Empire: The Rise of the English-Speaking Empires from the Fifteenth Century to the 1780s* (London: Jonathan Cape, 1981).

ANTHONY PAGDEN, *Lords of All the World: Ideologies of Empire in Spain, Britain and France, c.1500–c.1800* (New Haven: Yale University Press, 1995).

DAVID B. QUINN, *England and the Discovery of America, 1481–1620* (New York: Knopf, 1974).

G. V. SCAMMELL, *The First Imperial Age: European Overseas Expansion c.1400–1715* (London: Unwin Hyman, 1989).

IAN K. STEELE, *The English Atlantic, 1675–1740: An Exploration of Communication and Community* (Oxford; New York: Oxford University Press, 1986).

## THE EMPIRE AND SLAVERY

R. ANSTEY, *The Atlantic Slave Trade and British Abolition, 1760–1810* (London: Macmillan, 1975).

K. G. DAVIES, *The Royal African Company* (London; New York: Longmans, Green, 1957).

CLARE MIDGLEY, *Women Against Slavery: The British Campaigns, 1780–1870* (London; New York: Routledge, 1992).

KENNETH MORGAN, *Bristol and the Atlantic Trade in the Eighteenth Century* (Cambridge: Cambridge University Press, 1993).

HOWARD TEMPERLEY, *British Antislavery, 1833–1870* (London: Longman, 1972).

JOHN THORNTON, *Africa and Africans in the Making of the Atlantic World, 1400–1680* (Cambridge: Cambridge University Press, 1992).

J. R. WARD, *British West Indian Slavery, 1750–1834* (Oxford: Oxford University Press, 1988).


## THE 'DOMINIONS'

JAMES BELICH, *Making peoples: a history of the New Zealanders, from Polynesian settlement to the end of the nineteenth century* (Honolulu: University of Hawaii Press, 1996).

GEOFFREY BOLTON, ed., *The Oxford History of Australia*, 5 vols. (Melbourne; New York. Oxford University Press, 1986– ).

J. M. BUMSTED, *A history of the Canadian peoples* (Don Mills, ON: Oxford University Press, 1998).

JOHN EDDY and DERYCK SCHREUDER, eds., *The Rise of Colonial Nationalism: Australia, New Zealand, Canada, and South Africa First Assert their Nationalities, 1880–1914* (Sydney. Allen & Unwin, 1988).

RICHARD ELPHICK and HERMANN GILIOMEE, eds., *The Shaping of South African Society, 1652–1840*, 2nd edn. (Middletown, CN: Wesleyan University Press, 1989).

TIMOTHY KEEGAN, *Colonial South Africa and the Origins of the Racial Order* (Toronto: Canadian Scholars' Press, 1997).

J. M. WARD, *Colonial Self-Government: The British Experience 1759–1856* (London: Macmillan, 1976).


## INDIA AND THE TROPICAL EMPIRE

C. A. BAYLY, *Indian Society and the Making of the British Empire* (Cambridge: Cambridge University Press, 1988).

A. A. BOAHEN, *Africa under Colonial Domination 1880–1935* (London; Berkeley: James Currey, University of California Press, and UNESCO, 1990).

JUDITH M. BROWN, *Modern India: The Origins of an Asian Democracy*, 2nd edn. (Oxford: Oxford University Press, 1994).

N. CHARLESWORTH, *British Rule and the Indian Economy, 1800 to 1914* (London: Macmillan, 1982).

P. D. CURTIN, *The Image of Africa: British Ideas and Action, 1780–1850* (London: Macmillan, 1964).

PHILIP LAWSON, *The East India Company: A History* (London; New York: Longman, 1993).

W. David McIntyre, *The Imperial Frontier in the Tropics, 1865–75* (London: Macmillan, 1967).

W. P. Morrell, *Britain in the Pacific Islands* (Oxford: Oxford University Press, 1960).

R. Robinson and J. A. Gallagher with A. Denny, *Africa and the Victorians: The Official Mind of Imperialism*, 2nd edn. (London: Macmillan, 1981).

Nicholas Tarling, *Imperial Britain in South-East Asia* (Kuala Lumpur: Oxford University Press, 1975).


IMPERIAL BRITAIN

Patrick Brantlinger, *Rule of Darkness: British Literature and Imperialism, 1830–1914* (Ithaca: Cornell University Press, 1988).

Annie E. Coombes, *Reinventing Africa: Museums, Material Culture and Popular Imagination in Late Victorian and Edwardian England* (New Haven; London: Yale University Press, 1994).

John M. MacKenzie, ed., *Imperialism and Popular Culture* (Manchester: Manchester University Press, 1986).

Peter N. Miller, *Defining the Common Good: Empire, Religion, and Philosophy in Eighteenth-Century Britain* (Cambridge: Cambridge University Press, 1994).

P. B. Rich, *Race and Empire in British Politics*, 2nd edn. (Cambridge: Cambridge University Press, 1990).

B. R. Tomlinson, *Ideologies of the Raj* (Cambridge; New York: Cambridge University Press, 1994).

Kathleen Wilson, *The Sense of the People: Politics, Culture and Imperialism in England, 1715–1785* (Cambridge: Cambridge University Press, 1995).


THE END OF EMPIRE

M. Beloff, *Imperial Sunset*, 2nd edn., 2 vols. (London: Macmillan, 1987).

John Darwin, *Britain and Decolonisation: The Retreat from Empire in the Post-War World* (Basingstoke: Macmillan, 1988).

J. A. Gallagher, *The Decline, Revival and Fall of the British Empire* (Cambridge: Cambridge University Press, 1982).

John D. Hargreaves, *Decolonization in Africa*, 2nd edn. (London; New York: Longman, 1996).

R. F. Holland, *European Decolonization, 1918–1981: an introductory survey* (Basingstoke: Macmillan, 1985).

D. A. Low, *The Eclipse of Empire* (Cambridge: Cambridge University Press, 1991).

W. David McIntyre, *British Decolonization, 1946–1997* (New York: St. Martin's Press, 1998).

Nicholas J. White, *Decolonisation: the British experience since 1945* (London; New York: Longman, 1999).


THE COMMONWEALTH

Dennis Austin, *The Commonwealth and Britain* (London; New York: Routledge & Kegan Paul, 1988).

W. Dale, *The Modern Commonwealth* (London: Butterworths, 1983).

Nicholas Mansergh, *The Commonwealth Experience*, 2nd edn., 2 vols. (London: Macmillan, 1982).

W. David McIntyre, *The Significance of the Commonwealth, 1965–90* (Basingstoke: Macmillan, 1991).

# Acknowledgements

Achebe, Chinua, *Things Fall Apart* (Heinemann: London, 1984).

Beckles, Hilary McD., 'The "Hub of Empire": The Caribbean and Britain in the Seventeenth Century', in Nicholas Canny (ed.), *The Origins of Empire: British Overseas Enterprise to the Close of the Seventeenth Century*, vol. 1 of *The Oxford History of the British Empire* (Oxford and New York: Oxford University Press, 1998).

Bennett, George, *The Concept of Empire: From Burke to Attlee, 1774–1947* (London: A. and C. Black).

Bradley, Kenneth, *The Diary of a District Officer* (London: Thomas Nelson and Sons, 1947; orig. publ. 1943).

Charlton, Michael, *The Last Colony in Africa: Diplomacy and the Independence of Rhodesia* (Oxford: Oxford University Press, 1990).

Cressy, David, *Coming Over: Migration and Communication between England and New England in the Seventeenth Century* (Cambridge and New York: Cambridge University Press, 1987).

Darwin, John, *The End of the British Empire: The Historical Debate* (Oxford: Blackwell, 1991).

Fyfe, Christopher, *Sierra Leone Inheritance* (London: Oxford University Press, 1964).

Government of Rhodesia, *For the Record* (Salisbury: Government Printer, 1968).

Huxley, Elspeth, *The Flame Trees of Thika: Memories of an African Childhood* (London: Chatto and Windus, 1959).

Jeffrey, Keith, 'The Second World War', in Judith M. Brown and Wm. Roger Louis (eds.), *The Twentieth Century*, vol. 4 of *The Oxford History of the British Empire* (Oxford and New York: Oxford University Press, 1998).

Jordan, Winthrop D., *The White Man's Burden: Historical Origins of Racism in the United States* (New York: Oxford University Press, 1974).

Liberation Support Movement, *Zimbabwe: The Final Advance, Documents on the Zimbabwe Liberation Movement* (Oakland, CA: Liberation Support Movement Press, 1978).

Lynn, Martin, 'British Policy, Trade, and Informal Empire in the Mid-Nineteenth Century', in Andrew Porter (ed.), *The Nineteenth Century*, vol. 3 of *The Oxford History of the British Empire* (Oxford and New York: Oxford University Press, 1998).

McIntyre, David W., *The Significance of the Commonwealth, 1965–90* (London: Macmillan, 1991).

Mackenzie, John M., 'The Popular Culture of Empire in Britain', in Judith M. Brown and Wm. Roger Louis (eds.), *The Twentieth Century*, vol. 4 of *The Oxford History of the British Empire* (Oxford and New York: Oxford University Press, 1998).

Marshall, P. J., '1783–1870: An Expanding Empire' and '1870–1819: The Empire Under Threat' in Marshall, (ed.), *The Cambridge Illustrated History of the British Empire* (Cambridge: Cambridge University Press, 1996).

Moon, Penderel, *Divide and Quit: An Eyewitness Account of the Partition of India* (Delhi: Oxford University Press, 1998). © The Estate of Sir Penderel Moon, 1961.

Porter, Andrew, 'Trusteeship, Anti-Slavery, and Humanitarianism', in Andrew Porter (ed.), *The Nineteenth Century*, vol. 3 of *The Oxford History of the British Empire* (Oxford and New York: Oxford University Press, 1998).

Ray, Rajat Kanta, 'Indian Society and the Establishment of British Supremacy, 1765–1818', in P. J. Marshall, ed., *The Eighteenth Century*, vol. 2 of *The Oxford History of the British Empire* (Oxford and New York: Oxford University Press, 1998).

Richter, Daniel K., 'Native Peoples of North America and the Eighteenth-Century British Empire', in P. J. Marshall (ed.), *The Eighteenth Century*, vol. 2 of *The Oxford History of the British Empire* (Oxford and New York: Oxford University Press, 1998).

Rose, Deborah Bird, *Hidden Histories: black stories from Victoria River Downs, Humbert River and Wave Hill Stations* (Canberra: Aboriginal Studies Press, 1991).

Said, Edward W., *Orientalism* (New York: Pantheon, 1978).

Shy, John, 'The American Colonies, 1748–1783', in P. J. Marshall (ed.), *The Eighteenth Century*, vol. 2 of *The Oxford History of the British Empire* (Oxford and New York: Oxford University Press, 1998).

Strobel, Margaret, *White Women and the Second British Empire* (Bloomington: Indiana University Press, 1991).

Parliamentary copyright material is reproduced with the permission of the controller of Her Majesty's Stationery Office on behalf of Parliament.

# Index

# Approaches to curriculum management

OPEN UNIVERSITY PRESS

# Management in Education Series

## Editor
**Tony Bush**

Senior Lecturer in Educational Policy and Management
at The Open University

The series comprises five volumes which cover important topics within the field of educational management. The articles present examples of theory and practice in school and college management. The authors discuss many of the major issues of relevance to educational managers in the post-Education Reform Act era.

The five readers are components of The Open University M.A. in Education module *E818 Management in Education*. Further information about this course and the M.A. programme may be obtained by writing to the Higher Degrees Office, Open University, PO Box 49, Walton Hall, Milton Keynes, MK7 6AD.

# Approaches to curriculum management

EDITED BY
**Margaret Preedy**
at The Open University

OPEN UNIVERSITY PRESS
MILTON KEYNES · PHILADELPHIA
in association with The Open University

Open University Press
Celtic Court
22 Ballmoor
Buckingham
MK18 1XW

*and*
1900 Frost Road, Suite 101
Bristol, PA 19007, USA

First Published 1989
Reprinted 1992

**British Library Cataloguing in Publication Data**
Approaches to curriculum management. – (Management in
    education)
    1. Great Britain.   Schools.   Curriculum.   Planning
    I. Preedy, Margaret   II. Series
    375'.001'0941

    ISBN 0-335-09249-7
        0-335-09248-9 (paper)

**Library of Congress Cataloging-in-Publication Data**
Approaches to curriculum management / edited by Margaret Preedy.
        p.   cm. – (Management in education series)
    Includes indexes.
        ISBN 0-335-09249-7—ISBN 0-335-09248-9 (pbk.)
        1. Curriculum planning – United States.   2. Curriculum evaluation –
    – United States.   3. Educational law and legislation – United States.
    4. School management and organization – United States.   I. Preedy,
    Margaret.   II. Series.
    LB2806.15.A67   1989
    375'.001'0973—dc20                         89-34691 CIP

Typeset by Rowland Photosetting Ltd
Bury St Edmunds, Suffolk
Printed and bound in Great Britain by
Biddles Ltd, Guildford and King's Lynn

# Contents

# Acknowledgements

All possible care has been taken to trace ownership of the material included in this volume, and Open University Press would like to make grateful acknowledgement for permission to reproduce it here.

1. S. Maclure (1988). *Education Reformed*, pp. 1–33, London, Hodder & Stoughton.
2. Task Group on Assessment and Testing (1988). *National Curriculum: Task Group on Assessment and Testing – A Report*, London, DES. Reproduced with the permission of the Controller of Her Majesty's Stationery Office.
3. Further Education Unit (1989). *Towards a Framework for Curriculum Entitlement*, London, FEU.
4. K. Morrison and K. Ridley (1988). *Curriculum Planning and the Primary School*, London, Paul Chapman Publishing.
5. T. Becher (1989). Commissioned for this collection.
6. J. Campbell (1989). Commissioned for this collection.
7. A. McIntyre (1989). Commissioned for this collection.
8. J. Shackleton (1988). 'The professional role of the lecturer', *Planning the FE Curriculum* edited by B. Kedney and D. Parkes, London, FEU.
9. K. Reid, D. Hopkins and P. Holly (1987). *Towards the Effective School*, chapter 9, Oxford, Basil Blackwell.
10. E. Hoyle (1986). *The Politics of School Management*, pp. 51–73, London, Hodder & Stoughton.
11. M. Fullan (1987). 'Managing curriculum change', *Curriculum at the Crossroads* edited by M. O'Connor, London, School Curriculum Development Council. Also R. D. Laing (1970). *Knots*, London, Tavistock Publications.

12   D. Barnes, G. Johnson, S. Jordan, D. Layton, P. Medway and D. Yeomans (1988). 'TVEI and the school as a whole', *A Second Report on the TVEI Curriculum*, London, Training Agency. Reproduced with the permission of the Controller of Her Majesty's Stationery Office.

13   P. Ribbins (1986). 'Qualitative perspectives in research in secondary education: the management of pastoral care', *Research in the Management of Secondary Education* edited by T. Simkins, Sheffield Papers in Educational Management, No. 56, Sheffield City Polytechnic.

14   M. Wallace (1988). 'Towards a collegiate approach to curriculum management in primary and middle schools', *School Organisation*, Vol. 8, No. 1, Carfax Publishing Company.

15   S. Ball (1987). *The Micro-politics of the School*, chapter 9, London, Methuen & Company.

Grateful thanks are due to my secretary, Betty Russell, for her help in typing and other preparation work on this collection with great patience and good humour. Thanks are also due to members of the E818 course team for reading and commenting on drafts.

# Introduction

## Margaret Preedy

Curriculum management is a central activity for schools and colleges, creating the framework for effective teaching and learning to take place. This collection of papers examines various aspects of the curriculum management process and the context in which it occurs. The intention of this volume is to encourage greater reflection about and understanding of the elements of curriculum management.

The organizing framework and content of this book rest on a number of themes which are outlined below, followed by a brief review of the issues raised by the contributors. For our purposes here, curriculum management is taken to include organizing and co-ordinating curriculum planning; changing the curriculum in response to internal and external needs and demands; dealing with issues that arise in implementing curriculum change and evaluating the work of the school or college; and negotiating the curriculum in practice with the various groups and interests involved.

A major theme of the collection is the importance of the context in which curriculum management takes place. It is a truism now to suggest that external constraints and accountability demands play a large part in shaping curriculum decisions within the school or college. Yet it is not such a very long time ago (1959) since David Eccles (the then Minister of Education) described the curriculum as 'a secret garden', the preserve of professional teachers, into which politicians and the public at large strayed at their peril. The garden gate is now wide open. There has been a very significant increase in central control of the curriculum, accompanied by a growth in influence of other external groups – parents, school/college governors, employers. Much of the reduction in professional autonomy took place as a result of the radical legislation of the Conservative governments of the 1980s – particularly the 1986 (no. 2) Act, and the 1988 Education Reform Act (ERA), which set out the framework for the national curriculum and associated pupil assessment arrangements. The radical nature of these innovations contrasted with developments in education (and, indeed, other areas of public provision) in the 1950s, 1960s and 1970s when change had proceeded in a much more gradual and incremental way.

Lawton's (1983) model identifies five levels (national, regional or LEA, institutional, departmental, and individual) and three areas (aims, pedagogy, and evaluation) of curriculum control. In terms of this typology, the 1988 ERA brought about a significant increase in central control, a reduction in LEA control, and considerably circumscribed the area for curriculum decision-making within schools, especially in the areas of aims and evaluation. However, schools arguably retain a considerable degree of discretion in terms of *implementing* the national curriculum and assessment arrangements and also in the area of teaching/learning styles and approaches – pedagogical issues – which are not prescribed by the 1988 Act.

None the less, it can be argued that the cumulative impact of the assessment arrangements, together with other aspects of the ERA, all act as a strong constraint on the area of pedagogy in Lawton's typology. Thus the requirement to publish assessment results, coupled with the impact of parents acting as 'discriminating consumers' in comparing results between schools, and open enrolment, may provide a strong incentive to adopt forms of curriculum organization and teaching styles which maximize 'good' assessment results (see also Ranson's discussion of the impact of the publication of exam results as required by the 1980 Education Act: Ranson *et al.*, 1986). These and other aspects of curriculum control in the light of the ERA are explored by various chapters in this volume.

The ERA did not deal directly with curricular issues in further and higher education. None the less, in further education (FE) at least, there was by the end of the 1980s evidence of a move towards more overall planning and standardization of provision, and a national framework for vocational qualifications with the National Vocational Qualification (NVQ) due for implementation in the early 1990s. The ERA required each LEA to produce strategic plans for all its further education provision, for approval by the DES. The secretary of state also indicated a wish to move towards a core curriculum for further education.

External curricular control is thus an essential consideration when looking at curriculum decisions within the institution. Another major influence on curriculum management is formed by the *ideologies* or underlying sets of values and beliefs of those involved. Curriculum decisions are guided by these ideologies and by the interplay of the competing values which exist within and between the various decision-making levels identified by Lawton. Indeed, individuals may espouse elements of different ideologies with respect to various issues or at different times. Closely linked with individual and group ideologies are their perspectives of the management process. Until recently, the dominant perspectives in educational management were broadly functionalist or systems approaches which saw institutional decision-making as a generally rational and systematic process (see e.g. Cuthbert, 1984; Bush, 1986).

These approaches have however been increasingly questioned. An influential paper by Greenfield (1975) put forward the case for an alternative approach to the study of educational management. He and other writers argued for the insights offered by a phenomenological or interactionist approach, focusing on individual actors' meanings and interpretations rather than on organizational structures and goals. Similarly it has been argued that political, collegial, and organized anarchy perspectives can offer important insights into curriculum management (see Hoyle, 1986, and Reader 1 in this series).

The debate on alternative perspectives of management was paralleled by an increased concern for curricular *processes* as opposed to *products*. Kelly (1982) and others argued that traditional models of curriculum decision-making gave an undue emphasis to products or outcomes – especially in terms of test and exam results – and neglected processes: teaching and learning activities as perceived and negotiated by teachers and students themselves.

The later 1970s and the 1980s also saw a number of practical curriculum developments which promoted a greater emphasis on processes. These included work by the Further Education Unit (FEU) and further education colleges on pre-vocational courses, which included learner-centred elements such as negotiated curricula, the provision of guidance as an important curricular element, formative and profiled assessment. These, it was argued, developed greater student motivation. Hargreaves (ILEA, 1984) put forward similar points about the management of the school curriculum, arguing the need for a greater emphasis on learning processes and negotiation with the student, and approaches which would enable students to show attainments in broader areas than merely exam passes, and hence enhance their commitment to school. TVEI and CPVE incorporated elements of a student-centred process approach, and in some schools had a significant impact on teaching and learning styles (see e.g. Harland, 1987; DES, 1988). Profiling and records of achievement were also adopted in many secondary schools and their value widely endorsed (see e.g. Broadfoot *et al.*, 1988; TGAT, 1988).

Approaches to curriculum innovation and evaluation also saw a shift from top-down rationalist stances to a more interactionist school-based focus which stressed the importance of the user/classroom teacher in the design, review and evaluation of the curriculum (see e.g. Skilbeck, 1984 on school-based curriculum development; McMahon *et al.*, 1984). Empirical and theoretical studies increasingly recognized the importance of the implementation stage in effective curriculum innovation and the need to change teacher attitudes and values rather than just materials (see Fullan, 1982).

In many respects, recent large-scale top-down curriculum innovations by central government such as the national curriculum and GCSE can be seen as running counter to the school-based, process-focused, learner-centred approaches mentioned above. Many commentators, too, noted that in terms of content the national curriculum and assessment arrangements would tend to inhibit school-based developments, and to marginalize curriculum areas not included in the core and foundation subjects, as well as such developments as cross-curricular approaches and records of achievement (see Haviland, 1988).

None the less, while the framework of subjects and assessments are clearly defined by the Act and by the Orders of the secretary of state stemming from it, there is considerable scope for curriculum decision-making within schools. Indeed, in the light of the major implementation task, affecting all teachers and all schools in the maintained sector, flexible and responsive curriculum management in the schools is all the more important, with the need to phase in the new arrangements over a period of several years while maintaining existing provision, ensuring adequate staff preparation and resources, negotiating between internal school needs and external pressures, and coping with the impact of multiple changes.

The papers in this collection explore the themes outlined above from various angles. Section I (Chapters 1–3) looks at the policy framework for curriculum decision-making. Chapter 1 by Maclure outlines the main provisions of the ERA on the national curriculum and assessment, together with the TGAT proposals, looking at the main implications for local authorities, schools and parents. Maclure emphasizes that the curricular and assessment provisions of the Act create a clear framework for schools within which they are expected to become more open to the operation of market forces and consumer choice under the provisions of the Act dealing with LMS, open enrolment and grant-maintained status.

Chapter 2 comprises the conclusions and recommendations of the TGAT report. The extract shows the fairly 'liberal' approach taken by the task group, which went some way towards reassuring those who had grave doubts about a national system of testing. In particular the report stressed formative aspects, the combination of teacher assessments and standardized assessment tasks, a flexible system of levels of attainment to allow for children's differing rates of development, and the use of a range of methods of assessment, not just written tests.

Turning to further education, Chapter 3 outlines the FEU's general guidance for LEA and institutional staff who are involved in overall curriculum planning in the light of the requirements of the Education Reform Act. The document stresses the importance of considering student access and entitlement, and the essential elements that should be included in all learning programmes.

Section II (Chapters 4–11) looks at contextual factors for curriculum decision-making, particularly the ERA, and at various models of curriculum planning, change and evaluation. Morrison and Ridley (Chapter 4) identify and describe a number of educational ideologies, each suggesting a particular approach to the aims, outcomes, structure and content of the curriculum. A glance at the curricular aims of any school or college is likely to reveal elements of several of these ideologies, reflecting the demands of a pluralist society.

The next four chapters look at the implications of a major contextual factor – the Education Reform Act – for curriculum decision-making in the school or college. Chapter 5 by Becher examines a central issue confronting all schools in the early 1990s: putting in practice the major curriculum changes brought about by the ERA. Becher looks at the national curriculum in terms of the 'implementation gap' between policy objectives and their outcomes in practice, arguing that 'policy-makers cannot operate in isolation: what happens when their plans are put into action depends crucially on those who have to carry them out'. Although the national curriculum has been brought about by what the paper characterizes as a broadly coercive approach to policy change, schools, departments and individual teachers retain considerable scope for the exercise of professional autonomy. Approaches to implementation are likely to reflect the prevailing management styles of the institutions concerned. Becher identifies three broad approaches – coercive, manipulative and rational – and their implications for curricular policies and practice in the schools.

Curriculum diversity, standards and accountability and control are central issues in curriculum policy, at national and LEA levels as well as within the school. Campbell's (Chapter 6) discussion of the implications of the ERA for curriculum decision-making in primary schools assesses how far the Act has effectively addressed these issues. Campbell discusses three fundamental management tasks which the ERA raises for primary schools: curriculum implementation, assessment and public relations. All three, it is suggested, require a collegial approach with a key role for curriculum co-ordinators.

The impact of the ERA is also a central concern in Chapter 7, which looks at the management of curriculum and school evaluation. McInytre reviews various evaluation strategies and argues the need for a collaborative approach, involving groups inside and outside the school in meeting the demands of external accountability and internal school improvement within the framework created by the ERA.

Some of the curriculum management issues confronting the FE sector in the post-ERA period are reviewed in Chapter 8. Shackleton argues that colleges should move beyond a curriculum-led approach to institutional development, adopting instead a student-led perspective. In the context of changes brought about by the National Council for Vocational Qualifications, strategic planning of FE provision, and demographic trends, college managers need to develop a more flexible and responsive approach to client demands, perspectives and needs – to 'empower' the student.

The last three chapters in this section look more generally at curriculum management issues and perspectives. Reid, Hopkins and Holly (Chapter 9) argue that successful teaching needs 'thoughtful and systematic curriculum planning', in which the classroom teacher should occupy a central role. They trace the development of product and more recent process models of curriculum planning, and describe an approach which attempts to incorporate both product/outcome and process considerations.

Hoyle's paper (Chapter 10) raises a number of fundamental problems in the dominant rationalist or systems approach to curriculum decision-making. Focusing on the central rationalist concept of organizational goals, Hoyle discusses the 'organizational pathos' arising, he argues, from the 'chronic discrepancy between proclaimed organizational goals and their achievement'. This has considerable implications for the traditional approaches to curriculum planning which are evident in LEA and institutional planning models as well as in official documents. The ambiguity perspectives discussed by Hoyle may be particularly appropriate to institutions faced with rapid change and uncertainty in their environments – conditions which are confronting schools and colleges in the 1990s.

Finally in this section, the brief paper by Fullan (Chapter 11) looks at some general characteristics of curriculum change and proposes a number of strategies for the management of successful curriculum innovation. Fullan emphasizes the complexity of the change process, the importance of the implementation stage and the need to bring about alterations in teachers' fundamental beliefs and understandings, in order to achieve lasting and effective change.

Section III presents a number of empirically based papers illustrating the application of various approaches to curriculum management. Chapter 12, by Barnes *et al.*, is an extract from a University of Leeds evaluation report on the TVEI curriculum. Basing their analysis on case studies in 26 schools, the authors examine the impact of TVEI on the curriculum and on teachers. The study illustrates the wide diversity in the ways in which schools managed the implementation of TVEI. It explores some of the major issues raised by the innovation, in particular the problems and opportunities of modular curricula, the impact of TVEI on other areas of the curriculum and the perspectives of TVEI and non-TVEI teachers.

Ribbins (Chapter 13) describes the application of an interactionist or 'qualitative' approach to researching the management of pastoral care in secondary schools. Ribbins contrasts qualitative and quantitative approaches to educational research and demonstrates the strengths of an interactionist approach in revealing the differing meanings and interpretations of staff as to what constituted 'pastoral care' and how it was managed in the schools.

Wallace in Chapter 14 argues for a 'collegiate' approach to curriculum management in primary and middle schools. The case which he makes for a collegiate or democratic form of school organization is similar to that put forward by Campbell (1985) – see also Chapter 6 in this volume. Drawing on the experiences of the National Development Centre for School Management Training, Wallace proposes a 'management development' approach which he argues may help to implement collegiate management, despite the constraints and difficulties involved.

Finally, the extract from Ball's book, *The Micro-Politics of the School*, in Chapter 15 illustrates the application of a contrasting perspective, a political approach, in looking at examples of interdepartmental rivalry in schools, particularly over the issues of resource allocation and departmental status. Ball sees the department as a power base for the competing subject interests within the school, a political coalition which acts to promote the status and interests of its members against encroachments by other departments, the head and senior management.

This collection of papers is inevitably selective. It is hoped that it will encourage not only those who read it as part of an OU course, but also a wider readership, to reflect on the management of curriculum planning, evaluation and change within the framework of the ERA and other contextual factors, and to consider the applicability of various perspectives in understanding curriculum management processes. A flexible approach to curriculum decision-making, informed by an awareness of the 'competing rationalities' (Hoyle) of those involved, is essential in the context of the multiple changes currently confronting schools and colleges.

## References

Broadfoot, P., James, M., McMeeking, S., Nuttall, D. and Stierer, B. (1988) *Records of Achievement: Report of the National Evaluation of Pilot Schemes.* A report submitted to the DES and the Welsh Office, London, HMSO.

Bush, T. (1986) *Theories of Educational Management*, London, Harper & Row.

Campbell, R. J. (1985) *Developing the Primary School Curriculum*, London, Holt, Rinehart & Winston.

Cuthbert, R. (1984) Open University Course E324, *Management in Post-Compulsory Education*, Block 3, part 2, 'The management process', Milton Keynes, Open University.

DES (Department of Education and Science) (1988) *Report by HM Inspectors on a Survey of Courses leading to the Certificate of Pre-Vocational Education*, London, DES.

Fullan, M. (1982) *The Meaning of Educational Change*, Columbia University, New York, Teachers College Press.

Greenfield, T. B. (1975) 'Theory about organization: a new perspective and its implications for schools', in V. Houghton *et al.* (eds) *Management in Education: The Management of Organizations and Individuals*, London, Ward Lock.

Harland, J. (1987) 'The TVEI experience', in D. Gleeson (ed.) *TVEI and Secondary Education: A Critical Appraisal*, Milton Keynes, Open University Press.

Haviland, J. (ed.) (1988) *Take Care, Mr. Baker!*, London, Fourth Estate.

Hoyle, E. (1986) *The Politics of School Management*, London, Hodder & Stoughton.

ILEA (Inner London Education Authority) (1984) *Improving Secondary Schools*, The Hargreaves Report, London, ILEA.

Kelly, A. V. (1982) *The Curriculum: Theory and Practice*, 2nd edn, London, Harper & Row.

Lawton, D. (1983) *Curriculum Studies and Educational Planning*, London, Hodder & Stoughton.

McMahon, A., Bolam, R., Abbott, R. and Holly, P. (1984) *Guidelines for Review and Internal Development in Schools: Primary and Secondary School Handbooks*, London, Longman.

Ranson, S., Gray, J., Jesson, D. and Jones, B. (1986) 'Exams in context: values and power in educational accountability', in D. Nuttall (ed.) *Assessing Educational Achievement*, Lewes, Falmer Press.

Skilbeck, M. (1984) *School-Based Curriculum Development*, London, Harper & Row.

TGAT (Task Group on Assessment and Testing), DES (1988) *National Curriculum Task Group on Assessment and Testing: A Report*, London, DES and Welsh Office.

**Section I**

# Policy frameworks

# 1

# The national curriculum and assessment

**Stuart Maclure**

[This chapter provides a summary and analysis of the 1988 Education Reform Act's main provisions on the national curriculum and assessment, Sections 1–25 of the Act.]

> **1.** (1) It shall be the duty –
>
> > (a) of the Secretary of State as respects every maintained school;
> > (b) of every local education authority as respects every school maintained by them; and
> > (c) of every governing body or head teacher of a maintained school as respects that school;
>
> to exercise their functions (including, in particular, the functions conferred on them by this Chapter with respect to religious education, religious worship and the National Curriculum) with a view to securing that the curriculum for the school satisfies the requirements of this section.
>
> (2) The curriculum for a maintained school satisfies the requirements of this section if it is a balanced and broadly based curriculum which –
>
> > (a) promotes the spiritual, moral, cultural, mental and physical development of pupils at the school and of society; and
> > (b) prepares such pupils for the opportunities, responsibilities and experiences of adult life.

The Education Reform Act requires all maintained schools to provide for all pupils, within the years of compulsory schooling, a basic curriculum 'to be known as the national curriculum'. Section 1(2) notes that the curriculum for a maintained school 'satisfies the requirements of this section if it is a balanced and broadly based curriculum which:

(a) promotes the spiritual, moral, cultural, mental and physical development of pupils at the school and of society; and
(b) prepares such pupils for the opportunities, responsibilities and experiences of adult life.'

---

**2.** (1) The curriculum for every maintained school shall comprise a basic curriculum which includes –

(a) provision for religious education for all registered pupils at the school; and
(b) a curriculum for all registered pupils at the school of compulsory school age (to be known as 'the National Curriculum') which meets the requirements of subsection (2) below.

(2) The curriculum referred to in subsection (1)(b) above shall comprise the core and other foundation subjects and specify in relation to each of them –

(a) the knowledge, skills and understanding which pupils of different abilities and maturities are expected to have by the end of each key stage (in this Chapter referred to as 'attainment targets');
(b) the matters, skills and processes which are required to be taught to pupils of different abilities and maturities during each key stage (in this Chapter referred to as 'programmes of study'); and
(c) the arrangements for assessing pupils at or near the end of each key stage for the purpose of ascertaining what they have achieved in relation to the attainment targets for that stage (in this Chapter referred to as 'assessment arrangements') . . .

---

Section 3 designates three core subjects and seven foundation subjects which must be taught. The core subjects are mathematics, English and science. The foundation subjects are history, geography, technology, music, art, physical education and (at the secondary stage) a modern language. Welsh is a core subject for Welsh-speaking schools and a foundation subject in non-Welsh-speaking schools in Wales.

The curriculum includes religious education for all pupils (Section 2). It must specify in relation to each subject 'the knowledge, skills and understanding which all pupils of different abilities and maturities' are expected to have learned by the end of each 'key stage' – that is, by about the ages of 7, 11, 14 and 16 (the 'attainment targets'). It must also set out how pupils are to be assessed and tested at around the prescribed ages ('the assessment arrangements').

**3.** (1) Subject to subsection (4) below, the core subjects are –

   (a)   mathematics, English and science; and

   (b)   in relation to schools in Wales which are Welsh-speaking schools, Welsh.

  (2) Subject to subsection (4) below, the other foundation subjects are –

   (a)   history, geography, technology, music, art and physical education:

   (b)   in relation to the third and fourth key stages, a modern foreign language specified in an order of the Secretary of State; and

   (c)   in relation to schools in Wales which are not Welsh-speaking schools, Welsh . . .

**4.** (1) It shall be the duty of the Secretary of State . . .

   (a)   to establish a complete National Curriculum as soon as is reasonably practicable (taking first the core subjects and then the other foundation subjects); and

   (b)   to revise that Curriculum whenever he considers it necessary or expedient to do so.

  (2) The Secretary of State may by order specify in relation to each of the foundation subjects –

   (a)   such attainment targets;

   (b)   such programmes of study; and

   (c)   such assessment arrangements;

as he considers appropriate for that subject . . .

Note that although a list of subjects is specified in the Act, most of the implementation – such as, for example, the setting of attainment targets, the prescription of programmes of study and the outline arrangements for assessment – is by secondary legislation in the form of Orders. The original list of subjects, too, can be amended by Order.

All maintained schools are under a general duty to make sure the national curriculum is implemented (Section 10) – that is to say, a duty is placed on the local authority and school governors in respect of county and voluntary schools (other than aided schools) and on the governors of aided schools and grant maintained schools.

Religious worship and religious education are covered in Sections 6 to 13. Section 6 states the legal requirement for a single act of worship for all pupils, or separate acts of worship for pupils of different age groups or in different school groups. In county schools, responsibility for arranging the form of worship lies with the headteacher after consultation with the governors. In voluntary schools it is the other way round: the governors are meant to make the arrangements after consultation with the head.

---

*Religious education*

**6.** (1) . . . All pupils in attendance at a maintained school shall on each school day take part in an act of collective worship . . .

**7.** (1) . . . In the case of a county school the collective worship . . . shall be wholly or mainly of a broadly Christian character . . .

---

The Act adds the rider that in county schools the collective worship 'shall be wholly or mainly of a broadly Christian character' (Section 7(1)). This is qualified by giving schools some discretion to vary the form, provided that 'taking any school term as a whole' most assemblies comply. Among the considerations which may be taken into account (Section 7(5)) are the family background of the pupils. Where heads consider that insistence on a Christian act of daily worship should not apply, they can (Section 12) submit an application to the local Standing Advisory Council on Religious Education (SACRE), which body can decide whether or not the school should have exemption, having regard to the nature of the school community. (SACREs are committees set up by local authorities with representatives of the Churches to oversee the RE curriculum.)

Religious education continues to be non-denominational in character in county and controlled schools, based on Agreed Syllabuses. These, too, are the responsibility of the SACREs, and Section 8 lays down that they 'shall reflect the fact that the religious traditions in Great Britain are in the main Christian, ·while taking account of the teaching and practices of the other principal religions represented in Great Britain.'

The Act goes on (Section 14) to provide for two Curriculum Councils (one for England, one for Wales) and a School Examinations and Assessment Council to advise the secretary of state on matters relating to the curriculum and its assessment.

---

*Special cases*

**18.** The special educational provision for any pupil specified in a statement under section 7 of the 1981 Act of his special educational needs may include provision –

  (a) excluding the application of the provisions of the National Curriculum; or

  (b) applying those provisions with such modifications as may be specified in the statement.

**19.** (1) The Secretary of State may make regulations enabling the head teacher of any maintained school, . . .

  (a) to direct as respects a registered pupil . . . the provisions of the National Curriculum –

(i) shall not apply; or

(ii) shall apply with such modifications as may be so specified . . .

(2) The conditions prescribed by the regulations shall . . . limit the period that may be specified . . . to a maximum period specified in the regulations . . .

(3) Where a head teacher gives a direction under regulations made under this section . . . he shall give the information mentioned in subsection (4) below, . . .

(a) to the governing body; and

(b) where the school is a county, voluntary or maintained special school, to the local education authority;

and . . . also to a parent of the pupil,

(4) That information is the following –

(a) the fact that he has taken the action in question, its effect and his reasons for taking it;

(b) the provision that is being or is to be made for the pupil's education during the operative period of the direction; and

(c) either –

(i) a description of the manner in which he proposes to secure the full implementation in relation to the pupil after the end of that period of the provisions of the National Curriculum; or

(ii) an indication of his opinion that the pupil has or probably has special educational needs by virtue of which the local education authority would be required to determine the special educational provision that should be made for him (whether initially or on a review of any statement of his special educational needs the authority are for the time being required under section 7 of the 1981 Act to maintain). . . .

(6) It shall be the duty of a local education authority, on receiving information given to the authority under this section by the head teacher of any maintained school which includes such an indication of opinion with respect to a pupil, to consider whether any action on their part is required in the case of that pupil under section 5 of the 1981 Act (assessment of special educational needs).

All the members are nominated by [the secretary of state]. The Act specifically requires him/her (Section 20(2)) to refer proposed Orders relating to the subject requirements, attainment targets and programmes of study, to the National Curriculum Council, and obliges the Council to consult with local authorities, governors' representatives, teachers' organizations and others (subsection 3). The secretary of state must publish the advice he/she receives from the Council, and if he/she fails to follow it, state his/her reasons (subsection (5)(a)(ii)).

The secretary of state has also a general power to make regulations (Section 17) removing or modifying the provisions of the national curriculum in such circumstances as may be specified.

Certain exceptions to the provisions of the Act on the national curriculum are outlined in Sections 16–19. Section 16 sets out the limited conditions under which the secretary of state may issue a direction exempting a school from the requirements laid down in the national curriculum or modifying them. Such a direction can be given in a county, controlled or maintained special school on the application of the local authority with the agreement of the governing body, or vice versa; or of the Curriculum Council with the agreement of both the local authority and the governing body. In a grant maintained, aided or special agreement school, applications can be made by the governing body, or by the Curriculum Council with the governors' agreement.

Another exemption (Section 18) applies to pupils with special educational needs, for whom the national curriculum can be modified by a Statement under Section 7 of the 1981 Education Act.

An added flexibility is provided in Section 19, under which the secretary of state can make regulations enabling the headteacher of any maintained school to modify the national curriculum in respect of any pupil for a limited period.

In reporting such action to the parent, the governors and the local authority, the head can either press for a statement of special educational need, or signify how he or she intends to secure in due course that the pupil is brought back on to the full national curriculum course. The section provides for the parents to have right of appeal to the governors, in respect of any action by the head under these regulations.

An important aim of the introduction of a national curriculum is to give parents the maximum information about the programmes their children are following, and regular reports on their progress. Section 22 of the Act empowers the secretary of state to make regulations about the supply of public information which local authorities, governors and heads may be required to provide. Among the topics covered would be the details of how the national curriculum is to be interpreted, and the curriculum policy documents which all authorities and governing bodies are required to produce under the 1986 Education Act.

There is also a general power for the secretary of state to require the local education authorities, governors and heads to provide any other information about the education of pupils that he/she thinks fit.

The secretary of state's power to demand information also means that he/she can insist on the publication of results of assessment and testing, and determine the form which this must take.

Section 23 requires local authorities to establish their own procedures (approved by the secretary of state and therefore subject to his/her guidelines) for dealing with complaints about any maintained or county and voluntary or maintained special school, including complaints that the curriculum has not been followed, or that there has been a failure to provide all the information required under Section 22.

## A new orthodoxy

The powers which the secretary of state has taken to prescribe the curriculum are similar in effect to powers which existed under the Codes which governed elementary and secondary education under the 1902 Act. These powers continued till the 1944 Act, though from the mid-1920s their application was relaxed. When the 1944 Education Act was passed, legal control of the curriculum in maintained schools was ascribed to the local education authorities and the governors of aided schools. In practice, they never exercised their powers over the curriculum, which to all intents and purposes became the responsibility of heads and their senior staff. The external examinations exerted a strong influence in the upper forms. So too, in some local authorities, did the local advisers and other support staff.

In the decade before the introduction of the Education Reform Bill, the Department of Education and Science and successive secretaries of state showed increasing interest in the curriculum, and began to intervene by issuing a series of policy documents such as the *Organization and Content of the 5–16 Curriculum* (DES, 1984), *Science 5–16: A Statement of Policy* (DES, 1985a) and *Modern Languages in the School Curriculum* (DES, 1988a).

Her Majesty's Inspectors also increased their output of curriculum papers, and local education authorities were encouraged by DES circulars to review their own curriculum arrangements.

By the time Sir Keith Joseph (secretary of state, 1981–6) issued his White Paper on *Better Schools* (DES, 1985b), it had become clear that curriculum policy had to be considered at three levels: the *national* level in the form of statements of policy issued by the secretary of state; the *local authority* level in the form of each authority's policy statement, which would be expected to have regard to national aims and priorities; and the *school* level, where each governing body would be required to produce its own curriculum paper.

The 1986 Act, mainly concerned with reforming the composition of school governing bodies and extending their powers, demonstrated the potential danger of the three-way stretch which might arise if the secretary of state, the local authority and the school pulled in different directions. It seemed to leave the head in the invidious position of arbitrating between his or her governors and the local authority if a disagreement were to arise.

Though *Better Schools* (DES, 1985b: para. 37) stated that the government had no intention to introduce legislation redefining responsibility for the curriculum, shortly after Mr Kenneth Baker had succeeded Sir Keith Joseph in the early summer of 1986 he had begun to move towards a centrally controlled curriculum.

What had still been regarded as a highly controversial idea in the early 1980s had become commonplace by the time it figured in the Conservative election manifesto at the general election of June 1987. It soon became apparent that it enjoyed a wide measure of political support outside the Conservative party, and controversy concentrated not on *whether* there should be a national curriculum but on the mechanics of it and the setting of attainment targets and methods of assessment.

The 1988 Act made it clear exactly where the legal control of the curriculum lay – with the secretary of state. It removed the confusion built into the 1986 Act, while still insisting that both the local authority and the governing body must adopt curriculum policies to give effect to the national curriculum.

The local authority's curriculum role is downgraded. It is the national curriculum which provides the local authority, the governors and the headteacher with their marching orders. A school which is implementing the national curriculum is working within the law.

The distinction which the Act made in Section 3, between the core and foundation subjects, is more important as a guide to administrative action than as a fine legal distinction.

The core subjects, as their name implies, form the central part of the curriculum. It was with these subjects that the setting up of the national curriculum would begin. Working groups on mathematics and science had reported by August 1988 and the secretary of state had published these with his own proposals. [. . .]

The foundation subjects came afterwards. Technology was intended to be a priority but was not in the first batch. Modern languages differed from the other foundation subjects because they concerned only the secondary school stage. The introduction of a modern languages curriculum had to await some solution to the obvious staffing difficulties implicit in a demand for all pupils to be taught one or more languages *throughout* the compulsory period of secondary education.

[. . .]

The Act is at pains to describe the process by which the secretary of state is to arrive at his/her curriculum Orders, the documents which he/she must lay before Parliament for a positive resolution in both Houses. Any proposals have to be referred to the appropriate Curriculum Council. The Council then puts them out for consultation with local authorities, teachers' bodies, representatives of governing bodies and 'any other persons' thought to be worth consulting. The Council then reports back to the secretary of state, summarizing the views of those consulted and making its own recommendations. The Council can also add any other advice it thinks fit.

The secretary of state is then obliged to publish the Curriculum Council's report. He/she does not have to accept the advice, but if he/she fails to do so he/she must state his/her reasons for setting it aside. He/she then issues the draft Order, after which there has to be yet another period of at least a month for further consultation and representations from interested groups.

The reason for laying down such a detailed procedure was to make sure that the strong central powers vested in the secretary of state are constrained by a due process which ensures extensive consultation and requires the secretary of state to act publicly and explain him/herself. The effect may well be to hand the power over, within a relatively short time, to the powerful curriculum bureaucracy which the Act has created.

## Assessment and testing

The reliance placed on attainment targets and the testing and assessment of pupils at the key stages of 7, 11, 14 and 16 made this part of the Education Reform Act of great and controversial interest to those inside the education system. Testing and assessment were to be the public and visible way of enforcing the new curriculum.

It was a prime aim of the Act to make schools more accountable and give parents more and better information about their children's progress. Experience in the USA and elsewhere had shown the likelihood that the curriculum could become 'test-driven' if universal external testing were introduced in a simplistic or clumsy way. The English folk memory returned to Matthew Arnold's strictures on 'payment by results' and the three decades which followed the introduction of the New Code in 1862, spent in dismantling the disincentives to good teaching which that powerful administrative device instituted.

Teaching to the tests was a likely enough expectation. The question was: could sufficiently good tests be created to ensure that teachers who taught to them would do a good job?

Assessment is clearly an essential part of the teacher's job, and teachers regularly use standardized tests to help them. What sort of national scheme could be set up which would build on the best practice and make it the norm? How could it be ensured that assessment would avoid an excessive concentration on pencil and paper tests of a traditional kind?

The task of drawing up the outline of an assessment scheme fell to a group headed by Professor Paul Black of King's College, London, a scientist with considerable experience as a curriculum developer. His Task Group on Assessment and Testing (TGAT) produced a report at Christmas 1987 which became the basis of DES policy and a guide for the national curriculum subject working groups set up to consider attainment targets, programmes of study and assessment arrangements.

The scheme put forward by the Black Committee – generally known as the TGAT Report – envisaged a system of 'formative' assessment drawing heavily on teachers' observations as well as on 'standard assessment tasks' and other tests. The 'standard assessment tasks' could take the form of defined activity which was part of the normal teaching programme. In primary schools, the report suggested, children could undertake an assessment task without necessarily knowing it was a test which would be moderated and form part of a graded assessment.

The aim, according to TGAT, had to be to produce 'a full and well-articulated picture of the individual child's current strengths and future needs'. It was essential to build on good classroom practice:

> A system which was not closely linked to normal classroom assign-
> ments and which did not demand the professional skills and commit-
> ment of the teachers might be less expensive and simpler to implement
> but would be indefensible in that it could set in opposition the processes
> of learning, teaching and assessment.

(TGAT, 1988: para. 220)

This last is the key sentence in the report: it is all about trying to construct a *system* of assessment which runs in parallel with teaching and learning, and yet can be 'moderated' and 'standardized' to produce information about individual, class, school and local authority performance which can be usefully presented to parents and other 'consumers', teachers, adminis-trators, and so on.

TGAT assumed that the attainment targets which the Act required to be established for each subject would be divided up into groups, each group representing a different dimension of the subject. These groups of attainment targets would form what the TGAT Report called the 'profile components'. These components ('preferably no more than four and never more than six') would reflect 'the variety of knowledge, skills and understanding to which the subject gives rise'.

The assessments would be based on these profile components and would include the teachers' own estimates, based on classwork, as well as the performance of the pupils on 'standard assessment tasks' and in tests. Development which would have to be undertaken before the system could be introduced would include the creation of an item bank of test questions to be administered by teachers in connection with their teaching. An important assumption, especially at the primary level, was that there would be consider-able overlap of profile components, to reduce the number of separate assessments which individual teachers would be called upon to make, and to take account of cross-curricular themes.

The assessment of the various subject components would then be put together to form the complete assessment of the pupils' progress.

TGAT was anxious to devise a form of assessment which emphasized progression, and therefore constructed a framework of ten levels through which a pupil might be expected to climb.

At age 7 most (80 per cent) of pupils would achieve levels 1, 2 or 3 according to their assessed performance: 'Two years of learning represents one level of progress.' At age 11, 80 per cent would achieve levels 3 to 5. At age 14, the range would cover levels 4 to 7 and at age 16 there would be an overlap with the GCSE: levels 7 to 10 would, as the report put it, 'bear some relationship to upper GCSE grades'.

This ingenious scheme was intended to prevent pupils from moving through the various assessment points with a static or scarcely changing mark or grade. It would provide a sense of progression. It would also enable the wide spread of achievement in each age-group to be accommodated by the use of levels below or above the national average. The form of assessment would be criterion-referenced (that is, expressed as far as possible in terms of specified tasks) and directly linked to the programmes of study laid down in the national curriculum, thereby providing a flexible scheme with testing at more or less fixed ages which would nevertheless do justice to children of all performance standards.

How the results were to be reported outside the school was a matter of widespread concern. TGAT made a number of sensible recommendations.

Assessment results for *individual* pupils should be confidential to pupils, their parents and teachers.

> The *only* form on which results . . . for . . . a given school should be published is as part of a broader report by that school of its work as a whole.
>
> (TGAT, 1988: para. 227)

The group rejected the idea of 'scaling' results up or down to take account of social factors. It recommended that 'national assessment results for a class as a whole and a school should be available to the parents of its pupils'.

Much concern had been expressed about the impact of formal national assessment and testing on the primary schools. TGAT favoured starting the tests at age 7 to identify at an early stage any who were under-performing, but wished to restrict the number of standard assessment tasks at age 7 to three, each task being designed to give 'systematic assessment of competence in the range of profile components appropriate to age 7'. It opposed any requirement for the publication of school results for 7-year-olds.

By the time they reached the age of 11, TGAT assumed that children would need to be assessed on three or four standard tasks which covered a range of profile components, 'possibly supplemented by more narrowly focused tests for particular components'.

The report emphasized (as such reports usually do) that its recommendations had to be considered as a whole – including the far-reaching sections on in-service training, research and development, and resources in time and materials. The timetable attached to the report provided for a five-year run-in period in which the assessment procedures and the curriculum development would go hand-in-hand, with the first full reporting of the results in year 5, in 1993.

The TGAT Report was produced in five months – a feat in itself. It was an extremely skilful document in that it met the secretary of state's requirement for an assessment scheme which would satisfy the provisions of the Education Reform Act, while at the same time it won the confidence of many teachers who had been sceptical or hostile to the idea of universal testing and assessment. This in itself was enough to arouse suspicions in certain government quarters that the Group had subverted the radical intentions of the Act. A leaked letter from the prime minister's private office reported early doubts about the 'enormously elaborate and complex system' and the philosophy behind the scheme for formative and diagnostic rather than summative assessment. The central importance which the report placed on the role and judgements of teachers was also queried, along with the 'major role envisaged for the LEAs'. There were also doubts about the cost and the long lead time to bring the assessment and testing procedures into operation (*TES*, 1988).

These doubts appeared to be more muted as the Bill moved relentlessly forward to become an Act. It looked as if an attempt would be made, at some point, to simplify the working of the scheme and meet practical difficulties which might arise in its application. An assessment and testing scheme introduced in Croydon, independently of the Education Reform Act, appeared to produce a somewhat simpler method which might be expected to be easier for parents and employers to come to grips with. But the TGAT Report's proposals were the only national scheme on offer and, from the DES point of view, there was clearly a great deal to be said for mobilizing the widest possible support behind a scheme which would stand or fall on the cooperation of teachers.

The essential features of the scheme which the TGAT Report combined were

1  close interdependence between curriculum, teaching and assessment
2  full involvement of teachers
3  varied forms of assessment, including assessment via tasks which form a normal part of classroom activity
4  time for the development of assessment measures and for the training of teachers in their use
5  assessment at the primary level which was compatible with good primary practice
6  sensible ground rules for reporting results
7  a realistic timetable for the introduction of the scheme.

The government's formal response to the TGAT Report came in a parliamentary answer (*Hansard*, 7 June 1988) which set out the main principles on which assessment would be based:

(a) attainment targets will be set which establish what children should normally be expected to know, understand and be able to do at the ages of 7, 11, 14 and 16; these will enable the progress of each child to be measured against national standards.

(b) pupils' performance in relation to attainment targets should be assessed and reported on at ages 7, 11, 14 and 16. Attainment targets should be grouped for this purpose to make the assessment and reporting manageable.

(c) different *levels* of attainment and overall pupil progress demonstrated by tests and assessment should be registered on a ten-point scale covering all the years of compulsory schooling.

(d) assessment should be by a combination of national external tests and assessment by teachers. At age 16 the GCSE will be the main form of assessment, especially in the core subjects of English, mathematics and science.

(e) the results of tests and other assessments should be used both *formatively* to help better teaching and to inform decisions about next steps for a pupil, and *summatively* at ages 7, 11, 14 and 16 to inform parents about their child's progress.

(f) detailed results of assessments of individual pupils should be given in full to parents, and the Government attaches great importance to the principle that these reports should be simple and clear. Individuals' results should not be published, but aggregated results at the ages of 11, 14 and 16 should be, so that the wider public can make informed judgements about attainment in a school or LEA. There should be no legal requirement for schools to publish such results for seven-year-olds, though it is strongly recommended that schools should do so.

(g) in order to safeguard standards, assessments made by teachers should be compared with the results of the national tests and the judgement of other teachers.

The principles followed the general lines of the TGAT recommendations, with some significant differences in regard to the publication of results. TGAT wanted to insist that results should be published only within the context of a report on the work of the school as a whole. This proviso was ignored in the ministerial statement. The TGAT Report was opposed to any requirement for the formal publication of results at age 7. The ministerial statement stopped short of making publication at 7 compulsory, but added a strong recommendation that such results should be published, notwithstanding the TGAT's serious doubts about the usefulness of the comparisons to which this might give rise.

It was clear that the TGAT Report and the principles it adumbrated were only a beginning. A great deal would depend on how the scheme was developed, at every stage – from the setting of the attainment targets and the selection of the profile components, to the presentation of the results in detail and in aggregate. The commitment of human and physical resources which Professor Black's group assumed was great: if this commitment were not wholly forthcoming, the initial support for the TGAT approach could melt away.

[. . .]

## Applicability

The national curriculum is mandatory on all maintained schools – that is, county and voluntary schools, and the new category of grant-maintained schools. It does not have legal force in independent schools, though most independent schools will make sure they can satisfy parents that they offer it or something better. New independent schools seeking registration will have to bear this in mind. City technology colleges will have to provide 'a broad curriculum with an emphasis on science and technology'. The national curriculum does not apply to them, though the discussion document on the curriculum issued before the Bill was published indicated that the secretary of state would 'make adherence to the substance of the national curriculum' a condition of grant.

## Time allocation

The DES Consultative Paper on the national curriculum (DES, 1987), issued in advance of the Bill, gave an illustrative example of how the timetable for the last two years of compulsory education might work out under the constraints imposed by the national curriculum. This showed the ten compulsory subjects occupying some 75–85 per cent of the available time, with no allowance for religious education, or for additional science or mathematics. Subsequently ministers drew back from this draft illustration and in commending the Bill to Parliament in the Second Reading debate, Mr Baker contented himself with saying: 'it is our belief that it will be difficult if not impossible for any school to provide the national curriculum in less than 70 per cent of the time available.' In reality, nobody could say in advance of the publication of 'programmes of study' how much time would be required.

The first draft of the Bill was amended to underline the refusal to specify any particular periods of time. Section 4(3) makes this an explicit denial. In this it is unusual, in that it spells out what the secretary of state must *not* put in an Order, instead of what he/she must or may.

### Special educational need

There was considerable anxiety among those directly concerned with children with special educational needs that their interests might be prejudiced by the introduction of a national curriculum. At various points the Act acknowledges these concerns. Statemented children are exempt from the national curriculum, and headteachers have a procedure they can invoke for other pupils for whom the specified curriculum would be unsuitable.

The Act is clearly not designed to make it easy for schools to take the line of least resistance with pupils who are failing to make the grade. The effect of the legal changes may be to put pressure on local authorities to provide 'statements' for more pupils, and for the needs of slow learners to be considered more carefully because the Act will allow such children to be withdrawn from the regular course only in prescribed circumstances.

### Enforcement

The national curriculum is to be policed in local authority maintained schools by the governors, by the local authorities through their own inspectors, and by Her Majesty's Inspectors of schools.

*Local authority* inspectors are expected to play a key role. [. . .] The inspectors are the advisers who are in closest touch with the schools. It will fall to them, in many cases, to clarify, for the schools, points of difficulty arising from the mountain of curriculum material which is being generated by the DES, the National Curriculum Council and the subject working groups.

In addition to their formal in-service training activities, they will have much informal training to do in their regular school contacts. They will have to help the local authorities develop performance indicators by which schools can be judged. After 1989 they are expected to become increasingly involved in the introduction of teacher appraisal.

All this will be in addition to the essential part they play in matters of staff discipline. More intensive monitoring of performance is likely to increase the demand for reports from inspectors as a first step towards sanctions against ineffective staff and other, less extreme, remedial measures.

In addition to the monitoring functions undertaken by the local authority, direct intervention by parents is made possible through the complaints procedure. In terms of a market ideology, this gives the consumers (i.e. the parents, who throughout the Act are seen as surrogate consumers for their sons and daughters) a chance to act if they believe there is a failure to deliver the curriculum to which they are, by law, entitled. In an ideal market system, pressure by consumers would be all-important. Under the Act it seems unlikely to be of paramount significance, but dissatisfied parents who might otherwise feel impotent are given a weapon with which to fight back. It may also open up opportunities for barrack-room lawyers. Its main significance is likely to be to keep heads and their staff, and governing bodies, on permanent guard against the possibility of local challenge. They will watch their flanks with caution.

## Action

The national curriculum requires action from the secretary of state, from the local authorities, from governors, from headteachers and their staff, and from parents.

*The secretary of state* must activate the machinery to produce the programmes of study, attainment targets and procedures for testing and assessment. This means setting up working groups to prepare the programmes of study and attainment targets, subject by subject, for the ten-subject curriculum laid down in Section 3 of the Act. He/she must set up and keep in being a National Curriculum Council and a School Examinations and Assessment Council. The secretary of state's proposals for the Curriculum must be referred to the National Curriculum Council, starting with those for the core subjects. After receiving the advice of the Council (which must consult widely), the secretary of state must then make up his/her own mind. If the secretary of state rejects the advice, he/she must say why. Finally, the secretary of state must incorporate his/her decision in Orders which have to be approved by both Houses of Parliament.

It then becomes the continuing duty of the curriculum and examinations councils to keep the national curriculum under review. The councils must advise on matters referred to them by the secretary of state; they also have the right to give advice without waiting to be asked.

The timetable for the phased introduction of the national curriculum was set out in DES Circular 5/88:

(i) all primary schools will be required to teach all pupils, and secondary schools all 11–14-year-old pupils, core and other foundation subjects for a reasonable time from September 1989;

(ii) from September 1989 all primary schools will be required by Orders . . . to adopt for 5-year-old pupils the new attainment targets, programmes of study and assessment arrangements for mathematics, science and English;

(iii) Orders will similarly be made with effect from September 1989 for 11–12-year-olds in the third key stage for mathematics and science only;

(iv) Orders relating to technology for 5-year-olds, and to English and technology for 11–12-year-olds in the third key stage, will be introduced in 1990. Orders relating to mathematics and science and probably English and technology will be introduced for 7–8-year-olds in the second key stage in 1990;

(v) thereafter implementation arrangements for these subjects will proceed year by year as the first cohorts move through the first three key stages; requirements relating to the fourth key stage are unlikely to be introduced before Autumn 1992;

(vi) assessment arrangements for each key stage will be introduced alongside attainment targets and programmes of study but on a trial basis for the first year of operation. Thus the second cohort of pupils in a key stage will be the first for whom results of assessments are reported. In other words those who are 5 and 11 in Autumn 1989 will be assessed at the end of their key stage but it will be those who start key stages 1 and 3 in Autumn *1990* who will be formally assessed and *reported upon* in 1992 and 1993.

(DES, 1988b)

*Local education authorities* must implement the national curriculum (Sections 1 and 10) and have regard to it in undertaking their statutory duties. Under the 1986 Act, they must 'make, and keep up to date' a written statement of their curriculum policy.

How much initiative a local authority retains in regard to curriculum policy also depends on the working out of other parts of the Act (in particular those on financial delegation). In practice, it will mainly be through monitoring school performance and through in-service training and local authority support services that the local authority will be able to give expression to its own curriculum policy. There will also be the chance to take up or reject opportunities offered by government initiatives by way of in-service training grants, Education Support Grants and Training Agency programmes.

*Governing bodies* are (under the 1986 Act) responsible for the oversight of the curriculum at the school level and they must produce (and keep up to date) a curriculum policy document for parents, to show how they intend to meet the requirements of the national curriculum in the light of the local education authority's curriculum policy.

They have a specific responsibility with regard to sex education, which they have discretion to include in the curriculum or exclude; and they have the obligation to ensure that, if it is included, it is 'given in such a manner as to encourage those pupils to have due regard to moral considerations and family life'. They are also bound by the local authority's duty not to present homosexuality as a pretended family relationship.

*Headteachers* must see that the national curriculum policy is carried out. Schools will have to take the programmes of study which emerge from the Curriculum Councils and turn them into syllabuses and working timetables. The attainment targets will form the framework within which these syllabuses will have to be fitted together.

It will be for the schools to work out how the 'subjects' of the national curriculum are to be taught and to interpret them alongside the other demands made on them for the teaching of themes which stretch across the curriculum. Similarly, it will be for the schools to decide whether their statutory obligations are better met by strict timetabling of compulsory subjects, or by modular programmes which cover the ground in other ways.

In the case of grant-maintained schools, governing bodies and heads will have the same obligation to implement the national curriculum, but they will not have to have regard to the local authority's policy.

*Parents* are intended under the Act to become more discriminating consumers, watching school results, as published, and interpreting these results as best they can in the light of local circumstances. The assumption is that they will keep schools up to the mark by making their approval or disapproval known in informal contacts with governors and teachers, and through their formal opportunity to raise points (and pass resolutions) at the annual parents' meeting required by the 1986 Act. If complaints remain unanswered, parents can use the complaints procedure to force the school to deliver the national curriculum, or to force the local authority to use its powers to this end. If unable to get satisfaction, they can appeal to the Secretary of State. And, ultimately, parents have the power to remove their children from one school and send them to another. The procedures for doing so have been made marginally easier by the sections of the Act dealing with open enrolment.

### References

DES (1984) *Organization and Content of the 5–16 Curriculum*, London, HMSO.

DES (1985a) *Science 5–16: A Statement of Policy*, London, HMSO.

DES (1985b) *Better Schools*, Cmnd 9469, London, HMSO.

DES (1987) *The National Curriculum 5–16: A Consultation Document*, London, HMSO.

DES (1988a) *Modern Languages in the School Curriculum*, London, HMSO.

DES (1988b) Circular 5/88, London, DES.

TES (*Times Educational Supplement*) (1988) 'In dispute over whether to help parent or pupil' 18 March: 6.

TGAT (Task Group on Assessment and Testing) (1988) *National Curriculum Task Group on Assessment and Testing: A Report*, London, DES and Welsh Office.

# 2

# National curriculum: Task Group on Assessment and Testing Report: conclusions and recommendations

## Task Group on Assessment and Testing

[. . .]

Any system of assessment should satisfy certain general criteria. For the purpose of national assessment we give priority to the following four criteria:

1. the assessment results should give direct information about pupils' achievement in relation to objectives: they should be criterion-referenced;
2. the results should provide a basis for decisions about pupils' further learning needs: they should be formative;
3. the scales or grades should be capable of comparison across classes and schools, if teachers, pupils and parents are to share a common language and common standards: so the assessments should be calibrated or moderated;
4. the ways in which criteria and scales are set up and used should relate to expected routes of educational development, giving some continuity to a pupil's assessment at different ages: the assessments should relate to progression.

[. . .]

## Conclusions

While the system we propose draws on many aspects of good practice that are already established, it is radically new in the articulation and comprehensive deployment of methods based on such experience. We are confident that the system we describe is practicable and can bring benefits to work both within schools and outside them. In particular, we can see how provision of new types of support within a framework of a new set of procedures can replace much of the large volume of testing and assessment at present in use. A co-ordinated system will use resources to better effect and will complement and support the existing assessment work that teachers already carry out. Thus the system should contribute to the raising of educational standards so that the broad educational needs of individuals and the national need to enhance the resources and skills of young people can be met.

### Building on good classroom practice

The proposed procedures of assessment and testing bear directly upon the classroom practices of teachers. A system which was not closely linked to normal classroom assessments and which did not demand the professional skills and commitment of teachers might be less expensive and simpler to implement, but would be indefensible in that it could set in opposition the processes of learning, teaching and assessment.

### Formative assessment to support learning

Our terms of reference stress that the assessment to be proposed must be 'supportive of learning in schools'. The four criteria set out on p. 21 are essential if this support is to be secured and we believe that they necessarily follow from the aims expressed in the consultative document on the national curriculum. The formative aspect follows almost by definition. For the system to be formative it must produce a full and well-articulated picture of the individual child's current strengths and future needs. No simple label 1–6 will achieve this function, nor is any entirely external testing system capable of producing the necessary richness of information without placing an insuperable load of formal assessment on the child. The formative aspect calls for profile reporting and the exercise of the professional judgement of teachers.

### Raising standards

The system is also required to be formative at the national level, to play an active part in raising standards of attainment. Criterion-referencing inevitably follows. Norm-referenced approaches conceal changes in national standards. Whatever the average child accomplishes is the norm and if the average child's performance changes the reported norm remains the same figure. Only by criterion-referencing can standards be monitored; only by criterion-referencing can they be communicated. Formative assessment requires the involvement of the professional judgement of teachers. Criterion-referencing helps to inform these judgements. Group moderation will enable the dissemination of a shared language for discussing attainment at all levels: the central function of assessment. These three features will help to emphasize growth. They result in progression – a key element in ensuring that pupils and parents receive focused and evolving guidance throughout their school careers. Consistent and de-motivating confirmation of everything as it was at the previous reporting age can be avoided only if pupils and parents can have clear evidence of progress by use of the single sequence of levels across all ages in the way that we propose.

### The unity of our proposals

We have considered systems of assessment and testing which are very different from the one that we propose. All alternatives impoverish the relationships between assessment and learning, so that the former harms the latter instead of supporting it. Most of them give no clear information or guidance about pupils' achievement or progress, and they all risk interference with, rather than support of, teachers' work with pupils. Thus we cannot recommend any simpler alternative to our proposals. There is of course room for variation in their implementation: for example, using group moderation procedures for a restricted number of profile components, or not using all such procedures on every annual assessment cycle, or phasing in more slowly to spread the load on teachers and on the support systems. None of these marginal changes would destroy essential features of our system, although they might weaken its impact in the short term. However, any major change that we can envisage would destroy the linked unity of our proposals and lose most of the benefits which they are aimed to secure within and for the national curriculum.

### Securing teachers' commitment

The underlying unity of the three aspects of education – teaching, learning, and assessment – is fundamental to the strategy which informs our proposals. The strategy will fail if teachers do not come to have confidence in, and commitment to, the new system as a positive part of their teaching. Securing this commitment is the essential pre-condition for the new system to realize the considerable value that it could bring.

Amongst the conditions which will have to be met to secure this professional commitment will be the following:

1 Clear acceptance that the aim is to support and enhance the professional skills that teachers already deploy to promote learning.
2 Clear recognition that the focus of responsibility for operation of a new system lies with teachers within schools.
3 Stress on the formative aims and on giving clear guidance about progress to pupils and to their parents.
4 Widespread consultation and discussion before proposals are put into effect.
5 A realistic time-scale for phasing in a new system.
6 Adequate resources, including in-service provision.
7 Help with moderation procedures so that the system contributes to communication within schools, between schools, parents and governors,

and to the community as a whole about the realization and evaluation of the aims of schools.

8 Sensitive handling of any requirements for outside reporting, recognizing that simplistic procedures could mislead parents, damage schools, and impair relations between teachers and their pupils.

If there is one main motive to explain our support for the system we propose, it is that we believe that it can provide the essential means for promoting the learning development of children: support for teachers in enhancing the resources and professional skills which they deploy.

## A list of recommendations

The recommendations we have made in this report are listed below.

### *Purposes and principles*

1 The basis of the national assessment system should be essentially formative, but designed also to indicate where there is need for more detailed diagnostic assessment. At age 16, however, it should incorporate assessment with summative functions.

2 All assessment information about an individual should be treated as confidential and thus confined to those who need to know in order to help that pupil.

3 For summative and evaluative purposes results should be aggregated across classes or schools so that no individual performances can be separated out.

4 Assessment of attitudes should not form a prescribed part of the national assessment system.

5 To realize the formative purpose of the national assessment system, pupil results in a subject should be presented as an attainment profile.

6 An individual subject should report a small number (preferably no more than four and never more than six) of profile components reflecting the variety of knowledge, skills and understanding to which the subject gives rise. Wherever possible, one or more components should have more general application across the curriculum: for these a single common specification should be adopted in each of the subjects concerned.

7 The national system should employ tests for which a wide range of modes of presentation, operation and response should be used so that each may be valid in relation to the attainment targets assessed. These particular tests should be called 'standard assessment tasks' and they should be so designed that flexibility of form and use is allowed wherever this can be consistent with national comparability of results.

8 Assessment tasks should be reviewed regularly for evidence of bias, particularly in respect of gender and race.

9 Attainment targets should be exemplified as far as possible using specimen tasks. Such tasks can then assist in the communication of these
targets.

10 A mixture of standardized assessment instruments including tests, practical tasks and observations should be used in the national assessment
system in order to minimize curriculum distortion.

11 Teachers' ratings of pupil performance should be used as a fundamental
element of the national assessment system. Just as with the national tests
or tasks, teachers' own ratings should be derived from a variety of
methods of evoking and assessing pupils' responses.

12 When the subject working groups provide guidance on the aggregation of
targets into a small number of profile components, they should have
regard to the need for each component to lead to a report in which
reasonable confidence is possible.

13 Teachers' ratings should be moderated in such a way as to convey and to
inform national standards.

14 The national assessment system should be based on a combination of
moderated teachers' ratings and standardized assessment tasks.

15 Group moderation should be an integral part of the national assessment
system. It should be used to produce the agreed combination of moderated teachers' ratings and the results of the national tests.

16 An item bank of further assessment instruments should be available for
teachers to use in cases where they need additional evidence about
particular pupils.

17 The final reports on individual pupils to their parents should be the
responsibility of the teacher, supported by standardized assessment tasks
and group moderation.

18 Wherever schools use national assessment results in reports for evaluative
purposes, they should report the distribution of pupil achievements.

### The assessment system in practice

19 The ages for national assessment should be 7, 11, 14 and 16, with
reporting occurring near the end of the school year in which each cohort
reaches the age involved.

20 Each of the subject working groups should define a sequence of levels in
each of its profile components, related to broad criteria for progression in
that component. For a profile component which applies over the full
age-range 7 to 16, there should be ten such levels, with corresponding
reduction for profile components which will apply over a smaller span of
school years.

21 Levels 1 to 3 should be used for national assessments at age 7.

22 The formal relationship between national assessment and GCSE
should be limited, in the first instance, to this one reference point: and

accordingly the boundary between levels 6 and 7 should correspond to the grade F/G boundary for GCSE.

23 As they develop the upper four levels of their profile components, the subject working groups should adopt present practices for determining GCSE grades at A/B, C/D, mid-E, and F/G as a starting-point.

24 GCSE should be retained in its present form until the national assessment system is initiated at earlier ages.

25 Assessment and reporting for the national assessment system should be at the same ages for all pupils, and differentiation should be based on the use of the single sequence of levels set up to cover progression over the full age range.

26 Support items, procedures and training should be provided to help teachers relate their own assessments to the targets and assessment criteria of the national curriculum.

27 A review should be made of the materials available to schools for detailed diagnostic investigation of pupils' learning problems, and that the need for extra help with production or advice about such materials should be considered.

28 A working group should be established, with some shared membership between the subject working groups, to co-ordinate their proposals for assessment, including testing, at the primary stages, in the light of a comprehensive view of the primary curriculum and of the need to limit the assessment burden on teachers.

29 National assessment results for any individual pupil should be confidential, to be discussed between pupil, parents and teachers, and to be otherwise transmitted in confidence. National assessment results for a class as a whole and a school as a whole should be available to the parents of its pupils.

30 The *only* form in which results of national assessment for, and identifying, a given school should be published should be as part of a broader report by that school of its work as a whole.

31 Any report by a school which includes national assessment results should include a general report for the area, prepared by the local authority, to indicate the nature of socio-economic and other influences which are known to affect schools. This report should give a general indication of the known effects of such influences on performance.

32 National assessment results, for pupils at age 11, aggregated at school level, should be published as part of each primary school's report. There should be no requirement to publish results for pupils at age 7.

33 National assessment results for pupils at ages 14 and 16, aggregated at school level, should be published as part of each school's report.

34 At age 7 the standard assessment tasks for the national assessment should comprise a choice of three prescribed tasks for each child; each task should be designed to give opportunities for systematic assessment of competence in the range of profile components appropriate to age 7.

35 At age 11 the tests for national assessment should include three or four standard tasks which cover a range of profile components, possibly supplemented by more narrowly focused tests for particular components.

36 Records of Achievement should be used as a vehicle for recording progress and achievement within the national assessment system.

37 Eventually changes will be necessary to the GCSE and other criteria. Changes derived from the development of the national curriculum should have priority in an orderly process of amendment.

38 Like all children, those with special educational needs require attainable targets to encourage their development and promote their self-esteem. Wherever children with special educational needs are capable of undertaking the national tests, they should be encouraged to do so.

39 A special unit within a chosen test development agency should be dedicated to producing test materials and devising testing and assessment procedures sufficiently wide-ranging and sensitive to respond to the needs of these children.

*Implementation*

40 Each subject working group should decide on a limited number, usually four, of profile components in relation to which any pupil's performance will be assessed and discussed. A criterion-referenced set of levels should be set out for each component, to span the full range of performance over the ages for which the component is applicable.

41 Subject working groups should specify, in broad terms and for each profile component, the appropriate tests (standardized assessment tasks) which should be prepared, and the advice and help which should be given to teachers about their corresponding internal assessments.

42 Combination of profile component levels to give a subject level should be by a specified procedure. Uniform ways of describing profile components and the level within each should be specified in language that is helpful to pupils, teachers, parents, employers and other users.

43 Subject working groups should give general advice about the degree of novelty of the assessments they envisage, so that the construction of them and the provision of in-service support for teachers can be appraised.

44 The new assessment system should be phased in over a period adequate for the preparation and trial of new assessment methods, for teacher preparation, and for pupils to benefit from extensive experience of the new curriculum. This period needs to be at least five years from the promulgation of the relevant attainment targets.

# 3

# Towards a framework for curriculum entitlement

**Further Education Unit**

## Curriculum development

A useful starting-point for planning is to consider a model of curriculum development used by the Further Education Unit (FEU). A simplified version is shown in Figure 3.1. The model suggests that the adequacy of provision depends on the quality and appropriateness of all four processes shown in the outer circle, and the existence of the necessary systems required to support them. Thus, however well-resourced the implementation phase may be (for example), this cannot make up for inaccurate needs analysis or inappropriate programme design. This model also suggests that versions of all four processes are necessary at whatever level provision is being planned: from the level of the locality, via individual institutions, down to and including those concerned with specific programmes. Also, at each level, the clients as well as the providers need to be involved, whether the former be identifiable sections of the community or individual learners, vocational sectors or specific companies. Clients and providers need to be involved in the analysis of needs and judgements about priorities, the negotiation of learning programmes appropriate to these needs and priorities, and the evaluation of the extent to which the latter have been met. Implementation must also involve the active participation of the learner, and be flexible enough to adapt to different learning styles.

Like all models, this represents an ideal case. Nevertheless, it does illustrate the variety of factors which needs to be taken into account if the planning process is to achieve its purpose – the efficient provision of better learning opportunities. The role of the LEA is thus to design and support the development of the desired curriculum.

[. . .]

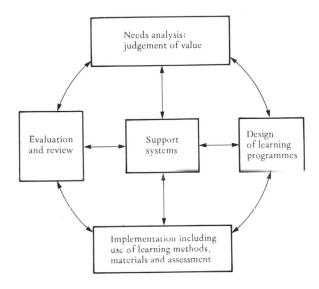

**Figure 3.1**    Processes of curriculum development

## Common curriculum framework

Over a period of many years, FEU has proposed and refined a framework within which the post-16 curriculum should be offered. The curriculum framework, in this sense, refers to the aims, principles and procedures within which all learning programmes should be designed and implemented.

*Aims*

FEU (1987a) suggests that the education service should aim to provide

1 appropriate learning opportunities, regardless of gender, race, age and ability;
2 opportunities for all learners to establish and develop a recognized competence base of knowledge, skills and experience, sufficient to facilitate progression into employment, further education, training, or other roles;
3 an understanding of the local and national economic and social environment, to promote an appreciation of the variety of available adult roles in society;
4 a basis for learners to increase their self-awareness, to appraise realistically their potential and prospects, and to become progressively responsible for negotiating their own personal development.

This set of generic aims can also be seen as a way of finding commonality across a diverse range of learning programmes.

These aims can be said to form the basis of an agenda of entitlement by providing individuals with equal opportunities to cope with change through progression, role competence and personal development. Alongside these aims, FEU suggests that there should be common learning themes applied to all learning programmes regardless of their content (FEU, 1987a; 1987b). These themes are

1 *relevance:* provided by analysing the needs of the learners and the receiving agencies; integrating education, training, work and other aspects of life; placing a value on experience; developing a negotiated curriculum; and ensuring a balance between competing needs;
2 *flexibility:* provided by timetabling to facilitate learning; allowing for individual differences in pace and style of learning; using formative, profiled assessment; introducing modularity to allow credit accumulation; and developing a curriculum to meet the needs of learners by negotiation and interaction;
3 *competence:* provided by designing programmes that deliver a broad range of skills, knowledge, experience and attitudes; ensuring that the programme is integrated and includes work-based learning; developing a better awareness of standards and the ability to recognize and encourage appropriate performance by learners.

### Principles

Value judgements made by providers often manifest themselves directly in the learning experiences which individuals have in schools and colleges. Learners tend to have quite different experiences according to the type of learning programme they are engaged in. This has happened partly because, particularly for 11- to 19-year-olds, we have generally worked to a deficit model of education in which the purpose of the service was to identify deficiency and remedy it, rather than to recognize proficiency and develop it. It is crucial that in developing a common curriculum framework, LEAs should encourage institutions to hold as fundamental principles that

1 learners are of equal value, regardless of their individual strengths and weaknesses;
2 learners have access to appropriate programmes in the locality, within the physical and financial constraints prevailing at the time;
3 learners have the opportunity and positive encouragement to maximize their own potential achievement;
4 all learners are treated equally and benefit from certain common experiences, regardless of the nature of their learning programmes.

*Procedures*

Over recent years, certain educational procedures have been recognized as effective and have been absorbed into practice. In 1981 FEU proposed (FEU, 1981) a set of connected procedures which can be summarized as: negotiation of the curriculum; provision of guidance; the opportunity to acquire relevant skills; formative and profiled assessment; valuing the experience of learners. This tended to be implemented only with a client group comprising learners with a variety of disadvantages who had previously not been well provided for. The DES supported these procedures but as an alternative to the academic and mainstream vocational curricula, rather than as a common framework for all learners over the age of 16.

The framework described above should be implemented with all learners. No one should be denied access to successful learning strategies and enriching curriculum elements and they should form part of the educational entitlement for everyone over the age of 14. These procedures are:

1  *learner-centredness:* this involves arranging educational provision so that learners are involved in negotiating the content, style, and targets for their programmes – this is often facilitated by valuing their experience and engaging in profiled formative assessment;
2  *maximized accessibility:* this is about ensuring that there are no artificial barriers to programmes, such as unnecessary entry requirements, and that every effort is made to provide for all of the potential learners in a locality;
3  *integrated curriculum:* this involves making connections between the various elements of learning – between the (subject) components of a programme, between activities in an institution and outside it, and between past, present and future experience;
4  *guidance and counselling:* this comprises a wide range of support for learners including educational, vocational and personal guidance provided as a part of both learning programmes and the institutional infrastructure;
5  *personal development:* an important consideration in the design of programmes is to ensure that there is both opportunity and encouragement for the development of personal qualities such as effectiveness and role awareness;
6  *optimized progression:* all learners should have the opportunity to achieve their own personal targets and maximize their progress on a particular programme in order to advance to another programme or employment;
7  *equality of opportunity and experience:* this is a starting-point, and implies that institutions should move from equality of access, through equality of treatment, towards equality of outcomes (having equal regard for different outcomes).

This set of procedures is an essential part of a learner's entitlement, and is about equitable access to learning and the quality of that learning.

[. . .]

## Learners' curriculum entitlement

*Content*

The curriculum framework described on pp. 29–31 is recommended as a starting-point, but LEAs will wish to require colleges to compose a curriculum statement which describes entitlement in more detail. For example, all learning programmes have components which may need to be specified for some contexts. FEU suggests that, in doing so, the content of a programme should be considered in terms of

1  *skills:* including performance-related (product skills) and activity-related (process skills);
2  *knowledge:* including theoretical and practical understanding;
3  *experience:* gained before and during a particular learning programme;
4  *learning support:* comprising the infrastructure surrounding learning programmes, including guidance.

Breadth and relevance are more likely to be provided by these components than by merely attempting a balance between subjects. The effectiveness of the combination is likely to be judged by its success in developing competence in a variety of vocational and other roles.

The need for a common curriculum within which learning is provided has led some to define a core, and much work has been undertaken by LEAs to design an 'entitlement core' within TVEI. In developing a core, it should be seen as only a part of the entitlement, and not the entitlement itself. A common core of learning content, defined in the national curriculum as single academic subjects, is a requirement up to the age of 16. Post-16, it may not be appropriate to categorize and deliver learning solely within a subject-based core, especially if it is both common and compulsory. It may be even less appropriate for individuals over 19.

HMI have encouraged a shift of emphasis from subjects to areas of experience in the context of the 11–16 curriculum (DES, 1983), and recommended a 'common framework which provides coherence, and, while taking into account individual needs and abilities, still ensures the provision of a broadly based experience'. A core based on learning experiences would seem to be appropriate for all learners, one to which they should all have access and which should form the basis for curriculum planning. It is not, however, something which all learners would necessarily choose to access all of the time.

For some curriculum planners, this core is expressed in the form of a checklist of activities, such as work experience and residential experience, while others use these and/or a list of areas of learning. This was first suggested by FEU in 1979. It describes groups of experiences and outcomes (including skills, knowledge and attitudes) capable of application in a variety of contexts, and has been helpful in providing the basis for consideration of core entitlement.

### Outcomes

Learners should be aware of the potential outcomes, as well as the content, of a programme. Some outcomes will be pre-specified according to external criteria, while others may be individually negotiated. An important outcome of all learning programmes will be competence. FEU has defined 'competence' as the possession and development of sufficient skills, knowledge, appropriate attitudes and experience for successful performance in life roles, thus embracing academic, vocational and personal competence.

Learners should also be informed of the range of opportunities following from an agreed programme if it is satisfactorily completed. Some colleges already provide this in the prospectus, but it also needs to be addressed at LEA level. Learners should be allowed to negotiate their own interim targets for achievement within nationally agreed parameters and mechanisms by which this will be checked.

### Progression

A comprehensive and impartial description of progression opportunities should form part of the contract between the institution and the learner, and will need to be supported by initial and continuing guidance. For some colleges, this may necessitate a shift of emphasis away from being provision-driven; that is to say, planning should begin with an analysis of clients' needs and not with an analysis of what teachers want to teach. This shift to a needs-driven approach may require colleges to update their staffing expertise. The role for LEAs will be to check that learners' needs are being met.

[. . .]

### Experience

Learners will often prefer to attend an institution in which they will feel comfortable rather than one which apparently best meets their extrinsic needs. This part of curriculum entitlement is about the kind of experience which learners have while they attend schools and colleges. Individuals should be able to expect equal and equitable treatment regardless of their individual needs.

An individual learner's entitlement may be described in the form of a learning contract, initially between the LEA and the learner, and then specifically between the learner and the providing institution, or a combination of them. This will, of course, be only a small part of the total provision on offer in a locality, but will be designed within the agreed overall LEA curriculum framework and underpinned by the prescribed principles. This contract may be in the form of a learning plan describing

1 *content:* this will be negotiated within the constraints of prevailing resources;
2 *outcomes:* these will be negotiated within the context of nationally agreed targets, and pre-specified by external bodies;
3 *progression:* this will be individual;
4 *experiences:* these will be common to all learners.

The equity of treatment and quality of experience which learners receive will be determined by the curriculum framework already described.

## Curriculum provision in institutions

Following the LEA curriculum statement, the various plans and policies may need to be synthesized into a coherent framework within which all post-14 education and training can be implemented. A development plan should be operationalized and implemented by institutions. This process of working from the LEA statement through a synthesis of plans and description of curriculum entitlement to institutional action plans will be followed by LEAs and colleges which place a value on the quality of provision and intend the curriculum to guide decisions about schemes of delegation. The process will also provide the basis of the framework within which the performance of institutions can be monitored and evaluated.

LEAs must design and monitor the implementation of the plan because they are accountable to constituents in a way that individual colleges are not. Colleges and their learning provision are part of the planned resources for those constituents. Greater institutional autonomy will not ensure coherence or comprehensiveness without LEA guidance. While an LEA will have an obligation to provide a curriculum entitlement in its institutions, a school or college will have an obligation to provide a service which meets local needs. Institutions and LEAs need to give equal attention to individual needs and collective community and employment needs.

### Institutional policy

An LEA may start this process by undertaking an audit of community and local employment needs. It will also be appropriate for many colleges to conduct such an audit, together with a thorough analysis of individual learners' needs, before finalizing provision. This will be particularly so if a college is in a large or geographically disparate LEA or intends to provide a comprehensive service. The audit would then become a continuous process. It would result in an institutional policy statement, sometimes called a 'mission statement' (agreed with the LEA), followed by an action plan (agreed with the governing body), and learning contracts (agreed with the individuals).

Colleges may wish to define a local entitlement, in addition to the LEA statement, including a core curriculum of outcomes and experiences for all learners, and may wish to ensure that a system of learner advocacy guarantees its delivery. This may be provided by LEA monitoring, or an external agency acting as an impartial broker, or by the learners taking responsibility for themselves following guidance. This overall process is shown in Figure 3.2.

### Equity

The tension between quality and cost-effectiveness will be most acute at college level, and managers will need to consider carefully not only the range of provision on offer but also the range of educational courses and services *not* on offer. The success of a college cannot be judged on high examination pass rates with a selective client group, as the true measure of effectiveness is the amount of progress made by all learners from their level of achievement at entry to their level at the point of exit. Nor is the successful college one which simply provides courses on demand. That student-led model, in which colleges exist to satisfy learners' wants, could lead to a proliferation of unsuitable programmes, reinforcing failure and lacking progression.

The role for the college is in mediating between learner aspiration, available and potential provision, and realistic progression opportunities. In this mediation process, the college entitlement policy will be the yardstick by which the equity of provision is judged. There should be scope for responding positively to an employer's request for short, full-cost recovery, programmes and providing for the individual needs of a disadvantaged student within the common curriculum framework of the college.

[. . .]

### Quality

The difference between the minimum and maximum entitlements will often comprise a variety of learning support mechanisms, including guidance, tutoring, individualized negotiated learning, and the package of curriculum

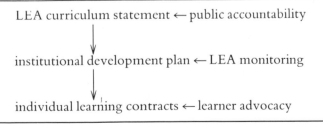

**Figure 3.2**   Putting the plan into action

enrichment elements described earlier. Enrichment is both expensive and cost-effective; it is not a marginal activity and cannot be provided cheaply. It is, however, investing in efficient learning and, if successfully implemented, it maximizes learning outcomes and optimizes progression. In reducing learning wastage it is a powerful and cost-effective weapon. Once this is realized, there may be a shift of resources from teaching activities to learning support systems.

Curriculum enrichment needs to be carefully marketed both inside and outside the college. Evidence of the intended benefits will need to be shown, and in this connection colleges may wish to work towards defining some performance indicators for curriculum quality. Elements of enrichment will be most effective when integrated into mainstream programmes rather than offered as 'bolt-on' packages or optional modules. In this way, the agreed curriculum principles are embedded in all programmes but specific content remains a non-compulsory (negotiated) element.

### Quantity

The preceding paragraphs have discussed curriculum quality as an essential component of entitlement. Another essential aspect is the quantity of provision. LEAs must consider their local staying-on rates and look closely at whether existing provision satisfies the overall needs of the community. The aim should be to ensure that all potential learners are enfranchized and that no one falls through the net. For LEAs, this will require a consideration of fee structures and cost implications. Some may wish to consider the possibility of providing two or three years of free education post-16 for everyone, which could be accessed at 16, or later, or over a period of time.

For a college, the issue of quantity means making some difficult decisions about *what* is offered and what is left out of the college provision. It is also about examining *who* is provided for, and whether that is equitable.
[. . .]
Further education is undergoing a process of modernization. Future developments are likely to encourage further multi-agency provision post-16 in which colleges are essential partners but not sole owners. More institutional autonomy, the growth of private provision, more demand for part-time and modular packages, accelerated technology and ever-changing skill needs could change further education quickly and profoundly. In terms of the curriculum model presented in Figure 3.1 the balance of a college's activities may shift to needs analysis, the tailor-making of learning programmes and evaluation, and away from implementation. Colleges may, therefore, be involved in a shift from being teaching centres to becoming learning resource, testing and accreditation centres. Managing the transition will be difficult and painful for further education staff. The purpose of the service, and changes to it, must be kept in mind at all times – simply, to provide better learning opportunities and experiences for everyone.

### References

DES (1983) *Curriculum 11–16: Towards a Statement of Entitlement*, London, HMSO.
FEU (1979) *A Basis for Choice*, London, FEU.
FEU (1981) *Vocational Preparation*, London, FEU.
FEU (1987a) *Relevance, Flexibility and Competence*, London, FEU.
FEU (1987b) *Supporting Vocational Change*, London, FEU.

# Contexts and perspectives

# 4

# Ideological contexts for curriculum planning

**Keith Morrison and Ken Ridley**

The curriculum is value based. It is founded on the principle of protection and neglect of selected values. Curriculum planners need to expose such values before evaluating how they are brought into the planning debate. A value or ideology can be defined as 'that system of beliefs which gives general direction to the educational policies of those who hold those beliefs' (Scrimshaw, 1983: 4). Different ideologies can coexist with a degree of harmony; different elements of the curriculum being built on different ideological foundations. Alternatively, one can adopt a less consensual line, seeing ideologies not as sets of beliefs of various social groups but – from a Marxian perspective – as that set of values issuing from the dominant powers in society which has imperceptibly permeated the whole class structure; this has the effect of sustaining the dominant class in power (Centre for Contemporary Cultural Studies, 1981).

The significance of this interpretation for curriculum planners is to direct attention to the power of certain groups to make major curriculum decisions, to ask 'whose values are protected in the curriculum?' Educational ideologies will contain values, beliefs and assumptions about children, learning, teaching, knowledge and the curriculum. A curriculum is taken to be all those activities designed or encouraged within the school's organizational framework to promote the intellectual, personal, social and physical development of its pupils. It includes not only the formal programme of lessons, but also the 'informal' programme of so-called extra-curricular activities as well as those features which produce the school's 'ethos'.

More specifically, Meighan (1981) contends that an ideology addresses seven components which concern curriculum planners:

1 A theory of knowledge: its content and structure – what is considered worthwhile or important knowledge, how it is organized (e.g. by subjects or integrated areas) and who shall have access to it.

2  A theory of learning and the learner's role – an active or a passive style, doing or listening, co-operative or competitive learning, producing or reproducing knowledge, problem-solving or receiving facts.
3  A theory of teaching and the teacher's role – formal or informal, authoritarian or democratic, interest in outcomes or processes, narrow or wide.
4  A theory of resources appropriate for learning – first hand or second hand.
5  A theory of organization of learning situations – criteria for grouping pupils.
6  A theory of assessment that learning has taken place – diagnostic or attainment testing, written or observational assessment, defining what is to be assessed.
7  A theory of aims, objectives and outcomes – a view of what is desirable for society, the child, and knowledge.

One can determine how characteristics of different educational ideologies will address these seven main components. Scrimshaw (1983), for example, suggests that ideologies differ in their emphasis on the individual learner, knowledge and society. While these are clearly not discrete, nevertheless the emphasis is useful, and is one way of organizing the potentially disparate number of ideologies which appear in educational literature. Many of these are substantially the same ideology under a different name and are presented in summary form in Table 4.1. The difference between knowledge (a) and knowledge (b) in Table 4.1 lies in the access to high status knowledge. Advocates of knowledge (a) would restrict high status knowledge to an elite minority, whereas advocates of knowledge (b) would make it accessible to all pupils. The difference between society (a) and society (b) lies in the perspec-

**Table 4.1**   Clusters of educational ideologies

| Ideology | Emphasis |
|---|---|
| Progressivism<br>Child-centredness<br>Romanticism | Individual child |
| Classical humanism<br>Conservatism<br>Traditionalism<br>Academicism | Knowledge (a) |
| Liberal humanism | Knowledge (b) |
| Instrumentalism<br>Revisionism<br>Economic renewal | Society (a) |
| Democratic socialism<br>Reconstructionism | Society (b) |

tives on society. Society (a) tends to regard the existing societal status quo as desirable and worth perpetuating and improving, while society (b) will look to its alteration, its future evolution.

### Ideologies emphasizing the individual learner

Ideologies in this sphere represent the 'developmental tradition' in primary education (Blyth, 1965). In them the transmission of knowledge is secondary to discovery and to following the child's impulses, needs and interests. Stress is laid on learning by doing, spontaneity, free expression and developing the child's own nature spontaneously: 'give your scholar no verbal lessons; he should be taught by experience alone' (Worthington, 1884: 56). Knowledge is not imposed from without, but is uncertain, pragmatic, tentative and provisional; it is that which the child discovers rather than reproduces.

Emphasis is placed, then, on originality and authenticity of the child's experience and awareness, on diversity of response and provision, on creativity, enjoyment and the development of the emotional side of the child's personality. The process of learning is as important as the outcomes of learning – the knowledge products. Hence education is seen as intrinsically worthwhile: valuable in itself rather than for what it leads to in later life.

In their challenge to rationalism, objectivity, abstract analysis and universalism, these ideologies celebrate empiricism, subjectivity, personal meanings and particularism. Childhood becomes a state in itself rather than a preparation for adulthood: 'The Child is father of the Man' (Wordsworth, 1807). Adults can learn from children and their childhood innocence (see also Aries, 1973). For curriculum planners such views refute the value of an imposed curriculum: 'put the problems before him and let him solve them himself . . . let him not be taught science, let him discover it' (Rousseau, quoted in Blenkin and Kelly, 1981: 19).

Schools have to protect children from the harmful and unpleasant aspects of the outside world (King, 1978) which might corrupt them. Hence they cocoon the child in a comfortable and secure environment separate from the vagaries of the world outside the classroom. If children fail at school then the school rather than the child is to be censured. One can detect the inspirational and optimistic rather than the analytic tenor of child-centred ideologies; indeed analysis reveals how dangerously loose these ideologies can be. For example, how can one derive and plan a curriculum from needs and interests which may be trivial, ephemeral, irrelevant or morally unacceptable? How will children judge what their needs are until they have a measure of knowledge? How can a curriculum be constructed from aims such as 'development', 'growth', or 'discovery' (Hirst and Peters, 1970)? Will it not lead to Bantock's (1980: 44) fears that 'temporary interest and immediate need are the guiding principle implicit in the attempt to "psychologize" learning; hence the emphasis on motivation and endogenous development too easily fosters a magpie curriculum of bits and pieces'?

Further, in sheltering children from the corruption of the outer world, how adequate an education is being provided for future citizens? How justified is the exclusion or neglect, however partial, of the world beyond the classroom or immediate environment, regardless of the desirability or undesirability of that world? Similarly, in concentrating on the 'here and now' of the child's existence, how fair or responsible are teachers being to the received wisdoms of prior generations? Children may want, and need, to know about conflict and change as well as consensus and stability.

In approaching child-centred ideologies, then, one has to pare away the romanticism and exhortation, address the criticisms, and then see how they can be usefully employed in curriculum planning, avoiding the curriculum myopia to which such ideologies are prone. The thrust of many of these ideologies towards practical discovery and experiential learning, problem-solving, a process approach to the curriculum, identifying, meeting and developing children's needs, abilities and individual personalities, flexibility rather than uniformity of teaching, and the provision of a stimulating environment, become the elements which curriculum planners can use.

### Ideologies emphasizing knowledge

In these ideologies one can detect a strong sympathy with conservative notions of protecting and perpetuating the best of the past as experienced in the present. Their antecedents lie in the 'preparatory' tradition (Blyth, 1965) of primary education and derive too from Plato's 'Republic' through Jesuit education, the mandarins of classical Chinese history (Weber, 1972), Matthew Arnold, T. S. Eliot and Bantock. They are unequivocally divisive and elitist, arguing for a separate and elite education into 'high culture' and a high cultural heritage for a chosen minority, giving them access to power and privilege:

> education should help to preserve the class and to select the elite. It is right that the exceptional individual should have the opportunity to elevate himself in the social scale and attain a position in which he can exercise his talents to the greatest benefit of himself and society. But the ideal of an educational system which would automatically sort out everyone according to his native capacities is unattainable in practice. . . . It would disorganize society, by substituting for classes, elites of brains, or perhaps only of sharp wits.
>
> (Eliot, 1948: 100–1)

Its curriculum is academic and intellectual, non-vocational even though its clients may go on to prestigious positions in employment; it recognizes the permanence of knowledge and of high status knowledge in particular. Children have to be initiated into the received wisdoms of their forebears, the initiation rites of passage often being formal examinations. Subject loyalty is strong, discipline oriented and reliant on instruction rather than experiential learning (Lawton, 1973). Standards are clear, excellence of academic achievement is emphasized, and stress is laid on the development of rationality through a curriculum marked by uniformity rather than diversity (Jenkins 1975). This curriculum runs counter to social justice and equality of opportunity (Lawton, 1983). For the masses who cannot aspire to this, a 'folk' curriculum (Bantock, 1975; 1976) is offered whose result is effectively to debar them from entering the corridors of privilege, providing what is often regarded as low status, practical, vocational and everyday knowledge. Ideologies in this area, then, emphasize a 'dual' curriculum (Scrimshaw, 1976).

Against this perhaps bleak picture an alternative ideology in this area advances a knowledge-based curriculum whose emphasis is less on a stratified than on a unified society, with egalitarian principles at its core. In liberal humanism high culture is to be accessible to all through a common curriculum:

> If, as Tawney said, we think the higher culture fit for solicitors, why should we not think it fit for coalminers? . . . Every child should be initiated into those forms of experience which together constitute this higher culture – the arts, mathematics, the human and physical sciences, philosophy.
>
> (White 1982: 26)

For curriculum planners the significance of debates about knowledge is to clarify which knowledge should be in the curriculum, how it should be organized and who should have access to it.


### Ideologies emphasizing society

The ideologies in this group share a common belief that education is valued for what it leads to rather than solely being an end in itself. One can discern two clear directions which society-oriented ideologies take. Instrumental ideologies – instrumentalism, revisionism, and those stressing economic renewal – emphasize the need for education to fit learners to society, particularly in economic terms. Education thus exists to provide a skilled work-force to expand the nation's economic strength; hence resources are developed for vocational (DES, 1985), scientific and technical education. Weight is laid on the relevance and utility aspects of education (Scrimshaw, 1983). The intentions of education are not to alter radically existing society, rather to improve the efficiency of existing organizations, institutions and economic structures (Oliver, 1982).

**Table 4.2** Ideologies interpreted by their component issues

| Ideology | Progressivism, child-centredness, romanticism | Classical humanism, traditionalism, academicism, conservatism | Liberal humanism | Instrumentalism, revisionism, economic renewal | Reconstructionism, democratic socialism |
|---|---|---|---|---|---|
| Emphasis | Individual child | Knowledge – unequal access | Knowledge – equal access | Society – status quo | Society – changed |
| Theory of knowledge | Empiricist, active, evolutionary, subjective, emphasis on processes, integrated curricula | Disciplines, non-vocational, academic, high culture, emphasis on products, rationalistic | Common culture curriculum | Utilitarian, economically relevant, vocational, scientific, technological | Revolutionary, problem-solving, active, socially relevant, vocational |
| Theory of learning and of the learner's role | Experiential, spontaneity, emphasis on skills and processes, co-operative, intrinsic motivation | Obedience, passivity, conformity, uniformity | Induction into key areas of experience, active and co-operative learning | Induction into vocationally relevant areas | Apprenticeship, practical, co-operative, problem-solving |
| Theory of teaching and of the teacher's role | Guide, provider of multiple resources, facilitator, catalyst of child's self-chosen curriculum | Instructor, information transmitter, authoritative, formal tutor | Guide, provider of resources, facilitator | Instructor, trainer, transmitter of vocationally relevant experiences | Guide, catalyst of social changes, disseminator of centralist philosophy, instructor, trainer |

|  | | | | | |
|---|---|---|---|---|---|
| Theory of resources | First-hand, diverse, extensive | Second-hand, restricted | First- and second-hand, multiple, extensive | Narrowly relevant to content, practical, vocational | Highly focused to task in hand, vocational |
| Theory of organization of learning situations | Diverse, flexible, informal, co-operative, group work, discovery methods | Class teaching, formal, uniform, competitive | Open, flexible, diverse | Narrow, practical, relevant to task, class and individual teaching, uniformity | Individual and group work as relevant to task |
| Theory of assessment | Diagnostic, multiple, criteria, informal, profiling | Written, formal, attainment testing, examinations | Diagnostic, norm and written, formal or informal | Formal, written and oral, practical | Flexible, formal or written as appropriate, attainment testing |
| Theory of aims, objectives and outcomes | Self-expression, individuality, creativity, development of whole personality | Received curricula, elitist, non-vocational, high culture | Equal access to key areas of knowledge, egalitarian | Extrinsic worthwhileness, relevant to economic good, efficient worker | Extrinsic worthwhileness, relevant to social good, citizenship, common good |

Contrasted to this are more radical society-oriented educational ideologies. Figuring high at times of social rebuilding or social upheaval, e.g. post-war renewal of society, reconstructionism posits a view of education as a major force for planned change rather than stability in society; what society ought to be rather than what it is (Scrimshaw, 1983). Society in need of reconstruction requires an educated populace whose curriculum has a strong social core with a stress on citizenship, egalitarianism, democracy and participation in decision-making. In this world teachers are catalysts and guardians of social change; creators rather than transmitters of knowledge. There are dangers in this approach. Such a vision is potentially unstable as it is always looking to the future; it is predicated for its success on an educated citizenry – which is perhaps both its greatest strength and its greatest weakness; it relies on a high level of control – running the risk perhaps of centralization or even indoctrination. Finally, one has to question the extent to which education can shoulder the burden of changing society. Do not macro changes require macro and manifold organizations and institutions to change? Reconstructionist ideology, with its positive, perhaps idealistic, tone and central role for education, requires curriculum planners to think from afresh the content, aims and pedagogy of curricula from the perspective of their benefit to society (Hewlett, 1986). From an analysis of key characteristics of different ideologies one can map their expression on to Meighan's (1981) components of ideologies outlined earlier, and they are presented thus in Table 4.2.

Ideological analysis affects primary curriculum planning extensively – at the levels of aims, content, pedagogy and evaluation. The analysis so far reveals the multiplicity of values which underpin the curriculum. There is no exclusive relationship between the ideologies and the everyday activities of primary schools; the same activity in school can support a variety of ideologies, just as one ideology can give rise to several activities. Further, different areas of the curriculum can, and will, serve different educational ideologies. The effect of this analysis is twofold: first, it reveals, importantly, that the curriculum is not a closed system, but that it is open, negotiable, problematic, and has to be constantly reviewed, questioned and discussed. Second, ideological analysis reveals potential conflicts in curriculum decision-making. If one queries why certain ideologies are over-represented or under-represented in the primary curriculum, one is thrust back on to an examination of the power structures operating in curriculum decision-making, to identify whose decisions are holding sway. As mentioned earlier, ideological investigation can reveal the nature of the power of dominant interest groups; ideological analysis is thus political analysis (Mannheim, 1936).

Schools and teachers are caught up in this, like it or not. The study of ideologies, while it separates artificially practices in the interests of conceptual clarity, assists teachers and planners to adopt the reflective and critical stance [which has been] advocated as a requisite of 'good' teaching.

Curriculum planners will need to ascertain the power behind curriculum proposals emanating from diverse sources.

## References

Aries, P. (1973) *Centuries of Childhood*, Harmondsworth, Penguin.

Bantock, G. H. (1975) 'Towards a theory of popular education', in M. Golby, J. Greenwald and R. West (eds) *Curriculum Design*, London, Croom Helm and the Open University.

Bantock, G. H. (1976) 'Quality and equality in curricular provisions', Appendix 1, in M. Skilbeck 'Ideologies and values', Unit 3, E203, *Curriculum Design and Development*, Milton Keynes, Open University.

Bantock, G. H. (1980) *Dilemmas of the Curriculum*, Oxford, Martin Robertson.

Blenkin, G. and Kelly, A. V. (1981) *The Primary Curriculum*, London, Harper & Row.

Blyth, W. A. L. (1965) *English Primary Education, Vol. 1*, London, Routledge & Kegan Paul.

Centre for Contemporary Cultural Studies (1981) *Unpopular Education*, London, Hutchinson.

DES (1985) *Better Schools*, Cmnd 9469, London, HMSO.

Eliot, T. S. (1948) *Notes towards the Definition of Culture*, London, Faber.

Hewlett, M. (1986) *Curriculum to Serve Society: How Schools can Work for People*, Loughborough, Newstead Publishing.

Hirst, P. H. and Peters, R. S. (1970) *The Logic of Education*, London, Routledge & Kegan Paul.

Jenkins, D. (1975) 'Classic and romantic in the curriculum landscape', in M. Golby, J. Greenwald and R. West (eds) *Curriculum Design*, London, Croom Helm.

King, R. (1978) *All Things Bright and Beautiful? A Sociological Study of Infants' Classrooms*, Chichester, Wiley.

Lawton, D. (1973) *Social Change, Educational Theory and Curriculum Planning*, London, University of London Press.

Lawton, D. (1983) *Curriculum Studies and Educational Planning*, Sevenoaks, Hodder & Stoughton.

Mannheim, K. (1936) *Ideology and Utopia*, London, Routledge & Kegan Paul.

Meighan, R. (1981) *A Sociology of Educating*, Eastbourne, Holt, Rinehart & Winston.

Oliver, D. (1982) 'The primary curriculum: a proper basis for planning', in C. Richards (ed.) *New Directions in Primary Education*, Lewes, Falmer Press.

Scrimshaw, P. (1976) 'Towards the whole curriculum', Units 9 and 10, E203, *Curriculum Design and Development*, Milton Keynes, Open University.

Scrimshaw, P. (1983) 'Educational ideologies', Unit 2, E204, *Purpose and Planning in the Curriculum*, Milton Keynes, Open University.

Weber, M. (1972) 'The Chinese literati', in B. Cosin (ed.) *Education Structure and Society*, Harmondsworth, Penguin.

White, J. (1982) 'The curriculum mongers: education in reverse', in T. Horton and P. Raggatt (eds) *Challenge and Change in the Curriculum*, Sevenoaks, Hodder & Stoughton.

Wordsworth, W. (1807) 'My heart leaps up', line 7.

Worthington, E. (1884) *Rousseau's Emile*, London, D.C. Heath.

# 5

# The national curriculum and the implementation gap

**Tony Becher**

## Introduction

At first sight, the prescription of a uniform national curriculum under the 1988 Act leaves little scope for curriculum decision-making at the classroom level. I want here to suggest that this is an unduly pessimistic view. Many of the most important choices will rest, as they have in the past, within the sphere of responsibility of the professional teachers in each school: curriculum management skills will be no less essential than they have always been.

It may be useful to begin with a reminder that the term curriculum can be interpreted in a number of different ways. At its narrowest, it may be used to stand for no more than a list of the subjects to be taught – the set of entries on the timetable. A slightly broader definition would equate 'curriculum' with 'syllabus', giving it the meaning of a formal list of the topics to be covered over a particular time-span within each subject area. Many people would accord it a wider sense than this, allowing the curriculum to refer to the totality of the planned provision through which any educational organization sets itself to achieve its educative purpose (a notion which would include what are often seen as 'extra-curricular activities'). And there are some who would argue that the concept should cover no less than the institution's total contribution to the student's learning experience (a definition which would embrace the 'hidden curriculum' as well).

Without choosing between these various possible interpretations, it is easy to see that the Education Reform Act itself does not go beyond the first, and most limited, of them. The national curriculum is identified as comprising ten timetable entries: three 'core subjects' (English, mathematics and science) and seven 'other foundation subjects' (history, geography, technology, music, art, physical education and a modern foreign language from age 11). It is only through the subsequently published 'Orders' by the secretary of state that any further specification is given of appropriate attainment targets, programmes of study and assessment arrangements for each of the foundation subjects. These, in effect, comprise the national syllabuses initially proposed by curriculum working groups and further refined through the consultative machinery of the National Curriculum Council (NCC) and the School Examinations and Assessment Council (SEAC).

From one standpoint, the national curriculum can be seen as marking an important educational advance, in that it offers the prospect of a universal entitlement to knowledge, breaking down the increasingly marked differentiation after the early secondary school years between the high-status courses followed by the abler pupils and the low-status offerings commonly provided for the less able. But it is also possible to take a more critical view, arguing that the list of approved items is too narrowly based on the traditional grammar school timetable, and that the curricular model adopted fails to look beyond the mere aggregation of a series of discrete subjects to a more holistic conception of what schools ought to be about.

Be that as it may, any broader view of what the curriculum comprises will remain open to local determination. The Act concedes various subsidiary powers over the individual school's curricular provision to other bodies, and notably the local authority and the governors; but even allowing for this, a large area of discretion remains to the teaching staff.

## The continuity behind the revolution

Even if the 1988 Education Reform Act is held to represent a far-reaching reform, the specific provisions it makes for the national curriculum are not especially radical. The seeds of that notion were, after all, sown in the mid-1970s by a Labour prime minister (reviving an older tradition which was enshrined in the Codes which governed elementary and secondary education under the 1902 Act, and which survived for more than twenty years afterwards). To the extent that no major political party voiced its dissent from the views expressed in James Callaghan's 1976 Ruskin speech, the idea of a publicly defined expression of 'the purpose of education and the standards that we need' could be said to be uncontentious.

In any case, there has always been a loose consensus among educationists and lay people about what curricular activities are important. At the upper secondary level, the curriculum in each subject has generally been constrained, if not determined, by national examination requirements; the overall range of subject offerings in schools has been limited by broad, if often unspoken, social expectations. Within the Act, neither the choice of a central core nor that of other foundation subjects is a matter for surprise. Particular interest groups might have wanted to argue for the inclusion of other themes, but there has been little suggestion that any of the existing ones are in-appropriate. So the national curriculum may be seen as giving explicit recognition to what many schools would claim they are in large part already doing.

Its symbolic significance should not however be overlooked. It rep-resents the culminating point of a growing sense of dissatisfaction with teachers and with schooling, whose origins lie in the late 1960s and early 1970s, but which was fuelled by more recent events, including the long-drawn-out industrial troubles of the mid-1980s. The imposition by Parlia-ment of a formal set of requirements on the schools may thus be interpreted as a rhetorical device, giving formal expression to a lack of confidence in the education service, though not in practice making a great deal of difference to schools' curricular offerings or policies.

But this line cannot be taken too far, because rhetoric may itself be an important means of enshrining new value assumptions, and hence changing operational practices. It would be as absurd to suggest that the national curriculum would have no noticeable impact on the classroom as it would be to contend that it removes any professionality that the teachers might previously have enjoyed. The truth, as so often, lies between the two extremes.

## The government's implementation strategy

It may be helpful to consider what room remains for decision-making within the prescribed curricular framework by standing back and looking at some characteristic ways in which policy initiatives are implemented. There are a number of relevant sources of research literature, each of them somewhat distinct from the others. There are, first, the early accounts of planned change, exemplified in Havelock (1969) and Bennis *et al.* (1969); there are studies of organization and management theory, usefully summarized in Bush (1986); there are the sociological writings on exchange theory, of which Archer (1981) is perhaps the most accessible; and there are the further sets of ideas developed in the context of policy analysis, of which a much-quoted exemplar is Pressman and Wildavsky (1973). None of these exactly catches the distinctions that I now want to make, although between them they give some support to the composite picture which I will try to describe.

There are, I suggest, three broad approaches to the business of putting an innovative idea into practice. The first is some form of coercion: it may be through the direct or indirect exercise of force, or it may rest on an invocation of superior authority. Bennis *et al.*'s (1969) power-coercive strategy approxi-mates to this, in identifying the particular way in which power is applied to limit alternatives for action or to shape its consequences. Archer's 'political' transaction is another variant on the same theme. This 'top-down' approach is perhaps most typically adopted within hierarchical, bureaucratic structures, in which orders are conveyed from central management to those concerned with the day-to-day running of the enterprise.

A second set of tactics encompasses bargaining and manipulation, often operating through emotionally charged appeals, or through a reference to self-interest. Havelock's social interaction model comes somewhere near to this, as does Archer's 'external' form of transaction. Manipulative styles of policy implementation tend to flourish in a setting characterized by rival interest groups.

The third mode of implementation depends on reasoned persuasion, impartial analysis or logical argument – what Bennis terms the empirical-rational approach. Here – though again the correlation is only a rough-and-ready one – one looks for examples most naturally within what Bush (1986) and others have characterized as a collegial or professional form of organization.

This summary of implementation strategies comprises a very simplified account of what is in reality a much more complex situation. It may however serve a useful purpose in bringing out the common structures underlying a number of diverse strands of inquiry into how policy change may be effected. The strategies in question can be illustrated by relatively recent attempts at large-scale curriculum reform.

The last of the three, depending upon the exercise of reason, and operating within a collegial framework, is typified by the Schools Council's approach to curriculum issues. The adoption of the projects it sponsored rested mainly on an appeal to teachers' professionalism, the attempt being to encapsulate existing good practice and to give it wider currency.

In contrast, the then Manpower Services Commission (MSC, now Training Agency) opted for an overtly manipulative technique: its curriculum proposals were supported by the promise of additional resources for schools which adopted them. The MSC's educational arguments were thus less central to the implementation process than the accompanying financial inducements. The context was uncompromisingly one of political bargaining, based on the strongly instrumental view of education characteristic of the MSC's parent agency, the Department of Trade and Industry.

The national curriculum rests for its adoption on the force of statute. Its requirements were promulgated with only a derisory show of consultation. No attempts were made, in the course of framing the Education Act which embodied such requirements, either to enlist professional support along the lines adopted by the Schools Council or to offer the special incentives characteristic of the curriculum schemes promoted by the MSC. It seems reasonable to argue that this particular aspect of the legislation was the product less of party political considerations than of a systematic campaign by the DES and HMI to win back some of the managerial power which had earlier been ceded to the local authorities and professional teacher interests (see Salter and Tapper, 1981). Accordingly it would appear that the national curriculum represents a coercive approach to the problem of adoption, in a context of bureaucratic and hierarchical (rather than collegial or pressure group) relationships between its initiators and those called upon to carry it out.

Coercion would seem a prompt and efficient means of putting any proposal into effect: it is less expensive in terms of money and effort than manipulation, and markedly quicker in its impact than reasoned argument. But its superiority in these regards over other approaches bears a cost. Because those who are required to carry out the resulting policies have no sense of ownership of them, they may – if they have any remaining freedom of action – elect to ignore them or at best to interpret them in ways that serve their own interests. The teaching profession, in so far as its members feel alienated and uninvolved in the process of devising the national curriculum, may well choose to deviate from it to any extent that enables them to avoid its inherent sanctions. Anyone who questions the distinction marked by Pressman and Wildavsky (1973) between policy as formulated and policy as practised has only to look at the provisions of the 1944 Act (reiterated in modified form in 1988) for a daily act of worship and for the teaching of an agreed syllabus of religious education in schools.

This phenomenon – the 'implementation gap' as it is often called – is not of course peculiar to the educational world. Numerous studies of policy analysis testify to its existence across a whole variety of contexts. Thus Lipsky (1971) was able to show how the intentions behind urban renewal policies in the USA could be significantly distorted by the 'street-level bureaucrats' – those relatively low-ranking officials who were charged with making the day-to-day decisions on which the fulfilment of the legislators' plans ultimately rested. More recently, and nearer home, Jordan and Richardson (1987), in their wide-ranging review of governmental policy-making in Britain, noted that 'the most desired goals cannot be secured simply by political will: they require the cooperation of other groups and institutions . . . in fact, the operationalization of policy is often difficult', and added, 'radical objectives [become] compromised in the process of bargaining and implementation'. The following section offers a reminder of the compromises that have already become evident in relation to some recently attempted reforms of national education policy.

## Compromise and counter-revolution

It is not, I think, unduly cynical to claim that 'the implementation game' (see Bardach, 1977) was played out with some skill and sophistication by educationists in the 1980s. A state system largely modelled on the liberal-democratic vision which lay behind the 1944 Act was confronted by a radically right-wing government set firmly on course to replace the ideology of the welfare state by a rival dedication to free market principles. At its extreme, that change – which, as we were often reminded, was sanctioned by the mandate of the electorate – resulted in a narrowly instrumental view of schooling. The view which prevailed was that the fundamental rationale for education's call on public funds lay in its contribution to the national economy. Contentions that it should also have intrinsic ends, serving as a source of personal development, and celebrating intellectual knowledge as a worthy goal in itself, were discounted. So, too, were considerations of social benefit, which seek to justify more broadly cultural arguments, along with those which call on humanistic notions of 'the good society'. Yet these reflect underlying values which many people, within the system and outside it, were deeply reluctant to abandon.

The potential here for counter-revolutionary conflict is evident enough: what is interesting is the way in which it gave place to a bargaining process in which the new values have been accommodated without any very drastic sacrifice of the old. By implication, if not explicitly, the proponents of the romantic vision conceded that they were wrong – or at least, that they were at odds with too many of their fellow-citizens – in appearing to scorn the pragmatic aspects of the education process. With the wisdom of hindsight, it was perhaps absurd to pretend, as was once fashionable, that education has nothing to do – and indeed ought to have nothing to do – with the world of work. The message seemed generally to have got home that the public funds on which a public service must depend are themselves the product of a sound economy: that the nation's schools, colleges and universities, if they are to survive in a healthy state, must play their part in contributing to the skilled labour force which such an economy needs. On one reading, the pendulum may – under the influence of the MSC and its successor, the Training Agency – have swung much too far the other way, reducing the concepts of learning and understanding to the narrower notions of job-related competence and entrepreneurial capability. But closer examination may encourage a less gloomy view.

A seemingly endless series of new national initiatives has been promoted in recent years, many of which have at first been greeted with widespread alarm and suspicion. TVEI provides a case in point. The nature of its sponsorship, the rhetoric behind its promotion, and the manner in which it was introduced, led to a quite reasonable expectation that it would have a damaging and restrictive effect on the pattern of teaching provision in the upper secondary years. On the whole, that expectation was not realized: the model it espoused was a fairly open one, and has indeed been compared favourably with the apparently much tighter and more dirigiste structure which underpins the national curriculum.

Teacher appraisal provides another example of an apparent threat which has, in the event, come to look more like a benefaction. Although it was conceived as part of Sir Keith Joseph's campaign to 'cut out the dead wood' in the schools, conjuring up visions of the root-and-branch pruning of classroom staff, the end result has instead been to create far more systematic opportunities than had previously existed for personal and professional development, and to open up (in theory, if not yet in practice) the possibility of a greater measure of career progression for teachers.

Examination reforms, too, have commonly been introduced in the name of 'raising standards', prompting fears that an already excessively competitive and meritocratic system, when judged in an international context, might become even more so. Yet the consequent changes looked very different from those which might reasonably have been predicted. The moves towards profiling and records of achievement represented a broadly enlightened view of the nature of the assessment process; and even the GCSE examination, whose advent at first gave rise to some concern, can now be seen to have provided an impetus for more adventurous methods of teaching and learning. Project work found its way into the secondary schools, filtering down from changes in tertiary education as well as up from long-standing practice in the primary schools; rewards geared solely towards the bookish skills of the academically able were supplemented by a wider recognition of other forms of accomplishment.

These apparent contradictions between what was initially proposed and what has eventually resulted call for some explaining. The transformation in each case is not, I suggest, due to a change in heart on the part of our political leadership, in which proposals intended as punitive measures have been turned miraculously into rewards. Nor can it plausibly be seen as a cunning conspiracy, in which a government in league with the teaching profession has deliberately set out to deceive its hard-line supporters by parading publicly in wolf's clothing, only to reveal itself in private as a wet and woolly sheep in disguise. The truth is likely to be more straightforward. It is that policy-makers cannot operate in isolation: what happens when their plans are put into action depends crucially on those who have to carry them out. However much it might wish to, no regime – whether based on Downing Street, the White House or the People's Palace – can dispense with the agents out there (on the ground, in the front line, at the coal-face) whose job it is to translate policy into practice. And translation is not, one should remember, a purely passive process: a translator has the power to change meanings in a variety of subtle ways.

In each of the examples noted above, one might argue that attempts from the centre to bring schooling into closer line with a 'back to the basics' philosophy were successfully hijacked by the liberal education establishment, who took the opportunity to infuse them with their own, predominantly progressive, ideals. Even where the elitists seem to have won out – as in the rejection of the Higginson Report, which attempted to instil some belated breadth into the sixth-form curriculum and examinations – their victory may have been a pyrrhic one; institutions of higher education, faced with the falling rolls that earlier hit the primary and secondary schools, are finding it expedient to call for a wider range of entry requirements, and hence to extol the virtues of reduced specialization. When one begins to look more closely, the underlying reality is hard to reconcile with the superficial appearance of right-wing radical reform.

## Implications for the individual school

If this reasoning is valid, it has obvious implications for the way in which the national curriculum is likely to affect the schools. In turning to consider this question, it must be acknowledged that those who drew up the legislation were in no sense naive enough to suppose that its provisions could be imposed without an accompanying system of checks and sanctions. The guarantee that the relevant provisions of the Act would be properly observed in every classroom, rather than subverted by a silently rebellious teaching force, was seen to lie in the imposition of universal testing at the ages of 7, 11, 14 and 16, whose scores should be published on a school-by-school basis. What was not so clearly foreseen was that the testing process would itself be subverted, in terms of the same liberal pedagogic sentiments that had already dulled the edge of earlier attempts to make education look more like industrial training.

The recommendations of the Task Group on Assessment and Testing must have come as a great disappointment to those who hoped it would give the national curriculum a sharp set of teeth. Although its report was eventually accepted, after some show of prime ministerial reluctance, it represented as forward-looking an approach to the issue as any child-centred educationist could have demanded in the circumstances, allowing a fair amount of scope for teacher involvement and building in a degree of complexity sufficient to defy any too-simplistic interpretation of the results.

To revert to the point with which this analysis began, the national curriculum will certainly impose some greater measure of uniformity on what is supposed to be learnt, and tested, at each given interval in the educational process. But that is about the limit of what can be said. Legislation is silent on how any particular part of the curriculum should be organized and taught; and even with respect to what are now fashionably termed outputs – the required goals at the end of the process – there is likely to be room for a good deal of slippage, since there is no foolproof way known to national legislators of closing tight the implementation gap. The pessimistic, neo-Orwellian vision of a uniform pattern of schooling with centrally controlled teachers, drilled in robot fashion into instilling a set item of the syllabus in exactly the same way at precisely the same moment of time, is a long way from realization.

It may indeed turn out to be almost true, if not intentionally so, that – as the first of the glossy DES bulletins on the Education Reform Act (DES 1988) claimed – 'The framework of the National Curriculum will build on best practice in schools with teachers continuing to have scope to decide what and how they teach, and to develop new approaches.' The 'what' looks pretty questionable, and the 'scope . . . to develop new approaches' may be somewhat more limited than it was before: but for the rest, it seems, *plus ça change* . . .

The room for curriculum decision-making at the level of the individual school ·may therefore be greater than many of us would initially have foreseen. The next, and final, section will consider some possible approaches to putting the national curriculum into practice, which are likely to reflect the existing management style of each institution concerned.

## Some alternative scenarios

Under the Education Reform Act, teachers – at least in principle – cease to have any major responsibility for determining the broad objectives of the curriculum. As an aside, it might reasonably be contended that they have no natural right to do so, nor yet any special expertise that entitles them to act as Platonic 'philosopher-kings' in the matter. Education is a matter for universal concern, and the opportunity to decide where its main emphases should be placed is one which, in a representative democracy, ought to rest with society as a whole.

Professionals, one might concede, should have a legitimate say in determining the most appropriate means to any generally desired end that has close relevance to their particular knowledge and skills: but their sovereignty does not properly extend to the determination of the ends themselves. Doctors cannot be entrusted to decide on behalf of society how the overall resources for medical research and hospital provision should be allocated – between, say, the general improvement of preventive medicine on the one hand and the development of highly esoteric surgical skills on the other; the police cannot be allowed to frame the criminal code or to determine the course of justice. No more should teachers expect to lay down the law on what ought and ought not to be taught in schools. The fact that, for a brief period in history, they were allowed to take this duty upon themselves is no good reason for saying that they ought to have done so. Indeed, one of the factors behind the political backlash of the mid-1970s, as manifested in an upsurge of demands for accountability, may have been the common perception that the teaching profession had begun to get too far above itself.

With this said, there is little sign of widespread public dissent from the view that the insiders should have the major role, if not in deciding what the curriculum comprises, then at least in working out how it can best – to use another revealingly modish term – be delivered. There still remains ample space for variety in this respect: the solutions are likely to remain as diverse as the schools themselves.

We may conveniently explore the implications of the 1988 Act for curriculum management by considering in turn the three structural levels of: the school as a whole, its constituent departments, and its individual staff members. At the school level, the distinction made earlier in relation to national curricular policies between coercive, manipulative and rational approaches to implementation may continue to be a useful one. It is possible to sketch out some likely differences in schools which adopt one such strategy at the expense of the others (though experience should remind us that, in real life, few pure copy-book cases can be found, since most institutions will – perhaps wisely – adopt a mixture of all three, changing the emphasis according to circumstance).

A school with a strongly hierarchical structure, one might predict, will opt to play safe, adopting a coercive managerial approach in which maximizing test scores and examination results becomes the most important consideration. It will be inclined to follow the stipulations of the national curriculum in a generally slavish manner, keeping rigidly to the specified subject boundaries and following the recommended time allocations for each. Little or no attention will be afforded to pastoral issues, the personal and social development of pupils, or any other issue not expressly sanctioned by the NCC and SEAC. Such a school will, in short, behave in much the manner that those who originally drew up the national legislation might have wished.

In contrast, a school in which a traditionally bureaucratic form of organization gives place to a pressure group system of operation is likely to follow a different pattern. Where the process of decision-making depends on constant jockeying for position among powerful departmental baronies and other coalitions of vested interest, the curriculum will in all probability be determined by political manipulation, on the basis of a continuing power struggle for timetable territory. Core subjects will have an in-built advantage; foundation subjects will chip in as best they can; most other activities will be brushed aside, unless a strong voice speaks for them. There will be little attempt at integration or coherence: curricular provision will remain balkanized.

A professionally oriented, collegially based school (a rare phenomenon, it must be said, in its unadulterated form) will incline towards a rational approach based on considerations of the pupils' own best interests. It is here that one might expect to find preserved some of the more valuable features of the previous system – including, for example, mixed ability teaching, cross-curricular integration, topic-based activity, and the fostering of a wide range of talents. In the most professionally confident schools, and perhaps in those alone, the testing process will not be given undue weight, or be allowed to determine the whole emphasis of the curriculum itself. It is such schools that will be least affected by the curricular provisions of the 1988 Act, and will remain distinctly different from the more examination-obsessed grammar and private schools of yesteryear.

If the Education Reform Act now prescribes the main objectives of the education process, one might conclude that it none the less remains to each school to determine the overall pattern of its curricular provision. As has been suggested, both a hierarchically organized institution and one in which pressure-group politics are rife will tend, for different reasons, to maintain a strongly classified, discipline-focused curriculum – the first because that is what the legislation points to and renders most administratively convenient, and the second because subject departments comprise the most obvious configuration of sectional interests. Collegiality, on the other hand, is capable of permitting weak classification – that is a less tightly structured, cross-curricular design in which subject boundaries, and the departments which act as their guardians, are not so strongly emphasized.

Turning next to the departmental level, the most straightforward cases will be those in which the department's ethos reflects that of the school. A hierarchical department in a hierarchical school will be liable to promote a strongly framed curriculum, in which the subject content is clearly laid down and fairly rigidly sequenced; a collegial department in a collegial school may accommodate weaker framing and a greater degree of choice for pupils in terms of curricular content; a department which embodies a diversity of competing factions will tend to allow a relatively unstructured sequence of topics, with little internal coordination.

Complexities are likely to set in when the department's managerial style is at odds with the school's: one may note that it is also possible for a gap to occur between institutional policy and departmental implementation. Thus one might occasionally find an internally contentious or even a collegial department in a hierarchical school; or – perhaps more rarely – a hierarchical or politically fragmented department in a collegial school; and a school organized in terms of baronial interest groups is in any case likely to leave room for a variety of constituent types. In such cases, although the scope for departure from the dominant institutional norms and the prevailing curriculum structure is limited, the department would in all likelihood continue to have a significant measure of sovereignty over the organization and planning of subject content.

Similar considerations apply at the individual level. Teachers who are in tune with their departmental values will present few problems: a traditionally didactic teaching mode will fit comfortably with a strongly subject- and test-oriented curriculum, and a progressive one with a more open, student-centred framework; in a school or department which has not got its own act together, and where the curriculum remains politically contentious, anything goes – though it helps if one can become part of a coterie of like-minded interests.

But perhaps especially here, at the front line of provision, those responsible for shaping the curriculum need to remember that their best-laid plans are vulnerable to the non-conformity of individual practice. The class-teacher may have little control over structure or content, but even in today's constraining climate still enjoys considerable autonomy in the matter of teaching style. At the end of the day, teachers who strongly dissent from existing national or school or departmental policy will retain the professional's scope to do things in their own way. The classroom is a private place, not easily invaded by opposing outside forces. As must always be the case in human affairs, even strongly coercive legislation has its limits.

## References

Archer, M. (1981) 'Educational politics: a model for their analysis', in P. Broadfoot *et al.* (eds) *Politics and Educational Change*, London, Croom Helm.
Bardach, E. (1977) *The Implementation Game*, Cambridge, Mass., MIT Press.
Bennis, W. G., Benne, K. D. and Chin, R. (1969) *The Planning of Change*, New York, Holt, Rinehart & Winston.
Bush, T. (1986) *Theories of Educational Management*, London, Harper & Row.
DES (1988) *Bulletin for School Teachers and Governors*, autumn 1988, issue 1, London, Department of Education and Science.
Havelock, R. G. (1969) *Planning for Innovation*, Ann Arbor, Mich., Center for Research on Utilization of Scientific Knowledge, University of Michigan.
Jordan, A. G and Richardson, J. J. (1987) *British Politics and the Policy Process*, London, Allen & Unwin.
Lipsky, M. (1971) 'Street-level bureaucracy and the analysis of urban reform', *Urban Affairs Quarterly*, 6, 4: 391–409.
Pressman, J. and Wildavsky, A. (1973) *Implementation*, Berkeley, University of California Press.
Salter, B. and Tapper, T. (1981) *Education, Politics and the State: The Theory and Practice of Educational Change*, London, Grant McIntyre.

# 6

# The Education Reform Act 1988: some implications for curriculum decision-making in primary schools

**Jim Campbell**

## The background: 1977–88

The decade that led to the publication of the 1987 Education Reform Bill was characterized by concern over three major issues in the primary school curriculum. These were curricular diversity, raising standards, and accountability and control. Taken together, these three factors provided the evidential and political base for the DES to assert (DES, 1987a), and to some extent to justify, the need for a national curriculum.

The issue of diversity in curriculum practice was in effect an argument about the limits of tolerance of discretion on curriculum matters, exercised either by an individual class-teacher, a school, or a local education authority. What counts as 'undue' diversity is in the end a matter of judgement, but the evidence in the Primary Survey (DES, 1978) had revealed very wide variation (for example, in the provision for science, and in progression and coverage in the humanities). This was used as a basis for arguing that much greater consistency, however defined, in curricular practice was required (Richards, 1983). Other evidence revealed a different kind of diversity, with dramatic variations in the time spent on mathematics and 'language' (even making allowances for definitional problems), by pupils in different schools and classes (Bennett *et al.*, 1980).

Drawing on arguments very similar to those offered for a common curriculum at secondary level (Lawton, 1975; Scottish Education Department, 1977) the Select Committee (House of Commons, 1986) called for an 'entitlement' curriculum for all children, and for the secretary of state to be given new powers to issue broad guidance on the curriculum. Variety, justified by reference to children's interests, local needs, and teacher initiative, lauded in the Plowden Report, had effectively been challenged on the basis of a moral claim that all children should experience a comparable range of curricular experiences. (DES, 1985a; DES, 1985b; Joseph, 1984).

The Primary Survey was also an important source of evidence about unsatisfactory standards in primary schools. It showed reading standards continuing to rise in the post-war period, while simultaneously revealing poor match between work set and pupil capacities, especially in respect of pupils considered able. The poor match was across the curriculum, and was attributed in part to low teacher expectations, with the problem most pervasive in inner-city schools, though there are methodological difficulties with the analysis (Bennett *et al.*, 1983). This general picture was painted more sharply by two school-based studies showing the nature of the mismatch of task to capacities, even in the classrooms of teachers regarded as good practitioners (Bennett and Desforges, 1984; Bennett *et al.*, 1987).

One of the oddest features of the public debate over standards has been its refusal to draw upon the above, rather damaging, evidence and to rely instead upon references to obscure international comparisons, which showed, for example, relatively low attainment in mathematics by low/ middle-ability children of secondary school age, compared to their German counterparts (Prais and Wagner, 1985).

However, the force of the evidence of the Primary Survey was implicitly acknowledged in the substantial shift in expectations for the role of curriculum co-ordinators as subject advisers to their colleagues (Campbell, 1985, ILEA, 1986, House of Commons, 1986). The extension of this role, while intended 'to support not undermine' class-teachers (Richards, 1986) was in effect addressing the problem of levels of teacher expertise across the curriculum (and, by implication, of standards expected of children). This shift was reinforced by in-service training (INSET) targeted on curriculum post-holders, and the widespread move to appoint advisory teachers through Education Support Grants and other mechanisms, which was also designed to strengthen the subject base of curriculum planning at school level.

The third strand, accountability and curriculum control, is more difficult to analyse, because of the way the admittedly rather broad concept has failed to secure a common meaning. One approach is to restrict its use to the idea of 'giving an account of' the curriculum to parents, governors and other interested parties. At the school level, accountability in this restricted sense has been built up from an ideal goal (Taylor Report, 1977) to a legal requirement in the Education Acts 1980 and 1986 (no. 2) and the Education Reform Act 1988, to enable parents to have a basis, however inadequate in reality, for judging how well a child, a teacher and a school are performing on a publicly known curriculum. The performance indicators to be used for this are assessments on attainment targets differentiated into ten levels for the 5–16 age range (see TGAT Report extract in Chapter 2).

At the local authority level, the casual attitudes to providing curricular statements revealed in Circular 14/77 (DES, 1977) have been transformed by the production of supportive and forward-looking curriculum statements by local authorities, many of them anticipating or following *Curriculum Matters 2* (DES, 1985a). In vivid contrast, accountability at the central authority level has shrunk, with the legal requirement of the 1944 Act that the secretary of state should produce an annual report (a duty still placed on chief education officers of the LEAs) abolished by the 1986 Education Act. This contrast between schools and local authorities moving towards greater account- ability, and central authority reducing accountability, has been powerfully illustrated in the recommendations from an ILEA inquiry into freedom of information about schools (Tomlinson. 1987).

But if we extend the concept to consider aspects of control over the curriculum that may flow from greater accountability, the analysis becomes both more interesting and more problematic. The new right has developed a rhetoric of consumer control as a market force to help to raise standards (CPC, 1986). If the information from accountability rights becomes com- bined with the right to choose schools, it is argued, parents will effectively become controlling consumers, as a counter to the producer-led system operating hitherto. (Producers in this analysis are LEAs, teachers and professional associations generally.) The real problem in a producer-led system is the tendency of corporate interests to dominate consumer interests (Shipman, 1984).

The problem for this analysis, however, is that the Education Reform Act goes against the market forces model in two obvious ways. First, it requires a national curriculum to be implemented in all maintained schools, whereas a market forces model would have allowed the curriculum to be negotiated locally according to parental and community wishes. The curricu- lum in Haringey would be different from the curriculum in Harrogate, if the parents in the two situations wanted different curricula. Second, although the Act effectively breaks much of the power of the corporate interest of the LEAs (the corporate power of the teachers' unions already having been broken under the imposition of the Teachers' Pay and Conditions Act 1987), the power is flowing up to the centre, not down to the localities or to the parents. For the Act gives over 400 new powers to the secretary of state (ACC, 1987). Of those concerned with the curriculum some are very specific (the ability to appoint membership of the National Curriculum Council (NCC) and School Examinations and Assessment Council (SEAC)), but others are catch-all general powers (the ability to redefine the national curriculum and the ages at which children are assessed). This paradox of a government committed to market forces taking greater unitary control over the curriculum has been characterized as a 'fundamental contradiction' in current policies (Campbell *et al.*, 1987).

However, even without the power base provided by a third substantial electoral victory, the Conservative government, by the middle of 1987, had sufficiently strong evidence, and probably wide endorsement amongst pro- fessionals, to enable the case for a national curriculum to be supported. Whether what was proposed in the consultation document on the national curriculum (DES, 1987a) and the Education Reform Act 1988 will deliver what was shown to be needed in terms of reduced diversity, raised teacher expectations and increased accountability and control by consumers is more problematic. The discussion that follows applies these three criteria to the government proposals.

### Curricular diversity

At its simplest, the national curriculum model is, for primary schools, a three-part one: religious education; the foundation subjects, including the 'core'; non-foundation subjects. There are three 'core' subjects, English, mathematics and science (plus Welsh for Welsh-speaking schools in Wales) which also form part of the 'foundation' group of subjects.

There are a further six subjects in the foundation, though outside the core. These are art, history, geography, physical education, music and technology (and Welsh for non-Welsh-speaking schools in Wales). (At the secondary stage a seventh subject – a modern foreign language – must be included.) Children's performance is to be assessed by arrangements that include nationally prescribed standard assessment tasks (SATs). A distinction made in the consultation paper was that music, physical education and art would have 'guidelines' rather than attainment targets. This distinction was not explicitly maintained in the Education Reform Act, although Clause 4(2) implies that the secretary of state would have discretion to make such distinctions. A further distinction is that attainment targets and programmes of study in the core subjects are to be specified, in the form of parliamentary orders, and implemented in schools, before those in the other foundations subjects.

Outside the foundation is religious education, which was required under the 1944 Education Act, and was given a distinctive position in the 1988 Act, and other subjects such as home economics, drama, etc., though in practice, aspects of home economics and health have been included in the programmes of study for science, and drama in those proposed for English.

Since the core and foundation and religious education are required by law, the national curriculum as specified appears effectively to address and to solve the problem of curricular diversity; children have a specified entitlement to a curriculum, which is not limited to a narrow basic skills core, and looks set to protect children from the vagaries of provision that has hitherto depended upon the personal inclinations of class-teachers, or particular enthusiasms of heads or governing bodies. Teachers who do not teach art or science or technology, because they do not feel confident or competent to do so, and governing bodies insisting upon a return to narrow basics, will alike find their curricular predilections illicit. Individual schools' practice in this respect is open to scrutiny, since the Act requires that schools' curriculum statements become public documents, available by law to interested parties.

There are two obstacles to the realization of this optimistic analysis. First, the decision to phase attainment targets in the core before the other foundation subjects, will create pressure upon teachers, parents and most importantly pupils, to perceive the core subjects as of greater significance than the others. This is likely to affect the perceived significance of the humanities and the arts adversely, especially as performance arts (Campbell *et al.*, 1987). Second, the Act has tried to clarify the position about which aspects of the curriculum may be subject to 'charges'. The attempt has not been entirely successful, but charges cannot be made for teaching the national curriculum, though voluntary contributions for things like field trips, visits, and swimming are not prohibited. The requirement to delegate financial responsibility to individual primary schools with over 200 pupils, and the possibility of doing so for smaller schools is likely to make parental contributions to school budgets, already a major item (Pring 1987), into a key factor in a school's ability to deliver a high-quality entitlement curriculum. If this happens, the main moral justification for the introduction of the national curriculum identified on p. 62–3 will have been subverted.

## Raising standards

The secretary of state, in his statement to the Select Committee in April 1987, gave raising standards as the main generalized justification for the introduction of the national curriculum. He stressed especially the role of attainment targets, which would identify what pupils should 'normally be able to know, understand and be able to do' at or around the ages of 7 and 11. It is difficult to see anyone objecting to the slogan 'raising standards', though logically the published attainment targets will have a chance of raising standards only if they are pitched at a higher level than the implicit targets that teachers previously set for their pupils.

However, we need to think of standards as broader than simply attainment. Educational standards include standards of provision, standards of treatment in school, as well as attainment. It is helpful to think of three related factors:

1 *inputs*: resources for staffing, building and equipment, and learning materials;
2 *within-school factors*: the nature of the curriculum, teaching and learning styles, teacher expectations, school atmosphere and ethos;
3 *outputs*: academic attainment, social and moral development.

At the level of inputs, standards have fallen in respect of building quality (DES, 1982; 1983; 1985c; NCPTA, 1985) to the stage where the neglect of plant and fabric has affected the quality of learning and the safety of staff and children.

In respect of resources for staffing, there has been an improvement in *per capita* spending, though a reduction in real terms in overall expenditure on primary education, between 1975 and 1985 (House of Commons, 1986). The *per capita* improvement is small and has been produced mainly by the impact of falling rolls. There has been an increase in teacher-training intakes for primary schools. This has been interpreted as a government commitment to increase the contact ratio in primary schools, as urged by the White Paper, *Better Schools* (DES, 1985b), and explicitly recommended by the Select Committee (House of Commons 1986). The latter report had obtained confirmation from Sir Keith Joseph that a figure of around 15,000 extra teachers (i.e. above what was necessary to maintain current pupil–teacher ratios) was needed to allow primary teachers to be free from normal class contact time in order to engage in school-based curriculum development, curriculum co-ordination, working with parents, and so on. In December 1987, however, the secretary of state, in a written memorandum, effectively dismissed this recommendation, along with most of the others that were not already built into his Education Reform Bill (DES 1987b). The government had, in effect, refused to endorse the resourcing of the kind of staffing levels which the Select Committee, with full cross-party support, had described as 'essential if any progress is to be made in the classroom' (House of Commons, 1986: para 12.19).

At the level of within-school factors, the specification of attainment targets promises to raise teacher expectations, especially of the more able children. The targets themselves are produced as 'proposals' by subject working groups, and following consultation, amended by the NCC if necessary; they are then sent as advice to the secretary of state who may alter them if he sees fit (and gives reasons). They finally appear as Orders of Parliament. The impact of these orders on teachers' control of the curriculum is discussed further below. A characteristic of the targets is that they are differentiated into ten levels, and thus promise not merely to raise expectations, but to help teachers overcome the problem, identified on p. 63, of classroom 'match' overall.

Two factors that may restrict the potential of such developments are teacher morale and the range of expertise in the overall teacher supply. Teacher morale has not been improved by the imposition of the Teachers' Pay and Conditions Act, or by the legal requirement in the Education Act 1986 and the 1988 Act for teacher appraisal, possibly linked to assessment results. Teacher perceptions of the intentions lying behind the Act are crucial here, and there is little indication that anything practical is planned to restore trust in the relationship between the DES and teachers in primary schools.

At the same time, the academic backgrounds of teachers in primary schools are badly matched to the academic needs created by the specification of the curriculum in subject terms, with severe shortages in mathematics, science and technology, and music, and over-supply in humanities. Even though there is no specification in the 1988 Act that the curriculum should be organized in any particular form, the national curriculum will increase the pressure identified earlier for curriculum-led or 'activity-led' staffing in primary schools, though not necessarily taking the form of curriculum co-ordination in each single subject of the national curriculum. (This point is taken up on p. 75.) The Select Committee anticipated the need for staff time that would follow from curriculum co-ordinators helping to develop whole school policies on aspects of the curriculum, and this need will be enlarged as the implications for developing appropriate assessment strategies in schools come to be realized. It is for this reason that the secretary of state's dismissal of the resource implications of the Select Committee Report is so damaging to the prospects for raising standards in primary schools.

The dismal scenario thus produced is of some schools with disaffected teachers, lacking in confidence to teach some subjects, and without the time for good school-based development, being forced to teach these subjects by premature implementation of parts of the national curriculum. If this comes to pass in only, say, 20 per cent of primary schools, it will undermine much of the potential of the opportunity, provided by the working groups, for raising expectations generally. The pressure for short-term political advantage gained from pressing on with the national curriculum to show results in time for an election, ought to be tempered by considerations of the educational advantages of a longer term development plan, with properly funded and directed in-service training to meet the needs of the schools.

At the level of outputs, the promise that the implementation of the Act will lead to raised attainment, and social and personal development (through the subjects) is unconvincing (if raised standards overall is meant) for three reasons.

First, the attainments of children with special needs have been virtually ignored in both the consultation paper, and the Act. For statemented children the Act seems to envisage the statement becoming a reason for excluding the children from some aspects of the national curriculum. It becomes, so to speak, a ground for withdrawing educational provision, in contrast to the conditions of the 1981 Act, which saw the statement as a claim on resources to meet needs.

Second, open enrolment and financial delegation may lead to raised output standards in popular schools, but may well lead to lower standards in unpopular schools, leading to a three-tier school system: well-resourced independent schools; well-resourced maintained sector schools, financially supported by parents; and unpopular schools, with falling rolls, teachers with low morale, resourced at a minimal level, unable to attract substantial financial support from their parent bodies (Campbell *et al.*, 1987).

Third, there is the logical problem that if targets and national assess-ment help to raise standards through their impact on teacher and pupil motivation, they will do so only in some subjects, and not in the rest of the curriculum, since art, physical education and music will not have attainment targets.

Thus, although some schools and some pupils may have attainment levels raised, the overall picture looks set to be very patchy. The gap between good and poor schools will widen. This may be intentional, as a market forces exercise to let the poor schools wither on the vine; but schools take a long time to wither, and even longer to close down, and in the mean time, children will still be attending the withering schools.

## Accountability and control

I have hinted (p. 63) at the conceptual vagueness involved in notions of accountability and control. At this stage it is helpful to separate out the idea of accountability from that of control, despite their interrelatedness, in order to analyse the Act's impact at school level.

### *Accountability*

The Education Reform Act, by its assessment arrangements and by the requirement to publish curriculum and assessment results, has required schools to give better accounts of the curriculum to parents as 'consumers', to help them to exercise their right to choose schools. For this to be effective, at least three conditions would need to be met.

First, there would need to be a sophisticated and informed constituency of parents able to use curriculum documents and assessment results in a sensitive and aware manner. The relatively low interest shown in the annual meetings for parents held by school governors does not suggest that this constituency is at a highly developed stage, nor that it is uniformly spread.

The second condition is that assessment results should be able to be technically aggregated in a way that does not do damage to the range of characteristics being assessed, and yet is easily comprehended by a lay audience. In addition, the scores would need to have built into them some calculation to take account of social characteristics in a school's intake. The assessment arrangements proposed by TGAT do not meet either of these conditions, since reporting will be based on results unadjusted for social background. Instead there will a broad statement of the work of the school as a whole as a background to the moderated results on assessment tasks.

A third condition concerns the relationship between parents and school that is envisaged in the Act, with its requirement on LEAs to set up complaints procedures. The last decade has been characterized by apparently effective attempts to involve parents in supporting the schools' efforts, and 'deprived' schools especially, in improving their children's progress. These developments, which began by focusing on parental involvement in reading

(Tizard and Hewitson, 1980; Hannon and Jackson, 1987; Widlake and Macleod, 1984), have moved into mathematics (Merttens and Vass, 1987). Although the quality of the evidence in these studies is variable, the fundamental shift in them all is towards co-operation between the parents and the school, with the common aim of raising standards. If parents are put into the role of inquisitorial consumers, such developments may be discouraged, either from teacher mistrust of how parental involvement may be exploited by unscrupulous parents, or because parents may see more benefit in moving school, as open enrolment comes in, than in the arduous and time-consuming work involved in participatory schemes. Thus it is possible to see the exercise of choice by parents becoming a reality as the provisions of the Act come in, but it is difficult to envisage such choice arising from more authentic forms of accountability.

### Curriculum control

The likelihood of an actual increase in central control of the curriculum in practice following the 1988 Act, was disputed by the then secretary of state (Baker, 1987) but a massive power base in principle has been established. Amongst other things, the secretary of state has power to appoint all the members of the NCC and SEAC, the bodies intended to give him/her independent advice on the curriculum; he/she has power to change the national curriculum, or to suspend it in order to allow a school to experiment. Above all, he/she has the power to change the recommendations of the NCC for attainment targets and programmes of study before they become incorporated into orders, and thus become the statutory specifications of the school curriculum, provided he/she gives reasons for doing so.

Thus on the face of it, there has been an enormous shift in power to define the curriculum, away from a *de facto* decision-making at school or classroom level to a *de jure* control at central government level. This shift, allied to other increases in power in the Act, has been so great as to raise serious constitutional issues, according to MacAuslan (1988).

From the point of view of control over the curriculum alone, however, Lawton (1983) has produced a simple model, with five system levels (central government, local government, school, department, and classroom) and three dimensions of curriculum (content, pedagogy, and assessment). This model is shown in Figure 6.1. If we use this model, power to define the curriculum appears to have been taken away from the local government level, and shifted to the central government. At the same time there has been some increase in power to regulate curriculum practice, within the centrally defined framework, through the delegation of responsibility to the governing body, and to parents through the complaints procedure referred to above. This applies both to content and assessment, though state control of pedagogy is intended to be excluded.

However, models are constructions invented to help in the analysis of

| Aspect / Level | Curriculum content | Pedagogy | Evaluation |
|---|---|---|---|
| 1 National | | | |
| 2 Regional | | | |
| 3 Institutional | | | |
| 4 Departmental | | | |
| 5 Individual | | | |

**Figure 6.1** A model of curriculum control

reality, and do not necessarily reflect the real world of decision-making on the curriculum, especially in situations where the system itself is being changed. The key question is how far decision-making over the curriculum at school and classroom level will effectively be controlled by the state, and how much will really remain *de facto* in the hands of the professionals – the teachers and headteachers. It is this issue that the following discussion attempts to analyse.

## The national curriculum and school-based decision-making

The crucible in which the range of power given to the central government will be most severely tested lies in the way in which targets of attainment are finally specified. The procedure is a three-step one. First, the subject working groups appointed by the secretary of state make proposals on which the NCC is statutorily obliged to consult. Second, on the basis of the consultation exercise, the NCC gives advice to the secretary of state, including rec-ommendations for draft orders. Third, on the basis of the advice, the secretary of state lays orders, containing programmes of study and attain-ment targets, which become the legally required specifications for the national curriculum. At the time of writing, we have evidence about the first two stages in mathematics and science and the first stage in English (DES, 1988a; 1988b; 1988c; NCC, 1988a; 1988b), as well as the changes made to the recommendations of the TGAT (DES, 1988c: Appendix 4). The evidence is all in the same direction, and suggests that the procedures are being used to try to curtail the scope for school-based decision-making on the curriculum.

The evidence is most substantial in respect of mathematics and science. In the case of mathematics, the working group's final report produced a recommendation that there should be three clusters of attainment targets (profile components: PC):

PC1 Knowledge, skills and understandings in number, algebra and measures;

PC2 Knowledge, skills and understandings in space and shape and handling data;

PC3 Practical applications of mathematics including personal qualities, communication skills and using mathematics.

For assessment purposes the working group recommended 30 per cent, 30 per cent and 40 per cent weightings respectively. The final report was published by the NCC, with a preamble in which the secretary of state's views of its recommendations were made clear. These included a request not to separate the attainment targets concerned with practical applications into a distinctive component, but to merge them into the knowledge-based targets, and an expression of disapproval about the relatively low weighting given to knowledge as against applications.

A similar fate befell the final report of the Science Working Group. It had proposed, for the primary stages, three profile components also, the first concerned with knowledge skills and understanding, and the other two with the exploration/investigation, and communication. Although welcoming the general approach, the secretary of state again expressed disapproval of the relatively low weighting for assessment purposes given to knowledge and understanding; and he proposed reducing the number of profile components in Exploration and Communication, and combining the latter with the knowledge and understanding components where possible. The NCC's response here was to recommend two profile components, one for Exploration in Science (one attainment target) and one for Knowledge and Understanding (sixteen targets), each component weighted for reporting assessment, 50/50 per cent at age 7, and 45/55 per cent respectively at age 11.

The interventions by the secretary of state in the consultation process, contained in a letter to the chairman of the NCC, were extraordinary in one particular sense. In addition to general directions (e.g. 'Are the proposals achievable bearing in mind the time that can be made available?') some requirements dealt with fine detail and, despite the promises in the consultation paper, were concerned with teaching *methods* (e.g. 'Is it justifiable to exclude the pencil and paper methods for long division and long multiplication from the attainment targets for mathematics?').

The impact of the interventions is difficult to assess without insider knowledge of the NCC, but on this particular point the NCC recommended:

that pupils should be able to use mental, paper and pencil methods and calculators as appropriate, and should be able to carry out the operations of multiplication and division using 2- and 3-digit numbers by paper and pencil methods.                              (NCC, 1988a: 16)

It is an irony that elsewhere the NCC refused to recommend a science attainment target called Working in Groups because, amongst other things, it prescribed 'too closely the teaching methods to be used by teachers' (NCC, 1988b: 20).

Likewise on the general points, about combining the profile components concerning Applications in Mathematics, and Investigation and Communication in Science, the NCC recommendations appear to give way to the secretary of state, despite its own evidence from the consultation exercise that 80 per cent of those responding wanted the profile components kept separate. The NCC recommendations were accepted by the secretary of state and became incorporated in draft orders (DES, 1988d). Thus, on the face of it, decision-making about the primary curriculum has been effectively removed from schools and teachers in respect of Lawton's content and assessment dimensions, and even to some extent in respect of pedagogy. About pedagogy it should be noted that the central control through specification of attainment targets implying a particular pedagogy is not directed only in favour of formal methods. Both the mathematics and science working groups specified targets that, at least by implication, and frequently explicitly, required 'progressive' approaches, especially those involving investigations and problem-solving methods, often using co-operative group work. It all makes the claim of the 1987 consultation document that there should be 'full scope for the enterprise and initiative of teachers' sound rather hollow.

### The need for collegial approaches

However, the above analysis takes too superficial a view of curriculum decision-making. This is because there is a world of difference between national policy and its delivery in schools. The national curriculum as specified in the Act (and to be specified in the orders) has created three fundamental management tasks for its delivery in primary schools. They concern the implementation of the curriculum, specified as subjects; assessment; and public relations. All three point toward the need for an approach to management, advocated and analysed throughout the 1980s, referred to as 'collegiality' (Coulson, 1976; Alexander, 1984; Campbell, 1985; House of Commons, 1986; Southworth, 1988). Although there are differences of interpretation, collegiality implies delegation of curriculum leadership to members of staff with designated curriculum responsibilities – curriculum co-ordinators – and distinctive subject expertise.

The effective implementation of this kind of role by curriculum co-ordinators is crucial in the three aspects mentioned above, and I shall now briefly illustrate the management issues in respect of each of them.

### Implementation of the curriculum specified as subjects

First, the attainment targets are fundamentally statements of objectives, and do not in general specify the means by which they should be achieved, which remain the responsibility of the school. For example, Attainment Target 3, concerned with the Processes of Life, in the statutory orders for Science (DES, 1989) is:

> Pupils should develop their knowledge and understanding of the organisation of living things, and of the processes which characterise their survival and reproduction.

> (DES, 1989: 8)

Part of the relevant programme of study for the 7–11-year-old stage is:

> Children should investigate some aspects of feeding, support, movement and behaviour in relation to themselves and other animals. They should be introduced . . . to basic ideas about the processes of breathing, circulation, growth and reproduction.

> (DES, 1989: 69)

Even when the general attainment target is specified in ten levels (e.g. Level 4 'be able to name the major organs and organ systems in flowering plants and mammals': p. 8), it remains a framework of objectives, not a strait-jacket of content and/or method. It is still a fundamental task of the school's curriculum management to organize progression in the sequence of learning experiences within the Key Stage 2 (7–11-year-olds) by which children come to such understandings, and to create a through-school policy on curriculum organization, for example, whether learning of science is integrated into cross-curricular topics and themes, or is dealt with in separate subject lessons.

### Assessment

Second, the responsibility for creating systematic assessment of children's performance against the attainment targets also remains with the school. The *requirement* to assess is part of the Act and legally enforceable. An element of the assessment arrangements is nationally specified through the externally developed standard assessment tasks (SATs), and administered at the end of each key stage. Even here, the schools are able to choose SATS from an item bank, to take account of local needs. But assessment through teachers' classroom judgements ('teacher ratings' in TGAT-speak), ongoing throughout each year in each key stage, will be an important contribution to the assessment alongside the SATs.

A key management task in this respect is to ensure that such classroom-based judgements are made consistently through the school, and systematically related to the attainment targets. The recording of such judgements, and their match or mismatch with pupil performance on the SATs, also need to be taken into account, probably through the adoption by the school of an LEA-wide information technology system.

### Public relations

The third reason relates to the need for school management to be accountable for its curriculum practice, the way it 'delivers' its version of the national curriculum to those with an interest in it. Interested groups include governors and parents, of course, who have a right to information about the curriculum, and also the staff and governors of other schools. For primary schools, this latter set of relations comprise its 'cluster' of primary schools, through which the choice and moderation of SATs are effected, and its receiving secondary school, which will be concerned not only to recruit primary pupils, but also to ensure curricular progression and continuity across Key Stages 2 and 3. In addition, of course, the need to account for the curriculum in practice to annual meetings of parents, and to show the quality of a school's curriculum to a consumer-oriented constituency of parents, with free choice of school, will become even more pressing.

Not all these co-ordination tasks are simple subject responsibilities. They illustrate one change affecting the management of the curriculum in primary schools, from the earlier collegiality models. They represent a shift from the allocation of responsibility for curriculum subjects exclusively (a curriculum-led management model) to responsibility for curriculum-related activities (an activity-led management model). Where the former specified subjects or clusters of subjects, such as topic work, as the key organizational responsibilities, the latter identifies key tasks or activities related to the curriculum, but not necessarily subject specific. For example, responsibility for assessment and public relations as discussed above might be regarded as more important than responsibility for, say, geography. In infant schools, home–school liaison, or learning through play, might take precedence over some subject responsibilities. The actual tasks would have to be agreed by the governors and staff, but activity-led management is likely to be the way that school management responds to the new political context of education, brought about by the 1988 Act. This kind of model, originally devised by the Audit Commission for secondary schools (Audit Commission 1986) and called activity-led staffing, should prove applicable by primary schools, both as a management model and as a basis for calculating a more appropriate staffing formula than the simple pupil–teacher ratio.

Thus the three curriculum management tasks identified earlier, together with others, have been turned, by the passing of the 1988 Act, into imperatives for schools that wish to flourish in the new political situation.

Collegiality was advocated in the early 1980s as a means of responding to the pressure for both democratic decision-making and higher standards across a broader curriculum in primary schools. But in the 1990s schools in which a collegial approach has been adopted, in which staff are accustomed to collective decision-making, and in which curriculum co-ordinators already exercise effective leadership in their subject or 'activity', will be better placed than most others to deliver the curriculum to which children and their parents are now entitled by law.

## References

ACC (Association of County Councils) (1987) 'Annex E, agenda item 2, Education Committee', 17 December, London, ACC.

Alexander, R. (1984) *Primary Teaching*, London, Holt, Rinehart & Winston.

Audit Commission (1986) *Towards Better Management of Secondary Education*, London, HMSO.

Baker, K. (1987) speech to the North of England Conference, Nottingham.

Bennett, N. and Desforges, C. (1984) *The Quality of Pupil Learning Experiences*, London, Lawrence Erlbaum Associates.

Bennett, N., Andrae, J., Hegarty, P. and Wade, B. (1980) *Open Plan Schools: Teaching, Curriculum and Design*, Windsor, NFER for the Schools Council.

Bennett, N., O'Hare, E. and Lee, J. (1983) 'Mixed age classes in primary schools', *British Educational Research Journal*, **9**(1), 41–56.

Bennett, N., Roth, E. and Dunne, R. (1987) 'Task processes in mixed and single ages classes', *Education 3–13*, **15**(1), 43–51.

Campbell, R. J. (1985) *Developing the Primary School Curriculum*, London, Holt, Rinehart & Winston.

Campbell, R. J., Little, V. and Tomlinson, J. R. G. (1987) 'Multiplying the divisions?', *Journal of Education Policy*, **2**(4), 369–78.

Coulson, A. A. (1976) 'The role of the primary head', in R. Peters (ed.) *The Role of the Head*, London, Routledge & Kegan Paul.

CPC (Conservative Political Centre) (1986) *Save Our Schools*, London, CPC.

DES (1977) *Circular 14/77*, London, DES.

DES (1978) *Primary Education in England: A Survey by HM Inspectors*, London, HMSO.

DES (1982) *Report by HMI on the Effects on the Education Service of Local Authority Expenditure Policies*, London, HMSO.

DES (1983) *Report by HMI on the Effects on the Education Service of Local Authority Expenditure Policies*, London, HMSO.

DES (1985a) 'The curriculum from 5–16', *Curriculum Matters 2*, London, HMSO.

DES (1985b) *Better Schools*, Cmnd 9469, London, HMSO.

DES (1985c) *Report by HMI on the Effects on the Education Service of Local Authority Expenditure Policies*, London, HMSO.

DES (1987a) *The National Curriculum 5–16: A Consultation Document*, London, HMSO.

DES (1987b) 'Memorandum by the Secretary of State for Education and Science on the Third Report from the Education, Science and Arts Committee,

Session 1985–6 Achievement in Primary Schools', 16 December, London, HMSO.

DES (1988a) *National Curriculum Mathematics for Ages 5–16*, London, HMSO.

DES (1988b) *National Curriculum Science for Ages 5–16*, London, HMSO.

DES (1988c) *National Curriculum English for Ages 5–11*, London, HMSO.

DES (1988d) *National Curriculum: Draft Orders for Mathematics and Science*, London, HMSO.

DES (1989) *Science in the National Curriculum*, London, HMSO.

Hannon, P. and Jackson, A. (1987) *The Bellfield Reading Project: Final Report*, London, National Children's Bureau.

House of Commons (1986) '3rd Report of the Education, Science and Arts Committee, Session 1985–86', *Achievement in Primary Schools*, 1, London, HMSO.

ILEA (1985) *Improving Primary Schools*, London, Inner London Education Authority.

Joseph, Sir K. (1984) speech to the North of England Conference, Sheffield.

Lawton, D. (1975) *Class Culture and the Curriculum*, London, Routledge & Kegan Paul.

Lawton, D. (1983) *Curriculum Studies and Educational Planning*, London, Hodder & Stoughton.

MacAuslan, P. (1988) 'The Bill – Does it offend against the constitution?', in J. Haviland (ed.) *Take Care, Mr Baker!*, London, Fourth Estate.

Merttens, R. and Vass, J. (1987) 'Parents in school: raising money or raising standards?', *Education 3–13*, **15**(2), 23–8.

NCC (National Curriculum Council) (1988) *Consultative Report: Mathematics 5–16*, London, NCC.

NCPTA (National Confederation of Parent-Teacher Associations) (1985) *The State of Schools in England and Wales*, Gravesend, NCPTA.

Prais, S. J. and Wagner, K. (1985) 'Schooling standards in England and Germany: some summary comparisons bearing on economic performance', *National Institute Economic Review*, 112, 53–76.

Pring, R. (1987) 'Privatisation in education', *Journal of Educational Policy*, **2**(4), 289–300.

Richards, C. (1983) 'Curriculum consistency', in C. Richards (ed.) *New Directions in Primary Education*, Lewes, Falmer Press.

Richards, C. (1986) 'The Curriculum from 5–16: implications for primary teachers', *Education 3–13*, **14**(1), 2–8.

Scottish Education Department, Consultative Committee on the Curriculum (1977) *The Structure of the Curriculum in the Third and Fourth Years of the Scottish Secondary School*, Munn Report, Edinburgh, HMSO.

Shipman, M. (1984) *Education as a Public Service*, London, Methuen.

Southworth, G. (1988) 'Collegiality and the role of the head', in G. Southworth (ed.) *Readings in Primary School Management*, Lewes, Falmer Press.

Taylor Report (1977) *A New Partnership for our Schools*, London, HMSO.

Tizard, B. and Hewitson, J. (1980) 'Parental involvement and reading attainment', *British Journal of Educational Psychology*, **50**, 209–15.

Tomlinson, J. R. G. (1987) *Informing Education*, Report of a committee chaired by Tomlinson for ILEA, London, Inner London Education Authority.

Widlake, P. and Macleod, F. (1984) *Raising Standards*, Coventry, Community Education Development Centre.

# 7

# Evaluating schools in the context of the Education Reform Act

**Anne McIntyre**

## Introduction

This chapter is concerned with the problems, possibilities and implications of evaluating schools within the terms set by the 1988 Education Reform Act. School managers are faced with the task of planning and implementing school evaluation policies which satisfy two sets of demands. On the one hand, there are the requirements of outside agencies for judging how far and in what respects schools have met external demands for accountability. On the other hand, school evaluation policies must also serve the needs of school managers and staff for improving their own practices.

First, this chapter describes evaluation strategies which have been developed by professional educators to meet accountability demands. Second, some characteristics of economic accountability are defined. Third, major assumptions which appear to underlie the arrangements for implementation of the national curriculum, standard assessment tasks and publication of results are outlined. The final section formulates some evaluation questions, and suggests strategies by which such questions may be answered.

Requirements that schools be evaluated come from a wide variety of groups with differential powers to assert the importance of their own criteria and to demand the provision of evidence that such criteria are being met. *Performance Indicators For Schools* (SIS, 1988) discusses the nature of possible performance indicators for use by schools in meeting public accountability demands. For the purposes of making a distinction between professional and educationist interests and concerns for evaluation and those of non-professionals, this chapter draws on the SIS notions of 'professional accountability' and 'economic accountability'.

## Professional accountability

By professional accountability, I mean a form of accounting where the demands being made upon schools – for example, by local or national government, parents and employers – are interpreted and translated into action and criteria for success within the frames of reference of professional educators. Several different strategies adopted by schools for meeting the demands of accountability are distinguished according to their focus for evaluation, their purposes, their evaluation strategies, the positions adopted by the evaluators, and the audiences for whom reports are made available. The strategies dealt with here are: *school prospectuses*, accounts of *self-evaluation*; *validation* of institutions and programmes; and school *reports* to individual parents.

### School prospectuses

The main focus of the school prospectus tends to be on descriptions of aspirations, rationales, policies, curriculum plans, extra-curricular activities, expectations of standards of attainment, dress, behaviour, time-keeping, parental support, and so on. The purposes for circulating such descriptions are to recruit pupils and parents, and to alert them to expectations of the school. Prospectuses highlight what the school does well and can offer to different groups of pupils with different interests or needs. The evaluation strategies are those adopted by parents in comparing statements of school intent with their own experiences, and those of their children, as to what happens in the day-to-day running of the school, and what its achievements are. Parents also compare the concerns and claims of the school with those apparent in other school prospectuses. The evaluators are therefore the clients: parents and their children.

### Self-evaluation

In the recent past in this country, professional accountability in schools has been largely conceived within a tradition of 'self-evaluation' with the emphasis on critical examination by schools of their own plans and related processes and outcomes. Adelman and Alexander (1982) give some indication of their expectations in this respect, in a description of 'formal' approaches to institutional self-evaluation. Formal evaluation is

> distinct from 'informal' not so much in terms of judgemental process itself as by virtue of the accessibility of that process, the intentions which lie behind it and the uses to which it is put. By formal educational evaluation we mean the making of judgements of the worth and effectiveness of educational endeavours at a public level, sometimes as a matter of deliberate institutional policy. These judgements . . . may reasonably claim to be valid and fair.
>
> (Adelman and Alexander, 1982: 6)

The implications of making public school decision-making, its processes and outcomes, are explored, for example, by Elliott *et al.* (1981). Significant contributions to the debate had earlier been made by House (1972), who was reacting against his experience of what he calls the 'productivity model' of accountability in the USA based primarily on economic and administrative concerns for efficiency, tidiness and value for money. MacDonald (1978) and, more recently, Simons (1988) have also been actively engaged in promoting the idea of self-evaluation as an appropriate way for educationists to respond to demands for public accountability.

These authors, and many others within this tradition, agree that accountability procedures of the self-reporting kind which render educational practice 'open to view and responsive to critique' can usefully serve both improvement purposes in schools and those of public accountability. Within this same tradition, Elliott and others (Elliott, 1981; Brown and McIntyre, 1981; Carr and Kemmis, 1986) have adopted and developed the idea of 'action research' as one way to fulfil the requirements of an explicit approach to self-evaluation. Action research can be described as:

> research carried out by practitioners with a view to improving their professional practice and understanding it better.
>
> (Cameron-Jones, 1983)

### Validation

Professional accountability may also be served by the validation and accreditation of institutions and courses. The aims of the procedures instigated are to provide clear and informative descriptions of the nature of institutions, their planned activities, clear and convincing rationales for these activities and how they will be organized and presented. Validation strategies are derived from attempts to make educational planning more considered and more explicitly justified. They rely on the acceptance of the idea that professional educators with qualifications and experience can be relied on to uphold the standards of attainment required by institutions and those they aim to serve. Importantly, the nature of the information generated is made available to a validating group who are usually drawn from a number of institutions, expert, sympathetic, sensitive to practical realities, and in a position to make comparisons between institutions. Most importantly, their judgements are made from independent positions by professionals who have no personal vested interests either in the plans they are being asked to validate or in their costs, the viability and availability of which are assumed to be negotiated elsewhere.

### School reports: profiling and records of achievement

For some time now schools have been working to improve their reports to parents and to prospective employers in ways that avoid 'invidious comparisons' between pupils, and which give credit to the specific things that pupils know and can do over a range of activities and contexts. The thinking which has informed much of the work on profiles and records of achievement has been based on criterion-referencing which is described by Brown as

> assessment that provides information about the specific knowledge and abilities of pupils through their performances on various kinds of tasks that are interpretable in terms of what the pupil knows or can do, without reference to the performance of others.
>
> (Brown, 1980: viii)

Many teachers have responded enthusiastically to profiles and records of achievement and, to varying degrees, have attempted to build criterion-referenced assessment into their reporting schemes. Profiles and records of achievement have been seen as helping teachers to work to sustain the motivation of pupils who may otherwise have been classified as 'below average' on the basis of single aggregated scores on tests or examinations (norm-referencing). One of the early advocates described the principles underlying profiles and records of achievement as follows:

> Student profiles or records of achievement are documents constituted by professional teachers . . . , in conjunction with their students, describing as accurately and succinctly as possible the knowledge, skills and experiences of an individual relative to a particular curriculum. They are meant to be read in their final (summative) form by (amongst others) employers, parents and educational personnel. . . . In the formative stage they are a common focus for concern between teacher and taught, . . . a basis for face to face discussion and reflection, and an opportunity to appraise the suitability . . . of the learning programme.
>
> (Mansell, 1986: 25)

Criterion-referenced assessment can, of course, be used in the same way as norm-referencing. While pupils' responses to individual test items can be criterion-referenced, and at this detailed level, provide useful information for professional purposes, they can also be added together to give an overall score or grade by which pupils are accorded a status relative to other pupils. Not only is important information lost in this process, but also the tendency is once more to compare one pupil with another on the basis of their assessment grades.

While profiles and criterion-referenced reports are not intended primarily for school evaluation purposes, they do provide the evidence from which parents can evaluate the school's contribution to their children's education; when reports from a whole year group of pupils are collated, patterns of strengths and weaknesses can be identified for either summative or formative purposes.

All these strategies of professional accountability in their own ways, directly or indirectly, can serve the interests of the public and also those of teachers wishing to improve the quality of learning for their pupils. The effectiveness of professional accountability approaches for these contrasting purposes depends upon the selection of evidence and the presentation of accounts in such a way as to be responsive to the concerns of different audiences, and so as to enable each audience to make valid interpretations of what is presented. On the one hand, there is the danger, to which professionals are likely to be alert, that a naive public will interpret evidence in over-simplified and unfair ways. On the other hand, a danger of all professional accountability, to which members of the public are likely to be alert, is that the professionals will, unwittingly or deliberately, be self-serving in their selection of criteria or of evidence. It is primarily because of this danger that there are demands for economic accountability.

## Economic accountability

The demands for economic accountability are that schools demonstrate value for money in relation to the interests and concerns of those bearing the costs. At one extreme, it is conceivable that economic accountability requirements could be met through the explicit professional evaluation activities of schools outlined above, without any further measures. However, schools have clearly been under pressure to justify the costs entailed. Responses in terms of reports by professionals on the benefits and values of their plans and processes, have not been regarded as sufficient. It has also been argued (SIS, 1988) that schools should respond in strictly economic terms. At the other extreme then, taking as the starting-point the general concerns of accountants and economists, value for money may be conceived in terms of such easily quantified variables as pupil–teacher ratios, costs per pupil, occupancy rates, and standards of pupil performance in examinations.

From this perspective, emphasis is laid on objective evidence, standard-izable variables, ready quantification and simple answers. It is clear that there is a significant tension between such an emphasis and a concern for professional relevance and qualitative approaches to the benefits of schooling. The SIS report on 'performance indicators' reflects this tension. The report attempts to achieve a compromise which gives greater weight to the economic perspective, seeking 'a range of suggested quantified indicators in accordance with certain basic principles'. The indicators should be:

(a) related to the school's own aims and objectives;
(b) reliable so far as possible, and able to be standardized;
(c) as few as are needed to achieve their purposes;
(d) as acceptable as possible to those who need them;
(e) capable of conveying messages and throwing up warning signs.

(SIS, 1988: 4)

Economic accountability may be seen as involving four possible categories of variables:

1  outcome, or benefit, variables
2  cost variables
3  process variables
4  context and uncontrolled input variables.

### Benefit and cost variables

If schools were to operate in a competitive open market in accordance with a *laissez-faire* 'market' ideology (Lawton, 1988), evaluation of schools would be unnecessary because it would be implicit in the mechanisms of the market. Successful schools would be able to charge more, would attract more clients, and would therefore have high incomes in comparison to their costs: the measure of their success, their profits, would itself provide the 'natural' reward for their success.

However, so long as the state continues to meet even some of the costs of schooling, such a simple model is inadequate, and it is necessary to specify the outcomes of schooling which are valued. These may be very diverse, including the manifold understandings, skills and attitudes which it may be desirable for pupils to acquire, their enjoyment of school life, the contribution that the school makes to the life of the community, and the professional development of teachers working in the school. These various possible benefits may be difficult to describe, more so to quantify, and may differ subtly from school to school; but within an economic accountability framework they are more likely to be considered if they can be both quantified and standardized – for example, the 'simple' and 'objective' measures provided by publication of external examination results as required by the 1980 Education Act.

Within a state-funded system of schooling, it is the benefits and outcomes potentially provided by schools which are most likely to interest both general public and professional teachers. To politicians and administrators, however, costs are likely to be of equal concern. A school's performance in economic terms is a function of the benefits achieved for given costs and of the costs incurred in achieving given benefits. Again, a sensitive analysis of costs would include the stresses and difficulties experienced by teachers, and indeed by pupils and their parents; but unless these can be quantified, and qualified in financial terms, it is unlikely that an economic accountability analysis will include them.

### Process variables

While it is in terms of its outcomes or products that a school is likely to be judged within an economic framework, the school has greater control, over its own internal processes, and these may in some respects be more easily observed and measured. 'Process–product' research studies of teaching, and increasingly in recent years of the operation of whole schools, have sought to establish through correlational analyses across schools the processes which are conducive to the achievement of various desired outcomes (Rutter *et al.*, 1979). In so far as such work has been successful, it would seem possible for schools to be evaluated not only in terms of the outcomes they achieve, but also in terms of whether their internal processes are likely to facilitate such desired outcomes.

### *Context and uncontrolled input variables*

Research studies have tended to show that schools' performances, in terms of the outcomes achieved for given costs, correlate more highly with external factors over which schools seem to have no control than with any significant internal process variables (Coleman, 1969; Jencks, 1972). Prominent amongst such variables are characteristics of schools' catchment areas, and the measured abilities or attainments of pupils on entry to the school. In the light of these findings, it may very reasonably be argued that an adequate model of economic accountability would judge the outcomes achieved by schools, and even the processes in which they engaged, only after statistical account had been taken of such major uncontrollable variables.

These then are some of the major considerations which have informed strategies for evaluating schools during recent years, reflecting the diverse values and interests inside and outside schools. Given this diversity, evaluation strategies have been aimed very often at resolving the major problem of reconciling professional interests with those of the public at large.

To know how best to develop our thinking from here, we now turn to the 1988 Education Reform Act to examine some major assumptions which appear to underlie the arrangements for implementation of the national curriculum, assessment, and publication of results. These are outlined, and their possible implications for professional and economic accountability are discussed.

## The 1988 Education Reform Act: national curriculum and standard assessment tasks

The aim of this section is to identify the major shifts in power relations that were brought about by the Act. The discussion focuses on the arrangements which are being made for the implementation of the national curriculum and its associated testing programme. The notion of power is useful in understanding who is accountable for what, and what pressures can be brought to bear on different groups to take account of the needs or demands of other groups, and to provide evidence of meeting such demands. Three aspects of the changes are of special significance for a re-examination of professional and economic accounting procedures.

First, the shift in responsibility for development of curricular aims and objectives. Teachers have been relieved of much of the responsibility for decision-making about which 'subjects' might be important, how much time will be devoted to them and what aspects of these subjects are to be given special emphasis. Instead, various subject groups are developing broad curriculum outlines and guidelines which teachers will use to implement their own strategies.

Second, the shift in responsibilities for determining the standards to be achieved. Arrangements have been made for selected consortia to develop appropriate, valid and reliable ways to assess pupils' performance against predetermined standards (or statements of attainment) at various stages throughout their school career. Aggregated results, which must be published, allow comparisons to be made between groups of pupils and schools. (The exception is results for 7-year-old pupils, though it was 'strongly recommended' that these should also be published: *Hansard*, 7 June 1988.) Despite a growing literature on making fair, adjusted comparisons of school performance (Goldstein and Cuttance, 1988; Nuttall, 1988), the school-level results are not to be adjusted for context and uncontrolled variables, but set within a report of the school as a whole and accompanied by a description of the socio-economic characteristics of the school's community. Through publication, for example, in a school's prospectus, parents will have access to these unadjusted test scores so that they can evaluate schools and choose the one they prefer. Competition between schools was anticipated by the government as one outcome of these arrangements. It was argued that this competition could be expected to lead to a raising of standards, although the precise mechanisms through which testing and publication of results might lead to the benefits envisaged were not made explicit (Gipps, 1988).

Third, the shift of powers in favour of government, school governors and parents. Schools have the choice of opting out of local authority control to be maintained directly by central government. The local school management arrangements also gave much greater autonomy to secondary and larger primary schools that remain under LEA control. However, central control is fairly firmly in the hands of government through its control of the curriculum and the standards to be achieved.

What implications, then, do these radical changes have for school evaluation procedures? The first implication would seem to be that, in future, professional accountability operations will be constrained within an economic accountability framework. The powers and obligations of school governors, combined with opportunities for parental choice, mean that teachers and managers have to account for their activities increasingly in terms set by other people.

More specifically, in terms of the categories of variables suggested above in relation to economic accountability, the Education Reform Act would seem to have the following implications:

1 *Outcome variables*: The external prescription of the curriculum, imposition of standardized assessments, and the obligation on schools to publish the results of these assessments, will surely mean that schools will, from now on, be primarily held accountable in terms of their pupils' performance on these assessment tasks.

2 *Cost variables*: Whether or not schools opt out, their funding will be determined by standard and 'fair' formulae. The relative costs which may be appropriately incurred by schools as a result of their differing circumstances (e.g. disadvantaged catchment areas) will not be, one may guess, a major factor in the economic accountability demands made upon them.

3 *Process variables*: Because of local school management, schools will be able to use their resources in meeting the demands of the national curriculum and the standards set as they consider best, with substantially more freedom than before. It must be expected that *how* they use this freedom will be a primary focus of accountability concern.

4 *Context and uncontrolled input variables*: Despite considerable controversy over this aspect of the initial report of the Task Group for Assessment and Testing (TGAT, 1988), it is clear that no formal procedure has been initiated to take account of schools' contexts or recruitment in publishing or evaluating their pupils' performances. Schools will, of course, be able, for example, to explain away poor results at the 14-year-old stage by pointing to the poor results of 11-year-olds entering the school. Such excuses are not, however, likely to be very persuasive to parents. Parents rightly tend to believe that their children's chances of academic success are likely to be poorer in schools where the attainments of entrants are generally low (see e.g. Rutter *et al.*, 1979). The more that the school emphasizes such low attainments, the less the school is likely to be valued. Schools need to find other ways of coping with this central problem.

The 1988 Education Reform Act therefore puts schools within a narrow framework within which they are held accountable. Furthermore it would seem that the relative success of different schools will be largely determined, unfairly, by factors over which they have no control. That is a depressing scenario. It is therefore necessary to ask whether there is any more optimistic and fruitful way of construing the situation.

The narrowing of the accountability framework for schools is primarily in terms of the national curriculum with its imposed attainment targets. Within the core subjects for which these targets have been specified, however, it would be difficult to argue that the attainment targets are inherently inappropriate. Criticisms have been largely about relative emphasis or lack of flexibility. It can be argued that the main problem which schools faced in recent years was an over-extension of commitments that teachers were asked to undertake. The national curriculum with its imposed attainment targets may be seen positively as offering a welcome restriction of the increasingly unmanageable range of tasks for which teachers were previously held accountable.

The plausibility of such an argument depends, of course, on whether or not schools have a genuine opportunity to engage in solving the problems which have been defined by given curricula and attainment targets. In a number of respects they clearly do. As noted, local management of schools enhances the substantial freedom schools already have to use their resources in whatever ways they think most effective. Also, the framework provided by the national curriculum and related assessment tasks does at least provide opportunities for meaningful accounting to parents in terms of what specific aspects of the curriculum have or have not been attained by a pupil and to what standards. None of this is much use, however, unless schools have that most crucial prerequisite for effectiveness: a sense of efficacy on the part of their teachers. Teachers, as much as pupils, have to believe that the problems with which they are faced are problems which they have the power to solve.

The fundamental question then relates to the possibility of a school being able to give valid and positive accounts of its efforts when, as has been suggested, its achievements are likely to be very heavily dependent on input variables beyond its control. Any alternative to the pessimistic scenario painted previously has to be dependent on construing the reality with which schools are faced in some way other than in terms of uncontrollable variables.

One such alternative can be found in the writings of Benjamin Bloom. He is interested especially in interpreting the available process-product research evidence on effective teaching in order to maximize pupils' attainments. The current situation as described would justify a brief reconsideration of some of the points which inform his work. In his book, *Human Characteristics and School Learning* (1976), Bloom establishes a way of analysing causal influences on pupils' attainments. Three sets of variables are at the heart of his thesis:

1 cognitive entry characteristics (knowledge, skills and understanding);
2 affective entry characteristics (attitudes to subject and school, and academic self-concept); and
3 quality of teaching.

Two major assumptions inform his thinking about these variables:

> Each learner begins a particular course . . . with a history which has prepared him [her] differently from other learners . . . [and] that the characteristics of the learners as well as the characteristics of the instruction can be modified.
>
> (Bloom, 1976: 13–14)

Bloom argues that cognitive entry characteristics are the most important explanatory variable in accounting for differences in attainment. In doing so, he rejects more traditional views which assume that the most useful way of explaining differences of attainment is by attributing them to relatively stable ability characteristics of the pupil.

He explains cognitive entry characteristics as various kinds of knowledge, skills and understandings which pupils will need to benefit from a course, and which they may or may not have acquired. This implies that criterion-referenced assessments should have been recorded on previous occasions and that there will be a clear continuity between those assessed prior attainments and the objectives of each new section of the curriculum. Given that most schools have been working towards profiling and records of achievement of the kind required by Bloom's analysis, and that national subject curricula have been articulated to demonstrate required continuities, the above demands are consistent with established policy. The usefulness of standard assessment tasks (SATs), for example, is dependent on internal profiling arrangements of a criterion-referenced kind so that continuity between the various stages of the national curriculum and its related assessment procedures is assured.

Bloom argues on the basis of a review of research evidence, that most differences in pupil attainments can be explained in terms of these three sets of variables: cognitive and affective entry characteristics and quality of teaching. Most crucially he demonstrates that, in explaining differences in attainment, one does not need to refer to such global and unalterable variables as general intelligence or verbal reasoning ability. He argues that the 'cognitive entry characteristics' which are the major determinants of pupils' success in learning *are* alterable and therefore potentially within the control of the school.

If this is so, then schools need not despair about being held accountable for outcomes which depend very largely on input variables beyond their control. Instead they are faced with evaluating their work on the admittedly very demanding criterion, among others, that their pupils should start each new learning task with the skills and understandings necessary to attain the learning objectives for that task.

In the final section, I draw on Bloom's ideas in looking at the evaluation questions which it might be necessary or appropriate for schools to ask in responding to accountability demands in the light of the Education Reform Act.

### Evaluation questions and strategies

It is well established that the abilities of pupils entering school are closely related to their home backgrounds, most notably in terms of social class and ethnic group. Furthermore, differences in attainment amongst children from these groups tend to grow steadily wider throughout the years of compulsory schooling. At every stage of schooling, the extent to which children bring with them the abilities they need to benefit from school tasks are powerfully dependent on relationships between cultural experiences and these tasks. This being so, there can be little doubt that school effectiveness in taking account of cognitive and affective entry characteristics is largely dependent on the quality of collaboration which can be established between home, community and school in relation to these tasks. Evaluation questions about the quality and effectiveness of this collaboration would therefore have to be at the top of every school's evaluation agenda.

A second issue relates to the way differences among pupils are dealt with. If it is supposed that pupils differ widely in their inherent abilities and their potential for learning, then the increasingly wide variations in attainment predicted by TGAT (1988) in their report must be seen as inevitable; the focus for accountability will be on the adequacy with which schools *manage* the problems raised by these inevitable variations. If, on the other hand, all pupils are seen as having a similar potential for success on the national curriculum, the important evaluation questions are about how far the school has ensured that temporary differences do not become permanent, and has mobilized its resources to ensure success in tests and examinations for all pupils. To accept such a demanding responsibility may on the face of it seem rash. However, to accept anything else is to resign oneself to being held accountable for what one believes to be outside the school's control.

It is proposed therefore that schools think about their in-school development and evaluation initiatives within a *collaborative* framework:

1 teamwork incorporating groups outside the school.
2 teamwork incorporating groups within the school.

### *Teamwork: outside groups*

#### *Parents*
Strategies of accounting such as school prospectuses and reports to parents can be used entirely as school accounting devices, whereby the school sets up a one way form of written communication with parents. While parents may learn a great deal from prospectuses about the requirements of the school, and about how well their children are meeting these requirements from school reports, schools learn very little about the home, and parental attitudes towards their children's school work.

If the schools are to establish effective ways of working with parents, much more information of this kind is required. Parent–school links have been established in some schools over such matters as reading and home-work, especially with groups of parents whose children are seen to be 'at risk'. Very often, however, such innovative attempts to engage parents in the work of the school have been developed without much regard for under-standing parents' perspectives or for the costs and benefits experienced by teachers, parents and pupils. If such measures were to be institutionalized as a part of school life, and in such a way as to attempt to maximize all pupils' attainments, then it would be necessary for the school to evaluate more carefully parental understandings, to evaluate existing provision and, on the basis of evaluation, to develop frequent and regular opportunities for exchange of views.

Because school prospectuses and reports are important ways of representing the work of the school to parents, and provide sources of evidence from which parents can make decisions about school effectiveness in and between schools, they are an important focus for school evaluation. If schools set out to recruit parents and to persuade parents of their collaborative intentions both prospectuses and reports can be used to communicate these aims. Thus, for example, prospectuses would include descriptions of the procedures through which the school proposes to maximize pupils' attainments and of the ways parents and teachers can collaborate (e.g. through homework) to make sure this happens. Neither prospectuses nor reports would refer to explanations which are beyond the powers of teachers or parents to change. They would concentrate instead on making explicit the standards to be met and the positive measures that can be taken by teachers in collaboration with parents to ensure that these standards are met. Evaluation of prospectuses and reports would set out to establish to what degree and in what respects they reflect such aspirations.

### Other professional groups

The idea of teamwork can be extended to include other professional groups. Many schools, for example, have links with local industry and with community groups including local health and social services. While all these sources of help and support can be used to maximize pupil attainments, the schools' concerns have not always been focused on collaboration with a view to establishing prerequisites which pupils may need to meet future curriculum requirements. One useful kind of collaboration would be between primary and nursery schools, or between secondary and primary schools, where prerequisites are identified and negotiated, and the curriculum strategies in each school planned accordingly.

Schools can also make good use of professional educators from higher education, or teachers from other schools, to validate their plans for national curriculum implementation and for related assessment initiatives. The major aims of validation would be to raise consciousness amongst the planners in the school by identifying problems or gaps in the planned provision. The exercise would enable the identification of a focus for evaluation, the clarification of evaluation questions and the reconceptualization of the plans in the light of new information.

### Teamwork: within the school

Drawing on Bloom's ideas, the priorities for evaluation in the school would be those questions about how far and in what respects the school has managed to ensure that temporary differences between pupils do not become permanent, and has mobilized its resources to ensure success in tests and examinations for all pupils. It is towards these ends that the principles and procedures developed within the self-evaluation tradition can be most useful.

The literature on evaluation and research techniques is extensive and can be referred to in order to explore the possibilities. Once the school has established the specific nature of the questions to be asked, then the task of finding appropriate techniques for answering the questions is not so daunting. Action research, for example, lends itself well to whole-school developments with staff in various posts studying their own practices in relation to one aspect of school policy. If evaluations are intended to serve the purposes of economic accountability, then they must also fulfil the criteria for explicit and systematic self-evaluation. What is meant by 'explicit and systematic' in this context, is that the procedures adopted should explore the validity of underlying assumptions, interpretations, implementation of plans, achievement of goals, and also possible explanations of potential failure to achieve these goals. (However, if the evidence is for internal use only then some degree of shared understandings can be assumed, although the more closely evaluations meet the criteria outlined above, the more useful they can be for sensitizing school decision-making.)

It is in the classroom, however, that pupils' attainments can be most directly influenced. It is there that learning problems are most likely to be encountered on a day-to-day basis. Following Bloom's proposals, the teachers' task would not be a simple or an easy one. In general, heads and senior staff rely on teachers to identify and solve their own classroom problems. What school managers can do to facilitate evaluation at the classroom level is to initiate, sustain and support questioning attitudes and practices among staff throughout the school. They can most usefully take measures to find out what kinds of internal or external support would be most welcomed by classroom teachers or departments; and how extra time might be found for teachers engaging in problem-solving or action research activities where time for reflection is crucial. They can also attempt to minimize administrative demands on teachers by taking on many of these tasks themselves.

With an emphasis on teamwork, senior staff in their policy-making would have to be sensitive to teachers' varying needs. There will be, for example, differences in subject philosophies and so there are likely to be aspects of a department's work which would benefit by non-standard approaches. There may also be differences in the stages of development which various departments or individuals may have reached in their understandings of what is required. In view of the considerable demands on teachers of undertaking evaluations within the self-evaluation tradition, balancing the costs and rewards for teachers would be an important factor to take into account. For example, there are increasing opportunities for teachers to undertake school-based evaluations as a way of meeting the requirements of part-time, award-bearing courses in higher education. Evaluation projects can be negotiated to suit the purposes of the school, and the scope and quality of such evaluations would benefit from the help and support of higher education personnel and local education authorities.

## References

Adelman, C. and Alexander, R. (1982) *The Self-Evaluating Institution*, London, Methuen.

Bloom, B. (1976) *Human Characteristics and School Learning*, New York, McGraw-Hill.

Brown, S. (1980) *What Do They Know?*, a review of Criterion-Referenced Assessment, Edinburgh, HMSO.

Brown, S. and McIntyre, D. (1981) 'An action research approach to innovation in centralised educational systems', *European Journal of the Sociology of Education*, **3**(3), 243–58.

Cameron-Jones, M. (1983) 'A researching profession? The growth of classroom research', paper given at a day seminar, University of Glasgow.

Carr, W. and Kemmis, S. (1986) *Becoming Critical*, Lewes, Falmer Press.

Coleman, J. S. (1969) 'Summary of the Coleman Report', Equal Educational Opportunity, Cambridge, Mass., Harvard University Press.

Elliott, J. (1981) 'Action research: a framework for self evaluation in schools', Working Paper, Cambridge, Cambridge Institute of Education.

Elliott, J., Bridges, D., Ebbutt, D., Gibson, R. and Nias, J. (1981) *School Accountability*, SSRC Cambridge Accountability Project, London, Grant McIntyre.

Gipps, C. (1988) 'The debate over standards and the uses of testing', *British Journal of Educational Studies*, **36**(1), 21–36.

Goldstein, H. and Cuttance, P. (1988) 'A note on national assessment and school comparisons', *Journal of Educational Policy*, **3**(2), 197–201.

House, E. (1972) 'The dominion of economic accountability', *Educational Forum*, **37**(1).

Jencks, C. (1972) *Inequality*, New York, Harper & Row.

Lawton, D. (1988) 'Ideologies of Education' in D. Lawton and C. Chitty (eds) *The National Curriculum*, Bedford Way Papers/33, pp. 10–20, University of London, Institute of Education.

MacDonald, B. (1978) 'Accountability, standards and the process of schooling', in T. Becher and S. Maclure (eds) *Accountability in Education*, London, Holt, Rinehart & Winston.

Mansell, J. (1986) 'Records of achievement and profiles in further education', in P. Broadfoot (ed.) *Profiles and Records of Achievement*, London, Holt, Rinehart & Winston.

Nuttall, D. (1988) 'National assessment: complacency or misinterpretation?', lecture given at University of London, Institute of Education, March.

Rutter, M., Maughan, B., Mortimore, P. and Ouston, J. (1979) *Fifteen Thousand Hours*, London, Open Books.

Simons, H. (1988) *Getting to Know Schools in a Democracy*, Lewes, Falmer Press.

SIS (Statistical Information Services) (1988) *Performance Indicators for Schools*, London, Chartered Institute of Public Finance and Accountancy.

*TES* (*Times Educational Supplement*) (1989) 'A lump sum of low standards', reported by W. Norris, p. A17.

TGAT (Task Group on Assessment and Testing) (1988) *National Curriculum Task Group on Assessment and Testing: A Report*, London, DES and Welsh Office.

### *Acknowledgement*

I must thank my colleague, Caroline Gipps, for her helpful comments and suggestions throughout the drafting of this paper.

# 8

# Planning for the future in further education: beyond a curriculum-led approach

## Jenny Shackleton

### Introduction

The 1988 Education Reform Act is a large piece in a jigsaw of change, but not the only piece. [. . .] In 1987 it was still possible, and even easy, for many college lecturers not to know about, or to feel, the impact of curriculum trends, demographic trends, the needs of adults, the National Council for Vocational Qualifications (NCVQ), [. . .] performance indicators, the role of the Manpower Services Commission (MSC: later the Training Agency) in further education (FE), and the impending removal of barriers within the European Economic Community (EEC). [The year 1988 also saw the settlement of a new pay and conditions agreement for lecturers in further education.] The post-settlement world [. . .] includes all the above developments in more concrete form and pointed up by the Education Reform Act (ERA). If public sector FE is to have a positive role in education and training in the future, both college managers and lecturers now have a shared responsibility and an urgent need to engage in joint action which recognizes and responds to these new circumstances.

### The 1980s: a decade of change

*Students*

The 1980s brought changes for colleges in respect of their students, curriculum, delivery methods and resources. The scale, range, timing and complexity of these changes impinged upon college lecturers in very varied and uneven ways, and added to the differences which inevitably arise from the breadth and diversity of FE's role, and the range of expertise required. Since the 1970s the patterns of movement among 16- to 19-year-olds [. . .] have been subject to major changes. Certain options such as employment dramatically declined; others expanded. The nature of each option also changed. More young people than hitherto moved into full-time education and training post-16, and the Youth Training Scheme (YTS) established the credentials of work-based learning. Among the nations which have ensured substantial participation in education and training beyond the compulsory stage, much of that education and training is explicitly work based or work related. In the United Kingdom the movement towards greater participation in post-compulsory education and training, and the involvement in this of large numbers of employers and work-places, have been a relatively recent one which is still associated by many college lecturers with youth unemployment, exploitation, and short-term crisis measures.

The piecemeal fashion in which provision for 16- to 19-year-olds, and more recently for adults, has arisen, has created confusion and ineffectiveness which has largely not been of lecturers' or colleges' making. The regulations restricting and controlling young people's and adults' entitlements have often undermined that essential sense of partnership between and among clients and providers to which the curriculum has subscribed.

### Curriculum

The overwhelming majority of students and lecturers still expect their course or programme content and processes to be determined by the examining and validating bodies. The trend towards the validation of institutions by awarding bodies, and the greater involvement of staff in course design and in learning and assessment strategies is, however, having an important developmental effect upon college lecturers. In sponsoring the Technical and Vocational Education Initiative (TVEI) and YTS, the MSC (and later the Training Agency) has itself acted as validating body, but since it has had rather broader aims, and has normally not held for lecturers the esteem of an examining and validating body, it has needed to use resources, incentives and penalties to ensure compliance. The major changes which we are now witnessing in qualifying procedures have been inevitable since the MSC became involved in education and training and, in doing so, highlighted the damaging effect upon learning and achievement of a fragmented array of awards.

A number of curriculum principles have managed to survive the years of experimentation and short-term remedies, and have now achieved respectability. These include a core of learning for all students to address, together with understanding and skills for new technology.

The process of

1 induction and initial assessment
2 activity-based, individual and open learning opportunities
3 negotiation of learning programmes and targets

4  planned work or community experience
5  formative assessment and reviews
6  continuing guidance and personal support

are no longer rejected outright. However, they are subscribed to more readily than they are fulfilled. There is also broad agreement that vocational qualifications should comprise statements of attainment in competence form.

### Achievement and progression

College lecturers have considerable expertise in assessment but may have applied this outside their own colleges on behalf of the examining and validating bodies, rather than internally, because of the nature of the assessment procedure laid down. However, the 1980s saw a shift away from external assessment and examinations towards internal processes. Continuing assessment, leading to profiles of achievement, encouraged less reliance on traditional examination structures and a greater sharing of aims between students and lecturers. However, the scope of these practices varies widely, as do the techniques and procedures involved.

Since college lecturers are by and large still preoccupied with developing their expertise in formative and summative assessment, they have not addressed in an incisive way the major boundary issues which are highlighted once student achievement is put to use: the currency of vocational qualifications relative to general education ones, and the interfaces between pre-16 and post-16 education, and between FE and HE and training.

In the 1980s much was spoken and written about student access and progression, but with limited effect. Provision for non-traditional students is still managed and delivered as a marginal remedial activity. Most colleges have not yet been able to provide these students with equal attention, an equal curriculum, or qualifications with high currency. Most colleges have not yet found ways of redeploying their resources to provide adequate learner support. By and large, therefore, access has come to mean exceptional entry to elements of the normal curriculum for specified disadvantaged groups. Progression through FE colleges and onwards has not been tackled in a systematic way.

### A spectrum of perceptions and practices

As a result of a decade or more of frenetic change stimulated for many different reasons by a variety of agents, individual college lecturers vary dramatically in their attitudes, capability and performance. Some still live in a world which assumes student confidence and motivation, common starting-points for students, regards teaching as equating to learning, thinks only of vertical progression routes, uses set time-scales for learning and courses, uses traditional delivery methods, monitors course inputs and puts the institution first.

In the same colleges, though, increasing numbers of lecturers are acquiring the ability to

1 set achievement targets relative to assessed needs
2 accredit prior attainments
3 support individual pathways
4 apply learning and course time-scales provisionally and flexibly
5 use varied and flexible teaching and learning methods
6 provide personal support
7 monitor and review student outcomes.

To survive and be fully effective in the new circumstances, college lecturers need, consciously and collectively, to espouse and use these latter approaches.

### Curriculum-led institutional development

Enormous amounts of time have been spent during the 1980s in encouraging, coaxing, persuading and sometimes bribing colleges to change. During this time, the principles and techniques of curriculum-led institutional development have been invaluable since they take account of, and build upon, the culture of FE. To quote from early working papers:

> FE colleges are concerned with structured student learning. That is what they are there to provide. It is the justification for their existence. Structured student learning is that which is planned and intended, and it is expressed through the provision of a curriculum for the student. Students learn in many other random and unstructured ways, but the responsibility of the college for their learning is bounded by the provision of the curriculum.
>
> If the prime purpose of the college is to facilitate student learning, then it can be argued that all activities of the college should directly or indirectly be supporting that learning, or at the very least should not be making it more difficult. The fundamental proposition is that the organisation, operational activities, and development of the college should be determined by the needs of the student learning programmes. This is our definition of curriculum-led institutional organisation and development.
>
> It follows that the curriculum is as much about support systems as about learning content and pedagogy, and those support systems include not only counselling and guidance for the student, but also a comprehensive management support system. It is true to say that the whole college and all its operations are part of the curriculum. It all impacts upon the students' experiences and their learning. The belief is that the management and organisational structures of colleges are

frequently not perceived in this relationship to student learning and are not defined as part of the total curriculum. Consequently they are as likely as not to work against student learning, or at least do nothing to help it. A curriculum-led approach constantly and consciously tries to keep students and their learning at the heart of things.

### The adoption of a curriculum-led approach

Equally, the expression of a curriculum-led approach through seven areas of attention has enabled colleges to adjust their collective behaviour in order to become more sensitive providers of courses and more acute listeners to students' explicit or implicit messages. The headings used for applying a curriculum-led approach to

1 policy-making
2 selective resource allocation
3 managing boundary transactions
4 harnessing staff skills
5 innovative capacity
6 management systems and organizational structure

can be used to include college lecturers in audits of their collective behaviour and operations, and to achieve well-supported strategies for developing a college mission, righting historical imbalances in resourcing, structuring to encourage professional behaviour, training and support to enhance staff capability, introducing response mechanisms for change, using information for quality assurance and management, as well as for administration.

### Beyond a curriculum-led approach

Curriculum-led development has a virtuous and moderate air, and wins ready support among lecturers who, as the most direct representatives of students given this approach, are also put at the 'heart of things'. However, for the circumstances we now find ourselves in, we must move forward and beyond a curriculum-led approach. We must question the implicit assumption of a curriculum-led approach that the college lecturer and the student are one and the same, and give the student a separate identity and a greater degree of autonomy. An outright learner-led approach is essential in order to redefine the role and function of colleges, and of college lecturers.

The market-place in which we offer our services is increasingly competitive. Public sector colleges will be no less partisan and competitive than the private sector wherever local authorities do not or cannot exercise their powers of strategic management within the terms of the Education Reform Act, and this may well put some colleges' survival at risk. By and large the quality assurance measures of the MSC and Training Agency eliminated most of the worst private training organizations. Within the remainder there may be people of considerable talent whom we would, in different times, be pleased to employ in our colleges. Many of those who have found a career route within the private sector, or in non-college public sector education and training, did so because at an earlier point they themselves were prevented from advancement in FE colleges. The mystique with which we at times justified our fee levels, our grip on certain qualifications, and particular student attendance patterns, has been seen through, and we have to be more honest and careful about the reasons we advance for a favourable place in the market. Further than that, we have to start providing new services and benefits which are based upon our primary purposes – to educate and train – but which go well beyond the current offering.

### The lecturer-student relationship

Competitiveness in FE is being sharpened by both the fall in numbers among the younger students who are available for our traditional provision, and the impact of selective economic growth. Despite the normally very positive relationship between lecturers and students, the basic relationship is not an equal one. Younger students are not consistently viewed as clients requiring a service, and they in turn generally do not assert their rights to personal choice and respect. Our colleges may still be essentially custodial, and the physical accommodation, with its classrooms, canteens and peremptory notices, may reinforce this. The battle for access for students of all needs and abilities is being won, if to some extent because of demographic trends. However, the campaign to give students equality of esteem with lecturers is only just beginning.

The reasons for such equality are to do with the rights of an educated population, the good health of corporations and communities, and the necessary conditions for positive and recurrent learning. The pressure for a more balanced relationship is strong and irresistible, and stems from several sources. Changes in the school curriculum are, it is hoped, leading to more aware young learners who recognize that they have choices in terms of learning methods and environments, and clear rights to a wider range of services.

Alternatives to college are attractive, and have to be competed with on stronger grounds than future career prospects or HE. This is not to say that the relative powers of lecturers and students should be reversed, but that students should have assigned to them a responsibility for managing their own learning, and be equipped and expected to do so in both schools and colleges. Fortunately, in attempting to compensate for the loss of school-leavers, FE colleges are turning to the adult learner, and the services, environments and relationships which develop for older age-groups should attract and benefit the younger students also.

As the average age of our students increases, more is having to change besides the prevailing lecturer–student relationship and the setting within which they meet. Much FE provision lacks clarity of purpose either generally or in its elements. It can easily come to be seen as a good thing without further definition and evaluation. However, for adults, and increasingly for young people, education and training needs to be more overtly supportive and purposeful (though not necessarily serious) if it is to increase its attractiveness. To achieve this, purposes need to be expressed at a series of levels: the institution; the course team; the individual lecturer; the course or programme; and the learning encounter. To bring this about we must dispel the notion that by making purposes explicit we are embracing training and behaviourism. Greater clarity of purpose should include the recognition that we have a national deficiency of educational attainment, as well as of training, and the resolve to address that problem in an open manner.

### The impact of NCVQ

It is evident that examining and awarding bodies have exerted, and still exert, a very powerful influence upon college lecturers' perceptions and behaviour. As a result, the number and disparateness of examining and validating bodies and qualifications has been reflected in the variety and lack of co-ordination of qualification schemes in colleges. Hierarchized and other distinctions have developed in colleges, based on external qualification factors, and types of qualifications are often still used to define boundaries between various post-16 institutions. For this reason NCVQ seems set to have at least as large an effect upon lecturers' roles and activities as the Education Reform Act or demographic trends. NCVQ has the remit to

1  secure standards of occupational competence and ensure that vocational qualifications are based on these
2  design and implement a new national framework for vocational qualifications
3  approve bodies making accredited awards
4  obtain comprehensive coverage of all occupational sectors
5  secure arrangements for quality assurance
6  set up effective liaison with bodies awarding vocational qualifications
7  establish a national data base for vocational qualifications
8  undertake or arrange for others to undertake research and development to discharge these functions
9  promote vocational education, training and qualifications.

Its framework, comprising outcomes in competence form, units, aggregate qualifications and levels, is introducing some welcome order into the proliferation of awards. However, by not setting minima and maxima to the number of units which make up a qualification, or to each unit's specificity, NCVQ may exacerbate the problems for colleges attempting to introduce a large number of the new or revised qualifications quickly. Greater consistency in both units and qualifications would assist lecturers with the design, preparation and sharing of learning materials and environments, with assessment, and with the acceptance of units and qualifications for purposes of progression. Credit transfer is an unknown and unpractised concept for many lecturers who have generally been encouraged to emphasize the distinctions between awards.

Faced with the general need to raise the nation's educational base, and the specific requirement by both TVEI and the national curriculum 5–16 to provide a core of learning, it is essential to specify a series of achievement levels in core areas such as language, mathematics, science and technology, which can support progressive and flexible vocational education and training post-16. These levels or grades would contribute another element of consistency to the vocational qualifications, could support the guidance and counselling needed to underpin a credit transfer system, and also provide a foundation for higher levels of vocational attainment. However, to help lecturers to adjust their perceptions and activity in a really radical way, NCVQ also needs to help break down the major barriers mentioned above: the distinctions between vocational and general education qualifications, and between vocational and professional qualifications and university degrees.

Whatever it has not yet managed to address, NCVQ is none the less having an impact upon colleges, setting direct challenges for lecturers at the centre of their professional identity. The National Record of Vocational Achievement has been launched, bringing with it a new type of student expectation. A significant wave of competence-based qualification schemes is now with us in the colleges.

### The future?

FE tends to have been under-managed and fragmented locally, and there is a danger of its becoming more so. Concurrently, though, the service is being shaped in new ways at a national level. Alongside the less protected operating conditions for individual colleges, a stronger national framework for strategic planning for the post-16 age range emerged through NCVQ, WRNAFE and TVEI, and the provisions of ERA such as unit-based resourcing. Taken together, these devices touch all aspects of a college: its curriculum, delivery, organization, resourcing and relationships. It is essential that they are seen as a whole, and do not, in effect, cut across each other either locally or nationally. Given the pace and scale of the anticipated changes, college lecturers will be vulnerable to the effects of poor college or local management, and they need urgently to develop their means of influencing decision-making.

If we assume that the changes, trends and requirements which are evident remain and take effect, then FE colleges may in the future have the following characteristics:

1 The students' average age will be higher owing to the reduction in the number of 16- to 19-year-olds, the increase in the number of young adults, and a greater participation rate among adults of all ages. Their fees and other costs will come from a wider variety of sources, some of which the students will have needed to tap on their own behalf, with extensive assistance from colleges. Other funding sources will liaise directly with the colleges.

2 The students will regard colleges as learning centres in a broader sense, offering a variety of direct and indirect learning and qualification services. These will include information and advice, initial assessment, accreditation of prior learning, group and individual learning opportunities, assessments of achievement on demand, work learning placements, final assessments, and assistance with transfer and progression.

3 College environments will be trying to look more like other centres offering community or commercial services, with information and advice points, meeting and relaxation areas. Classrooms and workshops for group learning will take up rather less of the total available space than they do now, but supported study areas will be much in evidence for overall learning purposes, and particularly for the core curriculum.

4 More of the college's resources will be going towards its activity and image in its locality. Industry and commerce and the open community will have access to such college facilities as assessment centres, consultancies, exhibition space and publishing units as part of this. A wider range of staff will be employed, therefore, and the college will be open for the equivalent hours of a leisure or community centre.

5 A much-expanded admissions service will exploit every opportunity to recruit, offering a continuous information, assessment and advice service, and monitoring students until well into their programmes. Family classes, Saturday and Sunday opening, and summer schools will be regarded as normal and essential features of a life-long learning facility.

6 Back-up services for students and the community will include careers education and work placement facilities, information about job vacancies, and support for employment and self-employment projects.

Where will the college lecturers be in this? Perhaps they will maintain existing practices and conditions, be distinct and valued for the job done, but also less dominant within FE colleges. In this event the more autonomous student will spend more time with non-teaching staff trained in learner support techniques. Alternatively, lecturers may find ways of broadening their roles and modifying their conditions of service to take on, at a reasonable cost, a number of those support roles for which so many are ideally equipped through their insight, training and experience. Any such broadening and modification need not imply any deterioration in conditions, remuneration, effectiveness or respect. However, it does require acceptance of wholly new approaches, and also of the open, honest feedback from students, colleagues and others which is the hallmark of healthy, purposeful organizations.

To move from curriculum-led approaches to learner-led or student-led ones requires an enormous shift in the thinking and behaviour of many college lecturers, and of most colleges as a whole, including their managers. There are many good reasons as well as irrational ones to be cautious about separating learning and students from teaching and lecturers. None the less, it is time that we move on from affording students access to learning to the stage where we help to empower students and the public as a whole as responsible achievers. Such a mission could harness the considerable talents and potential of college lecturers, who are otherwise in danger of losing their confidence and creative energy in the face of accelerating change and discontinuity.

Responsible student empowerment is still some way ahead, and needs careful evolution. For the present, while most college lecturers realize and accept that changes are occurring, few have yet had the chance to grasp their significance in terms of freeing learning and personal achievement from lecturers and the act of teaching. Yet this is central to the future activities of colleges and their lecturers, and urgently calls for a shift in professional thinking and identity.

### Reference

*Curriculum-led Institutional Development* (1984) A working paper by the FE Staff College and NICEC for FEU, January.

# 9

# Beyond the sabre-toothed curriculum?

**Ken Reid, David Hopkins and Peter Holly**

One of the most entertaining and perceptive accounts of curriculum development is the parable of *New-Fist-Hammer-Maker*, New Fist, as he is more commonly known, lived in Chellean (early palæolithic) times and, according to Harold Benjamin (1939), was the first great curriculum theorist and practitioner. He is remembered best for the development of the sabre-tooth curriculum. The sabre-tooth curriculum had its origins in New Fist's aspirations for a better life for his children and, by the same token, for the tribe as a whole. Motivated by this vision he developed a curriculum that included activities such as sabre-tooth-tiger-scaring-with-fire which he taught in a practical way to his children. The benefits of such an induction into these forms of knowledge soon became evident. Despite initial objections by the more conservative and theologically minded members of the tribe (objections that New Fist, being a statesman as well as a curriculum theorist, deftly overcame), tiger-scaring and the other activities soon became accepted as the heart of true education.

All continued well for some generations until the approach of a new ice age drastically changed the environment. The skills acquired through the sabre-tooth curriculum were no longer appropriate to the new conditions in the cave realm and the prosperity and equanimity of the tribe suffered. The spirit of New Fist, however, lived on in the new generation, some of whom proposed a new curriculum more suited to the current situation. These radical proposals were ridiculed by the tribal elders as being mere training; the suggestion that the new activities required as much intelligence and skill as the traditional curriculum was regarded as facetious. Unlike New Fist the tribal elders were neither thinkers nor doers, theorists nor statesmen, as evidenced by statements like:

We don't teach tiger-scaring to scare tigers; we teach it for the purposes of giving noble courage which carries over into all the affairs of life . . . true education is timelessness. It is something that endures through changing conditions like a solid rock standing squarely and firmly in the middle of a raging torrent. You must know that there are some eternal verities and the sabre tooth curriculum is one of them.

The parable [. . .] raises so many issues that we would require another chapter at least to elucidate them. Issues such as education versus training; vocational relevance; transfer of learning; the implementation of innovation; and the calumny of vested interests . . . are all as important now as they were in 1939, let alone Chellean times. Space obviously precludes such discussions but there are three points that we want particularly to highlight. The first is that the term curriculum is an ambiguous one; it is open to many differing interpretations and can be put to many different purposes. The second is that successful teaching is related to thoughtful and systematic curriculum planning. The third is that the responsibility for curriculum development needs to be located close to the classroom. We begin with the sabre-tooth parable because it is entertaining and illuminating, the lessons one can derive from it provide a context for what follows – the attempt to see how far we have progressed in curriculum development since Chellean times.

[. . .]

## Perceptions and models

[. . .]

We must be aware of the distinction between the 'formal' and the 'hidden' curriculum. The formal curriculum comprises the academic intentions of the course of study; what is supposed to be taught and learned in school. The hidden curriculum, on the other hand, is concerned more with the social side of education; the values and expectations that pupils acquire as a result of going through the schooling process. Although not part of the formal intentions of schooling, the hidden curriculum has the most powerful and lasting impact on most children. We are inevitably concerned with the formal rather than the hidden curriculum but this does not reflect their respective importance, either in our eyes or in reality. As Cusick (1973) among others, has argued, high schools tend to spend over two-thirds of their time involved in maintenance (or hidden curriculum) activities rather than instructional (or formal curriculum) activities; and, of course, the two are inevitably connected. The derivation of content for the curriculum – what is taught or not taught (see Eisner's *Null Curriculum* (1979)), what subjects are accorded high and low status and who is taught what, are all arguably aspects of the hidden curriculum. So, too, is how we teach the content – because differing teaching styles imply differing classroom climates and levels of pupil participation. The 'nurturant conditions', to use Joyce and Weil's (1980) phrase, are associated with different models of teaching that have a wide and differential impact on pupils. [. . .]

Eisner (1979) points to five basic orientations to the curriculum that underlie the purposes of schooling. Others have described similar influences: Lawton (1983), for example, discusses three or four basic educational ideologies; and Carr and Kemmis (1983) identify eight traditions in the study of education.

The differences between these ideas are less important than the general point. Behind any educational enterprise there is an ideological or philosophical force or forces pushing it forward, which provide a context or set of parameters in which to consider that form of schooling. Schooling and education are always embedded in a set of wider values and although they are often vague, implicit and even contradictory, it is important for us to realize their existence, because to some extent they control and inhibit our freedom of action and inevitably our purpose.

The first of Eisner's orientations is the 'development of cognitive processes'. Here the emphasis is on developing pupils' intellectual capacity and helping them learn how to learn more effectively. The second, 'academic rationalism', refers to the induction of pupils into worthwhile activities and forms of knowledge. The goal is the developing of an educated person, one who is competent in and familiar with the products of humanity's highest achievements. By engaging with these ideas and achievements the individual will inevitably develop rationality and acquire wisdom. The third orientation is 'personal relevance', and its most common expression is the child–centred curriculum. This approach requires that the curriculum and the teacher are aware of each pupil's abilities, experience and predisposition, and that a course of study is developed which builds on those unique qualities. The fourth orientation is 'social adaptation and social reconstruction'. In this approach it is the society's needs that are paramount and the school's purpose is seen explicitly as serving these needs. The billion dollar investment in the USA in science and math curricula in the decade following the Soviet success with Sputnik in 1957 is an example of this. So, too, is the recent emphasis on vocational education in the UK and the instrumental nature of many national curricula in the Third World. Finally, Eisner points to the idea of 'curriculum as technology'. Here the emphasis is not so much on the aims or context of curricula but on the means of achieving them. It is an approach that values efficiency, the measurement of observable achievement, and making schools, teachers and curricula accountable. Mastery teaching, standardized tests, systematic instruction and school accountability are all examples of this tendency. The behavioural objectives model for curriculum planning that we will soon be discussing is perhaps the most common example of this orientation.

In this brief description of the five orientations [. . .] we have not claimed that one orientation is necessarily better than another. Each has been discussed because it enables us more clearly to analyse the purpose of schooling. They provide us with a context within which to consider our own practice and aspirations. Also, it is unlikely that any school or educational system will exhibit characteristics of just one orientation. They are more likely to be found in combination. A useful exercise is to create a matrix using the five orientations and contemporary examples of schooling in England and Wales. Such a matrix would look a little like Figure 9.1.

There are virtually as many models of how to go about developing the curriculum, as there are definitions of the term. Model development is a game that academics play and on the whole it is of little help to teachers, because many models tend to be descriptive rather than prescriptive or specific. They describe their originators' somewhat idiosyncratic views of the educational world, which may or may not be very interesting, and give little information to the practitioner on how to proceed. Naturally there are exceptions, and in the following section we describe a curriculum model that we believe possesses some practical utility. There are also a number of models that deserve mention on the grounds of tradition, usage or appositeness. To two of these we now briefly turn.

### The Tyler model

The best known of the curriculum models is that associated with Ralph Tyler, derived from his seminal book *Basic Principles of Curriculum and Instruction* (1949). So ubiquitous is Tyler's model that many claim that it is the *only* way to develop curricula. Somewhat dismayed by the capricious and whimsical, if not downright sloppy, approach to curriculum development

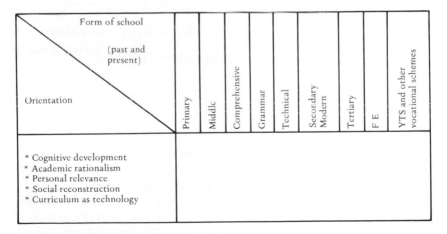

**Figure 9.1** The five orientations of schooling

that he witnessed in the USA in the 1940s, Tyler proposed as an antidote a systematic and beguilingly simple approach to curriculum planning based around four questions:

1  What educational purposes should the school seek to attain?
2  What educational experiences can be provided that are likely to attain these purposes?
3  How can these educational experiences be effectively organized?
4  How can we determine whether these purposes are being attained?

The so-called 'Tyler rationale' is often expressed in an even more simplified form:

Objectives
↓
Content
↓
Organization
↓
Evaluation

The Tyler model has been enormously influential, so much so that most curriculum or lesson plans appear to be based on this approach to some extent. Two points should be made about the model at the outset. The first is that by beginning with objectives one begs the question: where do they come from? Some of Tyler's students, who became important curriculum figures in their own right, provided some answers. Benjamin Bloom and his colleagues (1956) produced a taxonomy of educational objectives that provide a ready-made solution for the problem. Hilda Taba (1962) proposed a needs assessment stage that precedes the derivation of objectives. These solutions have served to satisfy most practitioners, but in many ways the problem still remains a real one. The second point relates to the evaluative aspect of the model. The only way to evaluate this type of curriculum scheme is through observing some change in behaviour on the part of the pupil that signifies achievement of the objective. In turn, that objective has to be expressed in behavioural terms so that the achievement can be observed and evaluated. In its pure form the model looks something like the diagram shown in Figure 9.2.

In the diagram, behavioural objectives result from some interaction between the general aim of the curriculum, the content to be taught, and the perceived pupil characteristics. The resulting list of objectives is then tested on the class and as a consequence possibly changed. This provides a base line measure of the pupils' achievement. The teaching/learning process then ensues and the curriculum episode ends with another test that serves to assess the overall pupil achievement on the curriculum. Rarely is the process like this. Testing, particularly the original test, is often omitted. So too is the revision of objectives. Also, the objectives are usually not established with

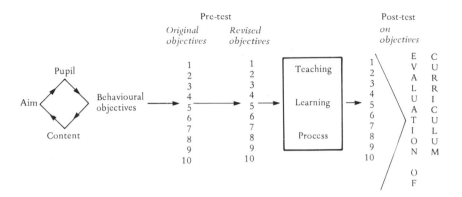

**Figure 9.2**  The flow of the Tyler model

any degree of precision. But the objectives approach is seen in one form or another in most curriculum designs.

Unfortunately, the objectives model is no panacea. Although it is suitable for certain teaching/learning situations its almost universal application is deleterious. There are a number of well-established critiques of the behavioural objectives model (e.g. Eisner, 1979; Stenhouse, 1975; Rudduck and Hopkins, 1985), but we will briefly rehearse some of the objections here. First, the objectives model trivializes the nature of knowledge. By fitting a subject into an objectives format there is the danger that the essence of, say, history will be reduced to a recitation of the Kings and Queens of England. It is very difficult to represent the deep structure of a subject – in this case, the historical method of inquiry, in an objectives format. How does one prepare an objective or series of objectives for appreciating *Hamlet*? So although the objectives approach may be very effective in transmitting information or skills it is unsuited to more complex forms of knowledge. Second, the objectives model tends to make for predictable pupil outcomes. This is to be welcomed when one is concerned with mathematical or scientific formulae, but to be regretted when one is concerned with poetry or art appreciation. Third, the model does not accord with reality. The teaching/learning process in general does not work like that. We teach in a more idiosyncratic and capricious way; often long periods of effort are followed by a sudden burst of understanding. It is only infrequently that we learn in carefully packaged, uniform and relatively short periods of time. Fourth, the approach, although it often increases the clarity of educational programmes, does little, for reasons already outlined, to increase the quality of educational performance. Finally, the model ignores the ethical, moral and political imperatives surrounding schooling. Questions such as 'Is this the appropriate content to teach?' are of no importance in this approach.

In discussing the objectives model we have tried to point both to its advantages and its drawbacks. It is the most common form of curriculum design. It has had enormous influence, but is appropriate only in certain, often instrumental, subject areas. Later we will propose a process model as a more appropriate means of dealing with more complex subject areas.

### Lawton's model

The other approach to curriculum design that we will briefly describe, although not as well known or as useful as Tyler's (being descriptive rather than prescriptive), is that associated with Denis Lawton (1973; 1983). His basic idea is of the curriculum as being a selection from the culture and he argues for a cultural analysis approach to curriculum. A slightly adapted version of his model appears in Figure 9.3.

Lawton has an eminently common-sense approach to curriculum in his writing. We find his 'selection from culture' notion very helpful, especially the tension or dialectic that exists between philosophical approaches, for example Hirst's forms of knowledge, and the sociological or relativist attitude of writers like Young.

Lawton originally envisaged psychology as operating on the selection from the culture, but given current constraints practical issues may be more appropriate. Certainly psychological considerations play (or should play) an

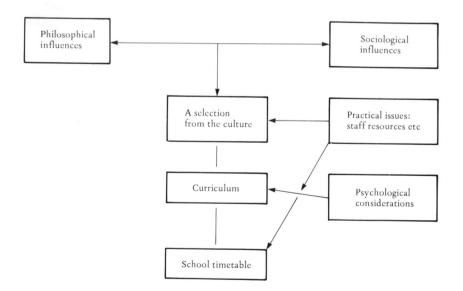

**Figure 9.3**  Lawton's model

important part in shaping the curriculum and in its presentation to pupils. To us Lawton's model has two main virtues: first, its central organizing concept of curriculum as a selection from the culture; second, the prominence it gives to philosophical, sociological and psychological factors in determining the curriculum. But as we said previously, it is a descriptive model and its utility is limited because it gives teachers no indication of how to proceed. It is to a curriculum development model that offers such practical advice that we now turn.

### A model for curriculum development

Figure 9.4 (see p. 113) represents our model for curriculum development (based on Gibbons, 1977: his work on self-directed learning has had a major impact on education in North America). There are seven major stages in the model; each stage has its own kind of task, its own kind of process and its own product (see Table 9.1).

**Table 9.1**   The seven stages in the curriculum development model

| Task | Process | Product |
| --- | --- | --- |
| 1 *Identify* what job the curriculum has to do | *Analyse* the situation | A clear *purpose* for curriculum development |
| 2 *Formulate* a means of achieving the purpose | *Design* a curriculum concept | A promising *theoretical model* of the curriculum |
| 3 *Select* an appropriate *teaching strategy* for the curriculum | *Establish* principles of procedure for students and teachers when using the curriculum | A specific *teaching/ learning strategy* |
| 4 *Produce* the curriculum delivery system | *Develop* the means required to present and maintain the curriculum | An *operational curriculum* |
| 5 *Experiment* with the curriculum on student learning and the school | *Refine* the model through classroom research and regular improvements | A *refined curriculum* |
| 6 *Implement* the curriculum throughout the school in other settings | *Change* general practice to the new curriculum | A *widely used curriculum* |
| 7 *Evaluate* the effects of the curriculum on student learning | *Evaluate* how effective the curriculum is | A *proven* curriculum |

At any point in curriculum development, difficulties may emerge which require returning to an earlier cycle and redoing the work. Alternatively, an opportunity for a major improvement may emerge which makes reconsideration of the earlier work desirable. When the whole cycle is successfully completed, so much will have been learned in the process that the curriculum developer will be well equipped to begin again.

Although the cycle has seven major stages it is, of course, not necessary to complete each stage in order to produce an effective product. An individual teacher might only engage in the Formulation, Teaching Strategy and Production stages if he or she simply wanted to design a new unit. Another teacher may start with classroom research, then find out that the teaching strategy needs altering and, having done that, go back to classroom research again. Alternatively, a fairly major curriculum innovation would most probably require work in each cycle. In a similar sense, the model is generic in so far as it applies to teachers wanting to develop a unit or a course as well as to curriculum developers on major national projects. The model is prescriptive because, as compared with the descriptive models discussed earlier, it provides a guide to action; it helps teachers and others become more systematic and reflective about the curriculum development task.

The model is also relatively value free, in so far as it represents no overt world view (except one that encourages systematic and self-conscious planning and reflection on the part of teachers). This enables the range of ideological perspectives on the curriculum to be accommodated.

An illustration of this last point is given in Table 9.2 (see p. 114), which summarizes a great deal of information about curriculum development. The first column contains the elements of the curriculum development cycle. The second column lists the activities that traditionally occur in each of the seven stages. These are activities that tend to underplay the teacher's role and occur mainly as the result of some external initiative by, for example, the Department of Education and Science. Most teachers will recognize these activities. The third column represents teacher-based activities that can also occur within each of these stages as an alternative to the traditional approach. The table clearly illustrates that teacher- or school-based approaches to curriculum development are both available and viable. The table is not supposed to be taken too literally (or seriously). It certainly does not imply a dichotomy between the two approaches. Its main purpose is to illustrate how a range of experiences, aspirations and activities can be contained within the model. In the following discussion of the stages, however, illustrations of different approaches will be discussed.

### Identification

The *identification* stage establishes a clear purpose for the curriculum. It is the rationale; if there is no purpose or rationale then there is no point in

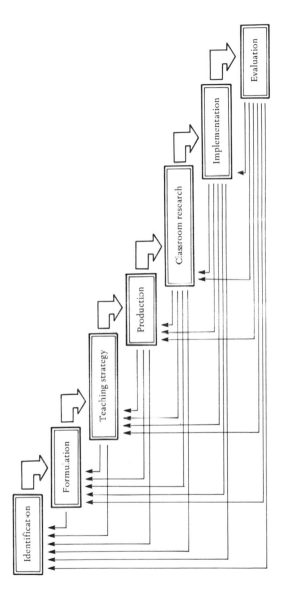

**Figure 9.4**  A curriculum development cycle

**Table 9.2**   Alternative approaches to curriculum development

| Stage | Traditional | Teacher-based |
|---|---|---|
| Identification | Prescribed curriculum/ forms of knowledge | Community based or pupil needs |
| Formulation | Behavioural objectives | Process model and principles of procedure |
| Teaching strategy | Teacher centred, didactic | Enquiry/discovery approaches, active learning etc. |
| Production | Centrally produced curricula | Locally developed programmes |
| Classroom research | Quantitative analysis | Doing research in your classroom |
| Implementation | Fidelity | Mutual adaptation |
| Evaluation | Quantitative, empirical and objective | Qualitative, illuminative and subjective |

proceeding. Curricula are, of course, open to varying purposes, a number of which we have already discussed. A well-known polarity within this stage is the distinction between classical and romantic approaches to the curriculum. Lawton's (1973) view of the debate is as follows:

| *Classical* | *Romantic* |
|---|---|
| Subject-centred | Child-centred |
| Skills | Creativity |
| Instruction | Experience |
| Information | Discovery |
| Obedience | Awareness |
| Conformity | Originality |
| Discipline | Freedom |

He continues:

> When it comes to questions of knowledge and curriculum the two views might be polarised as follows (but to subdivide in this way may be unfair to the Romantic view as the following list is set out in the Classical framework):

| *Classical* | *Romantic* |
|---|---|
| *Objectives:* | *Processes:* |
| Acquiring knowledge | 'Living' attitudes and values |
| *Content:* | *Experience:* |
| Subjects | Real-life topics and projects |

*Methods:*

| | |
|---|---|
| Didactic instruction | Involvement |
| Competition | Co-operation |

*Evaluation:*

| | |
|---|---|
| By tests (teacher set) and examinations (public and competitive) | Self-assessment (in terms of self-improvement) |

Inevitably these views are stereotypical but they do give an indication of the types of activities that can flow from such an orientation. The classical view has probably been best stated by Hirst in his concept of 'forms of knowledge'. Hirst (Hirst and Peters, 1970) argues that we can distinguish seven forms of knowledge:

1 Formal logic and mathematics
2 The physical sciences
3 'Our awareness and understanding of our own and other people's minds'
4 Moral judgement and awareness
5 Aesthetic experience
6 Religious
7 Philosophical

Lawton (1973) summarizes Hirst's position by saying that he justifies the categorization of knowledge into these seven forms on the grounds that all concepts belong to distinct categories, which are marked out by 'certain fundamental, ultimate or categorical concepts of a most general kind which other concepts in the category presuppose'. A good example of the influence of this is found in many DES/HMI publications on the curriculum.

The alternative notion, as represented by the 'romantic' argument, is that the curriculum should be based on the pupils' needs: that we must diagnose them and then build a curriculum around them. [. . .]

From even this brief discussion it can be seen that the identification stage is not only very important but also fraught with opposing views. Two other sources of curriculum purpose, relevant to the contemporary UK scene, need to be discussed. First is the function of curriculum in the eyes of central government. Curriculum innovations like TVEI began with the government (in this case the MSC) identifying the purpose of the curriculum and then allowing LEAs to complete the curriculum development cycle. The other very powerful source of curriculum initiative is the examination boards. Although times are changing a little, past examination papers still play an important part in the identification stage of curriculum development.

### Formulation

The formulation stage involves developing new ideas or improving old ones already developed which promise to fulfil the purpose already identified for the curriculum. In other words it offers strategies for answering the question: what is the best design which can be treated to fulfil the rationale for the curriculum?

As we have discussed already, behavioural objectives are the most commonly used method for formulating the curriculum; but teachers also realize that they are not the only way. Behavioural objectives are an excellent means for teaching skills or evaluating rote learning. However, they can be counter-productive in more complex and sophisticated content areas. For example, it is difficult to formulate behavioural objectives for a lesson on *Hamlet* or poetry appreciation and still remain faithful to the subject matter. The over-use of behavioural objectives has sometimes tended to reduce, say, the study of history to a series of dates or geography to a recitation of capes and bays. Stenhouse (1975) has said that 'Education as induction into knowledge is successful to the extent that it makes the behavioural outcomes of the students unpredictable.' In situations such as these it is better to put pre-specified behavioural objectives aside, and utilize some other organizing principle.

The process model is an alternative. This name was coined by Stenhouse to describe his alternative approach to curriculum development as exemplified in the *Humanities Curriculum Project* (Stenhouse, 1975; Rudduck and Hopkins, 1985). The process model does not specify the behaviour the student is to acquire after having engaged in a learning activity, rather it describes an educational encounter. It identifies a situation in which children are to work, a problem with which they are to cope, or a task in which they are to engage. By the use of the process model teachers can formulate educational encounters that respect both the child and the integrity of the knowledge with which they interact.

There are three basic approaches to developing a curriculum on a process model. The first is the approach identified with the work of Eisner (1979). Like many others Eisner was dissatisfied with the behavioural objectives approach, for reasons similar to the ones previously discussed. He advocated the use of expressive objectives in the areas where behavioural (or in his terms instructional) objectives were inappropriate. The expressive objective defines an educational encounter without specifying what the pupil is to learn from that encounter. Eisner (quoted in Stenhouse, 1975) says that 'an expressive objective provides both the teacher and the student with an invitation to explore, defer, or focus on issues that are of peculiar interest or import to the inquirer. An expressive objective is evocative rather than prescriptive.'

He continues by giving examples:

Statements of expressive objectives might read:

1 To interpret the meaning of *Paradise Lost*.
2 To examine and appraise the significance of *The Old Man and the Sea*.

3 To develop a three-dimensional form through the use of wire and wood.
4 To visit the zoo and discuss what was of interest there.

What should be noted about such objectives is that they do not specify what the student is to be able to do after he engages in an educational activity; rather they identify the type of encounter he is to have.

While entirely in sympathy with Eisner's argument we find his examples very loose: they provide no structure within which pupils or teachers can effectively explore their new-found freedom. The lack of structure, guidance or parameters is a serious drawback and will inevitably lead to aimless teaching and spasmodic learning.

A more satisfactory avenue for the process model is provided by Jerome Bruner and his concept of structure (Bruner, 1963; 1966). Following the logic of philosophers like Hirst, Bruner argues that each discipline has a structure which determines the way knowledge evolves or is produced within it. In history, for example, knowledge is produced through locating, analysing and making judgements based upon evidence. This historical method determines the way in which historical knowledge is developed. Similarly in science, knowledge advances through controlled experimentation commonly known as the scientific method. Bruner argues that this structure provides an effective model for teaching and learning. Curricula can be formulated by following the method of 'real' historians or scientists, using the historical or scientific method to structure the curriculum. Instead of teaching historical or scientific knowledge we teach how to do history or science and accumulate our knowledge in this way. Bruner would argue that we should introduce pupils to the process of knowledge. In his own words, 'Knowledge is a process not a product'. He further argues that 'any body of knowledge can be presented in a form simple enough so that any particular learner can understand it in a recognisable form'. The implication of this is that the historical or scientific approach to learning can and should be introduced in the primary school. These ideas and processes are then refined and become more sophisticated as one goes through the school: hence his notion of the spiral curriculum. [. . .] Many of the Schools Council curriculum projects were built on this model. The *History 13–16*, *Science 5–13* and, of course, Bruner's influential *Man, a Course of Study* (MACOS) were all examples of these. However, not all curriculum subjects are dignified by the label 'discipline' – so how does one proceed here?

'Principles of procedure' was the approach that Stenhouse and his colleagues adopted in the *Humanities Curriculum Project*. Faced with producing a curriculum on controversial issues for pupils of school leaving age in an area with no established tradition, they began by specifying the principles upon which the curriculum should be based. The following two extracts illustrate their approach.

The Humanities Curriculum Project, sponsored by the Schools Council and the Nuffield Foundation, was set up in September 1967 to extend the range of choice open to teachers working in the humanities with adolescent pupils.

The work of the Project has been based upon five major premises:

1 that controversial issues should be handled in the classroom with adolescents;
2 that teachers should not use their authority as teachers as a platform for promoting their own views;
3 that the mode of enquiry in controversial areas should have discussion rather than instruction as its core;
4 that the discussion should protect divergence of view among participants;
5 that the teacher as chairperson of the discussion should have responsibility for quality and standards in learning.

If teachers have reserves about any of these premises, the easiest procedure is to adopt them with due scepticism as an exploratory tactic. This will allow them to use the experimental findings of the project for support as they evaluate the likely effects of changing the premises.

The aim of the Project is to develop an understanding of social situations and human acts and of the value issues which they raise.

(Rudduck, 1983: 8)

In this project, discussion was the main mode of inquiry and the teacher acted as a neutral chairperson. Discussion was informed and disciplined by evidence: that is, items of material from history, journalism, literature, philosophy, art, photography, statistics might be introduced. . . . Here are summarised the kinds of demand which this curriculum project made on teachers, pupils and schools:

New skills for most teachers
1 Discussion rather than instruction.
2 Teacher as neutral chairperson – that is, not communicating his or her point of view.
3 Teacher talk reduced to about 15%.
4 Teacher handling material from different disciplines.
5 New modes of assessment.

New skills for most pupils
1 Discussion, not argument or debate.
2 Listening to, and talking to, each other, not just to the teacher.
3 Taking initiatives in contributing – not being cued in by teacher.

New content for many classrooms
1 Explorations of controversial social issues, often in the sensitive areas (e.g. race relations, poverty, family, relations between the sexes).

2 Evidence reproduced in an original form – no simplifications of language.

Organisational demands on schools
1 Small discussion groups, each with teacher chairperson.
2 Mixed ability groups found by many schools to be desirable.
3 Non-row formation of chairs – circle or rectangle appearing to be desirable.

(Rudduck 1984: 57–8)

From these considerations a set of highly specific principles was developed that provided a structure for both pupils and teachers despite the open-ended nature of the curriculum and the radical teaching/learning process it adopted.

In contrasting the behavioural objectives and process models we are not arguing that one is necessarily better than the other. They are complementary approaches; each has the potential of working well but in different areas.

### Teaching strategy

Implicit in the formulation stage is a teaching strategy that transmits the content of the curriculum. In our view the teaching strategy is equally as important as the content that the curriculum delivers. There was a time when many teachers felt that there was only one way to teach – the didactic or 'mug and jug' approach – but fortunately times change. We became increasingly aware that pupils learn in different ways and all are not amenable to a uniform approach. The Schools Council in their advocacy of enquiry/discovery learning, and the curriculum innovations like TVEI that promoted 'active learning', were all moves away from the traditional approach.

It is also important to consider at this stage of curriculum development the various assessment procedures associated with the curriculum. The adoption of profiling, for example, had a powerful impact upon teaching style.

Bruce Joyce *et al.* (1981) espoused 'flexibility' as a guiding principle for *professional* development. This represents

a view of humankind that envisions people-in-teaching and people-in-learning as the creators of themselves through their interaction. Flexibility from that stance, becomes an essential characteristic of the teacher as s/he creates her/himself, offers possibilities to his/her students, and creates the schools of the future.

A central component of flexibility is the teacher's ability intelligently to use a variety of teaching approaches, to match them to different goals, and adapt them to different student styles and characteristics. To quote Joyce again:

'Competence in teaching stems from the capacity to reach out to differing children and to create a rich and multi-dimensional environment for them.' In their *Models of Teaching* (1980), Joyce and Weil describe four families of teaching approaches: the information-processing, the personal, the social interaction, and the behavioural models. They argue that 'since no single teaching strategy can accomplish every purpose, the wise teacher will master a sufficient repertoire of strategies to deal with the specific kinds of learning problems he or she faces'. They suggest that teachers begin by mastering one model from each family, and then add others as they are found useful to each individual's particular teaching speciality. It is easier to learn models in collaboration with others (e.g. a colleague or student teacher), because the other person can help coach you (and vice versa) on the finer points of teaching style. [. . .]

## Production

Production is the stage where the ideas and aspirations are operationalized. At the end of this stage the curriculum is ready to go, ready to be used and shared. The scale of production will vary according to the size of the product, whether it be a teacher producing a new unit or a team working on a national curriculum project. Nevertheless, resources have to be collected and organized, staff trained in the new teaching methods and the timetable possibly altered.

The following extract from the original model – although somewhat 'North American' in style – gives a good indication of what is required at this stage (see Figure 9.5).

(*a*) production needs
- materials
- methods training
- role changes
- environments
- organisation

(*b*) organise for production:
- cover arranged to free teachers regularly for preparation
- time line for completion of materials and arrangements set
- working teams appointed

(*c*) produce materials and arrangements:
- planning committee receives materials and monitors arrangements
- critical examination of all materials and other elements of setting: they are revised

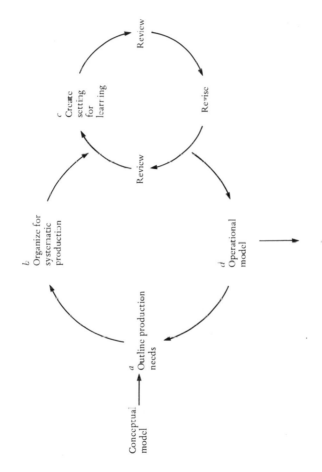

**Figure 9.5** The production model

> ● materials pilot-tested
> and modified from
> feedback; the gaps are
> filled and further
> revisions made

(d) operational model:    ● 'central planning' declares the curriculum
                             operational

Gibbons (1977) describes the strategies required for the production stage like this:

> *Production:* Strategies for making the curriculum operational; producing guides, texts and other materials; creating settings, training personnel, and organising the necessary support systems. Strategies for answering the questions, what must be prepared to make this curriculum design usable? How can this be done efficiently and effectively?

He then gives an example:

> The school's curriculum development committee outlined the tasks, divided the work among sub-committees and drew up a production schedule. A new space was found and set up like an editorial room. A teaching handbook of skills and content was written and reproduced. Teaching materials were prepared, reference libraries assembled, and training sessions on the teaching method were provided.

### Classroom research

The purpose of this stage is to field-test the curriculum in the classroom, and to refine it through regular improvement. It is important that teachers retain an enquiring and experimental attitude towards a curriculum, irrespective of whether they have produced it themselves or adapted it from elsewhere. A curriculum proposal should never be taken as given but rather regarded as a working hypothetical proposal. Stenhouse (1975) remarks that 'the proposal is not to be regarded as an unqualified recommendation but rather as a provisional specification claiming no more than to be worth putting to the test of practice. Such proposals claim to be intelligent rather than correct.' The ways in which teachers engage in systematic self-study *and* test theory in practice are essentially the same: through the use of classroom research methods.

Classroom research is normally associated with outside researchers measuring the effect and outcomes of classroom activity. In a teacher-based context the phrase has a very different meaning. It implies that the teacher is actively engaged in critically reflecting on his or her teaching by utilizing classroom-based research methods. This is a fundamental role for a teacher who takes professional development seriously, for it is only by understand-

ing our present behaviours, that we can expect to extend or change them.
[. . .]

The purpose of this stage is to revise the curriculum in the light of experience and consequently to produce a better curriculum and so improve the teaching/learning process. When we are dealing with larger curriculum projects then we need to consider the implementation and evaluation stages.

## Implementation

Implementation is an aspect of curriculum development that has recently received a great deal of attention. The predominant modality in the traditional approach is 'fidelity': the expectation that a new curriculum will be faithfully implemented and exactly reproduced in the receiving environment. The situation usually occurs when curriculum development begins centrally and then diffuses outwards. Often this expectation is not realized because the context of the local environment is not considered. Under the teacher-based paradigm there is the expectation that the curriculum will be adapted to the local situation. The norm of mutual adaptation implies that both the curriculum and the school or classroom will change as the process of implementation occurs. Thus, the teacher exercises control over the adoption of curriculum in his or her teaching situation.

The implementation process is multidimensional, involving change at a number of different levels. Five components of implementation can be identified. These involve changes in organization, materials, role and behaviour, knowledge, and beliefs.

Changes in organization (e.g. restructuring the timetable to accommodate new options) and materials (e.g. the introduction of a new published reading scheme) are achieved relatively easily. Indeed, it is these two components of implementation that are most often tackled; to the detriment of the others. Yet it is on the necessary changes in teaching style, understanding and commitment, that the success or failure of implementation depends. These are, of course, the most difficult to effect as they also require heavy involvement in time and inservice provision. Successful implementation depends on the meanings and attitudes that teachers give and have towards the curriculum. To recall Stenhouse's evocative phrase 'there is no curriculum development without teacher development'.

## Evaluation

A distinction is often made between formative and summative evaluation. The former is concerned with providing ongoing information to improve the quality of the curriculum. Summative evaluation is concerned to provide a judgement on the success of the curriculum. The formative aspects of evaluation occur in our model at the classroom research stage. This final stage is more concerned with summative judgement, on how good the curriculum is after it has been implemented for a period of time. [. . .]

After the conclusion of this cycle, the process of development begins again with the search for new opportunities for growth and new purpose in development.

### 'No curriculum development without teacher development'

The hidden curriculum behind the curriculum model is that it is a method that teachers can employ to make their curriculum planning more effective. It is a process not only for curriculum development but also for making teachers more skilful and more effective; of putting them more in control of the curriculum and the teaching/learning process. Only teachers can create good teaching, and thus it is imperative that they occupy a central role in developing the curriculum and that *they* develop with the curriculum.

Stenhouse adopted this principle as a central point of his work. As a conclusion to the discussion of the curriculum model, consider this quotation from the work of Lawrence Stenhouse:

> 'No curriculum development without teacher development', reads one of the poker-work mottoes we hung on our wall during the Humanities Project and haven't taken down. But that does not mean, as it often seems to be interpreted to mean, that we must train teachers in order to produce a world fit for curricula to live in. It means that by virtue of their meaningfulness, curricula are not simply instructional means to improve teaching but are expressions of ideas to improve teachers. Of course, they have a day-to-day instructional utility: cathedrals must keep the rain out. But the students benefit from curricula not so much because they change day-to-day instruction as because they improve teachers.
>
> A curriculum, if it is worthwhile, expresses in the form of teaching materials and criteria for teaching a view of knowledge and a conception of the processes of education. It provides a framework in which the teacher can develop new skills and relate them as he/she does so to conceptions of knowledge and of learning.
>
> Only in curricular form can ideas be tested by teachers. Curricula are hypothetical procedures testable only in classrooms. All educational ideas must find expression in curricula before we can tell whether they are day-dreams or contributions to practice. Many educational ideas are not found wanting because they cannot be found at all.
>
> We must be dedicated to the improvement of schooling. The improvement of schooling is bound to be experimental: it cannot be dogmatic. The experiment depends on the exercise of the art of

teaching and improves that art. The substantive content of the arts of teaching and learning is curriculum.

(Rudduck and Hopkins, 1985: 68–9)

## References

Benjamin, H. (J. A. Peddiwell 1939) *The Saber Tooth Curriculum*, New York McGraw-Hill.

Bloom, B. (ed.) (1956) *The Taxonomy of Educational Objectives: 1 The Cognitive Domain*, London, Longman.

Bruner, J. (1963) *The Process of Education*, New York, Random House.

Bruner, J. (1966) *Towards a Theory of Instruction*, Boston, Mass., Harvard University Press.

Carr, W. and Kemmis, S. (1983) *Becoming Critical: Knowing through Action Research*, Victoria, Australia, Deakin University Press.

Cusick, P. (1973) *Inside High School*, New York, Holt, Rinehart & Winston.

Eisner, E. (1979) *The Educational Imagination*, New York, Macmillan.

Gibbons, M. (1977) 'A model of curriculum development', British Columbia, Simon Fraser University, mimeograph.

Hirst, P. and Peters, R. (1970) *The Logic of Education*, London, Routledge & Kegan Paul.

Joyce, B. and Weil, M. (1980) *Models of Teaching*, 2nd edn, New York, Prentice-Hall.

Joyce, B. *et al.* (1981) *Flexibility in Teaching*, London and New York, Longman.

Lawton, D. (1973) *Social Change, Educational Theory and Curriculum Planning*, London, Hodder & Stoughton.

Lawton, D. (1983) *Curriculum Studies and Educational Planning*, London, Hodder & Stoughton.

Rudduck, J. (1983) *The Humanities Curriculum Project: An Introduction*, revised edn, Norwich, University of East Anglia/Schools Council.

Rudduck, J. (1984) 'Introducing innovation to pupils', in D. Hopkins and M. Wideen (eds) *Alternative Perspectives on School Improvement*, Lewes, Falmer Press.

Rudduck, J. and Hopkins, D. (1985) *Research as a Basis for Teaching*, London, Heinemann.

Stenhouse, L. (1975). *An Introduction to Curriculum Research and Development*, London, Heinemann.

Taba, H. (1962) *Curriculum Development: Theory and Practice*, New York, Harcourt Brace Jovanovich.

Tyler, R. (1949) *Basic Principles of Curriculum and Instruction*, Chicago, Ill., Chicago University Press.

# 10

# Organizational pathos and the school

**Eric Hoyle**

The trouble with school [teachers] is that they think all problems are soluble. They aren't.

(Stanley Middleton *The Daysman*)

There is a pathos inherent in all organizations which arises from the chronic discrepancy between proclaimed organizational goals and their achievement. The incumbent of any leadership role in any organization is a modern Sisyphus, constantly pushing uphill a backward-rolling boulder in an effort to mobilize people and resources and move them towards an ever-receding peak. To be sure, limited objectives are constantly being achieved by the organization as a whole or by particular groups within it. Without such achievements organizations would decay and members would remain acutely dissatisfied. But when one considers the goals which society attributes to organizations, and especially to the school, and the goals which organizations establish for themselves, the pathos is obvious.

There are a number of different reasons why this pathos is generated. One is that we tend to view organizations from a rationalistic perspective, the perspective which dominates management theory perhaps even more strongly than it dominates organization theory. This rationalistic ideal of organizational process assumes the establishment of a clear set of achievable goals, the total commitment of organizational members to these goals, the availability of all the necessary resources, the capacity of organizational members to co-ordinate their activities, and the unequivocal achievement of successful outcomes. In this direction lies neuroticism, if one takes neurotics to be people who are preoccupied with the discrepancy between an ideal world which they carry around in their heads and the imperfect world of everyday experience. Of course, the great majority of organizational members do not become neurotic. For many, the organizational world of work is not a central life interest, and problems other than malfunctioning organizations engage most of their attention. And even amongst the professional and administrative classes who invest more of themselves in their work organizations, most come to terms with the shortfall between goals and their achievement. Yet there will be none for whom the organizational pathos does not lead to daily irritations.

The sources of pathos are numerous. One is the fundamental notion of organizational *goal*. It is a term much in play when professionals and administrators discuss their organizations, yet it is a term which is at best problematic and at worst valueless as a guide to organizational processes. Another is that there are inherent limits to the effective co-ordination of organizational activities, partly because there are too many variables entailed to achieve fully a rational co-ordination and partly also because there are logical limits to rationality. Thus organizational members are invariably functioning in a world of imperfect rationality. A third reason, which relates to the empirical limits to rationality, is that contemporary, industrialized and modernized societies are becoming increasingly turbulent as the result of interrelated social, political, economic and technological changes so that the best-laid rational plans for an organization are constantly buffeted and knocked off course by the squalls created by uncontrollable external circumstances.

These themes will be explored in this chapter. To focus on the limits to organizational rationality is to adopt a perspective quite different from the conventional approach which posits an ideal form of rational organization. This focus might be dysfunctional with regard to the management of organizations since it is perhaps desirable that those studying management should not have their motivations impaired by considering the limits to what they can achieve. But here we are concerned with *understanding* organizations and hence with the limitations on what can be achieved.

## The problem of goals

The concept of *organizational goal* holds a powerful attraction for both administrators and theorists. One of the distinguishing characteristics of organizations as social units is that they are established for specific purposes. There can be no possible doubt that schools are established for the purpose of educating the young and school goals incorporate this purpose. The achievement of these goals is the administrator's *raison d'être*. They are the touchstone whereby the administrator can check the effectiveness of the various activities undertaken within the organization. The headteacher proclaims the goals of the school in the school brochure, in the staff handbook and to the assembled guests on speech night. Goals give meaning to what the school *does*. Organizational theorists, or those of a functionalist persuasion, find the concept of goal a useful aid to the understanding of organizational processes. Goals provide a focus for their enquiries and enable them to judge the contribution of a particular activity to the whole and, if goals can be operationalized, they provide the yardstick whereby the effectiveness of an organization can be judged both on its own terms (Is the organization achieving the goals which it set out to achieve?) or, taking a comparative view: Of organizations A, B and C, sharing the same goals, which has been the most successful in achieving them?

Goals may appear to offer a means of overcoming organizational pathos but in fact they actually contribute to that pathos, for the truth is that organizations need goals to give them meaning. However, when the goals *of the organization as a whole* are subjected to close scrutiny, their value as a guide to organizational practice becomes questionable. We can examine some of the problems relating to the concept itself, the content of goals and their operationalization.

The concept itself is extremely slippery. As Perrow (1968) puts it,

> The concept of organisational goal, like concepts of power, authority, or leadership, has been unusually resistant to precise, unambiguous definition. Yet a definition of goals is necessary and unavoidable in organisational analysis. Organisations are established to do something; they perform work directed toward some end. We must examine the end or goal if we are to analyse organisational behaviour.

This honest statement by a leading organizational analyst reveals the pathos discussed above: organizations have to have goals, we cannot quite say what they are, but we must endow them with some definition if we are to make any headway. One such definition is the following: 'By organisational goal we understand a state of the organisation as a whole toward which the organisa-tion is moving, as evidenced by statements persons make (intentions), and activities in which they engage' (Gross 1969). This is an adequate definition but reveals some of the difficulties inherent in the concept. One key problem is highlighted in the phrase *the organization as a whole*. A phenomenologically inclined theorist would question whether organizations as such can be said to have goals. It would be argued that this is an unwanted reification, the attribution of a reality to an organization which it does not have. The point would be that only *individuals* can have goals. The phenomenologist would concede that groups of individuals have common interests, and in confront-ing common problems can, through their interaction, come to recognize these mutual concerns and construct a set of shared goals. It is conceivable that all members of an organization, such as a school, could thus construct a common set of shared goals, but the point would be that these would be the constructed goals of a group of people and not goals which could be objectively ascribed to the organization as an abstract entity. In practice, it is unlikely that organizational goals would be shared to that extent. Although in the case of schools it is possible to conceive of all staff sharing the same goals, it is perhaps stretching credulity to believe that all pupils would share them as well. Thus a goals–model which assumes consensus is criticized by both phenomenologists and conflict theorists. Both argue that what are alleged to be the 'goals' of an organization are, in fact, the goals of those who hold most power in organizations and that these are continuously contested by groups which generate alternative sets of goals. Thus, from these perspectives, organizations are areas in which sets of goals are in conflict. Another problem inherent in Gross's definition is the potential gap between the ideal and reality which is concealed by linking 'statements persons make (intentions) *and* activities' (italics added). Intentions and activities will coincide only where there is either total consensus or total power to realize stated goals, a situation unlikely to occur in the real world. In the case of each of these problems we have the choice between treating a set of goals as an ideal remaining as such however far the activities of an organization fall short of their achievement, or defining goals operationally as the commitments which different sets of participants accept.

The phenomenological and conflict critique of goals has considerable theoretical validity. However, the main significance of this critique is to alert those who run organizations, and those who study them, that a rationalistic, consensual goal-oriented model of organizations can only be an ideal. It can thus sensitize them to limitations of the idea of a shared set of goals and alert them to the validity of the goals of different individuals and groups. The critique cannot, however, dispose of the goal as a symbolic concept for the organizational leader nor as an heuristic concept guiding one approach to the study of organizations. Organizations cannot be wholly devoid of an overall purpose if they are to fulfil the expectations which they are to meet.

If one accepts the paradox that in any strict sense organizations as such cannot have goals but that they cannot function effectively without them, then one is committed to exploring the problems involved in continuing to utilize the term. The major problems are that the goals which might be hypothesized for organizations are of different kinds, are frequently expressed in abstract and non-operational terms, and they often prove to be incompatible with each other. These problems can be explored in turn.

There is a tendency for goals to be initially conceptualized in terms of organizational *output*, not necessarily a physical output as in a factory but, in education, for example, in the skills, knowledge attitudes, etc. acquired by pupils. Yet organizations can have goals other than product goals of this sort. Gross (1969) identifies five kinds of organizational goal for a university, namely:

1 *Output goals*: the inculcation of knowledge, skills and values in students.
2 *Adaptation goals*: the attraction of staff and students, the procurement of resources and the validation of the activities of the university.
3 *Management goals*: the administration of the university, the assignment of priorities, the handling of conflict.
4 *Motivation goals*: the creation of satisfaction and commitment in both staff and students.

5 *Positional goals*: the maintenance of the university's standing in relation to other universities, the improvement on this, and its defence in the face of pressures likely to reduce this standing.

This list is illustrative and is not presented as an agreed list of organizational goals. Other lists could have been suggested, e.g. Perrow (1968) which, although different in some ways, would have made the same point: that there are organizational goals *other than* the obvious output goals. It might be suggested that all the listed goals other than output goals could be reformulated as 'means'. There is some merit in this. When one considers why organizations are established in the first place – in the case of schools for the education of children – only output goals can be the 'true' goals. This broad distinction is useful in pointing to what might be an organizational pathology – a preoccupation with goals other than output goals, particularly management goals – but substantively the distinction is difficult to sustain. Just two reasons can be noted. One is that output goals by no means exhaust the purposes which organizations serve. This is particularly true of schools. It is widely considered that the *process* of schooling is as important as its product. This is held to be so because of the significance for good or ill of the 'hidden curriculum', although this raises the nice point of whether what a child acquires through the hidden curriculum should be construed as an 'output goal' or as an unanticipated consequence. But this aside, it is also held that since children spend much of their time in schools the ethos or climate of a school has an importance independent of its outputs, although one can hardly think that the two would not be related if output is interpreted broadly to cover all changes brought about in the pupil. The other point is that the balance between the various kinds of goal will shift. Although one might expect output goals to be salient, there are situations in which they may be less crucial than other goals. For example, if a school is threatened with closure due to falling rolls, the school organization might be left to 'idle' in relation to the achievement of the output goals of pupil learning, as the goal of survival becomes salient and staff devote more of their energies toward mobilizing support, attracting additional pupils to the school and furthering the school's reputation.

When school goals are articulated they tend to be simultaneously both diverse and diffuse. They are diverse because education tends to be charged with a wide range of tasks to which schools seek to respond, and diffuse because schools seek to bring about changes in pupils which are more than a particular set of knowledge, skills and attitudes. In order to illustrate this point we can consider not the goals adumbrated by a particular school but those set out in the 1977 Green Paper *Education in Schools: A Consultative Document* (DES, 1977).

1 to help children develop lively, enquiring minds, giving them the ability to question and to argue rationally, and to apply themselves to tasks;

2 to instil respect for moral values, for other people and for oneself, and tolerance of other races, religions, and ways of life;

3 to help children understand the world in which we live, and the inter-dependence of nations;

4 to help children to use language effectively and imaginatively in reading, writing and speaking;

5 to help children to appreciate how the nation earns and maintains its standard of living and properly to esteem the essential role of industry and commerce in this process;

6 to provide a basis of mathematical, scientific and technical knowledge, enabling boys and girls to learn the essential skills needed in a fast changing world of work;

7 to teach children about human achievement and aspirations in the arts and sciences, in religion, and in the search for a more just social order;

8 to encourage and foster the development of the children whose social or environmental disadvantages cripple their capacity to learn, if necessary by making additional resources available to them.

We are not here concerned with whether these particular goals are appropriate to schools, but simply with taking them as examples of proclaimed goals in order to explore further the problems inherent in the concept. The first point to note is that they are both diverse and diffuse. As such they are completely open-ended. It would be impossible for schools to achieve these goals completely since they are infinite. This is made even more problematic since these goals, like the goals of most schools, are expressed in terms of the actions which the school will take and do not deal with the outcomes of the process, the notoriously difficult-to-measure changes which have occurred in pupils as a result of their schooling. Goals can be stated in terms of expected outcomes, but this is generally resisted in education because what can be readily assessed, namely the cognitive outcomes of schooling, is regarded as representing only a limited set of school goals which would distort the purpose of the school if confined to this domain. It can be readily seen that many of the goals listed above are not measurable in this way, or achievable in any total sense. Schools must always fall short of achieving these goals and here again we see the pathos of an inevitable gap between goals and achievement. A second point is that they stand in need of far greater specification if they are to become in any sense operational. As stated, they constitute only a general set of guides to action. However, it can be argued that in an organization such as a school which is staffed by professionals, it is sufficient for only the broadest goals to be established, thus leaving the professional with sufficient autonomy to interpret these goals in the interests of clients. A third point is that the goals may be inherently in conflict and that these conflicts will become manifest when the goals are given a specific form in terms of pedagogy and curriculum. From the list given above it could well be, for example, that inducing children to 'esteem the essential role of industry and commerce' when expressed in a curricular form, could be in conflict with the goal of 'the search for a more just social order'. These goals are not necessarily in conflict as they stand, but they could be if each is operationalized in certain ways.

The concept of *organizational goal* is invariably problematic but is particularly so in the case of schools for the reasons stated above: that proclaimed school goals tend to be diffuse, diverse, abstract and non-operational as they stand. If one accepts that proclaimed goals perform the function of guiding the organization, it becomes an interesting empirical problem to relate the avowed goals of a school to the activities undertaken by staff. Because of the diffuse nature of educational goals and the relative autonomy of the teacher, there is considerable opportunity for slippage between avowed goals and their implementation. A number of sources of such slippage can be noted. One is what might be called 'the strain to the instrumental'. There is a broadly accepted distinction within the social sciences between *instrumental* goals which are utilitarian and intermediate to the attainment of other goals, and *expressive* goals which are goals worthwhile in themselves. The avowed goals of many schools contain a strong expressive component, the worthwhileness in themselves of various components of the curriculum. However, because in a complex indus-trialized society schools perform a selecting and differentiating role in relation to the occupational structure, and since occupation is a central concern of pupils and their parents who expect schools to give some priority to this, there is a tendency for schools to give greater prominence to instrumental goals, as embodied in tests and examinations, than to expressive goals. There are few schools which give priority to expressive goals. A. S. Neill's Summerhill would be one.

Another problem is the substitution of control goals for educational goals. Control over pupils is a central organizational problem for schools. However, in so far as the control goal is stated at all, it is stated as an intermediate goal on the grounds that the end-goal of education cannot be achieved without pupil control. However, it is possible for control to become a major goal in its own right. The manner in which the substitution of goals can occur in educational organizations is neatly illustrated in *The Open Door College* by Burton Clark (1960). A junior college was established at San Jose in California with the major goal of providing a technical education for the majority of students who would enter the work-force at the end of their course, and with the minor goal of providing an academic education for a small number of students who would then transfer to a university. But because of the 'open-door' policy which prevailed, students were permitted to choose their own courses, and, in fact, the majority opted for the academic (transfer) courses and only a minority opted for the technical (terminal) courses. The official goals of the school thus changed to a major commitment to an academic education and a minor commitment to a technical education. But since, in the view of the teachers, many of the students enrolling for the academic course did not have the necessary aptitudes, the goal of 'cooling out' the students perceived as academically incompetent was substituted for the goal of teaching these students. A variety of techniques was evolved for persuading such students to drop academic courses in favour of technical courses. For example, counsellors used various kinds of data about students to convince them to withdraw from the transfer courses. 'Need for Improvement' notices were used (as Burton Clark put it: 'If the student did not seek advice, advice sought him'). A course entitled Psychology 5: Orientation to College, compulsory for all transfer students, was designed to encourage the students to make a careful appreciation of their capacity to achieve college entrance by inviting them to compare their own grade point averages and scores on various aptitude tests with those required by colleges.

It is clear from the above discussion of organizational goals in general and school goals in particular that the concept generates considerable theoretical and practical problems. Organizational pathos is inherent in schools since proclaimed goals are frequently unattainable, and thus all schools are thereby 'under-achieving'. There is a proclivity for proclaimed goals to be substituted by others through the everyday practices of teachers. In so far as there is a consciousness of this, it yields further scope for pathos. Moreover, as Musgrove (1971) has pointed out, schools are underpowered for the goals they are expected to achieve.

There is clearly much to be said for the phenomenological critique of the concept of organizational goals. Goals are declaimed by organizational élites who make efforts to have them accepted as operational guides to organizational activities. But since individual members of one organization may have their own contrary goals, and since there is great opportunity for slippage between proclaimed goals and operating norms, it is better to focus on the organization as an area of conflicting perspectives on what *ought* to be done, and to note only that certain 'goals' of certain individuals and groups emerge as dominant. Thus the problem of goals is transformed into a problem of power. And yet it is not wholly possible to dispose of goals in this way. Where the outcome of internal competition results in an organization pursuing 'goals' which are strongly at odds with the mandate bestowed by society, then sanctions might well be imposed. High-level abstract goals at least give some indication of a general expectation of what a school ought to be doing, and as such they at least give some broad direction to the organization.

## The limits to rationality

Organizational pathos is endemic because organizations are chronically incapable of achieving the goals which stakeholders and their own members set for them and because, except in relation to limited objectives or through the subjective sense of achievement of members, they are incapable of demonstrating their success in achieving these goals. An associated source of organizational pathos arises from the fact that there is a chronic discrepancy between the 'rational' model of organization, which holds considerable appeal for those who manage, and the less-than-rational reality of life in organizations. Three limitations of rationality can be considered: the *phenomenological* critique of rationality as a universal concept, the critique of those who note the *cognitive* limits to rationality, i.e. the limitations imposed by the limits to human capacities for ordering and relating data – advances in computing notwithstanding – and the *logical* limits to rationality wherein a 'rational' organization is inherently unattainable.

It is impossible in a relatively short section to mount a full discussion of the concept of rationality in its full philosophical splendour. It is perhaps sufficient to note here that the scientific means-ends rationality which underpins much organization theory, and particularly management theory, is widely contested. It is argued that this is not the only form which rationality can take. It is also argued that a distinction can be made between the form of rationality which may be appropriate for certain purposes, particularly scientific research and a different everyday or common-sense rationality which enables people to cope quite adequately with their lives. It is further argued that rationality is not universal and independent of interests but in fact flows from those interests. There are some enormously complicated issues here which have been much debated by philosophers and social scientists. One might dispute, for example, the rationality of the rain dance of the Hopi Indians and the witchcraft of the Azande tribe. These are not 'rational' activities according to the western scientific notion of rationality because there can be no scientific cause and effect relationship between witchcraft and the cure of disease, or between a tribal dance and the appearance of rain, but they may well be 'rational' when perceived from within the culture of the tribe since these activities have functions other than their manifest functions. From the perspective of management, the action of workers in taking strike action may well be irrational since the result could involve a loss of income by the workers. However, leaving aside the question of whether such a loss actually ensued, the strike might well have been 'rational' in terms of the workers' perceptions of their longer-term interests or in terms of their need to demonstrate solidarity. Likewise pupils behave highly 'irrationally' when their behaviour is viewed from the teachers' perspective in which rationality might be seen as the maximization of individual academic attainment. Pupils have other interests – the pleasures of 'messing about', prestige in the peer group, outside jobs, etc. – and their school behaviour may well be 'rational' in terms of these interests. Thus, leaving aside whether or not there is a single form of rationality founded on the principles of the natural sciences, there will be in all organizations competing 'rationalities' arising from differences of real interests or perceived interests which will lead to a gap between the goals of management and their achievement.

Even if one accepts the possibility of a rational model of organization, there are cognitive limits to rationality. This has been the main theme of the influential writings on organization by Simon (1964) and March and Simon (1958). Simon recognized that the model of 'economic man' [sic] who could be expected to optimize his interests by making rational choices was an inadequate account of organizational behaviour. He therefore substituted the concept of 'administrative man' [sic] whose rationality is bounded or limited and who, since he cannot know all the choice alternatives when making a decision 'satisfices' rather than maximizes. March and Simon write:

> Most human decision-making, whether individual, or organisational, is concerned with the discovery or selection of satisfactory alternatives, only in exceptional cases is it concerned with the selection of optimal alternatives.

March and Simon compare the two processes of *optimizing* and *satisficing* with looking for the sharpest needle in the haystack and looking for a needle which is sharp enough to sew with. The assumptions of the classical model are that all choice alternatives are known, that all the consequences of choosing each alternative are known, and that individuals can order these consequences in terms of utility. It is clear that all this is a well-nigh unattainable set of criteria and hence the actor is forced to 'satisfice'. This occurs according to the actor's necessarily limited definition of the situation which is only an approximate model of the 'real' situation. However, March and Simon do not deny rationality in organizational choice; they believe that the actor can achieve a *bounded rationality*. They hold that members work with simplified models which involve, for example, attending to a restricted range of situations and the pursuit of semi-independent or loosely-coupled actions. At the policy level, 'political' challenges to over-rationalistic 'economic' approaches were mounted in the 1950s and subsequently by Lindblom, in his notion of 'the science of muddling through', and others (cf. Dahl and Lindblom, 1953; Braybrooke and Lindblom, 1963; Lindblom, 1959; 1966; 1968). The empirical problem of rationality in organizations is exacerbated by the increasing turbulence of organizational environments. Organizations have long been recognized as being *open-systems* which entails their internal activities being open to influence to a greater or lesser degree by external circumstance. It is difficult to demonstrate that organizations are now, to a greater degree than in the past, subjected to more internal pressures from outside sources, but it would seem to be the case. Schon (1971) for example, argues that we have gone 'beyond the stable state'. He writes: 'Throughout our society we are experiencing the actual or theoretical dissolution of stable organisations and institutions, actions for personal identity and systems of values.' It does appear as though the rate of change, perhaps stemming mainly from technological development and the growing interdependence of social institutions, is accelerating and thus generating an increasingly turbulent environment in which organizations must function. This trend can be seen in relation to the schools. Once considered a 'domesticated' organization which could continue placidly to pursue its goals without need to compete in the market-place like the 'wild' organizations of the business world (Carlson, 1974), the declining birth-rate with consequently falling enrolments has put the continued existence of many schools in doubt. Moreover, schools have become more interdependent with other forms of organization and social institution – commercial, industrial, welfare, legal, community, political, etc. – and the once-strong boundary around the school has become more permeable. The school has become a more open system and has to take into account more, and frequently competing, factors in its decision-making. Thus the cognitive limits to rationality become more acute as the school seeks to take into account the expectations of various sets of stakeholders who are increasingly taking to forms of pressure group activity.

Finally, there is the question of the logical as well as cognitive limits to rationality. There is actually little work on the limits to rationality in schools, or indeed in organizations generally. The writers who have made the greatest contributions to this issue have been more concerned with the limits as they operate in the area of public policy (e.g. Olson, 1965; Hirschman, 1978; 1981). The most wide-ranging and fruitful discussion occurs in a series of books by Elster (1978; 1979). It is not possible to explore these ideas in detail, but essentially they are concerned with the ways in which the rational pursuit of ends by any single individual has an unanticipated outcome of preventing the achievement of those ends when all individuals in the relevant set pursue the same end in a rational manner. For example, in the context of high youth unemployment it is rational for the individuals to seek to improve their employability by enhancing their educational qualifications. However, if all school-leavers maximized their qualifications and no additional jobs were available, employers would increase their demand for qualifications and thus school leavers would be no better off. The individual can succeed only by increasing qualifications while others fail to do so.

A similar problem is that of promotion in a context of declining opportunities. Given the present salary structure and status differences, the teacher is in the same position as the school-leaver described above. Promotion will go to those who acquire the qualifications, using this term broadly to include not only academic qualifications but in-service training and experience of various kinds. But if all teachers pursue the 'rational' courses of obtaining qualifications, none will be better off.

Another fruitful area of analysis would be participation in decision-making. Without entering into a long discussion on the various connotations of *democracy*, it can be seen that in so far as individuals increase control over their own actions, the ultimate outcome may be a reduction of the capacity of all members to attain their individual ends. This can be seen to be the case in those schools which have been able to adapt thoroughgoing patterns of internal democracy. There has been a tendency for those schools to fall short of fulfilling the aspirations of members. It may be that this has been due to an inability to establish appropriate patterns of decision-making, or to respond to the pressures of a hostile environment, but the discrepancy between aspiration and achievement is logically inherent in the attempt to maximize organizational democracy. Elster (1978) quotes Simmel (1968) as stating: 'The all-and-out democrat will not be governed, even if this means that he cannot be served either.' Although Simmel made this statement in relation to the American political system, it can equally well apply to some attempts to democratise school. In Swidler's study (1979) of two highly democratized high schools in California, the power of the students was such that it negated the efforts of school leaders to meet the aspirations of the very same students.

## On garbage cans and organized anarchies

Because of the diversity and diffuseness of educational goals and the inevitable limits to rationality in all organizations, the conversion of goals into issues for discussion and decision-making becomes a highly problematic affair. The day-to-day problem of teaching provides the school with a basic stability and predictability, although this is not to say that teaching is an essentially routine process. But at the level of policy, issues emerge and disappear again in ways which are far from predictable. The source of an issue, how it becomes an agenda item, the range of people engaged in the issue, the intensity of the involvement, the direction of that intensity, and the fate of the issue – whether it leads to a decision, to the implementation of the decision, or to the demise of the issue without discernible effect upon the school – are matters which have been considered only rarely in the application of organizational theory to schools, and even less frequently have they been the subject for research. The prevailing model is still underpinned by rationalistic assumptions of goal-setting, decision-making and implementation. However, one theorist who has been attentive to the idiosyncratic nature of organizational decision-making is James March, whose work we can briefly consider as providing an appropriate backdrop to the discussion in the remainder of this chapter.

The collection of papers edited by March and Olsen (1976) questions the fit between the organizational theory and the real world of organizations. In particular, March and his colleagues question the received wisdom about how decisions are made and implemented. They note that this process hardly conforms to the rationalistic paradigm of management theory. The history of the decision-making process in organizations is extremely haphazard, with decisions keenly contested at some times but not at others, with disputes over participating rights sometimes more significant than the issues themselves, with decisions sometimes taken after lengthy and serious discussion, but at other times decisions taken matter-of-factly by a limited number of people. They note that the process of making an organizational choice is often an opportunity for much else, for fulfilling duties, for defining virtue, for distributing praise and blame, for discovering and expressing self-interests, and for the sheer pleasure of being involved in the occasion of making a choice as a decision.

This complexity is increased by the high degree of ambiguity which prevails in organizations, and it can be noted that the diverse goals of schools make them particularly prone to ambiguity. March and his colleagues identify four particular types of opaqueness or ambiguity in organizations: *intention* (i.e. existence of ill-defined and inconsistent objectives), *understanding* (i.e. the difficulty involved in interpreting the organizational world, its technology and environmental pressures), *history* (i.e. the difficulty in interpreting the organization's history and its present consequences) and *organization* (i.e. the variations in the time and attention which individuals give to decisions from one choice occasion to another). The problematic nature of organizational goals and individual preferences, the lack of clarity about how the organization 'works' and the fluidity of participation lead them to put forward the now-famous *garbage-can model of organizational choice*. Rather than decision-making following the apparently rational process of weighing alternatives between organizational goals and then between the different means of achieving these goals, a decision comes out of the 'garbage can' into which have gone four 'streams'. These are as follows:

1 *Problems*: Problems are the concern of people inside and outside the organization. They arise over issues of life-style: family; frustrations of work; careers; group relations within the organization; distribution of status, jobs, and money; ideology; or current crises of humanity as interpreted by the mass media or the next-door neighbour. All require attention. Problems are, however, distinct from choices, and they may not be resolved when choices are made.
2 *Solutions*: A solution is somebody's product. A computer is not just a solution to a problem in payroll management, discovered when needed. It is an answer actively looking for a question. The creation of need is not solely a curiosity of the market in consumer products; it is a general phenomenon of processes of choice. Despite the dictum that you cannot find the answer until you have formulated the question, you often do not know the question in organizational problem solving until you know the answer.
3 *Participants*: Participants come and go. Since every entrance is an exit somewhere else, the distribution of 'entrances' depends on the attributes of the choice being left as much as it does on the attributes of the new choice. Substantial variation in participation stems from other demands on the participants' time (rather than from features of the decision under study).
4 *Choice opportunities*: These are occasions when an organization is expected to produce behaviour that can be called a decision. Opportunities arise regularly and any organization has ways of declaring an occasion for

choice. Contracts must be signed; people hired, promoted, or fired; money spent; and responsibilities allocated.

They summarize the process as follows:

> The garbage can process, as it has been observed, is one in which problems, solutions and participants move from one choice opportunity to another in such way that the nature of the choice, the time it takes, and the problems it solves all depend on a relatively complicated intermeshing of the mix of choices available at any one time, the mix of problems that have access to the organisation, the mix of solutions looking for problems, and the outside demands on the decision makers.
>
> (March and Olsen, 1976)

The concept of the garbage can is linked to another concept which has become popular in the recent literature on organizations, presumably because it resonates with the experience of theorists and participants (and theorists-as-participants, for it must be remembered that organization theorists usually work in organizations). This is the concept of *organized anarchy*. Weiner writes:

> In these conceptions an organised anarchy is an organisation typified by unclear goals, poorly understood technology, and variable participation.
>
> (Weiner, in March and Olsen, 1976)

The above summary of some of the elements in March's approach to organization is necessarily concentrated and the reader should read March and Olsen's collection for an elaboration and for an account of case studies which explore organizational decision making with the aid of these concepts, case studies which deal mainly with educational settings of different kinds. Some critics of March claim that he has overemphasized the degree of ambiguity and anarchy in organizations. Against this, it must be said that March does not wholly throw out the baby with the bath water. He believes that rationality is present in organizational decision-making but simply notes that organizational choices get made sometimes in rather odd ways and always in conditions much more complex and adventitious than conventional theory allows. As such, it is an attractive and prima facie compelling view of organizations. Against this necessarily condensed theoretical background we can now consider some aspects of school decision-making.

### The succession of goals

This phenomenon has long had a place in the literature on organizations. However, it has usually been applied to organizations which survive by moving successively from one goal to another as each is fulfilled, or as particular goals become less significant for the supporting environment. The classic case in the literature is the American Infantile Paralysis Association which, as the cause for which it was founded ceased to be important when the incidence of infantile paralysis dramatically decreased, moved on to other charitable concerns (Sills, 1957). However, the 'succession of goals' concept has not been generally applied to 'domesticated' organizations, nor has it been informed by the insights of March and colleagues into organizational choice.

A school can be said to be characterized by a 'succession of goals'. As was noted in the previous section, schools have a very broad set of agreed goals which, whilst they are expressed at the most general level, are uncontroversial and schools can always claim to be pursuing these generalized goals as, indeed, they are. The issue of the succession of goals comes at the point where schools convert these goals into *commitments* (Corwin 1965), and make choices between the alternatives which are competing for attention at any given time. March's approach takes over when it becomes a question of determining by what process particular goals become salient and what factors lead to choices being made. There are enormous conceptual difficulties in such an enterprise, not least in defining what is an *issue*. The possible elements in what might be said to constitute an issue are its significance for the effectiveness of the school, the intensity of feelings amongst the staff, the number and hierarchical status of staff engaged in the making of choices, and the expectations of outsiders. Each of these is capable of independent variation. Thus one need not elaborate the difficulties entailed in understanding the ebb and flow of issues. There are very few studies of what can be termed 'the natural history of issues' from which generalizations, if such there are, can be drawn. The methodological problems involved in such a study need not be elaborated. Unless a researcher was immersed in a school over a long period of time and able to detect the first showings of what was to become an issue, studies would need to become *post hoc* with all the attendant problems of recall and reinterpretation by participants.

There are thus very few case studies of the natural history of an issue in schools, but one exception is Christensen's (1976) study of a Danish free school in which three apparently unequivocal decisions were made: to establish a 'Society of Friends of the School', to change the school to a non-graded pattern of organization for instruction, and to rehire a teacher who had been dismissed. Yet none of these decisions was implemented. In order to explain this rather surprising fact he calls upon the 'garbage can' model and makes the following points: that the *outcome* of a decision is often less important than the *process*, that implementation is in the hands of people who have the resources but who might not share the attitudes of the decision-making group. ('Votes count but resources decide': Rokkan, 1968.) The high level of attention to the making of a decision may not be sustained through to its implementation, and, finally, the fact that other problems come to absorb the allocation of the organization as new crises arise.

The unpredictable character of the natural history of issues in schools arises because they have the following characteristics:

1 The diffuseness and diversity of goals means that only a very limited number can have the attention of the school at any time.
2 The diversity of goals means that issues will arise from a variety of sources, e.g. LEA requirements, the imperatives of a national report or the report of an HMI visit, parental pressures, adventitious issues arising accidentally (perhaps literally arising from an accident), the head's identification of important issues, the emergence of an issue from a staff analysis of problems and needs, the persistence of an individual member of staff in pursuit of an interest which may sometimes take on the character of an *idée fixe*.
3 The ambiguous nature of the decision-making system of the school in which the head has a high degree of authority but generally establishes some pattern for involving colleagues. Since teacher involvement in consultation is voluntary, participation will be variable. There might be a high initial involvement which drops away as the daily imperatives of teaching reassert themselves, and as teachers 'discover' that their personal interests are not involved. On the other hand, there might be a limited initial involvement which grows as teachers recognize the significance of the issue. Or this might be an in-and-out involvement with a consequent loss of continuity and the introduction of new opinions, or the affirmation of new interests over time.
4 There is, as Christensen noted, often a division between those who decide upon a choice and those with executive power. It is usually the head who has the executive power and there may be a disjunction between decision and implementation (see Bailey, 1982).
5 The loosely coupled nature of the school means that although the head, as chief executive, can implement some decisions which have obvious school-wide and structural consequences, there are other decisions, usually affecting classroom practice, which are less easily implemented. A choice is made, but nothing happens. This is a situation of 'innovation without change'. There is a symbolic acceptance of a decision but practice remains the same.

### Conclusion

One volume of Isaiah Berlin's collected writings is entitled *Against the Current* (1979). The 'current' is the developing belief in the rationality, or the promise of rationality, in human affairs with the growing application to these affairs of the procedures of the natural sciences. The papers in that volume celebrate those writers who have perceived the inherent limits to scientific rationality and have stressed the idiosyncratic, adventitious, unpredictable and intractable nature of human action. The rationalistic 'current' has dominated management theory and, with some exceptions and until recently, organization theory. Yet anyone who observes organizations closely, or who tries to run an organization, is aware of their less-than-rational, even chaotic, nature and the unpredictable pebbles which derail the best-laid plans. The less-than-rational nature of policy-making and implementation even at the highest levels has been revealed in Allison's (1971) study of the Cuban missile crisis, and the comments by Zbigniew Brezinski, President Carter's adviser on national security, that history is the reflection of continuing chaos rather than consciously formulated policies (Urban, 1981). Of the less lethal level of the educational system Kogan (1975) has written that it is 'pluralistic, incremental and reactive'. And life in schools is certainly no more rational than in the educational system as a whole.

This chapter has explored the aleatory aspects of the school as an organization by pursuing two themes. One was the slippery concept of *organizational goal*. Although most schools will certainly move in some broad direction, the notion of a set of goals to which all the components are geared fails to correspond to the reality which is that in so far as a school has specific goals these will emerge from the interplay of interests within the school. A second was the inescapable limits to the particular kind of means-ends rationality which pervades the natural sciences in the contexts of social affairs. The limits arise from the fact that there are competing rationalities which are the outcome of different interests, the cognitive limits to rationality which arise because not all possibilities can be conceived in the planning process, and logical limits to rationality which arise because individual rationality can engender collective irrationality. These limitations were illuminated by reference to the work of March and others who have written 'against the current' in organization theory.

This rationality-questioning perspective raises a problem for those who run organizations and the management theory which is designed to guide their efforts. To *understand* organizations may be to detract from the task of *running* them. However, as noted, the work of Simon, March and Lindblom does not characterize organizations as wholly, or even mainly, irrational. They are probably more rational than they are adventitious and the quest for rational procedures is not misplaced. However, organizational pathos will remain and rationalistic approaches will always be blown off course by the contingent, the unexpected and the irrational.

## References

Allison, G. T. (1971) *Essence of Decision: Exploring the Cuban Missile Crisis*, Boston, Mass., Little, Brown.

Bailey, A. J. (1982) 'The question of legitimation: a response to Eric Hoyle', *Educational Management*, 10(2), 99–105.

Berlin, I. (1979) *Against the Current*, London, Hogarth Press.

Braybrooke, D. and Lindblom, C. E. (1963) *A Strategy of Decision*, New York, Free Press.

Carlson, D. (1974) 'Environmental constraints and educational consequences: the public school and its clients', in D. E. Griffiths (ed.) *Behavioural Science and Educational Administration*, 63rd NSSE Yearbook, Chicago, Ill., University of Chicago Press.

Christensen, S. (1976) 'Decision-making and socialization' in J. G. March and J. P. Olsen (eds) *Ambiguity and Choice in Organisations*, Bergen, Universitetforlaget,

Clark, B. R. (1960) *The Open Door College*, New York, McGraw-Hill.

Corwin, R. G. (1965) *A Sociology of Education*, New York, Appleton-Century-Croft.

Dahl, R. A. and Lindblom, C. E. (1953) *Politics, Economics and Welfare*, New York, Harper & Row.

DES (1977) *Education in Schools: A Consultative Document*, Cmnd 6869, London, HMSO.

Elster, J. (1978) *Logic and Society*, New York, Wiley.

Elster, J. (1979) *Ullysses and the Siren*, Cambridge, Cambridge University Press.

Gross, E. (1969) 'The definition of organizational goals', *British Journal of Sociology*, **20**, 277–94.

Hirschman, A. O. (1978) *Exit, Voice and Loyalty*, Cambridge, Mass., Harvard University Press.

Hirschman, A. O. (1981) *Essays in Trespassing: Economic Politics and Beyond*, Cambridge, Mass., Harvard University Press.

Kogan, M. (1975) *Educational Policy Making*, London, Allen & Unwin.

Lindblom, C. E. (1959) 'The science of muddling through', *Public Administration Review*, **19**

Lindblom, C. E. (1966) *The Intelligence of Democracy*, New York, Free Press.

Lindblom, C. E. (1968) *The Policy-Making Process*, Englewood Cliffs, NJ, Prentice-Hall.

March, J. G. and Olsen, J. P. (1976) (eds) *Ambiguity and Choice in Organisations*, Bergen, Universitetforlaget.

March, J. G. and Simon, H. A. (1958) *Organisations*, New York, Wiley.

Musgrove, F. (1971) *Patterns of Power and Authority in English Education*, London, Methuen.

Olson, M. (1965) *The Logic of Collective Action*, Cambridge, Mass., Harvard University Press.

Perrow, C. (1968) 'Organizational goals', in *International Encyclopaedia of the Social Sciences*, London, Macmillan.

Rokkan, S. (1968) 'Norway: numerical democracy and corporate pluralism', in R. A. Dahl, (ed.) *Political Opportunities in Western Democracies*, New Haven, Conn., Yale University Press.

Schon, D. (1971) *Beyond the Stable State*, Harmondsworth, Penguin.

Sills, D. L. (1957) *The Volunteers*, New York, Free Press.

Simmel, G. (1968) *The Conflict in Modern Culture and Other Essays*, New York, Teachers College Press.

Simon, H. (1964) *Administrative Behaviour: A Study of Decision-Making Processes in Administrative Organization*, 2nd edn, New York, Collier-Macmillan.

Swidler, A. (1979) *Organization without Authority*, Cambridge, Mass., Harvard University Press.

Urban, G. (1981) 'The perils of foreign policy: a conversation with Dr. Zbigniew Brezinski', *Encounter*, May, **98**, 12–30.

# 11

# Managing curriculum change

**Michael Fullan**

The purpose of studying the dynamics of curriculum change is to make the change process more explicit. This means identifying the key factors related to success, developing insights into the change process, and developing action programmes.

## Background

Studies of educational change have moved through several phases. In the 1960s research concentrated on tracing the adoption of innovations, for instance how many new schemes were actually in use in schools. It is obvious now, but it was not at that time that such research information was of limited value. For one thing, adoption by organizations tells us almost nothing about how individual members feel or act. For another, reported use by individuals does not indicate whether an innovation is actually in use, let alone the quality of use.

We do not need to dwell on the reasons why researchers and policy-makers were content to stop with adoption. Perhaps it relates to the symbolic value of having 'appeared' to change by launching a major reform effort; or to the naive optimism of the 1950s and early 1960s; or to the possibility that people were fully occupied with developing innovations and policies with little energy and resources for follow-through; or more basically to the fact that initiating projects is much more glamorous and visible than the time-consuming, laborious front-line work of implementing an innovation project; or more charitably to the possibility that worrying about implementation and actual use was a natural outgrowth of earlier adoption efforts that came with time.

Whatever the case, it was not until 1971 that the first works appeared analysing problems of implementing educational innovations (Sarason, 1971; Gross *et al.*, 1971).

The 1970s were concerned with classroom practice and essentially resulted in documenting failure (see Fullan and Pomfret, 1977 for a review). We learned more about what not to do than anything else (don't ignore local needs; don't introduce complex, vague innovations; don't ignore training needs; don't ignore local leaders and opinion makers, etc.).

The 1980s were concerned with identifying and analysing success and effectiveness in educational settings. Research provided some evidence on the factors related to success. Depending on the study, the latter were defined in terms of increases in student achievement, degree of institutionalization, or in more intermediate terms such as teaching skills, teacher change, teacher commitment.

We are now embarking on a new phase which can be called the management of change (or more accurately the management of change for achieving successful outcomes). At first glance one might think that the earlier descriptions of what constitutes success would have solved the management of change problem. But 'explanations' of situations are not the same as 'solutions' in new situations, although they can help. Our future efforts will need to concentrate on managing change and developing strategies for making it happen.

### Six basic observations about curriculum change

The six observations described in this section are ways of thinking or insights into the phenomenon of educational change that should give us pause for thought and provide important orientations prior to launching into any particular change project.

#### Brute sanity

The problem of brute sanity was identified by George Bernard Shaw when he observed that 'reformers have the idea that change can be achieved by brute sanity'. The tendency towards brute sanity on the part of change initiators or planners is natural. What could be more rational than advocating a change which one believes in and may be in a position to introduce? The use of sheer argument and sheer authority can get a change 'on the books', but it is, of course, not a very effective strategy for implementing change. Research has demonstrated that persistence, patience and attention to detail in putting something into practice is critical. Brute sanity is the tendency to overlook the complexity and detailed processes and procedures required, in favour of more obvious matters of stressing goals, the importance of the problem and the grand plan. Brute sanity over-promises, over-rationalizes and consequently results in unfulfilled dreams and frustrations which discourage people from sustaining their efforts and from taking on future change projects.

### Overload

The overload of change projects on implementers is well known and there are frequently conflicting priorities on the agenda. One could say that the initiation of change projects represents a mixture of political and educational merit. As such, (a) too many projects are launched, (b) implementation is often attempted too early, i.e. the political process often outstrips the educational development process, (c) overly ambitious projects are adopted, and (d) simultaneous multiple projects are introduced in an unco-ordinated way. The basic observation is: 'just because a change project is on the books does not mean that it should or could be implemented'. No theory or strategy can do the impossible, and the impossible in this case is to implement everything that is supposed to be implemented.

### Implementing the implementation plan

Many people have responded to the research of the 1970s, which documented implementation problems, by developing elaborate implementation plans designed to take into account factors known to affect success. This seems sensible enough on the surface but ironically has led to the problem of 'how do I implement the implementation plan?' It is useful to recognize that implementation plans, when they are first introduced, are *innovations* as much as, if not more than, curriculum innovations. Everything we know about the dos and don'ts of implementing curriculum innovations must be applied to the problem of developing implementation plans.

### Content versus process

It is also helpful to distinguish between the content of change and the process of change and to realize that each represents distinct bodies of knowledge and expertise and each needs an appropriate implementation strategy. They are independent in the sense that it is possible to have expertise in one and not the other. It is possible, in other words, to be highly knowledgeable about a particular curriculum or curriculum development programme but yet be a disaster in working with others to implement it. Indeed, those most committed to a particular innovation may be least effective in working with others to bring about the change. Both elements of expertise must be present and integrated in any given change project.

### Pressure and support

Research in recent years suggests that effective change, even if voluntarily pursued, rarely happens unless there is a combination of pressure and support. These are two important balancing mechanisms and success is usually accompanied by both. The positive role of pressure in change has been neglected until recently. Support without pressure can waste resources; pressure without support creates alienation (see Fullan, 1985).

### *Change = learning*

Successful change, or successful implementation, is none other than learning, but it is the adults in the system who are learning along with or more so than the students. Thus, anything we know about how adults learn and under what conditions they are most likely to learn is useful for designing and carrying out strategies for implementation.

## What is implementation?

Implementation means curriculum change. For teachers in classrooms, new materials are important, but are ineffective by themselves. Change also involves new behaviours and practices, and ultimately new beliefs and understandings. It involves changes in what people know and assume.

It is possible to obtain some degree of change through policy decision and the initial process of getting new structures and materials in place, but this represents the more obvious, structural aspects of change in comparison with the new skills and understandings required of front-line implementers. In the absence of the latter, only superficial change is achieved. The effectiveness of a change project stands or falls with the extent to which front-line implementers use new practices with degrees of mastery, commitment and understanding.

## Factors related to successful change

These can be grouped within the three broad project phases of initiation, implementation, and institutionalization.

### *Initiation factors*

There are four requirements

1 educational need should be linked to an agenda of political (high-profile) need
2 a clear model should exist for the proposed change
3 there needs to be a strong advocate for the change
4 there should be an early active initiation establishing initial commitment, as an elaborate planning stage is wasteful of energy.

### Implementation factors

Some critical needs include

1 careful orchestration: implementation requires the clear direction of many players; a group is needed to oversee the implementation plan and carry it through
2 the correct alchemy of pressure and support
3 early rewards for implementers
4 ongoing INSET, to maintain commitment as behaviours often change before beliefs.

### Institutionalization factors

An innovation will be more successful if

1 it becomes embedded into the fabric of everyday practice
2 it is clearly linked to classroom practice
3 it is in widespread use across several classrooms and schools
4 it is not contending with conflicting priorities
5 it is subject to continuing INSET for new staff, to consolidate commitment.


## Implications for action

I would offer finally the following eight basic guidelines or insights:

1 effective entrepreneurs exploit multiple innovations
2 overcome the 'if only . . .' problem, e.g. 'If only more heads were curriculum leaders . . .'; 'If only the government would stop introducing so many policies . . .'
3 manage multiple innovations: 'Do two well and the others as well as possible'
4 get better at implementation planning – more by doing than planning; start small but think big
5 beware of implementation dip, i.e. the risk of temporary de-skilling as innovators learn new skills
6 remember that research shows behaviour changes first and changes in belief follow
7 recognize that project leaders need to have a vision of content and process and the relationship between the two which will promote change; to have a vision of content change without a vision of process change is an example of 'brute sanity'
8 acknowledge the importance of ownership and commitment and that ownership is a process where commitment is increasingly acquired.

## Conclusion

The process of curriculum change is complex and the search to understand it continues. If the teachers are to be convinced, those in authority positions in LEAs and schools must believe and understand the change sufficiently to convey its meaning. The psychiatrist Ronald Laing has captured the essence of this in one of his poems:

> There is something I don't know
>     that I am supposed to know.
> I don't know *what* it is I don't know,
>     and yet am supposed to know,
> and I feel I look stupid
>     if I seem both not to know it
>        and not know *what* it is I don't know.
> Therefore I pretend I know it.
>     This is nerve-racking
>     since I don't know what I must pretend to know.
> Therefore I pretend to know everything.
>
>           (Laing, 1970)

## References

Fullan, M. (1985) 'Change processes and strategies at the local level', *Elementary School Journal*, **85**(3), 391–421.

Fullan, M. and Pomfret, A. (1977) 'Research on curriculum and instruction implementation', *Review of Educational Research*, **47**(1), 335–97.

Gross, N., Giaquinta, J. and Bernstein, M. (1971) *Implementing Organizational Innovations: a Sociological Analysis of Planned Educational Change*, New York, Basic Books.

Laing, R. D. (1970) *Knots*, London, Tavistock.

Sarason, S. (1971) *The Culture of the School and the Problem of Change*, Boston, Mass., Allyn & Bacon.

**Section III**

# Practices

# 12

# TVEI: curriculum issues and staff perspectives

**Douglas Barnes, George Johnson, Steven Jordan,
David Layton, Peter Medway and David Yeomans**

## Curriculum organization at school level: patterns of accommodation and the grouping of students

In our interim report (Barnes *et al.*, 1987, pp. 7–23), we used the categories, first suggested by Murray Saunders (1986), of *containment, accommodation* and *adaptive extension* to classify schools' responses to the Technical and Vocational Education Initiative (TVEI). We summarized these as follows:

1 Adaptive extension
  The school utilises TVEI as an opportunity to review and reshape the whole 14–18 curriculum.
2 Accommodation
  The school organizes a TVEI scheme with innovative elements but effects a compromise between TVEI goals and the claims of existing curricular arrangements.
3 Containment
  The effects of TVEI funding are almost entirely confined and absorbed by the school's existing practices which resist change.

We found that of the first twelve schools visited seven had contained TVEI, five had accommodated the initiative and there were no examples of adaptive extension. Of the remaining fourteen schools eight (A, D, L, P, S, X, Y, Z) had contained TVEI, five had accommodated it (G, J, M, N, V) and there was one example of adaptive extension (F). Thus the final distribution for the 26 schools is:

| | |
|---|---|
| Containment | 15 schools |
| Accommodation | 10 schools |
| Adaptive extension | 1 school |

This confirms our impression, reported previously, that the majority of the schools have not undertaken radical changes across the curriculum.

Interpretation of this finding has, of course, to be made cautiously. Given that the initiative was a pilot experiment which concentrated on a particular cohort of pupils only, schools could legitimately argue that a radical reshaping of the total 14–18 curriculum was an extravagant response.

A second potentially significant dimension of the way in which schools have responded to TVEI is whether they have decided to separate TVEI students from the others for their TVEI lessons or have chosen to integrate the two groups. We found that fifteen of the schools had mixed groups of TVEI and non-TVEI students taking TVEI designated courses. Twelve of the schools had discrete TVEI groups (school I had discrete groups in the fifth year and mixed groups in the fourth year). Table 12.1 combines the discrete/mixed dimension with the containment/accommodation/adaptive extension dimension.

We can now use the table to describe briefly the responses to TVEI made by the schools.

*Box 1*

This represents the most common responses to TVEI. These schools have used the initiative to add new subjects to their options list and to enhance some existing subjects. The basic core plus options structure of the curriculum remains unchanged. It is often an explicit aim of senior management in these schools that TVEI and TVEI students should not be seen as separate from the rest of the school, hence the decision to open the TVEI courses to all the fourth year and fifth year students. TVEI students are often only identified for monitoring purposes. Students do not opt for TVEI, they opt for subjects which may result in them becoming designated TVEI students. In some of the schools, however, TVEI students may have been on residentials or have had separate arrangements for work experience.

**Table 12.1**

|  | *Contained* | *Accommodated* | *Extended* |
|---|---|---|---|
| Discrete | $I^5$,K,X, Z,W,S<br><br>2 | B,R,O N,J,V<br><br>3 |  |
| Mixed | H,E,U,$I^4$,C P,A,L Y,D<br><br>1 | T,Q M,G<br><br>4 | F<br><br>5 |

*Box 2*

In this group of schools the core plus options structure is retained. Students are, however, required to opt for a distinct TVEI package which often includes some form of TVEI core. The result is that there is a discrete group of TVEI students.

*Box 3*

In this group of schools the TVEI curriculum has various novel features. In school B this was the Project Unit, in school R the system of workshops and assignments, in school J the modularization of the curriculum and in school V the establishment of consortium arrangements which led to TVEI being taught by a team of central teachers. In all cases, however, since the TVEI curriculum was provided to a discrete group of students who had opted for TVEI, influence on the mainstream curriculum was limited.

*Box 4*

Here again TVEI has led to the introduction of significant curriculum innovations. These included: in school T the spread of information technology (IT), profiling and counselling across the curriculum; major changes in the timetable in school Q; and modularization in schools M and G. In these schools there were opportunities for non-TVEI students to participate in parts of the TVEI curriculum.

*Box 5*

Only school F fell into this category. In this school a decision has been taken to modularize a large part of the 14–16 curriculum and a large proportion of fourth and fifth year students were involved in the modular courses.

Over half the schools, then, have adopted a contained version of TVEI. In these schools the initiative has not been allowed to substantially change the structure of the fourth and fifth year curriculum. We wish to make it clear that this does not necessarily reflect on the quality of the classroom experiences. We have seen a great deal of impressive teaching in individual subjects in these schools but this work has been carried on within a conventional subject-based 30–40 period per week curriculum structure.

There is some evidence that schools have felt more freedom to experiment where the TVEI students are a discrete group. The project unit in school B, the system of assignments and workshops in school R and the flexible modular structure in school J were among the most innovative approaches to curriculum organization and all were available only to TVEI students. A further advantage of this approach is that it makes possible the emergence of a distinctive team of TVEI teachers with its own ethos and common approach to teaching. Such teams were a strong feature of TVEI in schools B and R. However, this still leaves the task of extending such approaches to the rest of the 14–16 curriculum. In all three schools at the time of our visits little progress had been made in this direction and the mainstream curricula had scarcely been influenced by TVEI developments.

Five schools (F, G, K, Q, T) had embarked on changes which affected TVEI and non-TVEI students but in most cases these changes were less radical than those attempted in schools B, J. and R. In schools T and Q, despite the changes noted above, TVEI had not made a great impact upon the rest of the curriculum. In schools F and M, TVEI had encouraged the modularization of part of the 14–16 curriculum, this process having gone much further in school F than in school M. In both cases, however, the way in which the modular system was organized limited the extent to which there was a real change in the nature of the students' experience. Students were required to follow the courses they had chosen for two years and complete all the modules, the main change from conventional two year courses being that the content had been divided into free-standing units and shorter term learning objectives were spelled out to the students.

In school G a more flexible modular system had been established. Students took four compulsory modules in the fourth year and were then able to choose four further modules in the fifth year. This modular course was open to all fourth year students. There was also a clear intention in this school to extend the modular approach to other areas of the curriculum.

## Modularization of the curriculum

Considerable interest has been expressed in the development of modular curricula. Five of the schools in our sample (F, G, J, M, N) have responded to TVEI by modularizing parts of their 14–16 curriculum. In this section we examine the rationales which have been given for modularization, the forms which it has taken and the costs and benefits which have arisen.

### The structure of the modular curriculum

We do not offer any pre-emptive definition of modularization; rather we shall describe the operationalization of the concept in the five schools which claimed to have modularized parts of their 14–16 curriculum. It is *their* interpretations of a modular curriculum which will be presented here.

The length of modules varied between ten and eighteen weeks. In schools F, M and N once students had opted for a particular course they had to complete all the modules; mixing of modules from different courses was not allowed or was strongly discouraged (we heard of only one student in the three schools who had been allowed to mix modules). In these three schools modularization had resulted in the courses being broken up into smaller free-standing units. The intention was that these small units would have shorter term learning objectives and that this approach would help to motivate the students. The structure in schools G and J was considerably more flexible. In school J, 28 modules were offered; each student had to complete thirteen. There were two compulsory modules, but students could choose widely for their remaining eleven. Modules had to be clustered into groups of five for certification purposes and certain combinations were disallowed. Despite this the scheme was very flexible. The module on information processing, for example, could be used in five of the nine certification clusters as could the word processing modules. In school G students took four compulsory modules in the fourth year but in the fifth year they chose a further four from the 22 on offer although here also students had to choose combinations which could be certified.

### Rationales for Modularization

Modularization was said to greatly increase the motivation of the students. Here are just a few of the opinions expressed to us:

> Tremendous motivator of lower ability kids, may encourage them to carry on (with school).
> (Head, school N)

> Kids don't get bored with modules.
> (Teacher, school N)

> Modules more intense (than two year course) due to time constraints and that is a motivating factor. They take it a bit more seriously than they do the two year course.
> (Teacher, school J)

> It (the modular system) has advantages, the 16 week deadline is very stimulating. It has a sense of urgency.
> (Teacher, school M)

This increased motivation was linked to the setting of short-term objectives and the intensity of the teaching approach.

It was also claimed that modularization promoted changes in teaching style. The school co-ordinator in school J explained that:

> What we want to be distinctive about the modules is the active-based learning that gives them choice and responsibility, changes in teaching style, content, retraining teachers, developing relationships with pupils.

The head of school G argued that:

> Teachers *have* to identify learning objectives in modules so teachers know *why* they're teaching them.

In school F the head suggested that modularization had led to courses which were concept and process, rather than content, orientated. The rewriting of courses which modularization had necessitated had allowed teachers to rethink and bring syllabuses up to date. The claim that modular courses placed greater emphasis on concept and process was not always supported by teachers as we shall see below.

Modules were also linked with the development of continuous assessment. The modular courses did not have two year terminal exams, and this again was said to be a motivating factor as well as being a fairer method of assessment. Modularization was also said to make it easier to move to criterion-referenced assessment.

A further advantage claimed for the modular system was that it provided for balance, breadth and relevance. Students were able to taste modules from a wide range of subject disciplines and this would give a better basis for choice at sixteen. As one teacher said, 'the two year option choices are like joining the army, once you're in you can't get out'.

This argument only applied in schools G and J where students had some choice within the modular system. Modularization could also help to combat gender stereotyping. As was noted earlier, in school G all students had to take modules in community studies, technology, business studies and information technology; in school J there were compulsory modules in product development and computer literacy. In effect these schools had extended the compulsory core for those students opting for the modular courses. It was also hoped that students would be more adventurous in choosing modules if they knew they could always move into another area after, at most, a term. There was some evidence in school J that this had happened with some girls being prepared to try modules in electronics and technology although few of them pursued these subjects in later modules.

*Assessment in modular systems*

This was a major source of concern in the schools. In school N the modular courses had not been accepted by the examination board in May of the first year. In all five schools there had been a considerable amount of negotiation with the boards. This proved particularly difficult where there were proposals for the mixing of modules in cross-curricular courses. In schools M and N the uncertainties over certification had, in part, led the schools to discourage mixing of modules. In the project of which school J is part a deputy head had been seconded for a year to negotiate with the exam board and this perhaps accounted for the success of this project in achieving a flexible modular structure. While it was accepted that the boards had tried to be helpful there was a feeling that they were not geared up to deal with the assessment of modular courses. Moderators of one board were said to be more interested in product than process and the same board had been 'tardy' in agreeing to the modular scheme in which school G participated. The head of school F said of the boards:

> Boards are not staffed by innovators, they're staffed by administrators.

*Problems of modular systems*

In each of the five schools the modules had been written by groups of teachers. The staff involved had found this a stimulating and valuable experience. However it had also made very great demands on their time and caused a lot of stress. There was pressure to keep 'pumping stuff out' and this might be 'all right for five years but what about the next 35?' one teacher asked. The coursework and end of module tests associated with the assessment of modules also increased the pressure on teachers and some teachers were concerned that the amount of work associated with the assessment of modules might make the whole system unworkable.

A teacher in school J complained that 'too much time was spent on assessment' and that this was 'horrendous on project work'. This problem of time-consuming assessment practices had been exacerbated by GCSE with its increased emphasis on coursework and practical assessment. A teacher in school G explained the problems:

> GCSE assessment and practical work involves observing pupils working – how do you do that with 28 at the same time and ensure safety?

Another commonly noted problem was the overloading of modules with content. This was mentioned in all five schools and was often accompanied by complaints that the modules were too short to cover all the work. Thus it can be seen that some modules stressed content rather than process or concepts as was claimed.

Some teachers, particularly in science, were concerned that modular courses would not give a sound foundation for those wishing to go on to A-level physics, chemistry or biology. Their argument was that students would be able to mix the sciences and so not get sufficient background in any of them.

For the most part the modular systems were accommodated within conventional timetable structures, although in school J half day blocks had been created for the modules. The decision not to combine modularization with a restructuring of the timetable was a weakness for a teacher in school F:

> I'm not running a truly modular curriculum because we have not broken the timetable. As long as that continues we're not running a modular course, we just have modular assessment of parts of the course.

This teacher's argument was that since the structure of the timetable remained unchanged there had also been no major change in the students' overall curricular experience; the students' day continued to be broken up into a series of forty minute, relatively disconnected, lessons.

We felt that there was a tendency among some TVEI leaders, heads and teachers, to assume that because modularization had taken place changes in pedagogy, content and assessment techniques would follow. This is not necessarily the case. Controlled pedagogy is just as likely to take place in modules as in conventional courses. Modularity does not necessarily lead to greater realism or to assessments which reflect a wider range of skills, knowledge, attitudes and personal qualities. We suggest [. . .] that modularization also makes integration of curriculum content difficult to achieve. These issues remain to be tackled. Yet as a teacher in school F told us:

> We're under no pressure to change what we do except to modularize.

We tend to agree with the project co-ordinator who said that:

> I don't think there is anything intrinsically worthwhile about modularization, it's a fairly neutral device, it is only a device for using time more constructively, I suspect.

and

> Modules in themselves are not going to change the learning process.

## The disappearance or subordination of subjects

We investigated the extent to which the introduction of new subjects and the enhancement of existing subjects as a result of TVEI had affected the options offered to the students in the fourth and fifth years. Had any subjects disappeared from the curriculum or been significantly subordinated as a result of the changes which TVEI had brought in the 14–16 curriculum?

It is clear from the data that in many schools subjects had disappeared or attracted fewer students. Subjects affected included: commerce, woodwork, metalwork, geology, child care, traffic studies, geography, history, biology, Latin and RE. However the fact that these changes *coincided* with the introduction of TVEI does not allow us to say that they were *caused* wholly or in part by the initiative; often TVEI had accelerated changes in the patterns of option choice which were already in train. Other changes in the fourth and fifth year curriculum of the schools can clearly be attributed to TVEI. Some courses disappeared because they had been directly replaced by TVEI courses, for example the replacement of engineering science and economics by technology and business studies in school X or non-examination technology and electronics by electronics technology in school P. In schools D, H, K and Z the introduction of a TVEI core had meant that TVEI students lost time for PE and games. Careers was also affected in schools B, D and Q. Some claims were made that TVEI distorted class sizes and staffing elsewhere in the curriculum. In school U the Head of Science claimed that TVEI had made the policy of 20 per cent science for all more difficult to achieve by tying up teachers with small groups of TVEI students, and in school O groups in mathematics, English and science were said to be larger because of TVEI. Our data do not allow us to verify these claims. It is perhaps significant that some teachers and students blamed TVEI for changes for which the initiative was not responsible. In school Q, for example, students complained that they could not go to college to do typing and building studies because of TVEI. This was not true. These changes had come about because of the introduction of a course for the less able introduced independently of TVEI.

### Changes in the lower school curriculum

Care must again be taken in establishing causal links between the introduction of changes in the lower school curriculum and TVEI. Indeed in general terms mono-causal explanations for curriculum changes are likely to be over simplified.

However, it is clear that in several schools (I, K, T, and X) TVEI had contributed significantly to the introduction or expansion of information technology in the lower school. This had been made possible by the expansion of computing facilities as a result of TVEI. In schools K, W and X there had also been an extension of technology into the lower school. There seems to be a growing awareness that the teaching of technology needs to start lower down the school if fourth and fifth year technology is to be made more effective.

Not all changes in the lower school curriculum were seen as positive. In school Q we were told that performing arts in the second year had become 'just book reading' because of TVEI. In school M the commitments of teachers to TVEI had resulted in a part-time teacher being employed to teach lower school science and in most schools there must have been some redistribution of teachers among classes although our data allow us to say little on this.

### Resources

Schools were anxious that wherever possible TVEI resources were also used for non-TVEI lessons. Not only would this enhance teaching and learning in those lessons but, it was hoped, it would reduce resentment among non-TVEI staff at the scale of TVEI resourcing. As we shall see in the next section non-TVEI teachers were often quick to draw comparisons between the resources available through TVEI and those which they had received for their subjects. As was indicated in the previous section such changes as had taken place in the lower school curriculum in the schools had often come about as a result of TVEI resources.

Teachers expressed some concerns about the resource implications of TVEI. Several non-TVEI teachers were worried that when TVEI funding ended the maintenance of expensive subjects such as technology and computing, which had been expanded or introduced under TVEI, would affect the distribution of school capitation money to the detriment of non-TVEI subjects.

Some LEAs, in an attempt to ameliorate divisions between schools in and out of TVEI, had allocated all their funds for curriculum development to non-TVEI schools. The effect of this was that non-TVEI departments in TVEI schools were finding it impossible to obtain any money at all for curriculum development.

### Teachers' responses to TVEI

The potential 'enclave' effects of an educational experiment such as TVEI on teachers and other staff within schools and projects have been succinctly expressed in Saunders' triad of management responses to TVEI (Saunders 1986). [. . .] We shall here focus on the generalized implications of the initiative within the broader context of the school as a community. That is, we will be concerned [. . .] to outline a spectrum of effects on both TVEI and non-TVEI teachers within the 26 schools.

One of the most obvious and visible aspects of the introduction of TVEI into schools was the reduction of class sizes. In eight of the schools, the fact that TVEI finance was used to reduce group sizes generated a mixed response from teachers both inside and outside TVEI. In all the schools, TVEI teachers commented favourably on having smaller groups to teach. This was particularly the case with technology and PSE [personal and social education] teachers who felt that the success of their teaching strategies depended very much on group size. One only needs to comprehend the complexities of technology project work with, for example, a group of 25–30 (or more) to grasp the nature of the problem which teachers were referring to here. However, the fact that TVEI teachers had smaller groups sometimes had consequences for colleagues outside TVEI. In cases where there was a clearly defined cohort of students, taught in classes of smaller size than usual, non-TVEI teachers might have to contend with larger classes, a situation which caused resentment. Teacher shortages in certain subjects could be an exacerbating factor, as might a decision to use funding for equipment rather than teaching staff. On the other side of this coin is the phenomenon of non-viable student groups outside TVEI and disappearing subjects, on which we have already commented.

Teachers also compared the relatively lavish resourcing of TVEI courses with that of non-TVEI courses. For example an English teacher in school A speaking of a TVEI resourced media studies course said that:

Last year media studies obtained more resources for 27 children than English for 1200 children. That is ridiculous.

In addition to this uneven distribution of resources between the subjects, he also claimed that whereas there was provision made for INSET on TVEI courses, none at all had been made for English. A similar situation emerged in school O, where a considerable sum of money had been spent on purchasing four CNC lathes for technology classes but where in the science department, particularly in physics, equipment was becoming obsolete or was in short supply. The combined factors of smaller class sizes and privileged resourcing for TVEI in these schools was therefore the source and topic of some degree of tension between TVEI and non-TVEI staff.

Another issue that was a source of potential friction between TVEI and non TVEI staff could be traced to TVEI extra curricular activities for students and INSET for staff: both required cover from either full-time staff or supply teachers. This was a topic that featured prominently in at least seven schools. In school Q for example, non-TVEI staff commented on the fact that TVEI students 'were always out of school' engaging in surveys, residentials, or work experience. This led to some anxiety in 'academic' subjects such as English and mathematics, where teachers felt that TVEI students were missing out on large sections of the syllabus and would therefore have to 'catch up'. As a consequence of these activities and TVEI INSET, cover often had to be provided for classes. This gave rise to two related issues: that of cover itself and the quality of it. Teachers in these seven schools commented on the *extent* to which cover was required for TVEI classes from non-TVEI teachers, and secondly, that such cover in terms of its *quality*, particularly if it was supply cover, was often reduced to child-minding. TVEI was seen in these circumstances by non-TVEI teachers as being not only over-funded and privileged, but also parasitical on the school as a whole. It was drawing away much needed teacher time and finance from the general school curriculum. For TVEI teachers this was also a problem. In school M, a TVEI teacher stated that:

> There's a tension between my role as a teacher and a curriculum developer. My teaching has gone to pot . . .

In school C, a TVEI business studies teacher felt that 'I'm more marketable' as a result of TVEI but that TVEI was also 'A load of bloody hassle'. What both these teachers felt acutely, was that because of the extra time they had to devote to curriculum development as a result of being involved in TVEI, their non-TVEI teaching had been adversely affected. [. . .]

The fact that TVEI required extra time and attention from school staff within TVEI was particularly felt by school co-ordinators. Their position best exemplifies this issue of the contradictory demands placed on TVEI teachers in general: that is, at one level they are expected to pioneer and be responsible for the implementation and development of a broad range of new teaching practices and subject content, while also performing their existing teaching and administrative duties within the context of the school as a whole. In order that this could be achieved effectively, most school co-ordinators were on a senior scale or deputy head appointment. This was in recognition of the fact that TVEI, being a major curriculum development, required someone of seniority in the school to over-see it (the only exception here being school B). In school Z, an assistant co-ordinator had been appointed in support of the school co-ordinator, the holder of that post being already a senior teacher with responsibility for developing new GCSE Technology courses within the school. However, school O illustrated the problems which senior staff in schools who were given the role of school co-ordinator faced. The policy of the LEA in which school O was situated was to appoint deputy heads to the role of school co-ordinator (without any remuneration) and as a consequence 'overload' them. The deputy head here felt that because of the already demanding position he was in – 'going to meetings most evenings of the week' – he could not effectively deal with TVEI. As he put it, he felt 'remote from the chalkface'. In school C, the school co-ordinator, who was also director of studies, complained that despite the effort he put into TVEI curriculum development, he felt 'very bitter about the effect it's had on me' and that 'TVEI has done nothing for me at all'. In the project in which school S was situated, the school co-ordinator had been virtually ostracized by senior management within the school. In fact within the project as a whole, the extra pattern of management organization which TVEI had brought with it was generally viewed with some suspicion by other senior staff and management. It would seem appropriate to conclude that school co-ordinators must be given responsibility, authority and remuneration for their work in developing TVEI and where this is not adequately allocated, it might adversely affect TVEI curriculum development.

The fact that TVEI has brought with it not only resources to the classroom and encouraged major curriculum development, but also opened up a potential career route for teachers in terms of promotion, has, as the head of school K said, been 'very, very significant', or, as the head of school N put it, 'it's been a God-send'. The fact that heads of these schools have in most instances been able to offer extra scale points to induce staff to participate in TVEI curriculum development has been a very positive enabling factor in getting TVEI started within schools. We have already noted that this can, potentially, have negative side-effects in creating a TVEI enclave. It can also lead to what the school co-ordinator in school O described to us as 'poaching'. Given that TVEI has established a career route within schools, particularly amongst technology, electronics and IT staff, schools such as school O have found themselves in the position where staff have rapidly advanced their careers within the school as a result of TVEI, been offered a more senior position elsewhere, and left. This clash of career development, being offered more and better opportunities in a different position and school, and a teacher's loyalty to a school has been the cause of some friction within at least half the schools we visited, and indeed was probably more generalized than this finding suggests.

To conclude this section on teachers' attitudes towards TVEI, it is important to mention teachers' perception of the political factors which they saw surrounding the introduction of TVEI. In eight schools, teachers made reference to the haste with which TVEI was introduced. This was particularly resented by school co-ordinators, and senior management who were responsible for buying materials and equipment. Teachers felt that more time should have been allowed for consultation, dissemination of the principles on which TVEI was based as a curriculum initiative, resource selection and allocation, and staff INSET. Many of these teachers felt that the rush to establish TVEI had its cost in the quality and structure of provision made for students. The haste with which TVEI was implemented within these schools also appeared to affect communications, particularly between TVEI schools in a project and between TVEI and non-TVEI staff.

In half the schools we visited some staff viewed TVEI as a specifically vocational *training* initiative and *not* as being educational. This was a concern held particularly by non-TVEI staff where they counterpoised TVEI with liberal education: that is, they viewed TVEI's vocational emphasis as being a threat to liberal traditions and values in schools and especially the comprehensive principle. For example, the head of languages in school G criticized TVEI's vocational orientation because it had, by virtue of this fact, devalued the aesthetic, literary and creative aspects of the curriculum. The hidden curriculum for him and the head of school U was that humanities and the liberal-comprehensive ideal of developing the total attributes of the individual were to be subordinated to a narrowly technical and vocational curriculum producing equally narrow minded students. To this extent, teachers who expressed this opinion in schools perceived TVEI as producing an imbalance in the curriculum. However, it was common in the same schools to be told that although MSC provided the finance and framework for TVEI, many of the aims and objectives of TVEI had already been practised by teachers within schools for years. There was nothing 'new' about TVEI in this sense, they argued; it was merely TVEI taking credit for what they had been doing for several years, or what they had wanted to do but did not have the money or resources to do.

## Conclusion

In this chapter we have examined various aspects of the introduction of TVEI in the 26 schools. We have attempted to discover what effects TVEI has had on the organization of the curriculum and on staff. [. . .]

Involvement in TVEI has revitalized many teachers giving them opportunities to teach in new ways, participate in curriculum development and improve their professional knowledge and skill through INSET. The workload has been heavy, the rewards have sometimes seemed small and issues such as the provision of adequate and suitable supply cover remain to be tackled. Nevertheless, most teachers have thrown themselves into TVEI with gusto.

These are very considerable benefits, but there have been costs as well. For far too many teachers their introduction to TVEI was to an initiative, often imposed on the school, which had to be accommodated within a short space of time. First impressions are important and for many teachers their first impressions of TVEI were of a rushed and poorly managed scheme. As Pamela Young has pointed out:

> Thus once the decision was made [to adopt TVEI] things happened quickly – too quickly for effective implementation. Or, more precisely, planning for implementation was not recognised as an important component requiring more advanced attention.
>
> (Young, 1986, p. 60)

There is also much evidence that non-TVEI teachers and students have resented the additional resources with which TVEI students and teachers have been favoured. Many heads have attempted to minimize these enclave effects by spreading TVEI resources widely within their schools but even where this policy has been followed differentials have remained between areas of the curriculum.

There are two responses to complaints about the divisiveness of TVEI. First, it must be remembered that TVEI was a pilot scheme and this implies that a group of schools and students will be singled out for special attention. To attack this is to attack the very notion of a pilot. Second, TVEI did not create struggles for resources and status in schools. Such struggles are in the nature of organizational life. What TVEI has done in some schools has been to provide more resources and improve the status of traditionally low–status subjects such as craft, design and technology (CDT), business studies, catering and child care.

[. . .]

The data have confirmed our impression, reported in our interim reports (Barnes *et al.* 1987), that most schools have not engaged in major changes in the structure of their curriculum as a result of TVEI. Over half of the schools have contained TVEI within their existing structures. Let us again remember that TVEI was a pilot scheme affecting only a minority of fourth and fifth year students. It has perhaps been unrealistic to expect many schools to go through a major curriculum upheaval under these circumstances. Despite this a number of schools have experimented with new ways of organizing the 14–16 curriculum and there is evidence that many of these experiments have taken root. In particular there have been a number of examples of schools developing modular approaches. Modular systems have appeared to increase motivation among students and in some schools offer considerably greater choice to students than does the conventional two year options system. But it is important to remember that there is no necessary connection between the structure of the curriculum and the quality of teaching and learning experiences. Modular systems, block timetables and consortium arrangements may make certain teaching and learning situations easier to achieve but they do not guarantee that changes in content, pedagogy and assessment occur.

## References

Barnes, D., Johnson, G., Jordan, S., Layton, D., Medway, P. and Yeomans, D. (1987) *The TVEI Curriculum 14–16. An Interim Report Based on Case Studies in Twelve Schools.* London, Manpower Services Commission.

Saunders, M. (1986) 'The innovative enclave: unintended effects of TVEI implementation', in R. Fiddy and I. Stronach (eds) *TVEI Working Papers 1.* Norwich, CARE, University of East Anglia.

Young, P. (1986) 'An example of the management of change', in C. McCabe (ed.) *TVEI: The Organization of the Early Years of the Technical and Vocational Education Initiative.* Clevedon, Multilingual Matters.

# 13

# The management of pastoral care: a qualitative perspective

**Peter Ribbins**

## The 'conventional wisdom' and its alternatives

Much of the earliest literature on 'pastoral care' dating from the 1960s and early 1970s was dominated by practising managers within secondary schools who sought general principles based upon their own experience. From the work of Blackburn (1975), Haigh (1975), Marland (1974) and others, it is possible to identify what came to be called a 'conventional wisdom' in which the development of institutionalized pastoral care in the comprehensive school was seen as unproblematic and as having thoroughly worthwhile consequences for the individual, the school and for society as a whole. (For a summary of this view see Best and Ribbins, 1985.)

In the later 1970s this view began to be challenged by Best *et al.* (1977; 1980), Lang (1977) and others. [. . . They] questioned whether the wholly favourable impression of pastoral care presented by the conventional wisdom squared all that well with their own experiences as teachers or as teachers of teachers. On the basis of this experience they proposed explanations of the growth and functioning of pastoral care structures and processes which were much more sceptical and which had much more to do with the needs of teachers than with those of pupils (see Best and Ribbins, 1985).

Furthermore, [they] argued that the conventional wisdom failed to take account of the actual meanings which people in schools attach to what normally counted as 'pastoral care', and also failed to take account of the motives and interests of the different groups involved in the creation and operation of pastoral care structures. These, it was suggested, could be explored by focusing on the kinds of things which constituted problems for the relevant groups involved and by using qualitative methods of investigation.

This has meant looking at the perspectives and styles which teachers adopt to the pastoral dimension of their roles, how they perceive and enact those roles, and how they interpret and work the structures and processes through which institutionalized pastoral care is delivered. [. . .]

## The organization and management of pastoral care

I should like to illustrate the use of a qualitative approach to investigation by examining two related issues which have major implications for the management of pastoral care and which have received a good deal of attention – the first is concerned with structure (the 'pastoral–academic split'), and the second with process (the organization of the system of pupil referral within secondary schools). In doing this I shall draw mainly upon evidence from the case of Rivendell school, supplemented as necessary with, examples taken from Revelstone school. Before I turn to this perhaps I should say something about the two schools. They are both fairly large (1,200+) co-educational, 11–18 comprehensive schools located in the south-east and the Midlands respectively.

The dangers of institutionalizing artificial distinctions between the curricular and non-curricular aspects of the school worried a number of teachers at all the schools I have researched. This is a concern which has been the subject of a growing debate within the literature on the issue of the 'pastoral–academic split' (Best and Ribbins, 1983). At Rivendell various strategies were used by different heads to minimize the possible detrimental effects of such a split. The first head, 'Mr Barber', sought to implement a policy of curriculum development justified in terms of the school's fundamental task to educate the 'whole child'. Since this was central to his thinking, the objectives of pastoral care were broadly conceived as a concern for the total welfare of the child and, as such, not in any real sense seen as separate from the kind of total experience the curriculum ought to provide. To achieve this, pastoral, academic and behavioural responsibilities were combined in the same people:

> Heads of House were also Heads of Subject Departments and also had responsibility for a particular year located in a particular area of the building. Major responsibilities for all aspects of the child's welfare were thus concentrated in the hands of a small number of senior staff. Although a formal division existed in the separation of Houses from subject departments, there were strong connections between the two, with staff from the same subject departments being generally members of the same House. Moreover, the forms (tutor groups) were also the teaching groups, and this was justified in terms of making the pastoral and academic an undivided whole. . . . In these ways the Head claimed to create an organic unity.
>
> (Best *et al.*, 1983: 113)

Under the second head, 'Mr Sewell', a policy of rationalization of the organic structure, which was perceived as unclear and unspecified, led to the setting up of a highly complex structure (see Best *et al.*, 1983: 34, 35). In a sense, a 'dual academic and pastoral system' had been institutionalized but within a structure which contained four or even five substructures of authority and differentiation of task within the school. A curricular structure of eight faculties and heads of faculty and some twenty subject departments each with its head of subject, and a non-curricular system of schools-within-schools (lower, upper and sixth with a head and assistant head of lower and upper school and a head of sixth), four houses (each with its head and assistant head of house) and of five years (each with its head of year). Taken separately, each of these structures could be defended on the grounds that it catered for a particular type of pupil need and dealt with a particular type of problem. Problems of the provision and organization of learning situations were essentially a faculty and departmental responsibility, problems of a 'pastoral' nature were the main province of the houses, problems of general control and discipline were the defining task of the schools-within-schools, and problems of 'academic progress' were the particular task of the years. In theory any problem with which a class-teacher or a form tutor could not deal could be referred to the appropriate faculty/department head, house head/assistant house head, head of school/assistant head of school, or year head. As we remarked at the time

> It is fairly easy to think of a justification for such a complex and highly sophisticated set of structures. It can be argued that, together, they represent all the major aspects of the teacher's role as an imparter of knowledge, a supporter and counsellor of children with personal and academic problems, a disciplinarian and custodian of children, a monitor of educational progress, and, finally, as an administrator. The rationale for the system, as more than one teacher remarked, was that it constituted a 'net through which no problem could fall'.
>
> (Best *et al.*, 1983: 46)

Such remarks had considerable rhetorical force, but there were also those who felt that all was not well with the net, particularly in regard to what came to be thought of as the 'dual' structure of years and houses. In particular, many teachers were uncertain about what was involved in the role of the year head and doubted the validity of the distinction between the 'pastoral' concerns of the houses and the 'academic' concerns of the years.

Another reason for lack of confidence in the 'net' was the apparent absence of any systematic relationship between the curricular structure of faculties or departments and the 'non-curricular' systems of houses and years. Except in relatively minor ways, house heads and year heads both seemed to regard the content and organization of the curriculum and its pedagogy as something separate and beyond their legitimate concern or influence. Conversely, some of the faculty heads were amongst the most dismissive critics of the 'dual' structure of houses and years, and of what they saw as the 'burgeoning bureaucracy of pastoral care'. Three main sets of related criticisms emerged. The first of these questioned the relevance, even the reality, of the distinctions the system seemed to entail between 'pastoral', 'academic' and 'disciplinary' problems. Those who took this line, commonly argued, for example, that disciplinary problems could stem from academic ones, or from genuinely pastoral ones, such as family difficulties, while academic performance could be adversely affected by personal problems or disciplinary problems. Ironically, these kinds of views were also likely to be expressed by those who had been appointed to posts of responsibility as house heads, year heads or heads of school:

> Although I am more on the academic side, I don't believe you can distinguish between academic and pastoral, although I have been told that I should.
>
> (head of year)

> The academic problem should go to the form teacher, then the year head. If it is a behaviour problem, then it goes to the head of house, or the assistant head of house. It's very difficult, a behaviour problem may stem from an academic problem or a pastoral problem so that the year staff may pass it on to the house staff, or they may get together on it.
>
> (head of lower school)

The second kind of criticism followed from the first. Thus it was said that, if the sort of overlaps identified above do exist and if it is very difficult to distinguish these problems from each other, this must make for serious difficulties for heads of house and heads of year, and for subject teachers and for form tutors attempting to use the system. The 'dual system' of houses and years was an especial source of confusion and even quite senior and experienced staff sometimes seemed to founder in what was widely seen to be a situation rife with the possibility of demarcation disputes and problems of procedure and protocol as the following remarks from three quite experienced staff show:

> It clashes too much having a dual system. Both positions, that is head of year and head of house, are weakened by the existence of the other. It is not so much that they are in competition, but that there are problems of who you should go to . . .

> I certainly feel that at times it's clumsy, having two alternative systems of pastoral care/discipline, in that it's quite conceivable you tread on somebody's corns because you didn't refer them to them, and you referred them to somebody else.

> Having a vertical and a horizontal system is a mistake and sometimes people get caught between the two. Sometimes people don't know whether to go to the head of house or the head of year.

These kinds of difficulties could be especially serious for the inexperienced teacher, particularly if they were allocated to a year or a house where the pastoral leader was not prepared to make much effort to help them to settle in.

The third set of criticisms concerned the sheer scale of the structural hierarchies to be found at Rivendell – several staff described the school as a 'bureaucratic nightmare'. For some this was true of the structure of the school as a whole, others felt that this was also true of the curricular structure of faculties and subject departments but the greatest number reserved their most forceful comments for the 'dual system' within the non-curricular structure. This was said to create imbalances between subordinate and superordinate positions, foul-ups in communications and referrals, as well as the kinds of problems of role definition and of role conflict discussed above. The following comment by a senior member of staff may be taken to represent a widely held view:

> There are too many chiefs to the point of having no indians. It should not be necessary to have more than 20 people in positions of authority (within the non-curricular structure), and in some schools it is starting to look like everybody is . . . they cease to be teachers and become bureaucrats. Whether you do it vertically or horizontally, it needs to be clear cut. For example, eight or ten people as pastoral heads and deputies, whether as year heads or house heads wouldn't matter much.

As one might expect, many staff began to bypass the formal system or to 'work it' in ways that met their own perceived needs but which had little to do with officially designated procedures as such. As one probationary teacher said of the non-curricular structure:

> I have a pretty decent idea of the outline but some of the intricacies are not too clear to me. I find that I know who to go to to get something done but I don't know their titles and precise positions. I've got enough idea to know who deals with what sort of problem. For example, for class problems I go to the head of house, for discipline problems I go to the form tutor, or, more usually, to the head of that section of the school.

However, simplicity is no absolute guarantee that staff will not try to ignore formal systems when it suits them to do so. They did at Revelstone, where the pastoral system was much simpler. This was admitted by both junior and senior staff, particularly with reference to the 'official' system of referral to which we shall return shortly.

For some staff, the fact that formal structures and processes were sometimes circumvented simply did not matter very much. Rather, they believed that, since all systems were always more or less imperfect, what really matters is the attitudes and commitments of the people who work them. However, for others, the problems that result from intrinsically unsatisfactory systems cannot be so easily discounted. For example, one of the deputy heads at Rivendell took the view that if the pastoral system was being regularly bypassed this did not demonstrate that no system could work, rather what was necessary was that the system itself should be changed. Finally, many staff at Rivendell seemed to believe that much that was worthwhile in both the curricular and the non-curricular activities of the school happened as much in spite of as because of the structures which had been institutionalized there. Some of these spoke of the dangers of setting up artificial distinctions in the organization of the school:

> The main effect of having a horizontal system of years as well as the house system was to create a grey area, such that when there is praise to be given both heads of year and house staff can claim the kudos, but when there are problems both may be able to deny responsibility.

Clearly all was not well with the non-curricular net through which 'no problems could fall'. Regardless of the best intentions of teachers, some pupils and their problems got lost within these grey areas:

> The school's idea of a cross-structure of houses and years is that there is a net to catch people, but in fact things tend to get overlooked. Each person thinks someone else is taking care of it.

A further change of head, 'Mr Lucas', brought further sweeping changes. The discredited 'tripartite' system of houses, years and schools was replaced with a pastoral structure based upon a 'lower school', 'middle school' and 'upper school', each with its own head and assistant head of school. Role descriptions for these staff were set out in a staff handbook, and seemed very much a combination of the duties expected of the heads of house, school and year in the past. The role description for heads of subject departments was laid out in great detail whereas that for heads of faculty was very brief indeed. This, along with the promise that the faculty/department structure would be examined and if necessary revised, signalled a further rationalization in which the subject heads of department would be given greater prominence within the curricular structure and a consequent phasing out of the role of the faculty heads. The motives for these changes can be interpreted in different ways. Their effect was to create structures within the school which were both administratively more simple and which enabled tighter hierarchic control. As Mr Lucas put it:

> The structure has to be much more clearly set out and much simpler. The responsibilities people have must be more clearly set out and the sanctions that can be applied by different people in different positions have to be much more clearly specified.

But these were not the only justifications he offered for the new system which he had implemented. He also claimed to justify it in terms of the contribution it made to overcoming the 'pastoral–academic split' which he felt had been institutionalized under Sewell. As one senior member of staff remarked:

> The head's view, which I don't completely share, is that if you are going to overcome the dichotomy between academic and pastoral care you have to emphasize the academic people as being pastoral. The head of department now has a dual role which reduces the academic–pastoral split, therefore the heads of department underpin the heads of school.

This 'enhanced' role for the head of subject department could be seen in the part they were to play in a new process of referral which he introduced at the time (Figure 13.1). Although Mr Lucas defended the changes he had made in terms of the contribution which they made to overcoming the 'pastoral–academic split', the 'pastoral' aspect he seems to have emphasized has much to do with 'discipline'. This interpretation was shared by a number of senior staff, not all of whom were hostile to the new system. Thus one commented 'in terms of pastoral, in Mr Lucas's terms, read disciplinary'; and another, a former head of house and a head of school in the new system, when asked what part he saw pastoral care as playing within the school replied, 'Being a buffer state, a discipline state. Pastoral care is another word for discipline'. A head of department, describing what the new system could mean for him, and in particular its referral aspect, put it bluntly:

> [It] puts a premium on incompetence. For example these [referring to a bundle of referral slips] are the forms I have had from one particular teacher this week. Instead of creating his own discipline he has referred to me. The onus of forcing discipline falls on me. . . . What is happening is that the weak teacher is pushing his problems of discipline on to the head of department.

At Rivendell, and to a greater extent at Revelstone, the issue of the 'pastoral–academic split' has given rise to significant conflict between the curricular and the non-curricular systems and their respective subject heads and pastoral leaders. With a pastoral structure of four houses, each with a head and assistant head of house, and an academic structure of subject departments, with one or two quasi faculties such as science (which does not operate as a faculty) and design studies (which does), Revelstone has possessed for a number of years the kind of managerial and professional system at which the latest regime at Rivendell seems to be aiming.

Both house and subject department structures at Revelstone can be traced back to its grammar school origins but as one of the deputies points out:

> Well, of course, in the grammar school days there were houses but they were very much used for sporting and other competitive activities. . . . When we went comprehensive the whole structure of the house system was strengthened . . . by the time I came (in 1969) the 'dual-management system' had been set up. I think there was a quite considerable amount of friction between heads of department, who were well established in the grammar school, and this new system.

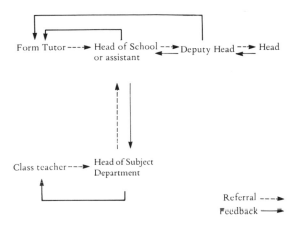

*Source*: Best *et al*. 1983: 51

**Figure 13.1** The new referral process

This was much as the head remembered things. He also recalled an earlier experience:

> When I was at . . . we had enormous arguments between the heads of department and the heads of house as to who was running the show, was the tail wagging the dog? This kind of thing . . . and when I came here there was clearly some bitter feeling between the two.

In the years since then some of these problems, he felt, had to some extent been resolved or, at least, diminished. Thus although the houses 'were given very much greater importance when the comprehensive system came in', since then 'perhaps the emphasis has changed slightly. I have shifted things back a little towards the heads of department because I think the house heads were tending to be regarded as the only people who could keep the place together'. Furthermore,

> I have set things out fairly clearly as to who does what. . . . I have not been aware that there has been a major split. . . . I do not accept that any head of department, as such, does not have any pastoral responsibility. What these may be is not so easy to define. But most heads of department at some time are going to be tutors of certain groups for which they are responsible to a head of house. By the same token every house [head] is responsible to some head of department for his academic work.

For all these reasons he felt that he could 'assume that most of the antipathies which were there at the beginning are not there now. This is not to say that every now and again something does not surface'.

Not all staff share his optimism. One head of house rejected the idea that the house system had ever been in the ascendent. Rather, at Revelstone:

> We put the pastoral side as of less importance than the academic . . . the academic is the strong side of the school and the pastoral side is of less importance. It's the weaker side. Up until the present time this has been agreed upon but there is a wind of change taking place and people are beginning to realize that there are more and more problems.

While he rejected the idea that a significant 'pastoral–academic split' existed at the school, he did think that some of the heads of department did take the view that the school put too much emphasis on pastoral care:

> But those very same people are the first to come running for help . . . [some] are hostile because they can't see any immediate results . . . somebody comes to me and says that little Billy has not been doing any homework this term and what am I going to do about it? Next week they find that the boy is still not doing homework and are critical. They expect immediate action and because it does not happen they assume the system is not working. Also, a lot of them are against pastoral care because they don't want to do it themselves.

Some heads of department were, indeed, very critical of aspects of the house system. As one put it:

> I feel that the pastoral system is weak at this school and it has no reason to be. It is very heavy on scale points, there is a scale four and a scale three in charge of every house. . . . Which in a school of 1,200 kids is far too many. . . . I don't feel that the second houseperson is necessary. I think there is only one strong house [head] . . . he will act on what is told to him. The other three are weak. I have taken discipline problems to them and have realized that the way they have dealt with it is far milder than the way that I have dealt with it before I took it to them. In that case you rarely go back. You need to feel that 'when I have exhausted my resources', I can go on to them. They are the bigger guns . . . there are serious holes in the pastoral structure, consequently there is a tendency for staff to hop over them and go straight to the deputies.

Similar points were made by other staff at Revelstone:

> The most effective houses are 'Milton' followed by 'Keats'. . . . They both have strong house staff who are helpful and support you if you have a discipline problem. . . . The others are less useful.

Such references to pastoral leaders as being more or less 'strong' or 'mild' in the way in which they deal with problems of discipline referred to them, as 'big guns' of the final resort, and to their 'usefulness' or 'helpfulness' as agents of control as the criteria for judging their 'effectiveness' are all characteristic of the discipline-centred perspective. Although more staff at Revelstone were likely to adopt such an attitude than at Rivendell, they were certainly not absent from the latter:

> As far as I can see, there is little in the way of distinguishing features between [the house structure and the year structure]. In individual cases the head of house may be stronger than the head of year, so you go to the former. At least this arrangement gives you two bites at the cherry: if one doesn't pay off the other does.

> When a teacher needs an ultimate deterrent they send the child to me. If it is a serious problem . . . I make contact immediately with the parents. In such cases I contact the house head to put together information on the case. . . . I have a thirty-year reputation as a disciplinarian, known to be firm and fair. The children know it's a 'fair cop'.
>
> (assistant head of upper school)

The last remark shows that some pastoral leaders also shared such attitudes to their responsibilities. These comments quoted from the staff at the two schools lead us to a problem which can be stated as two questions. First, 'What is pastoral care?' Second, 'What do the staff of particular schools actually mean by pastoral care and how do they enact those meanings?' As we have seen from the cases of Rivendell and Revelstone there are no simple answers to these questions. This is a hard but crucial lesson for those concerned with the management of pastoral care. But it is one they must take seriously.

### How can research help the pastoral manager?

As a prescription for what 'pastoral care' ought to be, I have a great deal of sympathy for the kinds of views expressed by the authors of the 'conventional wisdom'. But I am less happy about some of the assumptions they make when they turn to the management of the pastoral care. To put it simply, they all too often start from the wrong place. For an example of this we may turn to Keith Blackburn's (1983) fine and often useful treatise on the role of the pastoral leader. In his introduction he writes 'I have assumed throughout that the school has a developed idea of what will be achieved through its pastoral structures, and that those who hold a post of responsibility have in fact real areas of responsibility and leadership within the school' (1983: 1). The cases of Rivendell, Revelstone, and of other in-depth studies in schools (see 'Bishop McGregor', Burgess, 1983; 'Marshland Castle', Lang, 1982; 'Deanswater', Ribbins and Ribbins, 1986; 'Oakfield', Woods, 1983) all suggest that these are just the kinds of assumptions that ought not to be made.

To summarize, systematic research by 'professional researchers' and by 'practitioners as researchers' calls into question many of the central tenets of the 'conventional wisdom' in so far as these:

1 consider pastoral care as one aspect of the teacher's role on the tacit assumption that teachers are, or ought to be, 'child centred' in all aspects of their role – some clearly are not;
2 fail to take account of the meanings which teachers give to 'pastoral care', the construction they put on formal pastoral structures and processes and their responsibilities within these, and the extent to which the perspectives, styles and ideologies they adopt are essentially 'teacher centred' rather than 'child centred';
3 ignore the importance of teachers' own interests as instructors, disciplinarians and administrators in the perspectives and styles they adopt towards pastoral purposes, systems and practices;
4 ignore the problem of institutionalizing something which may have quite different meanings for different teachers and groups of teachers in the same school.

This last is very much a key idea of the conventional wisdom, that the absence of some kind of formal structure for the provision of 'pastoral care' leaves it to 'blind chance and sentiment'. In short, as Marland (1974) puts it, 'it is really a truism of school planning that what you want to happen must be institutionalised'. This is a popular idea; but what was it which was actually institutionalized at the schools listed above? What, for example, had Rivendell institutionalized? What was written in the staff handbook and in other official documents, and what staff said on public occasions looked a lot like the things to be found in the conventional wisdom. But from our observations and from the things teachers at the school told us, we concluded that:

1 only two of the houses worked really effectively;
2 the role of the head of year was nowhere clearly specified and most teachers were pretty uncertain about what they were expected to do;
3 teachers were therefore frequently uncertain as to whom they should go, or to whom they should refer children with problems;
4 problems of protocol resulted;
5 many teachers used the system for passing on their own problems, particularly as a means of buttressing their own discipline;
6 many teachers complained of communications problems and others that the system was so complicated that some children fell through the net anyway;
7 the form periods were often not used for pastoral care;
8 the 'induction programme' was inadequate and largely served purposes not too obviously connected with the needs of children;
9 there was nothing remotely like a pastoral curriculum;
10 teachers often evaluated the system as an unsatisfactory use of scarce

establishment points, an administrative nightmare, or an ineffectual disciplinary machine;

11 finally, when the system was 'rationalized' the rationale for the reorganization seemed to have little to do with the advantages and disadvantages of alternative systems for the care of children.

We concluded that there was some truth in our own conception of pastoral care systems as having as much to do with the problems of teachers as disciplinarians and as administrators, as with the needs and interests of pupils.

This does not mean that the teachers at Rivendell did not care about children. Many of them did – some superbly! But some of them saw 'caring' through formal-traditional eyes as instructors and disciplinarians. Yet others, and these teachers are quite numerous at Rivendell (and elsewhere), are so preoccupied with their own problems of classroom survival that they seem to have little time or energy left over to think about the individual problems of identity, adjustment and happiness of their pupils.

Finally, what passed for the institutionalization of pastoral care in the form of a highly elaborate 'net' through which no problem could fall, turned out to be a bureaucratic nightmare and an ineffective control hierarchy. When the system was drastically rationalized and simplified it did probably become a more efficient disciplinary instrument but at the cost of being even less successful at meeting the caring needs of children. It is not that there were no caring teachers at Rivendell; rather it is the case that such caring teachers were often caring *despite* the established systems. None the less, in the case of two of the houses and, perhaps, two of the years, the structure did provide a framework in which some effective caring was facilitated. To some extent, it also facilitated the activities of a wonderfully effective school counsellor, although, in his case, much of his success had little to do with the system itself. Finally, the shortfall between the stated objectives of the conventional wisdom – reproduced by senior staff on public occasions and written up in the official documents of the school – and actual practice were considerable. In regard to this school at any rate, the conventional wisdom is used, to a significant extent, for rhetorical purposes.

[. . .]

The following proposals are intended to suggest possible strategies which those seeking to improve the organization and management of pastoral care might consider rather than a detailed recipe appropriate to all needs and circumstances. These suggestions are designed to achieve two main outcomes:

1 To ensure that as many members of the teaching staff as reasonably possible reach a common understanding of the nature of pastoral care and of how it relates to the other facets of a school's provision;

2 To ensure that such an understanding is translated into effective practice through the setting up of appropriate organizational and managerial arrangements.

The Rivendell experience shows clearly that 'without a substantial degree of consensus about what it is that both people and structures are supposed to be doing the opportunities for inefficiency, misunderstanding, tension, conflict, and personal antagonism are enormous' (Best *et al.*, 1983: 282). Once some agreement on this has been achieved it is necessary to deliver this through structures appropriate to such purposes. Unnecessary complexity may be a barrier but one should not be fooled into thinking that complexity alone was the cause of Rivendell's problems. 'Rather, the system was mystifying and counter-productive because it was created in the absence of a clear understanding of precisely how different aspects of the school were to operate' (Best *et al.*, 1983: 282).

Improving the character of pastoral provision will raise different problems in different schools and in different contexts. The plan of attack, for example, of the senior staff of a new school might be both different and easier than those in a long established school. With these qualifications in mind, the following sequence of seven phases for the improvement of the management of pastoral care is proposed:

1   An initial and substantial period of discussion and consultation involving as many staff as possible aimed at achieving as high a level of consensus as practicable as to what pastoral care is and how it ought to be achieved.
2   In such planning or reorganizing of the pastoral provision of a school it is necessary to consult and listen carefully to the views of individual teachers and groups of teachers in order to be clear about what they expect and want from the various facets of the school's organization.
3   Those concerned with the management of pastoral care at the level of the school as a whole, and to some extent with the management of pastoral divisions as well, might find it helpful to compile a list of what it is they want their pastoral care provision to achieve, and also a second list of what it is that other teachers expect the pastoral system to do for them.
4   A great deal of thought needs to be given to the geographical and social conditions of the school, and to the relationships between teachers and teachers and between teachers and pupils in the setting up of appropriate pastoral structures and systems. Hard decisions will also be needed in determining the scope and scale of the changes to be attempted.
5   Change for the sake of change has little to recommend it. Those who seek to improve the provision of an existing or established pastoral system at the level of the school as a whole or of some part of it should undertake a careful evaluation of what already exists. At the level of the whole school this may entail examining a wide range of its pastoral, academic, disciplinary and administrative arrangements. Such an evaluation would take as its point of departure the recognition of the fact that aims and functions are not the same thing. The prospective innovator would need both to assess existing arrangements in terms of stated objectives and to establish as precisely as

possible what functions these existing arrangements are performing as a prelude to any worthwhile change.

6 Once decisions are made about the kinds of changes which are necessary the system to be aimed for should be the simplest which will achieve the stated objectives. But however 'simple' it is, it must not be assumed that teachers or pupils will necessarily understand it. Effort will have to be put in to ensure that this happens.

7 Finally, schools need to devise some strategy for ongoing evaluation. Successful achievement of some of the earlier phases are a necessary prelude to this exercise. Thus if a clear understanding of what is being attempted under the heading of pastoral care, some statement of specific objectives however difficult it is to give them expression, and some set of agreed performance indicators do not exist it is hard to see what useful purposes would be served by such an evaluation or by what criteria it should be accomplished. Without these things, of course, the existence of effective and worthwhile pastoral structures and systems within a school would be a matter of chance and good fortune.

### References

Best, R. and Ribbins, P. (1983) 'Rethinking the pastoral–academic split', *Pastoral Care in Education*, **1**(1); 11–18.

Best, R. and Ribbins, P. (1985) 'Research in education: pastoral care in the comprehensive school' (unpublished paper).

Best, R., Jarvis, C. and Ribbins, P. (1977) 'Pastoral care: concept and process', *British Journal of Education Studies*, **25**(2), 124–35.

Best, R., Jarvis, C. and Ribbins, P. (1980) *Perspectives on Pastoral Care*, London, Heinemann.

Best, R., Ribbins, P., Jarvis, C. and Oddy, D. (1983) *Education and Care*, London, Heinemann.

Blackburn, K. (1975) *The Tutor*, London, Heinemann.

Blackburn, K. (1983) *Head of House/Head of Year*, Oxford, Blackwell.

Burgess, R. (1983) *Experiencing Comprehensive Education*, London, Methuen.

Haigh, G. (1975) *Pastoral Care*, London, Pitman.

Lang, P. (1977) 'It's easier to punish us in small groups', *Times Educational Supplement*, 6 May, p. 17.

Lang, P. (1982) 'Pastoral care: concern or contradiction?', MA thesis (unpublished), University of Warwick.

Marland, M. (1974) *Pastoral Care*, London, Heinemann.

Ribbins, P. and Ribbins, P. (1986) 'Developing a design for living course at 'Deanswater' Comprehensive School', *Pastoral Care in Education*, **4**(1), 23–37.

Woods, E. (1983) 'The structure and practice of pastoral care at Oakfield School', M.Ed. dissertation (unpublished), University of Birmingham.

14

# Towards a collegiate approach to curriculum management in primary and middle schools

**Mike Wallace**

The purpose of this chapter is to explore how the process of management development may assist the professional staff of primary and middle schools in moving towards collegiate management of the curriculum. It is argued that HMI and other informed professionals have put forward a model of good management practice which appears not to have been implemented in many schools because it contains certain contradictions. Some ways are suggested of facilitating its implementation.

### The official model of good practice

In England and Wales during recent years the way in which professional staff in schools organize the curriculum has been subjected to the criticism of HMI, the DES, the Welsh Office and other informed groups within the education service. Implicit within the plethora of policy statements, surveys, inquiries and inspection reports lies a model of good management practice. Evidence of the 'official' model is contained in positive statements and may be inferred from criticisms expressed about schools. A broadly consistent view is set out in, for example, major national surveys conducted by HMI (DES, 1978; 1979; 1982a; 1983a; 1985a; Welsh Office, 1978); HMI inspection reports published since 1983 and their summaries (DES, 1984a; 1984b; 1985b); other surveys and occasional papers by HMI (e.g. DES, 1977; 1980a; 1982b; Welsh Office, 1984; 1985); official publications informed by HMI reports (e.g. DES, 1980b; 1981; 1983b; 1985c; 1986); the reports of national (Bullock, 1975; Cockcroft, 1982) and local committees of inquiry (e.g. ILEA, 1984; 1985); and the working papers of the Schools Council (1981; 1983). In essence, good curriculum management is seen as a process where all professional staff participate actively in negotiating an agreed curriculum and contribute jointly to planning, implementing and evaluating its delivery (including evaluating and giving feedback upon each other's performance as managers and class-teachers). Where the model is implemented, it is held to be a contributory factor in ensuring that pupils receive a desirable, consistent and progressive educational experience.

The model is to some extent consistent with the principles of 'collegial authority', defined by Lortie (1964) as the form of authority in which professional equals govern their affairs through democratic procedures. According to the sources mentioned, managerial roles and tasks should be shared out among professional colleagues who work collaboratively through various consultation procedures. While a management hierarchy exists, [. . .] there is a degree of overlap between the spheres of responsibility which is very different from the models of 'line-management' prevalent outside education (e.g. Handy, 1981).

The greatest overlap between responsibilities occurs in primary and middle schools, where most teachers operate in a range of curriculum areas where they are not designated as a specialist or expert, most significantly in their role as teachers responsible for a class. This arrangement of overlapping responsibilities may be interpreted as approximating to a model of management based on principles of collegiality.

Figure 14.1 is a simple framework for analysing the official interpretation of good practice. Pupil learning is influenced by individual teachers' classroom performance in delivering the curriculum within the climate of the school. The latter term refers to the general conditions surrounding learning which reflect the values of the various groups of people within the school as expressed in, for example, expectations about pupil behaviour (inside and outside the classroom) and about levels of achievement. Teachers' actions are influenced, in turn, by how all members of the professional staff organize themselves so as to bring about effective teaching within a climate supportive of learning. Organization is achieved through management tasks performed by individuals occupying various roles. Incumbents of particular roles are expected to act in certain ways in carrying out tasks associated with the areas of school life for which they are responsible. The key role which affects management of the curriculum is that of the headteacher, who is legally responsible for the day-to-day work of the school. Heads' behaviour in retaining or sharing the tasks of curriculum management has a bearing upon colleagues' performance of their roles. As the 'gatekeepers' of their schools, heads respond to various external influences, most immediately through the governors. Influence runs in two directions since the response of pupils and of heads and teachers in their class-room management roles has a bearing upon the actions of others at each level.

In the official documents good practice is seen to be based upon the clear differentiation of roles within the professional staff. Individuals occupy two or more roles, some of which, such as the leader of a group of classes, appear

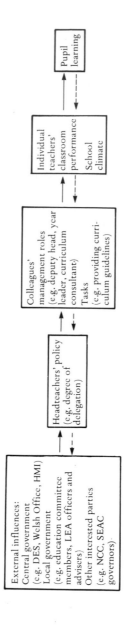

**Figure 14.1**  Management of the curriculum at school level

**Table 14.1** Roles, curriculum responsibilities and associated tasks

| Role | Curriculum responsibility | Major task area |
|---|---|---|
| Headteacher | Overall responsibility for curriculum management | Consulting with colleagues<br>Developing staff through structure of delegated responsibilities<br>Clarifying roles and tasks through job descriptions<br>Managing the staff development policy<br>Evaluating pupils' progress and the work of professional staff |
| Deputy headteacher | Leading staff in formulation of curriculum policy | Arranging for curriculum planning<br>Supporting curriculum consultants<br>Devising timetable |
| Leader of groups of classes | Co-ordinating day-to-day work of a group of classes | Co-ordinating teaching within and between year groups<br>Liaising with other schools |
| Teacher/ tutor | Induction of probationary teachers and oversight of staff development | Guiding probationary teachers within curriculum policies<br>Managing staff development policy |
| Curriculum consultant | Oversight throughout the school for an area of the curriculum | Planning a programme of work<br>Consulting colleagues during planning<br>Organizing study groups<br>Initiating dialogue during implementation<br>Giving demonstration lessons and working alongside colleagues<br>Procuring resources<br>Observing classes or analysing test results and evaluating colleagues' work<br>Arranging school-based INSET<br>Liaising with other schools |
| General class or specialist teacher | Teaching the agreed curriculum | Working according to guidelines<br>Using agreed resources<br>Contributing to planning and consultation procedure<br>Evaluating pupils' progress |

only in larger schools. Each role carries responsibilities associated with the curriculum, achieved through specific tasks. These tasks are held to contain both a content dimension, in so far as individuals should engage in certain activities, and a process dimension – an idea of how the activities should be carried out using certain skills. The roles, responsibilities and tasks outlined in Table 14.1 are mentioned in one or more of the official guidelines; there appear to be no major inconsistencies between statements in different documents. Particular importance is attached to the contribution of curriculum consultants as subject specialists or advisers to their colleagues.

### A gulf between the model and reality

There is ample evidence quoted within the documents mentioned and available from other sources (e.g. Bornett, 1980; Rushby and Richards, 1982; Williams, 1982; PSRDG, 1983; Rodger, 1983; Campbell, 1984; Robinson, 1983; ILEA, 1986) to suggest that, in perhaps the majority of primary and middle schools, the model has not been fully implemented. Some incumbents of each role are criticized in this literature: heads often fail to: delegate management responsibility, set up procedures for curriculum planning or give colleagues enough time to carry out their delegated management activities. Deputy heads are frequently excluded from sharing the overall management of the school, to the detriment of those who are preparing for future headship. Leaders of groups of classes may be unclear how their sphere of influence articulates with that of curriculum consultants. The latter are rarely given the support necessary to enable them to take the initiative in supporting their colleagues. Many class-teachers lack the expertise necessary to teach a broad curriculum effectively. Many heads do not delegate enough and their colleagues do not engage in the process of communication implied by the collegiate model of curriculum management.

HMI reports indicate that it is possible to implement the model and research (ILEA 1986) suggests that it is associated with effective pupil learning. If we accept the plausibility of the model, it is important to ask why it has consistently proved difficult to implement.

### Unpacking collegiate management

From a management perspective, it is possible to identify within the model several tensions or contradictions related to the way the professional staff are expected to organize themselves so as to manage the curriculum effectively. 'Good practice' is more complex than it might initially appear.

First, there is considerable overlap between the curriculum responsibilities accorded to the various roles. All members of professional staff (except perhaps probationary teachers) are expected to carry out at least two roles, one or more of which entails influencing the work of colleagues. For example, the House of Commons Education, Science and Arts Committee (1986) recommends that the requirement for heads to teach pupils should be established in legislation and suggests that most heads should act as co-ordinator for one aspect of the school's work. If the logic of the model is carried through, conflict may arise between overlapping responsibilities carried out by different people (or occasionally by the same person). Where consensus exists over the shape of the curriculum, such tensions will not be apparent; but when people hold different views, the issue arises over who has the right to define what should actually take place during the processes of planning, implementation and evaluation. It is widely recognized in middle schools that those with 'horizontal' responsibility for a year group and those with 'vertical' responsibility for an area of the curriculum throughout the school must negotiate the degree of influence each is to hold over the curriculum, occasionally giving rise to conflict (e.g. Bornett, 1980).

Second, potential tension is also embedded in the relationship between the roles of curriculum consultant and class-teacher. Many teachers expect a high degree of autonomy over the delivery of the curriculum in their classrooms, yet their professional judgement may conflict with that of the consultant. Campbell (1984: 353) gives an example of a curriculum con-sultant responsible for language who experienced strain in her role because she perceived that working alongside colleagues, advising them and moni-toring the progress of the curriculum policy throughout the school would be perceived by her colleagues as 'inspecting' the quality of their response to the language policy. She preferred to avoid potential conflict by waiting for staff to seek advice.

Third, it is only since the revised salary scales were introduced in the Teachers' Pay and Conditions Act of 1987 that the salary structure has come to reflect the management structure of schools (Wallace, 1986a). Prior to that, the number of posts available that carried salary scale 2 or above was dictated by the size of the school and the age range of the pupils. The number of these posts did not necessarily coincide with the school's management structure. Consequently, 'anomalies' were common: for example, Jefferson (1984) mentions several cases of joint curriculum responsibility including a situation where curriculum development in mathematics was shared between two teachers, one on scale 1 and the other on scale 3. In smaller schools, teachers often have more than one responsibility in order to cover curriculum and organizational areas. The salary structure has been revised but most of the roles set out in Table 14.1 continue to exist. Many 'middle management' roles fall to teachers on the main salary scale, only some of whom receive an incentive allowance.

Fourth, in the literature there are few if any accounts of tension between the headteachers (or deputies) in their class-teaching roles and curriculum consultants or leaders of groups of classes. Yet according to the logic of the model, when headteachers are undertaking their regular class-teaching they come under the jurisdiction of the curriculum consultant for the area in which they are teaching, and in larger schools they may also be working with pupils within the influence of the leader of those classes. It is possible that in small schools some of the heads' teaching lies within the sphere of influence of teachers on the main scale who are acting as curriculum consultants. According to the official model, these teachers might be recently trained and well versed in new ideas on curriculum content and pedagogy. Are such teachers likely to feel comfortable in asking to observe heads' classwork so as to evaluate their teaching performance? The model may not have been implemented in many cases because the hierarchy of curriculum influence contradicts the formal hierarchy supported in recent years by differential salaries.

Fifth, problems related to overlapping roles are expressed in the associated tasks: the boundaries of responsibilities must be negotiated at the level of quite detailed activities. For instance, according to the official model, curriculum consultants are expected to procure resources for their colleagues to use. It is debatable who is to prepare resources once they have arrived in school.

Sixth, the task of evaluating the curriculum is potentially highly sensitive. Some years ago, HMI stated that holders of posts of special responsibility should assess the effectiveness of the guidance and resources they provide, and this may involve visiting other classes in the school to see the work in progress (DES, 1978). Many teachers do not find this task amenable – whether as curriculum consultants (PSRDG, 1983; Rodger, 1983) or as year leaders (Robinson, 1983). It is not clear how many headteachers observe, evaluate, and give feedback to colleagues. Such action may be seen to transgress teachers' rightful classroom autonomy as professionals. Yet unless steps are taken to discover whether an agreed curriculum has been implemented in the way that was intended by the person responsible, or whether there have been unanticipated consequences, there is no guarantee that curriculum guidelines will actually influence practice.

Finally, it is apparent that achievement of the tasks of curriculum management recognized within the official model requires a considerable amount of time to be set aside during the school day. HMI has noted this necessity on many occasions (e.g. DES, 1986). Assigning time depends upon various factors including headteachers' and colleagues' perception of the need, staffing levels which are influenced by national and local government policies, and LEA policies for provision of supply cover. Southworth (1985) points out that many primary school heads are frequently forced to act as supply teachers, to the detriment of the management aspects of their work. Some proponents of the official model may not have understood the amount of time needed to manage the curriculum management process – the dialogue required to plan, negotiate, introduce, implement and evaluate what, for the staff of many schools, is a new way of working together, contradicting many deeply ingrained habits and deeply held beliefs, according to a sophisticated and complex model.

In sum, the new way of working presupposed in the model appears often to have been implemented at a superficial level. In many schools the professional staff appears to go through the motions of collegiate management without integrating the full implications of the model into everyday practice – a situation of innovation without change. Many heads seem to make what Lortie (1969) calls 'low constraint decisions': it is tacitly accepted that colleagues have considerable choice in practice over the extent to which they implement formally agreed policies, and it is mutually understood that there will be no follow-up to check that decisions are actually put into effect. Moreover, there are different zones where those with formal authority to make decisions are perceived to have the necessary power in practice. It is generally accepted that curriculum consultants may produce guidelines and procure resources, but monitoring colleagues' work and commenting upon their pedagogy tends to lie outside their decision-making zone. Through reliance on low-constraint decisions and variable zoning, decision-makers avoid the vulnerability which could stem from colleagues' reactions in sensitive areas.

### Collegiate management: nightmare or worthwhile innovation?

To many managers outside education, the collegiate model would probably appear to be a nightmare – too many overlapping fingers in the management pie! But shared management accords with the value of collaboration associated with teaching as a profession (Hoyle, 1975), although collegiality is limited by heads' legal authority for the work of their schools and differential salaries currently awarded for senior levels of management responsibility (Hoyle, 1986). There is evidence, largely from North America, that schools which practise a broadly collegiate style of management are effective in implementing all kinds of curriculum and organizational innovations. On the basis of a synthesis of the literature, Fullan (1985: 400–4) has identified four factors that underlie successful school improvement efforts:

1 a feel for the complexity, turbulence and demands of the improvement process on the part of the leadership
2 an explicit guiding value system which favours collegiality, clear rules, genuine caring about individuals and commitment to examination of detail
3 intense interaction and communication which provide positive pressure and support and give rise to new understanding
4 collaborative planning and implementation within schools and among those involved in their support.

These factors have much in common with the collaborative process by which the incumbents of various roles are expected to achieve their tasks within the official conception of collegiate management outlined in earlier sections of this chapter.

If the model is broadly accepted in principle as a means of improving pupil learning through a process which accords with professional values, we may usefully explore further how schools which do not practise collegiate management might work towards that aim. It seems that each person involved must come to understand what is entailed, know how to perform the necessary tasks with skill and tact, value collegiality and develop a positive attitude towards learning to work in this way. As Fullan (1982) identified, attitude change is particularly difficult to bring about. These analytic categories of conceptual knowledge, skills, values and attitude cannot, in the view of the present writer, be tackled sequentially in reality. Activities may, however, focus upon particular aspects of necessary knowledge, skills, values or attitudes while implicitly helping to develop others. From personal experience it seems valuable for staff to develop together:

1  awareness of individuals' educational values
2  acceptance of the need to agree upon school aims
3  clarity about rights, responsibilities and their boundaries in respect of each other
4  acceptance that people are likely to have different, and possibly conflicting, interests
5  understanding that different perceptions of the same situation are likely to exist – no one has a monopoly on truth
6  acceptance of the need therefore to give and receive constructive evaluation and feedback
7  specific skills needed to carry out tasks effectively
8  mutual trust and respect
9  willingness to give and take in order to achieve consensus or to implement an agreed compromise once majority agreement has been obtained.

The implementation strategy for the development implied by this innovation is likely to take a long time, since the people involved, the challenges they face and the experience upon which they draw are continually changing. It would be unwise to regard the model as a 'blueprint for perfection' as experience suggests that any innovation becomes modified in the light of the implementation attempt through mutual adaptation (Dalin and Rust, 1983). The model is merely what the term 'model' implies – a simplified vision which gives us something to aim for.

### Management development

A strategy that may support the joint development process is conceived by the National Development Centre for School Management Training as 'management development', or that part of staff development concerned with those who have, or aspire towards management responsibility. In essence, it is 'the process whereby the management function of an organization becomes performed with increasing effectiveness' (Bolam, 1986: 261). This definition implies that individual 'manager development' is organized so that, over time, those with or aspiring towards management responsibility develop in such a way that the organization as a whole develops. In order to ensure that co-ordinated management development takes place it is necessary for each school to develop a management development policy and associated programme of activities as part of its concern for staff development. A review of individual needs is conducted, through appraisal interviews or a staff questionnaire, for example. These needs are balanced with group and school-wide needs, identified by the headteacher or by participative means such as a school self-evaluation exercise. Once priorities are established, suitable activities are selected, implemented and evaluated, leading to the identification of new needs. Within the wide range of activities more or less closely related to the normal job available (see Wallace, 1986b) there are several which seem to be particularly appropriate for promoting a collegiate approach to curriculum management, including:

1 an exercise in role, responsibility and task clarification through negotiation of job descriptions
2 training in specific skills, such as active listening, counselling and assertiveness
3 practice in carrying out structured classroom observation and review procedures
4 a team-building exercise to help staff members to articulate their views and feelings and to promote mutual trust
5 school-based, in-service workshops organized by curriculum consultants
6 opportunities to try out other roles in the school (see Wallace 1985)
7 self-development exercises designed to raise individuals' awareness of their personal values and their assumptions about colleagues
8 development of critical friendships for mutual and confidential support
9 shadowing exercises involving observing colleagues and giving feedback upon their management performance
10 techniques such as brainstorming or the use of flipcharts which encourage participation in meetings
11 evaluation of staff meetings
12 school-wide monitoring of the use of each person's time
13 organization development activities to improve the school's ability for problem-solving (e.g. Schmuck and Runkel, 1985).

For management development to be effective in all schools within an LEA, it is necessary for the needs identified by schools to be matched with those relating to the LEA's policy. LEA policies may include curriculum initiatives such as home language teaching or equal opportunities in physical education whose implementation must be managed by staff in schools. They may also refer directly to management concerns: forming clusters of primary schools or the preparation of deputy heads for a possible headship, for example. Therefore, it is also necessary for a management development policy and programme for schools to be developed at LEA level within its framework for staff development. Management development needs of school staff must be identified in relation to LEA policies and according to groups at similar points in their career across the teaching force, such as newly appointed headteachers. Surveys of LEA advisers' informed opinion, questionnaires sent to schools or the development of a data base containing details of teachers' individual career stages throughout the LEA are among the methods that may be employed to identify these needs. The LEA's management development policy and a programme may be articulated with that of the schools through a consultative process such as a scheme of bids for support or a joint committee representing schools and the LEA so that priorities for meeting needs may be established and activities designed within available resources, implemented and evaluated (see McMahon and Bolam, 1987).

One priority for LEAs may be to promote a collegiate approach to curriculum management in primary and middle schools. It will be necessary to identify the needs of individuals, groups and whole schools across the LEA by the various means outlined and to develop a suitable programme of activities, possibly including financial support for the school-based activities listed earlier. LEAs are required by central government to articulate a policy and programme of in-service training for their teaching force (DES, 1985b). Management development forms a part of that policy and programme within the framework of the LEA training grants arrangements.

[. . .] The House of Commons Education, Science and Arts Committee recommended that there should be additional primary teachers to enable schools to benefit both from additional curriculum expertise and from more flexible staffing with more teachers than registration classes. LEA arrangements for in-service training coupled with the influx of extra teachers if these were to materialize would provide a golden opportunity for LEAs to promote collegiate management in primary and middle schools. We are in a period of rapid change as the government implements its radical programme for educational reform. Heads and staff have to manage the implementation of multiple innovations – from a national curriculum with regular testing, through new conditions of service to local financial management in larger schools. Since each of these innovations has implications for managing the curriculum in schools in the primary sector, the government's programme suggests that developing collegiality as a means of managing change is now a matter of urgency.

## References

Bolam, R. (1986) 'The National Development Centre for School Management Training', in E. Hoyle and A. McMahon (eds) *The Management of Schools*, London, Kogan Page.

Bornett, C. (1980) 'Staffing in middle schools: the roots and routes of hierarchy', in A. Hargreaves and L. Tickle (eds) *Middle Schools*, London, Harper & Row.

Bullock, Sir A. (1975) *A Language for Life*, Report of a Committee of Inquiry chaired by Sir Alan Bullock, London, HMSO.

Campbell, R. J. (1984) 'In-school development: the role of the curriculum post-holder', *School Organization*, **4**(4), 345–57.

Cockroft, W. H. (1982) *Mathematics Counts*, Report of a Committee of Inquiry chaired by Sir William Cockcroft, London, HMSO.

Dalin, P. and Rust, V. (1983) *Can Schools Learn?*, Windsor, NFER–Nelson.

DES (1977) *Ten Good Schools: A Secondary School Enquiry*, London, HMSO.

DES (1978) *Primary Education in England*, London, HMSO.

DES (1979) *Aspects of Secondary Education in England*, London, HMSO.

DES (1980a) *A View of the Curriculum*, HMI series: Matters for Discussion, London, HMSO.

DES (1980b) *A Framework for the School Curriculum*, London, HMSO.

DES (1981) *The School Curriculum*, London, HMSO.

DES (1982a) *Education 5 to 9: An Illustrative Survey of 80 First Schools in England*, London, HMSO.

DES (1982b) *The New Teacher in School*, London, HMSO.

DES (1983a) *9–13 Middle Schools*, London, HMSO.

DES (1983b) *Teaching Quality*, London, HMSO.

DES (1984a) *Education Observed*, London, DES.

DES (1984b) *Education Observed 2*, London, DES.

DES (1985a) *Education 8–12 in Combined and Middle Schools*, London, HMSO.

DES (1985b) *Education Observed 3*, London, DES.

DES (1985c) *Better Schools*, Cmnd 9469, London, HMSO.

DES (1986) *Report by Her Majesty's Inspectors on the Effects of Local Authority Expenditure Policies on Education Provision in England – 1985*, London, DES.

Fullan, M. (1982) 'Research into educational innovation', in H. L. Gray (ed.) *The Management of Educational Institutions*, Lewes, Falmer Press.

Fullan, M. (1985) 'Change processes and strategies at the local level', *Elementary School Journal*, **85**(3), 391–421.

Handy, C. (1981) *Understanding Organizations*, 2nd edn, Harmondsworth, Penguin.

House of Commons Education, Science and Arts Committee (1986) *Achievement in Primary Schools*, London, HMSO.

Hoyle, E. (1975) 'Professionality, professionalism and control in teaching', in V. Houghton, R. McHugh and C. Morgan (eds) *Management in Education*, London, Ward Lock Educational.

Hoyle, E. (1986) *The Politics of School Management*, London, Hodder & Stoughton.

ILEA (1984) *Improving Secondary Schools*, Report of the Committee of Inquiry chaired by D. Hargreaves, London, Inner London Education Authority.

ILEA (1985) *Improving Primary Schools*, Report of the Committee of Inquiry chaired by N. Thomas, London, Inner London Education Authority.

ILEA (1986) *The Junior School Project*, Summary of Main Report, London, Inner London Education Authority Research and Statistics Branch.

Jefferson, C. (1984) 'The responsibility of scale post holder primary-schools', in L. Watson (ed.) *Aspects of Primary School Management*, Education Management Department, Sheffield Polytechnic.

Lortie, D. (1964) 'The teacher and team teaching', in J. Shaplin and H. Olds (eds) *Team Teaching*, New York, Harper & Row.

Lortie, D. (1969) 'The balance of control and autonomy in elementary school teaching', A. Etzioni (ed.) *The Semi-Professions and their Organization*, New York, Free Press.

McMahon, A. and Bolam, R. (1987) *School Management Development: A Handbook for LEAs*, Bristol, NDC.

PSRDG (1983) *Curriculum Responsibility and the Use of Teacher Expertise in the Primary School: Five Studies*, Birmingham, Primary Schools Research and Development Group, University of Birmingham.

Robinson, M. (1983) 'The role of the year leader: an analysis of the perceptions of year leaders and deputy heads in 8–12 middle schools', *School Organization*, **3**(4), 333–44.

Rodger, I. (1983) *Teachers with Posts of Responsibility in Primary Schools*, Durham, University of Durham.

Rushby, T. and Richards, C. (1982) 'Staff development in primary schools', *Educational Management and Administration*, **10**(3), 223–31.

Schmuck, R. and Runkel, P. (1985) *The Third Handbook of Organization Development in Schools*, Palo Alto, Calif., Mayfield.

Schools Council (1981) *The Practical Curriculum*, London, Methuen.

Schools Council (1983) *Primary Practice*, London, Methuen.

Southworth, G. (1985) 'The headteacher as supply teacher', *Education*, 1 March: 189.

Wallace, M. (1985) 'Promoting careers through management development', *Education 3–13*, **13**(2) 12–16.

Wallace, M. (1986a) 'The rise of scale posts as a management hierarchy in schools', *Educational Management and Administration*, **14**(3), 203–12.

Wallace, M. (1986b) *A Directory of Management Development Activities and Resources*, Bristol, National Development Centre for School Management Training.

Welsh Office (1978) *Primary Education in Wales*, Cardiff, Welsh Office.

Welsh Office (1984) *Departmental Organization in Secondary Schools*, Cardiff, Welsh Office.

Welsh Office (1985) *Leadership in Primary Schools*, Cardiff, Welsh Office.

Williams, A. (1982) 'Physical education in the junior school', *Education 3–13*, **10**(2) 36–40.

# 15

# The micro-politics of the school: baronial politics

**Stephen Ball**

## Baronial politics

In the middle ages the conflicts between English barons were essentially concerned with two matters: wealth and power. In the school the concerns and interests of academic and pastoral barons are fundamentally the same: allocations from the budget, both in terms of capitation moneys and in relation to appointments, timetable time and control of territory (teaching rooms, offices, special facilities), and influence over school policies. Clearly, to a great extent, in the micro-political process these concerns are inseparable: 'If politics is regarded as conflict over whose preferences are to prevail in the determination of policy, then the budget records the outcomes of this struggle' (Wildavsky, 1968: 192).

[. . .]

Here I want to deal with the disputes and struggles between subject departments, particularly in and around the concomitant issues of resource allocation and departmental status.

In the secondary school, leaving aside the pastoral-care structure, subject departments are usually the most significant organizational divisions between teachers as colleagues. On the one hand, the department provides and maintains a special sense of identity for the teacher: it can be a basis for communality. 'The pedagogic subject department forms an epistemic and spatial boundary-maintaining community that its members share as an experience of being a common "kind" of teacher' (Smetherham, 1979: 1), they share a speciality. On the other hand, as I have indicated, the department is the basis for special interests and internecine competition; it is a political coalition:

> definitions of centrality and marginality arise through the super-imposition of departmental boundaries on speciality boundaries. One of the significant consequences of this is a budgetary separation which creates competitive groups. Boundaries are rationalized through decisions taken about what is central and what is peripheral as they are exemplified in allocation of time, money, and staff and even students.
>
> (Esland, 1971: 106)

Thus budgets forge and perpetuate (and occasionally change) a pattern of status and a distribution of influence. The competition between departments is a competition between unequals. Relative status and influence become embedded in the curriculum structure of the school and more immediately in the timetable. (Once established, this fixed structure is difficult to alter, either by outside agencies or internal interest groups.) In practice the 'voice' of any particular department, both in relation to policy issues and/or resource decision-making, is effectively limited by whether it is expanding, remaining static or on the defensive.

The specific distribution of the strong baronies and weak baronies will differ between institutions and will change over time; it is the outcome of ongoing conflicts and rivalries. None the less there are typical patterns, and clearly the expectations of influential outside audiences do enhance the claims made by certain subjects and detract from those of others. Richardson gives a flavour of strengths and weaknesses in her account of Nailsea Comprehensive:

> Two of the most persistent images that I carried . . . concerned the modern languages and science departments on the one side and the geography and history departments on the other. The former I saw as the 'giant' departments which seemed able to make their own con-ditions regardless of changes elsewhere in the system – almost, at times, to be holding the staff up to ransom. In contrast to my impression of power and independence in these areas, the departments of geography and history seemed to me to be suffering more than any others (except perhaps classics) from the problems of encroachment, erosion and loss of wholeness.
>
> (Richardson, 1973: 90)

The metaphor of baronial politics seems particularly apt in this case. As Richardson expresses the situation at Nailsea, it is the curriculum that is at stake. With curriculum control comes influence and control over resources; without it there is political impotence. In addition, the strength of modern languages and science also raises the question of the state of their mutual relations as well as their disposition towards weaker departments:

> Were their departments allies, rivals, or equally powerful independent forces in the school? Both were staffed almost entirely by specialist teachers; neither did any appreciable sharing of personnel with other

departments; both insisted, or appeared to insist, on finer setting by ability throughout the school than any other departments did; both were concerned with the development of new methods of teaching that involved the purchase, control and maintenance of expensive technical equipment.

(Richardson, 1973: 92)

However, as Richardson goes on to point out, there were occasions when the giants clashed, but these clashes did little to weaken their entrenched positions. It was the geography and history departments that seemed to be continually losing out in the battle for resources and control over the timetable:

> I began to think of geography as a department that was trapped – or perhaps suspended – between the arts and the sciences, having allegiances to both sides and a visible link with both sides through geology, but fearing encroachment from the arts side because of the uncertainty about where the subject was rooted. In the recurring discussions about the humanities course, geography was always linked (uneasily perhaps) with history, as mathematics seemed, in the recurring discussions about mixed-ability grouping, to be uneasily linked with science.
>
> If I saw geography as an area that was being crushed between opposing forces or being stretched in opposite directions, I saw history as an area that felt itself to be shrinking. The encroachments on its territory from humanities in the lower school, from social studies in the middle school, from general studies in the upper school, and perhaps also to a lesser extent from ancient history through classics, had to do partly with the loss of recently acquired subject matter, even of new approaches first worked out in terms of history, and partly with a loss of contact with younger children.

(Richardson, 1973: 95–6)

Several processes affecting the status and political 'voice' of subject departments are evident in the examples drawn from Richardson's study. It is apparent that the fortunes of certain departments are rising while others are in decline. In some areas, like humanities, new empires are being carved out. In others, like history, declarations of independence are undermining status claims which previously seemed inviolate. In the first case, smaller, weaker subjects areas are being swallowed up in expanding conglomerates. In the second, smaller subjects are emerging as separate entities to make their own claims for time, territory, money and personnel.

The impetus for the emergence of new subjects can take several different forms but is inevitably surrounded by political struggle and intrigue. In some cases the arrival of a new subject, and its struggle for departmental status, is shortlived. Goodson (1987) provides one example in his examination of the birth pangs of European studies. The 'subject', such as it was, developed from a combination of idealism, what Bucher and Strauss refer to as a sense of mission, in this case the creation of European consciousness among British school-children, and pragmatism, 'as a vehicle for motivating the less able in languages lessons' (1961: 9). In schools it was the latter that was the main driving force; Goodson (1987) quotes a number of examples, among them:

> Well you see . . . I think as far as we are concerned this was a conscious turning away from what was beginning to develop and then people were starting to say 'what are we going to do with the youngsters who are not learning French or German?' . . . From the point of view of timetable convenience they ought to be doing something associated . . . 'let them learn about Germany, you know and what you have for tea in Brussels or something' . . . we were so frightened that this was what European studies was going to become, some sort of dustbin . . . I think we have consciously turned away from that and although we haven't got to lose sight of it eventually, I think we've got to come back to terms with this after we've done the other things. . . . I think we've got to go ahead from our middle school into our sixth form first and get that thing right and get the subject established with status . . . then we may be able to add on these less able youngsters.

> Well, when I became Head of Humanities they also made me Head of European Studies . . . which had been taught on and off for several years to the 'dumbos' in languages. . . . So I organised a meeting to discuss it as a subject – only the young assistant teachers were interested. I went to the Head and asked for money. I was given £150.

> (Goodson, 1987: 215)

Here we have both the strengths and weaknesses of an assertive claimant for subject status. On the one hand, European studies teachers can claim to be heard and make demands on school resources in so far as they take responsibility for problematic groups of pupils, the less able. On the other hand, one crucial measure of subject status is taken from access to the most able pupils, particularly in the establishment of sixth-form A-level courses. Here European studies has a problem. The first teacher clearly recognizes this and is suggesting a strategy which will distance the 'subject' from its less able clients and go instead for recruits in the sixth form. But this is exactly the sort of strategy that is likely to meet with opposition from other subjects. To capture sixth-formers for European studies means luring them away from other subject choices. This threatens access to sought-after teaching allocations, capitation, status and perhaps chances of promotion within other departments. The second quotation also suggests contradictory pressures and possibilities. The interest of young teachers can provide important inputs of energy and commitment necessary for the development of new ideas and materials. However, these teachers lack institutional status; there may be considerable political disadvantage as a result of this and not having friends in high places. None the less, from the point of view of the young adherents, a new 'subject' area can offer the potential of career enhancement and increased promotion possibilities, although these possibilities clearly rest upon the successful establishment of that 'subject'. Again Goodson provides a clear example of the problems:

> I'm very disillusioned about my future. Well it hasn't given me a future after five years so I can't see that it will suddenly give me a future in the next few years. I don't think I could have done much more than I have done. I got involved with the County syllabus, had a lot of contacts with the European Resources Centre, one thing and another, and I thought this can only be of benefit to my career. But it's been going on and I've been doing things and doing things and it's done me no good whatsoever. You know I'm still where I was when I came here seven years ago. I just don't know really . . . obviously I've become disillusioned, disheartened.
>
> (Goodson, 1987: 17)

This teacher clearly sees his career tied closely to the development of his subject. The success of work put in is measured in terms of creating a 'future'. To a great extent the teacher is the subject. Their fortunes are inextricably linked.

The conflict potential posed by the rise of a new 'subject' like European studies is increased further if claims are made which actually involve encroachment into the subject matter of other departments. This is often a problem for the 'subjects' which, like European studies, have an interdisciplinary orientation. Much of the failure of interdisciplinarity in the 1960s and 1970s can be accounted for in terms of micro-political resistance While in content and pedagogical terms interdisciplinary work makes perfect sense, in micro-political terms it looks like empire-building, and it is rational for those who see their interests threatened to resist, to defend their patch. Again Goodson's European studies teachers recognized the problems:

> In a place like this departments are huge and they like to keep their legality. It's [i.e. the construction of a new subject] all a problem of trying to cross barriers which have been there for a long time. However well you get on with people it's still a thought in the back of their mind that their empire could be chipped away at. Interdisciplinary studies are always going to be in that situation.
>
> (Goodson, 1987: 220)

When attempts are made to separate off a new subject from its parent discipline – European studies from languages, drama from English, humanities from history – there are material interests at stake. The new boundaries involve a new distribution of resources – someone gets more and someone else less. Many a proposed innovation has floundered upon the opposition of potential losers in subject restructuring. Change cannot usefully be examined without attention to institutional micro-politics.

When structural change does occur the new divisions are quickly reinforced by new allegiances. New identities are forged:

> What ties a man more closely to one member of his profession may alienate him from another: when his group develops a unique mission, he may no longer share a mission with others in the same profession.
>
> (Bucher and Strauss, 1961: 227)

Where relationships between teachers are poor almost any attempt at innovation can be seen in terms of the political motivations or career aspirations of the instigators. One of the headteachers I interviewed described a group of teachers who had pressed for the school to become involved in PGCE work with the nearby university as 'suffering from frustrated ambition'.

European studies provides one example of a 'failed' innovation, a 'subject' which, with a few exceptions, was unable to establish itself as an independent department with its own resources and career structure. In contrast, classics provides a case where a once great subject has declined and virtually disappeared from the timetables of most comprehensive schools. Stray (1985) offers a case study of the declining fortunes of classics in Llangarr Comprehensive. The department and its teachers experienced a series of setbacks during the 1970s, which marked a gradual loss of political credibility and status for the subject. The first blow came when Latin was made optional:

> In the head of departments' meeting . . . the head confronted us with a sheet of paper which showed the options . . . we were horrified to see that Latin had been put against History. Whereas at present in the third form it was a class subject for the top two classes.
>
> (Stray, 1985: 39)

Such a change has both practical and symbolic implications. Symbolically, it indicates the removal of Latin from the assured status position of being a compulsory subject, a crushing blow. Access to pupil numbers is threatened and valued teaching, to the top classes, is at risk. Politically, two points are significant: first, the lack of consultation – the department was faced with a *fait accompli*; second, the inability of the department to mount a serious defence or call upon support from colleagues in other departments. The classics teachers were soon to find themselves further beleaguered. To add insult to injury, the reorganization of the option system also redefined classical studies as a subject for the less able, for those pupils who were prevented from continuing with French or Welsh:

> We get the poorer children, the difficult children. Now in a sense you may say this is justice, since we've had the cream in the past . . . but by virtue of the choice, the pupils we're getting, they're the rejects.
>
> (Stray, 1985: 216)

As noted already, a critical indicator of the status of a subject is the status of those it teaches. Once again the fortunes of the subject must be associated with the career opportunities of the teachers. The classicists began to find themselves under pressure in this regard from unsympathetic colleagues:

> One remarked that there were 'several people who don't see why a subject they think is on the decline should have two graded posts'; points are taken away from their own departments such as . . . practical subjects. They see themselves as more relevant to the comprehensive set-up than Classics.
>
> (Stray, 1985: 41)

Stray notes that the rivalry over promotion in Llangarr became ingrained in the micro-political processes of the school. The processes of influence were through these informal channels discussed above:

> The merger of the three different staffs and the tensions caused by 'overpointing' and the scarcity of promotions, in particular, discouraged open discussion; instead points were made via sarcastic jokes, the mutter in the corridor, separate trips into the 'administrative suite'.
>
> (Stray, 1985: 42)

Classics was often the subject and butt of these informal pressures and behind-the-scenes manoeuvrings. It was clearly a subject on the slide. There were few collegial scruples preventing the subject from being kicked when it was down. By 1974 Stray notes that 'The Llangarr classicists had thus suffered successive dislodgements towards an uncertain and marginal position. Underlying this process was a shift in the relations, and relative power, of the knowledge, occupation and organization systems' (Stray, 1985: 44).

In many schools both classics and European studies teachers have found themselves locked into a rather precarious and often unrewarding existence on the periphery of the curriculum. Their 'missions' (Bucher and Strauss, 1961) have failed and in the battle for institutional status they have been, for the present at least, routed. Falling rolls, a teacher who leaves, or any other contingency might extinguish the subject entirely. But clearly, in contrast, some new 'subjects' do make it, do establish themselves as secure and (relatively) permanent, taken-for-granted parts of the school curriculum.

Here again we must recognize that the rise and fall of subjects and departments is not solely dependent upon the outcomes of micro-political manoeuvring. The impact of changing patterns of external legitimation is also significant, Reid makes the point that

> For while it may appear that the professionals have power to determine what is taught (at school, district or national level, depending on the country in question), their scope is limited by the fact that only those forms and activities which have significance for external publics can, in the long run, survive.
>
> (Reid, 1984: 68)

While I would accept this statement in general terms, I would still want to argue that the legitimation of external publics is essentially a constraint upon or opportunity for the interest-groups and coalitions at work in the school. These constraints and opportunities are mediated through the micro-politics of the institution.

The impressive growth of computer studies is a good example. The high level of public awareness of 'high-technology', the massive infusion of government support and moneys, and programmes to get computers into every school during the 1980s provided a powerful base for the take-off in computing courses. Certainly in some schools, departments of computer studies emerged, in others such initiatives remain under the auspices of the mathematics departments. In some schools battle ensued to ensure that computing is seen to be relevant across a range of subjects; in others it is a specialist subject in its own right; in still others the impact of new technology has been minimal. The differences between schools can be explored and explained in terms of micro-political factors. The control of expensive, high-status hardware is at stake. So too are the reputations and futures of departments. The ability to respond to and cope with the new technologies may be critical in the long-term survival of certain subjects. This is not simply a matter of responding effectively but being seen to be able to respond. Once again it must be said that new curriculum initiatives like computing or TVEI or CPVE provide new career avenues; they also threatened established patterns of preferment. Indeed, a whole range of scarce and valued resources are subject to renegotiation. New skills are in demand, older skills are threatened with extinction. Interestingly, newer, younger teachers may be better trained and prepared, while others, keen to exploit the new opportunities, may turn to in-service courses. Awareness of new developments and up-to-date contacts, especially those which might provide equipment or money, are themselves important resources in the ebb and flow of status and influence.

External legitimation, or delegitimation, is just one factor at work in affecting the standing of departments and teachers. Innovations can be stifled by established interests or 'knowledgeable' young teachers may find themselves being sponsored by older, more influential colleagues. Outcomes, in terms of curriculum change cannot be assumed to be the result of rational, bureaucratic procedures. The departmental barons will not concede control easily. To a great extent, change or resistance to change will depend upon the relative influence of protagonists over organizational decision-making.

### Influence at court

The complex political calculus which underpins the actual distribution of status, and resources, in the school is by no means easy to unpick. One way to begin is by examination of those cases which fall outside the typical pattern.

For example, where mathematics, science or English departments have failed to achieve status and resource preferment, or where departments like drama, CDT or music have done so.

Oak Farm Comprehensive (Ball and Lacey, 1980) provides a case of the former kind. Here the English department is to be found in a marginal position. The head of department explained his predicament:

> We have three full-time English teachers including myself. . . . So that at the moment we have ten people who are teaching partly in the department or wholly. I've been fighting for more full-time English specialists since I've been here. We ranged from 22 teaching English, for a while it was 17, now it's 10.
>
> (Ball and Lacey, 1980: 42)

Despite the improvements, the head of department faces a difficult situation: he is unable to draw upon the support of a group of teachers committed fully to the English department in any negotiations over resources. Indeed, the status of English as a department in its own right is questionable. Most of his staff have major commitments elsewhere:

> it involved one trying to bring as much pressure as possible to bear on the Head and Deputy Head and other influential people in the school to make them see that English was being too much fragmented. And the most important subject, at least I consider it so. . . . I know that every teacher is a teacher of English, the old tag, but it doesn't work out that way.
>
> (Ball and Lacey, 1980: 158)

The head of department seems to acknowledge his own lack of influence in the school and the failure among those who have influence to recognize his case as valid. English has failed to acquire the infrastructural base which accompanies and underpins subject status:

> It's only for three years that I've had a second in charge. It was thought that there were other priorities. And also physical things like an office. Which is quite a sore point, it hasn't been recognised in that way. But this was determined not so much by a positive opposition but by the circumstances which prevail in the school which make it difficult. I just asked in this financial year that some provision be made whereby I could get a base to work from, but although it appeared on the list of requests, when it was sorted into priorities, it missed the priorities and was shelved again.
>
> (Ball and Lacey, 1980: 159)

Without a group of specialist teachers English cannot establish its credibility and assert demands for resources and facilities. There is a vicious circle. While the head of English continues to have no influence over the definition of new appointments, there is little possibility of such specialists being appointed.

English will continue to be regarded as something that anyone can teach. Once established in the culture and history of the institution, collective assumptions of this kind are difficult to break down. As the head of department sees it, the preferences and background of the headteacher are crucial factors at work here:

> it so largely depends on the background and previous careers of Headmasters. My present Headmaster has done quite a lot since he's been here for the science department; which is a good thing. But I feel that English is not recognised as firmly and as widely as it ought to be.
>
> (Ball and Lacey, 1980: 159)

In the same vein, St John Brooks (1983) provides as account of an English department in a Bristol comprehensive which as a result of ideological differences with the headteacher is also excluded from influence over school policy. Indeed, to a great extent the department was unwilling to engage with the accepted procedures of debate and policy-making.

> The department as a whole could not defend their position in a manner comprehensible or acceptable to most of the other teachers, especially the Headmaster. By rejecting the bureaucratic world of institutions and the realm of public argument and debate, along with the kind of justification it demands, such romantic individuals or groups are destined to remain forever marginal.
>
> (St John Brooks, 1983: 56)

By opting out of school micro-politics, the department marginalized itself and put itself under pressure. Sponsorship by the head can clearly do much to advance the position of a department both in terms of status and resources. An antagonistic head can make life very difficult. The relationship between headteacher and head of department will to a great extent rely on mutual obligation. The head will expect efficiency or loyalty or both, in return for continued support. This relationship will thus depend not only upon the *quality* of personal relationships, but also upon a matching of styles and some sharing of goals and ideologies. However, this is not the only relationship to be attended to: the head of department must face in three directions, towards the headteacher and senior management and a concern with whole-school policy, towards the interpersonal arena of departmental relationships and the specific policy interests of the department, and across towards other heads of department as colleagues with shared problems or competing interests. Taafe quotes a head of creative arts from a London comprehensive on the qualities of a head of faculty required by his headteacher:

> To be a senior head you must be very flexible and devious. Flexible to fit in with the headmaster, back off if necessary. Devious, to get your faculty to do what the headmaster wants.
>
> (Taafe, 1980: 23)

Careful tending of their patch, positive support from colleagues and positive indicators of department success can put the head of department in a powerful political position. In some cases, from the headteacher's point of view, heads of department can become too powerful. From Taafe's study again, the head of mathematics explains:

> If you look at the staff overall, forgetting creative arts for the moment, you will not find any large departments. I think this is a conscious effort on the part of the Head to break down influential bodies on the staff. Certainly maths has no influence.
>
> (Taafe, 1980: 39)

The head of languages takes up the point:

> Look at Science, you have specialists there, it is probably the largest department in the school. The last Head of Department was very strong, utterly ruthless, out for what he could get for his department. Science was a potent influence in the school. I don't think the Head liked it. Look at the new appointment, he's wet, the exact opposite. The result is science now is not an influential body.
>
> (Taafe, 1980: 40)

Two major themes of the analysis emerge here. One is the role of influence: here we see the problematic nature of *too much* influence, at least as far as the head is concerned. The other is the crucial importance of control of appointments and promotions: heads can do a great deal to bolster their position politically by the appointments that they make. However, it should not be assumed that it is the headteacher who is always successful in power struggles with departments. Latus offers the following account of ground gained by a head of department against opposition from 'the hierarchy':

> The English department is led by an academically strong Head of Department who in addition to taking over in difficult circumstances also had to assert his authority over his own specialism. This involved challenging the deputy headmaster, a member of the department, who was exercising positional power and thus depriving Mr Jenks [the HOD] of authority and status. In ousting his rival Mr Jenks also secured hitherto unknown autonomy for the department and this in turn led to gains on other fronts e.g. the right to be present at departmental appointments, and also a policy change: English specialists are appointed rather than general subject teachers offering some English.
>
> (Latus, 1977: 36)

Here the head of department gained ground in exactly those areas which proved so intractable for the head of English at Oak Farm.

The political role of the head of department is clearly significant not only in relations with the head but also in dealings with their own department members. If the heads of department are unable to produce and maintain at least an outward display of unity and coherence within their departments, then it becomes extremely difficult to mount a convincing case for new initiatives, additional resources or changes to the timetable. Both ideological and interpersonal tensions can arise to undermine the unity of a department, and heads of department find themselves more or less able to deal with the difficulties which ensue. (See Jago, 1983: ch. 8, for a discussion of leadership problems in subject departments.) If strong heads of department can create problems, so too can weak ones. If matters threaten major disruption, then the headteacher may step in.

Meadows (1981) describes a situation at Millrace Comprehensive where an existing head of department is eased out of her position and replaced, through a series of manoeuvres carefully managed by members of the department and the headteacher. Clearly, the head of department was not well regarded by her colleagues:

> Mary Standen gave the impression of perpetual bewilderment. She had a narrow, Scots', rigorous view . . . but she was out of her depth. Her qualities just weren't right. . . . The department was put in charge of an incompetent. (Colleague 1)
>
> (Meadows, 1981: 14)

> At the interviews some were even worse and so she got the job. She was administratively conscientious, but never well organized. She tended to listen to the last person, therefore the department's autonomy went. (Colleague 2)
>
> (Meadows, 1981: 14)

The members of department attempted their own solution to the problems created for them. Informal arrangements, a negotiated order of sorts, were brought into play to fill and to circumvent the formal vacuum:

> things tended to get done via the back door . . . she was prepared to let me get on, but I was a senior teacher in her eyes. She was very conscious of protocol. But she wouldn't give Victor responsibility for the middle school course. So, last year, the conspirators explored ways of moving things along. Victor produced a job description. It accepted Mary's nominal control, but the responsibility for English was split between different people. The head accepted the job description. (Colleague 1)
>
> (Meadows, 1981: 14–15)

With the retirement of the school librarian, despite the appointment of a temporary replacement, the head saw a solution to the English department difficulties:

> He saw the situation and worked out a way of getting a new head of department. He created a department – Library and Resources – and moved Mary Standen into it. (Colleague 3)
>
> (Meadows, 1981: 16)

The temporary incumbent was understandably not pleased: she had believed that the head had promised the permanent library post to her.

> Abruptly he pushed Mary Standen sideways into my job. He took five minutes to tell me. I was shocked but I went back and argued with him for half-an-hour. I told him he was unfair. He is incapable of running a school. He has no feelings. He will walk over people. (Colleague 4)
>
> (Meadows, 1981: 16)

Once again the interplay between institutional politics and individual careers is in evidence. Political solutions tend to dispense advantage to some and disadvantage to others.

What I have been attempting here is to establish some of those factors which enter into the making and breaking of departmental reputations and subject status, concentrating on the degree of influence that may be available to a department in varying circumstances. Certainly, however, as the case of classics illustrates, there are a number of objective indicators which enter into the appraisal of any department. The inability to attract option choices, a poor teaching or disciplinary record and poor examination results will, over time, undermine the position of even the most well entrenched subject. This is evident in the following interview extract where a headteacher explains his view of the mathematics department in his school:

> Their track record now is one which says 'No I'm not going to do this'. In the summer they wanted to have single-sex maths. Well, I said no to that. I had already given them £2,000 above their normal capitation to invest in SMILE. So they had this heavy investment in SMILE and immediately, within one year, they wanted to move on to something else. The difficult thing is why is it that the English results are good and the maths results are so appalling. It's roughly 10 per cent O-level in mathematics and 58 per cent in English, across the fifth-year group. It must be to do with the teaching, and with the organization. Now, the maths department has a problem because of the head of maths.

In the contemporary jargon, heads of departments are 'middle managers', with all the implications of 'line' responsibility that that suggests. It may be that baronial politics and the feudal relationships through which they have worked are being replaced by the bureaucratic procedures and relationships of management theory. On the other hand, the pristine language of management may only serve to obscure the real struggles over policy and budgets – who gets what, when and how?

[. . .]

### References

Ball, S. J. and Lacey, C. (1980) 'Subject disciplines and the opportunity for group action: a measured critique of subject sub-cultures', in P. E. Woods (ed.) *Teacher Strategies*, London, Croom Helm.

Bucher, R. and Strauss, A. (1961) 'Professions in process', *American Journal of Sociology*, 66, January: 325–34.

Esland, G. (1971) 'Teaching and learning as the organization of knowledge', in M. F. D. Young (ed.) *Knowledge and Control*, London, Collier-Macmillan.

Goodson, I. F. (1987) *The Making of Curriculum: Essays in the Social History of Education*, Lewes, Falmer Press.

Jago, W. (1983) 'Teachers at work: a study of individual and role in school', unpublished Ph.D. thesis, Falmer, University of Sussex, Education Area.

Latus, E. (1977) 'Seatown High School', unpublished MA project in Education, Falmer, University of Sussex, Education Area.

Meadows, E. (1981) 'Politics and personalities', unpublished MA project in Education, Institutional Profile, Falmer, University of Sussex, Education Area.

Reid, W. A. (1984) 'Curricular topics as institutional categories', in I. F. Goodson and S. J. Ball (eds) *Defining the Curriculum: Histories and Ethnographies*, Lewes, Falmer Press.

Richardson, E. (1973) *The Teacher, the School and the Task of Management*, London, Heinemann.

St John Brooks, C. (1983) 'English: a curriculum for personal development?', in M. Hammersley and A. Hargreaves (eds) *Curriculum Practice: Some Sociological Case Studies*, Lewes, Falmer Press.

Smetherham, D. (1979) 'Identifying strategies', paper given at SSRC-funded conference, 'Teacher and Pupil Strategies', Oxford, September.

Stray, C. (1985) 'From monopoly to marginality: classics in English education since 1800', in I. F. Goodson (ed.) *Social Histories of the Secondary Curriculum*, Lewes, Falmer Press.

Taafe, R. (1980) 'Charisma and collegiate: conflict or harmony?' Unpublished MA minor project in education, Education Area, University of Sussex.

Wildavsky, A. (1968) 'Budgeting as a political process', in D. Sills (ed.) *International Encyclopaedia of the Social Sciences*, 2, 192–9, New York, Cromwell, Collier Macmillan.

# Author index

# Subject index